MANAGING HUMAN RESOURCES

PRODUCTIVITY, QUALITY OF WORK LIFE, PROFITS

MCGRAW-HILL SERIES IN MANAGEMENT

CONSULTING EDITORS

Fred Luthans
Keith Davis

Arnold and Feldman: *Organizational Behavior*
Bartol and Martin: *Management*
Bernardin and Russell: *Human Resource Management: An Experiential Approach*
Boone and Bowen: *Great Writings in Management and Organizational Behavior*
Boone and Kurtz: *Management*
Bounds, Yorks, Adams, and Ranney: *Beyond Total Quality Management: Toward the Emerging Paradigm*
Bovée, Thill, Wood, and Dovel: *Management*
Cascio: *Managing Human Resources: Productivity, Quality of Work Life, Profits*
Davidson and de la Torre: *Managing the Global Corporation: Case Studies in Strategy and Management*
Dess and Miller: *Strategic Management*
Dilworth: *Operations Management: Design, Planning, and Control for Manufacturing and Services*
Dilworth: *Production and Operations Management: Manufacturing and Services*
Dobler, Burt, and Lee: *Purchasing and Materials Management: Text and Cases*
Feldman and Arnold: *Managing Individual and Group Behavior in Organizations*
Fitzsimmons and Fitzsimmons: *Service Management for Competitive Advantage*
Frederick, Post, and Davis: *Business and Society: Corporate Strategy, Public Policy, Ethics*
Gaynor and Kirkpatrick: *Introduction to Time Series Modeling and Forecasting for Business and Economics*
Hodgetts and Luthans: *International Management*
Hoffman and Moore: *Business Ethics: Readings and Cases in Corporate Morality*
Jauch and Glueck: *Business Policy and Strategic Management*
Jauch and Glueck: *Strategic Management and Business Policy*
Jauch and Townsend: *Cases in Strategic Management and Business Policy*
Katz and Kochan: *An Introduction to Collective Bargaining and Industrial Relations*
Koontz and Weihrich: *Essentials of Management*
Kopelman: *Managing Productivity in Organizations: A Practical, People-Oriented Perspective*
Kuriloff, Hemphill, and Cloud: *Starting and Managing the Small Business*
Levin, Rubin, Stinson, and Gardner: *Quantitative Approaches to Management*
Luthans: *Organizational Behavior*
Luthans and Thompson: *Contemporary Readings in Organizational Behavior*
Miles: *Theories of Management: Implications for Organizational Behavior and Development*

WAYNE F. CASCIO

Graduate School of Business, University of Colorado, Denver

MANAGING HUMAN RESOURCES

PRODUCTIVITY, QUALITY OF WORK LIFE, PROFITS

FOURTH EDITION

McGraw-Hill, Inc.

New York   St. Louis   San Francisco   Auckland
Bogotá   Caracas   Lisbon   London   Madrid
Mexico City   Milan   Montreal   New Delhi
San Juan   Singapore   Sydney   Tokyo   Toronto

MANAGING HUMAN RESOURCES
PRODUCTIVITY, QUALITY OF WORK LIFE, PROFITS

Copyright © 1995, 1992, 1989, 1986 by McGraw-Hill, Inc. All rights reserved. Printed in the United States of America. Except as permitted under the United States Copyright Act of 1976, no part of this publication may be reproduced or distributed in any form or by any means, or stored in a data base or retrieval system, without the prior written permission of the publisher.

Illustration Credits and Photo Credits appear on page 635 and on this page by reference.

 This book is printed on recycled, acid-free paper containing 10% postconsumer waste.

1 2 3 4 5 6 7 8 9 0 DOW DOW 9 0 9 8 7 6 5 4

ISBN 0-07-011154-5

This book was set in Janson by Better Graphics, Inc.
The editors were Lynn Richardson, Dan Alpert, and Linda Richmond;
the designer was Joan Greenfield;
the production supervisor was Friederich W. Schulte.
The photo editor was Anne Manning.
New drawings were done by Vantage Art.
R. R. Donnelley & Sons Company was printer and binder.

Cover Art
Full Circle by Michael James, © 1993; photo by David Caras.

Library of Congress Cataloging-in-Publication Data

Cascio, Wayne F.
    Managing human resources: productivity, quality of work life,
profits / Wayne F. Cascio. —4th ed.
        p.   cm.— (McGraw-Hill series in management)
    Includes index.
    ISBN 0-07-011154-5
    1. Personnel management.   I. Title.   II. Series.
HF5549.C2975   1995
658.3—dc20   94-3480

INTERNATIONAL EDITION

Copyright 1995. Exclusive rights by McGraw Hill, Inc., for manufacture and export. This book cannot be re-exported from the country to which it is consigned by McGraw-Hill. The International Edition is not available in North America.

When ordering this title, use ISBN 0-07-113886-2.

ABOUT THE AUTHOR

WAYNE F. CASCIO earned his B.A. degree from Holy Cross College in 1968, his M.A. degree from Emory University in 1969, and his Ph.D. in industrial/organizational psychology from the University of Rochester in 1973. Since that time he has taught at Florida International University, the University of California-Berkeley, and the University of Colorado-Denver, where he is at present Professor of Management.

Professor Cascio is past president both of the Human Resources Division of the Academy of Management and of the Society for Industrial and Organizational Psychology. He is a Fellow of the American Psychological Association and a Diplomate in industrial/organizational psychology of the American Board of Professional Psychology. His editorial board memberships have included the *Journal of Applied Psychology, Academy of Management Review, International Journal of Selection and Assessment, Human Performance, Organizational Dynamics,* and *Asia-Pacific Journal of Human Resources.* He has consulted on five continents with a wide variety of organizations in both the public and private sectors on HR matters, and periodically he testifies as an expert witness in employment discrimination cases. Professor Cascio is an active researcher and is the author or editor of five books on human resource management.

TO DOROTHY AND JOE,
the choicest blessings life has provided;
constant reminders of what really counts.

CONTENTS

CHAPTER 6   RECRUITING   **164**

PART FIVE

LABOR-MANAGEMENT ACCOMMO-DATION

455

CHAPTER 16   SAFETY, HEALTH AND EMPLOYEE ASSISTANCE PROGRAMS

PART SIX

SUPPORT, EVALUATION, AND INTERNATIONAL IMPLICATIONS

529

CHAPTER 18   INTERNATIONAL DIMENSIONS OF HUMAN RESOURCE MANAGEMENT   597

LIST OF ETHICAL DILEMMAS, COMPANY EXAMPLES, PRACTICAL EXAMPLES, AND INTERNATIONAL APPLICATIONS

PREFACE

This book was not written for aspiring human resource management (HRM) special-ists. It was written for the student of general management whose job inevitably will involve responsibility for managing *people*, along with other organizational assets. A fundamental assumption, then, is that all managers are accountable to their organiza-tions in terms of the impact of their HRM activities. They also are accountable to their peers and to their subordinates in terms of the quality of work life they are pro-viding.

As a unifying theme for the text, there is explicit linkage in each chapter of the three outcome variables—productivity, quality of work life, and profits—to the HRM activity under discussion. This relationship should strengthen the student's percep-tion of HRM as an important function affecting individuals, organizations, and soci-ety.

Each of the six parts that comprise the text includes a chart that illustrates the orga-nizing framework for the book. The specific topics covered in each part are high-lighted for emphasis.

Each chapter incorporates the following distinguishing features:

■ A split-sequential vignette, often from the popular press, that illustrates "Human Resource Management in Action." Events in the vignette are designed to sensitize the reader to the subject matter of the chapter. The events lead to a climax, but then the vignette stops—like a two-part television drama. The reader is asked to predict what will happen next and to anticipate the impact of alternative courses of action.

In keeping with the general management orientation of the book, the vignette is then followed by a section entitled "Questions This Chapter Will Help Managers Answer." This section provides a broad outline of the topics to be covered in the chap-ter. Then the text for the chapter appears, replete with concepts, theories, research findings, company examples, and international comparisons that illustrate current practices. Ultimately we are trying to teach prospective managers to *make decisions* based on accurate diagnoses of situations that involve HRM issues. Where relevant, it is important to see those issues in a global context. Students' ability to do this is enhanced by familiarity with theory, research, and practice.

At the end of the chapter we continue the vignette introduced at the outset, to see what happened. This dynamic design allows the student to move back and forth from concept to evidence to practice—then back to evaluating concepts—in a continuous "learning loop."

■ Relevant research findings plus clippings from the popular press (Company Examples) provide real world applications of concepts and theories. It has often been said that experience is a hard teacher because it gives the test first and the lessons afterward. Actual company examples, plus numerous international applications, allow the student to learn from the experience of others.

■ Near the end of the chapter, before the summary and discussion questions, there is a new section called "Ethical dilemma." Its purpose is to identify issues relevant to the topic under discussion where different courses of action may be desirable and possible. Students must choose a course of action and defend their reasons for doing so. As in the third edition, the section called "Implications for Management Practice" provides concrete, no-nonsense advice on how to manage the issues that have been discussed.

HRM texts have sometimes been criticized for overemphasizing the HR practices of large businesses. There is often scant advice for the manager of a small business who "wears many hats" and whose capital resources are limited. To address this issue explicitly, we have made a conscious effort to provide examples of effective HRM practices in small businesses in almost every chapter.

This was no cosmetic revision. We examined every topic and every example, in each chapter, for its continued relevance and appropriateness. In addition to adding a new chapter—Chapter 3, "Diversity at Work"—11 of the 18 split-sequential vignettes are new, there are many new company examples, and fully one-third of the references are new since the last edition of the book.

As in the previous editions, we have tried to make the text readable, neither too simplistic nor too complex.

NEW TOPICS IN THE FOURTH EDITION

■ Key characteristics and forms of the modern organization and of today's business environment (e.g., downsizing), as well as a discussion of Total Quality Management, corporate culture, and firm performance (Chapter 1).

■ Discussion of a fourth growth stage for HRM—strategic partnership—and the linkage of strategic HRM to general business strategy. The linkage is shown by a company example that illustrates how Federal Express and United Parcel Service use their human resources for competitive advantage (Chapter 2).

■ New Chapter 3, "Diversity at Work," focuses on the business reasons why managers should pay attention to managing diversity effectively. Practices at leading companies such as Xerox, Pacific Bell, J. C. Penney, Bankers Trust, and Levi Strauss & Co. illustrate diversity as an essential component of HR strategy.

■ Extensive discussion of the legal requirements and HR implications of the Americans with Disabilities Act of 1990, the Civil Rights Act of 1991, and the Family and Medical Leave Act of 1993, together with new case law on sexual harassment, overqualified applicants, and "English-only" rules at work (Chapter 4).

■ Job analysis under the ADA, together with a company example of changing business and human resource needs at Apple computer, illustrate the role of job analysis and HR planning in the 1990s and beyond (Chapter 5).

■ Diversity-oriented recruiting, enhanced discussion of job search strategies (i.e., how to find a job), and a company example that shows how Bristol-Myers Squibb uses computer technology to find top MBA graduates (Chapter 6).

- The impact of strategy and organizational culture on staffing decisions, as well as revised discussions of reliability, validity, and employment interviews (Chapter 7).

- Expanded and updated discussion of training trends and macro-level issues, plus a company example of a business–school partnership—Stihl, Inc. (Chapter 8).

- New section: Total Quality Management and the performance appraisal process (Chapter 9).

- Updated discussion of the meaning of career success in the 1990s, plus new research findings on dual-career couples, mentoring, and plateaued workers (Chapter 10).

- Strategic integration of compensation plans and business plans, difficulties in linking internal pay relationships to market data caused by "at-risk" forms of pay, and alternatives to job-based pay systems—market-based pay and skill/knowledge-based pay (Chapter 11).

- Strategic use of severance pay, controlling the costs of workers' compensation and health care, and a company example of how Nike matches people with the benefits they want and need (Chapter 12).

- Two updated company examples: North American Tool & Die and Lincoln Electric, plus an expanded section on designing jobs for teams (Chapter 13).

- Update on the changing nature of industrial relations in the United States, current tactics of labor and management, and discussion of conditions under which labor-management teams might violate federal law (Chapter 14).

- New section on procedural justice in action—employee voice systems, final-offer arbitration in major league baseball, and fair information practices in the computer age (Chapter 15).

- New section on violence at work, plus updated treatment of AIDS and business, Levi Strauss & Co.'s AIDS-related corporate policies, and the costs to small businesses for cutting corners on safety (Chapter 16).

- Firm-level assessments of the financial impact of high-performance work practices (Chapter 17)

- Globalization as a growth strategy, implications of the North American Free Trade Agreement (NAFTA) for HR practices, and new company examples on cultural differences among IBMers worldwide, interviewing potential expatriates at AT&T, and the pros and cons of working for a foreign-owned company in the United States (Chapter 18).

ORGANIZATION AND PLAN OF THE BOOK

The chart below provides an organizing framework for the book. It will appear again at the opening of each of the six parts that comprise the book. Each component of the organizing framework will be highlighted for the student as it is discussed. The organization of the parts is designed to reflect the fact that human resource management (HRM) is an integrated, goal-directed set of managerial functions, not just a collection of techniques.

The text is founded on the premise that three critical strategic objectives guide all HRM functions: productivity, quality of work life, and profits. The functions (employment; development; compensation; labor-management accommodation; and

| STRATEGIC OBJECTIVES, ENVIRONMENTS, FUNCTIONS | RELATIONSHIP OF HRM FUNCTIONS TO HRM ACTIVITIES |

STRATEGIC OBJECTIVES, ENVIRONMENTS, FUNCTIONS

PARTS ONE – SIX / STRATEGIC OBJECTIVES / CHAPTERS 1 – 18
- Productivity
- Quality of Work Life
- Profits

PART ONE / ENVIRON-MENTS / CHAPTERS 1 - 4
- Competitive
- Legal
- Social
- Organizational

PARTS TWO – SIX / FUNCTIONS / CHAPTERS 5 – 18
- Employment
- Development
- Compensation
- Labor-Management Accommodation
- Support, Evaluation, International Implications

RELATIONSHIP OF HRM FUNCTIONS TO HRM ACTIVITIES

FUNCTIONS	ACTIVITIES
Part Two **Employment**	Job Analysis, Human Resource Planning, Recruiting, Staffing (Chapters 5 - 7)
Part Three **Development**	Orienting, Training, Performance Appraisal, Managing Careers (Chapters 8 - 10)
Part Four **Compensation**	Pay, Benefits, Incentives (Chapters 11 - 13)
Part Five **Labor-Management Accommodation**	Union Representation, Collective Bargaining, Procedural Justice, Ethics (Chapters 14, 15)
Part Six **Support, Evaluation, International Implications**	Job Safety and Health, Costs/Benefits of HRM Activities, International Dimensions of HRM (Chapters 16 - 18)

support, evaluation, and international implications) in turn are carried out in the context of multiple environments: competitive, social, legal, and organizational.

Part 1, "Environment," includes Chapters 1 through 4. It provides the backdrop against which to appreciate the nature and content of each HRM function. These first four chapters paint a broad picture of the competitive, social, legal, and organizational environments of HRM. They also describe key economic and noneconomic factors that affect productivity, quality of work life, and profits. The remaining five parts (14 chapters) in the book are presented in the context of this conceptual framework.

Logically, "Employment" (Part 2) is the first step in the HRM process. Job analysis, human resource planning, recruiting, and staffing are key components of the employment process. Once employees are "on board," the process of "Development" (Part 3) begins with orientation and is sustained through continuing training, performance appraisal, and career management activities.

Parts 4, 5, and 6 are all concurrent processes. That is, "Compensation" (Part 4), "Labor-Management Accommodation" (Part 5), and "Support, Evaluation, and International Implications" (Part 6) are all closely intertwined conceptually and in practice. They represent a network of interacting activities, such that a change in one of them (e.g., a new pay system or collective bargaining contract) inevitably will have an impact on all other components of the HRM system. It is only for ease of exposition that they are considered separately in Parts 4, 5, and 6. Chapter 18 of Part 6, "International Dimensions of HRM," is a capstone chapter. That is, each of the topics we considered throughout the book is addressed in the special context of international business practices. It forces the student to consider the broad spectrum of HR activities across countries, across cultures, and across economic systems. The need to "fit" HRM practices to the company and country cultures in which they are embedded, in order to achieve the strategic objectives of enhancing productivity, quality of work life, and profits, is an important concept for students to understand and to apply.

In teaching HRM courses at both graduate and undergraduate levels, we use this model as a "road map" throughout the course. We believe that it is important for students to grasp the "big picture," as well as to understand how the topics in question fit into the broader scheme of HRM functions. We have found that by presenting the model frequently throughout the course, showing students where we have been and where we are going, students are better able to adopt a more systematic, strategic perspective in addressing any given HRM issue.

ACKNOWLEDGMENTS

Many people played important roles in the development of this edition of the book, and I am deeply grateful to them. Ultimately, of course, any errors of omission or commission are mine, and I bear responsibility for them.

Four people at McGraw-Hill were especially helpful. Senior Associate Editor Dan Alpert and Senior Sponsoring Editor Lynn Richardson provided continual advice, support, and encouragement. Senior Editing Supervisor Linda Richmond is a true professional and was a pleasure to work with on this edition, as on previous editions, of the book. Mike Elia, Developmental Editor and friend, keeps me updated with news clippings and humble as a practitioner of the craft of writing. His lessons are timeless. Finally, the many reviewers of various portions of the fourth edition provided important insights that helped to improve the final product. They deserve special thanks: Richard Alpert, Esq., Employment Discrimination Specialist; Christy L. DeVader, Loyola College in Maryland; Diane Dodd-McCue, University of Virginia; Jeremy Fox, Appalachian State University; David A. Gray, University of Texas at Arlington; W. Roy Johnson, Iowa State University; Allen I. Kraut, Baruch College; Glenn M. McEvoy, Utah State University; Carolyn Wiley, University of Tennessee at Chattanooga; and Kevin C. Wooten, University of Houston—Clear Lake.

Wayne F. Cascio

MANAGING HUMAN RESOURCES

PRODUCTIVITY, QUALITY OF WORK LIFE, PROFITS

A CONCEPTUAL VIEW OF
HUMAN RESOURCE MANAGEMENT

STRATEGIC OBJECTIVES, ENVIRONMENTS, FUNCTIONS

PARTS ONE - SIX
STRATEGIC OBJECTIVES
CHAPTERS 1 - 18

Productivity

Quality of
Work Life

Profits

PART ONE
ENVIRON-MENTS
CHAPTERS 1 - 4

Competitive

Legal

Social

Organizational

PARTS TWO - SIX
FUNCTIONS
CHAPTERS 5 - 18

Employment

Development

Compensation

Labor-Management
Accommodation

Support, Evaluation,
International Implications

RELATIONSHIP OF HRM FUNCTIONS TO HRM ACTIVITIES

FUNCTIONS	ACTIVITIES
Part Two **Employment**	Job Analysis, Human Resource Planning, Recruiting, Staffing (Chapters 5 - 7)
Part Three **Development**	Orienting, Training, Performance Appraisal, Managing Careers (Chapters 8 - 10)
Part Four **Compensation**	Pay, Benefits, Incentives (Chapters 11 - 13)
Part Five **Labor-Management** **Accommodation**	Union Representation, Collective Bargaining, Procedural Justice, Ethics (Chapters 14, 15)
Part Six **Support,** **Evaluation,** **International** **Implications**	Job Safety and Health, Costs/Benefits of HRM Activities, International Dimensions of HRM (Chapters 16 - 18)

PART ONE

ENVIRONMENT

In order to manage people effectively in today's world of work, it is essential to understand and appreciate the significant competitive, legal, and social issues. The purpose of Chapters 1, 3, and 4 is to provide insight into these issues. Chapter 2 considers the historical development and current status (role, strategic orientation, and evaluation) of the human resource management function in organizations.

CHAPTER 1

HUMAN RESOURCES IN A GLOBALLY COMPETITIVE BUSINESS ENVIRONMENT

PARADIGMS FOR POSTMODERN MANAGERS*

If we don't change our direction, we might end up where we're headed—ancient Chinese proverb

The modern corporation is a thing of the past. The twentieth-century enterprise was defined by Alfred P. Sloan, the legendary chairman of General Motors Corporation and the most influential professional manager of our time. His classic work, *My Years with General Motors,* set forth a management philosophy that has dominated U.S. corporations for decades. Company success, he argued, was based on efficiency and economies of scale—he never once mentioned the words creativity or flexibility. Large, efficient organizations, he theorized, must decentralize manufacturing while centralizing corporate policy and financial controls in hierarchical structures.

For decades, that model remained intact—even as managers challenged, debated, and refined it. Today, so many management gurus and corporate executives have abandoned Sloan's tenets that they are increasingly speaking of a "paradigm shift" in management thought—a dramatic change in the way we think about business problems and organizations.

Key Values. This new paradigm values teamwork over individualism, seeks global markets over domestic ones, and focuses on customers rather than on short-term profits. It views *time,* rather than a single-minded focus on *costs,* as the key competitive advantage. It recognizes the value of a multicultural workforce in an increasingly diverse labor

*Adapted from: Paradigms for postmodern managers, *Business Week*, 1992 Bonus Issue (Nov. 30), "Reinventing America," pp. 69 ff. Reprinted from November 30, 1992 issue of Business Week by special permission, copyright ©1992 by McGraw-Hill, Inc.

3

pool and customer base. The new form of organization is based on a network of alliances and partnerships, not Sloan's self-sufficient hierarchy. It is governed by an independent board with a broad view of the company's constituents—not just shareholders, but also employees, suppliers, customers, and the local community. A synopsis of these changes is presented in Table 1-1.

If GM once defined the shape of the old model, no existing organization serves as the prototype of this twenty-first-century corporation. And no company is likely to assume the ideal shape, because the successful company of the future will be an adaptive one in which change replaces stability as a key trait. What's right today isn't likely to be right tomorrow or the next day. Says a senior consultant, "There's an awareness that the re-invention of the corporation is going to go on forever. That's a new feeling. Not long ago, executives thought this thing called change was an event."

If no one corporation does it all, certain innovators have come up with exceptionally effective approaches to managing some aspects of change. These are the strategies that will help their practitioners thrive in the global economy of the twenty-first century. In the case conclusion at the end of the chapter, we will see what some of these strategies look like.

Challenges

1. In Table 1-1, which dimensions of the twenty-first-century prototype model require effective skills in managing people?

2. If change is viewed as a process rather than as an event, what must managers and employees do to deal effectively with change?

■ TABLE 1 . 1
REINVENTING THE CORPORATION

What shape will the twenty-first-century corporation take? How will its culture and the way it competes differ from today's model? Here are a dozen characteristics common to most organizations, and how many theorists and management experts expect them to change.

Current model		Twenty-first-century prototype
Hierarchy	ORGANIZATION	Network
Self-sufficient	STRUCTURE	Interdependencies
Security	WORKER EXPECTATIONS	Personal growth
Homogeneous	WORKFORCE	Culturally diverse
By individuals	WORK	By teams
Domestic	MARKETS	Global
Cost	ADVANTAGE	Time
Profits	FOCUS	Customers
Capital	RESOURCES	Information
Board of directors	GOVERNANCE	Varied constituents
What's affordable	QUALITY	No compromises
Autocratic	LEADERSHIP	Inspirational

3. If the twenty-first-century prototype model of organizations is to be successful, how must companies change their approach to managing people?

Questions This Chapter Will Help Managers Answer

1. Given the changes in workforce demographics, what can our firm do to be a beneficiary, rather than a victim, of these changes?

2. What people-related problems are likely to arise as a result of changes in the form of organizations? How can we avoid these problems?

3. How are the various factors of production affected by global competition? How is the role of the human resource professional different in a globally competitive environment?

4. How might the productivity of the workforce be affected by changes in the quality of work life?

5. As a general manager, what do I need to do in order to make total quality management work? What are the human resource management implications of such a change?

THE ENTERPRISE IS THE PEOPLE

Organizations are managed and staffed by people. Without people, organizations cannot exist. Indeed, the challenge, the opportunity, and also the frustration of creating and managing organizations frequently stem from the people-related problems that arise within them. People-related problems, in turn, frequently stem from the mistaken belief that people are all alike, that they can be treated identically. Nothing could be further from the truth. Like snowflakes, no two people are exactly alike, and everyone differs physically and psychologically from everyone else. Sitting in a sports arena, for example, will be tall people, small people, fat people, thin people, black people, white people, elderly people, young people, and so on. Even within any single physical category there will be enormous variability in psychological characteristics. Some will be outgoing, others reserved; some will be intelligent, others not so intelligent; some will prefer indoor activities, others outdoor activities. The point is that these differences demand attention so that each person can maximize his or her potential, so that organizations can maximize their effectiveness, and so that society as a whole can make the wisest use of its human resources.

Some managers place greater emphasis than others on developing employees' potential. For example, Mr. Konosuke Matsushita, founder of the giant electronics firm that bears his name and markets its products under the brand names National, Panasonic, Technics, and Quasar, was a lifelong believer in the notion that "the enterprise is the people." Here is a brief excerpt from his written philosophy of management.

> When my company was still small I often told my employees that when customers asked, "What does your company make?" they should answer, "Matsushita Electric is making men. We also make electrical appliances, but first and foremost our company makes men."[1]

This book is about managing people, the most vital of all resources, in work settings. Rather than focus exclusively on issues of concern to the human resource specialist, however, we will examine human resource management issues in terms of their impact on management in general. A changing world order has forced us to take a hard look at the ways we manage people. Research has shown time and again that human resource management practices can make an important, practical difference in terms of three key organizational outcomes: productivity, quality of work life, and profit. This is healthy. Each chapter in this book considers the impact of a different aspect of human resource management on these three broad themes. To study these impacts, we will look at the latest theory and research in each topical area, plus examples of actual company practices.

In this chapter we will examine some general issues related to productivity and quality of work life. In the next chapter we will focus on the relationship between competent human resource (HR) practices and profits. Let's begin by considering some basic ideas about organizations.

ORGANIZATIONS: WHY DO THEY EXIST AND HOW DO THEY WORK?

As our wants and needs grow, so do the ways of satisfying them. Consider the growth of the home-computer industry, for example, and how the firms within it are racing to deliver software—games, puzzles, educational exercises—to meet consumer demands for such products. None of our wants and needs is satisfied randomly or haphazardly. When you go to a store that sells computers, for example, the store will be open, and you will be able to buy the product of your choice even though the salesperson who helped you last time has the day off. In the process of satisfying needs and wants, *continuity* and *predictability* are essential in the delivery of goods and services. In modern society, continuity and predictability are made possible by *organizations*.

Some of the organizations that accommodate our wants and needs are fast-food restaurants, movie theaters, sporting goods stores, hospitals, universities, accounting firms, and antique stores, to name just a few. Each of these organizations exists because consumers demand its products or services, and because what must be done, the task to be accomplished, is too large or complex for one person to accomplish alone. So a number of people are gathered together, and each is assigned a part of the total task. It is most efficient to divide a large task (such as building a house) into its component parts so that specially qualified individuals can perform the subfunctions. *Specialization* by subfunction and *coordination* among all the tasks to be accomplished make the largest-scale task possible.

Although there are great differences among the organizations in our society, they also have much in common. Every organization is (1) made up of people (2) who perform specialized tasks (3) that are coordinated (4) to enhance the value or utility (5) of some good or service (6) that is wanted by and provided to a set of customers or clients.

The Traditional Approach to Organizing. In the simplest terms, a formal organization exists by virtue of two factors: the work it does and the technology it embraces to do that work. However, these are not the only elements of a formal organization. The key elements of a formal organization, in the traditional view, are related as follows (Figure 1-1). All organizations have objectives (e.g., to provide high-quality goods and services at competitive prices) that are based on some perceived unfulfilled demand in the outside environment. To attain these objectives, certain tasks must be done (e.g., processing canceled checks, assembling parts of an appliance, checking a

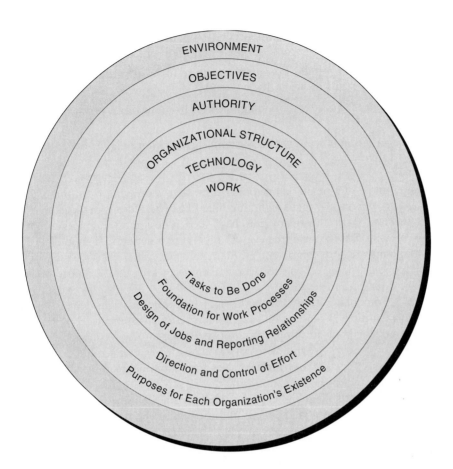

FIGURE 1-1
Key elements of formal organization, from specific to general.

patient's vital signs). Indeed, formal organizations are defined by the kind of work they do. Technology determines the nature of the work processes since it includes all the aspects of knowledge that are related to the attainment of a firm's objectives (e.g., employee skills, machines, and facilities). Organizational structure supports and facilitates technology by designing jobs and grouping tasks in order to optimize control, coordination, and productivity. This, for example, is why some firms are organized by function—production, marketing, sales, and distribution. To attain the benefits of specialization and efficiency, authority is used to ensure adequate role performance and direction of efforts. Some workers are bosses (in whom authority is formally vested by the organization), while others are subordinates. Today, these key elements are being redefined.

New Forms of Organization. In today's world of fast-moving global markets and fierce competition, the windows of opportunity are often frustratingly brief.[2] "Three-C" (i.e., command, control, compartmentalization) logic dominated industrial society's approach to organizational design throughout the nineteenth and twentieth centuries, but trends such as the following are accelerating the shift toward new forms of organization for the twenty-first:[3]

■ Smaller companies that employ fewer people
■ The shift from vertically integrated hierarchies to networks of specialists

- Technicians, ranging from computer repair persons to radiation therapists, replacing manufacturing operatives as the worker elite
- Pay tied less to a person's position or tenure in an organization and more to the market value of his or her skills
- A change in the paradigm of doing business from making a product to providing a service
- The redefinition of work itself: constant learning, more higher-order thinking, less nine-to-five

One example of a new organizational form that is evolving from these changes is the *modular corporation*—that's right, modular. The basic idea is to focus on a few core competencies—those a company does best, such as designing and marketing computers or copiers—and to outsource everything else to a network of suppliers.[4] If design and marketing are core competencies, then manufacturing or service units are modular components. They can be added or taken away with the flexibility of switching parts in a child's Lego set.

Does the modular corporation work? As an example, let's consider Dell Computer, currently returning 35 percent on shareholders' equity—up from 18 percent in 1991. Dell prospers by concentrating on only two aspects of the business: marketing and service. It owns no plants and leases two small factories to assemble computers from outsourced parts. Dell takes in $35 of sales for every dollar of fixed assets. For rival Compaq, the figure is $3.

Instead of spending heavily on plants, Dell lavishes money on training salespeople and service technicians and on furnishing them with the best computers, databases, and software. Those investments generate terrific returns. Dell sells IBM-compatible personal computers (PCs) in competition with Compaq, Digital, and IBM, but while others rely primarily on computer stores or dealers, Dell sells directly to consumers, who read about the products in newspaper ads or catalogues. Buyers call a toll-free number and place their orders with a staff of 560 well-trained salespeople. By eliminating intermediaries—and the retailer's typical 13 percent markup—Dell can charge lower prices than its rivals.

That's not all. Instead of selling a standard machine, Dell sells custom PCs. Customers can choose a color Mitsubishi monitor, a powerful Intel microprocessor, or a host of other options. Dell also offers everything you can buy in a computer store—650 software programs, a variety of modems, and other products—but here's the kicker: *it doesn't make or even stock the products.* Rather, it simply orders them from Merisel, a big distribution company. Merisel often delivers directly to the buyers, who find that dealing with a single supplier means fewer invoices and better service.[5]

Modular companies are flourishing in two industries that sell trendy products in a fast-changing marketplace: apparel (Nike and Reebok are modular pioneers) and electronics. Such companies work best when they accomplish two objectives: (1) collaborating smoothly with suppliers and (2) choosing the right specialty. Companies need to find loyal, reliable vendors they can trust with trade secrets, and they need the vision to identify what customers will want, not just what the company is technically good at.

Is this just a fad? Hardly. Such a streamlined structure fits today's tumultuous, fast-moving marketplace. According to the CEO of defense contractor and auto parts producer Rockwell International: "Without a doubt—focusing on a core competency—and outsourcing the rest—is a major trend of the 1990s."[6]

Organizations Need People, and People Need Organizations

Without people, organizations could not function. Even in highly automated plants, such as the one designed and built by Yamazaki (a large Japanese company that makes machine tools) to run smoothly using only 12 workers, people are nevertheless required to coordinate and control the plant's operations. Conversely, people need organizations so that they can satisfy their needs and wants, so that they can maintain their standard of living (by working in organizations), and so that modern society can continue to function.

These needs (organizations for people, people for organizations) will be ever more difficult to satisfy in the context of today's competitive business environment. That environment is defined by characteristics such as the following.

SOME KEY CHARACTERISTICS OF THE COMPETITIVE BUSINESS ENVIRONMENT OF THE 1990S

Demographic Changes and Increasing Cultural Diversity

From now until the end of the century, 88 percent of workforce growth in the United States will come from these groups: women, African Americans, and people of Hispanic or Asian origin, including immigrants. White men, meanwhile, account for most retirees and are leaving the workforce in record numbers. These trends are shown graphically in Figure 1-2.

With the aging of the baby boom generation (those born between 1946 and 1964), the growth of the labor force will slow, but its diversity will increase. While the number of men in the labor force is projected by the Bureau of Labor Statistics to increase by 16 percent between 1990 and 2005, the number of women is projected to increase by 26 percent, the number of African Americans by 32 percent, those of Asian origin by 74 percent, and those of Hispanic origin (who may be either dark- or light-

FIGURE 1-2
The changing labor pool.

THE CHANGING LABOR POOL

White men still dominate the workforce . . . . . . but more women and minorities are entering . . . . . . and more white males are leaving . . . . . . producing a more diverse workforce.

White men   White women   Minority men*   Minority women*

*Includes Hispanics

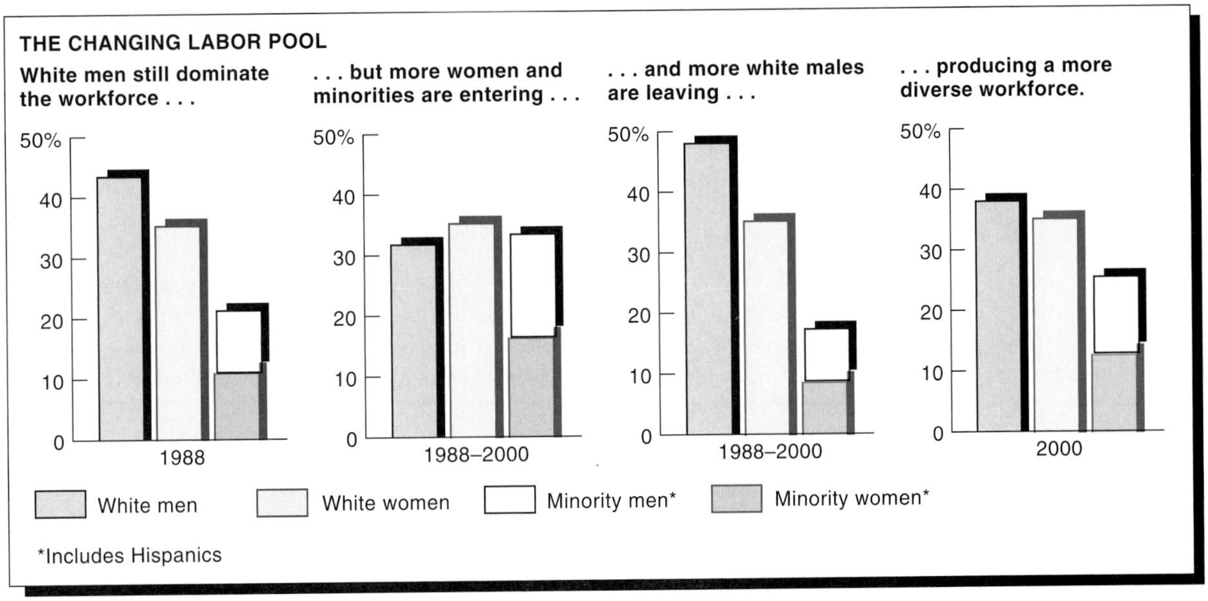

ETHICAL DILEMMA: SHOULD SCHOOLS TEACH ATTITUDES?[7]

A survey of small employers by the Committee for Economic Development revealed that their top priority in seeking applicants was "a sense of responsibility, self-discipline, pride, teamwork, and enthusiasm." Dedication to work and discipline in work habits were the biggest deficits that employers saw in high school graduates who were applying for jobs. Another survey by Towers Perrin found that the most common reason for rejecting job applicants (other than a lack of prior work experience) was the belief that they did not have the work attitudes and behaviors to adapt successfully to the work environment. The most common reasons for firing new hires were absenteeism and failure to adapt to the work environment. Only 9 percent of workers were dismissed because of difficulties in learning how to perform their jobs.

In the opinion of many employers, the most significant deficit in new entrants to the workforce is in their attitudes, not their skills. Indeed, the influential SCANS report (Secretary's Commission on Achieving Necessary Skills),[8] issued in 1991, identified a set of personal qualities (e.g., responsibility, sociability) that comprise one-third of the basic skills foundation required for a quality workforce.

Should the schools teach values? Opponents object on philosophical grounds (government-induced paternalism), and they question which set of values should be taught. Proponents counter that characteristics such as consistency and prosocial behavior ("going the extra mile" for the good of the organization or for those in it) are of broad benefit to individuals and society and do more than simply aid employers. What do you think?

skinned) by 75 percent, relative to their numbers in 1990. The overall increase in the labor force between 1990 and 2005 is projected to be 21 percent.[9]

These trends have two key implications for managers: (1) The reduced supply of entry-level workers will make finding and keeping employees a top priority in the decade ahead. Companies that once grudgingly shoehorned women and minorities into their ranks now find them indispensable.[10] (2) The task of managing a culturally diverse workforce, of harnessing the motivation and efforts of a wide variety of workers, will present managers with one of their biggest challenges throughout the 1990s and beyond.

The Crisis in Education

Consider this fact: between now and the year 2000 more than 50 percent of all new jobs will require an education beyond high school, and of those, 30 percent will require a college degree.[11] Unfortunately, however, dropout rates in U.S. high schools range from 10 to over 50 percent! Not surprisingly, therefore, a 4-year federal study of more than 26,000 Americans revealed a bleak picture. More than 40 million American adults are functionally illiterate, which means that they cannot write a bank check, fill out a job application, or identify a deduction for Social Security on a wage statement. Some 40 million others are barely competent in those skills. While some of these figures can be attributed to immigrants whose native language is not English, if current trends continue, by the year 2000, half of adult Americans will be functionally illiterate.[12]

Although in the last decade the overall education level of Americans has increased in terms of schooling and even fundamental literacy, so also have the demands of the workplace. As a group, therefore, the American workforce is simply not keeping pace with the kinds of skills required in the new economy.

U.S. firms are feeling these effects now. Thus 20 to 40 percent of job applicants at Motorola flunk an entry-level exam that requires seventh- to ninth-grade English and fifth- to seventh-grade mathematics. Southwestern Bell processed more than 15,000 applications last year just to find 3700 people to test. As a manager at Absorbent Cotton Company, a small business in Valley Park, Missouri, commented: "You look at the parade of people who are completely unqualified to hold even a simple job and you think, 'This is the future?' "[13]

To deal with these problems, business is following two broad strategies. One of these is illustrated by the Boston Compact, an agreement in which 600 Boston-area companies joined with the public schools to form a compact that provides jobs to be reserved for high school graduates who meet academic and attendance requirements. Seven other cities followed Boston's example and now have similar compacts in existence.[14]

A second strategy is in-house training for current or prospective employees. Thus Motorola spends an average of $1350 per person per year for six basic skills courses to get workers to a point where they can be retrained. Planters Nuts in Suffolk, Virginia, spent $40,000 to improve the reading and writing skills of 48 employees. Unisys in Mission Viejo, California, spent $150,000 to teach 125 workers how to read, write, and speak English. Hewlett-Packard spent $22,000 at its Spokane, Washington, plant to teach high school mathematics to 30 production supervisors. These investments are relatively modest. Polaroid, on the other hand, spent $700,000 at its Cambridge, Massachusetts, operation to teach basic English and mathematics to 1000 new and veteran employees.[15]

Although both of these strategies are expensive, the alternative—not having a competent workforce that will enable firms to compete in world markets—is unthinkable. For U.S. business, this is a "must-win" situation. Our standard of living and our very way of life are at stake.

Global Competition

As citizens of the twentieth century, we have witnessed more change in our daily existence and in our environment than anyone else who ever walked the planet. But if you think the pace of change was fast in this century, fasten your seat belts. The twenty-first century will be even more complex, fast-paced, and turbulent. It will also be very different.

Just as wars—two world wars, the Korean conflict, Vietnam, and Desert Storm—dominated the geopolitical map of the twentieth century, economics will rule the twenty-first. The competition that is normal and inevitable among nations increasingly will be played out not in aggression or war, but in the economic sphere. The weapons used will be those of commerce: growth rates, investments, trade blocs, imports and exports.[16]

What's behind all of this change? Global competition—the single most powerful economic fact of life in the 1990s. In the relatively sheltered era of the 1960s, a mere 6 percent of the U.S. economy was exposed to international competition. In the 1980s, that number zoomed past 70 percent, and it will keep climbing.[17] U.S. exports now generate one in six jobs; as recently as 1986, it was only one in eight.[18]

To be sure, the fall of communism has accelerated the forces of global competition.

As an ideology, communism began to unravel with the June 1989 elections in Poland—the first Communist state to evolve into a democracy. Subsequently, Communist regimes all across central and eastern Europe began to fall like dominoes.

The results of accelerated global competition have been almost beyond comprehension—free political debate throughout the former Soviet empire, democratic reforms in South and Central America, the integration of the 12-member European Community on January 1, 1993, peace pacts between Israel and her neighbors, the signing of the North American Free Trade Agreement, and an explosion of free-market entrepreneurship in southern China. In short, the free markets and free labor markets that we in the United States have enjoyed throughout our national history have now become a global passion.[19]

In fact, as nations around the world make the transition from wartime to peacetime economies, from industrial societies to information-based societies, we are witnessing profound, wrenching structural changes brought about by a number of factors. In the United States, four such factors are:

1. *The defense contraction.* Hundreds of thousands of high-wage production workers are being displaced at a rate that is taking an enormous personal toll on the workers and their families. According to the Bureau of Labor Statistics, an estimated 2 million civilian jobs are expected to be lost as a result of the reduction in federal expenditures for defense between 1987 and 1997. This figure is conservative, because it does not include jobs that would be affected by the so-called "multiplier effect," such as retail jobs in communities where military bases are closed.[20] Many with specialized defense industry skills will be structurally unemployed and will require retraining on a massive scale. For example, there isn't much demand in civilian life for people who make tanks, submarines, or complex weapons systems.

2. *Falling real wages.* As global competition has increased and productivity growth has slowed, Americans have suffered a steady decline in their average income for nearly two decades. After adjustment for inflation, the real incomes of U.S. workers have declined about 13 percent from 1972 to 1992.[21] In short, over the past 20 years, economic growth has been a spectator sport for most working Americans.

3. *The health care cost explosion.* The costs of this runaway system have been rising at triple the rate of inflation, costing U.S. companies an average of 26 percent of their net income.[22] The per capita cost? Over $2500 for every man, woman, and child in the United States. This is more than twice the level of most of the world's industrialized economies, it adds 15 percent to the sticker price of every new car produced in the United States, and it single-handedly threatens to wipe out all the cost advantages achieved by Ford and Chrysler as a result of employee involvement, total quality management, and improved manufacturing processes.

4. *Downsizing.* Some of the terms used to describe this phenomenon (i.e., the planned elimination of positions or jobs) are actually oxymorons—building down, deorganization, growth in reverse—but they all mean the same thing: layoffs. Across the total economy in the mid-1980s, managers were actually more vulnerable than nonmanagers to displacement as a result of streamlining and plant closings.[23] In manufacturing, 70 percent of the jobs lost since 1989 have been white-collar jobs.[24] As a result of flattening organizational hierarchies and new developments in information technology, most of those white-collar jobs are gone for good. Across the total economy, more than 6 million people lost permanent jobs between 1987 and 1993.[25] In good times as well as bad, companies large and small are slashing jobs at a pace never before seen in American economic history.

Unfortunately, many of the downsizings are reactive rather than proactive.[26] *Reactive downsizing* is characterized by processes such as the following:

- It occurs in a compressed time frame.
- Companies use simplistic criteria (e.g., across-the-board cuts) to reduce their workforces.
- They fail to consider strategically relevant competencies.
- The overall process is unmanaged.

In contrast, *proactive downsizing* is:

- Viewed as a long-term process that incorporates a number of strategies (e.g., attrition, voluntary redeployment, and involuntary redeployment)
- Linked to long-range, strategic objectives
- Targeted to preserve distinctive and critical competencies
- Carefully monitored through HR interventions

Perhaps the most disquieting result of downsizing is that our views of organizational life, managing as a career, hard work, rewards, and loyalty will never be the same.[27]

Impact and Effect of the Economic Changes

These structural burdens have made the most profound impact in terms of jobs. The highly touted job gains of the 1980s were, for the most part, in low-wage positions paying $250 per week or less. More than 25 percent of the U.S. workforce now holds this class of job, up from less than 19 percent in 1979. Laid-off workers who must return to the job market often must take huge pay cuts. According to the director of human resources for General Motors, "Only 10 percent are likely to find a job as good as they had before."[28] As a result, both their spending power and their standard of living have dropped.

What's happening here? In a nutshell, as an executive in the pharmaceutical industry noted recently, we're moving from an economy in which there are a lot of hard-working people to one in which there are fewer, smarter-working people.[29] Jobs aren't being lost *temporarily* because of a recession; rather, they are being wiped out *permanently* as a result of computerization, improved machinery, and new ways of organizing work. Most of the job losses are occurring at large firms. Only 16 percent of job losses in the early 1990s were from small businesses, which employ 57 percent of Americans. Not surprisingly, therefore, laid-off executives are gravitating to four areas: franchising, consulting, new start-ups, and small and family-owned businesses.[30]

In fact, some industries, such as computers and computer software, now swing through technological change so rapidly that they have become basically unstable. No one quite knows which companies, much less which employees, will be around next year. Such an environment hardly encourages corporate loyalty and could breed attitudes that actually diminish productivity.

Here's the problem: displaced workers must now reintegrate themselves into an economy that increasingly rewards only highly skilled labor. What has happened to the United States is not that people are a lot less educated than they were 20 years ago, it's that we live in a very different world. New technology, the pace of change, and global competition have "raised the bar"—that is, jobs require a higher level of skill development.

While part of the problem of increasing productivity is on the supply side—the quality of the workforce—the more subtle story is on the demand side. How can industry upgrade jobs, making them more challenging and better paying?

Many of the jobs in the new high-tech economy can be divided into two groups: routine work—entering data, following rote manufacturing systems, and the like—or far more demanding jobs requiring problem-solving skills, diagnostic skills, teamwork, and decision making. Machines can replace boring, repetitive jobs, but society's challenge is to reemploy the humans at more rewarding work.[31] This challenge is even more compelling, given the global competition for high-quality workers.

Global Competition for High-Quality Workers. As every advanced economy becomes global, a nation's most important competitive asset becomes the skills and cumulative learning of its workforce.[32] Globalization, almost by definition, makes this true. Virtually all developed countries can design, produce, and distribute goods and services equally well and equally fast. Every factor of production other than workforce skills can be duplicated anywhere in the world. Capital moves freely across international boundaries, seeking the lowest costs. State-of-the-art factories can be erected anywhere. The latest technologies move from computers in one nation, up to satellites parked in space, and back down to computers in another nation—all at the speed of electronic impulses. It's all fungible—capital, technology, raw materials, information—all except for one thing, the most critical part, the one element that is unique about a nation: its workforce. A workforce that is knowledgeable and skilled at doing complex things keeps a company competitive and attracts foreign investment.

In fact, the relationship forms a virtuous circle: well-trained workers attract global corporations, which invest and give the workers good jobs; the good jobs, in turn, generate additional training and experience. Let's face it: regardless of the shifting political winds in Tokyo, Berlin, Washington, Beijing, or Budapest, the shrunken globe is here to stay. Today Tokyo is closer than the town 100 miles away was 30 years ago (after all, routine long-distance phone use didn't begin until the 1970s).

And tomorrow? Our networks of suppliers, producers, distributors, service companies, and customers will be so tightly linked that we literally won't be able to tell one locale from another. No political force can stop, or even slow down for long, the borderless economy. The lesson for managers is clear: be ready or be lost.[33]

We noted at the beginning of this section that people make organizations go. How the people are selected, trained, and managed determines to a large extent how successful an organization will be. As you can certainly appreciate by now, the task of managing people in today's world of work is particularly challenging in light of the changes we have discussed. Indeed, one of the most pressing concerns that organizations face is productivity improvement.

PRODUCTIVITY: WHAT IS IT?

A popular buzzword in American industry today is "productivity." Although people talk about it as though they know precisely what it means, it is surprisingly difficult to define and measure, especially in highly diversified firms. How can or should we compare the productivity of a secretary whose boss dictates letters that take hours to edit against one whose boss produces clean copy? How can we measure accurately the productivity of a salesperson who fills her order book every day, but with customers whose subsequent service requirements far outweigh the investment returned?[34] What about a computer factory, where every year the products improve and the prices drop, or a hospital, where no one is even sure what output means? Even more perplexing, how does one identify the productivity improvement associated with outsourcing— that is, turning to outside service firms for work that ultimately raises output?[35]

Theorists generally agree that productivity concepts, definitions, and measures are arbitrary. Their relevance depends on the purpose for which they are developed—for example, comparing individuals, work groups, companies, or the competitive positions of nations.[36]

In general, however, productivity is a measure of the output of goods and services relative to the input of labor, material, and equipment. The more productive an industry, the better its competitive position because its unit costs are lower. When productivity increases, businesses can pay higher wages without boosting inflation. That is the way standards of living improve.[37] Improving productivity simply means getting more out of what is put in. It does not mean increasing production through the addition of resources, such as time, money, materials, or people. It is doing better with what you have. Improving productivity is not working harder, it is working smarter. Today's world demands that we do more with less—fewer people, less money, less time, less space, and fewer resources in general. These ideas are shown graphically in Figure 1-3.

Productivity Growth and National Competitiveness

The United States led the world in annual rate of productivity improvement for decades, but since the 1950s its productivity growth rate has slowed, while Japan and other industrial nations have kept gaining. Thus, in 1972, the average Japanese worker was 63 percent as productive as his American counterpart; by 1988 he was 80 per-

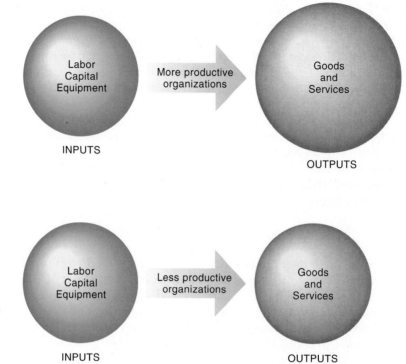

FIGURE 1-3
More productive
organizations get more
goods and services out of a
given amount of labor,
capital, and equipment
than do less productive
organizations.

cent as productive. In and of itself, a contracting lead is not so worrisome, because productivity growth rates tend to converge as countries that were late to industrialize (such as Japan and South Korea) catch up. Of far greater concern is a fall in the growth rate of productivity, which plagued the United States until the early 1990s. Consider what this implies.

Beginning in the late nineteenth century, for example, the yearly rise in the productivity of England, then the world's foremost industrial nation, was just slightly less (1 percent) than that of its industrial rivals, mainly the United States and Germany. But by the mid-twentieth century that seemingly small difference proved to be enough to tumble England from its previously undisputed industrial prominence.[38]

In the United States, productivity growth slowed to an average of 1.3 percent from 1970 to 1990. However, since the bottom of the recession in 1991, productivity gains have been outpacing overall economic growth. In 1992, productivity rose nearly 3 percent, its best showing in 20 years (see Figure 1-4). In part, this was due to the fact that, after adjusting for inflation and productivity gains, employers spent 3.8 percent less in 1992 for pay and benefits per unit of output than they did in 1988.[39] Most encouraging, though, was that service-sector productivity finally sprang to life, matching the gains in manufacturing in the 1980s. The $1 trillion that U.S. businesses invested in information technology throughout the 1980s may be paying off as databases and computer networks perform work faster, better, and more cheaply.

Increasing Productivity in Services. Certainly it is easier to measure the output of the blue-collar sector than it is to measure the output of people who work in marketing, engineering, human resources, and the rest of the white-collar sector, where outputs may be less tangible. Tangible or not, information technology, coupled with the redesign of work, has led to some spectacular gains.

Aetna Life & Casualty Co., for example, has completely overhauled its policy-issuing process. In 1992, Aetna had 22 business centers, with a staff of 3000. It took about 15 days to get a basic policy out of the office, in part because 60 different employees had to handle the application. Now the operation has been pared down to 700 employees in 4 centers—and customers get their policies within 5 days. How? Because a single rep sitting at a personal computer tied to a network can perform all the work necessary—accessing an actuarial database, for example—to process an application immediately. When all the relevant information is gathered, the policy is passed along the network to headquarters in Hartford, where it's printed and mailed within a day.[40]

Like Aetna, many companies are rethinking completely how they produce goods or deliver services to their customers. Their approach, called "total quality management" (TQM), may well be a long-term solution to the problems of productivity enhancement and global competitiveness. In the next section, therefore, we will consider TQM in more detail.

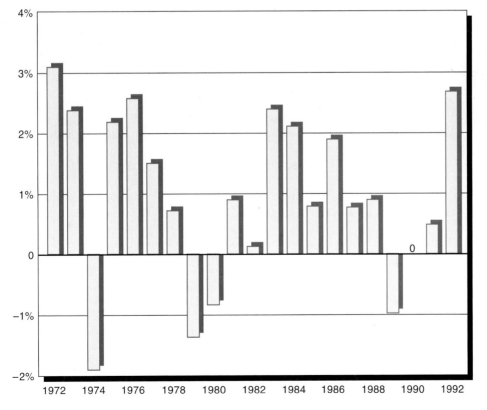

FIGURE 1-4
Annual percentage change in nonfarm business sector productivity: 1972–1992. (*Source*: U.S. Department of Labor.)

TOTAL QUALITY MANAGEMENT (TQM)

For many years, the traditional way of achieving quality was through systematic final inspection. This approach is called "inspecting-in quality." Intense foreign competition in general, and Japanese competition in particular, has led some U.S. companies to adopt TQM practices that are prevention-based. This approach is often referred to as "building-in quality."[41] "Quality" is the extent to which products and services conform to customer requirements. The Federal Quality Institute defines quality as meeting the customer's requirements the first time and every time, where customers can be internal as well as external to the organization. For example, products or services may flow to a person at the next desk or work area rather than to people outside of the immediate organization. Many managers once saw quality in terms of what they could afford. Now they see it as an issue on which they can't afford to compromise. TQM, a philosophy and a set of guiding principles that represent the foundation of a continuously improving organization, includes seven broad components:[42]

1. A *focus on the customer* or user of a product or service, ensuring that the customer's needs and expectations are satisfied consistently

2. *Active leadership* from top executives to establish quality as a fundamental value to be incorporated into a company's management philosophy

3. *Quality concepts* (e.g., statistical process control or computer-assisted design, engineering, and manufacturing) that are thoroughly integrated throughout all activities of a company

4. A *corporate culture*, established and reinforced by top executives, that involves all employees in contributing to quality improvements

5. A *focus on employee involvement*, teamwork, and training at all levels in order to strengthen employee commitment to continuous quality improvement

6. An *approach to problem solving* that is based on continuously gathering, evaluating, and acting on facts and data in a systematic manner

7. *Recognition of suppliers* as full partners in the quality management process

Each of these components has significant implications for human resource management, as shown in Table 1-2.[43]

Table 1-2 shows that HRM practices in a TQM organization must "fit" a corporate culture built on the shared assumptions of employee dedication to quality and customer service. Here's how the chairwoman of Xerox's Quality Forum described the need for such a cultural transformation:[44]

TQM requires a change in organizational culture, a fundamental change in the way individuals and groups approach their work and their roles in the organization, that is, from an environment of distrust and fear of reprisal to one of openness and trust where creativity can flourish; from working as individuals to working as teams; from protection of organizational turfs to the breakdown of departmental barriers; from an autocratic management style of direction and control to a softer style of team leader and coach; from power concentrated at the top to power shared with employees; from a focus on results to a focus on continuous improvement of the processes that deliver the results; and finally a change from making decisions based on gut-feel to an analytic, fact-based approach to management.

■ **TABLE 1 . 2**

IMPACT ON HUMAN RESOURCE MANAGEMENT SYSTEMS OF CHANGING FROM
TRADITIONAL PRACTICES TO TQM

Corporate context dimension	Traditional paradigm	Total quality paradigm
Corporate culture	Individualism Differentiation Autocratic leadership Profits Productivity	Collective efforts Cross-functional work Coaching/enabling Customer satisfaction Quality
Human resource characteristics	Traditional paradigm	Total quality paradigm

Communications	Top down	Top down,
		    horizontal, lateral,
		    multidirectional

Voice and involvement	Employment-at-will Suggestion systems	Due process Quality circles Attitude surveys
Job design	Efficiency Productivity Standard procedures Narrow span of control Specific job descriptions	Quality Customization Innovation Wide span of control Autonomous work teams Empowerment
Training	Job-related skills Functional, technical Productivity	Broad range of skills Cross-functional Diagnostic, problem solving Productivity and quality
Performance	Individual goals	Team goals

Measurement and
    evaluation
	Supervisory review
	
	Emphasize financial
	    performance
		Customer, peer, and supervisory
		    review
		Emphasize quality and service

Rewards	Competition for
	    individual merit
	    increases and benefits
		Team/group based rewards
		Financial rewards, financial
		    and nonfinancial recognition

Health and safety	Treat problems	Prevent problems Safety programs Wellness programs Employee assistance

Selection/promotion,
    career development
	Selected by manager
	Narrow job skills
	Promotion based on
	    individual
	    accomplishment
	Linear career path
		Selected by peers
		Problem-solving skills
		Promotion based on
		    group facilitation
		Horizontal career path

Source: R. Blackburn & B. Rosen. Total quality and human resources management: Lessons learned from Baldridge Award–winning companies, *Academy of Management Executive, 7*(3), 1993, 51.

To engineer such a massive change in corporate culture requires a radical break with tradition. Table 1-2 highlights these changes by contrasting traditional and TQM paradigms with respect to the following human resource systems: communications, voice and involvement, job design, training, performance, measurement and evaluation, rewards, health and safety, selection/promotion, and career development.

To monitor such changes, managers might consider using the following checklist, answering each question on a five-point "Agree/Disagree" scale:[45]

- Top management initiates and supports a vision of a total quality culture.
- This vision is clarified and communicated to the remainder of the organization in a variety of ways.
- Systems that allow upward and lateral communications are developed, implemented, and reinforced.
- TQM training is provided to all employees, and top management actively supports it.
- Employee involvement or participation programs are in place.
- Processes that bring multiple perspectives to bear on quality issues are working well (e.g., self-managing work groups).
- Jobs are designed so that employees are empowered to make quality-based decisions at their discretion.
- Rather than focusing exclusively on past performance, managers use performance reviews to find out what they can do to assist employees in their future job-related quality efforts.
- Compensation systems reflect team-related quality contributions, including mastery of additional skills.
- Nonfinancial recognition systems for individuals and work groups reinforce small wins as well as big victories in the quest for total quality.
- Employees at all levels can make known their concerns, ideas, and reactions to quality initiatives (e.g., open-door policies, skip-level policies, attitude surveys).
- Safety and health issues are addressed proactively, rather than reactively, and they incorporate employee participation.
- Recruitment, selection, promotion, and career development programs reflect the new reality of working and managing in a TQM environment.

How Does TQM Affect Company Performance?

A General Accounting Office study of 20 large and small (500 or fewer employees) companies found no "cookbook" approach to implementing a TQM system. Nevertheless, these companies improved their performance in about 2.5 years, on average (range: 1–5 years). The study considered four types of performance indicators: employee relations, operating procedures, customer satisfaction, and financial performance.[46]

In terms of five employee relations indicators, all-company averages changed as follows on an annual basis:

■ Job satisfaction: +1.4 percent
■ Attendance: +0.1 percent
■ Voluntary employee turnover: −6 percent
■ Lost workdays due to injury and illness: −1.8 percent
■ Number of quality-improvement suggestions: +16.6 percent

In terms of eight operating indicators, all-company averages changed as follows on an annual basis:

■ Reliability of products or services (i.e., freedom from error or breakdown while in use by the customer): +11.3 percent
■ Percentage of on-time delivery: +4.7 percent
■ Order processing time: −12 percent
■ Errors or defects: −10.3 percent
■ Product lead time (cycle time, or time in years from design of a new product or service until it is available to the customer): −5.8 percent
■ Inventory turnover rate: +7.2 percent
■ Costs of avoiding quality failures or defects (e.g., by inspection, testing, training): −9 percent
■ Cost savings as a result of employee suggestions: $1.3 million to $116 million per year

All-company averages for three customer satisfaction indicators changed as follows on an annual basis:

■ Overall customer satisfaction: +2 percent
■ Customer complaints: −11.6 percent
■ Customer retention: +1 percent

Finally, in terms of financial performance, all-company averages changed as follows on an annual basis:

■ Average increase in market share: +13.7 percent
■ Sales per employee: +8.6 percent
■ Return on assets (earnings before interest and taxes divided by average gross assets): +1.3 percent
■ Return on sales (earnings before interest and taxes divided by net sales): +0.4 percent

We hasten to add a note of caution, namely, that the profitability of a particular company can also be affected by a variety of external factors. These might include, for example, the general state of the economy; supply-and-demand conditions within a particular industry; and, for exporters, the relative value of the U.S. dollar in foreign markets. Nevertheless, the overall impact of TQM on long-term company performance is encouraging. We emphasize "long-term," because one lesson is very clear: *managers must recognize that it will take time to achieve sustained operating results.* Short-term profit is not the objective.

Problems in Implementing TQM

TQM is no "magic bullet" for productivity problems. In fact, changing to a TQM-oriented culture, according to industry experts, often is a frustrating and expensive process characterized by high front-end costs, extensive training time, possible restructuring of jobs and departments, and a complete shift away from short-term perspectives. Getting CEOs and bottom-line-oriented financial officers to do that requires strong motivation.[47]

To appreciate the scope of the problem—and the potential perils—consider what AT&T Global Business Communication Systems had to do in 2 years as part of its change effort. It rewrote job descriptions for hundreds of people, invented new recognition and reward systems, revamped its computer system, retrained massively, and made extensive changes in its financial reporting systems, its systems for writing proposals and contracts, and its approach to dealing with suppliers, manufacturing, installation, and billing.[48] Whew!

It should be clear by now that an all-out commitment to quality is anything but simple. It requires companies to uproot entrenched habits and business methods and virtually start over. Further, no single formula works for everyone. In fact, simply playing "copycat," trying to apply what world-class quality leaders such as Xerox Corp. are doing, may be a big waste of time and money. That's one insight uncovered by the International Quality Study, a two-year research project by Ernst & Young and the American Quality Foundation.[49] That study examined 945 management practices in 580 organizations in four industries on three continents (North America, Europe, and Asia).

Perhaps the major finding of the International Quality Study is that the changes necessary to master quality vary depending on a firm's experience and level of performance with respect to its quality-improvement efforts. Take employee involvement, for example. For firms that are novices in this area, the advice from the study is clear: train heavily, promote teamwork, but forget self-managed work teams, which take lots of preparation. Limit employee empowerment to resolving customer complaints. For journey-level firms in the quality-improvement area, the advice is to encourage employees at every level to find ways to do their jobs better—and to simplify core operations. Set up a separate quality-assurance staff. For master-level firms, the best advice is to use self-managed, multiskilled teams that focus on horizontal processes such as logistics and product development. Limit training, mainly to new hires. This kind of an approach, what we might call a "contingency model" of quality improvement efforts, is a sensible way to proceed.

PRODUCTIVITY IMPROVEMENT: LESSONS WE HAVE LEARNED

Among the hundreds of economists, think tanks, professors, politicians, and management consultants who ponder this issue full time, there is a surprising convergence of views, regardless of their political persuasion. Most would agree that we need:

- Solutions designed to have some definite payoff in the long run, whether or not they pay off immediately.

- Steps by the government to allow and encourage businesses to make capital investments and to be more flexible as a result of less government regulation.

- To make both unionized and nonunionized workers, as well as managers, aware that their rewards ultimately depend on production.

- Recognition that there is no "quick fix" approach. Worker training, work redesign, product reengineering—all must be linked to the priorities of the business plan and integrated into a comprehensive productivity improvement strategy.

- Recognition of the crucial importance of continuous improvements in quality (an important aspect of productivity improvement) through prevention. Doing so requires a reshaping of attitudes from the boardroom to the loading dock, so that quality becomes more important than simply getting a product out the door.

- Public investment in highways, bridges, railways, and airports, which will raise productivity by reducing transportation delays and costs.

Labor Secretary Robert Reich described the challenge clearly: "If we have an adequately educated and trained workforce and a state-of-the-art infrastructure linking them together and with the rest of the world, then global capital will come here to create good jobs. If we don't, the only way global capital will be invested here is if we promise low wages."[50]

Is this just academic theory? Hardly. Well-trained trades workers who can adapt to change are a big attraction to the more than 200 German companies that have invested over $4 billion in North and South Carolina.[51] As we noted earlier, greater productivity benefits organizations directly (i.e., it improves their competitive position relative to that of rivals), and it benefits workers indirectly (e.g., in higher pay and improved purchasing power). But many workers want to see a tighter connection between working smarter and the tangible and psychological rewards they receive from doing their jobs well. They want to see significant improvements in their quality of work life.

QUALITY OF WORK LIFE: WHAT IS IT?

There are two ways of looking at what *quality of work life (QWL)* means.[52] One way equates QWL with a set of objective organizational conditions and practices (e.g., promotion-from-within policies, democratic supervision, employee involvement, safe working conditions). An example of this approach is shown in Figure 1-5. The other way equates QWL with employees' perceptions that they are safe, relatively well satisfied, and able to grow and develop as human beings. This way relates QWL to the degree to which the full range of human needs is met.

In many cases these two views merge: workers who like their organizations and the ways their jobs are structured will feel that their work fulfills them. In such cases, either way of looking at one's quality of work life will lead to a common determination of whether a good QWL exists. However, because of the differences between people and because the second view is quite subjective—it concedes, for example, that not everyone finds such things as democratic decision making and enriched jobs to be important components of a good QWL[53]—we will define QWL in terms of employees' perceptions of their physical and mental well-being at work.

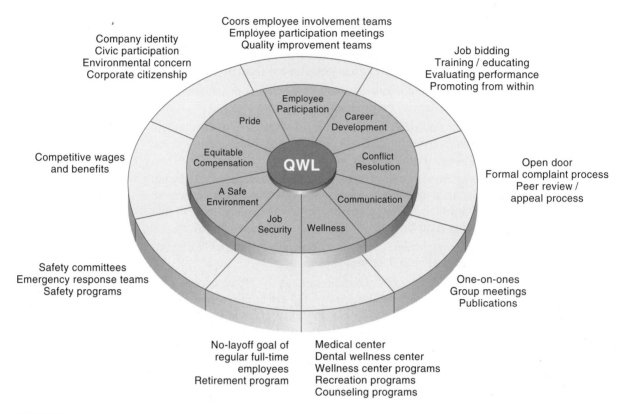

FIGURE 1-5
Quality of work life through quality relationships, as practiced by the Adolph Coors Company of Golden, Colorado.

Current Status of Quality of Work Life Efforts

In theory, QWL is simple—it involves giving workers the opportunity to make decisions about their jobs, the design of their workplaces, and what they need to make products or to deliver services most effectively. It requires managers to treat workers with dignity on the job. Its focus is on employees and management operating the business together.

In practice, its best illustrations can be found in the auto, steel, food, electronics, and consumer products industries, in plants characterized by self-managing work teams, flat organizational structures, and challenging roles for all. It requires a willingness to share power, extensive training for workers and managers, and considerable patience by all involved. Workers must get to know the basics of cost, quality, profits, losses, and customer satisfaction by being exposed to more than a narrowly defined job. Managers must come to understand their new role: leaders, helpers, and information gatherers. None of this is simple or easily done.

One reviewer found that QWL efforts often require 3 to 10 years or more to become fully integrated into a business.[54] Here are some other things that successful QWL efforts require. Do you see the parallel with TQM efforts?

- Managers must become leaders and coaches, not bosses and dictators.
- Openness and trust are necessary. QWL can't be used as a tool to break unions or keep them out. It must remain separate from the collective bargaining contract. And it can't be used by unions as a tool against management.
- Information typically held by management alone must be shared, and suggestions made by nonmanagers must be taken seriously.
- QWL must change continually and go forward from initial problem solving to an actual partnership between management and workers.
- QWL cannot be mandated unilaterally by management.

PARTICIPATION: THE ESSENCE OF QUALITY OF WORK LIFE

As we have noted, the common denominator of QWL experiments is joint worker-management participation for the purpose of identifying problems and opportunities in the work environment, making decisions, and implementing changes. The results of these undertakings are beginning to appear in the literature.[55] Critics say that participation will not work over time because it requires managers to give up too much power; this is why 75 percent of all such programs failed in the early 1980s.[56] On the other hand, advocates point to a study that examined 101 industrial companies and found that the participatively managed companies outscored the others on 13 of 14 financial measures.[57] The advocates argue that we are just beginning to understand what is required in order to bring about large-scale social change in organizations.

The term "participation" is a broad one, for it includes at least five types of participative methods:

1. Employee problem-solving groups
2. Union-management cooperative projects
3. Participative work design
4. Gain sharing, profit sharing, and Scanlon plans (these are methods for sharing profits with employees according to some formula)
5. Worker ownership or employee stock ownership

Do these methods work? In our next section we will consider the evidence.

Does Participation Work?

Although it is still premature to state which approaches are definitely effective and which are not, it is possible to detect trends in the emerging literature. Some of these are as follows:[58]

1. Worker participation programs that are tied directly to financial incentives for employees tend to result in productivity increases for the organization. For example, of 72 companies using Improshare[59]—production standards based on time-and-motion studies, plus a sharing of productivity gains 50/50 between employees and the company—38 companies were nonunion, and 34 were represented by 18 different international unions. The average gain in productivity over all companies using the plan after 1 year was 22.4 percent. Productivity gains tended to be larger if workers

were provided with training and information; gains tended to be smaller, nonexistent, or negative (that is, productivity deteriorated) if workers perceived that there was "nothing in it" for them.

For example, at Whirlpool's Benton Harbor, Michigan, plant, interactive training designed to improve quality, coupled with a gain-sharing plan, helped produce a 19 percent gain in productivity between 1988 and 1992, from 92.8 parts manufactured per worker hour to 110.6. Moreover, the number of parts rejected sank to a world-class 10 per million from 837 per million. To each of the plant's 265 employees, that meant an extra $2700 of pay in 1992, lifting the average blue-collar compensation to more than $26,400. And that has changed the workers' attitude from contentiousness to cooperation.[60]

2. Participation programs are generally perceived positively by those who directly participate but negatively by workers who do not.[61] In one case nonparticipating union members pressured management to terminate a large union-management work redesign effort because of perceived salary inequities.[62]

3. Participative strategies that alter the job itself tend to have a lasting impact on attitudes and productivity if the new job involves substantial increases in responsibility and autonomy. Worker participation in problem solving that does not alter the job itself, or job rotational schemes that do not add responsibility and challenge, tend to motivate employees only over the short term.[63]

4. Worker participation programs die out eventually if the organization does not change in a manner consistent with the democratic values and behaviors of the participation programs. Here are some of the ways to kill worker participation:

- Middle and upper management cease responding to workers' suggestions after the initial enthusiasm, if there was any, is over.

- The pay system fails to acknowledge the new activities and contributions of workers.

- Supervisors resent the increased attention to workers and undermine the program by not cooperating with the groups.

- Participating workers develop distorted perceptions of their own promotability and value to the company, and they become disillusioned when they do not advance.

- Many U.S. organizations embody a hierarchical, departmentalized structure, a set of management assumptions, and a set of norms that discourage employees from taking initiative, accepting responsibility, and cooperating with one another.[64] The unlearning of these assumptions and norms requires a conscious attempt to alter the culture of the organization, something that organizations such as IBM, Cummins Engine, and Westinghouse are systematically setting out to do.

5. Many participative programs underestimate the amount of training and learning necessary to support worker involvement. Workers need exposure to problem solving, group processes, and business concepts. Managers need training in the listening and feedback skills necessary to work with groups of workers who are taking responsibility for decision making. Both workers and managers need to learn the basic interpersonal skills necessary to treat others with dignity and respect.[65] Participation as an effort to improve QWL requires that managers treat lower-level employees as

mature individuals, for participation implies a redistribution of power within the organization.

6. Workers sometimes reject the participation program. Often this reaction reflects the official position of a union, which sees a threat to its long-term strength in dealing with management. Union and nonunion employees often perceive participation programs as management manipulation in which workers are expected to contribute something for nothing.[66] Managers frequently perceive a participation program as something they are doing "for" the workers. Workers detect this attitude and judge it to be patronizing at best, deceptive at worst.

7. There are interactions among different forms of participation. Thus it appears that informal participation works best when other formal mechanisms for participation already exist.

8. Performance or productivity effectiveness is associated with participation that is direct (as opposed to indirect through representatives) and long-term.[67]

IMPACT OF IMPROVED PRODUCTIVITY AND QUALITY OF WORK LIFE ON THE BOTTOM LINE

Attempts to enhance worker productivity through sharing rewards and implementing joint programs may well be worth the effort. To appreciate this, consider the contrast between management actions at General Motors and Ford during the 1980s. General Motors experienced tense relations with its workers and only modest gains in productivity, in part because management inconsistency and plunging market share undermined collaborative programs to boost quality and output. Meanwhile, Ford enjoyed placid relations with its union, the United Auto Workers, along with dramatic increases in productivity, because it made its workers feel rewarded, secure, and involved in its success. Those were two key findings in a 1990 report on the U.S. auto industry.[68]

GM began the 1980s by fighting with its union over its plan to open nonunion component plants in the South. It espoused collaborative plans slowly and at different rates in different parts of the organization. It relied heavily on symbolic joint appearances with union leaders and on wholesale reorganization of existing contracts. When GM's market share eroded, it couldn't offer workers job security or profit sharing on a par with Ford. The report also noted that GM failed to engineer products and work methods to help boost productivity and instead launched shop-floor efficiency campaigns that to many workers resembled traditional assembly line speedups.

Ford, conversely, enjoyed placid relations with the UAW because the company: (1) communicated a consistent, high-level commitment to joint programs; (2) offered gain sharing in the form of steady work, profit sharing, and extensive overtime; (3) maintained clear distinctions between joint programs and traditional collective bargaining structures; and (4) achieved much of its productivity gains through product design and work method changes that in many cases did not increase the everyday workload of workers. The bottom line: since the inception of the employee involvement process in 1980, Ford has improved its assembly productivity by 36 percent (compared to GM's 11 percent), and it requires 51 percent fewer people per vehicle produced in its domestic assembly plants than does GM.[69] In addition, Ford's product quality has improved more than 50 percent for cars and 47 percent for trucks.[70] High quality, in turn, has led to high profits for the company, and both employees and managers have shared in those benefits, which average 11 percent of their annual paychecks.[71] These are some of the key factors that have contributed to the 40 percent improvement in Ford's break-even point for its North American automotive operations.

PARADIGMS FOR POSTMODERN MANAGERS

In the twenty-first-century prototype corporation, a key component of managing people will be empowering them to make decisions that affect them. And when it comes to employee empowerment, it is Saturn Corporation—a GM division, ironically enough—that is leading the way. Saturn's teams of workers manage everything from budgets to inventory control, often without direct oversight from top management.[72] Both Levi Strauss & Co. and Corning, Inc., are demonstrating that recruiting, retaining, and promoting a culturally diverse work-force is a strategic advantage in serving culturally diverse markets.[73]

As for the global focus that will be needed in a worldwide economy, Loctite Corporation, a small maker of adhesives and sealants, is showing all companies why they should never define their markets narrowly.[74] Loctite earns $8 of every $10 of profit outside its U.S. base. For focus on the customer, 7-Eleven Japan Co. has few rivals. It took an American con-cept, the convenience store, and made it an overwhelming success in Japan. A $200 mil-lion computer system monitors inventory and tracks customer preferences. Clerks even key in the sex and approximate age of each customer to monitor buying patterns. Orders are transmitted instantly via satellite to distribution centers and manufacturers. Anything that doesn't move is discontinued immediately: of the 3000 items each franchisee carries, 70 percent are replaced annually. A bare-bones inventory saves money by allocating shelf space to only what local shoppers really want.[75]

Each of these companies has mastered at least one of the attributes of the organization of tomorrow. What many of them have found, however, is that even a single change poses new challenges to management and has implications that reach far beyond the concept itself. Perhaps the most basic element of the new paradigm is *quality*. Most senior man-agers now view quality not as a competitive advantage but as a competitive necessity. Says the CEO of Wausau Paper Mills: "Quality is your ticket into the stadium. You can't even come to the game unless you have a quality product and process in place. You have to compete on other dimensions." [76] As you can see from this case, managing twenty-first-century organizations will be fast-paced, exciting, and full of people-related business chal-lenges.

IMPLICATIONS FOR MANAGEMENT PRACTICE

The trends we have reviewed in this chapter suggest that the old approaches to managing people may no longer be appropriate responses to economic or social reality. A willingness to experiment with new approaches to managing people is healthy. To the extent that the newer approaches do enhance productivity and QWL, everybody wins. The competitive problems facing us cannot simply be willed away, and because of this we may see even more radical experiments in organizations. The traditional role of the manager may be blurred further as workers take a greater and greater part in planning work, doing it, and controlling it. For example, under its "Work-Out" program, General Electric holds corporate "town meetings" at which lower-level blue- and white-collar employees and even customers grill bosses and suggest ways to improve efficiency. The boss is supposed to approve or deny most suggestions immediately. The aim isn't to cut head counts but to get every employee involved in improving efficiency. Jack Welch, CEO of General Electric, con-tends that "Work-Out" is the key to the company's 4 percent productivity growth in 1992, more than twice the rate during the recession of 1981–1982.[77] Programs such as these suggest that human resource management, an essential part of the jobs of all managers, will play an even more crucial role in the future.

SUMMARY

In a fast-paced, globally competitive economy, efforts to boost productivity and quality never end. To make organizations more responsive to the demands of the marketplace, new organization forms, such as the modular corporation, are appearing. The new forms imply a redistribution of power, greater participation by workers, and more teamwork. This is necessary, for the competitive business environment of the 1990s will be characterized by factors such as an aging and changing workforce—one with more minorities, women, and low-skilled workers—in a high-tech workplace that demands and rewards ever-increasing skill; many workers who have been scarred by the unpleasant side effects of downsizing; and increasing global competition in almost every sector of the economy. The challenge of managing people effectively has never been greater.

One of the most pressing demands we face today is for productivity improvement—getting more out of what is put in, doing better with what we have, and working smarter, not harder. A major thrust in this area is total quality management (TQM), a philosophy and a set of guiding principles that represent the foundation of a continuously improving organization. Evidence indicates that TQM can improve employee relations and operating results, but changing to a TQM-oriented culture is often a frustrating, expensive process, for it requires extensive training, possible restructuring of departments, and a complete shift away from short-term perspectives. Nevertheless, increased productivity does not preclude a high quality of work life (QWL).

QWL may be defined and operationalized in terms of employees' perceptions of their physical and psychological well-being at work. It involves giving workers the opportunity to make decisions about their jobs, the design of their workplaces, and what they need to make products or to deliver services most effectively. Its focus is on employees and management operating a business together. Joint labor-management cooperation is the very essence of QWL efforts, but participation can take several forms. The most effective of these seem to be those that combine (1) financial rewards to workers for productivity improvements, (2) job changes that involve substantial increases in worker responsibility and autonomy, and (3) substantial training of workers and managers in order to support greater worker involvement. Although there are many pitfalls associated with instituting a productivity improvement or QWL program, the potential financial gains may well justify the effort.

DISCUSSION QUESTIONS

1·1 How are the demographic trends of the 1990s, the education crisis, downsizing, and the global competition for high-quality workers interrelated?

1·2 Discuss alternative strategies for harnessing the energies of workers concerned with TQM issues.

1·3 What common characteristics do the following organizations share: a hospital, a school, an auto repair shop, a baseball team?

1·4 Considering everything we have discussed in this chapter, describe management styles and practices that will be effective for U.S. businesses in the next decade.

1·5 What difficulties do you see in shifting from a hierarchical, departmentalized organization to a leaner, flatter one in which power is shared between workers and managers?

REFERENCES

1. Matsushita, K. (1978). *My management philosophy.* Tokyo: PHP Institute, Inc., p. 45.
2. Byrne, J. A. (1993, Feb. 8). The virtual corporation. *Business Week*, pp. 98–103.
3. Kiechel, W., III (1993, May 17). How we will work in the year 2000. *Fortune*, pp. 38–52.
4. Tully, S. (1993, Feb. 8). The modular corporation. *Fortune*, pp. 106–108; 112–114.
5. Ibid.
6. Beall, D., ibid., p. 106.
7. Material in this section is based on Cappelli, P. (1992). *Is the "skills gap" really about attitudes?* Philadelphia: National Center on the Educational Quality of the Workforce.
8. Secretary's Commission on Achieving Necessary Skills (SCANS) (1991). *What work requires of schools: A SCANS report for America 2000.* Washington, DC: U.S. Department of Labor.
9. Fullerton, H. N., Jr. (1991, Nov.). Labor force projections: The baby boom moves on. *Monthly Labor Review*, pp. 31–44.
10. Solomon, J. (1989, Nov. 7). Firms grapple with language barriers. *The Wall Street Journal*, pp. B1, B12.
11. Johnston, W. B. (1987). *Workforce 2000: Work and workers for the 21st century.* Indianapolis, IN: Hudson Institute.
12. Celis, W., 3rd (1993, Sept. 9). Study says half of adults in U.S. can't read or handle arithmetic. *The New York Times*, pp. A1; A22.
13. Richards, B. (1990, Feb. 9). Wanting workers. *The Wall Street Journal*, pp. R10, R11.
14. Kruger, P. (1990, Jan.). A game plan for the future. *Working Woman*, pp. 67–71.
15. The literacy gap (1988, Dec. 19). *Time*, pp. 56, 57.
16. Nelan, B. W. (1992, Fall). How the world will look in 50 years. *Time* (Special Issue: Beyond the Year 2000), pp. 36–38.
17. Gwynne, S. C. (1992, Sept. 28). The long haul. *Time*, pp. 34–38.
18. Farney, D. (1992, Oct. 28). Turning point: Even U.S. politics are being reshaped by a global economy. *The Wall Street Journal*, pp. A1, A8.
19. Doyle, F. P. (1992, June). Keynote address, National Academy of Human Resources, Santa Fe, NM.
20. Loss of two million civilian jobs seen from defense cutbacks by 1997 (1993, Apr. 14). *Daily Labor Report*, pp. A3, A4.
21. Gwynne, loc. cit.
22. Winslow, R. (1991, Feb. 1). Medical experiment: Some companies try "managed care" in bid to curb health care costs. *The Wall Street Journal*, pp. A1; A6.
23. Cappelli, P. (1992). Examining managerial displacement. *Academy of Management Journal*, **35**(1), 203–217.
24. Outlook (1992, Sept. 14). *The Wall Street Journal*, p. A1.
25. Baumohl, B. (1993, Mar. 15). When downsizing becomes "dumbsizing." *Time*, p. 55.
26. Kozlowski, S. W. J., Chao, G. T., Smith, E. M., & Hedlund, J. (1993). Organizational downsizing: Strategies, interventions, and research implications. *International Review of Industrial and Organizational Psychology*, 8, 263–332.
27. Cascio, W. F. (1993). Downsizing: What do we know? What have we learned? *Academy of Management Executive*, **7**(1), 95–104.
28. Hain, T., in Adler, T. (1993, Aug.). Layoffs just part of downsizing formula. *Monitor*, p. 23.
29. Pilon, L. J. (1993, Feb. 22). Quoted in "Jobs, Jobs." *Business Week*, p. 74.
30. Corporate refugees (1993, Apr. 12). *Business Week*, pp. 58–65.
31. Kuttner, R. (1993, Mar. 8). Training programs alone can't produce $20-an-hour workers. *Business Week*, p. 16.
32. Reich, R. B. (1990, Jan.–Feb.). Who is us? *Harvard Business Review*, pp. 53–64.
33. Peters, T. (1989, Oct. 17). Global thinking mandatory for companies in the 1990s. *Rocky Mountain News*, p. 52.

34. Preaching the gospel of productivity (1982, Mar. 21). *The Washington Post*, pp. F3–F5.

35. Malabre, A. L., Jr., & Clark, L. H., Jr. (1992, Aug. 12). Dubious figures: Productivity statistics for the service sector may understate gains. *The Wall Street Journal*, pp. A1, A5. See also Wildstrom, S. H. (1993, June 14). Gauging output: It's not just counting widgets anymore. *Business Week*, p. 68.

36. Mahoney, T. A. (1988). Productivity defined: The relativity of efficiency, effectiveness, and change. In J. P. Campbell & R. J. Campbell (eds.), *Productivity in organizations.* San Francisco: Jossey-Bass, pp. 13–39. See also Pritchard, R. D., Jones, S. D., Roth, P. L., Stuebing, K. K., & Ekeberg, S. E. (1989). The evaluation of an integrated approach to measuring organizational productivity. *Personnel Psychology, 42,* 69–115.

37. Nye, J. S., Jr. (1991, Oct.). We can stay on top. *Money,* pp. 160, 161.

38. Working smarter (1984, June 4). *Time,* p. 53.

39. Bernstein, A. (1993, July 12). Don't blame the slow job growth on labor costs. *Business Week,* p. 120.

40. The technology payoff: A sweeping reorganization of work itself is boosting productivity. (1993, June 14). *Business Week,* pp. 57–79.

41. U.S. General Acounting Office (1991, May). *Management practices: U.S. companies improve performance through quality efforts.* Washington, DC: U.S. Government Printing Office.

42. For more information about TQM, see, for example, Scott, W. B. (1989, Dec. 4). TQM expected to boost productivity, ensure survival of U.S. industry. *Aviation Week & Space Technology,* pp. 64–70. See also Deming, W. E. (1986). *Out of the crisis.* Boston: Center for Advanced Engineering Study, MIT. See also Walton, M. W. (1986). *The Deming management method.* New York: Perigee. See also A note on quality: The views of Deming, Juran, and Crosby (1986). Cambridge, MA: Harvard Business School (HBS) 9-687-011.

43. Blackburn, R., & Rosen, B. (1993). Total quality and human resources management: Lessons learned from Baldridge Award–winning companies. *Academy of Management Executive, 7*(3), 49–66.

44. Brody, P., in ibid., p. 50.

45. Blackburn & Rosen, loc. cit..

46. U.S. General Accounting Office, loc. cit.

47. Scott, loc. cit.

48. Stewart, T. A. (1993, Aug. 23). Reengineering: The hot new managing tool. *Fortune,* pp. 41–48.

49. Ernst & Young, & American Quality Foundation (1992). *The international quality study: Best practices report.* Cleveland: Author. See also Quality (1992, Nov. 3.). *Business Week,* pp. 66–75.

50. Reich, R., in Greenhouse, S. (1992, Feb. 9). Attention, America! Snap out of it! *The New York Times,* pp. 1F, 8F.

51. McCarthy, M. J. (1993, May 4). Unlikely sites: Why German firms choose the Carolinas to build U.S. plants. *The Wall Street Journal,* pp. A1, A6.

52. Lawler, E. E., & Mohrman, S. A. (1985, Jan.–Feb.). Quality circles: After the fad. *Harvard Business Review,* pp. 65–71.

53. Lawler, E. E. (1973). *Motivation in work organizations.* Monterey, CA: Brooks/Cole.

54. Moskal, B. S. (1989, Jan. 16). Quality of life in the factory: How far have we come? *Industry Week,* pp. 12–16.

55. Griffin, R. W. (1988). Consequences of quality circles in an industrial setting: A longitudinal assessment. *Academy of Management Journal, 31,* 338–358. See also Ledford, G. E., Jr., Lawler, E. E., III, & Mohrman, S. A. (1988). The quality circle and its variations. In J. P. Campbell & R. J. Campbell (eds.), *Productivity in organizations.* San Francisco: Jossey-Bass, pp. 255–294. See also Marks, M. L., Mirvis, P. H., Hackett, E. J., & Grady, J. F., Jr. (1986). Employee participation in a quality circle program: Impact on quality of work life, productivity, and absenteeism. *Journal of Applied Psychology, 71,* 61–69.

56. Saporito, B. (1986, July 21). The revolt against "working smarter." *Fortune,* pp. 58–65.

57. Ibid.

58. Cotton, J. L., Vollrath, D. A., Froggatt, K. L., Lengnick-Hall, J. L., & Jennings, K. R. (1988). Employee participation: Diverse forms and different outcomes. *Academy of Management Review*, **13**, 8–22.

59. Fein, M. (1982, Aug.). Improved productivity through worker involvement. Paper presented at the annual meeting of the Academy of Management, New York.

60. Wartzman, R. (1992, May 4). Sharing gains: A Whirlpool factory raises productivity—and pay of workers. *The Wall Street Journal*, pp. A1, A4.

61. Nurick, A. J. (1982). Participation in organizational change: A longitudinal field study. *Human Relations*, **35**, 413–430. See also Macy, B., & Peterson, M. (1981, Aug.). Evaluating attitudinal change in a longitudinal quality of work life intervention. Paper presented at the annual meeting of the Academy of Management, San Diego.

62. Goodman, P. S. (1979). *Assessing organizational change: The Rushton quality of work life experiment.* New York: Wiley.

63. Lawler, E. E., & Ledford, G. E. (1982). Productivity and the quality of work life. *National Productivity Review*, **2**, 2.

64. Kilduff, M. (1993). Deconstructing organizations. *Academy of Management Review*, **18**(1) 13–31.

65. Argyris, C., & Schon, D. A. (1978). *Organizational learning: A theory of action perspective.* Reading, MA: Addison-Wesley.

66. Templin, N. (1992, Dec. 15). Team spirit. *The Wall Street Journal*, pp. A1, A6.

67. Cotton et al., loc. cit.

68. Ford policies avoid labor strife (1990, Jan. 8). *Denver Post*, p. 3C.

69. White, J. B. (1992, Oct. 6). GM's labor cost disadvantage to Ford is placed at $4 billion a year by study. *The Wall Street Journal*, pp. A2, A6.

70. Banas, P. A. (1988). Employee involvement: A sustained labor/management initiative at the Ford Motor Company. In J. P. Campbell & R. J. Campbell (eds.), *Productivity in organizations.* San Francisco: Jossey-Bass, pp. 388–416.

71. Schroeder, M. (1988, Nov. 7). Watching the bottom line instead of the clock. *Business Week*, pp. 134, 136.

72. Where employees are management (1992, Nov. 30). *Business Week* Bonus Issue, "Reinventing America," p. 66.

73. See, for example, Hymowitz, C. (1989, Feb. 16). One firm's bid to keep blacks, women. *The Wall Street Journal*, p. B1.

74. Why ignore 95% of the world's market? Loctite thinks globally, profits locally (1992, Nov. 30). *Business Week* Bonus Issue, "Reinventing America," p. 65.

75. Listening to shoppers' voices: 7-Eleven Japan's common sense principles (1992, Nov. 30). *Business Week* Bonus Issue, "Reinventing America," p. 62.

76. Nemirow, A., in Paradigms for postmodern managers (1992, Nov. 30). *Business Week* Bonus Issue, "Reinventing America," p. 70.

77. Peterson, T. (1992, May 18). Can corporate America get out from under its overhead? *Business Week*, p. 102.

CHAPTER 2

HUMAN RESOURCE MANAGEMENT: A FIELD IN TRANSITION

THE 1990S CHALLENGE: MANAGING PEOPLE-RELATED BUSINESS ISSUES*

Blame it on a demographic firestorm that gathered force in the 1980s and is likely to reach full strength during the 1990s. No longer can companies rely on an endless supply of young, homogeneous workers, ready to join up for a lifetime with a single company. Now they have to worry about the working mother with day-care needs, the middle-aged executive who has to care for an elderly parent, an influx of workers who can't speak, or read, English.

If mishandled, "human resources" can be a source of corporate distress; if handled well, they can provide a competitive advantage. As a senior partner at an international consulting firm noted, "You have to be the village idiot not to see how critical these issues are to a company's future."

The upshot is that companies, inspired by fear and opportunity, are taking human resources executives more seriously. Median total cash compensation for top HR executives in large companies (those with more than 10,000 employees) was $221,000 in 1992, with those in manufacturing companies making somewhat more than those in for-profit service companies.[1] Many HR executives now report directly to the chief executive officer and serve on the executive committee.

---

*Adapted from: J. Solomon, People power, *The Wall Street Journal*, Mar. 9, 1990, p. R33. Reprinted by permission of *The Wall Street Journal*, © 1990 Dow Jones & Company, Inc. All rights reserved worldwide.

This is not the way things always were. Rather, it was "Let's run the business, and, by the way, we need somebody to take care of the people problem," says the vice president of human resources at Scott Paper Company. "People were viewed as a constraint to strategy and human resources as a cost in itself."

Today the challenge is to use the "human factor" creatively in planning and problem solving. HR executives are expected to be at the management table initiating ideas to make their companies more productive. Moreover, the rank and file aren't the only employees now considered to be "human resources." More and more HR means "management of managers," with the top HR executive sitting in judgment on who will be the future leaders of the organization at every level.

Another familiar—yet transformed—HR role involves labor relations. At Scott Paper, the HR department traditionally had a simple task: representing management's adversarial role in contract negotiations. Now that has changed. Last summer the HR vice president and other senior executives fashioned a new agreement with Scott's biggest union. At Scott's Somerset, Maine, mill, which is introducing new machinery, the agreement gives labor a say in the promotion and training of machinery operators. And in white-collar areas, HR executives are helping traditional antagonists—such as engineers and marketers—learn to communicate.

If all this sounds a bit, well, *too perfect,* you're right. Clearly an increasing number of top executives think these changes are essential to improving productivity. But the changes aren't coming easily.

Challenges

1. What is the difference between "people issues" and "people-related business issues"? How might this affect the operation of the HR function?

2. Aside from demographic changes, what are some other reasons why "people-related business issues" are becoming more and more important to a company's long-term success?

3. Can you suggest reasons why some line managers are resisting these changes?

Questions This Chapter Will Help Managers Answer

1. What should be the role, objectives, and responsibilities of the HR function?

2. How can HR professionals help managers to be more effective?

3. From a strategic perspective, how should the HR function be used?

4. What key questions should be asked in evaluating the HR function?

5. What specific people-related business issues provide the greatest opportunity for HR executives to add value to their firms?

THE EVOLUTION OF HUMAN RESOURCE MANAGEMENT

To appreciate where the HRM field is going, let's consider where it has come from. Doing so will help today's line manager gain a better insight and understanding of this aspect of business. Modern HRM has emerged from nine interrelated sources:

1. Rapid technological change, which increased the specialization of labor associated with the industrial revolution

2. The emergence of free collective bargaining, with constraints established for both unions and employers

3. The scientific management movement

4. Early industrial psychology

5. Government personnel practices growing out of the establishment of the Civil Service Commission

6. The emergence of personnel specialists and the grouping of these specialists into personnel departments

7. The human relations movement

8. The behavioral sciences

9. The social legislation and court decisions of the 1960s and 1970s[2]

Let us now consider the first eight of these; the ninth is the subject of Chapter 4.

The Industrial Revolution

Three characteristics of the industrial revolution were the development of machinery, the linking of human power to the machines, and the establishment of factories in which a large number of people were employed. The result was a tremendous increase in job specialization as well as in the amount of goods workers could produce. "Division of labor" became the rallying cry of this revolution.

Clearly, the industrial revolution greatly accelerated the development of business and commerce. Owners and entrepreneurs generally did quite well for themselves, but the average citizen fared poorly in comparison to today's workers in terms of purchasing power and working conditions. Labor was considered a commodity to be bought and sold, and the prevailing political philosophy of laissez faire resulted in little action by governments to protect the lot of workers.[3]

The Emergence of Free Collective Bargaining

Because of the way workers were abused, it was inevitable that they would organize to protect themselves and to improve their lot in life. From the perspective of workers, the industrial revolution fostered specialization and fostered the need for workers within each specialization to organize themselves against its abuses. Trade unions, also called "labor unions," spread rapidly, and so did the incidence of strikes (e.g., in 1886 by employees at the McCormick Reaper Works in Chicago, who went on strike for an 8-hour day).[4]

Until 1935, courts tended to side with management and adopted a decidedly anti-union stance. However, in that year the Wagner Act, technically called the National Labor Relations Act, was passed. The act focused largely on labor's right to organize, and it provided that a majority of employees in an appropriate "bargaining unit" (as determined and certified by the National Labor Relations Board, which the act created) could obtain exclusive collective bargaining rights for all the employees in that unit. It became an unfair labor practice for an employer to coerce or restrain employees in the exercise of their rights, to dominate or interfere with a labor organization, or to refuse to bargain collectively with a legal representative of the employees. Administration of the act was the responsibility of the National Labor Relations

Board. Subsequent legislation refined, broadened, and set legal limits on the scope of management and union activities.

Viewed through the perspective of labor, the development of free collective bargaining and the U.S. labor movement created the need for what we now recognize as effective human resource management.

Scientific Management

Viewed through the perspective of management, the scientific management movement also created a need for effective human resource management. Frederick Winslow Taylor was the prophet of scientific management, and his "Bible" was the stopwatch.[5]

Taylor was a pioneer in the scientific study of jobs ("time-and-motion" study). In addition, he argued that individuals selected to do a job should be as perfectly matched, physically and mentally, to its demands as possible and that *overqualified* individuals should be excluded.

Employees should be trained carefully by supervisors (whose own work was also divided into specialties) to ensure that they performed the work exactly as specified by prior scientific analysis. In no case, however, should employees ever be called upon to work at a pace that would be detrimental to their health.

Finally, to provide an incentive for employees to follow the detailed procedures specified (which were closely supervised by line supervisors on the shop floor), Taylor felt that they should receive an addition of 30 to 100 percent of their ordinary wages whenever the task was done right and within the time limits specified—labor's first piecework incentive systems. Taylor was also interested in the social aspects of work, although he saw little good emerging from social interaction within work groups. He felt that work groups fostered a level of individual efficiency equal to the level of the least productive worker in the group. In other words, he believed that the efficiency of the group would not be any greater than the efficiency of the least productive member.

Overall, there is little doubt that application of the principles of scientific management has resulted in much higher productivity than would otherwise have been possible. What is remarkable is not that Taylor was "correct in the context of his time" but that many of his insights are still valid today.[6]

Early Industrial Psychology

In 1913 Hugo Munsterberg's book *Psychology and Industrial Efficiency* described experiments in selecting streetcar operators, ship's officers, and telephone switchboard operators. Munsterberg's contributions to human resource management are noteworthy for his emphasis on the analysis of jobs in terms of (1) the abilities required to do them and (2) the development of testing devices—aptitude tests as well as work-sample tests.[7]

Paralleling these developments were advances in checking references given by workers, in the use of rating sheets for interviewers, and in statistical methods for estimating validity (the extent to which selection devices accurately forecast job performance). World War I accelerated the development of intelligence tests (the Army Alpha and the Army Beta) so that each individual could be matched more effectively with job requirements. Other kinds of psychological measures also appeared during and after World War I, such as measures of aptitude, interest, and personality.

The U.S. Civil Service Commission

The Pendelton Act of 1883 established the U.S. Civil Service Commission (today known as the U.S. Office of Personnel Management). A forerunner in progressive human resource policies, the act provided that competitive examinations be administered as a basis for employment in the public service. It also provided a measure of employment security for those selected, prohibited discharge for refusing to engage in political activity, encouraged a nonpartisan approach to appointments, and mandated that a commissioner administer the act.[8] Perhaps the major impact of this act was to foster employment promotion policies in the federal government on the basis of merit. Over the years, however, the progressive human resource policies of the civil service (e.g., by 1900, entrance criteria were developed for the majority of federal positions) have influenced human resource practices in state and local governments as well as in private industry.

Private Industry's Approach to Personnel Management

Historians consider 1912 the approximate date of the emergence of the modern personnel department.[9] The term "personnel," with its modern connotation of managing people in organizations, began to appear about 1909. It was used as a major item in the index of the Civil Service Commission's report of that year, and in 1910 the secretary of commerce and labor used the term in a major heading in his annual report. Between 1900 and 1920, while advances were being made in scientific management, industrial psychology, and the federal civil service, a number of *personnel specialists* emerged in companies such as B. F. Goodrich, National Cash Register, and Standard Oil of California. The specialists managed such areas as employment, employee welfare (financial, housing, medical, and educational), wage setting, safety, training, and health. This kind of specialization formed the basis for the organization of the modern human resource department.

The Human Relations Movement

Beginning in 1923, and continuing until the early 1930s, the Hawthorne Works of the Western Electric Company in Chicago provided the setting for one of the most famous behavioral research efforts of all time. The purpose of the research was to identify factors in the work situation that led to high productivity.

The results of these experiments indicated to some observers that productivity was directly related to the degree of group teamwork and cooperation. The level of teamwork and cooperation, in turn, seemed to be related to the interest of the supervisor and the researchers in the work group, the lack of coercive approaches to productivity improvement, and the participation afforded the workers in changes affecting them.[10] These relationships are shown in Figure 2-1. In short, the researchers came to view the organization of workers as a *social system*, in contrast to Taylor's view of the organization as a technical-economic system.

The conviction that group behavior and workers' feelings were associated with morale and productivity characterized much of the research and theorizing in the human relations movement for the next two decades. Unfortunately, these new concepts, popularized as the "Pet Milk theory," were widely misunderstood and misapplied. The Pet Milk Company advertised that it had better milk because Pet Milk came from contented cows. A similar idea, that happy workers are productive workers, provided the rationale for trying to improve workers' social environment with

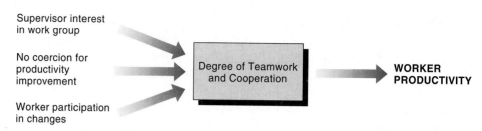

FIGURE 2-1
Conclusion of the
Hawthorne experiments
regarding the antecedents
of high worker productivity.

company picnics, newly created status symbols, employee coffee rooms, and other gimmicks.

The "Pet Milk" approach was widely discredited during the late 1950s. The 1957 recession led to a severe curtailment of human relations training programs. Failure to find evidence that these programs made a difference in workers' satisfaction or that happy workers were productive workers helped kill this approach to human resource management.[11] Many managers seemed to use human relations for the short-term purpose of manipulating workers to increase output rather than for the long-term goal of satisfying worker needs while meeting organizational needs. By 1960, the "happy worker" fad had largely ended.

The Behavioral Sciences

The behavioral science approach to managing people is an outgrowth of the human relations studies, although it embraces a wider base of academic and applied disciplines and is concerned with a wider range of problems.[12] *Behavioral sciences* refers to the social and biological sciences concerned with the study of human behavior (see Figure 2-2).

Much of the knowledge about HRM and many of its practical applications have come from such behavioral science disciplines as the following:

Industrial/organizational psychology—the study of the behavior of people at work

Social psychology—the study of how people affect and are affected by one another

Organization theory—basic philosophies about why organizations exist, how they function, how they should be designed, and how they can be effective

Organizational behavior—the study of the causes of individual and group behavior and of how this knowledge can be used to make people more productive and satisfied in organizational settings

Sociology—the study of society, social institutions, and social relationships

Needless to say, much behavioral science research cuts across these disciplines. As a result we now know that the ways people behave in organizations cannot be explained simply by human relationships. The organization itself, through its unique "culture," molds, constrains, and modifies human performance. The way the organization is structured, the authority attached to different positions, and job and technology requirements clearly affect behavior. Given the massive changes in organizations brought about by restructurings, downsizings, and changes in work relationships as a function of the information age (electronic mail, local area networks, on-line information services), the ways in which individuals relate to each other have changed dramatically in the 1990s. Even though our present understanding of the determinants and effects of behavior in organizations is incomplete, we do have a better sense of the ways in which separate influences interact with one another to affect individuals.

FOUR GROWTH STAGES OF HUMAN RESOURCE MANAGEMENT

The foundation for modern HRM rests on the nine factors listed earlier. Beyond that, HRM developed in four stages.

The first stage may be called the "file maintenance" stage, for it typified HRM activities up through the mid-1960s and the degree of emphasis placed on employee concerns. The first part of the chapter opening vignette illustrates some typical HRM responsibilities at this stage of the field's development. "Personnel" was the responsibility of a special department. These responsibilities included screening applicants, conducting orientation for new employees, collecting and storing personal data on each employee (date of birth, years of company service, education), planning the company picnic, and circulating memos "whose impertinence was exceeded only by their irrelevance."[13]

The second growth stage of HRM began soon after the Civil Rights Act of 1964 was passed. This is considered the "government accountability" stage. Antidiscrimination laws, pension laws, health and safety laws, federal regulatory agencies and their interpretive guidelines, and court rulings affecting virtually every aspect of employment—all of these accelerated the rise in importance of the HRM function. Class action suits and the large financial settlements for the winning suits illustrated the costs of *mismanaging* people. Thus, at American Telephone & Telegraph, a 1973 con-

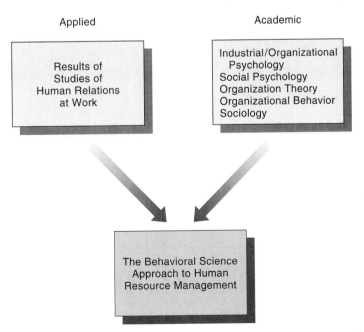

FIGURE 2-2
Academic and applied disciplines that contribute to the behavioral science approach to managing people at work.

sent agreement with the federal government to bring the starting pay of women promoted to managerial positions up to the starting pay of men who were so promoted cost the company over $30 million.

Managers outside the HRM function began to take notice because top management let it be known that ineptitude in this area simply would not be tolerated. Staying out of federal court became a top organizational priority. These trends also signaled the need for particular competence in each aspect of the HRM field.

Within HRM there began to appear specialties in compensation and benefits, affirmative action (the promotion of minority concerns in all aspects of employment), labor relations, and training and development. Considerable resources were devoted to compliance activities, for example, filing government-required reports on the numbers of minorities and nonminorities recruited, selected, and promoted by job class. Many top executives viewed these activities as nonproductive drains on overall organizational performance.

In the late 1970s and 1980s, when many firms were struggling simply to survive, a combination of economic and political factors (high interest rates, growing international competition, shrinking U.S. productivity growth) led to a demand for greater accountability in dollar terms of all the functional areas of business. Human resource management activities were not exempted from this emphasis on accountability. Hence this third stage may be termed "organizational accountability." Although methods of assessing the costs and benefits of human resource programs are available, they are not widely known.[14] In addition, social trends (more women in the workforce, as well as more minorities, immigrants, older workers, and poorly educated workers) accelerated demands for improving the quality of work life, for managing cultural and ethnic diversity, and for continual training and retraining.

In the 1990s, HRM has evolved to a fourth growth stage as it assumes a central role in the struggle of both large and small firms to gain and sustain a competitive advantage in the worldwide marketplace. This stage may be termed "strategic partnership." Top management looks to the HR department, as it does to line managers, to control costs, to enhance competitiveness, and to add value to the firm in everything it does. The following practical example illustrates how such a partnership might work in practice.

PRACTICAL EXAMPLE

GLOBAL PRODUCT AND SERVICE MARKET STRATEGIES— DEVELOPING A STRATEGIC HR—SENIOR MANAGEMENT PARTNERSHIP*

As companies look to world markets more aggressively, they are faced with developing world-class products and services at world-class costs. This means changes in design, production, distribution, and marketing. There are multiple HRM implications, including developing new forms of design teams, making better use of strategic sourcing, and estab-

---

*Adapted from: N. M. Tichy, Setting the global human resource management agenda for the 1990s, *Human Resource Management, 27,* 1–18 (1988). Copyright 1988 by John Wiley & Sons, Inc. Reprinted by permission of John Wiley & Sons, Inc.

lishing world-class standards for design, service, and performance. To accomplish these objectives, it is necessary to build complementary agendas for senior line executives and senior HR executives. Here are the basic elements of each one.

AGENDA FOR LINE EXECUTIVES

■ Clearly articulate why "going global" is needed.

■ Determine what markets the firm *must* be in in order to be a strong player 10 years from now.

■ Identify major competitors worldwide—which the firm needs to beat and which it needs to join (preempt).

■ Define the competitive imperatives, such as mastering economies of scale, technological advantage, access to markets, distribution, and so forth.

■ Identify the skills required and where they exist in the organization.

■ Determine how to create organizational processes that treat globalization as an ongoing experiment with deliberate learning and redirection as necessary.

AGENDA FOR HR EXECUTIVES

■ Ensure HR involvement as an integral partner in formulating the global strategy.

■ Develop competencies among senior HR staff in order to be a contributing partner.

■ Take the lead in developing processes and concepts for top managers as they develop global strategy. These might include information scanning, decision making, or learning processes.

■ Develop a framework to help top management fully understand the organizational structure and human implications of globalization.

■ Facilitate the implementation phase by identifying key skills required, assessing current competencies, and developing strategies for locating whatever outside talent may be required.

Note how the two agendas complement each other—as they must in order to make the strategic partnership work.

Consider an appraisal of the strategic importance of HRM by *Business Week:*

It is the most dramatic change in a managerial function since financial executives rose to power in the 1960s conglomerate era. . . . At a time when companies are constantly acquiring, merging, and spinning off divisions, entering new businesses and getting out of old ones, management must base strategic decisions more than ever on HR considerations—matching skills with jobs, keeping key personnel after a merger, and solving the human problems that arise from introducing new technology or closing a plant.[15]

The responsibility for effective management of people, along with the effective management of physical and financial resources, is squarely on the shoulders of line

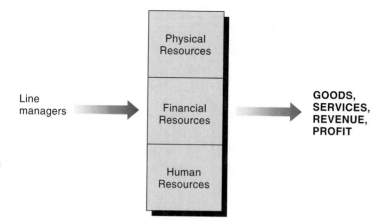

FIGURE 2-3
Line managers are responsible for optimizing the use of all three kinds of resources—physical, financial, and human—in order to generate useful output.

managers—those directly responsible for the operations of the business (Figure 2-3). In terms of the discussion in Chapter 1 about changes in the technical and social environments, we now know that productivity improves most when all three factors of production—equipment, capital, and labor—are used most wisely; we cannot emphasize any one factor (e.g., computer equipment) to the exclusion of the rest (since, for example, it takes people who are properly selected, trained, and motivated to operate and maintain the computers).

Organizations in the 1990s are flatter than ever before. In 1980, the ratio of managers to workers was about 1 to 10. Today it's more like 1 to 15.[16] That's (on average) a 50 percent increase in each manager's span of control! As a result of large-scale downsizing, which has eliminated layers of middle managers, self-managing work teams often have primary responsibility for planning, implementing, or controlling the production of products or the delivery of services. Team members work closely with HR representatives on issues such as rewards, discipline, and conflict resolution. For example, at Hewlett-Packard's Singapore plant, HR representatives work directly *on the plant floor* with the self-managing work teams.

In the contemporary view, therefore, managers and work team members, no matter what their line of responsibility (production, marketing, sales, or finance), are expected to add value by optimizing *all their resources*—physical, financial, and human. This suggests that the most effective approach to HRM may result from close interaction between the department charged with the administration of HRM and those directly responsible for the operations of the business. The HR department is still responsible for file maintenance, government accountability, and organizational accountability, but HRM in general is now viewed as a strategic partnership. Indeed, the chances for genuine cooperation between HR professionals, line managers, and members of independent work groups have never been better.[17] A summary of the ideas presented in this section is shown in Figure 2-4.

Strategic Human Resources Management

In practical terms, strategic HRM means getting everybody from the top of the organization to the bottom doing things to implement the strategy of the business effectively. The idea is to use people most wisely with respect to the strategic needs of the organization. This doesn't just happen. An integrative framework that systematically links HR activities with strategic business needs can help. Such a framework, termed the "5-P" model, is shown in Figure 2-5.[18]

Strategic business needs set the 5-P model in motion. Typically organizations define (or redefine) such needs during times of turbulence. They reflect management's overall plan for survival, growth, adaptability, and profitability. Such needs (or competitive strategies) might be described in terms of innovation, quality enhancement, cost control, speed, or a combination of these. They are affected by characteristics that are internal to the organization (e.g., culture, nature of the business) as well as external (e.g., state of the economy, critical success factors in the industry). To trigger specific actions, business needs are often translated into statements of strategic business objectives. For example, at PepsiCo International, strategic business objectives are:

- Committed bottling organization
- Uncompromising dedication to quality
- Development of talented people
- Focus on growth
- Quality business plans

Such statements clearly influence *human resources philosophy* (the first "P" shown in Figure 2-5). A firm's HR philosophy is generally a broad statement about how it regards its people, the role they play in the overall success of a business, and how they are to be treated and managed. For example, part of PepsiCo International's HR philosophy includes "Leadership in People." That is,

- Empowering people to drive the business from the closest point to the market
- Developing the skills to be the best in the business
- Building career opportunities

Stage I: File maintenance

Stage II: Government accountability

Stage III: Organizational accountability

Stage IV: Strategic partner

FIGURE 2-4
Development of the HR field over the course of the twentieth century.

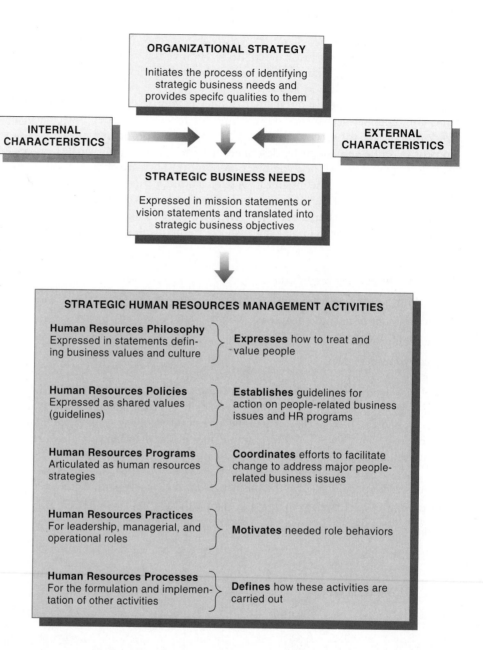

FIGURE 2-5
The 5-P model. (*Source:* R. S. Schuler, Strategic human resources management: Linking the people with the strategic needs of the business, *Organizational Dynamics,* Summer 1992, p. 20.)

■ Building teamwork (with bottlers; among area, division, and headquarters staff; and across markets to share best practices)

■ Helping people succeed by building an environment with high integrity, strong and consistent values, and continuous improvement

Human resources policies (the second "P") follow from the HR philosophy. They provide guidelines for action on people-related business issues (those that affect the success of the business and involve people). For example, to develop communication skills that will foster high performance in a decentralized international environment,

PepsiCo International (which operates in 150 different national cultures) instituted a policy of "instant feedback." That is, if an employee had a problem or an idea about any aspect of the business or about an individual's performance, then the organization demanded that he or she raise the issue and discuss it maturely. A 20-minute video-tape explained how instant feedback could be applied in an international environment. Over time, instant feedback became the connecting link in a chain of feedback systems designed to improve and maintain high levels of personal performance—and, with some cultural modifications, it worked in every nation.[19]

Human resources programs (the third "P") are developed to initiate and sustain efforts by the organization to change in a manner consistent with its strategic business needs. For example, HR programs (or strategies) might be developed to deal with projected skill shortages or surpluses, or external challenges to the survival of a business. Thus, after IBM spun off its printer business into a subsidiary operation (Lexmark), it initiated a large retraining effort for its former production workers in Boulder, Colorado. It taught them to be logistics specialists (knowledge workers) who electronically track the movement of IBM goods across international boundaries and deal with customers in particular regions of the world. Top management had identified the need for expertise in logistics as a strategic business need, and the retraining program was designed to meet that need.

Human resources practices (the fourth "P") are developed to cue and reinforce leadership, managerial, or operational roles (i.e., patterns of expected behavior). For example, at Honda's Marysville, Ohio, plant, an analysis of the roles and responsibilities of first-level supervisors (e.g., induction training, keeping production records, team briefing, discipline) revealed that many of these could be reallocated to teams and team members in order to accommodate a more self-directed, self-managed approach.[20] The reallocation reinforced the increased responsibility and accountability that the work teams were expected to assume.

Human resources processes (the fifth "P") deal with "how" all the other HR activities are identified, developed, and implemented. HR processes may vary along a continuum of high involvement/high participation by all employees to no involvement/no participation by any employees. Whichever approach is taken, there is a need for consistency across all strategic HRM activities. All such activities influence human behavior, and if they do not send the same messages to everyone about what is expected and rewarded, the organization is likely to be little more than an aggregation of people pulling in different directions. Frameworks such as the 5-P model are designed to keep this from happening. Human resource strategy is naturally related to the kinds of things managers and HR professionals actually do. In our next section we will consider how such practices may differ, even among successful firms in the same industry.

USING HUMAN RESOURCES FOR COMPETITIVE ADVANTAGE AT FEDERAL EXPRESS (FEDEX) AND UNITED PARCEL SERVICE (UPS)[21]

COMPANY EXAMPLE

Explanations for what makes firms competitive are turning more frequently to the notion of "core competencies" that are unique to firms.[22] In this example, let us consider how distinctive human resource philosophies, policies, programs, practices, and processes (all

5 Ps) help to create unique competencies that differentiate services and, in turn, drive the competitiveness of the two firms in question.

Although both FedEx and UPS are in the shipping business, it is difficult to find two companies with people management practices that are more different. FedEx has no union, and its workforce is managed using the latest HRM tools. For example, both individual and group performance are assessed, and both influence pay. The company has pay-for-suggestion systems, quality-of-work-life programs, and a variety of other arrangements that empower employees and increase their involvement. Employees at FedEx have played an important role in helping to design the organization of work and the way technology has been used.

UPS, on the other hand, uses none of these HRM practices. Employees have no direct say over issues regarding how work is organized. Their jobs are designed by industrial engineers according to time-and-motion studies. The performance of each employee is measured and evaluated against company standards for each task, and employees receive daily feedback on their performance. The only effort at employee involvement is collective bargaining over contract terms through the Teamsters' Union, which represents drivers. Management, rather than the union, appears to be the force maintaining this system of work organization. It has shown little interest in moving towards work systems such as the kind used at FedEx.

The material rewards for working at UPS are substantial, and may more than offset the low levels of job enrichment and tight supervision. The company pays the highest wages and benefits in the industry. It also offers employees gain-sharing and stock ownership plans. UPS is privately held and is owned by its employees. In contrast to FedEx, virtually all promotions (98 percent) are filled from within the company, offering entry-level drivers excellent long-term prospects for advancement.

As a result of these material rewards, UPS employees are highly motivated and loyal to the company. The productivity of UPS drivers, the most important work group in the delivery business, is about three times higher (measured by deliveries and packages) than productivity at FedEx.

Why does it make sense for UPS to rely on highly engineered systems that are generally thought to contribute to poor morale and motivation, but then to offset the negative effects with strong material rewards? FedEx, in contrast, offers an alternative model with high levels of morale and motivation and lower material rewards. Differences in technology don't explain it. FedEx is known for its pioneering investments in information systems, but UPS has responded recently with its own wave of computerized operations. Yet the basic organization of work at UPS has not changed.

In fact, the employment systems in these two companies are driven by their business strategies. FedEx is much the smaller of the two, operating until recently with only one hub in Memphis and focusing on the overnight package delivery service as its platform product. UPS, in contrast, has a much wider range of products. While its overnight delivery volume is only 60 percent of FedEx's, its total business is nine times as large (11.5 million deliveries per day at UPS versus 1.2 million at FedEx).

The scale and scope of business at UPS demand an extremely high level of coordination across its network of delivery hubs, coordination that may be achievable only through a highly regimented and standardized approach to job design. Changes in practices and procedures essentially have to be systemwide to be effective. Such coordination is compatible with the systemwide process of collective bargaining but not with significant levels of autonomy of the kind associated with shop-floor decision making by employees.

FedEx, on the other hand, historically had only one hub, which meant that there were fewer coordination problems. This allowed considerable scope for autonomy and participation in shaping work decisions at the group level.

What is the lesson in this example? When it comes to managing people, there may be no single set of "best practices" for all employers. Firms that are in competition with one another work hard to differentiate their products and services and to find niches in markets where they are protected from competition. Differentiating products and services is one of the essential functions of strategic management. Distinctive human resource practices encourage that by shaping the core competencies that determine how firms compete.

THE RESPONSIBILITIES AND OBJECTIVES OF HUMAN RESOURCE MANAGEMENT

When it comes to managing people, all managers must be concerned to some degree with the following four activities: staffing, retention, development, and adjustment.

Staffing comprises the activities of (1) identifying the job requirements within an organization, (2) determining the numbers of people and the skills mix necessary to do these jobs, and (3) recruiting, selecting, and promoting qualified candidates.

Retention comprises the activities of (1) rewarding employees for performing their jobs effectively, (2) ensuring harmonious working relations between employees and managers, and (3) maintaining a safe, healthy work environment.

Development is a function whose activities are aimed at preserving and enhancing employees' competence in their jobs through improving their knowledge, skills, abilities, and other characteristics; HR specialists use the abbreviation KSAOs to refer to these items.

Adjustment comprises activities intended to maintain compliance with the organization's HR policies (e.g., through discipline), and business strategies (e.g., downsizing).

Needless to say, these activities can be carried out at the individual, work team, or larger organizational unit (e.g., department) level. Sometimes they are initiated by the organization (e.g., recruitment efforts or management development programs), and sometimes they are initiated by the individual or work team (e.g., voluntary retirement, safety improvements). Whatever the case, the responsibilities for carrying out these activities are highly interrelated. Together they comprise the HRM system.

To illustrate how each of the major activities within HRM relates to every other one, consider the following scenario.

As a result of a large number of unexpected early retirements, the Hand Corporation finds that it must recruit extensively to fill the vacated jobs. The firm is well aware of the rapid changes that will be occurring in its business over the next 5 to 10 years, so it must change its recruiting strategy in accordance with the expected changes in job requirements. Selection procedures must therefore be developed that will identify the kinds of KSAOs required of future employees. Compensation policies and procedures may have to change because job requirements will change, and new incentive systems will probably have to be developed. Since the firm cannot identify all the KSAOs that will be required 5 to 10 years from now, new training and development programs will have to be offered to satisfy those needs. Assessment procedures will necessarily change as well, since different KSAOs will be required in order to perform the jobs effectively. As a result of carrying out all this activity, the firm may need to discharge, promote, or transfer some employees to accomplish its mission.

It is surprising, isn't it, how that single event, an unexpectedly large number of early retirees, can change the whole ball game? Can you see how each of the "5 Ps" of strategic HRM (HR philosophy, policies, programs, practices, and processes) might be affected by these changes?

So it is with any system or network of interrelated components. Changes in any single part of the system have a reverberating effect on all other parts of the system. Simply knowing that this will occur is healthy, because then we will not make the mistake of confining our problems only to one part. We will recognize and expect that whether we are dealing with problems of staffing, training, compensation, or labor relations, they are interrelated. In short, the *systems approach* provides a conceptual framework for integrating the various components within the system and for linking the HRM system with larger organizational needs.

As noted above, the activities of staffing, retention, development, and adjustment are the special responsibilities of the HR department. But these responsibilities also lie within the core of every manager's job throughout any organization—and because line managers have authority (the organizationally granted right to influence the actions and behavior of the workers they manage), they have considerable impact on the ways workers actually behave. This implies two things: (1) a *broad objective* of HRM is to optimize the usefulness (i.e., the productivity) of all workers in an organization, and (2) a *special objective* of the HR department is to help line managers manage those workers more effectively. The HR department accomplishes this special objective through policy initiation and formulation, advice, service, and control in resonance (close communication, understanding, and aims) with line managers when it comes to managing people. To be sure, each of the responsibilities of HRM is shared by the HR department and the line managers, as shown in Table 2-1.

In the context of Table 2-1, note how line and HR managers share people-related business activities. Generally speaking, HR provides the technical expertise in each area, while line managers (or, in some cases, self-directed work teams) use this expertise in order to manage people effectively. In a small business, however, line managers are responsible for both the technical and managerial aspects of HRM.

For example, in the area of retention, line managers are responsible for treating employees fairly, resolving conflicts, promoting teamwork, and providing pay increases based on merit. In order to do these things effectively, however, it is the HR department's responsibility to devise a compensation and benefits system that employees will perceive as attractive and fair, to establish merit increase guidelines that will apply across departments, and to provide training and consultation to line managers on all employee relations issues—such as conflict resolution and team building.

THE ROLE AND MISSION OF THE HR DEPARTMENT: A TOP-MANAGEMENT VIEW

There is a perception among some people that this small department, with no revenue or profit-and-loss responsibility, somehow manages the human resources of the cor-

■ TABLE 2■1
HRM ACTIVITIES AND THE RESPONSIBILITIES OF LINE MANAGERS AND THE HR DEPARTMENT

Activity	Line management responsibility	HR department responsibility
Staffing	Providing data for job analyses and minimum qualifications; integrating strategic plans with HR plans at the unit level (e.g., department, division); interviewing candidates, integrating information collected by the HR department, making final decisions on entry-level hires and promotions	Job analysis, human resource planning, recruitment; compliance with civil rights laws and regulations; application blanks, written tests, performance tests, interviews, background investigations, reference checks, physical examinations
Retention	Fair treatment of employees, open communication, face-to-face resolution of conflict, promotion of teamwork, respect for the dignity of each individual, pay increases based on merit	Compensation and benefits, employee relations, health and safety, employee services
Development	On-the-job training, job enrichment, coaching, applied motivational strategies, performance feedback to subordinates	Development of legally sound performance appraisal systems and morale surveys; techincal training, management and organizational development, career planning, counseling, HR research
Adjustment	Discipline, discharge, layoffs, transfers	Investigation of employee complaints, outplacement services, retirement counseling

poration. As noted earlier, this is not true, for *all managers*, regardless of their functional specialty, are responsible not only for managing capital and equipment but also for managing people. Another common perception is, in effect, that "Employees should be viewed as costs, not as assets." This also is not true, for, as Bruce Ellig, Pfizer's top HR executive, noted: "You cut costs; you develop assets. The renaming of the personnel function to Human Resources in most organizations is at least an outward indication of that."[23]

Recent in-depth interviews of 71 chief executive officers (CEOs) of major corporations indicated that in general, they subscribe to neither of these views. The HR department does not have the sole responsibility for managing people, and people are seen as assets, not just as costs. CEOs see HRM as one of the most important corporate functions—one to which they look for help in forging a competitive edge for the business. They cite quality of talent, flexibility and innovation, superior performance or productivity, and customer service as key factors in accomplishing this.[24] However, the CEOs also say that they expect more of the HRM function than they are getting. Despite such advances as HR planning, improved information systems, and new approaches to compensation and benefits, the function is often viewed as following, rather than leading, change. Often it is "responsive" rather than "proactive" (that is, anticipating events, not just reacting to them).

Using the HRM Function Strategically

Chief executive officers need HR executives who have a clear sense of strategic direction, know the services required by the business, and understand the initiatives it should be taking toward organizational change.[25] In order to use the HRM function most effectively as a corporate resource, therefore, top management should consider doing the following things:

1. Require that HR executives be experienced businesspeople, for example, through job rotation policies and by extensive interaction with managers in all other functional areas. Unless these executives are perceived as equals by their corporate peers, their ability to make significant contributions to the firm will be diminished.

2. Require the senior HR executive to report directly to the CEO. At present this occurs in about 70 percent of companies nationwide. Consider whether any corporate resource is more important than its people. Suppose a fire destroyed all the plant and equipment of a 1000-employee firm; how long would it take to rebuild the plant and replace the equipment? A year? Now suppose the same firm lost all its employees; how long would it take to replace the same level of competence and commitment? Considerably longer. Indeed, is any management function more important than managing the people who compose the organization? HR policy cannot have any real meaning unless the CEO is intimately involved in its development.

3. Ensure that the top HR officer is a key player in the development and implementation of business plans—providing early warning regarding their acceptance and serving as the CEO's "window" on the organization and as a sounding board.

4. Define the HR department's responsibility as the maximization of corporate profits through the better management and use of people. The key issues are time and

money. Concentrate the HRM function on ways to make people more productive—especially on ways of improving the employees' job skills, improving their motivation by improving their quality of work life (QWL), and improving the professional skills of managers.

5. Do not dilute the HRM function by saddling the HR department with unrelated responsibilities, such as the mailroom and public relations. Consider moving productivity functions, such as industrial engineering, into the HR department.

In today's climate of increased competition and cost control, there is simply no room for people who cannot have a significant impact on the firm's productivity and profitability. HR is no exception.[26]

HR INITIATIVES: CONSIDER THE POSSIBILITIES

Study after study has shown that top management wants the HRM function to concentrate on people-related business issues involving productivity and cost containment. Here are some typical initiatives:[27]

- Containing the costs of employee health care and other benefits
- Redesigning compensation programs, tying them more closely to performance
- Improving productivity through employee involvement and meaningful performance appraisal

HR staff should help plan and implement changes in organizational structure or management practices, such as:

- Staffing changes resulting from downsizing, restructuring, mergers, or acquisitions
- Increasing the innovation, creativity, and flexibility necessary to enhance competitiveness; proactive HR departments are doing this by designing and facilitating the application of new approaches to job design (e.g., promoting entrepreneurship), succession planning, career development, and lateral mobility
- Managing the implementation of technological changes through improved staffing, training, and communications with employees
- Promoting changes in relations with unions, particularly those that will enhance cooperation, productivity, and flexibility
- Anticipating and influencing the management impact of new legislation and court decisions

KEY MANAGEMENT QUESTIONS TO ASK IN EVALUATING THE HRM FUNCTION

Just as it does when evaluating any other function, a company's management should ask tough questions, such as:

- How many HR managers, professionals, and support staff does the company employ this year? How much does this cost the company? (Considering the total cost per person of salaries and benefits, equipment, supplies, computer time, heat, light, water, depreciation, and rent, employees actually cost about three times their annual salaries.[28])

- How do these numbers (people and dollars) relate to company revenues and to the employee population?

- How do these ratios compare with those of competitors and/or with national figures?

- What trends can be identified in the HR department over the past 5 years? What ratios would it be desirable to maintain in the future?

Evaluation from the HR Perspective

It has been said many times that if HR people are to make meaningful contributions to an enterprise, they must think and act like businesspeople. To promote this sort of outlook, it is useful to ask "How much profit must a profit center make to keep an HR department going?"

Suppose you run an HR department for a firm that makes bicycles. Last year the total cost to the company for your department's services was $1 million. How many bikes does the company have to sell to pay your way? Let's say that on a $200 bicycle, your company makes a profit of $20. Dividing this $20 into $1 million shows that 50,000 bikes must be sold to keep the HR department in business!

The point of this exercise is not to argue for the abolition of HR departments in order to save profits or to save selling more bikes. Certainly, if the HR department was not doing its work, somebody else would be doing much of it. Rather, the point is that there is an important connection between human resource management and profits. It is seldom discussed, but it should be in order to promote increased awareness of how time and money are spent. Imagine an HR director asking how many bikes will have to be sold to support a new orientation program!

A second important question that management should ask and that HR people should be prepared to answer is "How much more product can be sold because of your services?" While many HR contributions are not related directly to the bottom line, it is important to promote increased awareness of how HR activities relate to the purposes of the organization. Here are some possible HR department responses in six key areas:[29]

- "Here's what we did for you [in recruiting, say], here's what it cost, and here's what you would have done without us and what it would have cost you."

- "Here's how much money we saved you by changing insurers in our benefits package."

- "Here's an idea that workers developed in a training program we were leading. It's now working and saving you $50,000 per year."

- "If you had not asked us to do this executive search, you would have had to go outside, at a cost of $30,000. We did it for $5000."

- "You used to have an unhappy person doing this job for $40,000 per year. As a result of our job redesign, you now have a motivated person doing the same work for $20,000."

- "In working with the union on a new contract, we found a new way to reduce grievances by 30 percent, saving the company 6429 hours per year in management time."

Even though precise bottom-line numbers might be hard to come by for many HR activities, it is important to encourage HR people to think in these terms. As an example, consider rewards-based suggestion systems.

REWARDS-BASED SUGGESTION SYSTEMS

COMPANY EXAMPLE

Suggestion systems designed to improve the quality or speed of goods and services have gotten quite a bad reputation of late. Most managers are convinced that they simply do not work. Perhaps they do not because of faulty suggestion-system design and implementation.

One exception is Honeywell's Defense Systems and Avionics Division, based in Minneapolis.[30] One year this company division received more than 18,000 suggestions (3.66 per employee) that resulted in a saving of more than $1 million. The Honeywell Suggestion System rewards employees who offer cost-saving suggestions by recognizing them and paying them an amount based on how much their suggestions save the company.

Cash is awarded to employees equal to one-sixth of the total first year's anticipated savings. The more valuable the suggestion, the greater the reward—a clear application of "pay for performance." Here's another example. At Ford Motor Co.'s Walton Hills metal stamping plant outside Cleveland, Bob Kubec, a metal-press operator at the plant, figured out a way to save 4 inches of sheet metal on every floor panel part he makes. His innovation will save Ford $70,000 every year; it won him a $14,000 reward.[31]

The trend in this area is for companies to provide more top prizes with higher cash awards. For example, Pitney Bowes Business Systems raised its top prize from $30,000 paid over 3 years to $50,000 paid over 2 years. Ford Motor Company now allows *groups* of hourly workers, instead of just an *individual,* to win its top award. Recently, Eastman Kodak paid $3.6 million in awards, up 8.7 percent from the previous year, and figures it saved $16 million as a result of the suggestions.[32]

Some of the major areas in which HRM can demonstrate measurable cost savings, productivity increases, and turnover reductions are shown and described briefly in Table 2-2.

This has been just a brief glimpse into several areas where effective HRM can make a substantial contribution to the improvement of productivity, the quality of work life, and the bottom line. Although each area has been discussed separately, the overall objective is to develop a uniform financial reporting system for the entire HRM subsystem. Significant and timely information can be produced, both line managers and HR staff can see how their work is interconnected, and over time such a measurement system can become a very powerful tool.

■ **TABLE 2 ▪ 2**

THE CONTRIBUTION OF EFFECTIVE HRM TO PROFITS—SOME AREAS AND EXAMPLES

Compensation policies	Development of a structured pay plan that accurately reflects labor market worth in each job to avoid the problem of overpayment or underpayment for specific jobs.
Employee benefits administration	Finding the greatest value for the money in health and life insurance, employee assistance, and pension plans; monitoring the costs of benefits paid out against premiums contributed; requesting a dividend when premiums exceed payouts.*
Payroll tax management	Monitoring federal and state unemployment tax rates. Since the rates charged are a function of claims by former employees, the rates drop as turnover is reduced—and potential savings can be significant.
Selection and training	To the extent that more valid selection procedures help to reduce the attrition and increase the retention of newly hired employees, savings may be huge. For example, at a cost of $1 million to train a navy fighter pilot† and a loss of $250,000 for each unsuccessful candidate, a reduction of five unsuccessful candidates would save the navy $1.25 million *per year*.
Recruiting and retaining a diverse workforce	Given the demographic changes looming on the horizon, affirmative action to find and retain the best talent from the pool of women and racial and ethnic minorities makes more economic sense than ever. "Tokenism" is dead; managing cultural and ethnic diversity effectively can add genuine value to a firm. With regard to older workers, consider that the odds are 5 to 1 that a recent college graduate will leave within the first 3 years of employment. The odds of a 50-year-old recruit staying with an organization for 15 or more productive years are far better.††
Control of turnover costs	Using proper accounting procedures to compute the real cost of turnover (i.e., separation, replacement, and training costs) reveals that six- or seven-figure annual turnover costs are common for large firms.§ Controlling such costs through joint HR and line management efforts (e.g., through job redesign, retraining, changes in compensation)—even to a modest degree—can represent considerable savings.

*M. M. Markowich, 25 ways to save a bundle, *HRMagazine,* Oct. 1992, pp. 48–57.
†Navy worried over growing jet losses, *Honolulu Star Bulletin & Advertiser,* Mar. 23, 1986, pp. A1, A4.
††C. H. Driessnack, Financial impact of effective human resources management. *The Personnel Administrator,* **4,** 1979, 62–66.
§W. F. Cascio, *Costing human resources: The financial impact of behavior in organizations* (3d ed.), Boston: PWS-Kent, p. 19.

Current Status of HRM Activities

Progressive organizations are rotating their best managers through the various specialized HRM functions as a required part of their development and as a way of bringing line experience to HRM problems. Higher levels of education and experience are required for individuals who are given such HRM assignments. In fact, the vice president of human resources frequently reports directly to the chief executive officer and sits on the board of directors and the planning committee. As the chapter's opening vignette indicated, salaries for top HR executives also reflect this increased stature.

What are firms getting for this money? The best HR talent executes six roles well:[33]

IMPACT OF EFFECTIVE HRM ON PRODUCTIVITY, QUALITY OF WORK LIFE, AND THE BOTTOM LINE

Employees are well aware that the U.S. workplace is in a state of turbulence. Many have been through multiple waves of downsizing, and they have seen careers and work lives jolted from stability to uncertainty. As a result, according to a recent survey, employees are less loyal to their companies, and they tend to put their own needs and interests above those of their employers. More often they are willing to trade off higher wages and benefits for flexibility and autonomy, job characteristics that allow them to balance their lives on and off the job. Almost 9 out of every 10 workers live with family members, and nearly half care for dependents, including children, elderly parents, or ailing spouses. Among employees who switched jobs in the last 5 years, pay and benefits rated in the bottom half of 20 possible reasons why they did so. Factors rated highest were "nature of work," "open communication," and "effect on personal/family life." What are the implications of these results for organizations that depend on workforces made docile by fear? When companies fail to factor in quality-of-work-life issues and quality-of-life issues when introducing any of the popular schemes for improving productivity, the only thing they may gain is a view of the backs of their best people leaving for friendlier employers.[34]

- Businessperson
- Shaper of change
- Consultant to the organization and partner to line managers
- Strategy formulator and implementor
- Talent manager (i.e., networker with professional colleagues, including recruiters, line managers, and other HR professionals)
- Asset manager and cost controller (based on understanding financial and accounting procedures)

As the director of HR planning at Bank of America noted, "The perception used to be that human resources thought about the happiness of employees, and line managers thought about costs. Now both realize that the overriding concern is the yield from employees."[35]

Indeed, as people-related business issues continue to increase, the importance of professional *certification* in the HR field is becoming more important. Individuals become certified by demonstrating mastery of the defined body of knowledge required for success in a field. In HRM, two designations are available: Professional in Human Resources (PHR) and Senior Professional in Human Resources (SPHR). Each requires one comprehensive exam that covers six areas: staffing, labor relations, compensation, training, safety, and management practice. Other types of certification are available (see Figure 2-6) within more specialized areas in HR and related fields. Certification has enhanced the credibility of the profession, and today more than 10,000 HRM professionals have completed the certification process.[36]

CERTIFYING AGENCY	CERTIFICATION DESIGNATION
Human Resource Certification Institute	Professional in Human Resources
	Senior Professional in Human Resources
American Compensation Association	Certified Compensation Professional
International Foundation of Employee Benefit Plans	Certified Employee Benefit Specialist
Board of Certified Safety Professionals	Associate Safety Professional
	Certified Safety Professional
American Board of Industrial Hygiene/Board of Certified Safety Professionals	Occupational Health and Safety Technologist

FIGURE 2-6
Options for professional certification in human resource management. (*Source:* C. Wiley, The certified HR professional, *HRMagazine*, Aug. 1992, p. 79.)

ETHICAL DILEMMA: WHOM TO REPRESENT?

Earlier we noted that one of the roles that the HR professional plays is "consultant to the organization and partner to line managers." As a consultant to the organization, the HR professional often represents employees, for example, in mediating conflicts between employees and managers or in investigating claims of improper or unfair treatment. On the other hand, as a partner to line managers, the HR professional's job is to work with managers to help them be successful. Are there situations where the roles of consultant to the organization and partner to line managers might conflict and therefore pose ethical dilemmas for the HR professional?

IMPLICATIONS FOR MANAGEMENT PRACTICE

According to Robert Galvin, chief executive officer of Motorola:

> Generally we're seeing the HR manager and HR department being offered the opportunity to be transformed from a functional specialist to management team member, and it is expected that the shift from "employee advocate" to "member of the management team" will continue throughout the 1990s. Human resource professionals will be called upon to think and act like line managers and to address people-related business issues. Management will increasingly expect HR to think and act, and to view human resource activities, from a business perspective.[37]

If this is the role of HR professionals, what will be the role of line managers in the HRM area? Predominantly it will be a set of activities that indicate an increased awareness of the implications of the phrase "human resources." Organizations and line managers will truly consider their employees as important resources "to be invested in prudently, to be used productively, and from whom a return can be expected—a return that should be monitored as carefully as is the return on any other business investment."[38] Human resource management is not only planning and controlling, manipulating numbers, and reporting to higher management; it is also relating on a daily basis to the employees of the company. All managers must emphasize the human side of the workforce and give more than lip service to honoring and understanding that side. This is the real challenge of managing people effectively.

THE 1990s CHALLENGE: MANAGING PEOPLE-RELATED BUSINESS ISSUES

In the opinion of many top managers, the only way to make "people-related business issues" credible is to support them with real assets—such as pay and promotions. At Scott Paper, managers are now evaluated on how their employees develop and on how well they interact with other departments.

Senior management also needs to send signals that HR issues and HR executives are major players. Unfortunately, however, some of the biggest problems are the HR executives themselves, many of whom are not willing, or able, to make the leap to being major players. Thus, when a new CEO took over Scientific-Atlanta, Inc., a communications company, he promptly dismissed the HR executive he inherited from the previous administration. Why? The man ran a "sleepy" department. Said the new CEO: "This can't be someone sitting in a back office looking at compensation schedules."

The new role also means unfamiliar visibility and accountability. Even more intimate contact with top management carries a price; since the fit with a chief executive is critical, job security is only as good as the boss's tenure. As a result, says one expert, "some good people just can't take the heat." Those who can "are in short supply because companies just haven't been growing this type of person."

Career tracks for the longtime HR executive have also changed. Bob Murphy, the top HR executive at Rockwell International Corporation, is typical. He went back to school to earn his master's in business administration at night and did stints overseas and in finance. In fact, when top executives were asked to rank the ideal skills needed by their chief executive officers in the year 2000, the top four were strategy formulation, marketing-sales, negotiation and conflict resolution, and human resource management. People-related business skills are essential ingredients for success as a manager now, and all indications are that they will continue to be so in the future.

SUMMARY

Modern HRM has evolved from nine interrelated sources: (1) the industrial revolution, (2) the emergence of free collective bargaining, (3) the scientific management movement, (4) early industrial psychology, (5) government HRM practices resulting from the establishment of the U.S. Civil Service Commission, (6) the emergence of personnel specialists and their grouping into personnel departments, (7) the human relations movement, (8) the behavioral sciences, and (9) the social legislation and court decisions of the 1960s and 1970s.

HRM as we know it today has evolved through four growth stages: file maintenance, government accountability, organizational accountability, and strategic partner. In fact, we use the term "strategic HRM" to refer to the wisest possible use of people with respect to the strategic needs of the organization. An integrative framework that systematically links HR activities (i.e., human resources philosophy, policies, programs, practices, and processes) with strategic business needs can ensure a good fit.

HRM involves four major areas: staffing, retention, development, and adjustment. Together they compose the HRM system, for they describe a network of interrelated components. Top management views the HRM function as an important tool to enhance competitiveness. To accomplish this purpose, the HRM function must be used strategically. Its responsibility is the maximization of productivity, quality of work life, and profits through better management of people. To fulfill this responsibility, the senior HR executive should report directly to the CEO, she or he should play a key role in the development of business plans, the HRM function should focus on productivity-related activities, and HR people should above all be businesspeople, accountable, just as employees from any other function, in terms of their overall contributions to enhancing productivity and controlling costs.

In today's flatter, more complex organizations, the best HR talent executes six roles well: businessperson, shaper of change, consultant to the organization and partner to line managers, strategy formulator and implementor, talent manager, and asset manager and cost controller. Finally, contributions to improved productivity, QWL, and the bottom line can come from more effective management of a number of areas. These include, but certainly are not limited to, compensation policies and procedures, benefits administration, payroll tax management, selection and training, recruiting and retaining a diverse workforce, and controlling turnover costs.

DISCUSSION QUESTIONS

2▪1 Discuss the contributions of the industrial revolution, scientific management, and early industrial psychology to the development of modern HRM.

2▪2 Describe the characteristics of the new role of the HR executive—that of "strategic partner" with top management.

2▪3 How do the responsibilities and objectives of HRM contribute to employee productivity and employee job satisfaction?

2▪4 In what ways can effective HRM contribute to profits?

2▪5 What changes do you see in HRM over the next 5 years?

REFERENCES

1. Beatty, L. K. (1992, June). The 1992 HR pay picture. *HRMagazine*, 62–64.
2. French, W. L. (1994). *Human resources management* (3d ed.). Boston: Houghton Mifflin.
3. Ibid.
4. Cohen, S. (1960). *Labor in the United States*. Columbus, OH: Charles E. Merrill.
5. Bell, D. (1972). Three technologies: Size, measurement, hierarchy. In L. E. Davis and J. C. Taylor (eds.), *Design of jobs*. London: Penguin.
6. Locke, E. A. (1982). The ideas of Frederick W. Taylor: An evaluation. *Academy of Management Review*, **7**, 14–24.
7. Landy, F. J. (1992). Hugo Munsterberg: Victim or visionary? *Journal of Applied Psychology*, **77**, 787–802. See also Moskowitz, M. J. (1977). Hugo Munsterberg: A study in the history of applied psychology. *American Psychologist*, **32**, 824–842.
8. Van Riper, P. P. (1958). *History of the United States Civil Service*. Evanston, IL: Row-Peterson.
9. Eilbert, H. (1959). The development of personnel management in the United States. *Business History Review*, **33**, 345–364.
10. Pennock, G. A. (1930, Feb.). Industrial research at Hawthorne and experimental investigation of rest periods, working conditions, and other influences. *Personnel Journal*, **8**, 296–309. See also Roethlisberger, F. J., & Dickson, W. J. (1939). *Management and the worker*. Boston: Harvard University Press.
11. Brayfield, A. H., & Crockett, W. H. (1955). Employee attitudes and employee performance. *Psychological Bulletin*, **52**, 396–424.
12. French, op. cit.

13. Meyer, H. E. (1976, Feb.). Personnel directors are the new corporate heroes. *Fortune*, **93**, 84–88.

14. Cascio, W. F. (1991). *Costing human resources: The financial impact of behavior in organizations* (3d ed.). Boston: PWS-Kent.

15. Human resources managers aren't corporate nobodies anymore (1985, Dec. 2). *Business Week*, pp. 58–59.

16. Gleckman, H. (1993, Sept. 13). Where to prune, where to hack away. *Business Week*, pp. 98–99.

17. Kiechel, W., III (1987, Aug. 18). Living with human resources. *Fortune*, pp. 99–100.

18. This model was first presented in Schuler, R. S. (1992, Summer). Strategic human resources management: Linking the people with the strategic needs of the business. *Organizational Dynamics*, 18–32.

19. Ibid.

20. Ibid.

21. Cappelli, P., & Crocker-Hefter, A. (1993). *Distinctive human resources are the core competencies of firms.* Philadelphia: National Center on the Educational Quality of the Workforce, Working Paper WP18.

22. Prahalad, C. K., & Hamel, G. (1990, May–June). The core competencies of the corporation. *Harvard Business Review*, pp. 79–91.

23. Holder, J. (1986). Regaining the competitive edge. *Personnel Administrator*, **31**, 35–41, 122, 124.

24. Walker, J. W. (1986). Moving closer to the top. *Personnel Administrator*, **31**, 52–57, 117.

25. Penezic, R. A. (1993, May). HR executives influence CEO strategies. *HRMagazine*, pp. 58–59.

26. Lengnick-Hall, C. A., & Lengnick-Hall, M. L. (1990). *Interactive human resource management and strategic planning.* New York: Quorum Books.

27. Markowich, M. M. (1992, Oct.). 25 ways to save a bundle. *HRMagazine*, 48–57. See also Penezic, op. cit.; Walker, op. cit.

28. Bellman, G. M. (1986). Doing more with less. *Personnel Administrator*, **31**, 46–52.

29. Ibid.

30. Zemke, R. (1980, July). Combine recognition and reward. *Training*, pp. 12–13.

31. Templin, N. (1992, Dec. 15). Team spirit: A decisive response to crisis brought Ford enhanced productivity. *The Wall Street Journal*, pp. A1, A6.

32. Labor letter (1984, May 15). *The Wall Street Journal*, p. 1.

33. Schuler, R. S. (1990). Repositioning the human resource function: Transformation or demise? *Academy of Management Executive*, **4**(3), 49–60.

34. Noble, B. P. (1993, Sept. 11). Quality-of-life is getting to be key work issue. *The New York Times*, p. A6.

35. Kiechel, op. cit.

36. Wiley, C. (1992, Aug.). The certified HR professional. *HRMagazine*, pp. 77–84.

37. Schuler (1990), op. cit., p. 50.

38. Briscoe, D. R. (1982, Nov.). Human resource management has come of age. *The Personnel Administrator*, **26**, 75–83.

CHAPTER 3

DIVERSITY AT WORK

ON MANAGING A MULTICULTURAL WORKFORCE*

■ A manager born and raised in the United States sees two Arab Americans in his group arguing—and figures he'd better stay out of it. What started as a small disagreement escalates into a conflict requiring formal disciplinary action. Both employees had in fact *expected* a third-party intermediary, or *wasta* in Arabic. Without one the incident blows up. This expectation goes back to the Koran and Bedouin tradition. The dominant American culture (that is, the one traditionally defined by the most populous group in organizations—white males) tends to assume an individualistic, win-lose approach and to emphasize privacy. What the manager doesn't understand is that Arab Americans tend to value a win-win result that preserves group harmony even if it requires mediation.

■ A Latino manager starts a budget-planning meeting by chatting casually and checking with his new staff on whether everyone can get together after work. His own boss frets over the delay and wonders why he doesn't get straight to the numbers. What his boss doesn't understand is that in the Latino culture building relationships is crucial to working together. It's the boss's American culture that wants the manager to "get right down to business."

■ An Asian-American woman is being interviewed for employment. Deferring to authority, she keeps her eyes down, rarely meeting the interviewer's eyes. The interviewer, a white American male, thinks, "She's not assertive, not strong enough, maybe she's hiding

---

*Adapted from: J. Solomon, As cultural diversity of workers grows, experts urge appreciation of differences, *The Wall Street Journal*, Sept. 12, 1990, pp. B1, B12. Reprinted by permission of *The Wall Street Journal*, © 1990 Dow Jones & Company, Inc. All rights reserved worldwide.

something or is insecure." What the interviewer doesn't understand is that the Asian-American woman views the persistent eye contact of the interviewer as domineering, invasive, and controlling. The result: neither trusts the other.

■ In a corporate setting, one manager, who is African American, shows up a bit late for a meeting. Everyone notices. He is on time for the next meeting, when three other managers, who are white, are late. Their lateness is tolerated and not much of an issue. What is going on here is the exaggerated way in which the behavior of nonwhite people is often perceived, relative to that of white people.

These four scenarios are not blatant cases of unlawful discrimination. Nor are such incidents usually so overt as suggested here. But they do represent what happens every day in the workplace because cultural differences are not understood or appreciated.

Challenges

1. What is the objective of effective cross-cultural communication?

2. In light of the massive restructuring and downsizing that has occurred in large organizations, are employees from different cultures in a position to demand more flexibility from management?

3. What steps can you take to become more effective as a manager in a multicultural work environment?

---

1. Are there business reasons why I should pay attention to "managing diversity"?

2. What are leading companies doing in this area?

3. What can I do to reverse the perception among many managers that the growing diversity of the workforce is a problem?

4. How can I maximize the potential of a racially and ethnically diverse workforce?

5. What can I do to accommodate women and older workers?

Questions This Chapter Will Help Managers Answer

The United States workforce is diverse—and becoming more so every year.

■ More than half the U.S. workforce now consists of racial (i.e., nonwhite) and ethnic (i.e., people classified according to common traits and customs) minorities, immigrants, and women.

■ White, native-born males, though still dominant, are themselves a statistical minority. From 1983 to 1993, the percentage of white male professionals and managers dropped from 55 percent to 47 percent.[1]

■ Women will fill almost two-thirds of the new jobs created during this decade, and by the year 2000, nearly half the workforce will be female.

■ The so-called mainstream is now almost as diverse as the society at large. Today more than 20 million Americans were born in another country.[2]

■ White males will make up only 15 percent of the increase in the workforce over the next decade.[3]

These demographic facts do not indicate that a diverse workforce is something a company *ought* to have. Rather, they tell us that all companies already do have or soon will have diverse workforces.

Unfortunately, the attitudes and beliefs about the groups contributing to the diversity change only slowly. To some, workers and managers alike, workforce diversity is simply a problem that won't go away. Nothing can be gained with this perspective. To others, diversity represents an opportunity, an advantage that can be used to compete and win in the global marketplace, as we shall now see.

WORKFORCE DIVERSITY: AN ESSENTIAL COMPONENT OF HR STRATEGY

Managing diversity means establishing a heterogeneous workforce (including white men) to perform to its potential in an equitable work environment where no member or group of members has an advantage or a disadvantage.[4] Managing diversity is not the same thing as managing affirmative action. Affirmative action refers to actions taken to overcome the effects of past or present practices, policies, or other barriers to equal employment opportunity.[5] It is a first step that gives managers the opportunity to correct imbalances, injustices, and past mistakes. However, once the "numbers mistake" has been corrected (i.e., when the representation of each protected group in the workforce is proportional to its representation in the relevant labor market), the long-term challenge becomes to create a work setting in which each person can perform to his or her full potential and therefore compete for promotions and other rewards on merit alone. Key differences between managing diversity and managing affirmative action/equal employment opportunity are shown in Table 3-1.

There are five reasons why diversity has become a dominant activity in managing an organization's human resources (see Figure 3-1):

1. The shift from a manufacturing to a service economy

2. Globalization of markets

3. New business strategies that require more teamwork

4. Mergers and alliances that require different corporate cultures to work together

5. The changing labor market[6]

The Service Economy

As of 1993, 84 percent of U.S. employees worked in service-based industries (see Table 3-2).[7] Service-industry jobs, such as in banking, financial services, tourism, and retailing, imply lots of interaction with customers. Service employees need to be able to "read" their customers—to understand them, to anticipate and monitor their needs and expectations, and to respond sensitively and appropriately to those needs and expectations. In the service game, "customer literacy" is an essential skill. Racial- and ethnic-minority customers, in particular, represent a large market segment that accounts for $600 billion in purchases every year. Almost half of all *Fortune* 1000 companies have some type of ethnic-marketing campaign, and by the year 2000, minorities may account for 30 percent of the U.S. economy.[8]

A growing number of companies now realize that their workforces should mirror their customers. Similarities in culture, dress, and language between service workers and customers creates more efficient interactions between them and better business for the firm. Maryland National Bank in Baltimore discovered this when it studied the customer retention records for its branches. The branches showing highest customer loyalty recruited locally to hire tellers, who could swap neighborhood gossip. The best

■ TABLE 3 - 1

THE DIFFERENCES BETWEEN MANAGING DIVERSITY AND MANAGING AFFIRMATIVE ACTION/EQUAL EMPLOYMENT OPPORTUNITY (AA/EEO)

Managing diversity	Managing AA/EEO
Reason: Proactive—based on reality and anticipated needs	*Reason:* Reactive and based on law and moral imperatives (i.e., "it's the right thing to do")
1. Top management leads by example	1. Top management delegates the leading roles to AA/EEO administrators
2. AA/EEO is an important part of the strategy for managing a diverse workforce	2. AA/EEO is a separate activity
3. Strategic part of the business plan to help the organization survive, adapt (to changes in markets, customers, products, and services), and grow	3. Nonstrategic, not tied into the business plan
4. Strong link to managerial performance appraisals and rewards	4. No formal link to managerial performance appraisals and rewards
5. Linked to team building and quality efforts	5. Not linked to team building and quality efforts
6. Wide variety of programs that affect the organization's cultural values and norms (e.g., "family-friendly" policies, formal mentoring programs for all new hires)	6. Targeted special programs that have no significant impact on the organization's cultural values (e.g., "affirmative action recruiting")
7. Long-term linked commitments that use ongoing acquired knowledge as building blocks for future strategies, plans, and goals	7. Short-term, unlinked commitments with little building on acquired knowledge for the next steps
8. Emphasizes strategies to manage more effectively a diverse customer base, a more diverse employee body, and a more diverse stakeholder base	8. Emphasizes strategies to deal primarily with employees, not customers and stakeholders
9. Inclusive (focuses on all employees regardless of race, ethnicity, gender, age, religion, language, personality, sexual orientation, physical or mental limitations)	9. Exclusive (primarily focuses on women and people of color)
10. Respects, values, understands, appreciates differences	10. Attempts to make individuals conform to organizational norms
11. Produces significant change in reward, recognition, and benefit programs	11. Rewards, recognition, and benefit programs not changed
12. Both an internal and external strategy, that is, actively involved in community and societal issues involving diversity	12. Primarily an internal strategy, that is, only a limited involvement in community and societal issues to meet governmental requirements

Source: Adapted from J. P. Fernandez, with M. Barr, *The diversity advantage.* New York: Lexington Books, 1993, pp. 294, 295.

of 20 branch managers was located in a distant suburb and was described as dressing "very blue collar. She doesn't look like a typical manager of people. But this woman is totally committed to her customers."[9]

When companies discover they can communicate better with their customers through employees who are similar to their customers, those companies then realize they have increased their internal diversity. And that means they have to manage and retain their new, diverse workforce. There is no going back; diversity breeds diversity. Managing it well is an essential part of HR strategy.

The Globalization of Markets

As organizations around the world compete for customers, they offer customers choices unavailable to them domestically. With more options to choose from, customers have more power to insist that their needs and preferences be satisfied. To satisfy them, firms have to get closer and closer to their customers. Some firms have established a strong local presence (e.g., advertisements for Japanese-made cars that

FIGURE 3-1
Increased diversity in the
workforce meshes well with
the evolving changes in
organizations and markets.

showcase local dealerships and satisfied American owners); others have forged strategic international alliances (e.g., Apple Computer and Sony). Either way, diversity must be managed: by working through domestic diversity (local presence) or by merging national as well as corporate cultures (international alliances).

New Business Strategies That Require More Teamwork

To survive, to serve, and to succeed, organizations need to accomplish goals that are defined more broadly than ever before (e.g., world-class quality, reliability, and customer service). That means carrying out strategies that no one part of the organization can execute. For example, if a firm's business strategy emphasizes speed in every function (in developing new products, producing them, distributing them, and responding to feedback from customers), the firm needs to rely on teams of workers. Teams mean diverse workforces, whether as a result of drawing from the most talented or experienced staff or through deliberately structuring diversity to stimulate creativity.

■ **TABLE 3 - 2**

THE SHIFT FROM MANUFACTURING TO SERVICE JOBS,
1973–1993

Year	Manufacturing jobs (%)	Service jobs (%)
1973	26	74
1983	20	80
1993	16	84

Firms have found that only through work teams can they execute newly adopted strategies stressing better quality, innovation, cost control, or speed. For example, Ford Motor Company was able to execute its "Quality Is Job One" strategy by getting its employees' commitment to this strategy through team-based work that gave shop-floor workers the opportunity to suggest and implement changes that would improve the quality and efficiency of the production process. Companywide profit sharing has given the teams an incentive to be more efficient. To produce quality products, Ford believes, employees must be involved in and committed to their jobs, and team-based work fosters such commitment.[10] Indeed, thousands of companies, such as General Mills, Corning, Federal Express, Westinghouse, and Dana Corporation, have found that work teams promote greater flexibility, reduced operating costs, faster response to technological change, fewer job classifications, better response to new worker values (e.g., empowerment of lower-level workers, increased autonomy and responsibility), and the ability to attract and retain top talent.[11] Teams also facilitate innovation by bringing together experts with different knowledge bases and perspectives,[12] such as in concurrent engineering—a design process that relies on teams of experts from design, manufacturing, and marketing.

Diversity is an inevitable by-product of teamwork, especially when teams are drawn from a diverse base of employees. Young and old, male and female, American-born and non-American-born, better and less well educated, these are just some of the dimensions along which team members may differ. Coordinating team talents to develop new products, better customer service, or ways of working more efficiently is a difficult, yet essential, aspect of business strategy.

Mergers and Strategic International Alliances

The managers who have worked out the results of all the mergers, acquisitions, and strategic international alliances occurring over the past 20 years know how important it is to knit together the new partners' financial, technological, production, and marketing resources.[13] However, the resources of the new enterprise also include people, and this means creating a partnership that spans different corporate cultures.

The main source of problems in mergers, acquisitions, and strategic international alliances is differences in corporate cultures, according to a *Harvard Business Review* survey of 12,000 managers from 25 different countries.[14] It has created problems in 59 percent of the companies creating such alliances. Corporate cultures may differ in many ways, such as the customs of conducting business, how people are expected to behave, and the kinds of behaviors that get rewarded.

When two foreign businesses attempt a long-distance marriage, the obstacles are national cultures as well as corporate cultures. Fifty percent of U.S. managers either resign or are fired within 18 months of a foreign takeover.[15] Many of the managers report a kind of "culture shock." As one manager put it, "You don't quite know their values, where they're coming from, or what they really have in mind for you."[16] Both workers and managers need to understand and capitalize on diversity as companies combine their efforts to offer products and services to customers in far-flung markets.

The Changing Labor Market

The report *Workforce 2000*[17] predicts that the U.S. workforce will comprise more women, more immigrants, more people of color, and more older workers as we move into the twenty-first century. Our workplaces will be characterized by more cultural diversity. The first step to attaining the advantages of diversity is to teach *all* employees to understand and value different races, ethnic groups, cultures, languages, religions, sexual orientations, levels of physical ability, and family structures. Skeptical managers, supervisors, and policymakers need to understand that *different* does not mean *deficient*.[18] For example, in attempting to resolve a conflict between two employees, workers or managers from different cultures might: (1) dictate a solution; (2) serve as referees, issuing rulings only after hearing from both sides; or (3) stay out of the conflict altogether. Each of these strategies can work under certain circumstances. Different styles do not mean that one is necessarily better than another. Only when employees understand these things will the corporation they work for be able to build the trust that is essential among the members of high-performance work teams. Such teams incorporate practices that provide their members with the information, skills, incentives, and responsibility to make decisions that are essential to innovate, to improve quality, and to respond rapidly to change.[19]

DIVERSITY AT WORK—A PROBLEM FOR MANY ORGANIZATIONS

Recent studies of the U.S. workforce indicate widespread perceptions of racial and sexual discrimination in the workplace—perceptions that take a heavy toll on job performance.[20] More than 1 in 4 workers report that they personally have experienced racially motivated discrimination on the job. Reports of discrimination correlate with a tendency to feel "burned out," a reduced willingness to take initiative on the job, and a greater likelihood of planning to change jobs. And despite the increase of women in the workforce every year for the past 20 years or more, the women managers surveyed were more than twice as likely as men to rate their career advancement opportunities as "poor" or "fair." Moreover, women who said they saw little opportunity for career advancement also tended to be less loyal, less committed, and less satisfied on the job—hardly the way to build a productive workforce, as we saw in Chapter 1.

These studies challenge the notion that younger workers cope better with a more diverse workplace. Workers under 25 years of age show no greater preference than older workers do for working with people of other races, ages, or ethnic groups. Just over half of surveyed workers of all ages said they prefer to work with people of the same race, ethnic group, gender, and education. However, employees who had already lived or worked with people of other races, ethnic groups, or ages showed a stronger preference for diversity in the workplace. Unfortunately, few employees have had this experience. Even workers under 25 had little contact with people of different ethnic and cultural backgrounds in the neighborhoods where they grew up. All this suggests that the workplace is the main arena for racial and social interaction. If employers want to promote healthy, cooperative interaction, *they* must assume the leadership to do so.

To begin to do this, it is necessary to understand the concept of culture and its impact on thought and action. Culture is the foundation of group differences, and in the following sections we will examine the concept of culture and then focus briefly on some key issues that characterize three racial/ethnic groups (African Americans, Hispanic Americans, and Asian Americans), women, and the four generations that make up the U.S. workforce. As in other chapters, we will present examples of companies that have provided progressive leadership in this area.

Culture—The Foundation of Group Differences

Culture refers to the characteristic behavior of people in a country or region. Culture helps people make sense of their part of the world. It provides them with an identity—one they retain even when they emigrate and that is retained by their children and grandchildren as well.[21]

When we talk about culture, we include, for example, family patterns, customs, social classes, religions, political systems, clothing, music, food, literature, and laws.[22] Understanding the things that make up a person's culture helps diverse peoples to deal more constructively with one another. Conversely, misunderstandings among people of goodwill often cause unnecessary interpersonal problems and have undone countless business deals. We will examine the concept of culture more fully in Chapter 18.

"Accepting diversity" means more than feeling comfortable with employees whose race, ethnicity, or gender differ from your own.[23] It means more than accepting their accents or language, their dress or food. What it does mean is learning to value and respect cultural styles and ways of behaving that differ from your own. To manage cultural diversity, there is no room for inflexibility and intolerance—they must be totally displaced by adaptability and acceptance.

African Americans in the Workforce

African Americans make up 12 percent of the U.S. civilian workforce.[24] Since the early 1970s, the economic status of African Americans, relative to that of white Americans, has stagnated or deteriorated.[25] Studies indicate that some of the reasons are:

1. A shift in the industrial base of the U.S. economy from blue-collar manufacturing to service industries

2. A falling percentage of employed African Americans of all ages, relative to whites

3. An enormous increase in nonworkers among African American men in the prime working age group

4. An increase in poverty rates associated with an increase in the number of African-American families headed by females (in 1890, 80 percent of African-American families with children were headed by married couples; in 1990, that percentage was down to 39 percent[26])

5. Large occupational differences between African Americans and white Americans, with proportionally more African Americans in low-wage–low-skill jobs

This last factor is a key reason why African Americans suffered a disproportionately high loss of jobs during the 1990–1991 recession. As Figure 3-2 shows, the percentage change in employment of African Americans was negative in every EEOC job

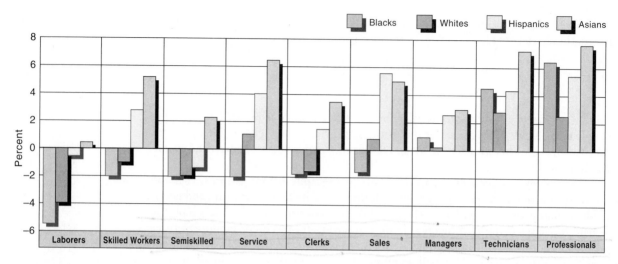

FIGURE 3-2

Percentage change in employment in nine job categories by race and job category, 1990–1991. (*Source:* R. Sharpe. Losing ground, *The Wall Street Journal*, Sept. 14, 1993, p. A14.)

category except for three: managers, technicians, and professionals. Even in these three categories, African Americans make up just 5.2% of the total for all races.

One big reason for this is lack of education. According to the 1990 census, only 13.1 percent of African Americans in the workforce have college degrees, compared with 24.6 percent of whites and 38.6 percent of Asian Americans. With comparably little education, African Americans get stuck in lower-skilled and blue-collar jobs. In the event of layoffs, seniority often determines who stays and who goes. Since African Americans are often the last hired for these kinds of jobs (for a variety of reasons ranging from a lack of knowledge of job opportunities to the recency of outreach recruitment programs in some companies to outright discrimination), they are the first to be laid off. At USX Corporation, for example, employees at some plants had to have almost 20 years' experience to keep their jobs through the 1990–1991 recession. African Americans lost nearly 20 percent of the total number of jobs eliminated at the company, even though they made up just 12.6 percent of the workforce going into the recession.[27] And the abandonment by companies of inner-city offices, factories, and franchise outlets hasn't helped keep African Americans in jobs.

To a large extent, their disproportionate loss in jobs is due to a shift in the way affirmative action programs operate. The Department of Labor's Office of Federal Contract Compliance Programs (the government enforcement agency that audits the affirmative action plans of government contractors) decides which companies to audit by analyzing their records on *overall minority employment*, not by individual ethnic or racial groups.

To see this, consider what happened at Dial Corporation. African Americans lost 43.6 percent of the jobs cut, even though they represented 26.3 percent of Dial's workforce going into the recession. But Dial's overall record of minority employment still looked good. That's because Dial had increased its hiring of Asian Americans and American Indians and had laid off a disproportionately small percentage of white women.[28]

Just the opposite happened at Louisiana-Pacific Corporation. The African-American workforce grew by 7.7 percent in 1991, even as the company cut its overall staff by 6.1 percent. The reason for the gain? Geography. The company eliminated jobs in its plants in rural northern California, which had few minorities, while adding workers in southern states with large populations of African Americans.

Why is this happening? Don't companies know about the underrepresentation of African Americans in their ranks? The answer is that companies are offering equitable, not preferential, treatment. Managers are held accountable for their overall minority employment record and for attaining workforce diversity, rather than for the representation of specific racial- or ethnic-minority groups.

Nevertheless, younger, educated African Americans are finding employment in skilled jobs that bring higher earnings. Others have gained from the expanded opportunities resulting from the enforcement of antidiscrimination laws and litigation in the federal courts. Yet only 24 percent of African-American families have attained the middle-class living standards specified by the U.S. Bureau of Labor Statistics, compared with 50 percent of white American families.[29]

Several options have been proposed to reduce barriers to occupational advancement among African Americans and other minorities. These include public- and private-sector investments in training to enhance skills and productive capabilities, promotion of economic growth and new job opportunities (for example, through tax incentives to businesses that invest in inner-city enterprise zones), and a reduction in discrimination (including subtle racism at work and in social situations)[30] and involuntary segregation.

COMMITMENT TO DIVERSITY AT XEROX[31]

COMPANY EXAMPLE

The philosophy at Xerox is simple: "If you don't value diversity, you can't manage it." This attitude can be traced to Joseph C. Wilson, who founded Xerox and who regularly stressed its social responsibilities and community involvement. David Kearns, the firm's former CEO, expressed its stance: "At Xerox, affirmative action is not a platitude, nor is it a special program. It is a clear-cut, plainly stated corporate business objective." One of the ways in which the company supports diversity is in its recognition and encouragement of a network of local and regional caucus groups (for African Americans, women, and Hispanic Americans). The groups meet on their own time and set their own rules and agendas, serving their members in these ways: (1) as a communication link between the members and upper management; (2) as a vehicle for personal and professional development (e.g., through workshops on topics such as presentation skills or how to run a meeting); (3) as a forum for networking and support within the caucus group (e.g., women relating to women on issues of common concern), (4) by giving members a chance to serve as role models to majority employees for managing diversity, and (5) by representing the corporation in community activities, such as outreach recruitment or presentations to schools or civic associations.

Another diversity strategy at Xerox focuses on how to get minority employees and women into jobs that are pivotal to further advancement. The idea here is to examine the backgrounds of all top executives and identify the key positions they held at lower levels—

that is, positions that get people noticed—and to set goals for getting minorities and women into these jobs.

A third goal at Xerox is to transform its total employment from male-dominated to a fully diverse workforce. This means that Xerox is actively striving to achieve and then maintain equitable representation of all employee groups—majority males and females as well as minority males and females—at all grade bands, in all functions, and in all organizations. To accomplish this, Xerox has incorporated these objectives into its corporate human resource planning and especially into all decisions regarding hiring, developing, and moving employees at all levels. As a result of what it has achieved through its commitment to diversity, Xerox's approach has been used as a benchmark by many other *Fortune* 500 firms.

Hispanics in the Workforce

Hispanics, who account for 9 percent of the civilian labor force,[32] experience many of the same disadvantages as African Americans. Hispanics are the second largest minority group in the United States. However, the term *Hispanic* encompasses a large, diverse group of people who come from distinctively different ethnic and racial backgrounds and who have achieved various economic and educational levels. For example, a third-generation educated, white Cuban American has little in common with an uneducated Central American immigrant of mainly Native American ancestry who has fled civil upheaval and political persecution. Despite the fact that their differences far outweigh their similarities, both are classified as Hispanic. Why? Largely because of the language they speak (Spanish) or because of their surnames or because of their geographical origins.

Mexicans, Puerto Ricans, and Cubans constitute the three largest groups classified as Hispanic.[33] They are concentrated in four geographic areas: Mexican Americans reside mostly in California and Texas, Puerto Ricans mostly in New York, and a majority of Cuban Americans in Florida. Labor force participation rates for Hispanics (as a group) are growing rapidly (as Figure 3-3 shows), although in the best-paid and most prestigious professions they are at present woefully underrepresented.

Hispanics currently hold less than half of their proportional share (7.5 percent) of the best-paying types of jobs (managerial and professional occupations). Take engineering, for example. In 1991, only 2.4 percent of engineers in the United States were Hispanics, up slightly from 2.2 percent in 1983. That means, of course, that they are overrepresented in service and blue-collar jobs.

FIGURE 3-3
Growth of the civilian Hispanic labor force (in millions), 1980–2000. (*Source: Statistical Abstract of the United States, 1992,* Table 609.)

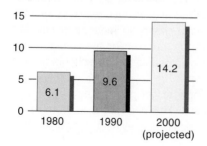

Other occupations in which there are relatively few Hispanics include physicians (4.4 percent), college and university professors (2.9 percent), dentists (2.7 percent), computer systems analysts and scientists (2.6 percent), authors (1 percent), and geologists (0.6 percent). However, there are some bright spots. By 1991, for example, 25 percent of Cuban Americans in the labor force were employed as managers, executives, or professionals.[34]

To encourage greater representation of Hispanics throughout the corporate structure, companies like Pacific Bell have initiated aggressive recruitment and retention programs.

MANAGEMENT DIVERSITY AT PACIFIC BELL[35]

Pacific Bell, a telecommunications company operating in California, realized for two basic reasons that it had to change the way it traditionally recruited employees and managers. For one, the population of Hispanics, African Americans, and Asian Americans was increasing rapidly in California, but only a small percentage of these minorities attended college. If Pacific Bell continued to hire only through college and university campuses, its minority employees as a percentage of its total employees would most likely shrink. This would be especially true for Hispanics, because their population was growing at the fastest rate. Hence while the percentage of Hispanics in California was growing, the percentage of Hispanics on the payroll of Pacific Bell was decreasing.

The other reason Pacific Bell decided to change its recruitment was based on forecasts by the company's planners that its largest growth in management jobs would be in the high-technology areas of engineering, marketing, and data systems. The work in these management jobs requires advanced technical skills and formal education, and they had traditionally been filled via promotion from lower levels. But the company recognized that promotions could not produce the number of skilled managers needed in the near future. So Pacific Bell developed a new recruitment strategy comprising four components:

1. Internal networking by a group called the Management Recruitment District designed to generate employee referrals, to establish networks of employees who had contacts in the minority communities, to identify employees who could serve as guest speakers for external presentations, and to make presentations at regularly scheduled departmental staff meetings.

2. Advertising directed toward specific ethnic groups. The advertisements showed a diverse group of people employed in marketing, engineering, and management positions. These ads were placed in local and national publications serving the targeted minority communities on a regular basis to demonstrate the company's interest in minority hiring and the fact that it valued employee diversity. The same ads were placed in campus publications to announce appointments for employment interviews.

3. Establishment of contact with small institutions in the California State University system, which tended to enroll a higher proportion of minority students, as well as with Arizona State University and the University of New Mexico, both of which have large Hispanic enrollments. The company established relationships with minority student organizations and faculty (particularly those identified with business or technical fields) to identify issues and to offer support. For example, Pacific Bell developed a video, "Engineering

Your Management Future," to tell engineering majors about career paths in management.

4. At the local or national level of professional minority organizations, such as the National Hispanic Council for High Technology Careers, Pacific Bell sought advisors to help develop management candidates. The company even hosted a 2-day conference to address the alarming underrepresentation of Hispanics in the teaching and practice of sciences and engineering.

Pacific Bell also established an internship program (the Summer Management Program) for third-year college students, making them student ambassadors representing Pacific Bell's career opportunities. For managers from minority groups who were already employed, Pacific Bell offered 6-day, off-site training programs conducted by external consultants and designed to help further develop their skills. The programs also provided a safe place for participants to talk about sensitive issues such as covert racism and prejudice, topics not likely to be discussed in the work setting.

RESULTS

Over the program's first 10 years, 1980–1990, minority managers increased from 17.5 percent to 28.2 percent (even after the significant downsizing that followed the AT&T divestiture in 1984). The company has won many awards for its recruitment among minorities. In 1990, Pacific Bell received the Exemplary Voluntary Efforts (EVE) award from the Department of Labor's Office of Federal Contract Compliance Programs for its long-term commitment to equal employment opportunity.

Women in the Workforce

Over the past 30 years, women have raised their expectations and levels of aspiration sharply higher, largely because of the women's movement (sparked by Betty Friedan's 1963 book, *The Feminine Mystique*), coupled with landmark civil rights legislation and well-publicized judgments against large companies for gender discrimination in hiring, promotion, and pay. Feminism was the last focus of the civil rights movement. Its constituency was the broadest and deepest, and so were the problems it addressed. In 1972, women questioned the possibility of having a family and holding a job at the same time. By the mid-1980s, they took it for granted that they could manage both. Five forces account for the changes:

1. *Changes in the family.* Legalized abortion, contraception, divorce, and a declining birthrate have all contributed to a decrease in the number of years of their lives most women devote to rearing children. Of all women, 85 percent have babies,[36] but 55 percent of mothers with children under 3 years of age now work, as do 75 percent of those whose youngest child is under 18.[37] Women are now also providers of family income.

The proportion of single-parent family groups with children under age 18 has increased, from 12.9 percent in 1970 to 28.9 percent in 1991. That 28.9 percent is a weighted average, based on the following statistics: 23.1 percent of whites, 62.5 per-

cent of African Americans, and 33.1 percent of Hispanics are single parents with children under 18 years of age. Most single-parent families are headed by women, and
most working women have little choice except to work. The stunning demographic
fact is that more than half of all children born in the United States after 1980 will
probably spend some time living in a single-parent household before reaching age
18.[38]

2. *Changes in education.* Since World War II, increasing numbers of women have
been attending college. Women now earn 52 percent of all undergraduate degrees, 55
percent of all undergraduate accounting degrees, 51 percent of all masters degrees,
and 35 percent of MBAs.[39]

3. *Changes in self-perception.* Many women juggle work and family roles. This often
causes personal conflict, and the higher they rise in an organization, the more that
work demands of them in terms of time and commitment. Many women executives
pay a high personal price for their organizational status in the form of broken marriages or never marrying at all. These kinds of personal conflicts have been termed the
"mommy wars."[40] Thus *a major goal of EEO for women is to raise the awareness of these
issues among both women and men so that women can be given a fair chance to think about
their interests and potential, to investigate other possibilities, to make an intelligent choice, and
then to be considered for openings or promotions on an equal basis with men.*[41]

4. *Changes in technology.* Advances in technology, both in the home (e.g., frozen
foods, microwave ovens) and in the workplace (e.g., robotics), have reduced the physical effort and time required to accomplish tasks. Through technology more women
can now qualify for formerly all-male jobs.

5. *Changes in the economy.* Although there has been an increasing shift away from
goods production and toward service-related industries, there are increasing numbers
of female employees in all types of industries. Here are some statistics characterizing
these changes:[42]

- 54 million businesses (28 percent of all U.S. companies) are owned and managed
  by women.
- Women-owned businesses include the same types of industries as are in the *Fortune*
  500.
- The number of jobs in businesses owned by women now surpasses the number of
  jobs in the businesses represented on the Fortune 500 list.
- Women held 30.5 percent of managerial jobs in 1992, compared with 21.7 percent
  in 1982.
- Only 7 percent of working women now drop out of the workforce in any given
  year, down from 12 percent in the mid-1970s.
- Of families having annual incomes that reach $40,000 to $50,000, 70 percent have
  working wives.
- In the mid-1990s, fully 30 percent of working women are professionals and managers, the same proportion as men.[43]
- By the year 2001, women are expected to hold about a third of the top jobs in major
  concerns and to head 10 percent of all companies.

The statistics presented thus far imply that women have made considerable economic gains over the past three decades. However, there are also some disturbing facts that moderate any broad conclusions about women's social and economic progress:

■ A 1992 report by the U.S. Department of Labor[44] indicated that little progress had been made by women in breaking through to senior management positions in the country's 1000 largest corporations. Women therefore failed to crack the "glass ceiling" (i.e., while they can see the top jobs, they can't actually reach them). Women represented less than 2 percent of all corporate officers and accounted for only 2.6 percent of executives (vice president and up) at *Fortune* 500 firms. Of 1315 board members of the 100 largest American corporations, only 7.5 percent were women. And only 11.5 percent of top union leaders were women!

■ In 1992, U.S. women made only 72 cents for every dollar earned by men. At the current rate of increase, women will not reach wage parity with men until 2017. Although the gap is decreasing, at every educational level women make less than men at the same level, and female-dominated fields do not pay as well as male-dominated fields.[45]

■ As a group, women who interrupt their careers for family reasons never again make as much money as women who stay on the job. A study of over 2400 women aged 30 to 64 (each with one or more gaps in work of at least 6 months) found that those who took a break of 1 year or so lost the same ground in salary as women who dropped out for longer periods. Compared with women who stayed on the job, women who took breaks earned 33 percent less, on average, during the year they returned to work. And the stigma persists: despite working continuously for 11 to 20 years after the dropout interval, these women still earned 10 percent less.[46] (For women who stay on the job, the accumulation of more experience accounts for as much as a quarter of the narrowing of the gender gap in pay.[47])

■ Women in paid jobs still bear most of the responsibility for family care and housework.

Conclusions Regarding Women in the Workforce

The clearest picture we need to see from the data reflecting all these changes is this: if all the United States' working women were to quit their jobs tomorrow and stay at home to cook and clean, businesses would disintegrate. There is no going back to the way things were before women entered the workforce. What many people tend to think of as "women's issues" really are business issues, competitiveness issues. Examples: Companies that routinely don't offer child care and flexibility in work scheduling will suffer along with their deprived workers.[48] Women are not less committed employees; working mothers especially are not less committed to their work. Three-quarters of professional women who quit large companies did so because of lack of career progress; only 7 percent left to stay at home with their children.[49] Businesses should react to the kinds of issues reflected in these examples based not on what is the right or wrong thing to do but on what makes economic sense to do—which usually also is the right thing to do.

The people who make the decisions about what makes economic sense from the perspective of their new workforces have to learn how to be more creative. For example, not many executives understand that skillfully managing time between the needs and responsibilities of the home and the needs and responsibilities of the office can provide enhanced productivity, which certainly makes good economic sense. It is important that executives see that creative responses to work/family dilemmas are in the best interests of both employers and employees. Adjustments to work schedules (flextime), extended maternity *and* paternity leaves, and quality day care based near the job come a little closer to workable solutions. Chapter 10 will consider this issue in greater detail, but for now let's consider some practical steps that two companies are taking.

WOMEN'S ADVISORY COMMITTEES AT J. C. PENNEY AND BANKERS TRUST[50]

Women employees first began to form groups within their firms during the feminist movement of the mid-1970s. Initially, management perceived them to be adversarial and discouraged them, but eventually management accepted the groups, once it understood why they were formed and that there are solid business reasons for their existence. Here are two examples:

■ Sometime during 1990, J. C. Penney realized there were few women in its senior management positions. So the firm assembled a women's advisory committee, comprising women employees from all departments. They meet regularly to discuss issues ranging from long-term career goals to the details of how they balance job and family. As a result of listening to what the women had to say at these meetings, there are now four additional women in senior management positions at Penney, and the firm has regular programs to train its store managers and executives in all aspects of a diverse workforce.

■ At Bankers Trust in New York City, a women's group started at about the same time, for the same purposes, and developed in the same way. At many of the regularly scheduled meetings, the group speakers and seminars addressed issues of special relevance to women, such as mentoring, career management, and creative approaches to work/family dilemmas. Membership has grown to 600 and has the full support of management because "Management believes that to be successful the company has to be global, that workforce demographics are changing, and we have to be diverse. Diversity breeds creativity."

Age-Based Diversity

At present, the U.S. workforce is populated by four different generations of workers, each with different, often conflicting values and attitudes.[51] Here is a brief sketch of each.

■ The *swing generation* (born roughly 1910–1929) struggled through the Great Depression, fought the good war (World War II), and, following that war, rebuilt the American economy, which would dominate the world for more than 30 years. Most, but not all, members of the swing generation have retired.

■ The *silent generation* (born 1930–1945) is demographically smaller. Born in the middle of the Great Depression, too young to have fought in World War II, they were influenced by the swing generation. Because its members represented a scarcer resource (i.e., they were in relatively short supply), they were more heavily in demand. Many went to the best colleges, were courted by corporations, rose rapidly, and were paid more than any other group in history. In return they embraced their elders' values and became good Organization Men (i.e., they gave their hearts and souls to their employers and made whatever sacrifices were necessary to get ahead; in return, employers gave them increasing job responsibility, pay, and benefits).[52] The silent generation currently holds most positions of power (e.g., corporate leaders, members of Congress).

■ The *baby-boom generation* (born 1946–1964) currently accounts for 78 million people and 55 percent of the workforce. Boomers do not share their parents' attitudes about much of anything. "Big business" still carries a negative connotation among many baby boomers. They believe that the business of business includes leadership in redressing social inequities.

The boomers believe in rights to privacy, due process, and freedom of speech in the workplace; that employees should not be fired without just cause; and that the best should be rewarded without regard to age, gender, race, position, or seniority. Downsizing (the planned elimination of positions or jobs) has shocked and frustrated many boomers over shrinking advancement opportunities for themselves and created a sense of betrayal as their parents were fired or rushed into early retirement. They vowed, "You can fire me, but you can't hurt me because I'm not giving you my loyalty."[53] This attitude resulting from the downsizing frenzy will cause problems for years to come.

■ The *baby-bust generation's* members (born 1965–1976), 44 million strong, are distinctly divided between those who have knowledge and skills and expect to do well and those who do not have knowledge and skills and have no hopes for the future. Nevertheless, this is a computer-literate generation. It is the most skeptical about society's institutions and their ability to solve problems. Busters do not invest loyalty in a large corporation, they see work as a means to an end, and they seek jobs more than careers. Raised in shopping malls, which were the centers of their social lives, they are rabid consumers.[54] The generation most affected by divorce, busters are marrying later than any previous generation this century has (26.5 years for men, 24.1 years for women in 1992).[55] Nevertheless, they believe strongly in the family, particularly that family comes before work. They probably will be conscientious parents and spend lots of time with their children. Baby busters' greatest value is quality of life.

MANAGING DIVERSITY

Racial and ethnic minorities, women, and immigrants will account for 80 percent of the growth in the U.S. labor force by the year 2000. And there is another large and growing minority—older workers—that will soon affect the overall makeup of the workforce. Businesses that want to grow will have to rely on this diversity.[56] Let us consider some practical steps that managers can take to prepare for these forthcoming changes.

Racial and Ethnic Minorities

To derive value from workforce diversity, not merely to tolerate it, an organization must do three things: *communicate diversity*, *cultivate diversity*, and *capitalize on diversity*.

Communicating diversity means providing an opportunity for all workers and managers to become aware of the different values of the various subgroups making up the workforce. This can be done through awareness training in different forms, by releasing news articles announcing significant achievements by workers from those subgroups, and by integrating diversity into the firm's advertising. Communicating diversity also means addressing its polar opposite, unlawful discrimination; it does not mean exercising what might amount to not much more than public relations "hype."

To *cultivate diversity*, workers and managers need to support and encourage each other's success at every opportunity. The objective is to enhance each individual's self-esteem, to make people feel confident in their abilities. Channels for doing this include committees composed of diverse members, associations of managers, women's groups, and vehicles for evaluating and addressing complaints. To measure its progress in cultivating diversity, the firm should periodically survey employee attitudes and conduct audits of promotions (who was considered, on what basis, and who got the job). The surveys and audits should reflect how the internal environment of the organization is changing over time.

To *capitalize on diversity*, management must install a formal process that regularly examines and focuses on identifying each individual's strengths, weaknesses, and options for development and points out potential job opportunities for candidates to consider. Diversity should be linked to every business strategy—e.g., recruiting, selection, placement (after identifying high-visibility jobs that lead to other opportunities within the firm), succession planning, performance appraisal, and reward systems.[57] Northern States Power in Minneapolis is an example of a company that is communicating, cultivating, and capitalizing on the diversity of its workforce by linking diversity to every business strategy, including succession planning, reengineering, employee development, performance management and review, and reward systems.[58]

None of these approaches will work unless a majority of employees wants them to work and their cooperative efforts are spearheaded by top management. Here's an example of one company that's done just that.

LEVI STRAUSS & COMPANY—DIVERSE BY DESIGN[59]

COMPANY EXAMPLE

CEO Robert D. Haas is proud of Levi Strauss & Company's (LS&CO.'s) 7 consecutive years of record sales. But he's just as proud that the company today is recognized as one of the most ethnically and culturally diverse companies in the U.S., if not the world. At the end of 1991, 56 percent of its 23,000 U.S. employees belonged to minority groups. Its top management level was 14 percent nonwhite and 30 percent female.

Education is the cornerstone of Haas's efforts. The company invests in its employees through its "Valuing Diversity" educational programs, one of which includes a 3.5-day experience. The program is designed to get employees thinking about how to become more tolerant of personal differences and to see the importance of those differences.

A meeting of the "Diversity Council" at Levi Strauss & Co.

The company's ads for job openings encourage minorities and women to apply. When job seekers interview at the company, they often find a person who looks like them on the other side of the desk. Says the African-American manager of internal audits: "You get a feeling that there's opportunity here because of the diversity at senior levels."

LS&CO. also supports in-house networking groups of African Americans, Hispanics, Asian-Pacific Islanders, women, lesbians, and gay men. A "Diversity Council," made up of two members of every group, meets regularly with members of the executive committee to raise awareness of diversity issues. Finally, part of every manager's bonus is tied to specific activities and accomplishments that meet the goals of the company's "Aspiration Statement," which encourages all employees to aspire to appreciate diversity.

Promoting diversity in the workforce makes good marketing sense for LS&CO. too. As an Asian-American manager of corporate marketing noted: "It's tough to design and develop merchandise for markets you don't understand." On the flip side: when you make a point of valuing other people's contributions, some good ideas for products make their way back to headquarters. The company credits an Argentine employee for thinking up its Dockers® brand of casual pants, now with more than $1 billion a year in revenues.

Alas, diversity also has its downside: costly and time-consuming disagreements abound in a company where everyone's ideas are encouraged. And some managers who feel they need command and control become uncomfortable in a less structured, more open and egalitarian organization—which Haas thinks harnesses diversity—and they leave.

Female Workers

Here are six ways that firms today provide women with opportunities not previously available to them.[60]

1. *Alternative career paths.* This is especially popular in law and accounting firms that have sanctioned part-time work for professionals.

2. *Extended leave.* IBM, for example, grants up to 3 years off with benefits and the guarantee of a comparable job on return. However, leave takers must be on call for part-time work during 2 of the 3 years.

3. *Flexible scheduling.* At NCNB, a bank based in North Carolina, employees create their own schedules and work at home. After 6 months' maternity leave, new mothers can increase their hours at work gradually. Most who choose to cut their hours work two-thirds time and receive two-thirds pay.

4. *Flextime.* Although flextime may take a variety of forms, a common arrangement allows any employee the right to shift the standard workday forward or backward by 1 hour. Thousands of public and private employers now allow flextime.

5. *Job sharing.* This is not for everyone, but it may work especially well with clerical positions where the need for coordination of the overall workload is minimal. That is, activities such as filing, faxing, word processing, and photocopying are relatively independent tasks that workers can share. However, development of a new product or a new marketing campaign, for example, often requires a continuity of thought and coordinated action that cannot easily be assigned to different workers or managers. At Steelcase, the office equipment manufacturer, for example, two employees can share title, workload, salary, health benefits, and vacation.

6. *Telecommuting.* The high-tech facility for high-tech working moms. Employers such as the California-based telecommunications firm Pacific Telesis allow employees to limit the time they spend in the office and to work at home using personal computers, fax machines, and electronic mail. In 1993, more than 6.6 million employees of business or government agencies worked at home, either part-time or full-time.[61]

Flexible approaches like these will be enhanced, revised, and extended as firms compete to attract and retain top female talent.

Older Workers

Among workers aged 55–64, 67.7 percent were in the workforce in 1990. By the year 2005, that number will increase as more and more baby boomers join the ranks of older workers (those 55 and older).[62] In a 1993 survey, 72 percent of companies had no particular practices in place to encourage workers over 50 to remain on the job.[63] Yet their experience, wisdom, and institutional memories (memories of traditions, of how and why things are done as they are in an organization) represent important assets to firms. As important elements of the diversity "mix," these assets should continue to be developed and used effectively. Here are six priorities to consider in order to maximize the use of older workers:[64]

ETHICAL DILEMMA: DOES DIVERSITY MANAGEMENT CONFLICT WITH MAXIMIZING SHAREHOLDER VALUE?

The main objective of profit-making businesses is to maximize overall returns to shareholders (increases in stock prices plus dividends). Since earnings affect this objective, management needs to determine the extent to which *any* new program—including any new workforce program—will affect the bottom line. There are sound business reasons why having a diverse workforce and managing it properly can increase shareholder value. However, companies generally tend to measure success in these programs by looking at indicators other than the bottom line. Affirmative action programs have been criticized strongly for adding costs to firms but little or no financial benefits.[65] Given the costs involved, can diversity programs be justified over time *purely* on philosophical and moral grounds (i.e., it's the right thing to do)?

1. *Age/experience profile.* Executives should look at the age distribution across jobs, as compared with performance measures, to see what career paths for older workers might open in the future and what past performance measures have indicated about the kinds of knowledge, skills, abilities, and other characteristics necessary to hold these positions. Why do this? Because it's important to identify types of jobs where older workers can use their experience and talents most effectively.

2. *Job performance requirements.* Companies should then define more precisely the types of abilities and skills needed for various posts. While physical abilities decline with age, especially for heavy lifting, running, or sustained physical exertion (which are needed in jobs such as fire fighting and law enforcement), mental abilities generally remain stable well into the eighties. Clear job specifications must serve as the basis for improved personnel selection, job design, and performance appraisal systems. For example, jobs may be designed for self-pacing, may require periodic updating, or may require staffing by people with certain physical abilities.

3. *Performance appraisal.* Not only must a firm analyze the requirements of jobs better, there must also be improved ways of analyzing the performance of workers in those jobs. Age biases may be reflected in the format of the appraisal instrument. This can happen, for example, by focusing exclusively on *how* a job is done, rather than *what* gets done. Thus, while an older police officer may rely more on negotiation and interpersonal skills to apprehend a suspect, a younger officer may take a more physical approach to accomplishing the same objective. It would be a mistake to assume there is only one way to do the job.

Age biases may also be reflected in managers' attitudes. This is known as *age grading:* subconscious expectations about what people can and cannot do at particular times of their lives.[66] Management training programs should be developed to address and correct both of these biases. Both Banker's Life and Casualty Co. and Polaroid have teams that audit the appraisals of older workers to check for unfair evaluations. These teams also attempt to redress general age prejudice in the workplace by working with employees and managers at all levels to replace myths about older workers with facts based on evidence.

4. *Workforce interest surveys.* Once management understands the abilities its older workers have, it must determine what they want. The idea is to survey workers to determine their career goals so that the ones who are capable of achieving their goals won't stall. Not only must management decide that it wants to encourage selectively some older workers to continue with the organization, it must also consider encouraging turnover of workers it doesn't want to continue. And, of course, management must evaluate what effects different incentives will have on the workers it wants to continue and on the ones it doesn't.

5. *Training and counseling.* Terminated workers are concerned about the direction of their lives after they stop working. Counseling on retirement and on how to develop second careers is becoming common. IBM now offers tuition rebates for courses on *any* topic of interest within 3 years of retirement and continuing into retirement. To meet the needs of the workforce remaining on the job, firms need to develop training programs to avoid midcareer plateauing (i.e., performance at an acceptable but not outstanding level, coupled with little or no effort to improve one's current performance) as well as training programs to reduce obsolescence (the tendency for knowledge or skills to become out of date). These programs must reflect the special needs of older workers, who can learn but need to be taught differently (for example, by using self-paced programs instead of lectures).

6. *The structure of jobs.* To whatever degree management may consider changing older workers' work conditions, such as work pace, the length or timing of the workday, leaves of absence, and challenges on the job, those proposed changes should be explored jointly with the workforce. Especially in the case of a workforce represented by a labor union, for example, part-time workers may be feared as a threat to the power of organized labor.

As we have seen, the workforce is now and will continue to be more and more diverse. A list of actions that managers can take to deal with these changes is presented in Figure 3-4.

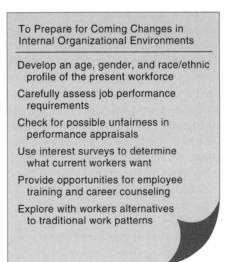

To Prepare for Coming Changes in Internal Organizational Environments

Develop an age, gender, and race/ethnic profile of the present workforce

Carefully assess job performance requirements

Check for possible unfairness in performance appraisals

Use interest surveys to determine what current workers want

Provide opportunities for employee training and career counseling

Explore with workers alternatives to traditional work patterns

FIGURE 3-4
Priority listing of suggested actions to manage effectively the internal organizational environment of the future.

IMPACT OF DIVERSITY ON PRODUCTIVITY, QUALITY OF WORK LIFE, AND THE BOTTOM LINE

All employees, no matter who, no matter at what level, want to be treated with respect. They want to know that their employer values the work they do. That's the most basic thing you must do in managing diversity. And when diversity is managed well, as at Avon, Xerox, Monsanto, and Levi Strauss & Company, productivity and the quality of work life improve. There is not yet a meaningful quantitative measure of how well diversity is managed. But there are other meaningful tests. For example, Northern States Power (NSP) won a major business contract in Australia because, in addition to cost and timeliness, competitors were judged according to how they treat their workers. NSP has won many awards for its progressive management of diversity issues (e.g., the Greater Minneapolis Chamber of Commerce, Minnesota Department of Jobs and Training, *Good Housekeeping* magazine). On the other side of this, we know that when workers do not feel respected for their individual talents nor valued at their work, the personal toll is high—more stress, more accidents, more grievances, and less that can be gained from the work they can contribute.

HUMAN RESOURCE MANAGEMENT IN ACTION: CONCLUSION

ON MANAGING A MULTICULTURAL WORKFORCE

Managing a diverse workforce to derive the benefits it is capable of producing depends on one fundamental thing—communication among the cultures that make up the diversity, communication that makes it possible for someone from each culture to understand the perspectives engendered by the culture of others and through that understanding to become comfortable with perspectives different from one's own. This is what managing a workforce is all about today—quite different from yesterday, when managers were taught to ignore differences or regard them as irrelevant. Today we recognize that cultural differences exist, that they are relevant, and that they reflect values. Rather than suppress cultural differences at work, managers are being taught how to respect them and how to work with them to maximize the contribution of each employee.

Today, both managers and employees are being encouraged to explore their own culture and the cultures of those around them, and to talk about the differences. Nevertheless, many people are uncomfortable doing this. They fear it will arouse suppressed tensions that could disrupt a system that appears to be functioning smoothly.

And when managers and employees do recognize differences, they have to be careful that they are perceived clearly and objectively. For example, during a training program on workforce diversity, a group of executives of a large oil company received kits containing, among other things, a *Harvard Business Review* article, "Black Managers: The Dream Deferred," which described African Americans' corporate experiences. Without reading the article, dozens of white managers sent their copies to the one African-American manager in the firm with the earnest thought that it would interest him. When the African-American manager glanced through the article, he thought, "Those white executives need to read this. I *know* what it's like."

Not only do managers need to learn about various cultures, they have to be aware of differences within a culture and also about personal idiosyncrasies and preferences. For example, many people assume that all Americans want to be recognized publicly for their accomplishments. Suppose, however, that the person who wants private recognition is a blond California woman who just happens to be shy. What's the bottom line in all of this? According to many experts it's simple: ask, don't just assume.

SUMMARY

More than half the U.S. workforce now consists of racial and ethnic minorities, immigrants, and women. White, native-born males, as a group, are still dominant in numbers over any other group, but women will fill almost two-thirds of the *new jobs* created during the 1990s, and by the year 2000, nearly half the *entire workforce* will be female. White males will make up only 15 percent of the increase in the workforce over the next decade.

Managing diversity means encouraging a heterogeneous workforce, which includes white men, to perform to its potential in an equitable work environment in which no one group enjoys an advantage or suffers a disadvantage. At least five factors account for the increasing attention companies are paying to diversity: (1) the shift from a manufacturing to a service economy, (2) the globalization of markets, (3) new business strategies that require more teamwork, (4) mergers and alliances that require different corporate cultures to work together, and (5) the changing labor market. Each of these factors can represent opportunities for firms whose managers and employees understand what culture is and the cultural differences among other employees and managers, and especially the firm's market.

Culture refers to characteristic ways of doing things and behaving that people in a given country or region have evolved over time. It helps people make sense of their part of the world and provides them with an identity. Culture is not just an issue for newly arrived immigrants; it continues to affect their children and grandchildren. Companies such as Xerox, Pacific Bell, J. C. Penney, Bankers Trust, and Levi Strauss have developed programs to raise all their employees' awareness and understanding of the impact of culture (e.g., African American, Hispanic American, Asian American), gender, and other workforce characteristics on job performance.

IMPLICATIONS FOR MANAGEMENT PRACTICE

1. Workforce diversity—for example, in gender, race, ethnicity, and age—is here to stay. There is no going back to the demographic makeup of organizations 20 years ago. To be successful in this new environment, learn to value and respect cultural styles and ways of behaving that differ from your own.

2. Recognize that there are tangible business reasons why managing workforce diversity effectively should be a high priority: (a) it's an opportunity to serve the needs of customers better and to penetrate new markets, and (b) diverse teams make it possible to enhance creativity, flexibility, and rapid response to change.

3. To maximize the potential of all members of the workforce, link concerns for diversity to every business strategy: recruitment, selection, placement, succession planning, performance appraisal, and rewards.

To attract and retain women, companies are making available to them alternative career paths, extended leaves, flexible scheduling, flextime, job sharing, and opportunities to telecommute. A different aspect of diversity is generational diversity—important differences in values, aspirations, and beliefs that characterize the swing generation, the silent generation, the baby boomers, and the baby busters. To manage older workers effectively, managers should develop an age profile of the workforce, monitor job performance requirements for the kinds of characteristics people need to do their jobs well, develop safeguards against age bias in performance appraisal, conduct workforce interest surveys, provide education and counseling, and consider modifying the structure of jobs. Finally, to manage diversity effectively, an organization must do three things well: communicate diversity, cultivate diversity, and capitalize on diversity.

DISCUSSION QUESTIONS

3■1 In your opinion, what are some key business reasons for emphasizing the effective management of a diverse workforce?

3■2 Discuss some possible reasons why deep divisions in the workforce still remain between and among racial and ethnic minorities, between women and men, and across generations.

3■3 What would the broad elements of a company policy include if the objective was to emphasize the management of diversity?

3■4 How should the outcomes of diversity programs be measured?

3■5 Suppose you were asked to enter a debate in which your task was to argue *against* any special effort to manage workforce diversity. What would you say?

REFERENCES

1. White, male, and worried (1994, Jan. 31). *Business Week*, pp. 50–55.
2. The new face of America: How immigrants are shaping the world's first multicultural society (1993, Fall). *Time* (Special Issue), p. 3.
3. Thomas, R. R., Jr. (1990, Mar.–Apr.). From affirmative action to affirming diversity. *Harvard Business Review*, pp. 107–117.
4. Torres, C., & Bruxelles, M. (1992, Dec.). Capitalizing on global diversity. *HRMagazine*, pp. 30–33.
5. Equal Employment Opportunity Commission (1979, Jan. 19). *Affirmative action guidelines*. Pub. no. 44 FR 4421. Washington, DC: U.S. Government Printing Office.
6. Jackson, S. E., & Alvarez, E. B. (1992). Working through diversity as a strategic imperative. In S. E. Jackson (ed.), *Diversity in the workplace*. New York: Guilford, pp. 13–35.
7. The data for Table 3-2 come from The Perplexing Case of the Plummeting Payrolls (1993, Sept. 20). *Business Week*, p. 27.
8. The new face of America, op. cit.
9. Sellers, P. (1990, June 4). What customers really want. *Fortune*, pp. 58–68.
10. Banas, P. A. (1988). Employee involvement: A sustained labor-management initiative at the Ford Motor Company. In J. P. Campbell and R. J. Campbell (eds.), *Productivity in organizations: New perspectives from industrial and organizational psychology*. San Francisco: Jossey-Bass, pp. 348–416.
11. Wellins, R. S., Byham, W. C., & Wilson, J. M. (1991). *Empowered teams*. San Francisco: Jossey-Bass.
12. Watson, W. E., Kumar, K., & Michaelson, L. K. (1993). Cultural diversity's impact on interaction process and performance: Comparing homogeneous and diverse task groups. *Academy of Management Journal*, **36**(3), 590–602.

13. Cascio, W. F., & Serapio, M. G., Jr. (1991, Winter). Human resources systems in an international alliance: The undoing of a done deal? *Organizational Dynamics*, pp. 63–74.

14. Kanter, R. M. (1991, May–June). Transcending business boundaries: 12,000 world managers view change. *Harvard Business Review*, pp. 151–164.

15. McWhirter, W. (1989, Oct. 9). I came, I saw, I blundered. *Time*, pp. 72, 77.

16. Ibid.

17. Johnston, W. B., & Packer, A. (1987). *Workforce 2000: Work and workers for the 21st century*. Indianapolis, IN: Hudson Institute.

18. Jackson, S. E. (1992). Preview of the road to be traveled. In S. E. Jackson (ed.), *Diversity in the workplace*. New York: Guilford, pp. 4–12.

19. *High-performance work practices and firm performance* (1993, Aug.). Washington, DC: U.S. Department of Labor.

20. Shellenbarger, S. (1993, Sept. 3). Work-force study finds loyalty is weak, divisions of race and gender are deep. *The Wall Street Journal*, pp. B1, B5. See also Hammonds, K. H. (1993, Sept. 13). Work: More complex than we thought. *Business Week*, p. 42.

21. Fugita, S. S., & O'Brien, D. J. (1991). *Japanese and American ethnicity: The persistence of the community*. Seattle: University of Washington Press. See also Mydans, S. (1991, June 30). For these Americans, Mexico not left behind. *The New York Times*, p. L12.

22. Harris, P. R., & Moran, R. T. (1990). *Managing cultural differences* (3d ed.). Houston: Gulf Publishing.

23. Fernandez, J. P., with Barr, M. (1993). *The diveristy advantage*. New York: Lexington Books.

24. Day, J. C. (1992). *Population projections of the United States by age, sex, race, and Hispanic origin: 1992 to 2050*. Washington, DC: U.S. Department of Commerce, Bureau of the Census.

25. Wallace, P. A. (1990). Affirmative action from a labor market perspective. *ILR Report*, **27**(2), 40–47.

26. Civil rights: The next generation. (1993, Aug. 31). *The Wall Street Journal*, p. A10.

27. Sharpe, R. (1993, Sept. 14). Losing ground: In latest recession, only blacks suffered net employment loss. *The Wall Street Journal*, pp. A1, A14, A15.

28. Ibid.

29. Wallace, op. cit.

30. Watts, R. A. (1993, Sept. 26). Subtle racism common, blacks say. *The Denver Post*, p. A3.

31. Sessa, V. J. (1992). Managing diversity at the Xerox Corporation: Balanced workforce goals and caucus groups. In S. E. Jackson (ed.), *Diversity in the workplace*. New York: Guilford, pp. 37–64.

32. Day, op. cit.

33. Fernandez, with Barr, op. cit.

34. Castro, M. J. (1993, Oct. 3). Hispanics and the new workforce. *Vista*, pp. 8, 10.

35. Roberson, L., & Gutierrez, N. (1992). Beyond good faith: Commitment to recruiting management diversity at Pacific Bell. In S. E. Jackson (ed.), *Diversity in the workplace*. New York: Guilford, pp. 65–68.

36. Schwartz, F. N. (1992, Mar.–Apr.). Women as a business imperative. *Harvard Business Review*, pp. 105–113.

37. Richardson, L. (1992, Sept. 2). No cookie cutter answers in "mommy wars." *The New York Times*, pp. B1, B5.

38. Lewin, T. (1992, Oct. 5). Rise in single parenthood is reshaping U.S. *The New York Times*, pp. B1, B6. See also Chira, S. (1992, Oct. 4). New realities fight old images of mother. *The New York Times*, pp. 1, 32.

39. Schwartz, op. cit.

40. Richardson, op. cit.

41. Boyle, M. B. (1975). Equal opportunity for women is smart business. *Harvard Business Review*, **51**, 85–95.

42. Sharpe, R. (1994, Mar. 29). The waiting game: Women make strides, but men stay firmly in top company jobs. *The Wall Street Journal*, pp. A1, A8. See also Nasar, S. (1992, Oct. 18). Women's progress stalled? Just not so. *The New York Times*, pp. 1F, 10F. See also Kleiman, C. (1992, Nov. 14). Women-owned firms creating most new jobs. *The Denver Post*, p. 4C.
43. Nasar, op. cit.
44. Pipelines of progress: A status report on the glass ceiling (1992). Washington, DC: U.S. Department of Labor.
45. Fernandez, with Barr, op. cit.
46. Rowland, M. (1992, Aug. 23). Strategies for stay-at-home moms. *The New York Times*, p. 16F.
47. Nasar, op. cit.
48. Schwartz, op. cit.
49. Garland, S. B. (1991, Sept. 2). How to keep women managers on the corporate ladder. *Business Week*, p. 64.
50. Genasci, L. (1993, Sept. 6). U.S. women at work organizing into groups. *The Denver Post*, pp. 1F, 4F.
51. The framework for this section was drawn from Managing generational diversity (1991, Apr.). *HRMagazine*, pp. 91, 92. See also Ratan, S. (1993, Oct. 4). Generational tension in the office: Why busters hate boomers. *Fortune*, pp. 56–70.
52. Huey, J. (1992, Jan. 27). The baby-boomers' latest whine. *Fortune*, pp. 56, 57.
53. Ibid.
54. Peterson, K. S. (1993, Sept. 23). Baby busters rise above elders' scorn. *USA Today*, pp. 1D, 2D.
55. Ibid. See also Deutschman, A. (1990, Aug. 27). What 25-year-olds want. *Fortune*, pp. 42–50.
56. Johnston & Packer, op. cit.
57. Weidenfeller, N. (1993, Oct. 8). Capitalizing on diversity. Presentation at Textbook Authors' Conference. Washington, DC: American Association of Retired Persons.
58. Northern States Power Company (1993). *Capitalizing on diversity*. Minneapolis: Author.
59. Cuneo, A. (1992, Nov. 15). Diverse by design: How good intentions make good business. *Business Week*, p. 72.
60. Schwartz, F. N. (1992). *Breaking with tradition: Women and work, the new facts of life*. New York: Warner. See also Garland, op. cit. See also The mommy track (1989, Mar. 20). *Business Week*, pp. 126–134. See also Trost, C. (1989, Nov. 22). Firms heed women employees' needs. *The Wall Street Journal*, pp. B1, B5.
61. Calem, R. E. (1993, Apr. 18). Working at home, for better or worse. *The New York Times*, pp. 1F, 6F.
62. *America's changing work force: Statistics in brief* (1992). Washington, DC: American Association of Retired Persons.
63. American Association of Retired Persons and Society for Human Resource Management (1993). *The older workforce: Recruitment and retention*. Washington, DC: AARP.
64. Shea, G. F. (1991). *Managing older employees*. San Francisco: Jossey-Bass. See also Andrews, E. S. (1992, Winter). Expanding opportunities for older workers. *Journal of Labor Research*, **13**(1), 55–65. See also Lefkovich, J. L. (1992, Spring). Older workers: Why and how to capitalize on their powers. *Employment Relations Today*, **19**(1), 63–79.
65. Brimelow, P., & Spencer, L. (1993, Feb. 15). When quotas replace merit, everybody suffers. *Forbes*, pp. 80–102.
66. Labor letter (1986, Dec. 2). *The Wall Street Journal*, p. 1.

CHAPTER 4

THE LEGAL CONTEXT OF EMPLOYMENT DECISIONS

DISABILITY DISCRIMINATION—CAN AN EMPLOYEE WHO SEEKS TREATMENT FOR ALCOHOL ABUSE BE FIRED?*

Shortly after the Exxon *Valdez* struck a reef off the Alaskan coast in 1989, Exxon Shipping Company adopted a new policy barring any employee who had ever participated in an alcohol rehabilitation program from holding designated jobs within the company. In accordance with this policy, Theodore Ellenwood, who had no connection to the *Valdez* incident, was removed from his position as chief engineer of another Exxon oil tanker, the Exxon *Wilmington*. Ellenwood voluntarily had entered, and successfully had completed, a month-long alcohol rehabilitation program a year before the *Valdez* accident. Despite his concerns about his drinking, Ellenwood had never had an on-the-job problem with alcohol. A psychiatrist who examined Ellenwood in connection with this case concluded that he had never been an alcoholic.

Relying primarily on the company's previous written policy that "no employees with alcoholism will have their job security or future opportunities jeopardized due to a request for help or involvement in a rehabilitation effort," Ellenwood and his wife brought suit against Exxon alleging that the company breached an agreement not to discriminate on the basis of Ellenwood's "disability" of alcohol abuse, as well as violations of state statutes prohibiting discrimination against the disabled. The Ellenwoods also alleged, among other claims, wrongful discharge in violation of the public policy promoting responsible treatment of alcoholism.

---

*Ellenwood et al. v. Exxon Shipping Co., U.S. Court of Appeals for the First Circuit, No. 92-1473, 1993 U.S. App. Lexis 362, January 14, 1993.

In response, Exxon raised three issues. First, it argued that Congress has a unique interest in regulating federal contractors like Exxon. It cited a passage from a Senate report that stated: "Congress intended that the federal Rehabilitation Act of 1973 be administered in such a manner that a consitent, uniform, and effective Federal approach to discrimination against disabled persons would result. Thus, Federal agencies and departments should cooperate in developing standards and policies so that there is a uniform, consistent Federal approach to these sections." Exxon claimed this passage demonstrated that Congress was seeking an exclusive approach to discrimination against the disabled by federal contractors (that is, there should be no "overlapping remedies"), and consequently, that it must have intended the federal law to displace parallel state laws governing the same conduct. Hence the Ellenwood's claim of violation of state laws prohibiting discrimination against the disabled should be dismissed.

Second, Exxon claimed that the area of discrimination against the disabled requires an extraordinary balancing of competing interests that distinguishes it from other types of employment discrimination, such as those involving race, gender, and age. In this area, Exxon maintained, the possibility of conflicitng judgments is much greater because courts in different jurisdictions could reach widely disparate conclusions on such basic questions as what constitutes a "disability" and which disabled persons are "qualified" to hold particular positions. Restricting individuals to the remedies specified under federal law would ensure that a federal contractor doing business in more than one state would face uniform obligations nationwide. Moreover, even if federal law does not preempt claims of violations of state law barring discrimination against the disabled, maritime law, which governs all issues surrounding Ellenwood's employment as a chief engineer on board ship, does.

Finally, Exxon contended that in allowing the jury to consider Ellenwood's claim of wrongful discharge in violation of the public policy promoting responsible treatment of alcoholism, the district court improperly created an exception to the well-established rule that maritime employment is terminable at will by either party in the absence of a contract setting a specific term.

Challenges

1. Should aggrieved parties be able to take advantage of "overlapping remedies" such as state *and* federal laws?

2. Is discrimination on the basis of disability different in kind from discrimination on the basis of age, race, gender, or religion?

3. In the interest of promoting safety in the operation of its tankers, should Exxon be allowed to terminate employees for substance abuse problems, even if treated?

Questions This Chapter Will Help Managers Answer

1. How are employment practices affected by the civil rights laws and Supreme Court interpretations of them?

2. What should be the components of an effective policy to prevent sexual harassment?

3. What obligations does the Family and Medical Leave Act impose on employers? What rights does it grant to employees?

4. In downsizing a company, what strategies can be used to avoid complaints of age discrimination?

5. What should senior management do to ensure that "reasonable accommodation" is provided to disabled job applicants or employees?

SOCIETAL OBJECTIVES

As a society, we espouse equality of opportunity, rather than equality of outcomes. That is, the broad goal is to provide for all Americans, regardless of race, age, gender, religion, national origin, or disability, an equal opportunity to compete for jobs for which they are qualified. The objective, therefore, is *EEO* (equal employment opportunity), not *EE* (equal employment, or equal numbers of employees from various subgroups). For Americans with disabilities, the nation's goals are to ensure equality of opportunity, full participation, independent living, and economic self-sufficiency.

As we saw in Chapter 3, the United States' population, as well as its workforce, is a diverse lot. Even among native-born English speakers, at least 22 different dialects of English are spoken in the United States! Whenever the members of such heterogeneous groups must work together, the possibility of unfair discrimination exists. Civil rights laws have been passed at the federal and state levels to provide remedies for job applicants or employees who feel they have been victims of unfair discrimination. From a managerial perspective, it is important to understand the rights as well as the obligations of employers, job candidates, and employees. Ignorance in this area can turn out to be very expensive. Let us begin, therefore, by considering the meaning of EEO and the forms of unfair discrimination.

EEO AND UNFAIR DISCRIMINATION: WHAT ARE THEY?

Civil rights laws, judicial interpretations of the laws, and the many sets of guidelines issued by state and federal regulatory agencies have outlawed discrimination based on race, religion, national origin, age, sex, and physical disability. In short, they have attempted to frame national policy on *equal employment opportunity* (EEO). Although no law has ever attempted to define precisely the term *discrimination*, in the employment context it can be viewed broadly as the giving of an unfair advantage (or disadvantage) to the members of a particular group in comparison to the members of other groups.[1] The disadvantage usually results in a denial or restriction of employment opportunities, or in an inequality in the terms or benefits of employment.

It is important to note that whenever there are more candidates than available positions, it is necessary to select some candidates in preference to others. Selection implies exclusion. And as long as the exclusion is based upon what can be demonstrated to be job-related criteria, that kind of discrimination is entirely proper. It is only when candidates are excluded on a prohibited basis not related to the job (e.g., age, race, sex) that unlawful and unfair discrimination exists. In short, EEO implies at least two things:

1. *Evaluation of candidates for jobs in terms of characteristics that really do make a difference between success and failure* (e.g., in selection, promotion, performance appraisal, or layoff)
2. *Fair and equal treatment of employees on the job* (e.g., equal pay for equal work, equal benefits, freedom from sexual harassment)

Despite federal and state laws on these issues, they represent the basis of an enormous volume of court cases, indicating that stereotypes and prejudices do not die quickly or easily. Discrimination is a subtle and complex phenomenon that may assume two broad forms:

1. *Unequal (disparate) treatment* is based on an *intention to discriminate*, including the intention to *retaliate* against a person who opposes discrimination, has brought charges, or has participated in an investigation or a hearing. There are three major subtheories of discrimination within the disparate treatment theory.

a. Cases that rely on *direct evidence* of the intention to discriminate. Such cases are proven with direct evidence of:

■ Pure bias based on an open expression of hatred, disrespect, or inequality, knowingly directed against members of a particular group.

■ Blanket exclusionary policies—for example, deliberate exclusion of an individual whose disability (e.g., walking) has nothing to do with the requirements of the job she is applying for (financial analyst).

b. Cases that are proved through *circumstantial evidence* of the intention to discriminate (see *McDonnell Douglas v. Green* test, p. 95), including those that rely on statistical evidence as a method of circumstantially proving the intention to discriminate systematically against classes of individuals.

c. *Mixed-motive* cases (a hybrid theory) that often rely on both direct evidence of the intention to discriminate on some impermissible basis (e.g., sex, race, disability) and proof that the employer's stated legitimate basis for its employment decision is actually just a pretext for illegal discrimination.

2. *Adverse impact (unintentional) discrimination* occurs when identical standards or procedures are applied to everyone, despite the fact that they lead to a substantial difference in employment outcomes (e.g., selection, promotion, layoffs) for the members of a particular group, *and* they are unrelated to success on a job. For example:

■ Use of a minimum height requirement of 5′8″ for police cadets. That requirement would have an adverse impact on Asians, Hispanics, and women. The policy is neutral on its face but has an adverse impact. To use it, an employer would need to show that the height requirement is necessary to perform the job.

These two forms of illegal discrimination are illustrated graphically in Figure 4-1.

THE LEGAL CONTEXT OF HUMAN RESOURCE DECISIONS

Now that we understand the forms that illegal discrimination can take, let us consider the major federal laws governing employment. Following this we shall consider the agencies that enforce the laws, as well as some important court cases that have interpreted them. The federal laws that we shall discuss fall into two broad classes:

1. Laws of broad scope that prohibit unfair discrimination

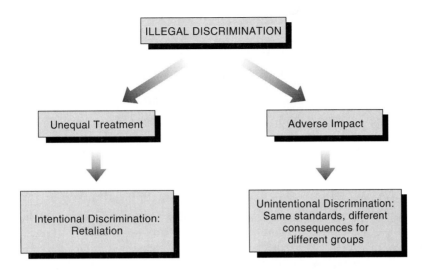

FIGURE 4-1
Major forms of illegal
discrimination.

2. Laws of limited application, for example, those that require nondiscrimination as a *condition* for receiving federal funds (contracts, grants, revenue-sharing entitlements)

The particular laws we shall discuss within each category are:

Laws of Broad Scope	**Laws of Limited Application**
Thirteenth and Fourteenth Amendments to the U.S. Constitution	Executive Orders 11246, 11375, and 11478
Civil Rights Acts of 1866 and 1871	Rehabilitation Act (1973)
Equal Pay Act (1963)	Vietnam Era Veterans Readjustment Act (1974)
Title VII of the 1964 Civil Rights Act	
Age Discrimination in Employment Act (1967), as amended in 1986	
Immigration Reform and Control Act (1986)	
Americans with Disabilities Act of 1990	
Civil Rights Act of 1991	
Family and Medical Leave Act of 1993	

The Thirteenth and Fourteenth Amendments

The Thirteenth Amendment prohibited slavery and involuntary servitude. Any form of discrimination may be considered an incident of slavery or involuntary servitude and thus be liable to legal action under this amendment.[2] The Fourteenth Amendment guarantees equal protection of the law for all citizens. Both the Thirteenth and Fourteenth amendments granted to Congress the constitutional power to enact legislation to enforce their provisions. It is from this source of constitutional power that all subsequent civil rights legislation originates.

The Civil Rights Acts of 1866 and 1871

These laws were enacted based on the provisions of the Thirteenth and Fourteenth amendments. The Civil Rights Act of 1866 grants all citizens the right to make and enforce contracts for employment, and the Civil Rights Act of 1871 grants all citizens the right to sue in federal court if they feel they have been deprived of any rights or privileges guaranteed by the Constitution and laws.

Until recently, both of these laws were viewed narrowly as tools for solving Reconstruction-era racial problems. This is no longer so. In *Johnson v. Railway Express Agency, Inc.*, the Supreme Court held that while the Civil Rights Act of 1866 on its face relates primarily to racial discrimination in the making and enforcement of contracts, it also provides a federal remedy against racial discrimination in private employment.[3] It is a powerful remedy. The Civil Rights Act of 1991 amended the Civil Rights Act of 1866 so that workers are protected from intentional discrimination in all aspects of employment, not just hiring and promotion. Thus racial harassment is covered by this civil rights law. The Civil Rights Act of 1866 allows for jury trials and for compensatory and punitive damages* for victims of intentional racial and ethnic discrimination, and it covers both large and small employers, even those with fewer than 15 employees.

The 1866 law also has been used recently to broaden the definition of racial discrimination originally applied to African Americans. In a unanimous decision, the Supreme Court ruled in 1987 that race was equated with ethnicity during the legislative debate after the Civil War, and therefore Arabs, Jews, and other ethnic groups thought of as "white" are not barred from suing under the 1866 act. The Court held that Congress intended to protect identifiable classes of persons who are subjected to intentional discrimination solely because of their ancestry or ethnic characteristics. Under the law, therefore, race involves more than just skin pigment.[4]

The Equal Pay Act of 1963

This act was passed as an amendment to an earlier compensation-related law, the Fair Labor Standards Act of 1938. For those employees covered by the Fair Labor Standards Act, the Equal Pay Act requires that men and women working for the same establishment be paid the same rate of pay for work that is substantially equal in skill, effort, responsibility, and working conditions. Pay differentials are legal and appropriate if they are based on seniority, merit, systems that measure the quality or quantity of work, or any factor other than sex. Moreover, in correcting any inequity under the Equal Pay Act, employers must raise the rate of lower-paid employees, not lower the rate of higher-paid employees.

Hundreds of equal-pay suits were filed (predominantly by women) during the 1970s and the 1980s. For individual companies the price can be quite high. For example, at Chicago's Harris Trust, the company agreed to pay $14 million in back wages to thousands of female workers in order to settle a 12-year-old lawsuit. The women claimed they had been treated differently solely because of their sex (i.e., unequal treatment discrimination). For example, female trainees were required to type, but male trainees were not.

---

*Punitive damages are awarded in civil cases to punish or deter a defendant's conduct and are separate from compensatory damages, which are intended to reimburse a plaintiff for injuries or harm.

Even before the decision, however, the bank had come a long way. When the suit was filed in 1977, Harris had 5 female vice presidents. By 1989, 102 out of 380 vice presidents were female.[5]

Title VII of the Civil Rights Act of 1964

The Civil Rights Act of 1964 is divided into several sections, or titles, each dealing with a particular facet of discrimination (e.g., voting rights, public accommodations, public education). Title VII is most relevant to the employment context, for it prohibits discrimination on the basis of race, color, religion, sex, or national origin in all aspects of employment (including apprenticeship programs). Title VII is the most important federal EEO law because it contains the broadest coverage, prohibitions, and remedies. Through it, the Equal Employment Opportunity Commission (EEOC) was created to ensure that employers, employment agencies, and labor organizations comply with Title VII.

Some may ask why we need such a law. As an expression of social policy, the law was passed to guarantee that people would be considered for jobs not on the basis of the color of their skin, their religion, their gender, or their national origin, but rather on the basis of the individual abilities and talents that are necessary to perform a job.

In 1972, the coverage of Title VII was expanded. It now includes almost all public and private employers with 15 or more employees, except: (1) private clubs, (2) religious organizations (which are allowed to discriminate on the basis of religion in certain circumstances), and (3) places of employment connected with an Indian reservation. The 1972 amendments also prohibited the denial, termination, or suspension of government contracts (without a special hearing) if an employer has followed and is now following an affirmative action plan accepted by the federal government for the same facility within the past 12 months. "Affirmative action" refers to *those actions appropriate to overcome the effects of past or present policies, practices, or other barriers to equal employment opportunity.*[6]

Finally, back-pay awards in Title VII cases are limited to 2 years prior to the filing of a charge. For example, if a woman filed a Title VII claim in 1988, and the matter continued through investigation, conciliation, trial, and appeal until 1993, she might be entitled to as much as seven years back pay, from 1986 (two years prior to the filing of a charge) until the matter was resolved in her favor. The 2-year statute of limitations begins with the *filing* of a charge of discrimination.

Elected officials and their appointees are excluded from Title VII coverage, but they are still subject to the Fourteenth Amendment, to the Civil Rights Acts of 1866 and 1871, and to the Civil Rights Act of 1991. The following are also specifically exempted from Title VII coverage:

1. *Bona fide occupational qualifications (BFOQs)*. Discrimination is permissible when a prohibited factor (e.g., gender) is a bona fide occupational qualification for employment, that is, when it is considered "reasonably necessary to the operation of that particular business or enterprise." The burden of proof rests with the employer to demonstrate this. (According to one HR director, the only legitimate BFOQs that she could think of are sperm donor and wet nurse!) Both the EEOC and the courts interpret BFOQs quite narrowly.[7] The preferences of the employer, coworkers, or clients are irrelevant and do not constitute BFOQs. Moreover, BFOQ is not a viable defense to a Title VII race claim.

2. *Seniority systems.* Although there are a number of legal questions associated with their use, Title VII explicitly permits bona fide seniority, merit, or incentive systems "provided that such differences are not the result of an intention to discriminate."

3. *Preemployment inquiries.* Inquiries regarding such matters as race, sex, or ethnic group are permissible as long as they can be shown to be job-related. Even if not job-related, some inquiries (e.g., regarding race or sex) are necessary to meet the reporting requirements of federal regulatory agencies. Applicants provide this information on a voluntary basis.

4. *Testing.* An employer may give or act upon any professionally developed ability test. If the results demonstrate adverse impact against a protected group, then the test itself must be shown to be job-related (i.e., valid) for the position in question.

5. *Preferential treatment.* The Supreme Court has ruled that Title VII does not require the granting of preferential treatment to individuals or groups because of their race, sex, religion, or national origin on account of existing imbalances:

> The burden which shifts to the employer is merely that of proving that he based his employment decision on a legitimate consideration, and not an illegitimate one such as race. . . . Title VII forbids him from having as a goal a work force selected by any proscribed discriminatory practice, but it does not impose a duty to adopt a hiring procedure that maximizes hiring of minority employees.[8]

6. *National security.* Discrimination is permitted under Title VII when it is deemed necessary to protect the national security (e.g., against members of groups whose avowed aim is to overthrow the U.S. government).

Initially it appeared that these exemptions (summarized in Figure 4-2) would blunt the overall impact of the law significantly. However, it soon became clear that they would be interpreted very narrowly both by the EEOC and by the courts.

FIGURE 4-2
The six exemptions to
Title VII coverage.

**EXEMPTIONS TO
TITLE VII COVERAGE**

Bona Fide Occupational
Qualifications

Seniority Systems

Preemployment Inquiries

Testing

Veteran's Preference Rights

National Security

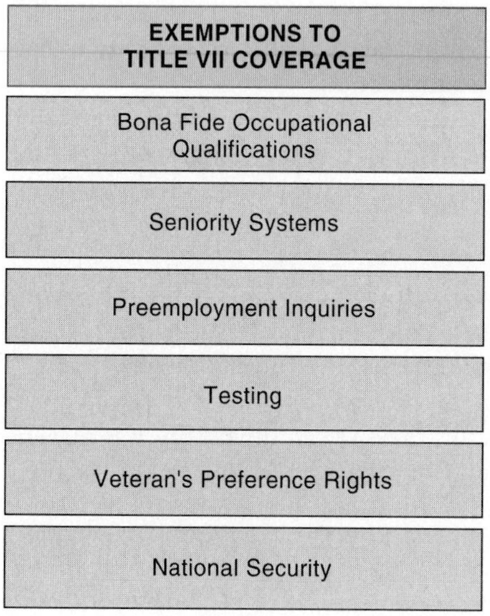

Litigating Claims of Unfair Discrimination. In bringing suit under Title VII, the first step is to establish a prima facie case of discrimination (i.e., a body of facts presumed to be true until proven otherwise). However, the nature of prima facie evidence differs depending on the type of case brought before the court. If an individual alleges that a particular employment practice had an *adverse impact* on all members of a class that he or she represents, prima facie evidence is presented when adverse impact is shown to exist. Usually this is demonstrated by showing that the selection rate for the group in question is less than 80 percent of the rate of the dominant group (e.g., white males) and that the difference is statistically significant. If the individual alleges that he or she was treated differently from others in the context of some employment practice (i.e., *unequal treatment discrimination*), a prima facie case is usually presented either through direct evidence of the intention to discriminate or by circumstantial evidence. The legal standard for circumstantial evidence is a four-part test first specified in the *McDonnell Douglas v. Green* case,[9] wherein a plaintiff must be able to demonstrate that:

1. She or he has asserted a basis protected by Title VII, the Age Discrimination in Employment Act, or the Americans with Disabilities Act.
2. She or he was somehow harmed or disadvantaged (e.g., by not receiving a job offer or a promotion).
3. She or he was qualified to do the job or to perform the job in a satisfactory manner.
4. Either a similarly situated individual (or a group other than that of the plaintiff) was treated more favorably than the plaintiff, *or* that the matter complained of involved an actual (rather than a nonexistent) employment opportunity.

Once prima facie evidence is accepted by the court, the burden of producing evidence shifts back and forth from plaintiff (the complaining party) to defendant (the employer). First the employer is given the opportunity to articulate a legitimate, nondiscriminatory reason for the practice in question. Following that, in an unequal treatment case, the burden then shifts back to the plaintiff to show that the employer's reason is a pretext for illegal discrimination. In an adverse impact case, the plaintiff's burden is to show that a less discriminatory alternative practice exists and that the employer failed to use it. A similar process is followed in age discrimination cases.

The Age Discrimination in Employment Act of 1967 (ADEA)

As amended in 1986, this act prohibits discrimination in pay, benefits, or continued employment for employees age 40 and over, unless an employer can demonstrate that age is a BFOQ for the job in question. Like Title VII, this law is administered by the EEOC. A key objective of the law is to prevent financially troubled companies from singling out older employees when there are cutbacks. However, the EEOC has ruled that when there are cutbacks, older workers can waive their rights to sue under this law (e.g., in return for sweetened benefits for early retirement). Under the Older Workers Benefit Protection Act, which took effect in 1990, employees have 45 days to consider such waivers, and 7 days after signing to revoke them.

Increasingly, older workers are being asked to sign such waivers in exchange for enhanced retirement benefits. For example, at AT&T Communications, Inc., employees who signed waivers received severance pay equal to 5 percent of current pay times the number of years of service. For those without waivers, the company offered a multiplier of 3 percent.

The Immigration Reform and Control Act of 1986 (IRCA)

This law applies to *every* employer in the United States, even to those with only one employee. It also applies to every employee—whether full-time, part-time, temporary, or seasonal. This act makes the enforcement of national immigration policy the job of every employer. While its provisions are complex, the basic features of the law fall into four broad categories:[10]

1. Employers may not hire or continue to employ "unauthorized aliens" (that is, those not legally authorized to work in this country).
2. Employers must verify the identity and work authorization of every new employee. Employers may not require any particular form of documentation but must examine documents provided by job applicants (e.g., U.S. passports for U.S. citizens; "green cards" for resident aliens) showing identity and work authorization. Both employer and employee then sign a form (I-9), attesting under penalty of perjury that the employee is lawfully eligible to work in the United States.
3. Employers with 4 to 14 employees may not discriminate on the basis of citizenship or national origin. Those with 15 or more employees are already prohibited from national origin discrimination by Title VII. However, this prohibition is tempered by an exception that allows employers to select an applicant who is a U.S. citizen over an alien when the two applicants are equally qualified.
4. Certain illegal aliens have "amnesty" rights. Those who can prove that they resided in the United States continuously from January 1982 to November 6, 1986 (the date of the law's enactment), are eligible for temporary, and ultimately permanent, resident status.

Penalties for noncompliance are severe. For example, for failure to comply with the verification rules, fines range from $100 to $1000 for *each* employee whose identity and work authorization have not been verified. The act also provides for criminal sanctions for employers who engage in a pattern or practice of violations.

This became obvious in 1989 when the government imposed a record fine of $580,000 against a South Carolina pillow factory accused of hiring more than 100 illegal aliens, including a 12-year-old boy. Further, the company, its owners, and nine managers were indicted by a federal grand jury on charges of illegally recruiting and harboring 117 illegal aliens. Such charges carry maximum prison terms of 653 years and fines totaling $5.1 million.[11]

The Americans with Disabilities Act of 1990 (ADA)

Passed to protect the estimated 43 million Americans with disabilities, this law became effective in July 1992 for employers with 25 or more employees and in July 1994 for employers with 15 or more employees. Persons with disabilities are protected from discrimination in employment, transportation, and public accommodation.

As a general rule, the ADA prohibits an employer from discriminating against a "qualified individual with a disability." A qualified individual is one who is able to perform the "essential" (i.e., primary) functions of a job with or without accommodation. "Disability" is a physical or mental impairment that substantially limits one or more major life activities, such as walking, talking, seeing, hearing, or learning. Persons are protected if they currently have an impairment, have a record of such impairment, or if the employer *thinks* they have an impairment (e.g., a person with diabetes under control). Rehabilitated drug and alcohol abusers are protected, but current drug abusers may be fired. The alcoholic, in contrast, is covered and must be reasonably accommodated by being given a firm choice to rehabilitate himself or herself or face career-threatening consequences. The law also protects persons who have tested positive for the AIDS virus.[12] Here are five major implications for employers:

1. Any factory, office, retail store, bank, hotel, or other building open to the public will have to be made accessible to those with physical disabilities (e.g., by installing ramps, elevators, telephones with amplifiers). "Expensive" will be no excuse, unless such modifications will lead an employer to suffer an "undue hardship."

2. Employers must make "reasonable accommodations" for disabled job applicants or employees (e.g., by restructuring job and training programs, modifying work schedules, or purchasing new equipment that is "user friendly" to blind or deaf people). Qualified job applicants (i.e., disabled individuals who can perform the essential functions of a job with or without reasonable accommodation) must be considered for employment. Practices such as the following may facilitate the process:[13]

- Expressions of commitment by top management to accommodate workers with disabilities
- Assignment of a specialist within the "EEO/Affirmative Action" section to focus on "equal access" for the disabled
- Centralizing recruiting, intake, and monitoring of hiring decisions
- Identifying jobs or task assignments where a specific disability is not a bar to employment
- Developing an orientation process for disabled workers, supervisors, and coworkers
- Publicizing successful accommodation experiences within the organization and among outside organizations
- Providing in-service training to all employees and managers about the firm's "equal access" policy, and about how to distinguish "essential" from "marginal" job functions
- Outreach recruitment to organizations that can refer disabled job applicants
- Reevaluating accommodations on a regular basis

3. Preemployment physicals will now be permissible only if all employees are subject to them, and they cannot be given until after a conditional offer of employment is made. That is, the employment offer is made conditional upon passing of the physical examination. Further, employers are not permitted to ask about past workers' compensation claims or disabilities in general. However, after describing essential job functions, an employer can ask whether the applicant can perform the job in question. Here is an example of the difference between these two types of inquiries:

"Do you have any back problems?" clearly violates the ADA because it is not job-specific. However, the employer could state the following: "This job involves lifting equipment weighing up to 50 pounds at least once every hour of an 8-hour shift. Can you do that?"

4. Medical information on employees must be kept separate from other personal or work-related information about them.

5. Drug testing rules remain intact. An employer can still prohibit the use of alcohol and illegal drugs at the workplace and continue to give alcohol and drug tests.

Enforcement. This law is enforced according to the same procedures currently applicable to race, gender, national origin, and religious discrimination under Title VII of the Civil Rights Act of 1964. The enforcement agency is the Equal Employment Opportunity Commission (EEOC). In cases of *intentional* discrimination, disabled individuals may be awarded both compensatory and punitive damages up to $300,000 (depending on the size of the employer's workforce). In the first 11 months after the law took effect, 11,760 discrimination complaints were filed with the agency. Roughly 20 percent of the cases were resolved during that time period, and aggrieved persons collected more than $11 million.[14] As the chapter opening vignette illustrates, this area will be a "hot" one for allegations of illegal discrimination for some time to come.

What will the cost to employers be? According to the EEOC, making such accommodations will cost employers $16 million a year, while providing productivity gains of $164 million and reduced government support payments and higher tax revenues of $222 million a year.[15]

The Civil Rights Act of 1991[16]

This act overturned six Supreme Court decisions issued in 1989. Here are some key provisions that are likely to have the greatest impact in the context of employment.

Monetary Damages and Jury Trials. A major effect of this act is to expand the remedies in discrimination cases. Individuals who feel they are the victims of *intentional discrimination* based on race, gender (including sexual harassment), religion, or disability can ask for compensatory damages for pain and suffering, as well as for punitive damages, and they may demand a jury trial. In the past, only plaintiffs in age discrimination cases had the right to demand a jury.

Compensatory and punitive damages are available only from nonpublic employers (public employers are still subject to compensatory damages up to $300,000), and not for adverse impact (unintentional discrimination) cases. Moreover, they may not be awarded in an ADA case when an employer has engaged in good-faith efforts to provide a reasonable accommodation. The total amount of damages that can be awarded depends on the size of the employer's workforce:

Number of employees	Maximum combined damages per complaint
15 to 100	$ 50,000
101 to 200	$100,000
201 to 500	$200,000
More than 500	$300,000

As we noted earlier, victims of intentional discrimination by race or national origin may sue under the Civil Rights Act of 1866, in which case there are no limits to compensatory and punitive damages. Note also that since intentional discrimination by reason of disability is a basis for compensatory and punitive damages (unless the employer makes a good-faith effort to provide reasonable accommodation), the 1991 Civil Rights Act provides the sanctions for violations of the Americans with Disabilities Act of 1990.

Adverse Impact (Unintentional Discrimination) Cases. The act clarifies each party's obligation in such cases. As we noted earlier, when an adverse impact charge is made, the plaintiff must identify a specific employment practice as the cause of discrimination. If the plaintiff is successful in demonstrating adverse impact, the burden of producing evidence shifts to the employer, who must prove that the challenged practice is "job-related for the position in question and consistent with business necessity."

Protection in Foreign Countries. Protection from discrimination in employment, under Title VII of the 1964 Civil Rights Act and the Americans with Disabilities Act, is extended to U.S. citizens employed in a foreign facility owned or controlled by a U.S. company. However, the employer does not have to comply with U.S. discrimination law if to do so would violate the law of the foreign country. This provision overturned a 1991 Supreme Court decision, *EEOC v. Arabian American Oil Co. and Aramco Service Co.*[17]

Racial Harassment. As we noted earlier, the act amended the Civil Rights Act of 1866 so that workers are protected from intentional discrimination in all aspects of employment, not just hiring and promotion.

Challenges to Consent Decrees. Once a court order or consent decree is entered to resolve a lawsuit, nonparties to the original suit cannot challenge such enforcement actions.

Mixed-Motive Cases. In a mixed-motive case, an employment decision was based on a combination of job-related factors as well as unlawful factors, such as race, gender, religion, or disability. Under the Civil Rights Act of 1991, an employer is guilty of discrimination if it can be shown that a prohibited consideration was a motivating factor in a decision, even though other factors, which are lawful, also were used. This clarified the Supreme Court's 1989 decision, *Price Waterhouse v. Hopkins.*[18] However, if the employer can show that the same decision would have been reached even without the unlawful considerations, the court may not assess damages or require hiring, reinstatement, or promotion.

Seniority Systems. The act provides that a seniority system that intentionally discriminates against the members of a protected group can be challenged (within 180 days) at any of three points: (1) when the system is adopted, (2) when an individual becomes subject to the system, or (3) when a person is injured by the system. This provision overturned the Supreme Court's decision in *Lorance v. AT&T Technologies* (1989).[19]

"Race Norming" and Affirmative Action. The act makes it unlawful "to adjust the scores of, use different cutoff scores for, or otherwise alter the results of employment-related tests on the basis of race, color, religion, sex, or national origin." Prior to the passage of this act, within-group percentile scoring (so-called "race norming") had been used extensively to adjust the test scores of minority candidates to make them more comparable to those of nonminority candidates. When race norming is used, each individual's percentile score on a selection test is computed relative only to others in his or her race/ethnic group, and not relative to the scores of all examinees who took the test. However, a merged list of percentile scores (high to low) is presented to those responsible for hiring decisions.

Despite these prohibitions, another section of the act states: "Nothing in the amendments made by this title shall be construed to affect court-ordered remedies, affirmative action, or conciliation agreements that are in accordance with the law." Although it could be argued that the act would permit individual employers to make test score adjustments as part of court-ordered affirmative action plans, or where a court approves a conciliation agreement, it is not yet clear that courts will interpret it so broadly.[20]

Extension to U.S. Senate and Appointed Officials. The act extends protection from discrimination on the basis of race, color, religion, gender, national origin, age, and disability to employees of the U.S. Senate, political appointees of the President, and staff members employed by elected officials at the state level. Employees of the U.S. House of Representatives are covered by a House resolution adopted in 1988.

The Family and Medical Leave Act of 1993 (FMLA)

The FMLA covers all private-sector employers with 50 or more employees, including part-timers, who work 1250 hours over a 12-month period (an average of 25 hours per week). The law gives workers up to 12 weeks' unpaid leave each year for birth, adoption, or foster care of a child within a year of the child's arrival; care for a spouse, parent, or child with a serious health condition; or the employee's own serious health condition if it prevents him or her from working. Employers can require workers to provide medical certification of such serious illnesses and can require a second medical opinion. Employers also can exempt from the FMLA key salaried employees who are among their highest paid 10 percent. For leave takers, however, employers must maintain health insurance benefits and give the workers their previous jobs (or comparable positions) when their leaves are over. Enforcement provisions of the FMLA are administered by the U.S. Department of Labor.[21] The overall impact of this law was softened considerably by the exemption of some of its fiercest opponents—companies with fewer than 50 employees, or 95 percent of all businesses. According to the Small Business Administration, such companies employ 27 percent of the nation's civilian workforce, or about 25 million people.[22]

This completes the discussion of "absolute prohibitions" against discrimination. The following sections discuss nondiscrimination as a basis for eligibility for federal funds.

Executive Orders 11246, 11375, and 11478

Presidential Executive Orders in the realm of employment and discrimination are aimed specifically at federal agencies, contractors, and subcontractors. They have the force of law, even though they are issued unilaterally by the President without congressional approval, and they can be altered unilaterally as well. The requirements of these orders are parallel to those of Title VII.

In 1965, President Johnson issued Executive Order 11246, prohibiting discrimination on the basis of race, color, religion, or national origin as a condition of employment by federal agencies, contractors, and subcontractors with contracts of $10,000 or more. Those covered are required to establish and maintain a program of equal employment opportunity in every facility of 50 or more people. Such programs include employment, upgrading, demotion, transfer, recruitment or recruitment advertising, layoff or termination, pay rates, and selection for training.

In 1967, Executive Order 11375 prohibited discrimination in employment based on sex. Executive Order 11478, issued by President Nixon in 1969, went even further, for it prohibited discrimination in employment based on all of the previous factors, plus political affiliation, marital status, or physical handicap.

Enforcement of Executive Orders. Executive Order 11246 provides considerable enforcement power, administered by the Department of Labor through its Office of Federal Contract Compliance Programs (OFCCP). Upon a finding by the OFCCP of noncompliance with the order, the Department of Justice may be advised to institute criminal proceedings, and the secretary of labor may cancel or suspend current contracts as well as the right to bid on future contracts. Needless to say, noncompliance can be *very* expensive.

The Rehabilitation Act of 1973

This act requires federal contractors (those receiving more than $2500 in federal contracts annually) and subcontractors actively to recruit qualified handicapped people and to use their talents to the fullest extent possible. The legal requirements are similar to those of the Americans with Disabilities Act.

The purpose of this act is to eliminate *systemic discrimination*, i.e., any business practice that results in the denial of equal employment opportunity.[23] Hence the act emphasizes "screening in" applicants, not screening them out. It is enforced by the OFCCP.

The Vietnam Era Veterans Readjustment Act of 1974

Federal contractors and subcontractors are required under this act to take affirmative action to ensure equal employment opportunity for Vietnam-era (August 5, 1964, to May 7, 1975) veterans. This act is enforced by the OFCCP.

FEDERAL ENFORCEMENT AGENCIES: EEOC AND OFCCP

The Equal Employment Opportunity Commission is an independent regulatory agency whose five commissioners (one of whom is chairperson) are appointed by the President and confirmed by the Senate for terms of 5 years. No more than three of the commissioners may be from the same political party. Like the OFCCP, the EEOC sets policy and in individual cases determines whether there is "reasonable cause" to believe that unlawful discrimination has occurred. If reasonable cause is found, the EEOC can sue either on its own behalf or on behalf of a claimant. As far as the employer is concerned, the simplest and least costly procedure is to establish a system to resolve complaints internally. However, if this system fails or if the employer does not make available an avenue for such complaints, an aggrieved individual (or group) can file a formal complaint with the EEOC. The process is shown graphically in Figure 4-3.

Once it receives a complaint of discrimination, the EEOC follows a three-step process: investigation, conciliation, and litigation.[24] As Figure 4-3 indicates, complaints must be filed within 180 days of an alleged violation (300 days if the same basis of discrimination is prohibited by either state or local laws). If that requirement is satisfied, the EEOC immediately refers the complaint to a state agency charged with enforcement of fair employment laws (if one exists) for resolution within 60 days. If the complaint cannot be resolved within that time, the state agency can file suit in a state district court and appeal any decision to a state appellate court, the state supreme court, or the U.S. Supreme Court. Alternatively to filing suit, the state agency may redefer to the EEOC. Again voluntary reconciliation is sought, but if this fails, the EEOC may refer the case to the Justice Department (if the defendant is a public employer) or file suit in federal district court (if the defendant is a private employer). Like state court decisions, federal court decisions may be appealed to one of the 12 U.S. Courts of Appeal (corresponding to the geographical region or "circuit" in which the case arose). In turn, these decisions may be appealed to the U.S. Supreme Court, although very few cases are actually heard by the Supreme Court. Generally the Court will grant certiorari (discretionary review) when two or more circuit courts have reached different conclusions on the same point of law or when a major question of constitutional interpretation is involved. If certiorari is denied, the lower court's decision is binding.

EEOC Guidelines

The EEOC has issued a number of guidelines for Title VII compliance. Among these are guidelines on discrimination because of religion, national origin, gender, and pregnancy; guidelines on affirmative action programs; guidelines on employee selection procedures; and a policy statement on preemployment inquiries. These guidelines are not laws, although the Supreme Court indicated in *Albemarle Paper Company v. Moody* that they are entitled to "great deference."[25]

Information Gathering. This is another major EEOC function, for each organization in the United States with 100 or more employees must file an annual report (EEO-1) detailing the number of women and minorities employed in nine different job categories ranging from laborers to managers and professionals. In 1992, 38,059 organizations filed these forms with the EEOC.[26] Through computerized analysis of the forms, the EEOC is able to identify broad patterns of discrimination (systemic discrimination) and to attack them through class action suits. In any given year the EEOC typically receives more than 70,000 complaints and has about 500 class action suits in progress. In 1991, it won $188 million in benefits for victims of illegal discrimination.[27]

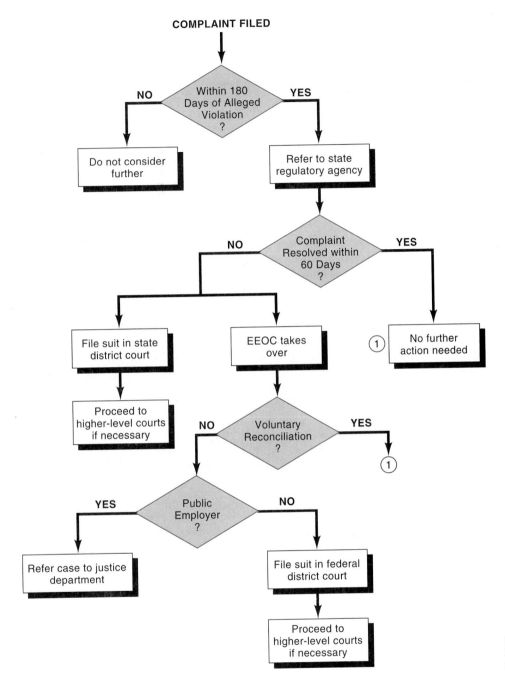

FIGURE 4-3
Discrimination complaints:
the formal process.

The Office of Federal Contract Compliance Programs (OFCCP)

Contract compliance means that in addition to quality, timeliness, and other requirements of federal contract work, contractors and subcontractors must meet EEO and
affirmative action requirements. As we have seen, these cover all aspects of employment.

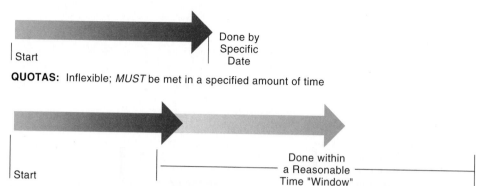

FIGURE 4-4
The distinction between
rigid quotas and goals and
timetables.

Companies are willing to go to considerable lengths to avoid the loss of government contracts. More than a quarter of a million companies, employing 27 million workers and providing the government with more than $100 billion in construction, supplies, equipment, and services, are subject to contract compliance enforcement by the OFCCP.[28] Contractors and subcontractors with more than $50,000 in government business and with 50 or more employees must prepare and implement written affirmative action plans.

In jobs where women and minorities are *underrepresented* in the workforce relative to their availability in the labor force, employers must establish goals and timetables for hiring and promotion. Theoretically, goals and timetables are distinguishable from rigid quotas in that they are flexible objectives that can be met in a realistic amount of time (Figure 4-4). Goals and timetables are not required under the Rehabilitation Act and Vietnam Veterans law.

When a compliance review by the Office of Federal Contract Compliance Programs indicates problems that cannot easily be resolved, it tries to reach a conciliation agreement with the employer. Such an agreement might include back pay, seniority credit, special recruitment efforts, promotion, or other forms of relief for the victims of unlawful discrimination.

The conciliation agreement is the OFCCP's preferred route, but if such efforts are unsuccessful, formal enforcement action is necessary. Contractors and subcontractors are entitled to a hearing before a judge. If conciliation is not reached before or after the hearing, employers may lose their government contracts, their payments may be withheld by the government, or they may be debarred from any government contract work. Debarment is the OFCCP's ultimate weapon, for it indicates in the most direct way possible that the U.S. government is serious about equal employment opportunity programs. Between 1965 and 1980, 24 companies were debarred from government work.[29]

Affirmative Action Remedies

In its 1986 ruling in *Local 28 Sheet Metal Workers v. E.E.O.C.*, the Supreme Court found that Congress specifically endorsed the concept of non-victim-specific racial hiring goals to achieve compliance.[30] Further, the Court noted the benefits of flexible affirmative action rather than rigid application of a color-blind policy that would deprive employers of flexibility in administering human resources. How do employers do in practice? One 7-year study of companies that set annual goals for increasing black male employment found that only one-tenth of the goals were achieved. Some may see this as a sign of failure, but it also reflects the fact that the goals were not rigid quotas. "Companies promise more than they can deliver, . . . but the ones that promise more do deliver more."[31]

EMPLOYMENT CASE LAW: SOME GENERAL PRINCIPLES

Although Congress enacts laws, the courts interpret the laws and determine how they shall be enforced. Such interpretations define what is called *case law*, which serves as a precedent to guide future legal decisions. And, of course, precedents are regularly subject to reinterpretation.

In the area of employment, a considerable body of case law has accumulated since 1964. Figure 4-5 illustrates areas in which case law is developed most extensively. Lawsuits affecting virtually every aspect of employment have been filed, and in the following sections we shall consider some of the most significant decisions to date.

Sex Discrimination

Suppose you run an organization that has 238 managerial positions—all filled by men. Suppose that only a 2-point difference in test scores separates the best-qualified man from the best-qualified woman. Only one promotional opportunity to a managerial position is available. What do you do? Until a landmark Supreme Court decision in 1987 (*Johnson v. Santa Clara Transportation Agency*[32]), if you promoted the woman you invited a lawsuit by the man. If you promoted the woman to correct past discrimination (thereby acknowledging past bias), you would invite discrimination suits by women. No longer. The Supreme Court ruled unambiguously that in traditionally sex-segregated jobs, a qualified woman can be promoted over a marginally better-qualified man to promote more balanced representation. The Court stressed the need for affirmative action plans to be flexible, gradual, and limited in their effect on whites and men. The Court also expressed disapproval of strict numerical quotas except where necessary (on a temporary basis) to remedy severe past discrimination.

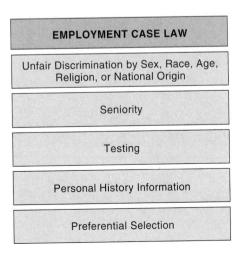

FIGURE 4-5

Areas making up the main body of employment case law.

Many employers are in similar positions. That is, they have not been proven guilty of past discrimination, but they have a significant underrepresentation of women or other protected groups in various job categories. This decision clearly put pressure on employers to institute voluntary affirmative action programs, but at the same time it also provided some welcome guidance on what they were permitted to do.

Pregnancy. The Equal Employment Opportunity Commission's guidelines on the Pregnancy Discrimination Act of 1978 state:

> The basic principle of the Act is that women affected by pregnancy and related conditions must be treated the same as other applicants and employees on the basis of their ability or inability to work. A woman is therefore protected against such practices as being fired, or refused a job or promotion, merely because she is pregnant or has had an abortion. She usually cannot be forced to go on leave as long as she can still work. If other employees who take disability leave are entitled to get their jobs back when they are able to work again, so are women who have been unable to work because of pregnancy.[33]

Each year, the EEOC receives about 3600 complaints related to pregnancy (about one out of every 50 complaints the commission receives).[34] However, this may be only the tip of the iceberg. For example, the National Association of Working Women in Cleveland handles 15,000 calls a year from women claiming gender-based discrimination, including pregnancy.[35]

Under the law, an employer is never *required* to give pregnant employees special treatment. If an organization provides no disability benefits or sick leave to other employees, it is not required to provide them for pregnant employees.[36] While the actual length of maternity leave is now an issue to be determined by the woman's and/or the company's physician, a 1987 Supreme Court decision in *California Federal Savings & Loan Association v. Guerra* upheld a California law that provides for up to 4 months of unpaid leave for pregnancy disability.[37]

Economic pressures on employers may make legal action unnecessary in the future. Evidence now indicates that many employers are doing their best to accommodate pregnant women through flexible work scheduling and generous maternity leave policies.[38] Given the number of women of childbearing age in the workforce and the fact that 85 percent of all women have children,[39] combined with the fact that two out of every three people who will fill the 15 million new jobs between 1993 and the twenty-first century will be women, there really is no other choice.

One large survey of company practices found that new mothers typically spend 1 to 3 months at home following childbirth, that job guarantees for returning mothers were provided by 35 percent of the companies, and that employers of 501 to 1000 employees are most likely to provide full pay.[40]

What percentage of women use disability benefits fully and then decide not to return to work? At Corning Glass, Inc., First Bank of Minneapolis, and Levi Straus & Co., more than 80 percent *do* return to work. Moreover, the provision of maternity leave benefits has helped to establish good rapport with employees.[41]

How much do these extra benefits cost? The Health Insurance Association of America estimated that the extension of health insurance coverage to pregnancy-related conditions of women employees and employees' spouses would increase premiums by an average of 13 percent.[42]

ETHICAL DILEMMA: SECRET TAPING OF SUPERVISORS: IT MAY BE LEGAL, BUT IS IT ETHICAL?

Employees who think a supervisor is out to get them have something new up their sleeves: hidden tape recorders. Secret tapings are on the rise, often by employees trying to protect their jobs, and aided by the availability of cheap, miniature recorders. Such taping, often done to support legal claims, outrages and exasperates employers. Defenders counter that secret recording sometimes is the only way to bring out the truth.

Federal law allows secret taping, as long as one of the people being recorded knows about it. At least a dozen states, including New York, have similar state laws. However, in about 14 other states, including California, the law requires that everyone being taped must know that he or she is being recorded.

Most companies confronted with a tape quickly settle out of court. In one case, for example, a pregnant saleswoman's coworkers told her outright that they would force her off the job by making life hard on her at work. The workers were afraid the pregnancy would stop the woman from racking up sales, and they all would lose a bonus as a result. Once the woman sued for pregnancy discrimination, the coworkers lied about threatening her. They said, "We were all happy for her—we gave her a big hug when we found out she was pregnant." But the woman produced a secret tape she'd made of the threats and won a $180,000 settlement.

What's a business to do? Issue a policy against covert recording. That way, employees who tape can be fired for breaking company rules. In states where secret taping is illegal, companies can turn the tables on employees by using the recordings against them. Employment lawyers also advise companies to hire experts to make sure the tapes are authentic and haven't been edited. How about coworkers and managers? The cheapest and best protection of all is to avoid saying things you would be embarrassed to go into on a witness stand . . . or to see on the evening news.[43]

Reproductive Hazards. Another way sex discrimination may be perpetuated is by barring women from competing for jobs that pose occupational health hazards to their reproductive systems. In a landmark 1991 decision (*UAW v. Johnson Controls, Inc.*) the Supreme Court ruled that such "fetal protection" policies, which had been used by more than a dozen major companies, including General Motors, Du Pont, Monsanto, Olin, Firestone, and B. F. Goodrich, are a form of illegal sex discrimination that is prohibited by Title VII. At issue was the policy of Johnson Controls, Inc., a car battery manufacturer, that excluded women of childbearing age from jobs involving exposure to lead.[44] The company argued that its policy was based on the BFOQ exception to Title VII, because it was essential to a safe workplace.

The high court disagreed, ruling that the BFOQ exception is a narrow one, limited to policies that are directly related to a worker's ability to do the job. "Women as capable of doing their jobs as their male counterparts may not be forced to choose between having a child and having a job. . . . Decisions about the welfare of future children must be left to the parents who conceive, bear, support, and raise them rather than to the employers who hire those parents," said the Court.[45]

What are businesses to do? Clearly, they will have to provide more complete information to inform and warn female (and male) workers about fetal health risks on the job. They may also urge women to consult their physicians before starting such assignments. However, the Supreme Court noted that it would be difficult to sue a company for negligence after it abandoned its fetal protection policy if (1) the employer fully informs women of the risk and (2) it has not acted negligently.[46] Mere exclusion of workers, both unions and managers agree, does not address chemicals remaining in the workplace to which other workers may be exposed. Nor are women more sensitive to reproductive hazards than men. Changing the workplace, rather than the workforce, is a more enlightened policy.

Sexual Harassment. This is not really about sex. It's about power—more to the point, the abuse of power.[47] In the vast majority of cases on this issue, females rather than males have suffered from sexual abuse at work. Such abuse may constitute illegal sex discrimination, a form of unequal treatment on the job. How prevalent is it? More than 12,500 complaints were filed with the EEOC in 1993, 90 percent of *Fortune* 500 companies have dealt with sexual harassment complaints, and more than a third have been sued at least once. The cost? An average of $200,000 on each complaint that is investigated in house and found to be valid. In fact, one consulting firm estimates that the problem costs the average large corporation $6.7 million a year.[48] It is perilous self-deception for a manager to believe that sexual harassment does not exist in his or her own organization.

What is sexual harassment? Although opinions differ,[49] perhaps the clearest definition is that provided by the EEOC: "unwelcome sexual advances, requests for sexual favors, and other verbal or physical conduct of a sexual nature when submission to or rejection of this conduct explicitly or implicitly affects an individual's employment, unreasonably interferes with an individual's work performance, or creates an intimidating, hostile, or offensive work environment."[50]

Actually, the "no-frills" definition can be put into one word: "unwelcome." According to the courts, for behavior to be treated as sexual harassment, the offender has to know that the behavior is unwelcome. If a person wants to file a grievance, therefore, it's important to be able to prove either that he or she told the perpetrator to back off or that the action was so offensive the harasser should have known it was unwelcome.

While many behaviors can constitute sexual harassment, there are two main types:

1. Quid pro quo (you give me this; I'll give you that)
2. Hostile work environment (an intimidating, hostile, or offensive atmosphere)

Quid pro quo harassment exists when the harassment is a *condition of employment*. For example, consider the case of *Barnes v. Costle:* The plaintiff rebuffed her director's repeated sexual overtures. She ignored his advice that sexual intimacy was the path she should take to improve her career opportunities. Subsequently the director abolished her job. The court of appeals found that sexual cooperation was a condition of her employment, a condition the director did not impose upon males. Therefore, sex discrimination occurred and the employer was liable.[51]

The courts have gone even further, holding employers responsible even if they knew nothing about a supervisor's conduct. For example, a federal appeals court held Avco Corporation of Nashville, Tennessee, liable for the sexually harassing actions of one of its supervisors against two female secretaries working under his supervision. The court found that the employer had a policy against sexual harassment but failed to enforce it effectively. Both the company *and* the supervisor were held liable. Regarding the company's liability, the court noted: "Although Avco took remedial action once the plaintiffs registered complaints, its duty to remedy the problem, or at

A smiling Patricia Harris (and her attorney) following the U.S. Supreme Court's 1993 decision in her favor.

a minimum, inquire, was created earlier when the initial allegations of harassment were reported."[52]

Hostile environment harassment was defined by the Supreme Court in its 1986 ruling *Meritor Savings Bank v. Vinson.*[53] Vinson's boss had abused her verbally as well as sexually. However, since Vinson was making good career progress, the district court ruled that the relationship was a voluntary one having nothing to do with her continued employment or advancement. The Supreme Court disagreed, ruling that whether the relationship was "voluntary" is irrelevant. The key question was whether the sexual advances from the supervisor were "unwelcome." If so, and if they are "sufficiently severe or pervasive to be abusive,"[54] then they are illegal. This case was groundbreaking because it expanded the definition of harassment to include verbal or physical conduct that creates an intimidating, hostile, or offensive work environment or interferes with an employee's job performance.

In a 1993 case, *Harris v. Forklift Systems, Inc.*, the Supreme Court ruled that plaintiffs in such suits need not show psychological injury to prevail. While a victim's emotional state may be relevant, she or he need not prove extreme distress. In considering whether illegal harassment has occurred, juries must consider factors such as the frequency and severity of the harassment, whether it is physically threatening or humiliating, and whether it interferes with an employee's work performance.[55]

As we noted earlier, the Civil Rights Act of 1991 permits victims of sexual harassment—who previously could be awarded only missed wages—to collect a wide range of punitive damages and attorney's fees from employers who mishandled a complaint.

Preventive Actions by Employers. What can an employer do to escape liability for the sexually harassing acts of its managers or workers? An effective policy should include the following features:

- A statement from the chief executive officer that states firmly that sexual harassment will not be tolerated
- A workable definition of sexual harassment that is publicized via staff meetings, bulletin boards, handbooks, and new-employee orientation programs
- An established complaint procedure to provide a vehicle for employees to report claims of harassment to their supervisors or to a neutral third party, such as the HR department
- A clear statement of sanctions for violators and protection for those who make charges
- Prompt, confidential investigation of every claim of harassment, no matter how trivial
- Preservation of all investigative information, with records of all such complaints kept in a central location
- Training of all managers and supervisors to recognize and respond to complaints, giving them written materials outlining their responsibilities and obligations when a complaint is made
- Follow-up to determine if harassment has stopped[56]

Age Discrimination

The Equal Employment Opportunity Commission's guidelines on age discrimination emphasize that in order to defend an adverse employment action against employees age 40 and over, an employer must be able to demonstrate a "business necessity" for doing so. That is, it must be shown that age is a factor directly related to the safe, efficient operation of a business. To establish a prima facie case of age discrimination with respect to termination, for example, an individual must show that:[57]

1. She or he is within the protected age group (40 years of age and over).
2. She or he is doing satisfactory work.
3. She or he was discharged despite satisfactory work performance.
4. The position was filled by a person younger than the person replaced.

For example, an employee named Schwager had worked for Sun Oil Ltd. for 18 years, and his retirement benefits were to be vested (i.e., not contingent on future service) at 20 years. When the company reorganized and had to reduce the size of its workforce, the average age of those retained was 35 years, while the average age of those terminated was 45.7 years. The company was able to demonstrate, however, that economic considerations prompted the reorganization and that factors other than age were considered in Schwager's termination. The local manager had to let one person go, and he chose Schwager because he ranked lowest in overall job performance among salespeople in his district and did not measure up to their standards. Job per-

"ENGLISH-ONLY" RULES – NATIONAL ORIGIN DISCRIMINATION?

Rules that require employees to speak only English in the workplace have come under fire in recent years. Employees who speak a language other than English claim that such rules are not related to the ability to do a job and have a harsh impact on them because of their national origin.

In a recent case, an employer applied an "English-only" rule while employees were on the premises of the company. Non-Spanish-speaking employees complained that they were being talked about by the plaintiff and others who spoke Spanish. The Eleventh Circuit Court of Appeals ruled in favor of the employer. The court noted that the rule in this case was job-related in that supervisors and other employees who spoke only English had a need to know what was being said in the workplace.

Employers should be careful when instituting an "English-only" rule. While it is not necessarily illegal to make fluency in English a job requirement, or to discipline an employee for violating an "English-only" rule, employers must be able to show there is a legitimate business need for it. (Conversely, many employers would be delighted to have a worker who can speak the language of a non-English-speaking customer.) Otherwise, the employer may be subject to discrimination complaints on the basis of national origin.[58]

formance, not age, was the reason for Schwager's termination. Employers can still fire unproductive workers, but the key is to base employment decisions on ability, not on age.[59]

"Overqualified" Job Applicants. Employers sometimes hesitate to hire an individual who has a great deal of experience for a job that requires few qualifications and may be only an entry-level job. They assume that an overqualified individual will be bored in such a job or is only using the job to get a foot in the door so he or she can apply for another job at a later time. Beware of violating the Age Discrimination in Employment Act! An appeals court recently ruled that rejection of an older worker because he or she is overqualified may be a pretext to mask the real reason for rejection—the employee's age. In the words of the court: "How can a person overqualified by experience and training be turned down for a position given to a younger person deemed better qualified?"[60]

Seniority

"Seniority" is a term that connotes length of employment. A "seniority system" is a scheme that, alone or in tandem with "nonseniority" criteria, allots to employees ever-improving employment rights and benefits as their relative lengths of pertinent employment increase.[61]

Various features of seniority systems have been challenged in the courts for many years.[62] However, one of the most nettlesome issues is the impact of established seniority systems on programs designed to ensure equal employment opportunity. Employers often work hard to hire and promote members of protected groups. If layoffs become necessary, however, those individuals may be lost because of their low seniority. As a result, the employer takes a step backward in terms of workforce diversity. What is the employer to do when seniority conflicts with EEO?

The courts have been quite clear in their rulings on this issue. In two landmark decisions, *Firefighters Local Union No. 1784 v. Stotts*[63] (decided under Title VII) and *Wygant v. Jackson Board of Education*[64] (decided under the equal protection clause of the Fourteenth Amendment), the Supreme Court ruled that an employer may not protect the jobs of recently hired African-American employees at the expense of whites who have more seniority.[65]

Voluntary modifications of seniority policies for affirmative action purposes remain proper, but where a collective bargaining agreement exists, the consent of the union is required. Moreover, in the unionized setting, courts have made it clear that the union must be a party to any decree that modifies a bona fide seniority system.[66]

Testing and Interviewing

Title VII clearly sanctions the use of "professionally developed" ability tests. Nevertheless, it took several landmark Supreme Court cases to clarify the proper role and use of tests. The first of these was *Griggs v. Duke Power Co.*, the most significant EEO case ever, which was decided in favor of Griggs.[67] The employer was prohibited from requiring a high school education or the passing of an intelligence test as a condition of employment or job transfer where neither standard was shown to be significantly related to job performance:

> What Congress has forbidden is giving these devices and mechanisms controlling force unless they are demonstrably a reasonable measure of job performance. . . . What Congress has commanded is that any tests used must measure the person for the job and not the person in the abstract.[68]

The ruling also included four other general principles:

1. The law prohibits not only open and deliberate discrimination but also practices that are fair in form but discriminatory in operation. That is, Title VII prohibits practices having an *adverse impact* on protected groups, unless they are job-related. This is a landmark pronouncement because it officially established *adverse impact* as a category of illegal discrimination.

For example, suppose an organization wants to use prior arrests as a basis for selection. In theory, arrests are a "neutral" practice since all persons are equally subject to arrest if they violate the law. However, if arrests cannot be shown to be job-related, and, in addition, if a significantly higher proportion of African Americans than whites is arrested, the use of arrests as a basis for selection is discriminatory in operation.

2. The employer bears the burden of proof that any requirement for employment is related to job performance. As affirmed by the Civil Rights Act of 1991, when a charge of adverse impact is made, the plaintiff must identify a specific employment practice as the cause of the discrimination. If the plaintiff is successful, the burden shifts to the employer.

3. It is not necessary for the plaintiff to prove that the discrimination was intentional; intent is irrelevant. If the standards result in discrimination, they are unlawful.

4. Job-related tests and other employment selection procedures are legal and useful.

The confidentiality of individual test scores has also been addressed. Thus the Supreme Court affirmed the right of the Detroit Edison Co. to refuse to hand over to a labor union copies of aptitude tests taken by job applicants and to refuse to disclose individual test scores without the written consent of employees.[69]

As is well known, interviews are commonly used as bases for employment decisions to hire or to promote certain candidates in preference to others. Must such "subjective" assessment procedures satisfy the same standards of job-relatedness as more "objective" procedures, such as written tests? If they produce an adverse impact against a protected group, the answer is yes, according to the Supreme Court in *Watson v. Fort Worth Bank & Trust*.[70]

As in its *Griggs* ruling, the Court held that it is not necessary for the plaintiff to prove that the discrimination was intentional. If the interview ratings result in adverse impact, they are presumed to be unlawful, unless the employer can show some relationship between the content of the ratings and the requirements of a given job. This need not involve a formal validation study, although the Court agreed unanimously that it is possible to conduct such studies when subjective assessment devices are used.[71] The lesson for employers? Be sure that there is a legitimate, job-related reason for every question raised in an employment or promotional interview. Limit questioning to "need to know," rather than "nice to know," information and monitor interview outcomes for adverse impact. Validate this selection method. It would be unwise to wait until the selection system is challenged.

Personal History

Frequently job qualification requirements involve personal background information. If the requirements have the effect of denying or restricting equal employment opportunity, they may violate Title VII. For example, in the *Griggs v. Duke Power Co.* case, a purportedly neutral practice (the high school education requirement that excluded a higher proportion of African Americans than whites from employment) was ruled unlawful because it had not been shown to be related to job performance. Other allegedly neutral practices that have been struck down by the courts on the basis of non–job relevance include:

- Recruitment practices based on present employee referrals, where the workforce is nearly all white to begin with[72]
- Height and weight requirements[73]
- Arrest records, because they show only that a person has been accused of a crime, not that she or he was guilty of it; thus arrests may not be used as a basis for selection decisions,[74] except in certain sensitive and responsible positions (e.g., police officer, school principal)[75]
- Conviction records, unless the conviction is directly related to the work to be performed—for example, a person convicted of embezzlement applying for a job as a bank teller[76]

Despite such decisions, it should be emphasized that personal-history items are not unlawfully discriminatory per se, but their use in each instance requires that job relevance be demonstrated. Just as with employment interviews, the employer should be collecting information on a "need to know," not on a "nice to know," basis.

Preferential Selection

In an ideal world, selection and promotion decisions would be "color-blind." That is, social policy as embodied in Title VII emphasizes that so-called reverse discrimination (discrimination against whites and in favor of members of protected groups) is just as unacceptable as is discrimination by whites against members of protected groups.[77] In an effort to improve the prospects for advancement of members of protected groups, such as African Americans, can an employer grant them preference in admission to a training program? The case of *United Steelworkers of America v. Weber* addressed this issue.

Brian Weber, a white lab analyst at Kaiser Aluminum & Chemical Company's Gramercy, Louisiana, plant, brought suit under Title VII after he was bypassed for a crafts retraining program in which the company and the union had jointly agreed to reserve 50 percent of the available places for African Americans.[78] Although there had been years of exclusion of African Americans from such training programs, there was no proven record of bias at the plant on which to justify such a quota. Thus the company and the union were caught in a dilemma. To eliminate the affirmative action plan was to run the risk of suits by minority employees and the loss of government contracts. To retain the plan when there was no previous history of proven discrimination was to run the risk of reverse discrimination suits by white employees. And to admit previous discrimination at the plant in order to justify the affirmative action plan was to *invite* suits by minority applicants and employees.

The Supreme Court ruled that employers can give preference to minorities and women in hiring for "traditionally segregated job categories" (i.e., where there has been a societal history of purposeful exclusion of these individuals from the job category). Employers need not admit past discrimination in order to establish voluntary affirmative action programs. The Court also noted that the Kaiser plan was a "temporary measure" designed simply to eliminate a manifest racial imbalance.[79]

Subsequent cases, together with the Civil Rights Act of 1991, have clarified a number of issues left unresolved by Weber:

1. Courts may order, and employers voluntarily may establish, affirmative action plans, including goals and timetables, to address problems of underutilization of women and minorities. Court-approved affirmative action settlements may not be reopened by individuals who were not parties to the original suit.

2. The plans need not be directed solely to identified victims of discrimination but may include general, classwide relief.

3. While the courts will almost never approve a plan that would result in whites *losing* their jobs through layoffs, they may sanction plans that impose limited burdens on whites in hiring and promotions (i.e., plans that postpone them).

4. Numerically based preferential programs should not be used in every instance, and they need not be based on an actual finding of discrimination.[80]

Social policy, as articulated in pronouncements by Congress and the courts, clearly reflects an effort to provide a "more level playing field" that allows women, minorities, and nonminorities to compete for jobs on the basis of merit alone.

As Eleanor Holmes Norton, former chair of the EEOC, noted: "Affirmative action alone cannot cure age-old disparities based on race or sex. But if Title VII is allowed to do its work, it will speed the time when it has outlived its usefulness and our country has lived up to its promises."[81]

IMPACT OF LEGAL FACTORS ON PRODUCTIVITY, QUALITY OF WORK LIFE, AND THE BOTTOM LINE

There are both direct and indirect costs associated with unlawful discrimination. For example, sexual harassment can create high levels of stress and anxiety for both the victim and the perpetrator. These psychological reactions can lead to outcomes that increase labor costs for employers. Job performance may suffer, and absenteeism, sick leave, and turnover may increase. Both internal discrimination against present employees and external discrimination against job applicants can lead to costly lawsuits. Litigation is a time-consuming, expensive luxury that few organizations can afford. Lawsuits affecting virtually every aspect of the employment relationship have been litigated, and many well-publicized awards to victims have reached millions of dollars.

The legal and social aspects of the human resource management process should not be viewed exclusively in negative terms. Most of the present civil rights laws and regulations were enacted as a result of gross violations of individual rights. In most instances, the flip side of unlawful discrimination is good HR practice. For example, it is good practice to use properly developed and validated employment selection procedures and performance appraisal systems. It is good HR practice to treat people as individuals and not to rely on stereotyped group membership characteristics (e.g., stereotypes about women, ethnic groups, older workers, disabled workers). Finally, it just makes good sense to pay people equally, regardless of gender, if they are equally qualified and are doing the same work. These kinds of HR practices can enhance productivity, provide a richer quality of work life, and contribute directly to the overall profitability of any enterprise.

CAN AN EMPLOYEE WHO SEEKS TREATMENT FOR ALCOHOL ABUSE BE FIRED?

HUMAN RESOURCE MANAGEMENT IN ACTION: CONCLUSION

"Overlapping Remedies." In its decision, the appeals court noted that in the Americans with Disabilities Act of 1990, which amended the Rehabilitation Act and extended remedies for discrimination on the basis of disability to many more private employers, Congress stated explicitly that the legislation did not "limit the remedies, rights, and procedures of any . . . law of any State . . . or jurisdiction that provides greater or equal protection for the rights of individuals with disabilities than are afforded by this chapter." The court noted: "While this provision obviously can have no effect on our view of Congressional intent in 1973, it is a particularly pertinent example of Congress's historical practice of allowing overlapping remedies for employment discrimination."

Disability Discrimination as a "Special Case." The court stated:

We think it unlikely that Congress has a special interest in immunizing federal contractors from obligations otherwise applicable to them under state [disability] discrimination statutes. These companies may do only $2500 in business with the federal government, with the bulk of their enterprise devoted to commerce within a single state. This division gives the state a substantial interest in protecting the employment interests of its disabled citizens. The developing nature of the issues raised in the field of disability discrimination strikes us as insufficient justification for excusing these employers from obligations imposed on others who differ only in that the federal government is not one of their customers.

In sum, the court found no "clear and manifest" intent on the part of Congress to treat disability discrimination claims against federal contractors any differently from other types of discrimination claims or to exempt them from state laws.

Maritime v. State Law. The court ruled that a state law claim should not be dismissed simply because it would result in differing remedies for plaintiffs in different parts of the country. "As a general matter, however, we conclude that state human rights statutes may be applied in maritime cases. Indeed, it would be anomalous for maritime law, which has always shown 'a special solicitude for the welfare of seamen and their families,' to reject such an employee-sensitive provision."

Wrongful Discharge of Ellenwood. The appeals court noted that the district court did not devise a new "wrongful discharge" cause of action on behalf of Ellenwood. It simply recognized the obvious fact that—notwithstanding the general rule that a seaman's employment is at will—a maritime employer may make a contractual agreement with, or an enforceable promise to, its employees:

In this case, Ellenwood claimed that Exxon had promised that his job security and future opportunities would not be jeopardized if he sought treatment for alcoholism. The jury found that the requirements for establishing a binding obligation were met. We see no reason why maritime law would invalidate this self-imposed obligation.

Ultimately the jury awarded Ellenwood a judgment of $677,648 for his claims.

SUMMARY

The following laws were enacted to promote fair employment. They provide the basis for discrimination suits and subsequent judicial rulings:

- Thirteenth and Fourteenth amendments to the U.S. Constitution
- Civil Rights Acts of 1866 and 1871
- Equal Pay Act of 1963
- Title VII of the 1964 Civil Rights Act
- Age Discrimination in Employment Act of 1967 (as amended in 1986)
- Immigration Reform and Control Act of 1986
- Americans with Disabilities Act of 1990
- Civil Rights Act of 1991
- Family and Medical Leave Act of 1993
- Executive Orders 11246, 11375, and 11478
- Rehabilitation Act of 1973
- Vietnam Era Veterans Readjustment Act of 1974

The Equal Employment Opportunity Commission (EEOC) and the Office of Federal Contract Compliance Programs (OFCCP) are the two major federal regulatory agencies charged with enforcing these nondiscrimination laws. The EEOC is responsible for both private and public nonfederal employers, unions, and employment agencies. The OFCCP is responsible for ensuring compliance from government contractors and subcontractors.

IMPLICATIONS FOR MANAGEMENT PRACTICE

As a manager, it is easy to feel "swamped" by the gauntlet of laws, court rulings, and regulatory agency pronouncements that organizations must navigate through. While it is true that in the foreseeable future there will continue to be legal pressure to avoid unlawful discrimination against protected groups, there will be great economic pressure to find and retain top talent from these groups.[82] Workforce diversity is a competitive necessity, and employers know it. Progressive managers recognize that now is the time to begin developing the kinds of corporate policies and interpersonal skills that will enable them to operate effectively in multicultural work environments.

A considerable body of case law has developed, affecting almost all aspects of the employment relationship. We discussed case law in the following areas:

- Sex discrimination, sexual harassment, reproductive hazards, and pregnancy
- Age discrimination
- National origin discrimination
- Seniority
- Testing
- Personal history (specifically, preemployment inquiries)
- Preferential selection

The bottom line in all these cases is that, as managers, we need to be very clear about job requirements and performance standards, we need to treat people as individuals, and we must evaluate each individual fairly relative to job requirements and performance standards.

DISCUSSION QUESTIONS

4.1 If you were asked to advise a private employer (with no government contracts) of its equal employment opportunity responsibilities, what would you say?
4.2 As a manager, what steps can you take to deal with the organizational impact of the Family and Medical Leave Act?
4.3 Prepare a brief outline of an organizational policy on sexual harassment. Be sure to include grievance, counseling, and enforcement procedures.
4.4 What steps would you take as a manager to ensure fair treatment for older employees?
4.5 Collect two policies on EEO, sexual harassment, or family and medical leave from two different employers in your area. How are they similar (or different)? Which aspects of the policies support the appropriate law?

REFERENCES

1. Jones, J. E., Jr., Murphy, W. P., & Belton, R. (1987). *Discrimination in employment* (5th ed.). St. Paul, MN: West.
2. Friedman, A. (1972). Attacking discrimination through the Thirteenth Amendment. *Cleveland State Law Review*, **21**, 165-178.
3. *Johnson v. Railway Express Agency, Inc.*, (1975). 95 S. Ct. 1716.

4. Civil rights statutes extended to Arabs, Jews (1987, May 19). *Daily Labor Report*, pp. 1, 2, A6.

5. Boys Club pays its dues (1989, Jan. 23). *Time*, p. 47.

6. Jones et al., op. cit. See also *Bakke v. Regents of the University of California* (1978). 17 FEPC 1000.

7. Privacy and sex discrimination (1992, Apr.). *Bulletin*. Denver: Mountain States Employers Council, Inc., p. 3.

8. *Furnco Construction Corp. v. Waters* (1978). 438 U.S. 567.

9. *McDonnell Douglas v. Green* (1973). 411 U.S. 972.

10. Bradshaw, D. S. (1987). Immigration reform: This one's for you. *Personnel Administrator*, **32**(4), 37–40.

11. Alien workers bring factory a $580,000 fine (1989, Dec. 14). *The New York Times*, p. A32.

12. Americans with Disabilities Act of 1990, Public Law No. 101-336, 104 Stat. 328 (1990). Codified at 42 U.S.C., Section 12101 *et seq.*

13. Cascio, W. F. (1993, Aug.). *The 1991 Civil Rights Act and the Americans with Disabilities Act of 1990: Requirements for psychological practice in the workplace.* Master lecture presented at the annual convention of the American Psychological Association, Toronto, Canada.

14. Labor letter (1993, July 27). *The Wall Street Journal*, p. A1.

15. Karr, A. R. (1991, Feb. 28). EEOC clarifies law on rights of handicapped. *The Wall Street Journal*, p. A12.

16. Civil Rights Act of 1991, Public Law No. 102-166, 105 Stat. 1071 (1991). Codified as amended at 42 U.S.C., Section 1981, 2000e *et seq.*

17. *EEOC v. Arabian American Oil Co. and Aramco Service Co.* (1991). 111 S. Ct., 1227, 113 L. Ed. 2d 274.

18. *Price Waterhouse v. Hopkins* (1989). 109 S. Ct. 1775.

19. *Lorance v. AT&T Technologies* (1989). 490 U. S. 900, 104 L. Ed. 2d 961, 109 S. Ct. 2261.

20. Arnold, D. W., & Thiemann, A. J. (1992, Dec.). Test scoring under the Civil Rights Act of 1991. *PTC Quarterly*, **8** (4), pp. 1, 2.

21. Family and Medical Leave Act—the regulations (1993, Aug.). *Bulletin*, Denver: Mountain States Employers Council, Inc., p. 1.

22. Most small businesses appear prepared to cope with new family-leave rules (1993, Feb. 8). *The Wall Street Journal*, pp. B1, B2.

23. Jackson, D. J. (1978). Update on handicapped discrimination. *Personnel Journal*, **57**, 488–491.

24. Ledvinka, J., & Scarpello, V. G. (1991). *Federal regulation of personnel and human resource management* (2d ed.). Boston: PWS-Kent.

25. *Albemarle Paper Company v. Moody* (1975) 442 U.S. 407 (1975).

26. Sharpe, R. (1994, March 29). The waiting game: Women make strides, but men stay firmly in top company jobs. *The Wall Street Journal*, pp. A1, A8.

27. Record settlements (1992, July). *Bulletin*. Denver: Mountain States Employers Council, Inc., p. 3.

28. Lublin, J. S., & Pasztor, A. (1985, Dec. 11). Tentative affirmative action accord is reached by top Reagan officials. *The Wall Street Journal*, p. 4.

29. Firestone Tire is barred from U.S. jobs as a result of job discrimination case (1980, July 16). *The Wall Street Journal*, p. 6.

30. *Wygant v. Jackson Board of Education* (1986). 106 S. Ct. 1842; *Local 28 Sheet Metal Workers v. E.E.O.C.* (1986). 106 S. Ct. 3019; *Local 93 Firefighters v. Cleveland* (1986). 106 S. Ct. 3063.

31. Pear, R. (1985, Oct. 27). The cabinet searches for consensus on affirmative action. *The New York Times*, p. E5.

32. *Johnson v. Santa Clara Transportation Agency* (1987, Mar. 26). 107 S. Ct. 1442, 43 FEP Cases 411; *Daily Labor Report*, pp. A1, D1–D19.

33. Equal Employment Opportunity Commission (1979, Mar. 9). Pregnancy Discrimination Act: Adoption of interim interpretive guidelines, questions, and answers. *Federal Register*, **44,** 13277–13281.

34. Cowan, A. L. (1989, Aug. 21). Women's gains on the job: Not without a heavy toll. *The New York Times*, pp. A1, A14.

35. Fernandez, J. P. (1993). *The diversity advantage.* New York: Lexington.

36. Trotter, R., Zacur, S. R., & Greenwood, W. (1982). The pregnancy disability amendment: What the law provides. Part II. *Personnel Administrator*, **27,** 55–58.

37. *California Federal Savings & Loan Association v. Guerra* (1987). 42 FEP Cases 1073.

38. Shellenbarger, S. (1993, Sept. 14). Concerns fight to be called best for moms. *The Wall Street Journal*, pp. B1; B11.

39. Schwartz, F. N. (1992, Mar.–Apr.). Women as a business imperative. *Harvard Business Review*, pp. 105–113.

40. *Pregnancy and employment: The complete handbook on discrimination, maternity leave, and health and safety* (1987). Washington, DC: Bureau of National Affairs.

41. Ibid.

42. Trotter et al., op. cit.

43. Woo, J. (1992, Nov. 3). Secret taping of supervisors is on the rise, lawyers say. *The Wall Street Journal*, pp. B1, B5.

44. Kilborn, P. (1990, Sept. 2). Manufacturer's policy, women's job rights clash. *Denver Post*, p. 2A.

45. Epstein, A. (1991, Mar. 21). Ruling called women's rights victory. *Denver Post*, pp. 1A, 16A. See also Wermiel, S. (1991, Mar. 21). Justices bar "fetal protection" policies. *The Wall Street Journal*, pp. B1, B8.

46. Fetal protection policy voided (1991, May). *Bulletin.* Denver: Mountain States Employers Council, p. 2.

47. Fisher, A. B. (1993, Aug. 23). Sexual harassment: What to do. *Fortune.* pp. 84–88.

48. Ibid. See also Court clears air on sexual harassment (1993, Nov. 10). *USA Today*, pp. 1, 2.

49. York, K. M. (1989). Defining sexual harassment in workplaces: A policy-capturing approach. *Academy of Management Journal*, **32,** 830–850.

50. EEOC (1980). *Guidelines on discrimination because of sex*, 29 C.F.R., Part 1604 (11)(a).

51. *Barnes v. Costle* (1977). 561 F. 2d 983 (D.C. Cir.).

52. Court holds employer liable for harassment by supervisor (1987, June 1). *Daily Labor Report*, pp. A1, D1-D5.

53. *Meritor Savings Bank v. Vinson* (1986). 477 U. S. 57.

54. Ibid.

55. Barrett, P. M. (1993, Nov. 10). Justices make it easier to prove sex harassment. *The Wall Street Journal*, pp. A3, A4.

56. Sexual harassment: Preventive measures. (1992, Jan.). *Bulletin.* Denver: Mountain States Employers Council, p. 2.

57. *Schwager v. Sun Oil Company of PA* (1979). 591 F. 2d 58 (10th Cir.).

58. *Garcia v. Gloor* (1980). 618 F. 2d 264 (5th Cir.); *Jurado v. Eleven-Fifty Corporation* (1987). 813 F. 2d 1406 (9th Cir.). See also English only (1993, July). *Bulletin.* Denver: Mountain States Employers Council, Inc., p. 3.

59. Miller, C. S., Kaspin, J. A., & Schuster, M. H. (1990). The impact of performance appraisal methods on age discrimination in employment act cases. *Personnel Psychology*, **43,** 555–578.

60. Over qualified (1991, Nov.–Dec.). *Bulletin.* Denver: Mountain States Employers Council, Inc., p. 3. See also Age discrimination—Overqualified (1993, July). *Bulletin.* Denver: Mountain States Employers Council, Inc., p. 2.

61. *California Brewers Association v. Bryant* (1982). 444 U.S. 598, p. 605.

62. See for example, *Franks v. Bowman Transportation Co.* (1976). 424 U.S. 747; *International Brotherhood of Teamsters v. United States* (1977). 432 U.S. 324; *American Tobacco Company v.*

Patterson (1982). 535 F. 2d 257 (CA-4). See also Gordon, M. E., & Johnson, W. A. (1982). Seniority: A review of its legal and scientific standing. *Personnel Psychology,* **35,** 255–280.

63. *Firefighters Local Union No. 1784 v. Stotts* (1984). 104 S. Ct. 2576.

64. *Wygant v. Jackson Board of Education* (1986). 106 S. Ct. 1842.

65. Greenhouse, L. (1984, June 13). Seniority is held to outweigh race as a layoff guide. *The New York Times,* pp. A1, B12.

66. Britt, L. P., III (1984). Affirmative action: Is there life after *Stotts? Personnel Administrator,* **29**(9), 96–100.

67. *Griggs v. Duke Power Company* (1971). 401 U.S. 424.

68. Ibid., p. 428.

69. Justices uphold utility's stand on job testing (1979, Mar. 6). *The Wall Street Journal,* p. 4.

70. *Watson v. Fort Worth Bank & Trust* (1988). 108 S. Ct. 299.

71. Bersoff, D. N. (1988). Should subjective employment devices be scrutinized? *American Psychologist,* **43,** 1016–1018.

72. *EEOC v. Radiator Specialty Company* (1979). 610 F. 2d 178 (4th Cir.).

73. *Dothard v. Rawlinson* (1977). 433 U.S. 321.

74. *Gregory v. Litton Systems, Inc.* (1972). 472 F. 2d 631 (9th Cir.).

75. *Webster v. Redmond* (1979). 599 F. 2d 793 (7th Cir.).

76. *Hyland v. Fukada* (1978). 580 F. 2d 977 (9th Cir.).

77. *McDonald v. Santa Fe Transportation Co.* (1976). 427 U.S. 273.

78. *United Steelworkers of America v. Weber* (1979). 99 S. Ct. 2721.

79. Beyond Bakke: High court approves affirmative action in hiring, promotion (1979, June 28). *The Wall Street Journal,* pp. 1, 30.

80. Replying in the affirmative (1987, Mar. 9). *Time,* p. 66.

81. Norton, E. H. (1987, May 13). Step by step, the Court helps affirmative action. *The New York Times,* p. A27.

82. Wallace, P. A. (1990). Affirmative action from a labor market perspective. *ILR Report,* **27**(2), 40–47.

PART TWO

EMPLOYMENT

A CONCEPTUAL VIEW OF
HUMAN RESOURCE MANAGEMENT

STRATEGIC OBJECTIVES, ENVIRONMENTS, FUNCTIONS

Productivity

Quality of Work Life

Profits

Competitive

Legal

Social

Organizational

Employment

Development

Compensation

Labor-Management Accommodation

Support, Evaluation, International Implications

RELATIONSHIP OF HRM FUNCTIONS TO HRM ACTIVITIES

FUNCTIONS	ACTIVITIES
Part Two **Employment**	Job Analysis, Human Resource Planning, Recruiting, Staffing (Chapters 5 – 7)
Part Three **Development**	Orienting, Training, Performance Appraisal, Managing Careers (Chapters 8 – 10)
Part Four **Compensation**	Pay, Benefits, Incentives (Chapters 11 – 13)
Part Five **Labor-Management** **Accommodation**	Union Representation, Collective Bargaining, Procedural Justice, Ethics (Chapters 14, 15)
Part Six **Support,** **Evaluation,** **International** **Implications**	Job Safety and Health, Costs/Benefits of HRM Activities, International Dimensions of HRM (Chapters 16 – 18)

PART TWO

EMPLOYMENT

Now that you understand the environmental context within which human resource management activities take place, it is time to address three major aspects of the employment process: analyzing jobs, determining their human resource requirements, and hiring employees. Logically, before an organization can select employees, it needs to be able to specify *what* work needs to be done, *how* it should be done, the *number* of people needed, and the *knowledge, skills, abilities,* and other characteristics required to do the work. Chapter 5 addresses these issues. Chapter 6 considers the planning, implementation, and evaluation of recruitment operations. Finally, Chapter 7 examines initial screening and personnel selection—why they are done, how they are done, and how they can be evaluated.

CHAPTER 5

JOB ANALYSIS AND HUMAN RESOURCE PLANNING

JOB ANALYSIS—FOUNDATION FOR EMPLOYMENT PRACTICES

Situation: You are Pat Evans, chief engineer at Western Water Company. Western Water is a small, investor-owned utility company that provides water treatment, water distribution, and water use planning for a small, but growing, area. Each year, Western hires about six junior civil engineers to work in any of the following areas: water service planning, wastewater treatment, facilities planning, design engineering, or construction engineering. However, the number of new hires among civil engineers is expected to grow larger in the coming years, as the population density (and thus the demand for water service) increases in the area served by Western Water.

As chief engineer, you are responsible for all hiring of new engineers. You are concerned that past hiring procedures have been pretty slack—basically a cursory review of courses taken in the engineering curriculum plus an unstructured interview. As a result, Western really doesn't know what its new junior civil engineers can do, what they are looking for in a company, and what particular assignments they are best suited for. To make matters worse, an average of 50 percent of the newly hired junior civil engineers leave the company within 3 years. You are determined to change current practices. As a start, you have asked your HR Department to analyze each of the possible job assignments for junior civil engineers and to report back to you with a list of "common denominators" that seem to cut across all the assignments. That study was begun in July, it is now November 1, and you have just received the results. Western will begin recruiting in earnest next February, and most hiring decisions will be made in March–April, primarily among engineering students who will graduate in May–June. Thus you have several months to develop new hiring procedures to be put into place before the screening and selection of the next group of candidates actually begin.

Here is a summary of the broad job dimensions of junior civil engineers, as well as the personal characteristics necessary to do each of them.

1. *Modeling and calculations*—applications of professional engineering knowledge in order to develop and test mathematical models of civil engineering activities (e.g., water distribution, quality, and treatment; hydraulic; structural). Knowledge required: civil engineering principles, including mathematics through advanced calculus, statics, dynamics, basic water and wastewater chemistry, engineering economics, structural systems, surveying principles, and construction methods.

2. *Computer software applications*—use and application of computer software tools ranging from word processing to spreadsheet-based economic analyses to modeling proposed projects. Abilities required: use of computer-based spreadsheets, graphics, word processing, and database management programs. Ability to use civil engineering modeling software, applications development software, project scheduling, and computer-aided drafting is desirable.

3. *Project planning and management*—identification of project objectives, scope, feasibility, milestones, and completion schedules, together with preparation of supporting documentation. Monitors and coordinates project activities in order to meet time and cost parameters. Knowledge and abilities required: engineering standard practices, formats of technical reports, water distribution systems, methods of effective presentations, whether oral or written. Must be able to develop cost analyses for projects, set priorities, and schedule activities in a logical, organized manner. Must be able to coordinate activities and work among other engineering sections, vendors, consultants, and contractors.

4. *Written communications*—preparation of memos, letters, and engineering reports designed to address a variety of audiences, including other engineers, staff members working in maintenance, operations, or clerical positions, public agencies, government bodies, and members of the general public. Knowledge and abilities required: proper English grammar, spelling, punctuation, and sentence structure; ability to organize and compile relevant information to be used in reports; ability to communicate effectively in English in a clear, concise, organized manner, taking into account the abilities and needs of the audience.

5. *Individual and group interactions*—provision of technical expertise, either by telephone or face to face, to contractors, other engineers, members of the board of directors, government agencies, and applicants for water service. Knowledge and abilities required: engineering terminology, ability to establish and maintain effective working relationships in a variety of contexts (one-on-one or group) and with people from a variety of backgrounds (technical as well as nontechnical); ability to communicate orally in English in a clear, understandable, concise manner, taking into account the needs and abilities of the audience.

6. *Data summary and synthesis*—integration of information from a variety of sources (e.g., maps, calculations, environmental reports, feasibility studies) in order to provide a basis for technical recommendations or project planning. Abilities required: ability to organize data in order to assemble a written memo; ability to modify existing maps to help visualize a site and surrounding conditions; ability to summarize assumptions used in project design in order to recommend a course of action to superiors.

7. *Problem resolution*—through technical and interpersonal skills in order to achieve workable solutions to civil engineering, economic, or people-related problems. Abilities required: ability to negotiate effectively with a variety of constituencies; ability to listen

actively in order to clarify issues and to ask for appropriate information; ability to express one's own position—verbally as well as in writing—including supporting logic and arguments, in order to communicate one's position to other parties.

Just as you finish reading the report, Tracy Garcia, a senior civil engineer at Western, knocks on your door. "Have you read that job analysis report on junior civils yet, Pat?" You reply, "I sure have, and boy, has it given me ideas about new ways of selecting, training, and judging the performance of our new hires."

Challenges

1. How might the information presented in the job analysis help Western do a better job of recruiting new junior civil engineers?
2. As Pat Evans, what specific selection procedures would you like to see put into place?
3. How might the information in the job analysis report be useful in judging the performance of new hires?

1. How can job analysis information be useful to the operating manager?
2. How can human resource planning be integrated most effectively with general business planning?
3. What should be the components of a fair information practice policy with regard to information about employees?
4. How can human resource forecasts be most useful?
5. What control mechanisms might be most appropriate to ensure that action plans match targeted needs?

Questions This Chapter Will Help Managers Answer

In order to make intelligent decisions about the people-related needs of a business, two types of information are essential: (1) a description of the work to be done, the skills needed, and the training and experience required for various jobs and (2) a description of the future direction of a business. Once these are known, it makes sense to forecast the numbers and skills mix of people required at some future time period. We consider the first of these needs, job analysis, in the sections to follow, and the second, human resource planning, in the latter part of the chapter.

ALTERNATIVE PERSPECTIVES ON JOBS

Jobs are frequently the subject of conversation: "I'm trying to get a job"; "I'm being promoted to a new job"; "I'd sure like to have my boss's job." Or, as Samuel Gompers, first president of the American Federation of Labor, once said, "A job's a job; if it doesn't pay enough, it's a lousy job."

Jobs are important to individuals: They help determine standards of living, places of residence, status (value ascribed to individuals because of their position), and even one's sense of self-worth. Jobs are important to organizations because they are the vehicles through which work (and thus organizational objectives) are accomplished. The way to manage people to work efficiently is through answers to such questions as:

- Who specifies the content of each job?
- Who decides how many jobs are necessary?
- How are the interrelationships among jobs determined and communicated?
- Has anyone looked at the number, design, and content of jobs from the perspective of the entire organization, the "big picture"?
- What are the minimum qualifications for each job?
- What should training programs stress?
- How should performance on each job be measured?
- How much is each job worth?

Unfortunately, there is often a tendency, even an urgency, to get on with work itself ("Get the job done!") rather than to take the time to think through these basic questions. But this tendency is changing as firms struggle to raise productivity and to cope with such problems as deregulation and global economic competition.

In the spirit of continuous improvement, firms in every developed country around the world are rethinking the fundamental principles that underlie the design of jobs and the required numbers and skills of people to do them. For example, in an effort to get a better return on its enormous capital investment, General Motors has instituted round-the-clock production and flexible, lean manufacturing at its Lordstown, Ohio, plant. To do so, it retrained workers to handle a variety of jobs, instead of endlessly repeating a few rote tasks.[1] Job analysis was essential to understand the relationships among the newly enlarged jobs.

The term *job analysis* describes the process of obtaining information about jobs. As the chapter opening vignette illustrates, this information is useful for a number of business purposes. Regardless of how it is collected, it usually includes information about the tasks to be done on the job, as well as the personal characteristics (education, experience, specialized training) necessary to do the tasks.

An overall written summary of task requirements is called a *job description*, and an overall written summary of worker requirements is called a *job specification*. The result of the process of job analysis is a job description and a job specification. In the past, such job definitions often tended to be quite narrow in scope. Today's organizations, however, emphasize flexibility and more thinking in jobs. As an example, consider a job description developed by Mazda executives of assembly line work at their Flat Rock, Michigan, plant:

> They want their new employees to be able to work in teams, to rotate through various jobs, to understand how their tasks fit into the entire process, to spot problems in production, to troubleshoot, articulate the problems to others, suggest improvements, and write detailed charts and memos that serve as a road map in the assembly of the car.[2]

Does that sound like a traditional description of assembly line work? Hardly. Yet it is typical of the increased mental demands being placed on workers at all levels. Instead of being responsible for simple procedures and predictable tasks, workers are now expected to draw inferences and render diagnoses, judgments, and decisions, often under severe time pressure.[3]

Why Study Job Requirements?

Sound human resource management practice dictates that thorough, competent job analyses always be done, for they provide a deeper understanding of the behavioral requirements of jobs. This in turn creates a solid basis on which to make job-related employment decisions.[4] Legally, job analyses play a major role in the defense of employment practices (e.g., interviews, tests, performance appraisal systems) that are challenged, for they demonstrate that the practices in question are "job-related." Unfortunately, job analyses are often done for a specific purpose (e.g., training design) without consideration of the many other uses of this information. Some of these other uses, along with a brief description of each, are listed below and shown graphically in Figure 5-1.

Organizational structure and design. By clarifying job requirements and the interrelationships among jobs, responsibilities at all levels can be specified, promoting efficiency and minimizing overlap or duplication.

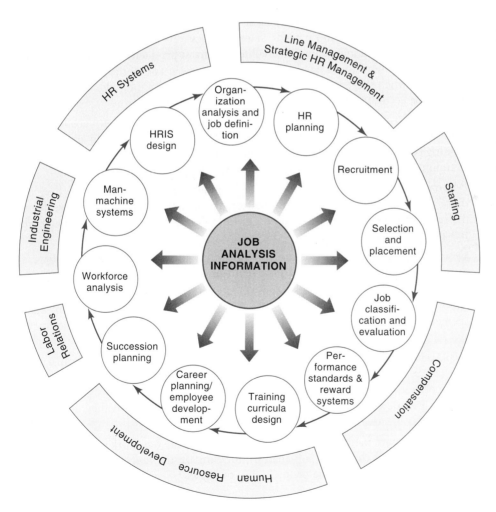

FIGURE 5-1
Job analysis is the foundation of many human resource management programs. (*Source:* R. C. Page and D. M. Van De Voort, Human resource planning and job analysis. In W. F. Cascio (ed.), *Planning, employment, and placement,* vol. 2. of the ASPA/BNA *Human resource management series.* Washington, DC: Bureau of National Affairs, 1989.)

Human resource planning. Job analysis is the foundation for forecasting the need for human resources as well as for plans for such activities as training, transfer, or promotion. Frequently, job analysis information is incorporated into a human resource information system (HRIS).

Job evaluation and compensation. Before jobs can be ranked in terms of their overall worth to an organization or compared to jobs in other firms for purposes of pay surveys, their requirements must be understood thoroughly. Job descriptions and specifications provide such understanding to those who must make job evaluation and compensation decisions.

Recruitment. The most important information an executive recruiter ("headhunter") or company recruiter needs is full knowledge of the job(s) in question.

Selection. Any method used to select or promote applicants must be based on a keen, meaningful forecast of job performance. An understanding of just what a worker is expected to do on the job, as reflected in job-related interviews or test questions, is necessary for such a meaningful forecast.

Placement. In many cases, applicants are first selected and then placed in one of many possible jobs. When there is a clear picture of the needs of a job and the abilities of workers to fulfill those needs, selection decisions will be accurate and workers will be placed in jobs where they will be the most productive. That is, selection and placement tend to go hand in hand. On the other side of the selection-placement coin, when there is a blurred picture of the needs of a job, selection decisions will not be accurate, and placement will probably be worse.

Orientation, training, and development. Training a worker can be very costly, as we shall see later. Up-to-date job descriptions and specifications help ensure that training programs reflect actual job requirements. In other words, "What you learn in training today you'll use on the job tomorrow."

Performance appraisal. If employees are to be judged in terms of how well they do those parts of their jobs that really matter, those that distinguish effective from ineffective performers, critical and noncritical job requirements must be specified. Job analysis does this.

Career path planning. If the organization (as well as the individual) does not have a thorough understanding of the requirements of available jobs and how jobs at succeeding levels relate to one another, effective career path planning is impossible.

Labor relations. The information provided by job analysis is helpful to both management and unions for contract negotiations, as well as for resolving grievances and jurisdictional disputes.

Engineering design and methods improvement. To design equipment to perform a specific task reliably and efficiently, engineers must understand exactly the capabilities of the operator and what he or she is expected to do. Similarly, any improvements or proposed new working methods must be evaluated relative to their impact on overall job objectives.

Job design. As with methods improvement, changes in the way work is accomplished must be evaluated through a job analysis, focusing on the tasks to be done and on the behaviors required of the people doing the tasks.

Safety. Frequently, in the course of doing a job analysis, unsafe conditions (environmental conditions or personal habits) are discovered and thus may lead to safety improvements.

Vocational guidance and rehabilitation counseling. Informed decisions regarding career choices may be derived meaningfully from comprehensive job descriptions and specifications.

Job classification systems. Selection, training, and pay systems are often keyed to job classification systems, also referred to as "job families." Without job analysis information, it is impossible to determine reliably the structure of the relationships among jobs in an organization.

Dynamic Characteristics of Jobs

There are two basic things to keep in mind when thinking about what job analysis is and what it should accomplish:

One, as time goes on, everything changes, and so do jobs. This has been recognized only recently; the popular view of a job was that what it required did not change; a job was a static thing, designed to be consistent although the workers who passed through it were different. Now we know that for a job to produce efficient output, it must change according to the workers who do it. In fact, the nature of jobs might change for three reasons:[5]

- *Time.* For example, lifeguards, ski instructors, and accountants do different things at different times of the year.

- *People.* Particularly in management jobs but also in teaching or coaching, the job is what the incumbent makes of it.

- *Environment.* Such changes may be technological—for example, word processing has drastically changed the nature of many secretarial jobs. Or the changes may be situational, as in a recent collective bargaining agreement between Gulf Oil Corp. and the Oil, Chemical, and Atomic Workers Union in which the company has "total flexibility" in assigning work across traditional craft lines; thus welders may be assigned as helpers to pipe fitters, boilermakers, and forklift operators.

Two, job analysis comprises job specifications and people requirements that should reflect *minimally* acceptable qualifications for job holders. Frequently they do not, reflecting instead a profile of the *ideal* job holder. For example, in evaluating positions for government and industry, the EEOC found that more than 65 percent of the jobs requiring a college degree could easily be handled by workers who are not college graduates.[6]

How are job specifications set? Typically by consensus among experts—immediate supervisors, job incumbents, and job analysts. Such a procedure is professionally acceptable, but care must be taken to distinguish between required and desirable qualifications. The term required denotes inflexibility; that is, it is assumed that without this qualification, an individual absolutely would be unable to do the job. Desirable implies flexibility; it is "nice to have" this ability, but it is not a "need to have" (see job dimension 2 in the chapter opening vignette). To be sure, required qualifications will exist in almost all jobs, but care must be exercised in establishing them, for such requirements must meet a higher standard.

Job Analysis and the Americans with Disabilities Act of 1990

Job analyses are not legally required under the ADA, but sound professional practice suggests that they be done for three reasons. One, the law makes it clear that job applicants must be able to understand what the essential functions of a job are before they can respond to the question "Can you perform the essential functions of the job for which you are applying?" Essential functions are those that require relatively more time and have serious consequences of error or nonperformance associated with them. A function may be essential because the reason the position exists at all is the performance of that function (e.g., a baggage handler at an airport must be able to lift bags weighing up to 70 pounds repeatedly throughout an 8-hour shift). Alternatively, the function may be so highly specialized that it cannot be shifted to others (e.g., in a nuclear power plant, a nuclear engineer must perform inspections, often by crawling through tight spaces). Job analysis is a systematic procedure that can help to identify essential job functions.

Two, existing job analyses may need to be updated to reflect additional dimensions of jobs, namely, the physical demands, environmental demands, and mental abilities required to perform essential functions. A portion of a checklist of physical demands is presented in Figure 5-2.

Three, once job analyses are updated as described, a summary of the results is normally prepared in writing in the form of a job description. What may work even better under the ADA, however, is a video job description, to provide concrete evidence to applicants of the physical, environmental (e.g., temperatures, noise level, working space), or mental (e.g., irate customers calling with complaints) demand of jobs. Candidates who are unable to perform a job because of a physical or mental disability may self-select out, thereby minimizing the likelihood of a legal challenge.

To ensure job-relatedness, be able to link required knowledge, skills, abilities, and other characteristics (measures of which candidates actually are assessed on) to essential job functions. Finally, recognize that under the ADA it is imperative that distinctions between "essential" and "nonessential" functions be made prior to announcing a job or interviewing applicants.[7] If a disabled candidate can perform the essential functions of a job and is hired, the employer must be willing to make "reasonable accommodations" to enable the person to work. Here are some examples that the ADA defines as "reasonable" accommodation efforts:

- Restructuring a job so that someone else does the nonessential tasks a disabled person cannot do
- Modifying work hours or work schedules so that a disabled person can commute during off-peak periods
- Reassigning a worker who becomes disabled to a vacant position
- Acquiring or modifying equipment or devices (e.g., a telecommunications device for the deaf)
- Appropriate adjustment or modification of examinations, training materials, or human resource policies
- Providing qualified readers or interpreters

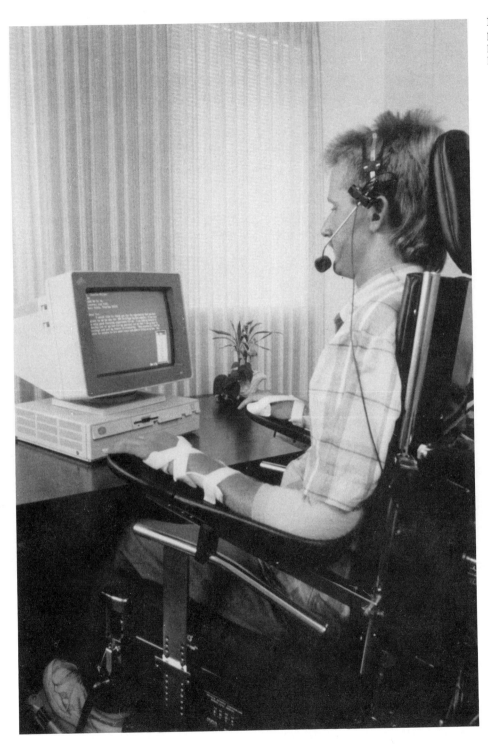

New developments in computer technology permit persons with disabilities to perform many types of jobs.

Use the symbols below to rate the following activities:

NP	Not present	Activity does not exist
O	Occasionally	Activity exists up to 1/3 of the time
F	Frequently	Activity exists from 1/3 to 2/3 of the time
C	Constantly	Activity exists 2/3 or more of the time

1a. Strength (also enter the percentage of time spent in each activity)

_____ Standing _____ percent

_____ Walking _____ percent

_____ Sitting _____ percent

1b. Also indicate the number of pounds that must be lifted, carried, pushed, or pulled.

_____ Lifting _____ (weight)

_____ Carrying _____ (weight)

_____ Pushing _____ (weight)

_____ Pulling _____ (weight)

2. Climbing _____

3. Balancing _____

4. Stooping _____

5. Kneeling _____

6. Crouching _____

7. Crawling _____

8. Reaching _____

9. Talking (Ordinary) _____ (Other) _____

10. Hearing (Ordinary conversation) _____ (Other) _____

FIGURE 5-2
Portion of a physical abilities checklist.

How Do We Study Job Requirements?

There are a number of methods used to study jobs. At the outset it is important to note that no one of them is sufficient. Some combination of methods must be used to obtain a total picture of the task and the physical, mental, social, and environmental demands of a job. Here are five common methods of job analysis:

1. *Job performance*. With this approach, an analyst actually does the job under study to get firsthand exposure to what it demands. (In the 1980 Florida governor's race, one of the candidates actually performed 100 different jobs so that he could better identify with the workers' concerns.)

2. *Observation.* The analyst simply observes a worker or group of workers doing a job. Without interfering, the analyst records the what, why, and how of the various parts of the job. Usually this information is recorded in a standard format.

3. *Interview.* In many jobs in which it is not possible for the analyst actually to perform the job (e.g., airline pilot) or where observation is impractical (e.g., architect), it is necessary to rely on workers' own descriptions of what is done, why it is done, and how it is done. As with recordings of observations, a standard format should be used to collect input from all workers to survey the requirements of a particular job. In this way all questions and responses can be restricted to job-related topics. But more important, standardization makes it possible to compare what different people are saying within the overall survey.

4. *Critical incidents.* These are vignettes comprising brief actual reports that illustrate particularly effective or ineffective worker behaviors. For example:

On January 14, Mr. Vin, the restaurant's wine steward, was asked about an obscure bottle of wine. Without hesitation, he described the place of vintage and bottling, the meaning of the symbols on the label, and the characteristics of the grapes in the year of vintage.

When a large number of these little incidents are collected from knowledgeable individuals, they are abstracted and categorized according to the general job area they describe. The end result is a fairly clear picture of actual job requirements.

5. *Structured questionnaires.* With this approach, the worker is presented with a list of tasks, a list of behaviors (e.g., negotiating, coordinating, using both hands), or both. Tasks focus on *what* gets done. This is a job-oriented approach. Behaviors, on the other hand, focus on *how* a job is done. This is a worker-oriented, or ability-requirements, approach. Each task or behavior is rated in terms of whether or not it is performed, and, if it is, it is further described in terms of characteristics such as frequency, importance, level of difficulty, and relationship to overall performance. The ratings provide a basis for scoring the questionnaires and for developing a profile of actual job requirements.[8] Numerical representation of job content also allows relatively precise comparisons of job content across different jobs.[9] One of the most popular structured questionnaires is the Position Analysis Questionnaire (PAQ).

The PAQ is a behavior-oriented job analysis questionnaire.[10] It consists of 194 items that fall into the following categories:

- *Information input*—Where and how the worker gets the information to do her or his job
- *Mental processes*—the reasoning, planning, and decision making involved in a job
- *Work output*—physical activities as well as the tools or devices used
- *Relationships with other persons*
- *Job context*—physical and social
- *Other job characteristics*—for example, apparel, work continuity, licensing, hours, and responsibility.

The items provide for either checking a job element if it applies or rating it on a scale, such as in terms of importance, time, or difficulty. An example of some PAQ items is shown in Figure 5-3. While structured job analysis questionnaires are growing in popularity, the newest applications use computer-generated graphics to help illustrate similarities and differences across jobs and organizational units.[11]

Code	Importance to This Job (I)
DNA	Does not apply
1	Very minor
2	Low
3	Average
4	High
5	Extreme

5.3 Personal and Social Aspects

This section includes various personal and social aspects of jobs. Indicate by code the *importance* of these aspects as part of the job.

148 | I | Civic obligations (because of the job the worker assumes, or is expected to assume, certain civil obligations or responsibilities)

149 | I | Frustrating situations (job situations in which attempts to deal with problems or to achieve job objectives are obstructed or hindered, and may thus contribute to frustration on the part of the worker)

150 | I | Strained personal contacts (dealing with individuals or groups in "unpleasant" or "strained" situations, for example, certain aspects of police work, certain types of negotiations, handling certain mental patients, etc.)

FIGURE 5-3
Sample PAQ items.

The preceding five methods of job analysis represent the popular ones in use today. Table 5-1 considers the pros and cons of each method. Regardless of the method used, the workers providing job information to the analyst must be experienced and knowledgeable about the jobs in question;[12] however, there seem to be no differences in the quality of information provided by members of different gender or race/ethnic subgroups,[13] or by high as opposed to low performers.[14] Nevertheless, it may well be that in relatively autonomous jobs, such as those of stockbrokers, high and low performers allocate their time quite differently.[15] In terms of the types of data actually collected, the most popular methods today are observation, interviews, and structured questionnaires.

Analyzing Managerial Jobs

There are a number of special considerations to be taken into account when analyzing managerial jobs. One is that managers tend to adjust the content of their jobs to fit their own style rather than to fit the needs of the managerial tasks to be done. The result of this is that when it comes to querying them about their work, they will describe what they actually do, having lost sight of what they should be doing. Another consideration is that it is difficult to identify what a manager does over time because her or his activity differs from time to time, perhaps one activity one month or week or day, and then some other activity the following day or week or month. Indeed, managers' activities change throughout the day. As immediate situations or general environments change, so will the content of a manager's job, and each such change will affect managers differently in different functional areas, different geographical areas, and different organizational levels (e.g., first-line supervisors versus divisional vice presidents). To analyze them, we must identify and measure the fundamental dimensions along which they differ and change. That is, we must identify what managers actually do on their jobs, and then we must specify behavioral differences due to time, person, and environmental changes.

Two methods of analyzing managerial jobs are based on questionnaires. They are the Management Position Description Questionnaire (MPDQ) and the Supervisor Task Description Questionnaire (STDQ).

■ TABLE 5 ▪ 1
ADVANTAGES AND DISADVANTAGES OF FIVE POPULAR JOB ANALYSIS METHODS

Job performance

Advantages With this method there is exposure to actual job tasks, as well as to the physical, environmental, and social demands of the job. It is appropriate for jobs that can be learned in a relatively short period of time.

Disadvantages This method is inappropriate for jobs that require extensive training or are hazardous to perform.

Observation

Advantages Direct exposure to jobs can provide a richer, deeper understanding of job requirements than workers' descriptions of what they do.

Disadvantages If the work in question is primarily mental, observations alone may reveal little useful information. Critical yet rare job requirements (e.g., "copes with emergencies") simply may not be observed.

Interviews

Advantages This method can provide information about standard as well as nonstandard activities and about physical as well as mental work. Since the worker is also his or her own observer, he or she can report on activities that would not be observed often. In short, the worker can provide the analyst with information that might not be available from any other source.

Disadvantages Workers may be suspicious of interviewers and their motives; interviewers may ask ambiguous questions. Thus distortion of information (either as a result of honest misunderstanding or as a result of purposeful misrepresentation) is a real possibility. For this reason, the interview should never be used as the sole job analysis method.

Critical incidents

Advantages This method focuses directly on what people do in their jobs, and thus it provides insight into job dynamics. Since the behaviors in question are observable and measurable, information derived from this method can be used for most possible applications of job analysis.

Disadvantages It takes considerable time to gather, abstract, and categorize the incidents. Also, since by definition the incidents describe particularly effective or ineffective behavior, it may be difficult to develop a profile of average job behavior—our main objective in job analysis.

Structured questionnaires

Advantages This method is generally cheaper and quicker to administer than other methods. Questionnaires can be completed off the job, thus avoiding lost productive time. Also, where there are large numbers of job incumbents, this method allows an analyst to survey all of them, thus providing a breadth of coverage that is impossible to obtain otherwise. Furthermore, such survey data often can be quantified and processed by computer, which opens up vast analytical possibilities.

Disadvantages Questionnaires are often time-consuming and expensive to develop. Rapport between analyst and respondent is not possible unless the analyst is present to explain items and clarify misunderstandings. Such an impersonal approach may have adverse effects on respondent cooperation and motivation.

The MPDQ is a 197-item, behaviorally based instrument for describing, comparing, classifying, and evaluating executive positions in terms of their content.[16] An example of one portion of the MPDQ is shown in Figure 5-4.

The STDQ describes 100 work activities of first-line supervisors in seven areas:[17]

■ Working with subordinates
■ Organizing work of subordinates

Part 8
Contacts

To achieve organizational goals, managers and consultants may be required to communicate with employees at many levels within the company and with influential people outside of the company. This part of the questionnaire addresses the nature and level of these contacts.

Directions:

Step 1 — Significance

For each contact and purpose of contact noted on the opposite page, indicate how significant a part of your position each represents by assigning a number between 0 to 4 to each block. Remember to consider both the importance and the frequency of the contact.

0—Definitely not a part of the position.

1—Minor significance to the position.

2—Moderate significance to the position.

3—Substantial significance to the position

4—Crucial significance to the position.

Step 2 — Other Contacts

If you have any other contacts, please elaborate on their nature and purpose below.

_____

_____

_____

_____

_____

_____

_____

_____

_____

_____

_____

Purpose of Contact

Internal Contacts	Share information regarding past, present, or anticipated activities or decisions.	Influence others to act or decide in a manner consistent with your objectives.	Direct the plans, activities, or decisions of others.
1. Executives.	10	11	12
2. Group Managers (managers report to position).	13	14	15
3. Managers (supervisors report to position).	16	17	18
4. Supervisors (no supervisors report to position).	19	'20	21
5. Professional/Administrative Exempt.	22	23	24
6. Clerical or Support staff (Nonexempt).	25	26	27
7. Other Nonexempt employees.	28	29	30

External Contacts	Provide/gather information or promote the organization or its products/services.	Resolve problems.	Sell products/ services.	Negotiate contracts/ settlements, etc.
8. Customers of the company's products or services.	31	32	33	34
9. Representatives of vendors/subcontractors.	35	36	37	38
10. Representatives of other companies or professional organizations and institutions.	39	40	41	42
11. Representatives of labor unions.	43	44	45	46
12. Representatives of influential community organizations.	47	48	49	50
13. Individuals such as applicants or shareholders.	51	52	53	54
14. Representatives of the media, including the press, radio, television, etc.	55	56	57	58
15. National, state, or regional elected government representatives and/or lobbyists.	59	60	61	62
16. Local government officials and/or representatives of departments such as: customs, tax, revenue, traffic, procurement, law enforcement, and environment.	63	64	65	66

FIGURE 5-4

Sample Management Position Description Questionnaire items.

■ Work planning and scheduling
■ Maintaining efficient quality and production
■ Maintaining safe and clean work areas
■ Maintaining equipment and machinery
■ Compiling records and reports

Responses from 251 first-line supervisors from 40 plants yielded few differences in the supervisors' jobs regardless of technology or function. These results imply that with the exception of the technical knowledge that may be required in a first-line supervisory job, organizations should be able to develop staffing, training, and performance appraisal systems for first-line supervisors that can be applied generally throughout the organization.

Job Analysis: Relating Method to Purpose

Given such a wide choice among available job analysis methods, the combination of methods to use is the one that best fits the purpose of the job analysis research (e.g., staffing, training design, performance appraisal). Table 5-2 is a matrix that suggests some possible match-ups between job analysis methods and various human resource management purposes. The table simply illustrates the *relative* strengths of each method when used for each purpose. For example, the job performance method of job analysis is most appropriate for the development of tests and interviews, training design, and performance appraisal system design.

COSTS AND BENEFITS OF ALTERNATIVE JOB ANALYSIS METHODS

Key considerations in the choice of job analysis methods are the method-purpose fit, cost, practicality, and an overall judgment of their appropriateness for the situation in question. Comparative research based on the purposes and practicality of these seven job analysis methods has yielded a pattern of results similar to that shown in Table 5-2.[18] In terms of costs, the PAQ (a behavior checklist) was the least costly method to use, while critical incidents was the most costly. However, cost is not the only consideration in choosing a job analysis method. Appropriateness for the situation is

■ **TABLE 5 ■ 2**
JOB ANALYSIS METHODS AND THE PURPOSE(S) *BEST* SUITED TO EACH

Method	Job descriptions	Development of tests	Development of interviews	Job evaluation	Training design	Performance appraisal design	Career path planning
Job performance		X	X		X	X	
Observation	X	X	X				
Interviews	X	X	X	X	X	X	
Critical incidents	X	X	X		X	X	
Questionnaires:							
Task checklists	X	X	X	X	X	X	
Behavior checklists			X	X	X	X	X

another. While the PAQ is used widely, unless a trained analyst actually interviews job incumbents, the PAQ may be more appropriate for analyzing higher-level jobs since a college-graduate reading level is required to comprehend the items.[19] Related to the issue of appropriateness is an awareness that *behavioral* similarities in jobs may mask genuine *task* differences between them. For example, on the surface the jobs performed by typists and belly dancers may appear quite similar—both require fine motor movements!

A thorough job analysis may require a considerable investment of time, effort, and money. Choices must be made among methods. If the choices are based on a rational consideration of the trade-offs involved, they will result in the wisest use of time *and* effort *and* money.

As an example, consider a job analysis approach called JobScope, used by Nationwide Insurance Companies. As a result of improved accuracy in job evaluation (assessment of the relative worth of jobs to the firm), the system is saving the company more than $60,000 in salary and benefits *each year*. The company recouped the entire cost of developing JobScope during its first 2 years of operation and used it as the basis for developing an integrated HR system.[20]

THE RELATIONSHIP OF JOB ANALYSIS TO HUMAN RESOURCE PLANNING

Having identified the behavioral requirements of jobs, the organization is in a position to identify the numbers of employees and the skills required to do those jobs, at least in the short term. Further, an understanding of available KSAOs is necessary to allow the organization to plan for the changes to new jobs required by corporate goals. This process is known as human resource planning (HRP). HRP is becoming more important in firms as a result of globalization, new technologies, organizational restructuring, and diversity in the workforce. All these factors produce uncertainty—and since it's difficult to be efficient in an uncertain environment, firms develop business and human resource plans to reduce the impact of uncertainty. The plans may be short-term or long-term in nature, but to have a meaningful impact on future operations, business plans and human resource plans must be integrally related to each other. To understand why that linkage is important, let's consider how HRP in the 1990s differs from HRP in earlier time periods.

HRP in the 1990s

In the past, HRP tended to be a reactive process because business needs usually defined human resource needs. For example, in the past a bank might decide to acquire a rival because it made good economic sense. Only after that decision was made would the bank worry about deploying talent in the two firms and integrating the two workforces. Today, major changes in business, economic, and social environments are forcing organizations to integrate business planning with HRP and to adopt a longer-term, proactive perspective.[21] For example, according to the vice president of human resources at Liz Claiborne, Inc.:

> Human resources is part of the strategic [business] planning process. It's part of policy development, line extension planning, and merger and acquisition processes. Little is done in the company that doesn't involve us in the planning, policy, or finalization stages of any deal.[22]

Change, as well as the pace of change, is accelerating. Thus, in a 1993 survey of 400 executives of large firms, 79 percent reported that change in their companies is rapid or extremely rapid, and 61 percent believed the pace of change will accelerate.[23] To address human resource concerns systematically, firms now recognize that they need short-term as well as long-term solutions. As usually practiced, job analysis identifies qualities that employees need to perform existing jobs. Yet rapid changes in technology mean that the jobs of the future will differ radically from those of the present.[24] Methods are available now for identifying skill and ability requirements for jobs that do not yet exist. These are known as future-oriented, or "strategic" job analyses.[25] They can provide additional, relevant information to general business plans. General business plans, in turn, may be strategic or tactical in nature. Let's consider them further in the following section.

Types of Plans: Strategic, Tactical, and Human Resources

Strategic planning. This is the process of setting objectives and deciding on the actions to achieve them.[26] Strategic planning for an organization includes:

Defining philosophy. Why does the organization exist? What unique contribution does it make?

Formulating statements of identity, purpose, and objectives. What is the overall mission of the organization? Are the missions of divisions and departments consistent with the mission of the organization?

Evaluating strengths and weaknesses. What factors may enhance or inhibit any future courses of action aimed at achieving the organization's objectives?

Determining design. What are the components of the organization, what should they do, and how should they relate to one another, toward achieving objectives and fulfilling the organization's mission?

Developing strategies. How will the objectives, at every level, be achieved? How will they be measured, not only in quantitative terms of what is to be achieved, but also in terms of time?

Devising programs. What will be the components of each program, and how will the effectiveness of each program be measured?

Strategic planning differs considerably from short-range tactical (or operational) planning. It involves fundamental decisions about the very nature of the business. Strategic planning may result in new business acquisitions, divestitures of current (profitable or unprofitable) product lines, new capital investments, or new management approaches.[27] It is long-range in scope, and it may involve substantial commitments of resources. Almost always it involves considerable data collection, analysis, and repeated review and reevaluation by top management.

Tactical, or Operational, Planning. This deals with the normal growth of current operations, as well as with any specific problems that might disrupt the pace of planned, normal growth. Purchasing new or additional office equipment to enhance production efficiency (e.g., word processors), coping with the recall of a defective product (e.g., defective brakes in cars), or dealing with the need to design tamper-proof bottle caps (e.g., in the pharmaceutical industry) are examples of tactical planning problems. Beyond the obvious difference in the time frames distinguishing strategic planning and tactical planning, the other difference between the two is the degree of change resulting from the planning—and hence the degree of impact on human resource planning.

Human resource planning (HRP) parallels the plans for the business as a whole. HRP focuses on questions such as: What do the proposed business strategies imply with respect to human resources? What kinds of internal and external constraints will (or do) we face? For example, restrictive work rules in a collective bargaining contract are an internal constraint, while a projected shortfall in the supply of college graduate electrical engineers (relative to the demand for them by employers) is an external constraint. What are the implications for staffing, compensation practices, training and development, and management succession? What can be done in the short run (tactically) to prepare for long-term (strategic) needs? To appreciate the interplay between business and HR planning, let's consider a company example.

COMPANY EXAMPLE

PHILIPS, THE DUTCH MULTINATIONAL CORPORATION

In Holland, the Philips Company recently decided to open a new plant to capitalize on its competitive advantages. One important advantage was that existing production facilities were already located in Holland. Another was that the Dutch workforce viewed Philips as an attractive place to work. Before building the new plant, elaborate strategic studies were made. Of course, one of the factors under study was the availability of qualified human resources. But the study especially focused on how to build in changes in the manufacturing technology to match the expected characteristics of the labor force 20 years ahead. Machines and methods used to produce the products efficiently by today's labor force may not be used efficiently as the labor force grows older. This is an important consideration because one of the cultural characteristics of Dutch workers is that they tend not to move from one location to another during their working careers. Hence it is difficult to transfer employees and almost impossible to replace them. So, to maintain its competitive advantage, Philips attempted to incorporate into the production planning process the characteristics of the future labor force. Since the planners anticipated that the future workforce will be better educated and more independent, they tried to design the manufacturing process in a way that might permit improved opportunities for job rotation, job sharing, and job enrichment. This represents a true integration of planning—strategic and human resource—to optimize overall company performance.[28]

More on Human Resource Planning

Although HRP means different things to different people, general agreement exists on its ultimate objective—namely, the most effective use of scarce talent in the interests of the worker and the organization. Thus we may define HRP broadly as *an effort to anticipate future business and environmental demands on an organization, and to provide qualified people to fulfill that business and satisfy those demands.*[29] This general view suggests several specific, interrelated activities that together comprise an HRP system. They include:

- *A talent inventory* to assess current human resources (skills, abilities, and potential) and to analyze how they are currently being used

- *A human resource forecast* to predict future human resource requirements (the number of workers needed, the number expected to be available based on labor market characteristics, the skills mix required, internal versus external labor supply)

- *Action plans* to enlarge the pool of people qualified to fill the projected vacancies through such actions as recruitment, selection, training, placement, transfer, promotion, development, and compensation

- *Control and evaluation* to provide feedback on the overall effectiveness of the human resource planning system by monitoring the degree of attainment of human resource objectives

THE RELATIONSHIP OF HUMAN RESOURCE PLANNING TO STRATEGIC AND TACTICAL PLANNING

A variety of HRP applications exists.[30] For example, HRP itself can be strategic (long-term and general) or tactical (short-term and specific). It may be done organization-wide, or it may be restricted to divisions, departments, or any common employee groups. Or it may be carried out on a recurring basis (e.g., annually) or only sporadically (e.g., when launching a new product line or at the outset of a capital expansion project). Regardless of its specific application, almost all experts agree that if HRP is to be genuinely effective, it must be linked with the different levels of general business planning, not as an end or *goal* in and of itself, but rather as a *means* to the end of building more competitive organizations. The overall process is directed by line managers. When line managers perceive that human resource practices help them achieve their goals, they are more likely to initiate and support HRP efforts. Furthermore, the process raises important human resource questions.[31] The relationship between business planning and HRP is depicted in Figure 5-5.

The long-range perspective (2 to 5 years or longer) of strategic planning flows naturally into the middle-range perspective (1 to 2 years) of operational planning. Annual budgeting decisions provide specific timetables, allocations of resources, and standards for implementing strategic and operational plans. As the time frame shortens, planning details become increasingly specific.

At the level of strategic planning, HRP is concerned with such issues as assessing the management implications of future business needs, assessing factors external to the firm (e.g., demographic and social trends), and gauging the internal supply of employees over the long run. The focus here is to analyze issues, not to make detailed projections.

At the level of operational, or tactical, planning, HRP is concerned with detailed forecasts of employee supply (internal and external to the organization) and employee demand (numbers needed at some future time period). Based on the forecasts, specific action plans can be undertaken. These may involve recruitment, changes in incentives, promotions, training, or transfers. Procedures must be established to control and evaluate progress toward targeted objectives.

Of necessity, Figure 5-5 is an oversimplification. As we noted in Chapter 2, in our discussion of the 5-P model of human resource strategy, business objectives (needs) may be long- or short-term in nature, and HR forecasts and programs (action plans) must address both types. As a simple example, consider that the personal characteris-

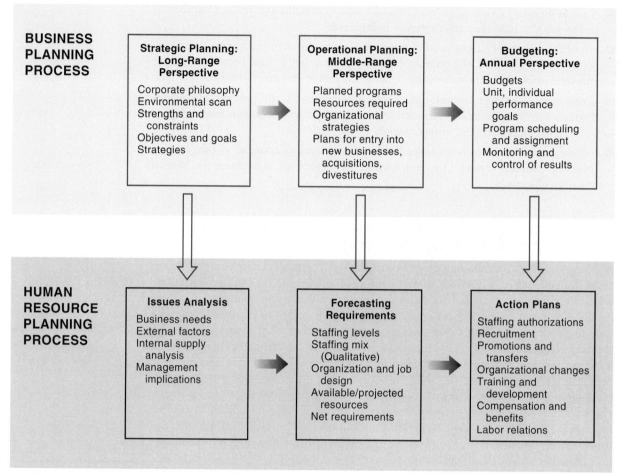

FIGURE 5-5
Impact of three levels of business planning on human resource planning.

tics of managers that lead to success during the start-up and early growth phases of an organization's life cycle (i.e., short- and intermediate-term horizons) may inhibit performance as the organization matures and stabilizes (i.e., the long-term horizon). To appreciate this, consider the experience of Apple Computer, Inc.

COMPANY EXAMPLE

CHANGING BUSINESS AND HUMAN RESOURCES NEEDS AT APPLE COMPUTER, INC.

Apple experienced dramatic changes as a company as it moved from an entrepreneurial start-up in the 1970s, through a high-growth phase in the 1980s tied to its Macintosh computers, to a mature, stable competitor in the globally competitive personal computer market in the mid-1990s. In the 1970s, Apple was launched by technical whizzes and young dreamers, led by Steven Jobs. The major objective was to produce a commercially viable product. In the 1980s, Apple hired John Sculley as CEO to provide marketing savvy and technological vision as the company showed the masses that computing with a graphical user interface could be fun. The Macintosh line had arrived, as had the need for professional marketing expertise. In the 1990s, however, Apple realized that it needed a CEO with a proven ability to cut costs, to shorten product development cycles, and to raise productivity. Thus, in June 1993, it turned to Michael Spindler, its German-born former head of European operations, as CEO. Apple's challenge in the 1990s, as it was in the 1970s, is once again to make and market commercially viable products—in a totally different business environment from that of the 1970s.[32]

As Figure 5-5 shows, human resource planning focuses on firm-level responses to people-related business issues over multiple time horizons. What are some examples of such issues, and how can managers identify them?

Such people-related business concerns, or issues, might include, for example, "What types of managers will we need to run the business in the early twenty-first century, and how do we make sure we'll have them?" At a broader level, issues include the impact of rapid technological change, more complex organizations (in terms of products, locations, customers, and markets), more frequent responses to external forces such as legislation and litigation, demographic changes, and increasing multinational competition. In this scenario, environmental changes drive issues, issues drive actions, and actions encompass programs and processes used to design and implement them.[33] Issues themselves may be identified with the aid of an HR strategy worksheet, such as that shown in Figure 5-6.

Realistically, HR concerns become business concerns and are dealt with by the line only when they affect the line manager's ability to function effectively. Such concerns may result from an immediate issue, such as downsizing or a labor shortage, or from a longer-term issue that can be felt as if it were an immediate issue, such as management development and succession planning.[34] On the other hand, HR issues such as workforce diversity, changing requirements for managerial skills, no-growth assumptions, mergers, retraining needs, and health and safety are issues that relate directly to the competitiveness of an organization and threaten its ability to survive. In short,

Human Resources Issue	Analysis: Evidence Options
What is the HR problem, gap, or opportunity identified a result of changes in the following? • Business environment • Business strategy • Organizational circumstances	What are the dimensions of the issue? • Evidence of the issue • Scope • Converage/applicability • Potential business impact • Alternative solutions and their pros and cons

Management Actions/Resources	Measures/Targets
What course of action will be implemented? • Strategy of 1–2 years • Specific action programs • Responsibility assigned • Timing for completion • Financial and staff resources required	How will the results be measured? • Outcomes • Measures/evidence • Target levels

FIGURE 5-6

Data to include on an HR strategy worksheet. (*Source:* R. S. Schuler & J. W. Walker, Human resources strategy: Focusing on issues and actions. *Organizational Dynamics,* Summer 1990, p. 14.)

progressive firms regard HR issues as people-related business issues that will have powerful impacts on their strategic business *and* HR planning throughout the 1990s.

Human Resource Objectives—Foundation for Human Resource Planning

Objectives can be expressed either in behavioral terms ("By the third week of training, you should be able to do these things . . .") or in end-result terms ("By the end of the next fiscal year, five new retail stores should be open, and each should be staffed by a manager, an assistant manager, and three clerks"). In the context of cost control in compensation, for example, the following questions should prove useful in setting human resource objectives:[35]

- What level will the wage rate for an occupation be?
- How many people will be employed?
- How much more will our firm have to pay to attract more employees?
- How would the number of people our company employs change if the wage were lower? If it were higher?

HR objectives vary according to such things as the type of environment a company operates in, its strategic and tactical plans, and the current design of jobs and employee work behaviors. As examples, consider some of McDonald's human resource objectives: define jobs narrowly so that they are easy to learn in a short period of time; pay minimum wages to most nonmanagement employees so that the cost of turnover is low; design jobs to minimize decision making by the human operator (e.g., computer-controlled cooking operations, item labeling on cash registers).[36]

As another example of HR objectives, consider again the Philips Company, which decided to build a futuristic plant in an area where the workforce is quite stable. The company focused its human resource objectives on minimizing turnover (since workers are so hard to replace), paying competitive wages, and designing jobs to challenge the workforce anticipated 20 years hence.

To be sure, objectives will differ depending on the time frame they represent. Examples of short-term HR objectives include increasing the breadth and depth of the applicant pool, increasing the length of time new hires stay with the organization, and decreasing the amount of time undesirable hires stay with the organization. In the longer term, HR objectives are more likely to include readjusting employees' skills, attitudes, and behaviors to fit major changes in the needs of the business. This happened, for example, as heavily regulated industries, such as cable television, were given the freedom to compete for business in open markets. Different kinds of KSAOs were needed. Of course, HR practices also must change to fit changes in the needs of employees.

In sum, differences in the types of objectives established for the short and long term reflect differences in the types of changes that are feasible with 2 or 3 additional years of time.[37] Setting human resource objectives is art as much as it is science. It requires conscious forethought based on the kind of future the firm wants to create for itself. It requires teamwork; it cannot be left to serendipity.

TALENT INVENTORIES

Once HR objectives are set, it then becomes useful to compare the numbers, skills, and experience of the current workforce with those desired at some future time period. A talent inventory facilitates assessment of the current workforce; HR forecasts of supply and demand help to determine future needs. In combination they provide powerful planning information for the development of action programs. In both large and small organizations, such information is often computerized. When combined with other databases, it can be used to form a complete human resource information system (HRIS) that is useful in a variety of situations.[38]

Information such as the following is typically included in a profile developed for each manager or nonmanager:

- Current position information
- Previous positions in the company
- Other significant work experience (e.g., other companies, military)
- Education (including degrees, licenses, certifications)
- Language skills and relevant international experience
- Training and development programs attended
- Community or industry leadership responsibilities
- Current and past performance appraisal data
- Disciplinary actions
- Awards received

Information provided by individuals may also be included. A major retailer, for example, includes factors that may limit an employee's mobility (e.g., health, family circumstances), as well as willingness to relocate. IBM includes the individual's expressed preference for future assignments and locations, including interest in staff or line positions in other IBM locations and divisions.[39]

Talent inventories and HR forecasts must complement each other; an inventory of present talent is not particularly useful for planning purposes unless it can be analyzed in terms of future human resource requirements. On the other hand, a forecast of human resource requirements is useless unless it can be evaluated relative to the current and projected future supply of workers available internally. Only at that time, when we have a clear understanding of the projected surpluses or deficits of employees in terms of their numbers, their skills, and their experience, does it make sense to initiate action plans to rectify projected problems. Such an integrated HRP system is shown in Figure 5-7.

Projected Uses. Although secondary uses of the talent inventory data may emerge, the primary uses must be specified at the concept development stage. This will provide direction and scope regarding who and what kinds of data should be included.

Some common uses of a talent inventory are: identification of candidates for promotion, management succession planning, assignment to special projects, transfer, training, workforce diversity planning and reporting, compensation planning, career planning, and organizational analysis.

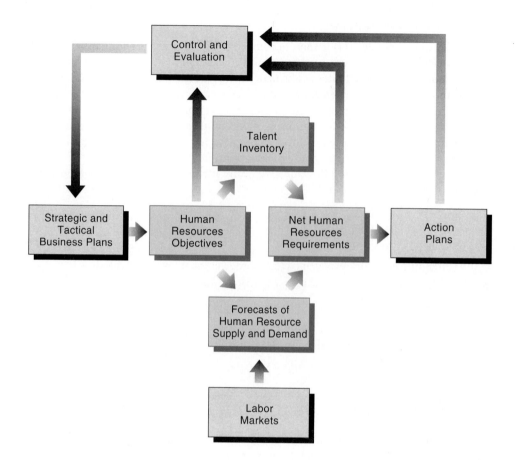

FIGURE 5-7
An integrated human
resource planning system.

Human Resource Information Systems and Personal Privacy

Given the wide availability of and easy access to personal computers, information networks, local databases, and user-friendly applications software, human resource information systems (HRIS) are more accessible (and potentially more useful) than ever. Today, emphasis is on effective use of information technology to reshape human resource functions to meet management needs.[40] However, two crucial issues that must be considered in setting up and maintaining an HRIS are data security and personal privacy. Data security is a technical problem that can be dealt with in several ways, including the use of passwords and elaborate codes. In the information age, personal privacy is both an ethical and a moral issue.

Unfortunately, many companies are failing to safeguard the privacy of their employees. Thus a recent study of 126 *Fortune* 500 companies employing 3.7 million people found that:

■ While 87 percent of the companies allow employees to look at their personnel files, only 27 percent give them access to supervisors' files on them, which often contain more subjective information.

- Fifty-seven percent use private investigative agencies to collect or verify information about employees, and 42 percent collect information without telling the employee.

- Thirty-eight percent have no policy covering release of data to the government; of those that do, 38 percent don't require a subpoena. Eighty percent of companies will give information to an employee's potential creditor without a subpoena, and 58 percent will give information to landlords.[41]

The results of a 1993 survey of top corporate managers of 301 businesses of all sizes and in a wide range of industries revealed another unsettling fact: fewer than one in five had a written policy regarding electronic privacy—that is, employee computer files, voice mail, electronic mail, or other networking communications. With respect to employee records contained in an HRIS, 66 percent of HR managers reported that they have unlimited access to such information, while 52 percent of executives do.[42] To establish a fair information practice policy, here are some general recommendations:

1. Set up guidelines and policies to protect information in the organization: types of data to be sought, methods of obtaining the data, retention and dissemination of information, employee or third-party access to information, release of information about former employees, and mishandling of information.

2. Inform employees of these information-handling policies.

3. Become thoroughly familiar with state and federal laws regarding privacy.

4. Establish a policy that states specifically that employees and prospective employees cannot waive their rights to privacy.

5. Establish a policy that any manager or nonmanager who violates these privacy principles will be subject to discipline or termination.[43]

Here are some specific recommendations:[44]

1. Avoid fraudulent, secretive, or unfair means of collecting data. When possible, collect data directly from the individual concerned.

2. Do not maintain secret files on individuals. Inform them of what information is stored on them, the purpose for which it was collected, how it will be used, and how long it will be kept.

3. Collect only job-related information that is relevant for specific decisions.

4. Maintain records of individuals or organizations who have regular access or who request information on a need-to-know basis.

5. Periodically allow employees the right to inspect and update information stored on them.

6. Gain assurance that any information released to outside parties will be used only for the purposes set forth prior to its release.

HUMAN RESOURCE FORECASTS

The purpose of human resource forecasting is to estimate labor requirements at some future time period. Such forecasts are of two types: (1) the external and internal supply of labor and (2) the aggregate external and internal demand for labor. The two types of forecasts should be considered separately because each rests on a different set of assumptions and depends on a different set of variables.[45]

Internal supply forecasts relate to conditions *inside* the organization, such as the age distribution of the workforce, terminations, retirements, and new hires within job classes. Both internal and external demand forecasts, on the other hand, depend primarily on the behavior of some business factor (e.g., student enrollments, projected sales, product volume) to which human resource needs can be related. Unlike internal and external supply forecasts, internal and external demand forecasts are subject to many uncertainties—in domestic or worldwide economic conditions, in technology, and in consumer behavior, to name just a few. The *Occupational Outlook Handbook*, published by the U.S. Department of Labor, focuses on macroforecasts of aggregate demand for various occupations. Figure 5-8 shows an excerpt of one such forecast for the fastest-growing occupations in the coming decade. In the following sections we will consider several micro- or firm-level human resource forecasting techniques that have proven to be practical and useful.

FIGURE 5-8
The fastest-growing occupations, 1991–2005. (*Source:* L. S. Richman, Jobs that are growing and slowing, *Fortune* July 12, 1993, p. 53.)

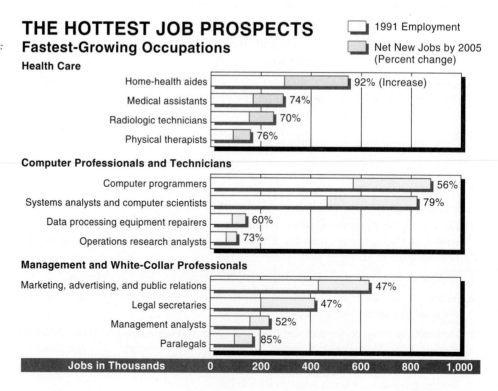

Forecasting External Human Resource Supply

Recruiting and hiring new employees are essential for virtually all firms, at least over the long run. Whether they are due to projected expansion of operations or to normal workforce attrition, forays into the labor market are necessary.

Several agencies regularly make projections of external labor market conditions and estimates of the supply of labor to be available in general categories. Included among these agencies are the Bureau of Labor Statistics of the U.S. Department of Labor, the Engineering Manpower Commission, and the Public Health Service of the Department of Health and Human Services. For new college and university graduates, the Northwestern Endicott-Lindquist Report is one of the most respected barometers of future hiring decisions. Organizations in both the public and private sectors are finding such projections of the external labor market to be helpful in preventing surpluses or deficits of employees.

Managers in Japan pay especially close attention to labor market forecasts, because among blue-chip employers, it is taboo to lay off workers. While Western governments give money to workers after they lose their jobs, the Japanese government pays distressed companies not to lay off workers.[46] It was no surprise, therefore, to find out that in a recent poll of senior HR executives taken in the United States and Japan, managers from both countries gave top priority to executive development and recruiting. However, while a third major concern of the Americans was compensation, for the Japanese it was workforce planning.[47]

Forecasting Internal Human Resource Supply

A reasonable starting point for projecting a firm's future supply of labor is its current supply of labor. Perhaps the simplest type of internal supply forecast is the *succession plan*, a concept that has been discussed in the planning literature for over 25 years.[48] Succession plans may be developed for management employees, nonmanagement employees, or both. The process for developing such a plan includes setting a planning horizon, identifying replacement candidates for each key position, assessing current performance and readiness for promotion, identifying career development needs, and integrating the career goals of individuals with company goals. The overall objective, of course, is to ensure the availability of competent executive talent in the future or, in some cases, immediately, as when a key executive dies suddenly.[49] Here is how one firm does it.

SUCCESSION PLANNING IN THE MINISTRY OF TRANSPORTATION AND COMMUNICATIONS (MTC), PROVINCE OF ONTARIO

COMPANY EXAMPLE

MTC, one of the leading transportation authorities in North America, is responsible for the management of a highway network comprising approximately 13,000 miles of provincial roads. It also manages the subsidy allocation for an additional 62,500 miles of municipal roads and is involved in the planning for provincial commuter rail and air services. Major operational activities include planning, design, construction, maintenance, and research related to transportation systems and facilities.

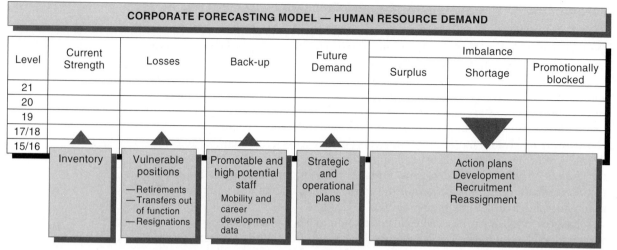

FIGURE 5-9

Corporate human resource demand forecasting model used at the Ontario Ministry of Transportation and Communications. See text for explanations of the data that go into each column.

The full-time workforce consists of approximately 2600 management and 7700 bargaining-unit employees, although for practical reasons, succession planning has been limited to middle and senior management (about 1300 positions). Succession planning is one of the responsibilities of every manager.

Current and future business plans and the assessed skills and potential of the management workforce provide the main inputs to the planning system. Meaningful forecasts can be done only for large job families. Hence, MTC's operations have been divided into five primary and eight secondary functions, and separate analyses are done for each of these functions. Figure 5-9 illustrates the various data that are used in the forecast to determine potential shortages, surpluses, numbers of promotable staff blocked from promotion (e.g., because there is no higher-level job to progress to in a particular job family), and annual training and development effort required to maintain backup strength.

- Current strength is determined from a talent inventory maintained by the corporate planning group.

- Losses are made up of resignations, dismissals, transfers, and retirements. Resignations, dismissals, and transfers are assessed from historical data, modified by current and future trends. Retirement figures are based on a review of individual retirement ranges.

- Backup is determined from two sources: (1) As part of the annual appraisal process, managers identify those employees who are considered promotable within the next 1-year planning cycle; and (2) in a separate annual process, managers identify high-potential individuals who have the ability to progress to two responsibility levels higher—in more than one function—during a 5-year forecast period.

- Future demand is forecast on the basis of current as well as future business plans. These are determined by MTC's strategic policy committee (comprised of the CEO and senior executives) with input from six planning groups.

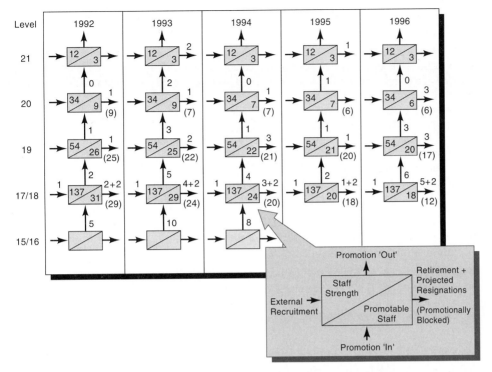

FIGURE 5-10
Management succession forecasting model used at the Ontario Ministry of Transportation and Communications. An explanation of the numbers in each box is contained in the lower right corner of the figure. For example, at job level 17/18 in 1994, staff strength is 137 persons, of whom 24 are promotable. Four persons were promoted "out," 8 were promoted "in," 1 was recruited externally, 3 retired, 2 were projected to resign, and 20 were promotionally blocked.

■ Finally, the data for succession planning for each function are manipulated by means of a computerized forecasting model (Figure 5-10). The model was chosen because it is simple to use and flexible enough to be able to analyze situations that vary according to staffing levels, turnover rates, and replacement strategies.[50]

What's different about succession planning in today's turbulent business environment? In a nutshell, in specifying position requirements companies are defining more generic competencies (e.g., ability to cut costs and to work with diverse constituencies), rather than specific knowledge and skills.[51] They also are making it clear to individuals that they are responsible for their own career development, with no explicit or implicit promises made to them about future opportunities by the firm.[52]

The previous company example illustrated succession planning in a large firm. But what about small firms, such as family-owned businesses? Only about 30 percent of family businesses outlive their founders, usually for lack of planning. Since many founders of small companies started in the post–World War II boom are now retiring, the question of succession is becoming more pressing. Here are some of the ways families are trying to solve the problem:

■ 35 percent plan to groom one child from an early age to take over.

■ 25 percent plan to let the children compete and choose one or more successors with help from the board of directors.

ETHICAL DILEMMA: SHOULD SUCCESSION PLANS BE SECRET?

This is a thorny issue. If firms keep HR planning information about specific candidates secret, planning may have limited value. Thus at a software company, a senior executive on her way out the door for a president's job at a competitor was told that the firm had expected her to be its next president. Her response? "If I'd known, I would have stayed."

A somewhat different course of events transpired at another firm whose policy was to talk openly about prospective candidates. There, employees learned what the company had in mind for them over the next 3 to 5 years. Subsequently, when they did not get the jobs they thought they were entitled to, employees felt betrayed. Some sued; other left. In your view, is it unethical to share planning information with employees and then not follow the plan? Conversely, do employees have a right to see such information?

- 15 percent plan to let the children compete and choose one or more successors without input from a third party.
- 15 percent plan to form an "executive committee" of two or more children.
- 10 percent plan to let the children choose their own leader, or leaders.[53]

Forecasting Human Resource Demand

In contrast to supply forecasting, demand forecasting is beset with multiple uncertainties—changes in technology; consumer attitudes and patterns of buying behavior; local, national, and international economies; number, size, and types of contracts won or lost; and government regulations that might open new markets or close off old ones, just to name a few. Consequently, forecasts of human resource demand are often more subjective than quantitative, although in practice a combination of the two is often used. One of the popular approaches to demand forecasting is the Delphi technique.

The Delphi Technique. Delphi is a structured approach for reaching a consensus judgment among experts about future developments in any area that might affect a business (e.g., the level of a firm's future demand for labor). Originally developed as a method to facilitate group decision making, it has also been used in human resource forecasting. Experts are chosen on the basis of their knowledge of internal factors that might affect a business (e.g., projected retirements), their knowledge of the general business plans of the organization, or their knowledge of external factors that might affect demand for the firm's product or service and hence its internal demand for labor. Experts may range from first-line supervisors to top-level managers. Sometimes experts internal to the firm are used, but if the required expertise is not available internally, then one or more outside experts may be brought in to contribute their opinions. To estimate the level of future demand for labor, an organization might select as experts, for example, managers from corporate planning, human resources, marketing, production, and sales.

The Delphi technique was developed during the late 1940s at the Rand Corporation's "think tank" in Santa Monica, California. Its objective is to predict future developments in a particular area by integrating the *independent* opinions of experts.[54]

Face-to-face group discussion among the experts is avoided since differences in job status among group members may lead some individuals to avoid criticizing others and to compromise on their good ideas. To avoid these problems, an intermediary is used. The intermediary's job is to pool, summarize, and then feed back to the experts the information generated independently by all the other experts during the first round of forecasting. The cycle is then repeated, so that the experts are given the opportunity to revise their forecasts and the reasons behind their revised forecasts. Successive rounds usually lead to a convergence of expert opinion within three to five rounds.

In one application, Delphi did provide an accurate 1-year demand forecast for the number of buyers needed for a retailing firm.[55] Here's a set of guidelines to make the Delphi process most useful:

■ Give the expert enough information to make an informed judgment. That is, give him or her the historical data that have been collected, as well as the results of any relevant statistical analysis that has been conducted, such as staffing patterns and productivity trends.

■ Ask the kinds of questions a unit manager can answer. For example, instead of asking for total staffing requirements, ask by what percentage staffing is likely to increase or ask only about anticipated increases in key employee groups, such as marketing managers or engineers.

■ Do not require precision. Allow the experts to round off figures, and give them the opportunity to indicate how sure they are of the forecasted figures.

■ Keep the exercise as simple as possible, and especially avoid questions that are not absolutely necessary.

■ Be sure that classifications of employees and other definitions are understood in the same way by all experts.

■ Enlist top management's and experts' support for the Delphi process by showing how good forecasts will benefit the organization and small-unit operations and how they will affect profitability and workforce productivity.[56]

How Accurate Is Accurate?

Accuracy in forecasting the demand for labor varies considerably by firm and by industry type (e.g., utilities versus women's fashions): roughly from 2 to 20 percent error. Certainly factors such as the duration of the planning period, the quality of the data on which forecasts are based (e.g., expected changes in the business factor and labor productivity), and the degree of integration of HRP with strategic business planning all affect accuracy. How accurate a labor demand forecast should be depends on the degree of flexibility in staffing the workforce. That is, to the extent that people are geographically mobile, multiskilled, and easily hired, there is no need for precise forecasts.[57]

Matching Forecast Results to Action Plans

Labor demand forecasts affect a firm's programs in many different areas, including recruitment, selection, performance appraisal, training, transfer, and many other types of career enhancement activities. These activities all comprise "action programs." Action programs help organizations adapt to changes in their environments. In the past decade or so, one of the most obvious changes in the business environment has been the large influx of women, minorities, and immigrants into the workforce. To adapt to these changes, organizations have provided extensive training programs designed to develop these individuals' management skills. Also, they have provided training programs for supervisors and coworkers in human relations skills to deal effectively with members of these underrepresented groups.[58]

Assuming a firm has a choice, however, is it better to *select* workers who already have developed the skills necessary to perform competently or to select workers who do not have the skills immediately but who can be *trained* to perform competently? This is the same type of "make-or-buy" decision that managers often face in so many other areas of business. Managers have found that it is often more cost-effective to buy, rather than to make. This is also true in the context of selection versus training.[59] Put your money and resources into selection. Always strive *first* to develop the most accurate, the most valid selection process that you can, for it will yield higher-ability workers. *Then* apply those action programs that are most appropriate in further increasing the performance of your employees. With high-ability employees, the productivity gain from a training program in, say, Lotus 1-2-3 might be greater than the gain from the same program with lower-ability employees. Further, even if the training is about equally effective with well-selected, higher-ability employees and poorly selected, lower-ability employees, the required training *time* may be reduced for higher-ability employees. Thus training costs will be reduced, and the net effectiveness of training will be greater when applied along with a highly valid personnel selection process. This point becomes even more relevant if one views training as a strategy for building sustained competitive advantage. Firms that *select* high-caliber employees, and then commit resources to develop them continually, gain a competitive advantage that no other organization can match: a deep reservoir of firm-specific human capital.

IMPACT OF JOB ANALYSIS AND HRP ON PRODUCTIVITY, QUALITY OF WORK LIFE, AND THE BOTTOM LINE

Earlier we noted that jobs are dynamic, not static, in their requirements. This is especially true of jobs at the bottom and at the top of today's organizations. Entry-level jobs now demand workers with new and different kinds of skills. Even simple clerical work now requires computer knowledge, bank tellers need more knowledge of financial transactions and sales techniques, and foreign competition means that assembly line workers need more sophisticated understanding of mathematics and better reading and reasoning skills in order to cut costs and improve quality.

Current information on the behavioral requirements of jobs is critically important if firms are to develop meaningful specifications for selecting, training, and appraising the performance of employees in them and if employees are to perform their jobs successfully. HR planning information is no less important so that firms can institute action plans now to cope with projected HR needs in the future.

What are firms actually doing? A recent survey of 2100 firms by the Hay Group found that HR planning was formal and well developed at only 21 percent of the firms. It was undeveloped or rudimentary at another 30 percent. Most firms said that finding and keeping key people is a top priority.[60] However, without solid planning they may miss seeing the need for new talent and the need to develop new ways of selecting and training that talent.

CONTROL AND EVALUATION OF HRP SYSTEMS

The purpose of control and evaluation is to guide HRP activities, identifying deviations from the plan and their causes. For this reason, we need yardsticks to measure performance. Qualitative and quantitative objectives can both play useful roles in HRP. Quantitative objectives make the control and evaluation process more objective and measure deviations from desired performance more precisely. Nevertheless, the nature of evaluation and control should always match the degree of development of the rest of the HRP process. In newly instituted HRP systems, for example, evaluation is likely to be more qualitative than quantitative, with little emphasis placed on control. This is because supply-and-demand forecasts are likely to be based more on "hunches" and subjective opinions than on hard data. Under these circumstances, human resource planners should attempt to assess the following:[61]

- The extent to which they are tuned in to human resource problems and opportunities and the extent to which their priorities are sound
- The quality of their working relationships with staff specialists and line managers who supply data and use HRP results (how closely do the human resource planners work with these specialists and line managers on a day-to-day basis?)
- The extent to which decision makers, from line managers who hire employees to top managers who develop long-term business strategy, are making use of HRP forecasts, action plans, and recommendations
- The perceived value of HRP among decision makers (do they view the information provided by human resource planners as useful to them in their own jobs?)

In more established HRP systems, in which objectives and action plans are both underpinned by measured performance standards, key comparisons might include the following:[62]

- Actual staffing levels against forecast staffing requirements
- Actual levels of labor productivity against anticipated levels of labor productivity
- Actual personnel flow rates against desired rates
- Action programs implemented against action programs planned (were there more or fewer? Why?)
- The *actual* results of the action programs implemented against the *expected* results (e.g., improved applicant flows, lower quit rates, improved replacement ratios)
- Labor and action program costs against budgets
- Ratios of action program benefits to action program costs

The advantage of quantitative information is that it highlights potential problem areas and can provide the basis for constructive discussion of the issues. Now let us examine an issue that has been all too common for many firms—managing a merger.

MANAGING THE MERGER BETWEEN HARRIS SEMICONDUCTOR (HSS) AND GENERAL ELECTRIC SOLID STATE (GESS)[63]

COMPANY EXAMPLE

Each year there are thousands of mergers among companies large and small. Mergers help companies to accelerate their growth by moving into new markets, gaining market share, enhancing technical expertise, increasing the products and services offered, or improving their financial performance. Successful mergers depend on the "fit" between the organizations coming together—in their product, technical, marketing and financial operations—and, most important, in their organizational and management fit. Partners must learn to accommodate each other's organizational cultures, structures, management systems, and processes. Difficulty in doing this accounts for the almost one-third of mergers that end in divestiture.[64]

In the case of HSS and GESS, the product, technical, market, and financial fit was excellent. While HSS was the second largest supplier of integrated circuits to the U.S. government, GESS had a much stronger presence in the commercial, industrial, and automotive/consumer markets. It also had a far greater presence in Europe and South Asia. Thus the merger would greatly increase sales in those markets and enable Harris to become the sixth-largest U.S. semiconductor company. The increase in size would enable HSS to achieve economies of scale from higher volumes in such areas as procurement, R&D, manufacturing, marketing, and distribution. The combined R&D talents would provide additional opportunities for new-product and other technology programs, such as computer-aided design and process development.

By far the most challenging aspect of the merger was the merger of people, for HSS, with its 4000 employees, was merging with the 10,000-employee GESS organization. Over a 3-year period, both organizations learned a great deal about managing a merger. HSS management put it simply: "We learned that merger integration is harder than it looks and takes longer than you think." Here are eight other lessons:

1. *Successful mergers require the management of many types of diversity.* HSS and GESS differed with respect to management philosophy, HR practices and policy, location, information systems, and organizational cultures. If the goal is to rebuild a new, unified organization, communication and joint problem solving are essential.

2. *One-shot interventions are insufficient.* Continued communication and learning are necessary, e.g., through workshops, symbols, and company newspapers.

3. *Managers from both organizations need high levels of commitment, tenacity, and patience.*

4. *Rebuild management teams as early as possible during the integration.*

5. *Failure to reconcile and integrate vital management information systems can undermine the companies' ability to conduct business.* Specifically, it makes it difficult for top management to empower managers and to hold them accountable for measured outcomes (e.g., profit margins).

6. *While the merger focuses on what's going on inside the new organization, don't ignore the fact that business is going on outside, in spite of the merger.* The last thing the new business needs is to become sluggish in its response to demands from the marketplace.

7. *In staffing decisions, strike a careful balance between perceived fairness and the capabilities of employees.*

8. *Learn as much as possible about your prospective partner prior to the consummation of the deal.*

JOB ANALYSIS—FOUNDATION FOR EMPLOYMENT PRACTICES

One of the new ideas that you, as Pat Evans, had for recruiting junior civil engineers was to develop a video that illustrated each of the seven essential functions of the job: modeling and calculations, computer software applications, project planning and management, written communications, individual and group interactions, summary and synthesis of data, and problem resolution. Using a narrator, a script, and actual engineers at Western, the video would, in your opinion, ensure that job applicants developed a realistic picture of what it's like to work. Since Western always seemed to have many more applicants than positions, you thought that perhaps the video might help to reduce turnover among new hires, if they could get a good idea ahead of time of what they'd be getting into. Just as the company was selective about who it chose to hire, the video would provide job applicants with information that would help them make informed decisions about their future employer.

Another application was in selection. You could visualize a "technical oral interview" in which candidates would be asked to describe their experiences in dealing with each of the seven major areas revealed by the job analysis. Interviewers would then ask follow-up questions in a systematic manner in order to elicit relevant information, and, based on the recruiting video job applicants had seen, they too could ask meaningful questions of the interviewers. Finally, it occurred to you that the very same job dimensions identified by the job analysis could, with a little elaboration, also be used as bases for judging the performance of junior civil engineers. You thought: "I love to mine information from a report, and that job analysis report has really been a gold mine for me and for engineering at Western."

IMPLICATIONS FOR MANAGEMENT PRACTICE

More and more, HR issues are seen as people-related business issues. This suggests that as a manager you should do the following:

■ Keep a management view, not an HR staff department view, of critical issues and opportunities. Consider a comment by the director of human resources at Merck & Co.:

Line managers are starting to address the needs of individual and organizational performance—e.g., they know why every job exists in the organization, who the people in these jobs are, and how competent they are; and they know it is important to keep their skills updated. There is a saying at Merck: "Human resources are too important to be left to the HR department." Fully one-third of the performance evaluation of line managers is related to people management.[65]

■ Plan within the context of managing the business strategically.

■ Execute the strategy—doing so requires effective management consensus, communications designed to educate, and involvement of all parties. This is not a "pie in the sky" recommendation. In a recent survey, only 37 percent of senior managers thought other key managers completely understood new business goals. Only 4 percent thought middle managers totally understood. Not surprisingly, as understanding drops, so does compliance.[66]

SUMMARY

We are witnessing vast changes in the very nature of work itself, as well as in the types and numbers of jobs available. To reduce uncertainty and increase efficiency, careful attention needs to be paid to a thorough understanding of the behavioral requirements of jobs and the determination of human resource needs.

A written summary of the task requirements for a particular job is called a job description, and a written summary of people requirements is called a job specification. Together they comprise a job analysis. This information is useful for a variety of organizational purposes ranging from human resource planning to career counseling.

Some combination of available job analysis methods (job performance, observation, interviews, critical incidents, structured questionnaires) should be used, for all have both advantages and disadvantages. Key considerations in the choice of methods are the method-purpose fit, cost, practicality, and an overall judgment of the appropriateness of the methods for the situation in question.

Job analysis provides one input to the human resource planning process. Strategic and operational planning provide others. Strategic business planning is the long-range process of setting organizational objectives and deciding on action programs to achieve those objectives. Operational, or tactical, planning deals with the normal, ongoing growth of current operations or with specific problems that temporarily disrupt the pace of normal growth. Annual budgeting decisions provide specific timetables, allocations of resources, and implementation standards. The shorter the planning time frame, the more specific the planning details must be.

Strategic and operational business objectives dictate what human resource objectives must be. So also do internal and external labor markets. Human resource planning (HRP) parallels general business planning. Broadly speaking, HRP is an effort to anticipate future business and environmental demands on an organization and to meet the human resource requirements dictated by those conditions. This general view suggests several interrelated activities that together comprise an integrated HRP system. These include (1) an inventory of talent currently on hand, (2) forecasts of human resource supply and human resource demand over short- and long-term periods, (3) action plans such as training or job transfer to meet forecasted human resource needs, and (4) control and evaluation procedures.

DISCUSSION QUESTIONS

5∎1 In your opinion, what are some of the key reasons for the deep changes we are seeing in the way jobs are done?

5∎2 For purposes of succession planning, what information would you want in order to evaluate "potential"?

5∎3 Discuss the pros and cons of alternative safeguards for employee information privacy.

5∎4 In your opinion, is it more cost-effective to "buy" or to "make" competent employees?

5∎5 Why should the output from forecasting models be tempered with the judgment of experienced line managers?

REFERENCES

1. General Motors: Open all night (1992, June 1). *Business Week*, pp. 82, 83.
2. Vobejda, B. (1987, Apr. 4). The new cutting edge in factories. *The Washington Post*, p. A14.
3. Goldstein, I. L., & Gilliam, P. (1990). Training system issues in the year 2000. *American Psychologist*, **45**, 134–143.

4. Schneider, B., & Konz, A. (1989). Strategic job analysis. *Human Resource Management*, **28**, 51–63.

5. A work revolution in U.S. industry (1983, May 16). *Business Week*, pp. 100–110.

6. Driessnack, C. H. (1979, December). Financial impact of effective human resource management. *The Personnel Administrator*, pp. 62–66.

7. Cascio, W. F. (1993, August). *The Americans with Disabilities Act of 1990 and the 1991 Civil Rights Act: Requirements for psychological practice in the workplace.* Master lecture presented at the annual convention of the American Psychological Association, Toronto, Canada.

8. Christal, R. E. (1974, January). *The United States Air Force Occupational Research Project.* Occupational Research Division, AFHRL-TR-73-75, Lackland Air Force Base, TX. See also Fleishman, E. A., & Mumford, M. D. (1991). Evaluating classifications of job behavior: A construct validation of the ability requirements scales. *Personnel Psychology*, **44**, 523–575.

9. Harvey, R. J. (1991). Job analysis. In M. D. Dunnette & L. M. Hough (eds.), *Handbook of industrial and organizational psychology.* Palo Alto, CA: Consulting Psychologists Press, pp. 71–163.

10. McCormick, E. J., Jeanneret, P. R., & Mecham, R. C. (1972). A study of job characteristics and job dimensions as based on the Position Analysis Questionnaire (PAQ). *Journal of Applied Psychology*, **56**, 347–368.

11. Page, R. C., & Van De Voort, D. M. (1989). Job analysis and HR planning. In W. F. Cascio (ed.), *Human resource planning, employment, and placement.* Washington, DC: Bureau of National Affairs, pp. 2-34 to 2-72. See also *Fleishman Job Analysis Survey* (1992). Palo Alto, CA: Consulting Psychologists Press.

12. DiNisi, A. S., Cornelius, E. T., III, & Blencoe, A. G. (1987). Further investigation of common knowledge effects on job analysis ratings. *Journal of Applied Psychology*, **72**, 262–268. See also Friedman, L., & Harvey, R. J. (1986). Can raters with reduced job descriptive information provide accurate Position Analysis Questionnaire (PAQ) ratings? *Personnel Psychology*, **39**, 779–789. See also Landy, F. J., & Vasey, J. (1991). Job analysis: The composition of SME samples. *Personnel Psychology*, **44**, 27–50.

13. Schmitt, N., & Cohen, S. A. (1989). Internal analyses of task ratings by job incumbents. *Journal of Applied Psychology*, **73**, 96–104.

14. Conley, P. R., & Sackett, P. R. (1987). Effects of using high- versus low-performing job incumbents as sources of job-analysis information. *Journal of Applied Psychology*, **72**, 434–437.

15. Borman, W. C., Dorsey, D., & Ackerman, L. (1992). Time-spent responses as time-allocation strategies: Relations with sales performance in a stockbroker sample. *Personnel Psychology*, **45**, 763–777.

16. Tornow, W. W., & Pinto, P. R. (1976). The development of a managerial taxonomy: A system for describing, classifying, and evaluating executive positions. *Journal of Applied Psychology*, **61**, 410–418.

17. Dowell, B. E., & Wexley, K. N. (1978). Development of a work behavior taxonomy for first-line supervisors. *Journal of Applied Psychology*, **63**, 563–572.

18. Levine, E. L., Ash, R. A., & Bennett, N. (1980). Exploratory comparative study of four job analysis methods. *Journal of Applied Psychology*, **65**, 524–535. See also Levine, E. L., Ash, R. A., Hall, H., & Sistrunk, F. (1983). Evaluation of job analysis methods by experienced job analysts. *Academy of Management Journal*, **26**(2), 339–348.

19. Ash, R. A., & Edgell, S. L. (1975). A note on the readability of the Position Analysis Questionnaire (PAQ). *Journal of Applied Psychology*, **60**, 765–766.

20. Page & Van De Voort, op. cit.

21. Jackson, S. E., & Schuler, R. S. (1990). Human resource planning: Challenges for industrial/organizational psychologists. *American Psychologist*, **45**, 223–239.

22. Connors, K., cited in Lawrence, S. (1989, April). Voice of HR experience. *Personnel Journal*, p. 70.

23. Changing, but not happy about it (1993, Sept. 20). *Business Week*, p. 44.

24. Richman, L. S. (1993, July 12). Jobs that are growing and slowing. *Fortune*, pp. 52–55.

25. Arvey, R. D., Salas, E., & Gialluca, K. A. (1992). Using task inventories to forecast skills and abilities. *Human Performance*, **5**, 171–190. See also Schneider, B., & Konz, A. M. (1989). Strategic job analysis. *Human Resource Management*, **38**, 51–64.

26. Olian J. D., & Rynes, S. L. (1984). Organizational staffing: Integrating practice with strategy. *Industrial Relations*, **23**, 170–183. See also Snow, C. C. (ed.) (1987). *Strategy, organization design, and human resources management.* Greenwich, CT: JAI Press.

27. Walker, J. W. (1992). *Human resource strategy.* New York: McGraw-Hill.

28. Alpander, G. C., & Botter, C. H. (1981). An integrated model of strategic human resource planning and utilization. *Human Resource Planning*, **4**, 189–208.

29. Cascio, W. F. (1991). *Applied psychology in personnel management* (4th ed.). Englewood Cliffs, NJ: Prentice-Hall.

30. Jackson & Schuler, op. cit.

31. Ulrich, D. (1986). Human resource planning as a competitive edge. *Human Resource Planning*, **9**(2), 41–50.

32. McCoy, C. (1993, Oct. 18). As Sculley leaves Apple, image lingers of a leader distracted by his vision. *The Wall Street Journal*, p. B10. See also Apple's Future (1993, July 5). *Business Week*, pp. 22–28.

33. Schuler, R. S., & Walker, J. W. (1990, Summer). Human resources strategy: Focusing on issues and actions. *Organizational Dynamics*, pp. 5–19.

34. Ibid.

35. Wallace, M. J., & Fay, C. H. (1988). *Compensation theory and practice* (2d ed.). Boston: PWS-Kent.

36. The man who McDonaldized Burger King (1979, Oct. 8). *Business Week*, pp. 132, 136.

37. Jackson & Schuler, op. cit.

38. See, for example, Kavanagh, M. J., Geutal, H. G., & Tannenbaum, S. I. (1990). *Human resource information systems: Development and application.* Boston: PWS-Kent.

39. Walker, op. cit.

40. Ibid.

41. Solomon, J. (1989, Apr. 4). As firms' personnel files grow, worker privacy falls. *The Wall Street Journal*, p. B1.

42. Piller, C. (1993, July). Bosses with X-ray eyes. *Macworld*, pp. 118–123.

43. A model employment-privacy policy (1993, July). *Macworld*, p. 121.

44. Cook, S. H. (1987). Privacy rights: Whose life is it anyway? *Personnel Administrator*, **32**(4), 58–65.

45. Walker, op. cit.

46. Schlesinger, J. M. (1993, Sept. 16). Japan begins to confront job insecurity. *The Wall Street Journal*, p. A20.

47. Labor letter (1990, May 22). *The Wall Street Journal*, p. A1.

48. Jackson & Schuler, op. cit. See also Perham, J. (1981). Management succession: A hard game to play. *Dun's Review*, **117**, 54–55, 58.

49. Bennett, A. (1988, Apr. 29). Many companies aren't prepared to deal with sudden death of chief executive. *The Wall Street Journal*, p. 25.

50. Reypert, L. J. (1981). Succession planning in the Ministry of Transportation and Communications, Province of Ontario. *Human Resource Planning*, **4**, 151–156.

51. Ibid.

52. For more on this issue, see Borwick, C. (1993, May). Eight ways to assess succession plans. *HRMagazine*, pp. 109–114.

53. Brown, B. (1988, Aug. 4). Succession strategies for family firms. *The Wall Street Journal*, p. 23.

54. Dalkey, N. (1969). *The Delphi method: An experimental study of group opinion.* Santa Monica, CA: Rand.

55. Milkovich, G. T., Annoni, A. J., & Mahoney, T. A. (1972). The use of the Delphi procedure in manpower forecasting. *Management Science*, **19**, 381–388.

56. Frantzreb, R. B. (1981). Human resource planning: Forecasting manpower needs. *Personnel Journal*, **60**, 850–857.

57. Ibid.

58. Mitchell, C. (1987, Sept. 28). Corporate classes: Firms broaden scope of their education programs. *The Wall Street Journal*, p. 35. See also Solomon, J. (1989, Nov. 7). Firms grapple with language barriers. *The Wall Street Journal*, pp. B1, B12.

59. Schmidt, F. L., Hunter, J. E., & Pearlman, K. (1982). Assessing the economic impact of personnel programs on workforce productivity. *Personnel Psychology*, **35**, 333–347.

60. Lopez, J. A. (1993, Jan. 5). Bosses seek ways to hold onto workers as recovery encourages job hopping. *The Wall Street Journal*, pp. B1; B4.

61. Walker, J. W. (1980). *Human resource planning*. New York: McGraw-Hill.

62. Dyer, L., & Holder, G. W. (1988). A strategic perspective of human resource management. In L. Dyer & G. W. Holder (eds.), *Human resource management: Evolving roles and responsibilities*. Washington, DC: Bureau of National Affairs. See also Dyer, L. (1982). Human resource planning. In K. M. Rowland and G. R. Ferris (eds.), *Personnel management*. Boston: Allyn & Bacon, pp. 52–77.

63. Schweiger, D. M., Ridley, J. R., Jr., & Marini, D. M. (1992). Creating one from two: The merger between Harris Semiconductor and General Electric Solid State. In S. E. Jackson (ed.), *Diversity in the workplace*. New York: Guilford, pp. 167–196.

64. Walker (1992), op. cit.

65. Schuler & Walker, op. cit., p. 13.

66. Labor letter (1990, May 1). *The Wall Street Journal*, p. A1.

CHAPTER 6

RECRUITING

HUMAN
RESOURCE
MANAGEMENT
IN ACTION

RÉSUMÉ DATABASES—RECRUITMENT METHOD OF CHOICE IN THE FUTURE?*

To many professionals in the recruitment industry, résumé databases are on the edge of an explosive growth in popularity. They believe that the cost- and time-efficient nature of the database will make most other recruiting methods obsolete. Says the director of communications for a Chicago-based database company that currently has more than 175,000 résumés on file: "Ten years from now, [résumé databases] will be the primary method of recruiting. I liken it to word processing software; 10 years ago, very few people used it."

Such databases have already begun to shape the ways that corporations approach recruiting college graduates. By using a database system, corporate recruiters can receive copies of students' résumés before they visit a campus. By specifying the kinds of characteristics they are looking for in successful candidates (e.g., bachelor's degree in chemistry, specialization in plastics), recruiters can use the power and speed of the computer to scan thousands of résumés to identify candidates who meet such criteria. Quickly and inexpensively, recruiters can make a list of which schools they want to visit and which students they want to interview. Not only are the numbers of people enrolling in résumé database systems growing, but so are the numbers of employers interested in using databases to conduct recruitment searches.

According to the president of University ProNet in Palo Alto, California (owned by the alumni associations of such top-tier universities as Stanford and MIT), employers' interest

---

*Adapted from: B. Leonard, Résumé databases to dominate field, *HRMagazine*, April 1993, pp. 59–60. Reprinted with the permission of *HRMagazine* published by the Society for Human Resource Management, Alexandria, VA.

in recruitment databases is increasing because they are realizing major cost savings in job searches. Although it typically costs a company $1000 to conduct a job search through a ProNet database, that search usually will net three or four qualified candidates. The cost of using an executive search firm can average between 20 and 30 percent of an employee's first-year salary, costing an employer as much as $30,000 to hire an executive at a salary of $100,000 per year.

"Even if the employer conducts 15 searches through the database, the cost of using a search firm only once is still 100 percent higher than using the database 15 times," he said.

Challenges

1. Proponents make the use of résumé databases sound almost too good to be true. Do you see any disadvantages to using this approach?

2. Are there aspects of recruitment for which résumé databases are not suitable?

3. In your opinion, is a résumé database search appropriate for jobs at all levels?

---

1. What factors are most important to consider in developing a recruitment policy?

2. Under what circumstances does it make sense to retain an executive search firm?

3. Do alternative recruitment sources yield differences in the quality of employees and in their "survival" rates on the job?

4. How can we communicate as realistic a picture as possible of a job and organization to prospective new employees? What kinds of issues are most crucial to them?

5. If I lose my current job in management, what's the most efficient strategy for finding a new one?

Questions This Chapter Will Help Managers Answer

Recruitment is a form of business competition. Just as corporations compete to develop, manufacture, and market the best product or service, so they must also compete to identify, attract, and hire the most qualified people. Recruitment is a business, and it is big business.[1] Yet each set of organizational circumstances differs, and the range of recruitment needs is broad. A small manufacturer in a well-populated rural area faces recruitment challenges that are far different from those of a high-technology firm operating in global markets. As Senator Bill Bradley has noted, in the global competition of the twenty-first century, the ability to forge international alliances and to relate to people different from ourselves will be critical assets.[2] Recruitment and selection of people with those abilities will be more important than ever. Let's begin our treatment by examining the "big picture" of the employee recruitment and selection process, along with some important legal issues. Then we'll focus specifically on the processes of planning, managing, and evaluating recruitment efforts.

THE EMPLOYEE RECRUITMENT/SELECTION PROCESS

Recruitment begins, as Figure 6-1 indicates, by specifying human resource requirements (numbers, skills mix, levels, time frame), which are the typical result of job analysis and human resource planning activities. Conceptually (and logically) job analysis precedes human resource planning in Figure 6-1, because, as we noted in

FIGURE 6-1
The employee recruit-
ment/selection process.

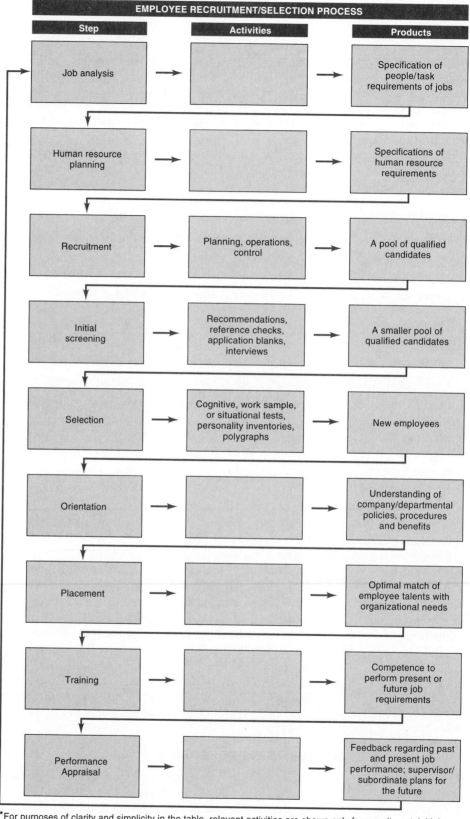

*For purposes of clarity and simplicity in the table, relevant activities are shown only for recruitment, initial screening, and selection — the topics of this and the following chapter.

166

Chapter 5, it is necessary to specify the work to be done (task requirements) and the personal characteristics necessary to do the work (knowledge, skills, abilities, and other characteristics) before one can specify the numbers and types of people needed to do the work. Not shown in Figure 6-1, although critically important to the overall recruitment-selection process, are strategic business objectives (see the 5-P model described in Chapter 2). For example, recruitment and selection strategies for new employees are likely to differ considerably depending on whether a company's objective in hiring, say, new salespeople, is to identify candidates who are able to execute "cold calls" for new customers as opposed to servicing existing, long-term clientele.

The step following recruitment is *initial screening*, which is basically a rapid, rough "selection" process. Sixty years ago, when line supervisors hired factory workers outside the gates of a plant, they simply looked over the candidates and then pointed to various people. "You, you, and you—the rest of you come back another day." That's an example of initial screening, and it was probably done only on the basis of physical characteristics. The *selection process* following initial screening is more rigorous. For example, physical characteristics alone do not provide many clues about a person's potential for management, or for any other kind of work for that matter. What is needed, of course, are samples of behavior, either through tests and personal interviews or through the testimony of others about a candidate, as with reference checks.

Past the selection stage, we are no longer dealing with job candidates, we are dealing with new employees. Typically, the first step in their introduction to company policies, practices, and benefits (technically, this is called "socialization") is an *orientation program*. Orientation may take up several hours or several weeks; it may be formal, informal, or some combination of the two. As we shall see in Chapter 8, orientation has more significant and lasting effects than most people might expect.

Placement occurs after orientation; placement is the assignment of individuals to jobs. In large firms, for example, individuals may be selected initially on the basis of their potential to succeed in general management. After they have been observed and assessed during an intensive management training program, however, the organization is in a much better position to assign them to specific jobs within broader job families, such as marketing, production, or sales. (There are instances in which employees are selected specifically to fill certain positions; these are so-called "one-shot" selection-placement programs.) The technical expertise and the resources necessary to implement optimal placement programs (select, orient, then place) are found mostly in very large organizations, such as the military.

Once new employees are selected, oriented, and placed, they can be *trained* to achieve a competent level of job performance. As we shall see in the next chapter, training is very big business.

Finally, *performance appraisal* provides feedback to employees regarding their past and present job performance proficiency, as well as a basis for improving performance in the future. The first time a new employee's performance is appraised, it is like pushing the button that starts a continuous loop, more precisely a continuous feedback loop comprising the employee's performance, the manager's appraisal of it, and the communication between the two about performance and appraisal.

Of course, all the phases of recruiting and selecting employees are interrelated. But the final test of all phases comes with the appraisal of job performance. There is no point in reporting that, say, 150 possible candidates were recruited and screened, that 90 offers were extended, and that 65 candidates were hired and trained if the first appraisal of their performance indicates that most were inept. You must always remember that when you evaluate the performance of new hires, you are doing so within the context of a system, a network of human resource activities, and you are really appraising recruitment, selection, and training, among other HRM activities.

Developing Recruitment Policies: Legal and Labor Market Issues

As a framework for setting recruitment policies, let us consider four different possible company postures:[3]

1. *Passive nondiscrimination* is a commitment to treat all races and both sexes equally in all decisions about hiring, promotion, and pay. No attempt is made to recruit actively among prospective minority applicants. This posture fails to recognize that discriminatory practices in the past may block prospective applicants from seeking present job opportunities.

2. *Pure diversity-based recruitment* is a concerted effort by the organization actively to expand the pool of applicants so that no one is excluded because of past or present discrimination. However, the decision to hire or to promote is based on the best-qualified individual, regardless of race or sex.

3. *Diversity-based recruitment with preferential hiring* goes further than pure diversity-based recruitment; it systematically favors women and minorities in hiring and promotion decisions. This is a "soft-quota" system.

4. *Hard quotas* represent a mandate to hire or promote specific numbers or proportions of women or minority-group members.

Both private and government employers find hard quotas an unsavory strategy for rectifying the effects of past or present unfair discrimination. Nevertheless, the courts have ordered "temporary" quotas in instances where unfair discrimination has obviously taken place and where no other remedy is feasible.[4] Temporary quotas have bounds placed on them. For example, a judge might order an employer to hire two African-American employees for every white employee until the number of African-American employees reaches x percent.

Passive nondiscrimination misses the mark. This became obvious as far back as 1968, when the secretary of labor publicly cited the Allen-Bradley Company of Milwaukee for failure to comply with Executive Order 11246 by not actively recruiting African Americans. The company was so well known in Milwaukee as a good place to work that it usually had a long waiting list of friends and relatives of current employees. As a matter of established business practice, the company preferred to hire referrals from current employees; almost no public recruiting was done for entry-level job openings. As a result, because almost all the present employees were white, so were almost all the referrals.

As noted in Chapter 4's discussion of legal issues in employment, preferential selection is a sticky issue. However, in several landmark cases the Supreme Court established the following principle:[5] *Staffing decisions must be made on a case-by-case basis; race or sex may be taken into account as one factor in an applicant's favor, but the overall decision to select or reject must be made on the basis of a combination of factors,* such as entrance test scores and previous performance. That leaves us with pure diversity-based recruitment as a recruitment and selection strategy. Indeed, in a free and open competitive labor market, that's the way it ought to be.

Recruitment policies ultimately depend on the structure and functioning of internal and external labor markets. Let us therefore discuss labor market issues in some detail.

A *labor market* is a geographical area within which the forces of supply (people looking for work) interact with the forces of demand (employers looking for people) and thereby determine the price of labor.[6] In a *tight labor market*, demand by employers exceeds the available supply of workers, which tends to exert upward pressure on wages. In a *loose labor market*, the reverse is true: the supply of workers exceeds employer demand, exerting downward pressure on wages. In recent years the labor market for electrical engineers, nurses, and aircraft mechanics has been fairly tight; wages for these jobs have been increasing steadily.[7] On the other hand, the labor market for lawyers, steelworkers, and unskilled labor has been fairly loose in recent years, reducing pressure for wage increases for these workers.

Unfortunately, it is not possible to define the geographical boundaries of a labor market in any clear-cut manner.[8] Employers needing key employees will recruit far and wide if necessary. From the perspective of job applicants, movement from a labor market in one geographical area to another is also quite restricted. There are exceptions: during 1982, in the depths of an economic recession, hundreds of unemployed auto workers left Detroit for Houston in the hope of finding work. In 1986, as oil prices plummeted, workers moved from Houston to other cities. Such movements reflect an underlying turbulence in the environment. In short, employers do not face a single, homogeneous market for labor, but rather a series of discontinuous, segmented labor markets over which supply-and-demand conditions vary substantially.[9] Economists focus on this fact as the major explanation for wage differences among occupations and among geographical areas.

Of practical concern to managers, however, is a reasonably accurate definition of labor markets for planning purposes. Here are some factors that are important for defining the limits of a labor market:[10]

- Geography
- Education and/or technical background required to perform a job
- Industry
- Licensing or certification requirements
- Union membership

Companies may use one or more of these factors to help define their labor markets. Thus an agricultural research firm that needs to hire four veterinarians cannot restrict its search to a local area since the market is national or international in scope. Union membership is not a concern in this market, but licensing and/or certification is. Typically a doctor of veterinary medicine degree is required along with state licensure to practice. Applicants are likely to be less concerned with where the job is located and more concerned with job design and career opportunities. On the other hand, suppose a hospital is trying to hire a journey-level plumber. The hospital will be looking at a labor market defined primarily by its geographic proximity and secondarily by people whose experience, technical background, and (possibly) willingness to join a union after employment qualify them for the job.

Internal versus External Labor Markets

The discussion thus far has concerned the structure and function of external labor markets. Internal labor markets also affect recruitment policies, in many cases more directly, because firms often give preference to present employees in promotions, transfers, and other career-enhancing opportunities. Each employing unit is a separate market. At Delta Air Lines, for example, virtually all jobs above the entry level are filled by internal promotion rather than by outside recruitment. Delta looks to its present employees as its source of labor supply, and workers look to this "internal labor market" to advance their careers. In the internal labor markets of most organizations, employees peddle their talents to available "buyers."[11] Three elements comprise the internal labor market:

- Formal and informal practices that determine how jobs are organized and described
- Methods for choosing among candidates
- Procedures and authorities through which potential candidates are generated by those responsible for filling open jobs

In an open internal labor market, every available job is advertised throughout the organization, and anyone can apply. Preference is given to internal candidates by withholding outside advertising until the job has been on the internal market for several days. Finally, each candidate for a job receives an interview.

Recruitment Policies and Labor Market Characteristics. A great deal of research suggests that employers change their policies in response to changes in market conditions.[12] For example, as labor becomes increasingly scarce, employers have been observed to change their policies in the following ways:

- Improving the characteristics of vacant positions, for example, by raising salaries or increasing training and educational benefits
- Reducing hiring standards
- Using more (and more expensive) recruiting methods
- Extending searches over a wider geographical area

Legal considerations are another important component of recruitment policies. Workforce utilization is a central issue in this area.

Workforce Utilization

Workforce utilization is simply a way of identifying whether or not the composition of the workforce—measured by race and sex—employed in a particular job category in a particular firm is representative of the composition of the entire labor market available to perform that job. To see what considerations this implies, let's consider this situation: There is a town where the percentage of qualified arc welders is 10 percent females and 15 percent African Americans. Now let's say that a firm in this town needs and has on staff 20 arc welders, of whom none are female and 3 are African American. If the representation of the workforce reflects the representation of qualified arc welders in the town, we should expect to find $20 \times 0.15 = 3$ African-American arc welders, and $20 \times 0.10 = 2$ female arc welders. Yet no female arc welders are employed at the firm. Now can you begin to see what workforce utilization is all about?

One of the main things that must be considered in workforce utilization is the available labor market, which the courts refer to as the "relevant labor market." In practice, some courts have defined the relevant labor market for jobs that require skills not possessed by the general population as *those living within a reasonable commuting or recruiting area for the facility who are in the same occupational classification as the job in question.*[13]

In computing workforce utilization statistics, a table such as Table 6-1, in which the job group "managers" is examined, is prepared. (Similar analyses must also be done for eight other categories of employees specified by the EEOC.) This table shows that of 90 managers, 20 are African American and 15 are female. However, labor market data indicate that 30 percent and 10 percent of the available labor market for managers are African American and female, respectively. Hence, for workforce representation to reach parity with labor market representation, 0.30 x 90, or 27, of the managers should be African American and 0.10×90, or 9, should be female. The recruitment goal, therefore, is to hire 7 more African Americans to reach parity with the available labor force. What about the 6 excess female managers? The utilization analysis serves simply as a "red flag," calling attention to recruitment needs. The extra female managers will not be furloughed or fired. However, they may be given additional training, or they may be transferred to other jobs that might provide them with greater breadth of experience, particularly if utilization analyses for those other jobs indicate a need to recruit additional females.

At this point, a logical question is, how large a disparity between the composition of the workforce employed and the composition of the available labor market constitutes a prima facie case of unfair discrimination by the employer? Fortunately the Supreme Court has provided some guidance on this question in its ruling in *Hazelwood School District v. United States.*[14] To appreciate the Court's ruling, it is necessary to describe the reasoning behind it. In examining disparities between workforce representation and labor force representation, the first step is to compute the difference between the *actual* number of employees in a particular job category (e.g., the 20 African-American managers in Table 6-1) and the number *expected* if the workforce were truly representative of the labor force (27 African-American managers). The

■ TABLE 6 ▪ 1

AFRICAN-AMERICAN AND FEMALE UTILIZATION ANALYSIS FOR MANAGERIAL JOBS

	Managers employed by the firm		Percent available in relevant labor market		Utilization*		Goal	
Total	African Americans	Females	African Americans	Females	African Americans	Females	African Americans	Females
90	20	15	30	10	−7 (22%)	+6 (17%)	27	9

*Under the "utilization" column, the −7 for African Americans means that according to the relevant labor market, the African Americans are underrepresented by 7 managers, and the +6 for females means that not only are the females adequately represented, but there are 6 more female managers than needed to meet parity according to the relevant labor market.

Court ruled that if the difference between the actual number and the expected number is so large that the difference would have only 1 chance in 20 of occurring by chance alone, it is reasonable to conclude that race was a factor in the hiring decisions made. If the odds of the difference occurring by chance alone are greater than 1 in 20 (e.g., 1 in 10), it is reasonable to conclude that race was not a factor in the hiring decisions. Statistical tests can be used to compute the probability that the differences occurred by chance.

RECRUITMENT—A TWO-WAY PROCESS

Recruitment frequently is treated as if it were a one-way process—something organizations do to search for prospective employees. This approach may be termed a "prospecting" theory of recruitment. In practice, however, prospective employees and managers seek out organizations just as organizations seek them out. This view, termed a "mating" theory of recruitment, appears more realistic. Recruitment success (from the organization's perspective) and job search success (from the candidate's perspective) are both critically dependent on timing. If there is a match between organizational recruitment efforts and a candidate's job search efforts, conditions are ripe for the two to meet.

In order for organizations and candidates actually to meet, however, three other conditions must be satisfied. There must be a common communication medium (e.g., the organization advertises in a trade journal read by the candidate), the candidate perceives a match between his or her personal characteristics and the organization's stated job requirements, and the candidate must be motivated to apply for the job. Comprehensive recruitment planning efforts must address these issues.

RECRUITMENT PLANNING

Recruitment begins with a clear specification of (1) the number of people needed (e.g., through human resource forecasts and workforce utilization analyses) and (2) when they are needed. Implicit in the latter specification is a time frame—the duration between the receipt of a résumé and the time a new hire starts work. This time frame is sometimes referred to as "the recruitment pipeline." The "flow" of events through the pipeline is represented in Table 6-2. The table shows that if an operating manager sends a requisition for a new hire to the Human Resources Department today, it

■ **TABLE 6 ∎ 2**
EVENTS AND THEIR DURATION
COMPRISING A HYPOTHETICAL
RECRUITMENT PIPELINE

Average number of days from	
Résumé to invitation	5
Invitation to interview	6
Interview to offer	4
Offer to acceptance	7
Acceptance to report for work	21
Total length of the pipeline	43

will take almost a month and a half, 43 days on average, before an employee fulfilling that requisition actually starts work. The HR department must make sure that operating and staff managers realize and understand information such as is represented by this pipeline.

One of the ways that operating and staff managers can be sure that their recruitment needs will fit the length of the recruitment pipeline is by examining the segments of the overall workforce by job group (e.g., clerical, sales, production, engineering, managers). For each of these job groups, the HR department, with the cooperation of operating managers who represent each job group, should examine what has occurred over the past several years in terms of new hires, promotions, transfers, and turnover. This will help provide an index of what to expect in the coming year, other things remaining equal.

INTERNAL RECRUITMENT

In deciding where, when, and how to implement recruitment activities, initial consideration should be given to a company's current employees, especially for filling jobs above the entry level. If external recruitment efforts are undertaken without considering the desires, capabilities, and potential of present employees (e.g., the six excess female managers shown in Table 6-1), both short- and long-run costs may be incurred. In the short run, morale may degenerate; in the long run, an organization with a reputation for consistent neglect of in-house talent may find it difficult to attract new employees and to retain experienced ones. This is why soundly conceived action plans (that incorporate developmental and training needs for employees and managers) and management succession plans are so important.

One of the thorniest issues confronting internal recruitment is the reluctance of managers to grant permission for their subordinates to be interviewed for potential transfer or promotion. As one reviewer put it, "Most supervisors are about as reluctant to release a current employee as they are to take a cut in pay."[15] To overcome this aversion, promotion-from-within policies must receive strong top-management support, coupled with a company philosophy that permits employees to consider available opportunities within the organization.

Among the channels available for internal recruitment, the most popular ones are succession plans (discussed in Chapter 5), job posting, employee referrals, and temporary worker pools.

Job Posting

Advertising available jobs internally began in the early days of affirmative action, as a means of providing equal opportunity for women and minorities to compete. It served as a method of getting around the "old boy" network, where jobs sometimes were filled more by "who you knew" than by "what you knew." Today it is an established practice in many organizations, especially for filling jobs up to the lower executive level.

Openings are published on bulletin boards or in lists available to all employees. Interested employees must reply within a specified number of days, and they may or may not have to obtain the consent of their immediate supervisors.[16] Some job posting systems apply only to the plant or office in which a job is located, while other companies will relocate employees.

An example of the latter practice occurred when the Gannett Company, Inc., inaugurated its national newspaper *USA Today*. It filled 50 positions at the new office with experienced people from the chain's other 133 newspapers. Employees who worked on the start-up had the option of staying with *USA Today* once it was under way or returning to their previous job assignments.

While there are clear advantages to job posting, potential disadvantages arise if employees "game" the system by transferring to new jobs in other company departments or locations that do not require different or additional skills, simply as a way of obtaining grade or salary increases. To avoid this problem, it is critical to establish consistent pay policies across jobs and locations. Further, if no limits are placed on the bidding process, job posting systems can impose substantial administrative costs. Thus, at some firms, employees cannot bid on a new job until at least 1 year after hire, and they must have accrued at least 6 months' tenure in their current jobs before becoming eligible to bid for new ones.[17]

Another problem might arise from poor communication. For example, if employees who unsuccessfully apply for open jobs do not receive feedback that might help them to be more competitive in the future, and if they have to find out through the grapevine that someone else got the job they applied for, a job posting program cannot be successful. The lesson for managers is obvious: regular communication and follow-up feedback are essential if job posting is to work properly.

Employee Referrals

Referral of job candidates by present employees has been and continues to be a major source of new hires at many levels, including professionals. It is an internal recruitment method, since internal rather than external sources are used to attract candidates. Typically such programs offer a cash or merchandise bonus when a current employee refers a successful candidate to fill a job opening. The logic behind employee referral is that "it takes one to know one." Interestingly, the rate of employee participation seems to remain unaffected by such efforts as higher cash bonuses, cars, or expense-paid trips.[18] This suggests that good employees will not refer potentially undesirable candidates even if the rewards are outstanding.

The Apple Bank for Savings in New York City has a typical referral program. Current employees who recruit new workers receive $250 after the new recruits have remained with the bank for 3 months and an additional $250 when the recruit has been employed for 1 year. The employee who recruits the new worker must also remain with the bank to receive the payment. Thus the program incorporates the twin advantage of attracting new employees and retaining old ones. The bank hires about 50 percent of the candidates referred by current employees.[19] At fashion retailer T. J. Maxx, employees receive a $100 bonus for each person they refer who is hired and remains for 60 days. To encourage other employees to refer people they know, managers often distribute the checks at staff meetings.[20]

Three factors seem to be instrumental in the prescreening process of referrals: the morale of present employees, the accuracy of job information, and the closeness of the intermediary friend.[21] While employee referrals clearly have advantages, it is important to note that from an EEO perspective, employee referrals are fine as long as the workforce is diverse in gender, race, and ethnicity to begin with.

Temporary Worker Pools

Unlike workers supplied from temporary agencies, in-house "temporaries" work directly for the hiring organization and may receive benefits, depending on the number of scheduled hours worked per week. Temporary workers (e.g., in clerical jobs, accounting, word processing) help meet fluctuating labor demands due to such factors as illness, vacations, terminations, and resignations. Companies save on commissions to outside agencies, which may be as high as 50 percent or more of a temporary employee's hourly wages.[22]

In the health-care field, Humana (now owned by Hospital Corp. of America) operates an internal pool of 2000 itinerant registered nurses who circulate among the company's 83 hospitals in 19 cities on 13-week assignments. The nurses get a $450-a-month housing allowance, even if they stay with their families or friends, and they keep accruing benefits and seniority rather than starting anew each time they take an assignment.[23]

The Travelers Corporation established a pool of temporaries made up of its own retirees. A recent survey showed the growing popularity of this practice. Almost half the firms surveyed used retirees under some contractual arrangement, about 10 percent allowed retirees to share jobs with other employees, and most retirees continued to receive pension and insurance benefits when they came back to work. About 40 percent of the respondents paid market rates for jobs performed by retirees, while 26 percent paid retirees what they had received at the time they retired.[24]

EXTERNAL RECRUITMENT

To meet demands for talent brought about by business growth a desire for fresh ideas or to replenish the stock of employees who leave, organizations periodically turn to the outside labor market. In doing so they may employ a variety of recruitment sources. In this section we will describe four of the most popular ones: university relations, executive search firms, employment agencies, and recruitment advertising.

University Relations

What used to be known as "college recruiting" is now considerably broader in many companies. The companies have targeted certain schools that best meet their needs and have broadened the scope of their interactions with them. Such activities may now include, in addition to recruitment, gifts and grants to the institutions, summer employment and consulting projects for faculty, and invitations to placement officers to visit company plants and offices.

Mobil is a good example of this trend. The company now deals with only about 50 colleges and universities, instead of the 200 or so on its list a few years ago. It also uses separate teams (made up of six to eight people from various Mobil units) for each school. Many of the team members are alumni or alumnae of the school they are assigned to, and they help plan the dozen or so campus activities each year, such as providing talent for student organizations, conducting career information days, holding receptions, and sponsoring ceremonies at which recruiters present Mobil

Foundation checks to support some campus activity. The recruitment team strategy has already helped to increase the number of graduates hired from targeted schools.[25]

HOW BRISTOL-MYERS SQUIBB USES COMPUTER TECHNOLOGY TO FIND TOP MBA STUDENTS

In order to get itself noticed by MBA students at some of the best schools in the country, Bristol-Myers Squibb distributed an interactive computer diskette that conveyed its recruitment message. That message includes information about the company, positions available at the company, and case histories of Squibb managers, specifically, case histories of difficult business problems faced by recent MBAs who worked for Squibb. After describing a problem, the diskette provides several options for solving it. Viewers are asked which solution they would choose. Subsequently they are told which option actually was chosen and why.

Squibb chose to use these interactive quizzes so that viewers would get involved in the recruitment information it provided. In designing the diskette, Squibb provided a menu so that MBAs could access the information they were interested in and skip the rest. To set itself apart from other companies, Squibb injected humor into its "otherwise information-laden message."

Was the recruitment diskette effective? Based on follow-up research, Squibb found that 33 percent of those who received the diskette viewed it once, 29 percent viewed it twice, and 18 percent viewed it three times or more.[26] As this example shows, employers are becoming more sophisticated in deciding where, when, and how to approach markets they have targeted.

To enhance the yield from campus recruitment efforts, employers should consider the following research-based guidelines:[27]

1. Establish a "presence" on college campuses beyond just the on-campus interviewing period (as Mobil has done).

2. Upgrade the content and specificity of recruiting brochures. Many are far too general in nature. Instead, provide more detailed information about the characteristics of entry-level jobs, especially those that have had a significant positive effect on prior applicants' decisions to join the organization.

3. Devote more time and resources to train on-campus interviewers to answer specific job-related questions of applicants.

4. For those candidates who are invited for on-site company visits, provide itineraries and agendas prior to their arrival. Written materials should answer candidates' questions dealing with travel arrangements, expense reimbursements, and whom to contact at the company and how.

5. Ensure that the attributes of vacant positions are comparable to those of competitors. This is as true for large as for small organizations. Some of the key job attrib-

utes that influence the decisions of applicants, according to a Roper poll of 1000 college students, are promotional opportunities, job security, and long-term income potential. They ranked starting salary in sixth place, after "opportunities for creativity or to exercise initiative" and employee benefits packages.[28]

Executive Search Firms

Such firms are retained typically to recruit for senior-level positions that command salaries over $50,000 and total compensation packages worth in excess of $100,000. The reasons for doing so may include a need to maintain confidentiality from an incumbent or a competitor, a lack of local resources to recruit executive-level individuals, or insufficient time. To use an executive search consultant most effectively requires time and commitment from the hiring organization. It must allow the consultant to become a company "insider," to develop knowledge and familiarity with the business, its strategic plans, and key players.[29] Despite its advantages, consider the following facts: only 55 to 60 percent of all contracts to search for qualified personnel are fulfilled; of those fulfilled, only 40 percent are fulfilled within the promised time estimate. Some 50 percent of the fulfilled searches take two or three times longer than originally estimated.[30] In short, many employers are being sold recruitment services that will never be provided. Employers evaluating a search firm should carefully consider the following indications that the firms can do competent work:[31]

- The firm has defined its market position by industries rather than by disciplines or as a jack-of-all-trades.
- The firm understands how your organization functions within the industries served.
- The firm is performance-oriented and compensates the search salesperson substantially on the basis of assignment completion.
- The firm combines the research and recruiting responsibilities into one function. Doing so allows the researcher-recruiter to make a more comprehensive and knowledgeable presentation to targeted candidates on behalf of the client.
- The firm uses primary research techniques for locating sources. Secondary research techniques in the form of computerized databases, files of unsolicited résumés, and directories can identify qualified candidates, but finding top performers requires a more personalized approach. In fact, only one in 300 unsolicited résumés is likely to be shown to a client, and only one in 3000 of these job seekers may get a job.[32]
- The firm is organized to function as a task force in the search for candidates, particularly where they are being recruited for multiple assignments or when placement speed is essential.

Compared to other recruitment sources, executive search firms are quite expensive. Total fees may reach 30 to 35 percent of the compensation package of the new hire. Fees are often paid as follows: a retainer amounting to one-third the total fee as soon as the search is commissioned; one-third 60 days into the assignment; and a final third upon completion. If an organization hires a candidate on its own prior to the completion of the search, it still must pay all or some portion of the search firm's fee, unless it makes other arrangements.[33]

Employment Agencies

These are some of the most widely available and used outside sources. However, there is great variability in size and quality across agencies. To achieve best results from this channel, cultivate a small number of firms and thoroughly describe the characteristics (e.g., education, training, experience) of candidates needed, the fee structure, and the method of resolving disputes.[34]

■ TABLE 6 ■ 3
DIFFERENCES BETWEEN EXECUTIVE SEARCH FIRMS AND EMPLOYMENT AGENCIES

Services	Executive search firms	Employment agencies
Financial arrangements	Fees based on 30 to 35 percent of candidate's salary and time needed to recruit, or a flat rate plus expenses.	Fees based on 20 to 35 percent of candidate's starting salary.
	Retainer fee required; payment due even if opening filled through other sources.	No retainer fee; fee due only if position filled by agency.
	Staff compensation may include salary, bonus, profit-sharing, and incentives for business generation.	Staff compensation usually depends on commissions for placements made.
Caseload	Personal consultant handles only three to five cases at once.	Agent works with many open job orders at one time.
	Firms usually handle openings at higher levels of organization.	Agencies typically assigned lower-level vacancies.
Relationship with clients	Firms represent employers only.	Agencies represent employers and job seekers.
	General management involved in decision to retain search firm.	HR department makes decision to use agency.
	Consultant thoroughly researches client organization and position requirements before search.	Agents spend less time on initial research and job specifications. Some assignments handled by phone with no personal contact.
	Firms conduct assignments on an exclusive basis.	Agencies compete with similar companies for placements.
Time commitment	Consultant invests 40 to 50 hours per month on each search.	Limited investment of time on any one client, due to lack of guaranteed payment.
Referral rates and guarantees	Two to four highly qualified candidates recommended to each client.	Large numbers of applicants referred to increase odds of a placement.
	Recruitment and evaluation efforts target broad range of candidates, most of whom are not in job market.	Recruitment focuses mainly on candidates actively seeking new employment.
	Process- and results-oriented.	Placement-oriented.
	Reputable firms offer a professional guarantee and commitment to thorough, ethical practices.	Contingency fee arrangement eliminates any obligation to produce results.
Level of client involvement	Minimal HR and management time involvement required.	Considerable HR time required to screen, interview, and evaluate candidates.

Source: J. S. Lord, External and internal recruitment. In W. F. Cascio (ed.), *Human resource planning, employment, and placement.* Washington, D.C.: Bureau of National Affairs, 1989, pp. 2-87, 2-88.

FIGURE 6-2
A Burger King franchise in
Michigan uses billboards to
advertise a benefit designed
to help employees earn
money for college tuition.

Agency fees generally vary from 10 percent of the starting salary for clerical and support staff to 20 to 30 percent of the starting salary for professional, exempt-level hires. Unlike executive search firms, however, employment agencies receive payment only if one of their referrals results in a hire. In addition, most agencies offer prorated refunds if a candidate proves unacceptable. For example, an agency might return 90 percent of its fee if a candidate leaves within 30 days, 60 percent if the new hire lasts between 30 and 60 days, and 30 percent if the new hire leaves after 60 to 90 days on the job.[35] Table 6-3 summarizes the differences between executive search firms and employment agencies.

Recruitment Advertising

When this medium is mentioned, most people think of want ads in the local newspaper. But think again. This medium has become just as colorful, lively, and imaginative as consumer advertising. In addition to newspapers, such advertising media include magazines, direct mail, radio and television, and even billboards (see Figure 6-2).

RECRUITMENT AS A LONG-TERM STRATEGY— THE CASE OF BURGER KING

**COMPANY
EXAMPLE**

A Burger King franchisee in western Michigan made recruitment part of his long-term strategy after experiencing turnover at his restaurants as high as 150 percent in 1 year. He hired a public relations firm to help target two groups of potential employees: working mothers and students. The recruitment program emphasized two things: a free day-care program and an education bonus program. The day-care program helped to increase the employee base by 30 percent within a year after it was started. Currently half the franchisee's employees participate in the day-care program.

The education bonus project allows students to earn $1 for every hour worked, up to $2500 a year, to further their education beyond high school. The same program is also offered to senior citizens—with a twist: they can either use the money themselves or else pass it along as a gift to younger members of their family.

To spread the word about these benefits, the franchisee and the public relations firm distributed posters and brochures to women's centers, high schools, adult education centers, colleges, and other locations where the target audiences of mothers and teenagers were likely to see the message. They also held news conferences and placed stories in newspapers.[36]

Themes in Advertisements

Fads in ads are common. At one time, employers of engineers stressed the recreational attractions of their locations, so many sandy beaches and sunny slopes appeared in recruitment materials. Today, however, the following trends are more evident:[37]

- Widespread use of employees in ads
- Emphasis on intangible benefits, such as room for creativity, alternative development paths, and independence
- Point-of-purchase advertising techniques, including returnable coupons and mini-résumés
- More reliance on entertainment—witty headlines and amusing illustrations that have nothing to do with the job

This is just a brief glimpse into external recruitment sources. Others include career fairs, outplacement firms, former employees, trade shows, co-op and work-study programs, government employment agencies, alumni associations, racial and ethnic organizations, and free-standing computer-based name banks. With respect to the latter, some, such as Career Placement Registry and College Recruitment Database, are generalized lists of job seekers. Others, such as Bank Executive Network, specialize. Both get used a lot; Career Placement says employers order 1800 résumés a month from it.[38]

SPECIAL INDUCEMENTS—RELOCATION AID, HELP FOR THE TRAILING SPOUSE, AND SIGN-ON BONUSES

Especially with higher-level jobs, newly recruited managers expect some form of relocation assistance. Such assistance may include disposal of the residence left behind, lease-breaking expenses, temporary living expenses, and moving costs, to name just a few. Such costs add up quickly. The average cost of relocating a homeowning employee is about $45,000.[39]

Prodded by the emergence of the dual-career family, firms are finding that many managers and professionals, men and women alike, are reluctant to relocate unless the spouse will be able to find suitable employment in a new location. One way that recruiters are dealing with this is to trade information informally. Thus, beginning in 1979, employment managers from Armco, National Cash Register, and Mead Corporation began meeting regularly to exchange information about trailing spouses who were seeking employment. By 1987, the group had expanded to include 38 companies. This type of network is not unusual in most metropolitan areas.[40]

Another recruiting inducement, independent of any relocation assistance, is the sign-on bonus. Originally used in the sports world, signing bonuses are now common among executives, professionals (particularly in high-technology firms), and other ranks as well. Sun Life of Canada pays $200 to $1000 to any employee who brings in a new worker. In New York, Personnel Pool, an office-temp firm, offers $50 finder fees.[41] The practice is even more widespread in health care, in the tight labor market for registered nurses. In large cities, nurses are receiving bonuses of $3000 to $4000 for coming aboard, bonuses for staying, bounties for finding recruits, freedom to set their own schedules, and free tuition for advanced courses. Some employers even offer maid service and free housing for those who are willing to shuttle from city to city to relieve the critical demand for medical care.[42]

Summary Findings Regarding Recruitment Sources

Now that we have examined some of the most popular sources for internal and external recruiting, it seems reasonable to ask "Which sources are most *popular* with employers and job applicants?" Among employers, evidence indicates that:

- Informal contacts are used widely and effectively at all occupational levels.
- Use of public employment services declines as required skills levels increase.
- The internal market is a major recruitment source except for entry-level, unskilled, and semiskilled workers.
- Larger firms are the most frequent users of walk-ins, write-ins, and the internal market.[43]

However, for recruiting workers from underrepresented groups, a study of 20,000 applicants in a major insurance company revealed that female and African-American applicants consistently used formal recruitment sources (employment agencies, advertising) rather than informal ones (walk-ins, write-ins, employee referrals). Nevertheless, informal sources produced the best-quality applicants for all groups (males, females, African Americans, Hispanics, and under and over 40 years of age), and led to proportionately more hires.[44]

Factors Affecting Recruitment Needs

A recent survey of 500 companies revealed how factors such as the source of résumés, type of position, geographic location, and time constraints all can influence recruitment success.[45] With regard to résumés, managers surveyed judged only about 7 percent of incoming résumés to be worth routing to hiring managers. However, those from employment agencies generated more qualified applicants than did general inquiries or advertisements.

The rate of invitations to visit varied markedly (from 8 to 60 percent), depending on the type of position in question. Generally, candidates for technical and lower-level positions had the highest invitation rates; the invitation rate fell as the level of position rose. About 40 percent of those interviewed received job offers, with candidates for lower-level positions earning the highest offer rates. Nontechnical positions generated twice as many acceptances (82 percent) as technical positions (41 percent).

With respect to geographical location, positions requiring relocation generated fewer acceptances to interview requests and (not surprisingly) fewer employment offers. A final factor that affects recruitment needs is time. Adequate assessment of recruitment needs begins with accurate staffing analysis and forecasting. However, a large number of unexpected retirements, resignations, or terminations may place unrealistic time demands on recruiters. Although time frames differ from job to job and industry to industry, 3 months from the receipt of a requisition to the new employee's start date is considered an acceptable time period for recruiting a journey-level professional.[46]

Diversity-Oriented Recruiting

Special measures are called for in diversity-oriented recruiting: employers should use women and members of underrepresented groups (1) in their HR offices as interviewers, (2) on recruiting trips to high schools, colleges, and job fairs, and (3) in employment advertisements.

Employers need to establish contacts in the groups targeted for recruitment based on credibility between the employer and the contact and credibility between the contact and the targeted groups. Allow plenty of lead time for the contacts in the targeted groups to notify prospective applicants and for the applicants to apply for available positions.

Various community or professional organizations might be contacted (e.g., Society of Mexican American Engineers and Scientists, National Society of Black Engineers), and leaders of those organizations should be encouraged to visit the employer and to talk with employees. As we saw in Chapter 3, this strategy was used successfully by Pacific Bell in its effort to recruit high-potential Hispanic candidates.[47] Another source is *The Black Resource Guide*, a compendium of over 3000 church leaders, political figures, educators, newspapers, radio stations, and national associations.[48]

For companies that use search firms to recruit executives, some offer an additional 5 percent of the first year's salary—in addition to the usual 30 percent fee—if the search consultant can find qualified minorities to fill a position.[49] Frequent use of the phrase "an equal opportunity–equal access employer" is a "must" in diversity-oriented recruiting. Finally, recognize two things: (1) it will take time to establish a credible, workable diversity-oriented recruitment program and (2) there is no payoff from passive nondiscrimination.

What are firms actually doing in this area to increase workforce diversity? Kraft General Foods, Phillip Morris, and Dun & Bradstreet are typical. They are revamping their decentralized recruitment systems in order to develop a coordinated recruitment effort. They have begun by gathering data on who, when, and where they recruit, and how they fare with different groups. The goal is to create a consistent corporate image that will support recruiting efforts across the board.[50]

MANAGING RECRUITMENT OPERATIONS

Administratively, recruitment is one of the easiest activities to foul up—with potentially long-term negative publicity for the firm. The following guidelines can help to avoid such snafus:

■ Incoming applications and résumés must be logged in at some central point (they have a way of getting lost in a hurry).

- Activities at important points in the recruitment pipeline must be recorded for each candidate at the same central point. It is truly embarrassing when a candidate appears for a company visit but no one at the company has been notified in advance.

- Acknowledgments and "no interest" letters must be entered against the candidates' central records. Failure to respond to an inquiry or formal application connotes one of two things: incompetence or snobbishness.

- Offers, acceptances, and terms of employment (e.g., salary) must be recorded and evaluated relative to open staffing requisitions. Drastically different salary offers to the same candidate by managers in different departments also signal confusion.

- Records of individuals who do not receive offers should be kept for a reasonable period of time (e.g., 1 year).

Evaluation and Control of Recruitment Operations

The reason for evaluating past and current recruitment operations is simple: to improve the efficiency of future recruitment efforts. To do this, it is necessary to analyze systematically the performance of the various recruitment sources. The following kinds of information should be considered:

- *Cost of operations*, that is, labor costs of company recruitment staff, operational costs (e.g., recruiting staff's travel and living expenses, agency fees, advertising expenses, brochures, supplies, and postage), and overhead expenses (e.g., rental of temporary facilities and equipment)
- *Cost per hire, by source*
- *Number and quality of résumés by source*
- *Acceptance/offer ratio*
- *Analysis of postvisit and rejection questionnaires*
- *Salary offered—acceptances versus rejections*

Evidence indicates, unfortunately, that the evaluation of recruitment activities by large organizations is honored more in the breach than in the observance. Few firms link their recruitment practices to posthire effectiveness, and evaluation is more subjective than quantitative.[51] In one study, for example, just over half the firms even bothered to calculate the average cost per hire in their college recruitment operations (over $2500 in 1994 dollars).[52] As a general benchmark, other research suggests one-third of annual first-year salary.[53] Given the rapid proliferation of human resource information systems, with at least a dozen that provide applicant-tracking features (e.g., PeopleSoft, Revelation Technologies, Resumix),[54] there is no excuse for not evaluating this costly activity.

Which recruitment sources are most *effective*? According to a survey of 245 firms, newspaper advertisements are the most effective sources for recruiting office/clerical, production/service, professional/technical, and commissioned sales workers. For recruiting managers, promotion from within is most effective, followed by newspaper ads. Walk-ins are the most popular method for recruiting production/service workers.[55]

However, a study of 10 different recruitment sources used by more than 20,000 applicants for the job of insurance agent showed that recruiting source explained only

5 percent of the variation in applicant quality, 1 percent of the variation in the survival of new hires, and none of the variation in commissions.[56] If sources do not differ appreciably on these important characteristics, organizations probably should rely on those that are less costly (e.g., newspaper ads) and produce higher-quality applicants (informal sources) than more expensive sources (employment agencies). Later research generally has supported these findings. Thus, regardless of the recruitment sources used to generate applicants, once a final applicant pool has been assembled, organizations can maximize the economic returns of selection by ignoring recruitment sources and using a top-down (i.e., rank order from best to least qualified) selection strategy.[57]

Several studies have examined the recruitment process from the perspective of applicants—how applicants regarded the various sources of information (on-campus interviewer-recruiter, friend, job incumbent, professor) about a job opportunity.[58] The studies investigated whether applicants regarded the information source as credible or not, which sources provided favorable or unfavorable job information, and which sources led to greater acceptances of job offers.

Findings indicated that the on-campus interviewer-recruiter, the first and often the only representative of a company seen by applicants, often was not liked, not trusted, and not perceived as knowing much about the job. Furthermore, applicants were more inclined to believe unfavorable information than favorable information, and they were more likely to accept jobs when the source of information about the job was not the interviewer. Other research has shown that job attributes (supervision, job challenge, location, salary, title) *as well as* recruitment activities (e.g., gender and educational characteristics of recruiter, behavior during the interview) are important to applicants' reactions. In short, recruitment may be viewed as a market exchange process in which employers attempt to differentiate their "products" (job opportunities) among "consumers" (job applicants) who vary in their levels of job-relevant knowledge, abilities, and skills.[59]

Timing issues in recruitment, particularly delays, are important factors in the job choice decisions of applicants.[60] Research indicates that (1) long delays between recruitment phases are not uncommon; (2) applicants react to such delays very negatively, often perceiving that "something is wrong" with the organization; and (3) regardless of their inferences, the most marketable candidates accept other offers if delays become extended. What are the implications of these findings for organizations? In a competitive marketplace, top talent disappears quickly. If you want to compete for it, streamline the decision-making process so that you can move fast.

A conceptual framework that might help explain these findings is that of the "realistic job preview" (RJP).[61] An RJP requires that, in addition to telling applicants about the nice things a job has to offer (e.g., pay, benefits, opportunities for advancement), recruiters must also tell applicants about the unpleasant aspects of the job. For example, "It's hot, dirty, and sometimes you'll have to work on weekends." Research in actual company settings has indicated consistent results.[62] That is, when the unrealistically positive expectations of job applicants are lowered to match the reality of the actual work setting *prior to hire*, job acceptance rates may be lower and job performance is unaffected, but job satisfaction and survival are higher for those who receive an RJP. These conclusions have held up in different organizational settings (e.g., manufacturing versus service jobs) and when different RJP techniques are used (e.g., plant tours versus slide presentations versus written descriptions of the work). In fact, RJPs improve retention rates, on average, by 9 percent.[63]

RECRUITERS AND COMPUTERS

A new computer-based requisition tracking system is giving recruiters at New England Medical Center more time for the professional aspects of their jobs and cutting the time needed for the purely clerical aspects of the operation by about 20 hours per week. The old system was built on three sets of logs. One was kept by the receptionist who took in job requisitions, the second was kept by the secretary who distributed the requisitions to the various recruiters, and the third was kept by the recruiters, who used the logs to keep track of their individual positions.

Every other week, the recruiters brought up to date a *jobs posting list* consisting of over 300 positions. These lists, often with illegible corrections, were given to the secretary for preparing an update. Another weekly report, *number of days to fill positions,* was prepared from the same information. *Offer letters* were typewritten forms with fill-in blanks, done by hand, for information such as name, salary, position, and title.

The new system involves a "master" station and three "slaves" networked together, one for each of the recruiters. The system tracks all position requisitions, logs the resulting hire information, and feeds back the information in various forms. It serves as an *automated logbook,* and it produces a series of reports, including the biweekly job postings, open requisition reports, new-hire orientation reports, and other management data. It also produces the offer letters.

The system provides a series of menus backed up with "Help" screens for each one so that people do not need a lot of technical knowledge to use it. With new network software becoming available, management expects the unit to be able to upload the data from this system directly into the mainframe computer, thereby saving another data entry.[64]

ETHICAL DILEMMA: MUST A COMPANY TELL A JOB APPLICANT ABOUT POTENTIAL LAYOFFS?

Does a company have an obligation to tell job applicants if it is on shaky financial ground and plans to cut back? Some managers argue that such disclosure is not necessary since the layoffs may never materialize. Moreover, they say, "You don't want to scare off top talent, do you?"

At least one state court disagrees with that logic. A woman who was offered a job with Security Pacific Information Services, Inc., relocated from New Orleans to Denver. Seven weeks after she started work, the unit she worked for collapsed for lack of business. A jury awarded her $250,000 for actual and punitive damages, and the Colorado Court of Appeals upheld the jury's verdict.[65] As a general matter, do you agree with the jury's verdict?

Longitudinal research shows that RJPs should be *balanced* in their orientation. That is, they should be conducted to enhance overly pessimistic expectations and to reduce overly optimistic expectations. Doing so helps to bolster the applicant's perceptions of the organization as caring, trustworthy, and honest.[66]

A final recommendation is to develop RJPs even when there is no turnover problem (proactively rather than reactively). They should employ an audiovisual medium and, where possible, show actual job incumbents.[67]

Nevertheless, RJPs are not appropriate for all types of jobs. They seem to work best (1) when few applicants are actually hired (that is, the *selection ratio* is low), (2) when used with *entry-level positions* (since those coming from outside to inside the organization tend to have more inflated expectations than those who make changes internally), and (3) when *unemployment is low* (since job candidates are more likely to have alternative jobs to choose from).[68]

THE OTHER SIDE OF RECRUITMENT—JOB SEARCH

At some time or another, whether voluntarily or otherwise, almost everyone faces the difficult task of finding a job. Much of this chapter has emphasized recruitment from the organization's perspective. But as we noted at the outset, a mating theory of recruitment—in which organizations search for qualified candidates just as candidates search for organizations—is more realistic. How do people find jobs? Research shows that 70 percent land a job through personal contacts, 15 percent through placement agencies, 10 percent through direct mailings of their résumés, and only 5 percent through published job openings.[69]

Consider the following scenario, which has happened all too frequently over the last decade (as a result of mergers, restructurings, and downsizings) and is expected to occur often this decade as economic conditions change.[70] You are a midlevel executive, well regarded, well paid, and seemingly well established in your chosen field. Then—whammo!—a change in business strategy or a change in economic conditions results in your layoff from the firm you hoped to retire from. What do you do? How do you go about finding another job? According to management consultants and executive recruiters, the following are some of the key things *not* to do.[71]

- Don't panic—a search takes time, even for well-qualified middle- and upper-level managers. Seven months to a year is not unusual. Be prepared to wait it out.
- Don't be bitter—bitterness makes it harder to begin to search; it also turns off potential employers.
- Don't kid yourself—do a thorough self-appraisal of your strengths and weaknesses, your likes and dislikes about jobs and organizations. Face up to what has happened, decide if you want to switch fields, figure out where you and your family want to live, and don't delay the search itself for long.
- Don't drift—develop a plan, target companies, and go after them relentlessly. Realize that your job is to find a new job. Cast a wide net; consider industries other than your own.
- Don't be lazy—the heart of a good job hunt is research. Use reference books, public filings, and annual reports when drawing up a list of target companies. If negotiations get serious, talk to a range of insiders and knowledgeable outsiders to learn about politics and practices. You don't want to wind up in a worse fix than the one you left.
- Don't be shy *or* overeager—since personal contacts are the most effective means to land a job, pull out all the stops to get the word out that you are available. At the same time, resist the temptation to accept the first job that comes along. Unless it's absolutely right for you, the chances of making a mistake are quite high.
- Don't ignore your family—some executives are embarrassed and don't tell their families what's going on. A better approach, experts say, is to bring the family into the process and deal with issues honestly.
- Don't lie—experts are unanimous on this point. Don't lie, and don't stretch a point—either on résumés or in interviews. Be willing to address failures as well as strengths. Discuss openly and fully what went wrong at the old job.

IMPACT OF RECRUITMENT ON PRODUCTIVITY, QUALITY OF WORK LIFE, AND THE BOTTOM LINE

A close fit between individual strengths and interests and organizational and job characteristics almost guarantees a happy "marriage." On the other hand, since the bottom line of recruitment success lies in the number of successful placements made, the effects of ineffective recruitment may not appear for years. For this reason alone, a regular system for measuring and evaluating recruitment efforts is essential. Moreover, it's difficult to manage what you can't measure.[72] With the cost of new college hires between $1500 and $6000 (and with the first-year turnover rate for new college graduates as high as 50 percent at some companies),[73] it seems more important than ever to assess whether such costs are outweighed by easier and improved selection procedures, better employee retention, lower training needs and costs, or higher levels of productivity. Finding, attracting, and retaining top talent is now and will continue to be an important management challenge with direct impacts on productivity, quality of work life, and the bottom line.

■ Don't jump the gun on salary—always let the potential employer bring this subject up first. But once it surfaces, thoroughly explore all aspects of your future compensation and benefits package.

Those who have been through the trauma of job loss and the challenge of finding a job often describe the entire process as a wrenching, stressful one. Avoiding the mistakes shown above can ensure that finding a new job need not take any longer than necessary.

RÉSUMÉ DATABASES—RECRUITMENT METHOD OF CHOICE IN THE FUTURE?

HUMAN RESOURCE MANAGEMENT IN ACTION: CONCLUSION:

Generally speaking, there are two disadvantages to such databases that should be recognized.[74] One, many individuals who currently are employed will not list themselves in a database to which the public can have access. The last thing they want their current employers to know is that they are looking for another job! Thus such databases might best be used to locate individuals who are not employed currently, such as new college graduates. Two, some employers do not use public-access databases because they believe that when the objective is to hire experienced individuals, the best candidates are those that aren't really "in the market." That is, they have to be "sold" before they will leave their current jobs.

Thus while résumé databases may become an integral part of recruitment cycles, they will probably supplement, but not replace completely, the recruitment systems that most employers now use. After all, no recruitment effort would be complete without an interview that allows a prospective employer to see and interact with a candidate and allows the candidate an opportunity to learn more about the prospective job and organization. Moreover, the terms and conditions of employment are usually negotiated face to face, not by computer.

According to the president of a résumé database firm in Boston, The Executives' Network, "We have found that our database works best in finding that elusive, qualified midlevel manager. Top-level management searches such as CEOs will always be politically sensitive and will need special handling. Those searches will likely remain in the realm of the executive search firm."

IMPLICATIONS FOR MANAGEMENT PRACTICE

Wave after wave of downsizings and restructurings, predominately at large firms, indicate quite clearly that job hunting has become a buyer's market in the mid-1990s. Nevertheless, given the substantial costs of recruitment and training competent employees, employers must consider the needs of employees if they wish to attract and retain top talent. American Express Travel-Related Services adopted this view in introducing its KidsCheque and FamilyCheque programs to subsidize child care and elder care for employees, over 70 percent of whom are female.[75] Its experience suggests that the following elements should be part of any successful recruitment program:

■ Always view recruitment as a long-term strategy.

■ Be responsive to employees' needs.

■ Develop benefits that genuinely appeal to the employees being hired.

■ Promote recruitment benefits to the target audience.

■ Audit the recruitment programs in place.

How did the senior HR officer at American Express Travel-Related Services sell the program to hard-nosed senior managers? By emphasizing its business advantages; that is, he presented it less like a typical human resources plan and more like a marketing plan—focusing on the goal of differentiating the company in the labor market and placing it ahead of the competition. He emphasized again and again the importance of acting immediately to obtain a first-mover advantage.

What were the results of the program? Within weeks of introducing the program in Jacksonville, Florida, for example, almost 80 percent of eligible employees had signed up. In addition, the company began to receive résumés from people who had heard about KidsCheque from the local media and who were interested in joining American Express as a result. It also received telephone calls from HR managers at other companies that were interested in instituting similar programs.[76]

SUMMARY

Recruitment begins with a clear statement of objectives, based on the types of knowledge, skills, abilities, and other characteristics that an organization needs. Objectives are also based on a consideration of the gender and ethnic-group representation of the workforce, relative to that of the surrounding labor force. Finally, a recruitment policy must spell out clearly an organization's intention to evaluate and screen candidates without regard to factors such as race, gender, age, or disability, where these characteristics are unrelated to a person's ability to do a job successfully. The actual process of recruitment begins with a specification of human resource requirements—numbers, skills mix, levels, and the time frame within which such needs must be met.

Recruitment may involve internal, external, or both kinds of labor markets. Internal recruitment often relies on succession plans, job posting, employee referrals, or temporary worker pools. Many external recruitment sources are also available. In this chapter we discussed four such sources: university relations, executive search firms, employment agencies, and recruitment advertising. In managing and controlling recruitment operations, consideration should be given to the cost of operations and to an analysis of the performance of each recruitment source, since recruitment success is determined by the number of hires who actually perform their jobs successfully.

DISCUSSION QUESTIONS

6▪1 What special measures might be necessary for a successful diversity-oriented recruitment effort?

6▪2 Discuss the conditions under which realistic job previews are and are not appropriate.

6▪3 How can college recruitment efforts be improved?

6▪4 Draft a recruitment ad for a trade journal to advertise a job opening at your company. Have a friend critique it, as well as, if possible, a knowledgeable HR professional from a local company. Summarize their suggestions for improvement and incorporate them into a final draft.

6▪5 You have just lost your middle-management job. Outline a procedure to follow in trying to land a new one.

REFERENCES

1. Lord, J. S. (1989). External and internal recruitment. In W. F. Cascio (ed.), *Human resource planning, employment, and placement.* Washington, DC: Bureau of National Affairs, pp. 2-73 to 2-102.

2. Bradley, B. (1993, Sept. 16). NAFTA opens more than a trade door. *The Wall Street Journal,* p. A14. See also The Mexican worker (1993, Apr. 19). *Business Week,* pp. 84–92.

3. Seligman, D. (1973, March). How "equal opportunity" turned into employment quotas. *Fortune,* pp. 160–168.

4. Replying in the affirmative (1987, Mar. 9). *Time,* p. 66.

5. *Officers for Justice v. Civil Service Commission* (1992). 979 F. 2d 721 (9th Cir.), cert. denied, 61 U.S.L.W. 3667, 113 S. Ct. 1645 (Mar. 29, 1993). See also Affirmative action upheld by high court as a remedy for past job discrimination (1986, July 3). *The New York Times,* pp. A1, B9.

6. Reynolds, L. G., Masters, S. H., & Moser, C. H. (1986). *Labor economics and labor relations* (9th ed.). Englewood Cliffs, NJ: Prentice-Hall.

7. Sharn, L. (1989, Sept. 7). Help wanted: Mechanics for busy airlines. *USA Today,* pp. 1, 2.

8. Reynolds et al., op. cit.

9. Sebastian, P. (1988, Sept. 16). Labor pains. *The Wall Street Journal,* pp. 1, 12.

10. Milkovich, G. T., & Newman, J. G. (1990). *Compensation* (3d ed.). Homewood, IL: Irwin. See also Wallace, M. J., & Fay, C. H. (1988). *Compensation theory and practice* (2d ed.). Boston: PWS-Kent.

11. Baron, J. N., Davis-Blake, A., & Bielby, W. T. (1986). The structure of opportunity: How promotion ladders vary within and among organizations. *Administrative Science Quarterly,* **31,** 248–273. See also Stewman, S. (1986). Demographic models of internal labor markets. *Administrative Science Quarterly,* **31,** 212–247.

12. For an excellent summary of this research, see Rynes, S. L. (1991). Recruitment, job choice, and post-hire consequences: A call for new research directions. In M. D. Dunnette & L. M. Hough (eds.), *Handbook of industrial and organizational psychology* (2d ed.). Palo Alto, CA: Consulting Psychologists Press, vol. 2, pp. 399–444.

13. *Wards Cove Packing Co. v. Antonio,* 109 S. Ct. 2115 (1989). See also Ledvinka, J., & Scarpello, V. G. (1991). *Federal regulation of personnel and human resource management* (2d ed.). Boston: PWS-Kent.

14. *Hazelwood School District v. United States* (1977). 433 U.S. 299.

15. Lord, op. cit.

16. Farish, P. (1989). Recruitment sources. In W. F. Cascio (ed.), *Human resource planning, employment, and placement.* Washington, DC: Bureau of National Affairs, pp. 2-103 to 2-134.

17. Breaugh, J. A. (1992). *Recruitment: Science and practice.* Boston: PWS-Kent.

18. Lord, op. cit.

19. Amante, L. (1989). Help wanted: Creative recruitment tactics. *Personnel*, **66**(10), 32–36.
20. Breaugh, op. cit.
21. Kirnan, J. P., Farley, J. A., & Geisinger, K. F. (1989). The relationship between recruiting source, applicant quality, and hire performance: An analysis by sex, ethnicity, and age. *Personnel Psychology*, **42**, 293–308.
22. Lord, op. cit.
23. Kilborn, P. T. (1990, May 6). Nurses get V.I.P. treatment, easing shortage. *The New York Times*, pp. 1, 28.
24. Farish, op. cit.
25. Ibid.
26. Koch, J. (1990, Winter). Desktop recruiting. *Recruitment Today*, **3**, pp. 32–37.
27. Kolenko, T. A. (1990). College recruiting: Models, myths, and management. In G. R. Ferris, K. M. Rowland, & M. R. Buckley (eds.), *Human resource management: Perspectives and issues* (2d ed.). Boston: Allyn & Bacon, pp. 109–121.
28. "Employee priorities shifting" (1992, Sept. 7). *The Denver Post*, p. 19A. See also Today's students say money isn't everything (1988, Sept. 7). *The Wall Street Journal*, p. 27.
29. Lord, op. cit.
30. Dee, W. (1983). Evaluating a search firm. *Personnel Administrator*, **28**(3), 41–43, 99–100.
31. Lord, op. cit. See also LoPresto, R. (1986). Ethical recruiting. *Personnel Administrator*, **31**(11), 90–91.
32. Labor letter (1988, May 10). *The Wall Street Journal*, p. 1.
33. Lord, op. cit.
34. Farish, op. cit.
35. Lord, op. cit.
36. Amante, op. cit.
37. Farish, op. cit.
38. Labor letter (1989, Dec. 5). *The Wall Street Journal*, p. A1.
39. Labor letter (1992, Apr. 14). *The Wall Street Journal*, p. A1.
40. Farish, op. cit.
41. Labor letter (1989, Apr. 4). *The Wall Street Journal*, p. A1.
42. Kilborn, op. cit.
43. Bureau of National Affairs (1988, May). *Recruiting and selection procedures* (PPF Survey 146). Washington, DC: Bureau of National Affairs.
44. Kirnan et al., op. cit.
45. Lord, op. cit.
46. Ibid.
47. Roberson, L., & Gutierrez, N. C. (1992). Beyond good faith: Commitment to recruiting management diversity at Pacific Bell. In S. E. Jackson (ed.), *Diversity in the workplace*. New York: Guilford, pp. 65–88.
48. *Black resource guide* (10th ed., 1992). 501 Oneida Place NW, Washington, DC 20011.
49. Labor letter (1989, Mar. 21). *The Wall Street Journal*, p. A1.
50. Employers go to school on minority recruiting (1992, Dec. 15). *The Wall Street Journal*, p. B1.
51. Kolenko, op. cit.
52. Rynes, S. L., & Boudreau, J. W. (1986). College recruiting in large organizations: Practice, evaluation, and research implications. *Personnel Psychology*, **39**, 729–757. See also Martin, S. L., & Raju, N. S. (1992). Determining cutoff scores that optimize utility: A recognition of recruiting costs. *Journal of Applied Psychology*, **77**, 15–23.
53. Breaugh, op. cit.
54. Polilli, S. (1992, February). Applicant tracking tools automate résumé review. *Software Magazine*, pp. 8–14.
55. Bureau of National Affairs, op. cit.
56. Kirnan et al., op. cit.

57. Williams, C. R., Labig, C. E., Jr., & Stone, T. H. (1993). Recruitment sources and posthire outcomes for job applicants and new hires: A test of two hypotheses. *Journal of Applied Psychology*, **78**, 163–172.

58. Rynes, S. L., Bretz, R. D., Jr., & Gerhart, B. (1991). The importance of recruitment in job choice: A different way of looking. *Personnel Psychology*, **44**, 487–521. See also Fisher, C. D., Ilgen, D. R., & Hoyer, W. D. (1979). Source credibility, information favorability, and job offer acceptance. *Academy of Management Journal*, **22**, 94–103.

59. Maurer, S. D., Howe, V., & Lee, T. W. (1992). Organizational recruiting as marketing management: An interdisciplinary study of engineering graduates. *Personnel Psychology*, **45**, 807–833.

60. Rynes et al., op. cit.

61. Popovich, P., & Wanous, J. P. (1982). The realistic job preview as a persuasive communication. *Academy of Management Review*, **7**, 570–578.

62. Breaugh, op. cit. See also Premack, S. L., & Wanous, J. P. (1985). A meta-analysis of realistic job preview experiments. *Journal of Applied Psychology*, **70**, 706–719.

63. McEvoy, G. M., & Cascio, W. F. (1985). Strategies for reducing employee turnover. A meta-analysis. *Journal of Applied Psychology*, **70**, 342–353.

64. Farish, P. (ed.) (1987, September). *Recruiting Trends*, p. 1.

65. Menter, E. (1990, Fall). Company must disclose problems to applicants. Denver: *The Legal Vantage* (Pryor, Garney and Johnson), p. 1.

66. Meglino, B. M., De Nisi, A. S., Youngblood, S. A., & Williams, K. J. (1988). Effects of realistic job previews: A comparison using an enhancement and a reduction preview. *Journal of Applied Psychology*, **73**, 259–266.

67. Wanous, J. P. (1989). Installing a realistic job preview: Ten tough choices. *Personnel Psychology*, **42**, 117–134.

68. Wanous, J. P. (1980) *Organizational entry: Recruitment, selection and socialization of newcomers*. Reading, MA: Addison-Wesley.

69. Falvey, J. (1991, Fall). A new set of rules for the "real world." *Managing Your Career*. Chicopee, MA: pp. 39, 41. See also Cohn, G. (1985, Nov. 19). Advice on what not to do as the search continues. *The Wall Street Journal*, p. 37.

70. Downsizers chalk up a record first half (1993, July 26). *Business Week*, p. 20.

71. Rigdon, J. E. (1992, June 17). Deceptive résumés can be door openers but can become an employee's undoing. *The Wall Street Journal*, pp. B1, B7. See also Cohn, op. cit.

72. Kolenko, op. cit.

73. Breaugh, op. cit.

74. Willis, R. (1990, May). Recruitment: Playing the database game. *Personnel*, **67**, 25–29.

75. Morrison, E. W., & Herlihy, J. M. (1992). Becoming the best place to work: Managing diversity at American Express Travel-Related Services. In S. E. Jackson (ed.), *Diversity in the workplace*. New York: Guilford, pp. 203–226.

76. Ibid.

CHAPTER 7

STAFFING

CEO SELECTION CRITERIA—IN THE THROES OF CHANGE*

According to management experts, many of today's top executives are the right people, but for the wrong time. The quickening pace of corporate change means growing numbers of managers who are well groomed for the wrong race. This, apparently, was the case for Robert Stempel, former chairman of General Motors Corporation, who resigned in 1992 under pressure from outside directors of the company.

By most accounts, Mr. Stempel was a competent manager who inspired strong loyalty in his staff. His grooming by the ponderous GM management system was thorough and meticulous. Yet the very skills that propel managers such as Mr. Stempel to the top of large, successful companies—conciliation, deliberateness, relationship building, loyalty—can prove to be their undoing. Boards often compound the problem by choosing chief executives groomed in yesterday's corporate cultures to solve yesterday's problems. The result? Boards often select the right leaders—but for the wrong time.

Mr. Stempel is not alone. At about the same time, both Tom H. Barrett of Goodyear Tire & Rubber Co. and Kenneth H. Olsen of Digital Equipment Corporation also resigned under intense pressure from their boards of directors. Like Mr. Stempel, who had been with GM for 34 years, both were old-time company men. Mr. Barrett had spent 38 years with Goodyear, and Mr. Olsen, who founded Digital, stayed with the company for 35 years. All three faced sharp changes in market demand and competition.

---

*Adapted from: A. Bennett, Many of today's top corporate officers are the right people for the wrong time, *The Wall Street Journal*, Oct. 27, 1992, pp. B1; B12. Reprinted by permission of *The Wall Street Journal*, © 1992 Dow Jones & Company. All rights reserved worldwide.

What's the problem? Management experts say that most CEOs of big companies are products of long, ponderous, and often very highly structured management succession systems. Especially at old-line industrial companies, these individuals often joined the company right out of school and worked their way up through the ranks, assuming greater and greater management responsibility along the way.

Such systems worked well during an epoch of stable markets and increasing consumer demand, but they may prove inadequate for a more rapidly changing environment. Leaders groomed in one business environment thus wind up ill prepared for another. Experts generally agree that there are three flaws in the current system: (1) the process takes too long, (2) the system produces leaders who are too insular in their contacts and their views, and (3) the current approach ties executives too closely to tradition.

Challenges

1. What kinds of experience and personal characteristics should boards be looking for in today's top executives?
2. How should companies address the flaws in the current system?
3. Are there "seasons" for leaders?

Questions This Chapter Will Help Managers Answer

1. In what ways do business strategy and organizational culture affect staffing decisions?
2. What screening and selection methods are available, and which ones are most accurate?
3. What should be done to improve preemployment interviews?
4. Can work-sample tests improve staffing decisions?
5. What are some advantages and potential problems to consider in using assessment centers to select managers?

The chapter opening vignette describes the sometimes wrenching process of selecting a top manager. In fact, management selection decisions are some of the most important and most difficult staffing decisions that organizations face. Compounding these difficulties is the constant need to align staffing decisions with business strategy and organizational culture. As we shall see in this chapter, there is a wide variety of tools for initial screening and selection decisions, and much is known about each one. We will examine the evidence of the relative effectiveness of the tools, so that decision makers can choose those that best fit their long- and short-range objectives.

ORGANIZATIONAL CONSIDERATIONS IN STAFFING DECISIONS

Business Strategy

Clearly, there should be a fit between the intended strategy of an enterprise and the characteristics of the people who are expected to implement it. Unfortunately, very few firms actually link strategy and staffing decisions in a structured, logical way. Nevertheless, we can learn how to effect such a fit by considering a two-dimensional

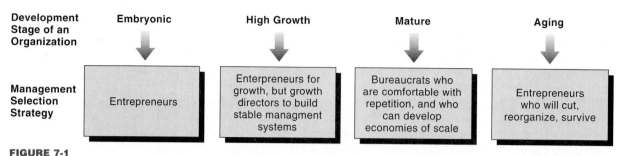

FIGURE 7-1

The relationship between the development stage of an organization and the management selection strategy that best "fits" each stage.

model that relates an organization's strategy during the stages of its development to the style of its managers during each stage.[1]

For strategic reasons, it is important to consider the stage of development of a business because many characteristics of a business—such as its growth rate, product lines, market share, entry opportunity, and technology—change as the organization changes. One possible set of relationships between the development stage and the management selection strategies is shown in Figure 7-1. While a model such as this is useful conceptually, in practice the stages might not be so clearly defined, and there are many exceptions.

Organizations that are just starting out are in the *embryonic* stage. They are characterized by high growth rates, basic product lines, heavy emphasis on product engineering, and little or no customer loyalty.

Organizations in the *high-growth* stage are concerned with two things: fighting for market share and building excellence in their management teams. Product lines are refined and extended, and customer loyalty begins to build.

Mature organizations emphasize the maintenance of market share, cost reductions through economies of scale, more rigid management controls over workers' actions, and the generation of cash to develop new product lines. In contrast to the "free-wheeling" style of an embryonic organization, there is much less flexibility and variability in a mature organization.

Finally, an *aging* organization struggles to hold market share in a declining market, and it demands extreme cost control obtained through consistency and centralized procedures. Economic survival becomes the primary motivation.

Different management styles seem to fit each of these development stages best. In the embryonic stage there is a need for enterprising managers who can thrive in high-risk environments. These are known as entrepreneurs (Figure 7-1). They are decisive individuals who can respond rapidly to changing conditions.

During the high-growth stage there is still a need for entrepreneurs, but it is also important to select the kinds of managers who can develop stable management systems to preserve the gains achieved during the embryonic stage. We might call these managers "growth directors."

As an organization matures, there is a need to select the kind of manager who does not need lots of variety in her or his work, who can oversee repetitive daily operations, and who can search continually for economies of scale. Individuals who fit best into mature organizations have a "bureaucratic" style of management.

Finally, an aging organization needs "movers and shakers" to reinvigorate it. Strategically, it becomes important to select (again) entrepreneurs capable of doing whatever is necessary to ensure the economic survival of the firm. This may involve divesting unprofitable operations, firing unproductive workers, or eliminating practices that are considered extravagant.

Admittedly, these characterizations are coarse, but they provide a starting point in the construction of an important link between the development stage of an organization and its staffing strategy. Such strategic concerns may be used to supplement job analyses as bases for staffing. This also suggests that job descriptions, which standardize and formalize behavior, should be broadened into role descriptions that reflect the broader and more changeable strategic requirements of an organization.

Organizational Culture

A logical extension of the mating theory of recruitment (i.e., concurrent search efforts for a match by organizations and individuals) is the mating theory of selection. That is, just as organizations choose people, people choose jobs and organizations that fit their personalities and career objectives and in which they can satisfy needs that are important to them.[2]

In the context of selection, it is important for an organization to describe the dimensions of its "culture." Culture is the pattern of basic assumptions a given group has invented, discovered, or developed in learning to adapt to both its external environment and its internal environment. The pattern of assumptions has worked well enough to be considered valid and, therefore, to be taught to new members as the correct way to perceive, think, and feel in relation to those problems. Organizational culture is embedded and transmitted through mechanisms such as the following:

1. Formal statements of organizational philosophy and materials used for recruitment, selection, and socialization of new employees
2. Promotion criteria
3. Stories, legends, and myths about key people and events
4. What leaders pay attention to, measure, and control
5. Implicit and possibly unconscious criteria that leaders use to determine who fits key slots in the organization

Organizational culture has two implications for staffing decisions. One, cultures vary across organizations; individuals will consider this information if it is available to them in their job search process.[3] Companies such as IBM and Procter & Gamble have a strong marketing orientation, and their staffing decisions tend to reflect this value. Other companies, such as Sun Microsystems and Hewlett-Packard, are oriented toward R&D and engineering, while still others, such as McDonald's, concentrate on consistency and efficiency. By linking staffing decisions to cultural factors, companies try to ensure that their employees have internalized the strategic intent and core values of the enterprise. In this way they will be more likely to act in the interest of the company and as dedicated team members, regardless of their formal job duties.[4]

Two, other things being equal, individuals who choose jobs and organizations that are consistent with their own values, beliefs, and attitudes are more likely to be productive, satisfied employees. This was demonstrated in a study of 904 college graduates hired by six public accounting firms over a 6-year period. Those hired by firms that emphasized interpersonal relationship values (team orientation, respect for people) stayed an average of 45 months. Those hired by firms that emphasized work-task values (detail, stability, innovation) stayed with their firms an average of 31 months. This 14-month difference in survival rates translated into an opportunity loss of at least $6 million for each firm that emphasized work-task values.

While the firms that emphasized interpersonal relationship values were uniformly more attractive to both strong and weak performers, strong performers stayed an average of 13 months longer in firms that emphasized work-task values (39 months versus 26 months for weak performers). The lesson for managers? Promote cultural values that are attractive to most new employees; don't just select individuals who fit a specific profile of cultural values.[5]

The Logic of Personnel Selection

If variability in physical and psychological characteristics were not so prevalent, there would be little need for *selection* of people to fill various jobs. Without variability among individuals in abilities, aptitudes, interests, and personality traits, we would expect all job candidates to perform comparably. Research shows clearly that as jobs become more complex, individual differences in output variability also increase.[6] Likewise, if there were 10 job openings available and only 10 qualified candidates, selection again would not be a significant issue since all 10 candidates would have to be hired. Selection becomes a relevant concern only when there are more qualified candidates than there are positions to be filled, for selection implies choice and choice means exclusion.

Since practical considerations (safety, time, cost) make job tryouts for all candidates infeasible in most selection situations, the relative level of job performance of each candidate must be *predicted* on the basis of available information. As we shall see, some methods for doing this are more accurate than others. However, before considering them, we need to focus on the fundamental technical requirements of all such methods—reliability and validity.

Reliability of Measurement

The goal of any selection program is to identify applicants who score high on measures that purport to assess knowledge, skills, abilities, or other characteristics that are critical for job performance. Yet we always run the risk of making errors in employee selection decisions. Selection errors are of two types: selecting someone who should be rejected (erroneous acceptance) and rejecting someone who should be accepted (erroneous rejection). These kinds of errors can be avoided by using measurement procedures that are reliable and valid.

A measurement is considered to be reliable if it is consistent or stable, for example:

- *Over time*—such as on a hearing test administered first on Monday morning and then again on Friday night

- *Across different samples of items*—say, on form A and form B of a test of mathematical aptitude; or on a measure of vocational interests administered at the beginning of a student's sophomore year in college and then again at the end of her or his senior year

- *Across different raters or judges* working independently—as in a gymnastics competition

As you might suspect, inconsistency is present to some degree in all measurement situations. In employment settings, people are generally assessed only once. That is, they are given, for example, one test of their knowledge of a job or one application form or one interview. The procedures through which these assessments are made must be standardized in terms of content, administration, and scoring. Only when that is done can the results of the assessments be compared meaningfully with one another. Those who desire more specific information about how reliability is actually estimated in quantitative terms should consult the technical appendix at the end of this chapter.

Validity of Measurement

Reliability is certainly an important characteristic of any measurement procedure, but it is simply a means to an end, a step along the way to a goal. Unless a measure is reliable, it cannot be valid. This is so because unless a measure produces consistent, dependable, stable scores, we cannot begin to understand what implications high versus low scores have for later job performance and economic returns to the organization. Such understanding is the goal of the validation process. From a practical point of view, validity refers to the job-relatedness of a measure—that is, the strength of the relationship between scores from the measure and some indicator or rating of actual job performance.[7]

Although evidence of validity may be accumulated in many ways, validity always refers to the degree to which the evidence supports *inferences* that are drawn from scores or ratings on a selection procedure. It is the inferences regarding the specific use of a selection procedure that are validated, not the procedure itself.[8] Hence a user must first specify exactly *why* he or she intends to use a particular selection procedure (that is, what inferences are to be drawn from it). Then the user can make an informed judgment about the adequacy of the available evidence of validity in support of that particular selection procedure when used for a particular purpose.

Scientific standards for validation are described in greater detail in *Principles for the Validation and Use of Personnel Selection Procedures,*[9] and legal standards for validation are contained in the *Uniform Guidelines on Employee Selection Procedures.*[10] For those who desire an overview of the various strategies used to validate employee selection procedures, see the technical appendix at the end of the chapter.

Quantitative evidence of validity is often expressed in terms of a correlation coefficient (that may assume values between -1 and $+1$) between scores on a predictor of later job performance (e.g., a test or an interview) and a criterion that reflects actual job performance (e.g., supervisory ratings, dollar volume of sales). In employment contexts, predictor validities typically vary between about .20 and .50. In the following sections we will consider some of the most commonly used methods for screening and selection decisions, together with validity evidence for each one.

SCREENING AND SELECTION METHODS
Employment Application Forms

Particularly when unemployment is high, organizations find themselves deluged with applications for employment for only a small number of available jobs. As an example, consider that a typical public utility company *receives* about 75 applications a day (each of which must be screened), *interviews* about 4 of the 75 applicants, and *selects* maybe

1 of the 4. Considerable staff-hours are required just for screening these applications. Alaska Airlines attempted to cause applicants to screen themselves before applying for 40 jobs as flight attendants. How did it do that? By charging applicants a $10 fee for filing an application for employment. More than 5000 people applied and paid the filing fee![11] Other airlines noticed. Now they too charge each job applicant a $10 "processing fee."[12] It is not clear whether such fees discourage any applicants, but at least the companies can recover some of the costs associated with screening them.

An important requirement of all employment application forms is that they ask only for information that is valid and fair with respect to the nature of the job. Studies of application blanks used by more than 200 organizations indicated that, for the most part, the questions required information that was job-related and necessary for the employment decision.[13] On the other hand, more than 95 percent of the forms included one or more legally indefensible questions.

Employment application forms should be reviewed regularly to be sure that the information they require complies with equal employment opportunity guidelines and case law. For example, under the Americans with Disabilities Act of 1990, an employer may not ask a general question about physical or mental disabilities on an application form. However, at a preemployment interview, after describing the essential functions of a job, an employer may ask if there is any physical or mental reason why the candidate cannot perform the essential functions. Here are some guidelines that will suggest what questions should be deleted:

- Any question that might lead to an adverse impact on the employment of members of groups protected under civil rights law
- Any question that cannot be demonstrated to be job-related or that does not concern a bona fide occupational qualification
- Any question that could possibly constitute an invasion of privacy

Some organizations have sought to identify statistically significant relationships between responses to questions on application forms and later measures of job performance (e.g., tenure, absenteeism, theft). Such "weighted application blanks" (WABs) are often highly predictive, yielding validities in the range of .25 to .50.[14] In one study, for example, 28 objective questions were examined for a random sample of the employment applications representing 243 current and former circulation route managers at a metropolitan daily newspaper.[15] A statistical procedure (multiple regression analysis) was used to identify which people were most likely to stay on the job for more than 1 year (the break-even point for employee orientation and training costs). Several interesting findings resulted from the study:

1. Questions on the WAB that best predicted time on the job at the beginning of the study did not predict time on the job several years later. Hence, WAB questions need to be rechecked periodically.

2. The statistical analysis showed that items that "conventional wisdom" might suggest or those used by interviewers did not predict employee turnover accurately.

3. An independent check of a new sample of job candidates showed that the WAB was able to identify employees who would stay on the job longer than 1 year in 83 percent of the cases.

4. The length of the time employees stayed on previous jobs was unrelated to their length of stay on their current job.

Yes, they're here—but maybe not to stay. With the popularity of videocassette recorders at home and at work, the video résumé may seem like an inevitable development. Candidates can look their best, rehearse answers to questions, and, in general, present themselves in the "best possible light."

These efforts, however, get mixed reviews from employers and recruiters, many of whom consider video résumés to be costly gimmicks that fail to provide as much useful information as an ordinary résumé. Here are some of their objections: answers are shallow rather than in depth, the videos take considerable time to review, and they could cause legal problems for employers who reject candidates from protected groups. As the director of human resources for Apple Computer noted: "We get 9000 résumés a month; we don't have time to watch videos when we're going through our screening process."[16] Stay tuned for future developments.

5. The best predictors were "experience as a sales representative," "business school education," and "never previously worked for this company."

Executives balk at spending time and money on human resources research. Nevertheless, poor hires are expensive. SmithKline Beecham Corporation spends an average of $10,000 to recruit and train each worker.[17] That's $1 million for every 100 workers hired. Those kinds of numbers often tend to cast new light on this neglected area.

Recommendations and Reference Checks

Recommendations and reference checks are commonly used to screen outside job applicants. They can provide four kinds of information about a job applicant: (1) education and employment history, (2) character and interpersonal competence, (3) ability to perform the job, and (4) the willingness of the past or current employer to rehire the applicant.

A recommendation or reference check will be meaningful, however, only if the person providing it (1) has had an adequate opportunity to observe the applicant in job-relevant situations, (2) is competent to evaluate the applicant's job performance, (3) can express such an evaluation in a way that is meaningful to the prospective employer, and (4) is completely candid.[18]

Unfortunately, evidence is beginning to show that there is little candor, and thus little value, in written recommendations and referrals, especially those that must, by law, be revealed to applicants if they petition to see them. Specifically, the Family Educational Rights and Privacy Act of 1974 (the Buckley amendment) gives students the legal right to see all letters of recommendation written about them. It also permits release of information about a student only to people approved by the student at the time of the request.

Recent research suggests that if letters of recommendation are to be meaningful, they should contain the following information:[19]

- Degree of writer familiarity with the candidate—time known, and time observed per week.
- Degree of writer familiarity with the job in question. To help the writer make this judgment, the reader should supply to the writer a description of the job in question.

- Specific examples of performance—goals, task difficulty, work environment, and extent of cooperation from coworkers.
- Individuals or groups to whom the candidate is compared.

When seeking information about a candidate from references, consider the following guidelines:[20]

- Request job-related information only; put it in written form to prove that your hire or no-hire decision was based on relevant information.
- Obtain job candidates' written permission to check references prior to doing so.
- Stay away from subjective areas, such as the candidate's *personality.*
- Evaluate the credibility of the source of the reference material. Under most circumstances, an evaluation by a past immediate supervisor will be more credible than an evaluation by an HR representative.
- Wherever possible, use public records to evaluate on-the-job behavior or personal conduct—e.g., records regarding criminal and civil litigation, driving, or bankruptcy.
- Remember that the courts have ruled that a reference check of an applicant's prior employment record does not violate his or her civil rights as long as the information provided relates solely to work behavior and to reasons for leaving a previous job.

What should you do if you are asked to *provide* reference information? Here are some useful guidelines:

- Obtain written consent from the employee prior to providing reference data.
- Do not blacklist former employees.
- Keep a written record of all released information.
- Make no subjective statements, such as "He's got a bad attitude." Be specific, such as "He was formally disciplined three times last year for fighting at work."
- So long as you know the facts and have records to back you up, you can feel free to challenge an ex-employee's ability or integrity. But official records are not always candid. A file might show that an executive "resigned," but not that the company avoided a scandal by letting him quit instead of firing him for dishonesty. When there is no supporting data, never even whisper about the employee's sticky fingers.[21]
- If you are contacted by phone, use a telephone "call back" procedure to verify information provided on a job application by a former employee. Ask the caller to give her or his name, title, company name, and the nature and purpose of the request. Next, obtain the written consent of the employee to release the information. Finally, call back the company by phone. Do not volunteer any information; say only whether or not the information the caller already has is correct.
- Release only the following general types of information (subject to written consent of the employee): dates of employment, job titles during employment and time in each position, promotions, demotions, attendance record, salary, and reason for termination (no details, just the reason).

Sweetening of résumés and previous work history is common. Key aspects of previous history should always be verified. How common? It has been reported that 20 to 25 percent of all résumés and job applications include at least one major fabrication.[22]

What is the current status of reference checking in practice? A 1993 survey found that fully two-thirds of companies reported that it has become harder to check applicants' references. Some 44 percent said that a former employer's reluctance to comment hurts applicants' chances of being hired.[23] In large measure this is due to a series of well-publicized suits for slander, such as the $25 million in punitive damages received by a former employee of John Hancock Co. and the $250,000 award upheld by a federal appeals court in Washington, D.C., against a construction company for giving a poor job reference based on hearsay.[24]

On the other hand, employers can be held liable for *negligent hiring* if they fail to check closely enough on a prospective employee who then commits a crime in the course of performing his or her job duties. The employer becomes liable if it knew, or should have known, about the applicant's unfitness to perform the job in question.[25]

Currently, an employer has no legal duty or obligation to provide information to prospective employers. However, if an employer's policy is to disclose reference information, providing false or speculative information could be grounds for a lawsuit. Reference checking is not an infringement on privacy when fair reference-checking practices are used. It is a sound evaluative tool that can provide objectivity for employers and fairness for job applicants. Figure 7-2 shows the kinds of employment information checked most often.

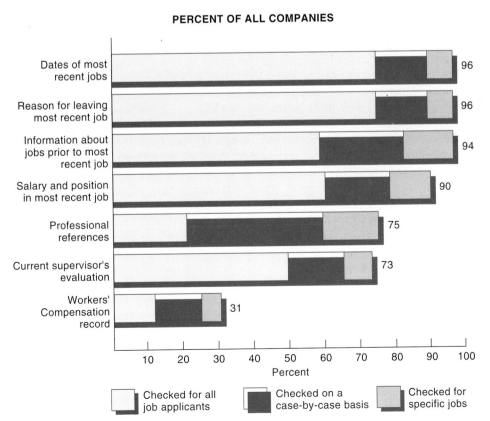

PERCENT OF ALL COMPANIES

FIGURE 7-2
Employment information most commonly checked. (*Source:* Bureau of National Affairs. *Recruiting and selection procedures.* PPF Survey 146, May 1988. Washington, DC: Bureau of National Affairs, p. 22.)

THE USE OF TESTS AND INVENTORIES IN SELECTION

Job candidates can be evaluated and selected on the basis of the results of psychological measurements. The term *measurements* is used here in the broad sense, implying tests and inventories. *Tests* are standardized measures of behavior (e.g., math, vocabulary) that have right and wrong answers, and *inventories* are standardized measures of behavior (e.g., interests, attitudes, opinions) that do not have right and wrong answers. Inventories can be falsified to present an image that a candidate *thinks* a prospective employer is looking for. Tests cannot be falsified. In the context of personnel selection, tests are preferable, for obvious reasons. Inventories are probably best used for purposes of placement or development because in those contexts there is less motivation for a job candidate to present an image other than what he or she really is. Nevertheless, as we shall see, inventories have been used (with modest success) in selection. What follows is a brief description of available methods and techniques, together with an assessment of their track records to date.

Drug Testing

Drug screening tests, which began in the military and spread to the sports world, are now becoming more common in employment. A survey by the American Management Association found that 85 percent of large companies used drug tests in 1993, compared to 74 percent in 1992.[26]

Critics charge that such screening violates an individual's right to privacy and that frequently the tests are inaccurate.[27] Employers counter that the widespread abuse of drugs is reason enough for wider testing.

Do the results of such drug tests forecast certain aspects of later job performance? In the largest reported study of its kind, the U.S. Postal Service took urine samples from 5465 job applicants. It never used the results to make hiring decisions and did not tell local managers of the findings. When the data were examined 6 months to a year later, workers who had tested positive prior to employment were absent 41 percent more often and were fired 38 percent more often. There were no differences in turnover between those who tested positive and those who did not. These results held up even after adjustment for factors such as age, sex, and race. As a result, the Postal Service is now implementing preemployment drug testing nationwide.[28]

Is such drug testing legal? In two rulings in 1989, the Supreme Court upheld (1) the constitutionality of the government regulations that require railroad crews involved in accidents to submit to prompt urinalysis and blood tests and (2) urine tests for U.S. Customs Service employees seeking drug enforcement posts. The extent to which such rulings will be limited to safety-sensitive positions has yet to be clarified by the Court. Nevertheless, an employer has a legal right to ensure that employees perform their jobs competently and that no employee endangers the safety of other workers. So if illegal drug use either on or off the job may reduce job performance and endanger coworkers, the employer has adequate legal grounds for conducting drug tests.

To avoid legal challenge, consider instituting the following commonsense procedures:[29]

1. Inform all employees and job applicants, in writing, of the company's policy regarding drug use.

2. Include the policy, and the possibility of testing, in all employment contracts.

3. Present the program in a medical and safety context. That is, state that drug screening will help improve the health of employees and will also help ensure a safer workplace.

4. Check the testing laboratory's experience, its analytical methods, and the way it protects the security and identity of each sample.

5. If drug testing will be used with employees as well as job applicants, tell employees in advance that it will be a routine part of their employment.

6. If drug testing is done, it should be uniform—that is, it should apply to managers as well as nonmanagers.

PERFORMANCE FACTORS INC. (PFI)

COMPANY EXAMPLE

PFI has designed an innovative, computer-based assessment program to determine an employee's fitness for work. PFI's Factor 1000 software, which tests a worker's hand-eye coordination, could provide an effective alternative to blood tests and urinalysis, which many regard as an invasion of personal privacy. The test, which demands considerable concentration and skill, requires the employee to center a moving object between two posts on the computer screen; employees are able to manipulate the object by turning a small knob while the computer monitors and records their performance. Results of each employee's performance are compared with a companywide baseline average.

One company that uses Factor 1000 is Silicon Valley's Ion Implant Services, Inc. Each day before work, delivery drivers line up to stand in front of a computer to play the short video game. But it's not a game. Unless the machine prints a receipt confirming that the drivers have passed the video test, they can't climb behind the wheel.

Does Factor 1000 work? According to *Business Week,* R. F. White, a California petroleum distributor, used Factor 1000 for a year and found that accidents dropped 67 percent, errors fell 92 percent, and workers' compensation claims declined 64 percent. Not surprisingly, PFI's business has been good. It now tests workers who perform a range of tasks, from machine tooling to driving tour buses to handling poisonous gases and high-voltage equipment.

TWO CONTROVERSIAL SELECTION TECHNIQUES

Handwriting Analysis

Handwriting analysis (graphology) is reportedly used as a hiring tool by 85 percent of all European companies.[31] In Israel, graphology is more widespread than any other personality measurement. Its use is clearly not as widespread in the United States, although sources estimate that more than 3000 U.S. firms retain handwriting analysts as employment consultants. Such firms generally require job applicants to provide a one-page writing sample. Experts then examine it (at a cost of $60 to $500) for 3 to 10 hours. More than 300 personality traits, including enthusiasm, imagination, and ambition, are assessed.[32] Are the analysts' predictions valid? In one study involving the prediction of sales success, 103 writers supplied two samples of their handwriting—one "neutral" in content, the second autobiographical. The data were then analyzed by 20 professional graphologists to predict supervisors' ratings of each salesperson's job performance, each salesperson's *own* ratings of his or her job performance, and sales productivity. The results indicated that the type of script sample did not make any difference. There was some evidence of interrater agreement, but there was no evidence for the validity of the graphologists' predictions.[33] Similar findings have been reported in other well-controlled studies.[34] In short, there is little to recommend the use of handwriting analysis as a predictor of job performance.

Polygraph Examinations

Polygraph (literally, "many pens") examinations are quick and inexpensive ($25 to $50 per person) in comparison to reference checks or background investigations ($100 to $500 and up, depending on the degree of detail required). Professional polygraphers claim their tests are accurate in more than 90 percent of criminal and employment cases *if* interpreted by a competent examiner. Critics claim that the tests are accurate only two-thirds of the time and are far more likely to be unreliable for a subject who is telling the truth.[35]

Prior to 1988, some 2 million polygraph tests were administered each year, 98 percent in private industry.[36] However, a federal law passed in 1988, the Employee Polygraph Protection Act, severely restricts the use of polygraphs in the employment context (except in the case of firms providing security services and those manufacturing controlled substances). Polygraph examinations of current employees are permitted only under very restricted circumstances. The prohibition is a huge setback for the polygraph industry, which is expected to lose about 85 percent of its $100 million in annual revenues.[37] Indeed, arbitrators had long held that the refusal of an employee to submit to a polygraph exam does not constitute "just cause" for discharge, *even* when the employee has agreed in advance (e.g., on a job application) to do so on request.[38]

INTEGRITY TESTS

It is estimated that white-collar crime costs businesses $67 billion per year, and, according to a congressional study, crime increases retail prices by 15 percent.[39] "Shrinkage"—an industry term for losses due to bookkeeping errors and employee, customer, and vendor theft—is estimated to make up almost 2 percent of annual sales.[40] With statistics like these, it should come as no surprise that written integrity tests are being used more frequently by employers. They are of two types.[41] *Overt integrity tests* (clear purpose tests) are designed to assess directly attitudes toward dishonest behaviors. The second type, *personality-based measures* (disguised purpose tests) aim to predict a broad range of counterproductive behaviors at work (disciplinary problems, violence on the job, excessive absenteeism, and drug abuse, in addition to theft).

Do they work? Yes—as a meta-analysis (a statistical cumulation of research results across studies) of 665 validity coefficients that used 576,460 test takers demonstrated. The average validity of the tests, when used to predict supervisory ratings of performance, was .41. The results for overt integrity and personality-based tests were similar. However, the average validity of overt tests for predicting theft per se was much lower—.13. For personality-based tests, there were no validity estimates available for the prediction of theft alone. Thus theft appears to be less predictable than broadly counterproductive behaviors, at least by overt integrity tests. Finally, since there is no correlation between race and integrity test scores, such tests might well be used in combination with general mental ability test scores to comprise a broader selection procedure.[42]

Mental Ability Tests

The major types of mental ability tests used in business today include measures of general intelligence; verbal, nonverbal, and numerical skills; spatial relations ability (the ability to visualize the effects of manipulating or changing the position of objects); motor functions (speed, coordination); mechanical information, reasoning, and comprehension; clerical aptitudes (perceptual speed tests); and inductive reasoning (the ability to draw general conclusions on the basis of specific facts). When job analysis shows that the abilities or aptitudes measured by such tests are important for successful job performance, the tests are among the most valid predictors currently available (see Figure 7-3 and Table 7-1). For administrative convenience and for reasons of efficiency, many tests today are administered on personal computers. While there are obvious advantages to computer-based tests, it is important to ensure that they measure the same characteristics as the paper-and-pencil versions of the same tests.[43]

With respect to the selection of managers, 70 years of research indicate that successful managers are forecast most accurately by tests of their intellectual ability, by their ability to draw conclusions from verbal or numerical information, and by their interests.[44] Further research has found two other types of mental abilities that are related to successful performance as a manager: fluency with words and spatial relations ability.[45]

Validity Generalization. A traditional belief of testing experts is that validity is situation-specific. That is, a test with a demonstrated validity in one setting (e.g., select-

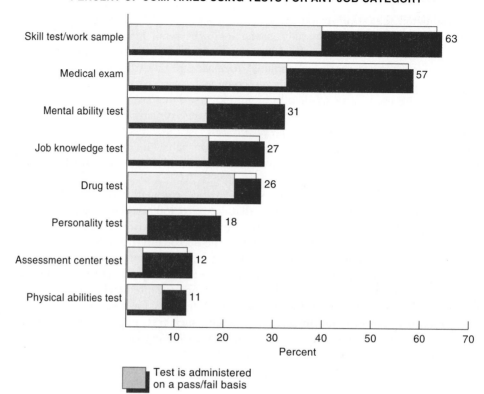

PERCENT OF COMPANIES USING TESTS FOR ANY JOB CATEGORY

FIGURE 7-3
Most common tests and examinations used for selection. (*Source:* Bureau of National Affairs. *Recruiting and selection procedures.* PPF Survey 146, May 1988. Washington, DC: Bureau of National Affairs, p. 18.)

Test is administered on a pass/fail basis

■ **TABLE 7■1**
AVERAGE VALIDITIES OF ALTERNATIVE PREDICTORS OF JOB PERFORMANCE

Entry-level + training		Current performance used to predict future performance	
Cognitive ability tests	.53	Work-sample tests	.54
Job tryout	.44	Cognitive ability tests	.53
Biographical inventories	.37	Peer ratings	.49
Reference checks	.26	Ratings of the quality of performance in past work experience (behavioral consistency ratings)	
Experience	.18		
Interview	.14		
Ratings of training and experience	.13	Job knowledge tests	.48
Academic achievement	.11	Assessment centers	.43
Amount of education	.10		
Interest	.10		
Age	−.01		

Source: J. E. Hunter & R. E. Hunter, Validity and utility of alternative predictors of job performance, *Psychological Bulletin, 96,* 1984, 72–98.

ing bus drivers in St. Louis) might not be valid in another, similar setting (e.g., selecting bus drivers in Atlanta), possibly as a result of differences in specific job tasks, duties, and behaviors. Thus it would seem that the same test used to predict bus driver success in St. Louis and in Atlanta would have to be validated separately in each city.

Almost two decades of research have cast serious doubt on this assumption.[46] In fact, it has been shown that the major reason for the variation in validity coefficients across settings is the size of the samples—they were too small. When the effect of sampling error is removed, the validities observed for similar test–job combinations across settings do not differ significantly. In short, the results of a validity study conducted in one situation can be generalized to other situations as long as it can be shown that jobs in the two situations are similar.

Since thousands of studies have been done on the prediction of job performance, validity generalization allows us to use this database to establish definite values for the average validity of most predictors. The average validities for predictors commonly in use are shown in Table 7-1.

Objective Personality and Interest Inventories

Objective personality and interest inventories provide a clear stimulus, such as statements about preferences for various ways of behaving, and a clear set of responses from which to choose. Here is an example of an objective measure of personality; the examinee's task is to select the alternatives that are most (M) and least (L) descriptive of herself or himself:

Prefers to get up early in the morning	M	L
Does not get enough exercise	M	L
Follows a well-balanced diet	M	L
Does not care for popular music	M	L

Ever since 1944, Sears has used objective personality and interest inventories as part of a larger "executive battery" of measures to predict management success. It has done so very successfully.[47] Measures of "general activity" have proven especially accurate, as have measures of conscientiousness, dependability, imagination, ambition, and sociability.[48] In fact, when job analysis information is used explicitly to select personality measures, their average validity is a respectable .38.[49]

Projective Measures

Projective measures present an individual with ambiguous stimuli (primarily visual) and allow him or her to respond in an open-ended fashion (Figure 7-4), for example, by telling a story regarding what is happening in the picture. Based on how the individual structures the situation through the story he or she tells, an examiner (usually a clinical psychologist) makes inferences concerning the individual's personality structure.

Basically, the difference between an objective and a projective test is this: in an objective test, the test taker tries to guess what the examiner is thinking; in a projective test, the examiner tries to guess what the test taker is thinking.[50]

FIGURE 7-4
Sample projective stimulus. Candidates are told to look at the picture briefly and then to write the story it suggests. Stories are scored in terms of the key themes expressed.

Although early research showed projective measures *not* to be accurate predictors of management success,[51] they can provide useful results when the examinee's responses are related to motivation to manage (e.g., achievement motivation, willingness to accept a leadership role).[52] Moreover, measures of intelligence are unrelated to scores on projective tests. So a combination of both types of instruments can provide a fuller picture of individual "can-do" (intelligence) and "will-do" (motivational) factors than can either one used alone.

Measures of Leadership Ability

At first glance, one might suspect that measures of leadership ability are highly predictive of managerial success since they appear to tap a critical management job requirement directly. Scales designed to measure two key aspects of leadership behavior, *consideration* and *initiating structure*, have been developed and used in many situations. Consideration reflects management actions oriented toward developing mutual trust, respect for subordinates' ideas, and consideration of their feelings. Initiating structure, on the other hand, reflects the extent to which an individual defines and structures her or his role and those of her or his subordinates toward task accomplishment.

Unfortunately, questionnaires designed to measure consideration and initiating structure have been inaccurate predictors of success in management.[53] This is not to imply that leadership is unimportant in managerial jobs. Rather, it may be that the majority of such jobs are designed to encourage and reward managing (doing things right) rather than leading (doing the right things).

Personal-History Data

Based on the assumption that one of the best predictors of future behavior is past behavior, biographical information has been used widely and successfully as one basis for staffing decisions. As with any other method, careful, competent research is necessary if "biodata" are to prove genuinely useful as predictors of job success.[54] For example, items that are more objective and verifiable are less likely to be faked.[55] Here is another example of this kind of effort.

Many professionals resist taking preemployment tests, arguing "My record speaks for itself." The *accomplishment record inventory*, a biodata instrument, lets those records speak systematically.[56] Job candidates describe their accomplishments, in writing, in each job dimension that job analysis shows to be essential (e.g., for attorneys, technical knowledge, research/investigating, assertive advocacy). Raters then use scales developed (by incumbents) for each dimension to evaluate the accomplishments. Research with five types of jobs (attorneys, librarians, economists, research analysts, and supervisors) yielded validities ranging from .22 to .45 and no adverse impact against protected groups.[57] The approach is legally defensible, results-oriented, and highly job-related, and it elicits unique, job-relevant information from each person. Not surprisingly, therefore, it is getting lots of attention.

Employment Interviews

Employment interviewing is a difficult mental and social task. Managing a smooth social exchange while instantaneously processing information about a job candidate makes interviewing uniquely difficult among all managerial tasks.[58] Researchers have been studying the employment interview for more than 60 years for two purposes: (1) to determine the reliability (consistency) and validity (accuracy) of employment decisions based on assessments derived from interviews and (2) to discover the various psychological factors that influence interviewer judgments. Hundreds of research articles on these issues have been published, along with periodic reviews of the "state of the art" of interviewing research and practice.[59] Until recently, the employment interview was considered an unreliable basis for employment decisions (note that in Table 7-1 the average validity for interviews is only .14). However, research is beginning to indicate that the interview works well when:

1. The interview is limited to information that a prior job analysis indicates is important for successful job performance.
2. Interviewers are trained to evaluate behavior objectively.
3. The interview is conducted along a specific set of guidelines.[60]

The interview was originally considered a poor basis for employment decisions because interviewers' decisions were influenced by such factors as first impressions, personal feelings about the kinds of characteristics that lead to success on the job, and contrast effects, among other nonobjective factors. *Contrast effects* describe a tendency among interviewers to evaluate a current candidate's interview performance relative to those that immediately preceded it. If a first candidate received a very positive evaluation and a second candidate is just "average," interviewers tend to evaluate the second candidate more negatively than is deserved. The second candidate's performance is "contrasted" to that of the first.

Finally, research indicates that when interviewers' evaluations of job candidates are in the form of specific predictions of job behavior rather than in terms of general impressions about each candidate, less distortion between actual and perceived interview behavior is found. Employers are therefore likely to achieve nonbiased hiring decisions if they concentrate on shaping interviewer behavior.[61]

One way to shape interviewer behavior is to establish a specific system for conducting the employment interview. Here are some things to consider in setting up such a system:[62]

- Determine the requirements of the job through a job analysis that considers the input of the incumbent along with the inputs of the supervisor and the HR representative.

- To know what to look for in applicants, focus only on the knowledge, skills, abilities, and other characteristics (KSAOs) necessary for the job. Be sure to distinguish between entry-level and full-performance KSAOs.

- Screen résumés and application forms by focusing on (1) key words that match job requirements, (2) quantifiers and qualifiers that show whether applicants have these requirements, and (3) skills that might transfer from previous jobs to the new job.

- Develop interview questions that are strictly based on the job analysis results; use "open-ended" questions (those that cannot be answered with a simple yes or no response); and use questions relevant to the individual's ability to perform, motivation to do a good job, and overall "fit" with the firm.

- Consider asking "What would you do if . . . ?" questions. Such questions comprise the *situational interview*, which is based on the assumption that a person's expressed behavioral intentions are related to subsequent behavior. In the situational interview, candidates are asked to describe how they think they would respond in certain job-related situations. Alternatively, in a *patterned behavior description interview* they are asked to provide detailed accounts of actual situations. For example, instead of asking "How would you reprimand an employee?" the interviewer might say, "Give me a specific example of a time you had to reprimand an employee. What action did you take, and what was the result?" Answers tend to be remarkably consistent with actual (subsequent) job behavior.[63] Validities for both types of interviews vary from about .22 to .28.[64]

- Conduct the interview in a relaxed physical setting. Begin by putting the applicant at ease with simple questions and general information about the organization and the position being filled. Throughout, note all nonverbal cues, such as lack of eye contact and facial expressions, as possible indicators of the candidate's interest in and ability to do the job.

- To evaluate applicants, develop a form containing a list of KSAOs weighted for overall importance to the job, and evaluate each applicant relative to each KSAO.

A systematic interview developed along these lines will minimize the uncertainty so inherent in decision making that is based predominantly on "gut feeling." Table 7-2 shows some examples of proper and improper interview questions, along with several examples of "situational"-type questions.

■**TABLE 7 ▪ 2**

SOME EXAMPLES OF PROPER AND IMPROPER QUESTIONS IN EMPLOYMENT
INTERVIEWS

Issue	Proper	Improper
Criminal history	Have you ever been convicted of a violation of a law?	Have you ever been arrested?
Marital status	None	Are you married? Do you prefer Ms., Miss, or Mrs.? What does your spouse do for a living?
National origin	None	Where were you born? Where were your parents born?
Disability	None	Do you have any disabilities or handicaps? Do you have any health problems?
Sexual orientation	None	Whom do you live with? Do you ever intend to marry?
Citizenship status	Do you have a legal right to work in the United States?	Are you a U.S. citizen? Are you an alien?
Situational questions	(Assumption: Job analysis has shown such questions to be job-related) How do you plan to keep up with current developments in your field? How do you measure your customers' satisfaction with your product or services? If you were a product, how would you position yourself?	

Peer Assessment

In the typical peer assessment procedure, raters are asked to predict how well a peer will do if placed in a leadership or managerial role. Such information can be enlightening, since peers evaluate managerial behavior from a different perspective than do managers themselves. Actually, the term *peer assessment* is a general term denoting three basic methods that members of a well-defined group use in judging each other's performance: *Peer nomination* requires each group member to designate a certain number of group members as highest or lowest on a performance dimension. *Peer rating* requires each group member to rate the performance of every group member. *Peer ranking* requires each group member to rank the performance of all other members from best to worst.

Reviews of more than 50 studies found all three methods of peer assessment to be reliable, valid, and free from bias.[65] Peer assessments do predict job advancement.[66]

ETHICAL DILEMMA: ARE WORK HISTORY OMISSIONS UNETHICAL?

Consider the following situation. A job applicant knowingly omits some previous work history on a company's application form, even though the form asks applicants to provide a complete list of previous jobs. However, the applicant is truthful about the dates of previous jobs he does report. He leaves it to the interviewer to discover and to ask about the gaps in his work history. The interviewer fails to ask about the gaps. Is the job applicant's behavior unethical?

However, since implicitly they require people to consider privileged information about their coworkers, it is essential that peers be thoroughly involved in the planning and design of the peer assessment method to be used.

Work-Sample Tests

Work-sample, or situational, tests are standardized measures of behavior whose primary objective is to assess the ability to do rather than the ability to know. They may be *motor*, involving physical manipulation of things (e.g., trade tests for carpenters, plumbers, electricians), or *verbal*, involving problem situations that are primarily language-oriented or people-oriented (e.g., situational tests for supervisory jobs).[67] Since work samples are miniature replicas of actual job requirements, they are difficult to fake, and they are unlikely to lead to charges of discrimination or invasion of privacy. Moreover, since the content of the test reflects the essential content of the job, the tests have content-oriented evidence of validity. Their use in one study of 263 applicants for city government jobs led to a reduction of turnover from 40 percent to less than 3 percent in the 9 to 26 months following their introduction. The reduction in turnover saved the city more than $650,000 in 1993 dollars.[68] Nevertheless, since each candidate must be tested individually, work-sample tests are probably not cost-effective when large numbers of people must be evaluated.

Two types of situational tests are used to evaluate and select managers: *group exercises*, in which participants are placed in a situation where the successful completion of a task requires interaction among the participants, and *individual exercises*, in which participants complete a task independently. The following sections consider three of the most popular situational tests: the leaderless group discussion, the in-basket test, and the business game.

Leaderless Group Discussion (LGD). The LGD is simple and has been used for decades. A group of participants is given a job-related topic and is asked simply to carry on a discussion about it for a period of time. No one is appointed leader, nor is anyone told where to sit. Instead of using a rectangular table (with a "head" at each end), a circular table is often used so that each position carries equal weight. Observers rate the performance of each participant.

For example, IBM uses an LGD in which each participant is required to make a 5-minute oral presentation of a candidate for promotion and then subsequently defend her or his candidate in a group discussion with five other participants. All roles are well defined and structured. Seven characteristics are rated, each on a 5-point scale of effectiveness: aggressiveness, persuasiveness or selling ability, oral communication, self-confidence, resistance to stress, energy level, and interpersonal contact.[69]

LGD ratings have forecast managerial performance accurately in virtually all the functional areas of business.[70] Previous LGD experience appears to have little effect on present LGD performance, although prior training clearly does.[71] Individuals in one study who received a 15-minute briefing on the history, development, rating instruments, and research relative to the LGD were rated significantly higher than untrained individuals. To control for this, all those with prior training in LGD should be put into the same groups.

In-Basket Test. A situational test designed to simulate important aspects of a position, the in-basket tests an individual's ability to work independently. In general, it takes the following form:

> It consists of the letters, memoranda, notes of incoming telephone calls, and other materials which have supposedly collected in the in-basket of an administrative officer. The subject who takes the test is given appropriate background information concerning the school, business, military unit, or whatever institution is involved. He is told that he is the new incumbent of the administrative position and that he is to deal with the material in the in-basket. The background information is sufficiently detailed that the subject can reasonably be expected to take action on many of the problems presented by the in-basket documents. The subject is instructed that he is not to play a role, he is not to pretend to be someone else. He is to bring to the new job his own background of knowledge and experience, his own personality, and he is to deal with the problems as though he were really the incumbent of the administrative position. He is not to say what he would do; he is actually to write letters and memoranda, prepare agenda for meetings, make notes and reminders for himself, as though he were actually on the job.[72]

Some sample in-basket items are shown in Figure 7-5.

Although the situation is relatively unstructured, each candidate faces the same complex set of materials. At the conclusion of the in-basket test, each candidate leaves behind a packet full of notes, memos, letters, etc., that provide a record of his or her behavior. The test is then scored by describing (if the purpose is development) or evaluating (if the purpose is selection for promotion) what the candidate did in terms of such dimensions as self-confidence, organizational and planning abilities, written communications, decision making, risk taking, and administrative abilities. The dimensions to be evaluated are identified through job analysis prior to designing or selecting the exercise. The major advantages of the in-basket, therefore, are its flexibility (it can be designed to fit many different types of situations) and the fact that it permits *direct* observation of individual behavior within the context of a job-relevant, standardized problem situation.

More than 25 years of research on the in-basket indicate that it validly forecasts subsequent job behavior and promotion.[73] Moreover, since performance on the LGD is not strongly related to performance on the in-basket, in combination they are potentially powerful predictors of managerial success.

Business Games. The business game is a situational test, a living case in which candidates play themselves, not an assigned role, and are evaluated within a group. Like the in-basket, business games are available for a wide variety of executive activities, from marketing to capital asset management. They may be simple (focusing on very specific activities) or complex models of complete organizational systems. They may be computer-based or manually operated, rigidly programmed or flexible.[74] They will

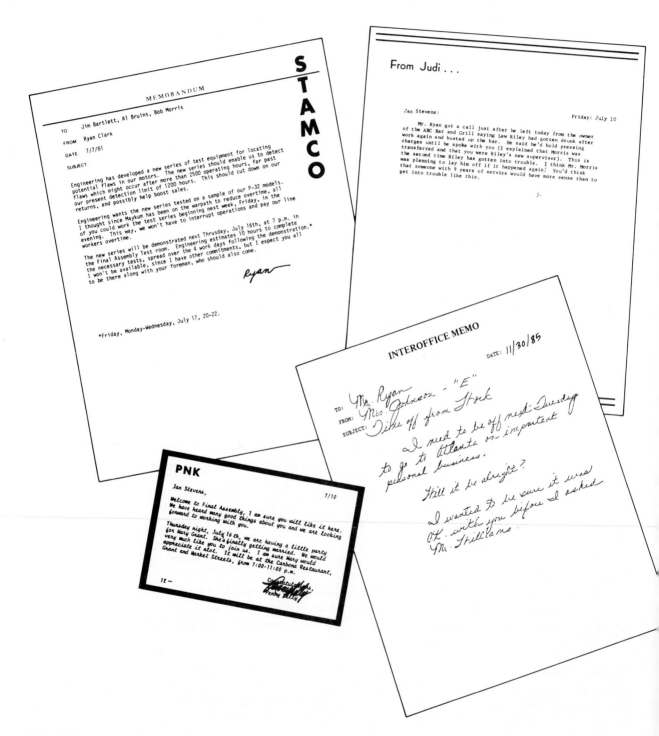

FIGURE 7-5
Sample in-basket items.

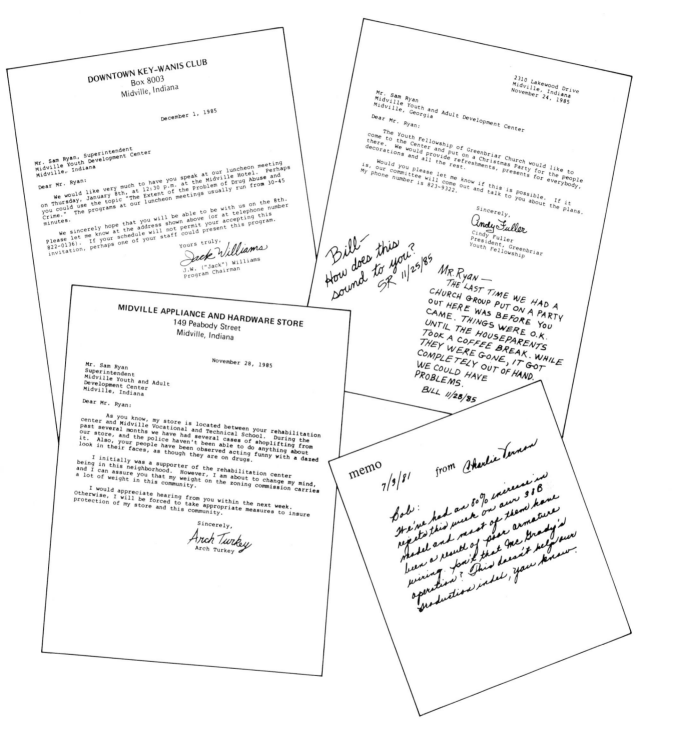

DOWNTOWN KEY-WANIS CLUB
Box 8003
Midville, Indiana

December 1, 1985

Mr. Sam Ryan, Superintendent
Midville Youth Development Center
Midville, Indiana

Dear Mr. Ryan:

We would like very much to have you speak at our luncheon meeting on Thursday, January 8th, at 12:30 P.m. at the Midville Hotel. Perhaps you could use the topic "The Extent of the Problem of Drug Abuse and Crime." The programs at our luncheon meetings usually run from 30-45 minutes.

We sincerely hope that you will be able to be with us on the 8th. Please let me know at the address shown above (or at telephone number 822-0136). If your schedule will not permit your accepting this invitation, perhaps one of your staff could present this program.

Yours truly,

Jack Williams

J.W. ("Jack") Williams
Program Chairman

2310 Lakewood Drive
Midville, Indiana
November 24, 1985

Mr. Sam Ryan
Midville Youth and Adult Development Center
Midville, Georgia

Dear Mr. Ryan:

The Youth Fellowship of Greenbriar Church would like to come to the Center and put on a Christmas Party for the people there. We would provide refreshments, presents for everybody, decorations and all the rest.

Would you please let me know if this is possible. If it is, our committee will come out and talk to you about the plans. My phone number is 823-9322.

Sincerely,

Cindy Fuller

Cindy Fuller
President, Greenbriar
Youth Fellowship

Bill—
How does this
sound to you?
SR 11/25/85

MR. RYAN —
THE LAST TIME WE HAD A
CHURCH GROUP PUT ON A PARTY
OUT HERE WAS BEFORE YOU
CAME. THINGS WERE O.K.
UNTIL THE HOUSEPARENTS
TOOK A COFFEE BREAK. WHILE
THEY WERE GONE, IT GOT
COMPLETELY OUT OF HAND.
WE COULD HAVE
PROBLEMS.
BILL 11/28/85

MIDVILLE APPLIANCE AND HARDWARE STORE
149 Peabody Street
Midville, Indiana

November 28, 1985

Mr. Sam Ryan
Superintendent
Midville Youth and Adult
Development Center
Midville, Indiana

Dear Mr. Ryan:

As you know, my store is located between your rehabilitation center and Midville Vocational and Technical School. During the past several months we have had several cases of shoplifting from our store, and the police haven't been able to do anything about it. Also, your people have been observed acting funny with a dazed look in their faces, as though they are on drugs.

I initially was a supporter of the rehabilitation center being in this neighborhood. However, I am about to change my mind, and I can assure you that my weight on the zoning commission carries a lot of weight in this community.

I would appreciate hearing from you within the next week. Otherwise, I will be forced to take appropriate measures to insure protection of my store and this community.

Sincerely,

Arch Turkey

Arch Turkey

---

memo   7/9/81   from *Charlie Vernon*

Bob:
We've had an 80% increase in
rejects this week on our 31B
model and most of them have
been a result of poor armature
wiring. Isn't that McGrady's
operation? This doesn't help our
production index, you know.

FIG. 7-5 (CONTINUED)

probably be used more frequently for training purposes, given the continued development and availability of personal computers and simulation software—for example, stock market simulations and battle simulations for military academies.

| COMPANY EXAMPLE | **IBM'S MANUFACTURING PROBLEM** |

In this exercise, six participants must work together as a group to operate a manufacturing company. They must purchase raw materials, manufacture a product, and sell it in the market. Included in the exercise are a product forecast and specific prices (that fluctuate during the exercise) for raw materials and completed products. No preassigned roles are given to the participants, but each one is rated in terms of aggressiveness, persuasiveness or selling ability, resistance to stress, energy level, interpersonal contact, administrative ability, and risk taking. In one IBM study, performance on the manufacturing problem accurately forecast changes in position level for 94 middle managers 3 years later.[75] When the in-basket score was added as an additional predictor, the forecast was even more accurate.

Business games have several advantages. One, they compress time; events that might not actually occur for months or years are made to occur in a matter of hours. Two, the games are interesting because of their realism, competitive nature, and the immediacy and objectivity of feedback. And three, such games promote increased understanding of complex interrelationships among organizational units.

Business games also have several drawbacks. One, in the context of training, some participants may become so engrossed in "beating the system" that they fail to grasp the underlying management principles being taught. And two, creative approaches to solving problems presented by the game may be stifled, particularly if the highly innovative manager is penalized financially during the game for her or his unorthodox strategies.[76]

Based on available research, a rough "scorecard" indicating the overall effectiveness of predictors commonly used to assess managerial potential is shown in Table 7-3.

Assessment Centers

The assessment center approach was first used by German military psychologists during World War II to select officers. They felt that paper-and-pencil tests took too narrow a view of human nature; therefore, they chose to observe each candidate's behavior in a complex situation to develop a broader appraisal of his reactions. Borrowing from this work and that of the War Office Selection Board of the British army during the early 1940s, the U.S. Office of Strategic Services used the method to select spies during World War II. Each candidate had to develop a cover story that would hide her or his identity during the assessment. Testing for the ability to maintain cover was crucial, and ingenious situational tests were designed to seduce candidates into breaking cover.[77]

After World War II many military psychologists and officers joined private companies, where they started small-scale assessment centers. In 1956, AT&T was the

■ **TABLE 7 ▪ 3**
ACCURACY OF VARIOUS PROCEDURES USED TO ASSESS POTENTIAL
FOR MANAGEMENT

Procedure	Accuracy
Mental ability tests	5
Objective personality and interest inventories	4
Projective techniques	3
Measures of leadership ability	1
Interviews	2
Personal history data	4
Peer assessment	4
Situational tests (when used in combination, as in an assessment center)	5

Procedures are rated on a 1-to-5 scale, where 1 = poor prediction and 5 = accurate prediction. It is important to stress, however, that no single procedure or combination of procedures is perfectly accurate. Even the most accurate procedures available account for only about 25 percent of the variability in actual job performance among managers. The following rating scheme was therefore used for each procedure, based on the average correlation between scores on the procedure and measures of actual job performance:

Average correlation	Accuracy score
.00 to .10	1
.11 to .20	2
.21 to .30	3
.31 to .40	4
.41 to .50	5

first to use the method as the basis of a large-scale study of managerial progress and career development. As a result of extensive research conducted over 25 years, AT&T found that managerial skills and abilities are best measured by the following procedures:[78]

1. *Administrative skills*—performance on the in-basket test

2. *Interpersonal skills*—LGD, manufacturing problem

3. *Intellectual ability*—paper-and-pencil ability tests

4. *Stability of performance*—in-basket, LGD, manufacturing problem

5. *Work-oriented motivation*—projective tests, interviews, simulations

6. *Career orientation*—projective tests, interviews, personality inventories

7. *Dependency on others*—projective tests

But assessment centers do more than just *test* people. The assessment center method is a process that evaluates a candidate's potential for management based on three sources: (1) multiple assessment techniques, such as situational tests, tests of mental abilities, and interest inventories; (2) standardized methods of making inferences from such techniques, because assessors are trained to distinguish between effective and ineffective behaviors by the candidates; and (3) pooled judgments from multiple assessors to rate each candidate's behavior.

Today assessment centers take many different forms, for they are used in a wide variety of settings and for a variety of purposes. Thousands of organizations in countries around the world are now using the assessment center method, and more are doing so every year. In addition to evaluating and selecting managers, the method is being used to train and upgrade management skills, to encourage creativity among research and engineering professionals, to resolve interpersonal and interdepartmental conflicts, to assist individuals in career planning, to train managers in performance appraisal, and to provide information for human resource planning and organization design.

The assessment center method offers great flexibility. The specific content and design of a center can be tailored to the characteristics of the job in question. For example, when used for management selection, the assessment center method should be designed to predict how a person would behave in the next-higher-level management job. By relating each candidate's overall performance on the assessment center exercises to such indicators as the management level subsequently achieved 2 (or more) years later or current salary, researchers have shown that the predictions for each candidate are very accurate. An accurate reading of each candidate's behavior *before* the promotion decision is made can help avoid potentially costly selection errors (erroneous acceptances as well as erroneous rejections).

As a specific example of the flexibility of the assessment center method in using multiple assessment techniques, consider the following six types of exercises used to help select U.S. Army recruiters:[79]

- *Structured interview.* Assessors ask a series of questions targeted at the subject's level of achievement motivation, potential for being a "self-starter," and commitment to the Army.
- *Cold calls.* The subject has an opportunity to learn a little about three prospects and must phone each of them for the purpose of getting them to come into the office. Assessor role players have well-defined characters (prospects) to portray.
- *Interviews.* Two of the three cold-call prospects agree to come in for an interview. The subject's job is to follow up on what was learned in the cold-call conversations and to begin promoting Army enlistment to these people. A third walk-in prospect also appears for an interview with the subject.
- *Interview with concerned parent.* The subject is asked to prepare for and conduct an interview with the father of one of the prospects that he or she interviewed previously.
- *Five-minute speech about the Army.* The subject prepares a short talk about an Army career that she or he delivers to the rest of the group and to the assessors.
- *In-basket.* The subject is given an in-basket filled with notes, phone messages, and letters on which he or she must take some action.

A third feature of the assessment center method is assessor training. Assessors are typically line managers two or more levels above the candidates, trained (from 2 days to several weeks depending on the complexity of the center) in interviewing techniques, behavior observation, and in-basket performance. In addition, assessors usually go through the exercises as participants before rating others. This experience, plus the development of a consensus by assessors on effective versus ineffective responses by candidates to the situations presented, enables the assessors to standardize their interpretations of each candidate's behavior. Standardization ensures that each candidate will be assessed fairly, that is, in terms of the same "yardstick."

Instead of professional psychologists, line managers are often used as assessors for several reasons:

1. They are thoroughly familiar with the jobs for which candidates are being assessed.
2. Their involvement in the assessment process contributes to its acceptance by participants as well as by line managers.
3. Participation by line managers is a developmental experience for them and may contribute to the identification of areas in which they need improvement themselves.[80]
4. Assessors can be more objective in evaluating candidate performance since they usually do not know the candidates personally.[81]

Despite these potential advantages, cumulative evidence across assessment center studies indicates that professional psychologists who are trained to interpret behaviors in the assessment center relative to the requirements of specific jobs provide more valid assessment center ratings than do managers.[82]

With the assessment center method, the judgments of multiple assessors are pooled in rating each candidate's behavior. The advantage of pooling is that no candidate is subject to ratings from only one assessor. Since judgments from more than one source tend to be more reliable and valid, pooling enhances the overall accuracy of the judgments made. Each candidate is usually evaluated by a different assessor on each exercise. Although assessor judgments are made independently, the judgments must be combined into an overall rating on each dimension of interest. A summary report is then prepared and shared with each candidate.

These features of the assessment center method—flexibility of form and content, the use of multiple assessment techniques, standardized methods of interpreting behavior, and pooled assessor judgments—account for the successful track record of this approach over the past four decades. It has consistently demonstrated high validity, with correlations between assessment center performance and later job performance as a manager sometimes reaching the .50s and .60s.[83] Both minorities and nonminorities and men and women acknowledge that the method provides them a fair opportunity to demonstrate what they are capable of doing in a management job.[84]

In terms of its bottom-line impact, two studies have shown that assessment centers *are* cost-effective, even though the per-candidate cost may vary from as little as $50 to more than $2000. Using the general utility equation (Equation 7-1 in the appendix to this chapter, page 227), both studies have demonstrated that the assessment center method should not be measured against the cost of implementing it but rather against the cost (in lost sales and declining productivity) of promoting the wrong person into a management job.[85] In a first-level management job, the gain in improved job performance as a result of promoting people via the assessment center method is about $3300 per year (in 1993 dollars). However, if the average tenure of first-level managers is, say, 5 years, the gain per person is about $16,500 (in 1993 dollars).

Despite its advantages, the method is not without potential problems. These include:[86]

- Adoption of the assessment center method without carefully analyzing the need for it and without adequate preparations to use it wisely
- Blind acceptance of assessment data without considering other information on candidates, such as past and current performance
- The tendency to rate only general "exercise effectiveness," rather than performance relative to individual behavioral dimensions (e.g., by using a behavioral checklist), as the number of dimensions exceeds the ability of assessors to evaluate each dimension individually
- Lack of control over the information generated during assessment: for example, "leaking" assessment ratings to operating managers
- Failure to evaluate the utility of the program in terms of dollar benefits relative to costs
- Inadequate feedback to participants

Here is an interesting finding: ratings of management potential made after a review of employee files correlated significantly (.46) with assessment ratings, suggesting that assessment might to some extent duplicate a much simpler and less costly process.[87] This conclusion held true for predictions made regarding each candidate's progress in management 1 and 8 years after assessment.[88] However, when the rating of management potential was added to the assessment center prediction, the validity of the two together (.58) was higher than that of either one alone. What does the assessment center prediction add? Not much if we are simply trying to predict each candidate's rate and level of *advancement*. But if we are trying to predict *performance* in management—that is, to clarify and evaluate the promotion system in an organization—assessment centers can be of considerable help, even if they serve only to capture the promotion policy of the organization.[89]

INTERNATIONAL APPLICATION: THE JAPANESE APPROACH TO PERSONNEL SELECTION

Soon after Toyota announced that it would build an auto assembly plant in Kentucky, some 90,000 job applications poured in for the 2700 production jobs and 300 office jobs available. To narrow the field, Toyota uses common tests to an uncommon degree. Even someone applying for the lowest-paying job on the shop floor goes through at least 14 hours of testing, administered on Toyota's behalf by state employment offices and Kentucky State University.

Rigorous testing is also standard procedure for the U.S. auto plants of Mazda Motor Corporation, for a joint venture of Isuzu Motors, Ltd., and Fuji Heavy Industries, Ltd., and for Diamond-Star Motors Corporation, a joint venture of Mitsubishi and Chrysler.

Initial tests cover reading and mathematics, manual dexterity, "job fitness," and, for skilled trades, technical knowledge. "Job fitness" is actually an attitude measure in which applicants are asked whether they agree or disagree with 100 different statements. Here are two examples: "It's important for workers to work past quitting time to get the job done when necessary"; "Management will take advantage of employees whenever possible."

Next come workplace simulations. Groups of applicants are assigned such problems as ranking the features of a hypothetical auto according to how well the market would accept them. As the job seekers discuss the options, trained assessors record their observations and later pool their findings in order to assess each candidate. Other problems focus on manufacturing and making repairs—though not of autos, since Toyota is interested in aptitude more than experience.

There are also mock production lines, where applicants assemble tubes or circuit boards. The objective is to identify applicants who can keep to a fast pace, endure tedious repetition, and yet stay alert. The tube-assembly procedure is intentionally flawed, and applicants are asked how they would improve it.

Only 1 applicant in 20 makes it to an interview, which is conducted by a panel representing various Toyota departments. By then, says an HRM staffer, "we're going to know more about these people than perhaps any company has ever known about people." The final steps are a physical examination and a drug test.

For all the testing being done by the Japanese auto makers, there are some that use other methods. Honda, for example, uses few tests at its Marysville, Ohio, plant. Instead it puts every potential hire through three interviews. And Nissan Motor Co., which has been operating in Smyrna, Tennessee, since the early 1980s, prefers to give probable hires at least 40 hours of "preemployment" training—without pay. The training is intended partly as a final check on whether the company and those in training are really right for each other.[90]

Choosing the Right Predictor

Determining the right predictor depends on the following:

- *The nature of the job*
- An estimate of the *validity of the predictor* in terms of the size of the correlation coefficient that summarizes the strength of the relationship between applicants' scores on the predictor and their corresponding scores on some measure of performance
- *The selection ratio*, or percentage of applicants selected
- *The cost of the predictor*

To the extent that job performance is multidimensional (as indicated in job analysis results), multiple predictors, each focused on critical knowledge, skills, abilities, or other characteristics, might be used. Other things being equal, predictors with the highest estimated validities should be used; they will tend to minimize the number of erroneous acceptances and rejections, and they will tend to maximize workforce productivity. Table 7-1 summarizes the accumulated validity evidence on a number of potential predictors. The predictors fall into two categories: those that can be used for entry-level hiring into jobs that require subsequent training and those that depend on the use of current job performance or job knowledge to predict future job performance.

It is important to take into account the selection ratio (the percentage of applicants hired) in evaluating the overall usefulness of any predictor, regardless of its validity. On the one hand, low selection ratios mean that more applicants must be evaluated; on the other hand, low selection ratios also mean that only the "cream" of the applicant crop will be selected. Hence predictors with lower validity may be used when the selection ratio is low since it is necessary only to distinguish the very best qualified from everyone else.

Finally, the cost of selection is a consideration, but not a major one. Of course, if two predictors are roughly equal in estimated validity, the less costly procedure should be used. However, the trade-off between cost and validity should almost always be resolved in favor of validity. Choose the more valid procedure, because the major concern is not the cost of the procedure but rather the cost of a mistake if the wrong candidate is selected or promoted. In management jobs, such mistakes are likely to be particularly costly.[91]

<table>
<tr><td>

**HUMAN
RESOURCE
MANAGEMENT
IN ACTION:
CONCLUSION**

</td><td>

CEO SELECTION CRITERIA—IN THE THROES OF CHANGE

Here are some suggested improvements to correct the flaws in the current systems for developing managers:

1. *The process takes too long.* Instead of identifying potential leaders early in their careers, perhaps limiting choices for chief executives later on, some boards of directors are building in more flexibility. That is, they are hiring search firms to identify new board members who can step in as CEO if necessary.

2. *The system produces leaders who are too insular.* As an engineer and longtime GM insider, Mr. Stempel was well respected inside the company. But he apparently lacked the outside contacts and experience to make him an effective peer to a strong board. The antidote? The experience of would-be CEOs should be broad enough to give them visibility outside the organization so that they don't have to rely only on their internal authority in the enterprise.

As an example, consider IBM's chairman, Louis Gerstner, Jr. After graduating from the Harvard Business School in 1965, he became one of the youngest directors ever of McKinsey & Co., a management consulting firm. A hard-charging corporate strategist, he moved to American Express Co. in 1978 and eventually rose to its presidency. In 1989, he left to take the chairman's job at RJR Nabisco, then in the spotlight as it went through the biggest leveraged buyout ever. Finally, in 1993, at the age of 51, Mr. Gerstner was named chairman of IBM.[92] No one would ever accuse him of being too insular!

3. *The method ties executives too closely to tradition.* Management experts say that the grooming process for CEOs should focus more on the ability to adapt to change than on a specific skill such as engineering or finance. Indeed, when major change is needed, it is almost impossible for long-term internal people to do it. Says a New York executive recruiter: "Sometimes they just can't see the solution. Sometimes they can see it but can't face it emotionally. The people whose lives and careers they are affecting are close friends. It is their entire network and support system."

What's the bottom line in all of this? According to Warren Bennis, an expert on leadership, "With the galloping changes that are taking place—demographic, geopolitical, global—if you think you can run the business in the next 10 years the way you did in the last 10 years, you are crazy." In short, there are seasons for leaders.

</td></tr>
</table>

IMPACT OF STAFFING DECISIONS ON PRODUCTIVITY, QUALITY OF WORK LIFE, AND THE BOTTOM LINE

Some companies avoid validating their screening and selection procedures because they think validation is too costly—and its benefits too elusive. Alternatively, scare tactics ("validate or else lose in court") have not encouraged widespread validation efforts either. However, recent research has shown that the dollar gains in productivity associated with the use of valid selection and promotion procedures *far* outweigh the cost of those procedures.[93] Think about that. If people who score high (low) on selection procedures also do well (poorly) on their jobs, high scores suggest a close "fit" between individual capabilities and organizational needs. Low scores, on the other hand, suggest a poor fit. In both cases, productivity, quality of work life, and the bottom line stand to gain from the use of valid selection procedures. Thus a 1993 study of firms in the service and financial industries reported correlations ranging from .71 to .86 between the use of progressive staffing practices (e.g., validation studies, use of structured interviews, biodata, and mental ability tests) and measures of organizational performance over a 5-year period (annual profit, profit growth, sales growth, and overall performance).[94]

IIMPLICATIONS FOR MANAGEMENT PRACTICE

The research evidence is clear: valid selection procedures can produce substantial economic gains for organizations. The implication for policymakers also is clear:

- *Select* the highest-caliber managers and lower-level employees, for they are most likely to profit from development programs.

- Do not assume that a large investment in training can transform marginally competent performers into innovative, motivated top performers.

- A wide variety of screening and selection procedures is available. It is your responsibility to ask "tough" questions of staff specialists about the reliability, job-relatedness, and validity of each one proposed for use.

- Recognize that no one predictor is perfectly valid and therefore that some mistakes in selection (erroneous acceptances or erroneous rejections) are inevitable. By consciously selecting managers and lower-level employees based on their "fit" with demonstrated job requirements, the strategic direction of a business, and organizational culture, mistakes can be minimized and optimum choices can be made

SUMMARY

In staffing an organization or an organizational unit, it is important to consider its developmental stage—embryonic, high growth, mature, or aging—in order to align staffing decisions with business strategy. It also is important to communicate an organization's culture, since research shows that applicants will consider this information to choose among jobs if it is available to them. In order to use selection techniques meaningfully, however, it is necessary to specify the kinds of knowledge, skills, abilities, and other characteristics necessary for success.

Applicants may be screened through recommendations and reference checks, information on application forms, or employment interviews. In addition, some firms use written ability or integrity tests, work-sample tests, drug tests, polygraph examinations, or handwriting analysis. In each case, careful attention must be paid to the reliability and validity of the information obtained. *Reliability* refers to the consistency or stability of scores over time, across different samples of items, or across different raters or judges. *Validity* refers to the job-relatedness of a measure—that is, the strength of the relationship between scores from the measure and some indicator or rating of actual job performance.

In the context of managerial selection, numerous techniques are available, but the research literature indicates that the most effective ones have been mental ability tests, objective personality and interest inventories, peer assessments, personal history data, and situational tests. Projective techniques and leadership ability tests have been less effective. The use of situational tests, such as the leaderless group discussion, the in-basket, and the business game, lies at the heart of the assessment center method. Key advantages of the method are its high validity and fair evaluation of each candidate's ability and its flexibility of form and content. Other features include the use of multiple assessment techniques, assessor training, and pooled assessor judgments in rating candidate behavior.

Recent research indicates, at least for ability tests, that a test that accurately forecasts performance on a particular job in one situation will also forecast performance on the same job in other situations. Hence it may not be necessary to conduct a new validity study each time a predictor is used. Recent research has also demonstrated that the dollar benefits to an organization that uses valid selection procedures may be substantial. In choosing the right predictors for a given situation, careful attention must be paid to four factors: the nature of the job, the estimated validity of the predictor(s), the selection ratio, and the cost of the predictor(s). Doing so can pay handsome dividends to organizations and employees alike.

DISCUSSION QUESTIONS

7 ∎1 How can the accuracy of preemployment interviews be improved?

7 ∎2 Why are reliability and validity key considerations for all assessment methods?

7 ∎3 How does business strategy affect management selection?

7 ∎4 "At lower levels, managers do basically the same things regardless of functional specialty." Do you agree or disagree with this statement, and why?

7 ∎5 As jobs become more team-oriented, assessment centers will be used more often for non-management jobs. Do you agree or disagree?

TECHNICAL APPENDIX

The Estimation of Reliability

A quantitative estimate of the reliability of each measure used as a basis for employment decisions is important for two reasons: (1) if any measure is challenged legally, reliability estimates are important in establishing a defense, and (2) a measurement procedure cannot be any more valid (accurate) than it is reliable (consistent and stable). To estimate reliability, a *coefficient of correlation* (a measure of the degree of relationship between two variables) is computed between two sets of scores obtained independently. As an example, consider the sets of scores shown in Table 7-4.

In Table 7-4, two sets of scores were obtained from two forms of the same test. The resulting correlation coefficient is called a *parallel forms reliability estimate*. By the way, the correlation coefficient for the two sets of scores shown in Table 7-4 is .93, a very strong relationship. (The word "test" is used in the broad sense here to include any physical or psychological measurement instrument, technique, or procedure.) However, the scores in Table 7-4 could just as easily have been obtained from two administrations of the same test at two different times (*test-retest reliability*) or from independent ratings of the same test by two different scorers (*interrater reliability*).

■ TABLE 7 ■ 4

TWO SETS OF HYPOTHETICAL SCORES FOR THE SAME INDIVIDUALS ON FORM A AND FORM B OF A MATHEMATICAL APTITUTE TEST

Person no.	Form A	Form B
1	75	82
2	85	84
3	72	77
4	96	90
5	65	68
6	81	82
7	93	95
8	59	52
9	67	60
10	87	89

The coefficient of correlation between these sets of scores is .93. It is computed from the following formula:

$$r = \frac{\sum Z_x Z_y}{N}$$

where r = the correlation coefficient
$\sum$ = sum of
Z_x = the standard score on form A, where
$Z = x$, each person's raw score on form A, minus $\bar{x}$, the mean score on form A, divided by the standard deviation of form A scores.
Z_y = the standard score on form B
N = the number of persons in the sample (10 in this case)

Finally, in situations where it is not practical to use any of the preceding procedures and where a test can be administered only once, a procedure known as *split-half reliability* is used. With this procedure, a test is split statistically into two halves (e.g., odd items and even items) after it has been given, thus yielding two scores for each individual. In effect, therefore, two sets of scores (so-called parallel forms) from the same test are created for each individual. Scores on the two "half tests" are then correlated. However, since reliability increases as we sample larger and larger portions of a particular area of knowledge, skill, or ability, and since we have cut the length of the original test in half, the correlation between the two half tests *underestimates* the true reliability of the total test. Fortunately, formulas are available to correct such underestimates.

Validation Strategies

Although a number of procedures are available for evaluating evidence of validity, three of the best-known strategies are *construct-oriented*, *content-oriented*, and *criterion-related*. The three differ in terms of the conclusions and inferences that may be drawn, but they are interrelated logically and also in terms of the operations used to measure them.

Evaluation of *construct-oriented evidence of validity* begins by formulating hypotheses about the characteristics of those with high scores on a particular measurement procedure, in contrast to those with low scores. For example, we might hypothesize that sales managers will score significantly higher on the managerial interests scale of the California Psychological Inventory (CPI) than will pharmacy students (in fact, they do), and that they will also be more decisive and apt to take risks as well. The hypotheses form a tentative theory about the nature of the psychological construct, or trait, that the CPI is believed to be measuring. These hypotheses may then be used to predict how people at different score levels on the CPI will behave on other tests or in other situations during their careers. Construct validation is not accomplished in a single study. It requires that evidence be accumulated from different sources to determine the meaning of the test scores in terms of how people actually behave. It is a logical as well as an empirical process.

Content-oriented evidence of validity is also a judgmental, rational process. It requires an answer to the following question: *Is the content of the measurement procedure a fair, representative sample of the content of the job it is supposed to represent?* Such judgments can be made rather easily by job incumbents, supervisors, or other job experts when job knowledge or work-sample tests are used (e.g., typing tests and tests for electricians, plumbers, and computer programmers). However, content-oriented evidence becomes less appropriate as the behaviors in question become less observable and more abstract (e.g., the ability to draw conclusions from a written sample of material). In addition, since such judgments are not expressed in quantitative terms, it is difficult to justify *ranking* applicants in terms of predicted job performance, and it is difficult to estimate directly the dollar benefits to the firm from using such a procedure. To overcome these problems, we need a criterion-related validity strategy.

The term *criterion-related evidence of validity* calls attention to the fact that the chief concern is with the relationship between predictor [the selection procedure(s) used] and criterion (job performance) scores, not with predictor scores per se. Indeed, the content of the predictor measure is relatively unimportant, for it serves only as a vehicle to predict actual job performance.

There are two strategies of criterion-related validation: *concurrent* and *predictive*. A *concurrent strategy* is used to measure job incumbents. Job performance (criterion) measures for this group are already available; so immediately after a selection measure is administered to this group, a correlation coefficient between predictor scores and criterion scores (over all individuals in the group) can be computed. A procedure identical to that shown in Table 7-4 is used. If the selection measure is valid, those employees with the highest (or lowest) job performance scores should also score highest (or lowest) on the selection measure. In short, if the selection measure is valid, there should exist a systematic relationship between scores on that measure and job performance. The higher the test score, the better the job performance (and vice versa).

When a *predictive strategy* is used, the procedure is identical, except that job candidates are measured. Methods currently used to select employees are used, and the new selection procedure is simply added to the overall process. However, candidates are selected *without using* the results of the new procedure. At a later date (e.g., 6 months to a year), when a meaningful measure of job performance can be developed for each new hire, scores on the new selection procedure can be correlated with job performance scores. At that point, the strength of the predictor–criterion relationship can be assessed in terms of the size of the correlation coefficient.

ESTIMATING THE ECONOMIC BENEFITS OF SELECTION PROGRAMS

If we assume that n workers are hired during a given year and that the average job tenure of those workers is t years, the dollar increase in productivity can be determined from Equation 7-1. Admittedly, this is a "cookbook recipe," but the formula was derived more than 40 years ago and is well established in applied psychology:[95]

$$\Delta U = ntr_{xy} \, SD_y \, \overline{Z}_x \qquad (7\text{-}1)$$

where ΔU = increase in productivity in dollars

n = number of persons hired

t = average job tenure in years of those hired

r_{xy} = the validity coefficient representing the correlation between the predictor and job performance in the applicant population

SD_y = the standard deviation of job performance in dollars (roughly 40 percent of annual wage)[96]

$\overline{Z}_x$ = the average predictor score of those selected in the applicant population, expressed in terms of standard scores

When Equation 7-1 was used to estimate the dollar gains in productivity associated with use of the Programmer Aptitude Test (PAT) to select computer programmers for federal government jobs, given that an average of 618 programmers per year are selected, each with an average job tenure of 9.69 years, the payoff per selectee was $64,725 over his or her tenure on the job. This represents a per-year productivity gain of $6679 for each new programmer.[97] Clearly, the dollar gains in increased productivity associated with the use of valid selection procedures (the estimated true validity of the PAT is .76) are not trivial. Indeed, in a globally competitive environment, businesses need to take advantage of every possible strategy for improving productivity.

The widespread use of valid selection and promotion procedures should be a priority consideration in this effort.

Valid selection and promotion procedures also benefit applicants in several ways. One is that a more accurate matching of applicant knowledge, skills, ability, and other characteristics to job requirements helps enhance the likelihood of successful performance. This, in turn, helps workers feel better about their jobs and adjust to changes in them, as they are doing the kinds of things they do best. Moreover, since we know that there is a positive spillover effect between job satisfaction and life satisfaction, the accurate matching of people and jobs will also foster an improved quality of life, not just an improved quality of work life, for all concerned.

REFERENCES

1. Snow, C. C., & Snell, S. A. (1993). Staffing as strategy. In N. Schmitt & W. C. Borman (eds.), *Personnel selection in organizations*. San Francisco: Jossey-Bass, pp. 448–478. See also Smith, E. C. (1982). Strategic business planning and human resources: Part I. *Personnel Journal*, **61**, 606–610.
2. Schneider, B. (1990) (ed.). *Organizational climate and culture*. San Francisco: Jossey-Bass. See also Schneider, B. (1987). The people make the place. *Personnel Psychology*, **40**, 437–453.
3. Power, D. J., & Aldag, R. J. (1985). Soelberg's job search and choice model: A clarification, review, and critique. *Academy of Management Review*, **10**, 48–58.
4. Snow & Snell, op. cit.
5. Sheridan, J. E. (1992). Organizational culture and employee retention. *Academy of Management Journal*, **35**, 1036–1056.
6. Hunter, J. E., Schmidt, F. L., & Judiesch, M. K. (1990). Individual differences in output variability as a function of job complexity. *Journal of Applied Psychology*, **75**, 28–42.
7. Guion, R. M. (1991). Personnel assessment, selection, and placement. In M. D. Dunnette & L. M. Hough (eds.), *Handbook of industrial and organizational psychology*. San Francisco: Jossey-Bass, vol. 2, pp. 327–397.
8. Schmitt, N., & Landy, F. J. (1993). The concept of validity. In N. Schmitt & W. C. Borman (eds.), *Personnel selection in organizations*. San Francisco: Jossey-Bass, pp. 275–309.
9. *Principles for the validation and use of personnel selection procedures* (3d ed., 1987). College Park, MD: Society of Industrial-Organizational Psychology.
10. Uniform guidelines on employee selection procedures (1978). *Federal Register*, **43**, 38290–38315.
11. Alaska Airlines sets job application handling fee (1983, Jan. 19). *Aviation Daily*, p. 1.
12. Labor letter (1988, Oct. 18). *The Wall Street Journal*, p. 1. See also Labor letter (1986, May 13). *The Wall Street Journal*, p. 1.
13. Lowell, R. S., & DeLoach, J. A. (1982). Equal employment opportunity: Are you overlooking the application form? *Personnel*, **59**(4), 49–55. See also Miller, E. C. (1980). An EEO examination of employment applications. *Personnel Administrator*, **25**(3), 63–69, 81.
14. Klimoski, R. J. (1993). Predictor constructs and their measurement. In N. Schmitt & W. C. Borman (eds.), *Personnel selection in organizations*. San Francisco: Jossey-Bass, pp. 99–134. See also Hunter, J. E., & Hunter, R. F. (1984). Validity and utility of alternative predictors of job performance. *Psychological Bulletin*, **96**, 72–98.
15. Lawrence, D. G., Salsburg, B. L., Dawson, J. G., & Fasman, Z. D. (1982). Design and use of weighted application blanks. *Personnel Administrator*, **27**(3), 47–53, 101.
16. Knowlton, J. (1987, June 22). Smile for the camera: Job seekers make more use of video résumés. *The Wall Street Journal*, p. 29.
17. Labor letter (1987, June 30). *The Wall Street Journal*, p. 1.
18. McCormick, E. J., & Ilgen, D. R. (1985). *Industrial psychology* (8th ed.). Englewood Cliffs, NJ: Prentice-Hall.

19. Knouse, S. B. (1987). An attribution theory approach to the letter of recommendation. *International Journal of Management*, **4**(1), 5–13.

20. Munchus, G. (1992, June). Check references for safer selection. *HRMagazine*, pp. 75–77. See also LoPresto, R. L., Mitcham, D. E., & Ripley, D. E. (1986). *Reference checking handbook*. Alexandria, VA: American Society for Personnel Administration. See also Rice, J. D. (1978). Privacy legislation: Its effect on pre-employment reference checking. *Personnel Administrator*, **23**, 46–51.

21. Job references: Handle with care (1987, Mar. 9). *Business Week*, p. 124.

22. Rigdon, J. E. (1992, June 17). Deceptive résumés can be door openers but can become an employee's undoing. *The Wall Street Journal*, pp. B1; B7. See also LoPresto et al., op. cit.

23. Reliable references are getting difficult to find (1993, Feb. 23). *The Wall Street Journal*, p. A1.

24. Weiner, T. (1993, May 16). Firms tighten reference policies. *The Denver Post*, p. 5G. See also Reference preference: Employers button lips (1990, Jan. 4). *The Wall Street Journal*, p. B1. See also Revenge of the fired (1987, Feb. 16). *Newsweek*, pp. 46, 47.

25. Ryan, A. M., & Lasek, M. (1991). Negligent hiring and defamation: Areas of liability related to pre-employment inquiries. *Personnel Psychology*, **44**, 293–319.

26. More U.S. companies test employees for drug use. (1993, Feb. 2). *The Wall Street Journal*, p. B4.

27. Morgan, J. P. (1989, Aug. 20). Employee drug tests are unreliable and intrusive. *Hospitals*, p. 42. See also Bogdanich, W. (1987, Feb. 2). False negative: Medical labs, trusted as largely error-free, are far from infallible. *The Wall Street Journal*, pp. 1, 14.

28. Wessel, D. (1989, Sept. 7). Evidence is skimpy that drug testing works, but employers embrace practice. *The Wall Street Journal*, pp. B1, B8.

29. Limit drug tests in the workplace (1991, Nov. 20). *The Rocky Mountain News*, p. 50. See also Stone, D. L., & Kotch, D. A. (1989). Individuals' attitudes toward organizational drug testing policies and practices. *Journal of Applied Psychology*, **74**, 518–521.

30. Boyer, J., Director of Marketing and Sales, Performance Factors Inc. (1994, Feb. 10). Personal communication. See also Hamilton, J. O'C. (1991, June 3). A video game that tells if employees are fit for work *Business Week*, p. 36. See also Holstein, W. L. (1993, Nov. 28). Finding a better way to test for drugs. *The New York Times*.

31. Levy, L. (1979). Handwriting and hiring. *Dun's Review*, **113**, 72–79

32. Gorman, C. (1989, Jan. 23). Honestly, can we trust you? *Time*, p. 44. See also McCarthy, M. J. (1988, Aug. 25). Handwriting analysis as personnel tool. *The Wall Street Journal*, p. B1.

33. Rafaeli, A., & Klimoski, R. J. (1983). Predicting sales success through handwriting analysis: An evaluation of the effects of training and handwriting sample content. *Journal of Applied Psychology*, **68**, 212–217.

34. Ben-Shakhar, G., Bar-Hillel, M., Bilu, Y., Ben-Abba, E., & Flug, A. (1986). Can graphology predict occupational success? Two empirical studies and some methodological ruminations. *Journal of Applied Psychology*, **71**, 645–653.

35. Kleinmutz, B. (1985, July–August). Lie detectors fail the truth test. *Harvard Business Review*, **63**, 36–42. See also Patrick, C. J., & Iacono, W. G. (1989). Psychopathy, threat, and polygraph test accuracy. *Journal of Applied Psychology*, **74**, 347–355. See also Saxe, L., Dougherty, D., & Cross, T. (1985). The validity of polygraph testing. *American Psychologist*, **40**, 355-356.

36. Polygraph testing hit (1986, October). *Resource*, p. 13.

37. Gorman, op. cit.

38. Susser, P. A. (1986). Update on polygraphs and employment. *Personnel Administrator*, **31**(2), pp. 28, 32.

39. Jacobs, S. L. (1985, Mar. 11). Owners who ignore security make worker dishonesty easy. *The Wall Street Journal*, p. 25.

40. Conner, C. (1992, Dec. 5). Shoplifting, theft losses decline but U.S. retailers still vigilant. *The Denver Post*, p. 4.

41. Camara, W. J., & Schneider, D. L. (1994). Integrity tests: Facts and unresolved issues.

American Psychologist, **49**(2), 112–119. See also Sackett, P. R., Burris, L. R., & Callahan, C. (1989). Integrity testing for personnel selection: An update. *Personnel Psychology,* **42,** 491–529.

42. Ones, D. S., Viswesvaran, C., & Schmidt, F. L. (1993). Comprehensive meta-analysis of integrity test validities: Findings and implications for personnel selection and theories of job performance. *Journal of Applied Psychology* (monograph), **78,** 679–703.

43. Burke, M. J. (1993). Computerized psychological testing: Impacts on measuring predictor constructs and future job behavior. In N. Schmitt & W. C. Borman (eds.), *Personnel selection in organizations.* San Francisco: Jossey-Bass, pp. 203–239.

44. Ghiselli, E. E. (1973). The validity of aptitude tests in personnel selection. *Personnel Psychology,* **26,** 461–467. See also Klimoski, R., & Brickner, M. (1987). Why do assessment centers work? The puzzle of assessment center validity. *Personnel Psychology,* **40,** 243–260. See also Lord, R. G., DeVader, C. L., & Alliger, G. M. (1986). A meta-analysis of the relationship between personality traits and leadership perceptions: An application of validity generalization procedures. *Journal of Applied Psychology,* **71,** 402–410.

45. Grimsley, G., & Jarrett, H. F. (1975). The relation of past managerial achievement to test measures obtained in the employment situation: Methodology and results—II. *Personnel Psychology,* **28,** 215–231. See also Korman, A. K. (1968). The prediction of managerial performance: A review. *Personnel Psychology,* **21,** 295–322. See also Kraut, A. I. (1969). Intellectual ability and promotional success among high-level managers. *Personnel Psychology,* **22,** 281–290.

46. Schmidt, F. L. (1992). What do data really mean? *American Psychologist,* **47,** 1173–1181. See also Schmidt, F. L., Pearlman, K., Hunter, J. E., & Hirsch, H. R. (1985). Forty questions about validity generalization and meta-analysis. *Personnel Psychology,* **38,** 697–798.

47. Bentz, V. J. (1985). Executive selection at Sears: An update. In H. J. Bernardin & D. A. Bownas (eds.), (1985). *Personality assessment in organizations.* New York: Praeger, pp. 82–144.

48. Hogan, R. T. (1991). Personality and personality measurement. In M. D. Dunnette & L. M. Hough (eds.), *Handbook of industrial and organizational psychology.* San Francisco: Jossey-Bass, vol. 2, pp. 873–919. See also Barrick, M. R., & Mount, M. K. (1991). The big five personality dimensions and job performance: A meta-analysis. *Personnel Psychology,* **44,** 1–26. See also Hough, L. M., Eaton, N. K., Dunnette, M. D., Kamp, J. D., & McCloy, R. A. (1990). Criterion-related validities of personality constructs and the effect of response distortion on those validities. *Journal of Applied Psychology Monograph,* **75,** 581–595.

49. Tett, R. P., Jackson, D. N., & Rothstein, M. (1991). Personality measures as predictors of job performance: A meta-analytic review. *Personnel Psychology,* **44,** 703–742.

50. Kelly, G. A. (1958). The theory and technique of assessment. *Annual Review of Psychology,* **9,** 323–352.

51. Kinslinger, H. J. (1966). Application of projective techniques in personnel psychology since 1940. *Psychological Bulletin,* **66,** 134–150.

52. Hogan, op. cit.

53. Kerr, S., & Schriesheim, C. (1974). Consideration, initiating structure, and organizational criteria—an update of Korman's 1966 review. *Personnel Psychology,* **27,** 555–568. See also Schriesheim, C., House, R. A., & Kerr, S. (1976). Leader initiating structure: A reconciliation of discrepant research results and some empirical tests. *Organizational Behavior and Human Performance,* **15,** 297–321.

54. Kluger, A. N., Reilly, R. R., & Russell, C. J. (1991). Faking biodata tests: Are option-keyed instruments more resistant? *Journal of Applied Psychology,* **76,** 889–896.

55. Becker, T. E., & Colquitt, A. L. (1992). Potential versus actual faking of a biodata form: An analysis along several dimensions of item type. *Personnel Psychology,* **45,** 389–406.

56. Hough, L. M. (1984). Development and evaluation of the "accomplishment record" method of selecting and promoting professionals. *Journal of Applied Psychology,* **69,** 135–146.

57. Hough, L. M. (1985, Nov.). The accomplishment record method of selecting, promoting, and appraising professionals. Paper presented at the conference on *Selection Guidelines,*

Testing, and the EEOC: An Update. Berkeley: University of California, Institute for Industrial Relations.

58. Hakel, M. D. (1989). Merit-based selection: Measuring the person for the job. In W. F. Cascio (ed.), *Human resource planning, employment, and placement*. Washington, DC: Bureau of National Affairs, pp. 2-135 to 2-158.

59. See, for example, Dipboye, R. L., & Gaugler, B. B. (1993). Cognitive and behavioral processes in the selection interview. In N. Schmitt & W. C. Borman (eds.), *Personnel selection in organizations*. San Francisco: Jossey-Bass, pp. 135–170.

60. Arvey, R. D., Miller, H. E., Gould, R., & Burch, P. (1987). Interview validity for selecting sales clerks. *Personnel Psychology*, **40**, 1–12. See also Campion, M. A., Pursell, E. D., & Brown, B. K. (1988). Structured interviewing: Raising the psychometric properties of the employment interview. *Personnel Psychology*, **41**, 25–42. See also Harris, M. M. (1989). Reconsidering the employment interview: A review of recent literature and suggestions for future research. *Personnel Psychology*, **42**, 691–726.

61. Dipboye & Gaugler, op. cit. See also Phillips, A. P., & Dipboye, R. L. (1989). Correlational tests of a prediction from a process model of the interview. *Journal of Applied Psychology*, **74**, 41–52.

62. Campion, et al., op. cit.

63. Dipboye & Gaugler, op. cit. See also Weekley, J. A., & Gier, J. A. (1987). Reliability and validity of the situational interview for a sales position. *Journal of Applied Psychology*, **72**,

64. Motowidlo, S. J., Carter, G. W., Dunnette, M. D., Tippins, N., Werner, S., Burnett, J. R., & Vaughan, M. J. (1992). Studies of the structured behavioral interview. *Journal of Applied Psychology*, **77**, 571–587.

65. Schmitt, N., Gooding, R. Z., Noe, R. A., & Kirsch, M. (1984). Meta-analysis of validity studies published between 1964 and 1982 and the investigation of study characteristics. *Personnel Psychology*, **37**, 407–422.

66. Shore, T. H., Shore, L. M., & Thornton, G. C., III. (1992). Construct validity of self- and peer evaluations of performance dimensions in an assessment center. *Journal of Applied Psychology*, **77**, 42–54.

67. Asher, J. J., & Sciarrino, J. A. (1974). Realistic work sample tests: A review. *Personnel Psychology*, **27**, 519–533.

68. Cascio, W. F., & Phillips, N. (1979). Performance testing: A rose among thorns? *Personnel Psychology*, **32**, 751–766.

69. Wollowick, H. B., & McNamara, W. J. (1969). Relationship of the components of an assessment center to management success. *Journal of Applied Psychology*, **53**, 348–352.

70. Bass, B. M. (1954). The leaderless group discussion. *Psychological Bulletin*, **51**, 465–492. See also Tziner, A., & Dolan, S. (1982). Validity of an assessment center for identifying future female officers in the military. *Journal of Applied Psychology*, **67**, 728–736.

71. Kurecka, P. M., Austin, J. M., Jr., Johnson, W., & Mendoza, J. L. (1982). Full and errant coaching effects on assigned role leaderless group discussion performance. *Personnel Psychology*, **35**, 805–812. See also Petty, M. M. (1974). A multivariate analysis of the effects of experience and training upon performance in a leaderless group discussion. *Personnel Psychology*, **27**, 271–282

72. Fredericksen, N. (1962). Factors in in-basket performance. *Psychological Monographs*, **76** (22, whole no. 541), p. 1.

73. See for example, Brass, G. J., & Oldham, G. R. (1976). Validating an in-basket test using an alternative set of leadership scoring dimensions. *Journal of Applied Psychology*, **61**, 652–657. See also Tziner, op. cit.

74. Goldstein, I. L. (1993). *Training in organizations: Needs assessment, development, and evaluation* (3d ed.). Monterey, CA: Brooks/Cole.

75. Wollowick & McNamara, op. cit.

76. Wexley, K. N., & Latham, G. P. (1991). *Developing and training human resources in organizations* (2d ed.). Glenview, IL: Scott, Foresman.

77. McKinnon, D. W. (1975). Assessment centers then and now. *Assessment and Development*,

2, 8–9. See also Office of Strategic Services (OSS) Assessment Staff (1948). *Assessment of men.* New York: Rinehart.

78. Bray, D. W. (1976). The assessment center method. In R. L. Craig (ed.), *Training and development handbook* (2d ed.): McGraw-Hill, pp. 16-1 to 16-15.

79. Borman, W. C. (1982). Validity of behavioral assessment for predicting military recruiter performance. *Journal of Applied Psychology,* **67,** 3–9. See also Pulakos, E. D., Borman, W. C., & Hough, L. M. (1988). Test validation for scientific understanding: Two demonstrations of an approach to studying predictor-criterion linkages. *Personnel Psychology,* **41,** 703–716.

80. Lorenzo, R. V. (1984). Effects of assessorship on managers' proficiency in acquiring, evaluating, and communicating information about people. *Personnel Psychology,* **37,** 617–634.

81. Byham, W. C. (1970). Assessment centers for spotting future managers. *Harvard Business Review,* **48,** 150–160.

82. Gaugler, B. B., Rosenthal, D. B., Thornton, G. C., III, & Bentson, C. (1987). Meta-analysis of assessment center validity. *Journal of Applied Psychology,* **72,** 493–511.

83. Ibid. See also Howard, A. (1974). An assessment of assessment centers. *Academy of Management Journal,* **17,** 115–134. See also Klimoski & Brickner, op. cit.

84. Thornton, G. C., III, & Byham, W. C. (1982). *Assessment centers and managerial performance.* New York: Academic Press. See also Huck, J. R., & Bray, D. W. (1976). Management assessment center evaluations and subsequent job performance of white and black females. *Personnel Psychology,* **29,** 13–30.

85. Cascio, W. F., & Ramos, R. A. (1986). Development and application of a new method for assessing job performance in behavioral/economic terms. *Journal of Applied Psychology,* **71,** 20–28. See also Cascio, W. F., & Silbey, V. (1979). Utility of the assessment center as a selection device. *Journal of Applied Psychology,* **64,** 107–118.

86. Klimoski, op. cit. See also Gaugler, B. B., & Thornton, G. C., III (1989). Number of assessment center dimensions as a determinant of assessor accuracy. *Journal of Applied Psychology,* **74,** 611–618. See also Reilly, R. R., Henry, S., & Smither, J. W. (1990). An examination of the effects of using behavior checklists on the construct validity of assessment center dimensions. *Journal of Applied Psychology,* **43,** 71–84.

87. Hinrichs, J. R. (1969). Comparison of "real life" assessments of management potential with situational exercises, paper-and-pencil ability tests, and personality inventories. *Journal of Applied Psychology,* **53,** 425–433.

88. Hinrichs, J. R. (1978). An eight-year follow-up of a management assessment center. *Journal of Applied Psychology,* **63,** 596–601.

89. Ibid.

90. Koenig, R. (1987, Dec. 1). Exacting employer: Toyota takes pains, and time, filling jobs at its Kentucky plant. *The Wall Street Journal,* p. 1, 31.

91. Cascio & Ramos, op. cit.

92. Miller, M. W. (1993, Aug. 2). Fate seemed to have a Gerstner in mind for top job at IBM. *The Wall Street Journal,* pp. A1; A13.

93. Boudreau, J. W. (1991). Utility analysis for decisions in human resource management. In M. D. Dunnette & L. M. Hough (eds.), *Handbook of industrial and organizational psychology.* San Francisco: Jossey-Bass, vol. 2, pp. 621–745.

94. Terpstra, D. E., & Rozell, E. J. (1993). The relationship of staffing practices to organizational-level measures of performance. *Personnel Psychology,* **46,** 27–48.

95. Cascio, W. F. (1991). *Costing human resources: The financial impact of behavior in organizations* (3d ed.). Boston: PWS-Kent. See also Boudreau, op. cit.

96. Hunter, J. E., & Schmidt, F. L. (1983). Quantifying the effects of psychological interventions on employee job performance and workforce productivity. *American Psychologist,* **38,** 473–478.

97. Schmidt, F. L., Hunter, J. E., McKenzie, R., & Muldrow, T. (1979). The impact of valid selection procedures on workforce productivity. *Journal of Applied Psychology,* **64,** 609–626.

PART THREE

DEVELOPMENT

A CONCEPTUAL VIEW OF
HUMAN RESOURCE MANAGEMENT

STRATEGIC OBJECTIVES, ENVIRONMENTS, FUNCTIONS

PARTS ONE – SIX · STRATEGIC OBJECTIVES · CHAPTERS 1 – 18

Productivity

Quality of Work Life

Profits

PART ONE · ENVIRON-MENTS · CHAPTERS 1 – 4

Competitive

Legal

Social

Organizational

PARTS TWO – SIX · FUNCTIONS · CHAPTERS 5 – 18

Employment

Development

Compensation

Labor-Management Accommodation

Support, Evaluation, International Implications

RELATIONSHIP OF HRM FUNCTIONS TO HRM ACTIVITIES

FUNCTIONS	ACTIVITIES
Part Two **Employment**	Job Analysis, Human Resource Planning, Recruiting, Staffing (Chapters 5 - 7)
Part Three **Development**	**Orienting,** **Training,** **Performance Appraisal,** **Managing Careers** **(Chapters 8 – 10)**
Part Four **Compensation**	Pay, Benefits, Incentives (Chapters 11 - 13)
Part Five **Labor-Management** **Accommodation**	Union Representation, Collective Bargaining, Procedural Justice, Ethics (Chapters 14, 15)
Part Six **Support,** **Evaluation,** **International** **Implications**	Job Safety and Health, Costs/Benefits of HRM Activities, International Dimensions of HRM (Chapters 16 - 18)

PART THREE

DEVELOPMENT

Once employees are "on board," their personal growth and development over time become a major concern. Change is a fact of organizational life, and to cope with it effectively, planned programs of employee orientation, development, and career management are essential. These issues are addressed in Chapters 8 through 10. Chapter 8 examines what is known about orienting and training management and nonmanagement employees. Chapter 9 is concerned with performance appraisal—particularly with the design, implementation, and evaluation of appraisal systems. Finally, Chapter 10 considers the many issues involved in managing careers—from the perspective of individuals at different career stages and from the perspective of organizational staffing decisions. The overall objective of Part Three is to establish a framework for managing the development process of employees as their careers in organizations unfold.

CHAPTER 8

ORIENTING AND TRAINING

THE NEW EDUCATORS: COMPANY-BASED SCHOOLS*

The news hit the floor of the Collins & Aikman Carpet plant in Dalton, Georgia, with a thud: the massive tufting machines and shearing equipment that lined the factory floor were being hooked up to computers. More than a third of the 560 workers at the plant were high school dropouts; a few couldn't read or write. The prospect of working with a computer was terrifying. Said a plant serviceman who depended on a pocket calculator to tally the weights of various yarns: "I was scared to death."

So are companies across the United States that are trying to join the race for global markets. They are discovering that many of their employees, as well as students fresh from the nation's schools, can't meet the demands of high-tech jobs. The consequences are not pleasant: declining productivity, an inability to generate new business, and a possible loss of existing business. Some firms have opted for cheap labor instead of advanced technology, moving across the border to Mexico or overseas to Taiwan.

But a growing number of businesses, including Collins & Aikman, are taking another tack: trying to do educational makeovers of their own workforces. Unable to wait for public schools or vocational schools to catch up with their corporate needs, these employers are taking on the role of educators. They are pouring millions of dollars and thousands of hours into high school equivalency courses and basic skill training. Much of it is being taught inside company walls on company time.

As recently as the early 1980s, education was hardly a priority at the carpet plants in the area. For decades, a strong back and nimble hands were enough. HR officers simply

---

*Adapted from H. Cooper, The new educators, *The Wall Street Journal*, Oct. 5, 1992, pp. A1, A6. Reprinted by permission of *The Wall Street Journal*, © 1992 Dow Jones & Company. All rights reserved.

smiled to themselves when applicants who were asked to fill out forms suddenly would say, "Can I take this home? I forgot my glasses." Then, because they actually were unable to read or write, they'd get someone else to fill out the forms for them.

By 1989, however, the smiles were disappearing fast. The company was buying more sophisticated equipment designed to meet the needs of a changing business. In addition to wanting more types of carpets and more colors in shorter periods of time, customers were demanding floor coverings, with, say, their company logos woven into the fabric. Collins & Aikman installed new tufting machines that can weave elaborate patterns, new automated shearers that work 80 times faster than their predecessors, and new yarn machines that spin out precisely the amount of material needed for each run—all controlled by computer keyboards and all thoroughly intimidating to many workers.

Meanwhile, management had done a study of educational backgrounds and found that fully one-third of the staff hadn't graduated from high school and only 8 percent of the laborers had the skills the company expected to need in the twenty-first century. These include the ability to analyze machine performance and to make on-the-spot production decisions, tasks that currently are performed by plant supervisors.

So a year ago the company hired an adult education teacher and set up classes on the plant floor. Eighty workers signed up. For 2 hours a day, 2 days a week, on each of three shifts, the new teacher taught reading, writing, science, social studies, and math. The company spent an average of $1200 for each worker's training, including lost work time. The employees themselves often found the task daunting. After a full day's work, they had to spend hours in the evening on homework. Was the effort worth it?

Challenges

1. What are the key distinguishing features of this approach to training?
2. How can the company determine whether or not its training is effective?
3. What obstacles to the success of a such a program can you identify?

Questions This Chapter Will Help Managers Answer

1. Why should we invest time and money on new employee orientation? Is there a payoff?
2. How should new-employee orientation be managed for maximum positive impact?
3. Why should firms expect to expand their training outlays and their menu of choices for employees at all levels?
4. What kind of evidence is necessary to justify investments in training programs?
5. What are the key issues that should be addressed in the design, conduct, and evaluation of training programs?

Change, growth, and sometimes displacement are facts of modern organizational life. The stock market crash of October 19, 1987, vividly illustrated this fact. In the wave of layoffs following the crash, more than 18,000 professionals in the financial services industry lost their jobs. As they found new jobs, they discovered what all new employees do: one has to "relearn the ropes" in the new job setting. Orientation, the subject of the first part of this chapter, can ease that process considerably, with positive results both for the new employee and for the company. Trends such as leased employees, disposable managers, and free-agent workers will make orientation even more important in the future. Like orientation, training helps deal with change—technological and social.

Traditionally, lower-level employees were "trained," while higher-level employees were "developed." This distinction, focusing on the learning of hands-on skills versus interpersonal and decision-making skills, has in practice become too blurry to be useful. Throughout the remainder of this chapter, therefore, the terms *training* and *development* will be used interchangeably. In the United States, as in many other countries, training is big business, and the second half of this chapter examines some current issues in the design, conduct, and evaluation of training programs.

NEW EMPLOYEE ORIENTATION: AN OVERVIEW

One definition of *orientation* is "familiarization with and adaptation to a situation or an environment." Eight out of every 10 organizations in the United States that have more than 50 employees provide orientation.[1] However, the time and effort devoted to its design, conduct, and evaluation are woefully inadequate. In practice, orientation is often just a superficial indoctrination into company philosophy, policies, and rules; sometimes it includes the presentation of an employee handbook and a quick tour of the office or plant. This can be a very costly mistake. Here is why.

In one way, a displaced worker from the factory who is hired into another environment is similar to a new college graduate. Upon starting a new job, both will face a kind of "culture shock." As they are exposed for the first time to a new organizational culture, both find that the new job is not quite what they imagined it to be. In fact, coming to work at a new company is not unlike visiting a foreign country. Either you are told about the local customs, or else you learn them on your own by a process of trial and error. An effective orientation program can help lessen the impact of this shock. But there must be more, such as a period of "socialization," or learning to function as a contributing member of the corporate "family."

The cost of hiring, training, and orienting a new person is far higher than most of us realize. For example, Merck & Co., the pharmaceutical giant, found that, depending on the job, turnover costs 1.5 to 2.5 times the annual salary paid for the job.[2] As another example, consider that in 1986 the U.S. Navy estimated that it would lose 550 fighter pilots as a result of attrition. Assuming each one is replaced, at a cost of $1 million to train one new fighter pilot, that adds up to an annual training cost of more than half a billion dollars![3]

Moreover, since the turnover rate among new college hires can be as great as 50 percent during the first 12 months, such costs can be quite painful. In the case of stockbroker trainees, it takes approximately 2 years for the average broker trainee to become fully productive.[4] Yet during this period, depending on the level of wage and how it is determined, the trainee may be drawing 100 percent of his or her wage before the organization can recoup its investment.

A new employee's experiences during the initial period with an organization can have a major impact on his or her career. A new hire stands on the "boundary" of the organization—certainly no longer an outsider but not yet embraced by those within. There is great stress. The new hire wants to reduce this stress by becoming incorporated into the "interior" as quickly as possible. Consequently, during this period an employee is more receptive to cues from the organizational environment than she or he is ever likely to be again. Such cues to proper behavior may come from a variety of sources; for example:

- Official literature of the organization
- Examples set by senior people
- Formal instructions given by senior people
- Examples given by peers
- Rewards and punishments that flow from the employee's efforts
- Responses to the employee's ideas
- Degree of challenge in the assignments the employee receives

Special problems may arise for a new employee whose young life has been spent mainly in an educational setting. As she approaches her first job, the recent graduate may feel motivated entirely by personal creativity. She is information-rich but experience-poor, eager to apply her knowledge to new processes and problems. Unfortunately, there are conditions that may stifle this creative urge. During her undergraduate days, the new employee exercised direct control over her work. But now she faces regular hours, greater restrictions, possibly a less pleasant environment, and a need to work *through* other people—often finding that most of the work is mundane and unchallenging. In short, three typical problems face the new employee:

1. *Problems in entering a group.* The new employee asks herself whether she will (a) be acceptable to the other group members, (b) be liked, and (c) be safe—that is, free from physical and psychological harm. These issues must be resolved before she can feel comfortable and productive in the new situation.

2. *Naive expectations.* Organizations find it much easier to communicate factual information about pay and benefits, vacations, and company policies than information about employee norms (rules or guides to acceptable behavior), company attitudes, or "what it really takes to get ahead around here." Simple fairness suggests that employees ought to be told about these intangibles. The bonus is that being up front and honest with job candidates produces positive results. As we saw in Chapter 6, the research on realistic job previews (RJPs) indicates that job acceptance rates will likely be lower for those who receive an RJP, but job survival rates will be higher.

3. *First-job environment.* Does the new environment help or hinder the new employee trying to climb aboard? Can peers be counted on to socialize the new employee to desired job standards? How and why was the first job assignment chosen? Is it clear to the new employee what she or he can expect to get out of it?

The first year with an organization is the critical period during which an employee will or will not learn to become a high performer. The careful matching of company and employee expectations during this period can result in positive job attitudes and high standards, which then can be reinforced in new and more demanding jobs.

PLANNING, PACKAGING, AND EVALUATING AN ORIENTATION PROGRAM[5]

New employees need specific information in three major areas:
- Company standards, expectations, norms, traditions, and policies

- Social behavior, such as approved conduct, the work climate, and getting to know fellow workers and supervisors
- Technical aspects of the job

Keep in mind that the most common reasons for firing new hires are absenteeism and failure to adapt to the work environment. Fewer than 10 percent of employees are dismissed because of difficulties in learning how to perform their jobs.[6] These results suggest two levels of orientation: company and departmental. There will be some matters of general interest and importance to all new employees, regardless of department, and there will also be matters relevant only to each department. The HR department should have overall responsibility for program planning and follow-up (subject to top-management review and approval), but the specific responsibilities of the HR department and the immediate supervisor should be made very clear to avoid duplication or omission of important information.

Approaches to orientation that should be avoided are:[7]

- *An emphasis on paperwork.* After completing forms required by the HR department, the new employee is given a cursory welcome. Then the employee is directed to his or her immediate supervisor. The likely result: The employee does not feel like part of the company.
- *A sketchy overview of the basics.* A quick, superficial orientation, and the new employee is immediately put to work—sink or swim.
- *Mickey Mouse assignments.* The new employee's first tasks are insignificant duties, supposedly intended to teach the job "from the ground up."
- *Suffocation.* Giving too much information too fast is a well-intentioned but disastrous approach, causing the new employee to feel overwhelmed and "suffocated."

We know from other companies' mistakes what works and what does not. For example, at the outset of orientation, each new employee should be given an information kit or packet prepared by the HR department to supplement the verbal and/or audiovisual orientation. Such a kit might include the materials and information shown in Table 8-1.

At the outset of a group orientation session, one or more representatives of top management should talk about company philosophy and expectations—describing exactly what employees can expect from management and vice versa. These statements can also be reinforced and made official policy when included in a prominent place in the employee handbook or orientation kit. Following this, HR department representatives should discuss issues that are of general importance to all departments. These issues might include an overview of the company (its history, traditions, and products and services), a review of key policies and procedures, a summary of employee benefits, an outline of safety and accident-prevention procedures, a discussion of employee–management and union–management relations, and a description of the physical facilities.

Obviously not all these topics will apply in every situation in every organization. The list should be tailored to fit the particular needs of the firm—be it a hospital, a manufacturing facility, a bank, or a service organization. The departmental or job orientation provided by supervisors will likely be even more variable, for it must describe the organization of the department, how it interfaces with other departments, depart-

■ TABLE 8 ▪ 1
SAMPLE ITEMS TO BE INCLUDED IN AN EMPLOYEE ORIENTATION KIT

A current company organization chart
Map of the facility
Key terms unique to the industry, company, and/or job
Copy of company policy handbook
Copy of union contract (if appropriate)
Copy of specific job goals and descriptions
List of company holidays
List of benefits
Copies of performance appraisal forms, dates, and procedures
Copies of other required forms (e.g., supply requisition and expense reimbursement)
List of on-the-job training opportunities
Sources of information
Detailed outline of emergency and accident-prevention procedures
Sample copy of each important company publication
Telephone numbers and locations of key people and operations
Copies of insurance plans

Source: W. D. St. John, The complete employee orientation program, *Personnel Journal,* May 1980, p. 375.

mental policies and procedures, job duties, standards of performance, and responsibilities. It must also include a tour of the department and introduce new employees to their coworkers.

Orientation Follow-up

The worst mistake a company can make is to ignore the new employee after orientation. Almost as bad is an informal open-door policy: "Come see me sometime if you have any questions." Many new employees are simply not assertive enough to seek out the supervisor or HR representative—more than likely, they fear looking "dumb." What is needed is formal and systematic orientation follow-up: for example, by the immediate supervisor after the new employee has been on the job 1 day and again after 1 week, and by the HR representative after the new employee has been on the job 1 month. Many of the topics covered during orientation will need to be explained briefly again, once the employee has had the opportunity to experience them firsthand. This is natural and understandable in view of the blizzard of information that needs to be communicated during orientation. In completing the orientation follow-up, a checklist of items covered should be reviewed with each new employee or small group of employees to ensure that all items were in fact covered. The completed checklist should then be signed by the supervisor, the HR representative, and the new employee.

Evaluation of the Orientation Program

At least once a year, the orientation program should be reviewed to determine if it is meeting its objectives and to suggest future improvements. To improve orientation, candid, comprehensive feedback is needed from everyone involved in the program. This feedback can be provided in several ways: through roundtable discussions with new employees after their first year on the job, through in-depth interviews with randomly selected employees and supervisors, and through questionnaires for mass coverage of all recent hires. Now let's consider one company's approach to the overall orientation process.[8]

NEW-EMPLOYEE ORIENTATION AT CORNING, INC.

In the early 1980s, Corning faced a problem similar to that found in many other firms: new people were getting the red-carpet treatment while being recruited, but once they started work, it was often a different story—a letdown. Often their first day on the job was disorganized and confusing, and sometimes this continued for weeks. One new employee said, "You're planting the seeds of turnover right at the beginning."

It became clear to managers at Corning that a better way was needed to help new employees make the transition to their new company and community. Corning needed a better way to help these new people get off on the right foot—to learn the how-tos, the wheres, and the whys, and to learn about the company's culture and its philosophies. And the company had to ensure the same support for newly hired secretaries in a district office, sales representatives working out of their homes, or engineers in a plant.

THE CORNING ORIENTATION SYSTEM AND HOW IT WORKS

Three features distinguish the Corning approach from others:

1. It is an orientation *process*, not a program.
2. It is based on guided self-learning. New people have responsibility for their own learning.
3. It is long-term (15 to 18 months), and it is in depth.

The new person learns with help and information from:

- The immediate supervisor, who has guidelines and checklists
- Colleagues, whom the new person interviews before starting regular assignments
- Attendance at nine 2-hour seminars at intervals during the first 6 months
- Answers to questions in a workbook for new employees

Figure 8-1 provides an overview of how the system works.

OBJECTIVES OF THE PROGRAM

Corning set four objectives, each aimed at improving productivity. The first was to reduce voluntary turnover in the first 3 years of employment by 17 percent. The second was to shorten by 17 percent the time it takes a new person to learn the job. The third was to foster a uniform understanding among employees about the company: its objectives, its principles, its strategies, and what the company expects of its people. The fourth was to build a positive attitude toward the company and its surrounding communities.

MEASURING RESULTS

After 2 years, voluntary turnover among new hires was reduced by 69 percent—far greater than the 17 percent expected after 3 years. Corning also anticipates a major payback on its investment in the orientation system: an 8:1 benefit/cost ratio in the first year and a 14:1 ratio annually thereafter. These computations are shown in Figure 8-2.

Material distribution. As soon as possible after a hiring decision is made, orientation material is distributed:

- The new person's supervisor gets a pamphlet entitled *A Guide for Supervisors.*
- The new person gets an orientation plan.

The prearrival period. During this period the supervisor maintains contact with the new person, helps with housing problems, designs the job, makes a preliminary MBO (management by objectives) list after discussing this with the new person, gets the office ready, notifies the organization that this has been done, and sets the interview schedule.

The 1st day. On this important day, new employees have breakfast with their supervisors, go through processing in the personnel department, attend a *Corning and You* seminar, have lunch with the seminar leader, read the workbook for new employees, are given a tour of the building, and are introduced to coworkers.

The 1st week. During this week, the new employee (1) has one-to-one interviews with the supervisors, coworkers, and specialists; (2) learns the how-tos, wheres, and whys connected with the job: (3) answers questions in the workbook; (4) gets settled in the community; and (5) participates with the supervisor in firming up the MBO plan.

The 2nd week. The new person begins regular assignments.

The 3rd and 4th weeks. The new person attends a community seminar and an employee benefits seminar (a spouse or guest may be invited).

The 2nd through 5th months. During this period, assignments are intensified and new people have biweekly progress reviews with their supervisors, attend six two-hour seminars at intervals (on quality and productivity, technology, performance management and salaried compensation plans, financial and strategic managment, employee relations and EEO, and social change), answer workbook questions about each seminar, and review answers with their supervisor.

The 6th month. The new employee completes the workbook questions, reviews the MBO list with the supervisor, participates in a performance review with the supervisor, receives a certification of completion for Phase I orientation, and makes plans for Phase II orientation.

The 7th through 15th months. This period features Phase II orientation: division orientation, function orientation, education programs, MBO reviews, performance reviews, and salary reviews.

FIGURE 8-1
Timetable of events in the Corning, Inc., orientation system.

LESSONS LEARNED

As a result of the 2 years it took to develop the system and Corning's 2 years of experience with it, the company offers the following considerations to guide the process of orienting new employees. They apply to any type of organization, large or small, and to any function or level of job:[9]

1. The impressions formed by new employees within their first 60 to 90 days on a job are lasting.

2. Day 1 is crucial—new employees remember it for years. It must be managed well.

3. New employees are interested in learning about the total organization—and how they and their unit fit into the "big picture." This is just as important as is specific information about the new employee's own job and department.

4. Give new employees major responsibility for their own orientation, through guided self-learning, but with direction and support.

5. Avoid information overload—provide it in reasonable amounts.

6. Recognize that community, social, and family adjustment is a critical aspect of orientation for new employees.

7. Make the immediate supervisor ultimately responsible for the success of the orientation process.

8. Thorough orientation is a "must" for productivity improvement. It is a vital part of the total

244

A. Benefit Estimate:

A 17 percent decrease in the number of voluntary separations among those with 3 years or less of service:	$ 852M
A decrease in the time required to learn the job — from 6 months to 5 months:	489M
	TOTAL $1,341M

B. Cost Estimate:

	First Year Only	Ongoing Annual
Materials and salaries of developers, instructors, administrators	$171M	$95M

C. Benefit/Cost Ratio:

First year: $1,341M : 171M = 8 : 1
Ongoing annual: $1,341M : 95M = 14 : 1

The following formula was used to estimate productivity gains per year.

Improved Retention Rate:

Number of voluntary separations (3 or fewer years' service) X 17% expected decrease with orientation X $30M investment in new hire = Annual productivity gain

Shorten Learning Curve from 6 Months to 5 Months:

1 month average base salary x 65% X Number of new hires per year = Annual productivity gain

FIGURE 8-2
Calculation of benefits and costs in the Corning, Inc., orientation program. Note: The term M denotes thousands.

management system—and therefore the foundation of any effort to improve employee productivity.

In summary, the results of Corning's research are exciting and provocative. They suggest that we should be at least as concerned with preparing the new employee for the social context of his or her job and for coping with the insecurities and frustrations of a new learning situation as with the development of the technical skills necessary for job performance. The question of how best to teach those technical skills is also critically important. The design, conduct, and evaluation of employee training programs are strategic issues that simply cannot be ignored.

EMPLOYEE TRAINING

What Is Training?

Training consists of planned programs designed to improve performance at the individual, group, and/or organizational levels. Improved performance, in turn, implies that there have been measurable changes in knowledge, skills, attitudes, and/or social behavior.

When we examine the training enterprise as a whole, it is clear that training issues can be addressed from at least two perspectives. At the structural level, one can examine issues such as the following, among others: the aggregate level of expenditures by the various providers of training (e.g., federal, state, and local governments, educational institutions, private-sector businesses), the degree of cooperation among the providers, incentives (or lack of incentives) for providing training, who gets training, and the economic impact of training. These are macrolevel concerns.

At the micro level, one may choose to examine issues such as the following: what types of training seem to yield positive outcomes for organizations and trainees (i.e., what "works"); how to identify *if* training is needed and, if so, what type of training best fits the needs that have been identified; how to structure the delivery of training programs; and how to evaluate the outcomes of training efforts.

Unfortunately, too much emphasis is often placed on the techniques and methods of training to be used and not enough on first defining what the employee should learn in relation to desired job behaviors. Furthermore, very few organizations place much emphasis on assessing the outcomes of training activities. That is, they overlook the need to determine whether the training objectives were met.

In the remainder of this chapter, we will do two things: (1) discuss several structural issues at the macro level and (2) illustrate research-based findings that might lead to improvements in the design, delivery, and evaluation of training systems. Before we do so, however, let's consider some important training trends.

Training Trends

Both economic and demographic trends suggest radical changes in the composition of the workforce of the 1990s.[10] Other factors that affect the number, types, and requirements of available jobs include automation; continuing worker displacement as a function of mergers, acquisitions, and downsizing; and the shift from manufacturing to service jobs.[11] In late 1993, for example, 84 percent of U.S. employees worked in service-based industries.[12]

These issues suggest five reasons why the time and money budgeted for training will increase during the next decade:[13]

1. The number of unskilled and undereducated youth who will be needed for entry-level jobs

2. Increasingly sophisticated technological systems that will impose training and retraining requirements on the existing workforce

3. The need to train currently underutilized groups of racial and ethnic minorities, women, and older workers

4. The need, as more firms move to employee involvement and teams in the workplace, for team members to learn behaviors such as asking for ideas, offering help without being asked, listening and feedback skills, and recognizing and considering the ideas of others[14]

5. Training needs stimulated by the internationally competitive environments of many organizations

Labor Secretary Robert Reich described the challenge clearly: "If we have an adequately educated and trained workforce and a state-of-the-art infrastructure linking them together and with the rest of the world, then global capital will come here to create good jobs. If we don't, the only way global capital will be invested here is if we promise low wages."[15]

These changes suggest a dual responsibility: the organization is responsible for providing an atmosphere that will support and encourage change, and the individual is responsible for deriving maximum benefit from the learning opportunities provided.

Indeed, as the demands of the second industrial revolution spread, companies are coming to regard training expenses as no less a part of their capital costs than plants and equipment. Total training outlays by U.S. firms are now $30 billion per year— and rising.[16] At the individual-firm level, Motorola is exemplary. It budgets about 1 percent of annual sales (2.6 percent of payroll) for training. It even trains workers for its key suppliers, many of them small- to medium-size firms without the resources to train their own people in such advanced specialties as computer-aided design and defect control. Taking into account training expenses, wages, and benefits, the total cost to Motorola amounts to about $90 million. The results have been dramatic, according to a company spokesperson: "We've documented the savings from the statistical process control methods and problem-solving methods we've trained our people in. We're running a rate of return of about 30 times the dollars invested—which is why we've gotten pretty good support from senior management."[17]

Retraining, too, can pay off. A study by the Work in America Institute found that retraining current workers for new jobs is more cost-effective than firing them and hiring new ones—not to mention the difference that retraining makes to employee morale.[18] And in "downsizing" industries where there are no alternatives to furloughs, unions are working with management to retrain displaced workers. Yet there are serious potential difficulties with retraining efforts, such as jobs not being available for newly retrained workers.[19] Here's another problem.

POTENTIAL PITFALLS IN WORKER RETRAINING

COMPANY
EXAMPLE

For years, conventional wisdom has held that the best way to help workers who lose their jobs when industry shrinks is to teach them to do something else. But in many cases retraining is more talked about than done. A critical problem, one that is almost uniquely American, is the way employers juggle their labor forces, laying people off when business dips and calling them back when it rises again. This practice has been going on for decades in some industries, especially automobile manufacturing and defense contracting.

Workforce juggling occurs most often in communities where a single employer dominates an economy and pays the highest wages. Consider Whirlpool Corporation, the biggest and highest-paying employer in Fort Smith, Arkansas. In 1988, the company employed 5400 people in Fort Smith. But with a series of big cuts in 1989, it chopped the payroll to 1900. Management says it doesn't expect to need 5400 workers again, but it did call back 500 workers in February 1990 and 1500 more through April. Many of those recalled were then let go in September. According to the company, the juggling is unavoidable because the company's business in Fort Smith, the manufacture of refrigerators, is historically seasonal and cyclical.

Whirlpool's struggle for survival plays havoc with a comprehensive community retraining program for 670 workers from the company and its suppliers. According to retraining experts, as long as workers think there is hope for a recall and a Whirlpool wage, they are unlikely to join the program. Many who might have enrolled will choose to take a Whirlpool paycheck instead, even though they are likely to lose it again. While retraining, the workers would collect only unemployment benefits and, if they qualify, an extra $50 a week.

To be sure, there have been some successes in retraining laid-off workers, especially young people, who are better able to handle major changes in their lives. But for most former workers, retraining is difficult because wages for new jobs can be half and even a third those of the old factory jobs, leaving them little incentive to seek retraining. As one retrainer said, "It almost seems you're playing with workers' lives."[20]

The lesson to be learned from this case is that even well-planned, well-executed retraining efforts may fail unless companies and communities help workers see retraining as a long-term investment in their own career success. The ups and downs of Whirlpool's economic fortunes suggest that this will pose an enduring challenge.

Structural Issues in the Delivery of Training

Despite compelling arguments for training, at least nine structural issues must be addressed if training systems are to reach their full potential. Here are some problems often identified at the macro level:[21]

1. *Corporate commitment is lacking and uneven.* Most companies spend nothing at all on training. Those that do tend to concentrate on managers, technicians, and professionals, not rank-and-file workers. Fully 89 percent of American workers never receive any formal training from their employers.[22] This must change, for as a result of the rapid pace of introduction of new technology, combined with new approaches to organization design and production management, workers have to learn three kinds of new skills: (1) the ability to *use* the new technology, (2) the ability to *maintain* it, and (3) the ability to *diagnose* system problems.[23] In an increasingly competitive marketplace, the ability to implement rapid changes in products and technologies is often essential for economic viability.

2. *Aggregate expenditures by business on training are inadequate.* Thus the American Society for Training and Development urges business to increase training expenditures to at least $44 billion annually, from the current $30 billion. To provide incentive, some experts recommend that all companies be required to invest 1 percent of their payrolls on training—and receive a tax advantage for doing so.

3. *Businesses complain that schools award degrees, but they are no guarantee that graduates have mastered skills.* As a result, business must spend large amounts of money to retrain workers in basic skills. Thus, as noted in Chapter 1:

■ Motorola spends an average of $1350 per person per year for six basic skills courses, simply so the worker can reach a point where he or she can be retrained.

■ Planters Nuts in Suffolk, Virginia, spent $40,000 to improve the reading and writing skills of 48 employees.

■ Unisys in Mission Viejo, California, spent $150,000 to teach 125 workers how to read, write, and speak English.

■ Hewlett-Packard spent $22,000 at its Spokane, Washington, plant to teach high school mathematics to 30 production supervisors.

These investments are relatively modest. Polaroid, on the other hand, spent $700,000 at its Cambridge, Massachusetts, operation to teach basic English and mathematics to 1000 new and veteran employees.[24]

4. *Poaching trained workers is a major problem for U.S. businesses, and provides a strong disincentive for training.* Unlike Germany, where local business groups pressure companies not to steal one another's employees, there is no such system in the United States.[25] To put the problem into a broader perspective, consider some relative comparisons between the United States and other countries.

According to the Organization for Economic Cooperation and Development (OECD), the United States has the second lowest rate of job tenure compared to 13 European countries and Japan.[26] The contrast in layoffs is even more extreme. Between 1971 and 1984, the rate of layoffs in the United States averaged 6 times that in Sweden and Italy and 15 times that in Japan.[27] And that was before the defense contraction and the major wave of downsizings that has swept the United States throughout the 1990s![28] This has profound consequences for "selling" senior managers on the value of training in the United States. As one researcher put it, "Because of the high inter-firm mobility of labor, only a small fraction of the economic benefits of a better-trained work force can be captured by the firm that invests in training."[29]

5. *Despite the rhetoric about training being viewed as an investment, current accounting rules require that it be treated as an expense.* Business might spend more on training if accounting rules were revised. Unlike investments in plant and equipment, which show up on the books as an asset, training expenditures are seen merely as expenses to be deducted in the year in which they are incurred.[30]

6. *Government is not providing enough funds for retraining to help workers who have been displaced as a result of downsizing or the defense contraction.* This issue is difficult to address objectively, for what is "enough"? Currently, the administration is earmarking $1.2 billion over 4 years to help create school-to-work transition programs, such as youth apprenticeships. Previously such programs did not even exist. In addition, about $5.8 billion was funneled through the Labor Department in 1993 for worker training.

7. *Businesses, with help from the government, need to focus on the 70 percent of non–college graduates who enter the U.S. workforce. At most, 30 percent of the future workforce will need a college degree.* Schools can help, for example, by developing curricula that focus on areas that are or will demonstrably be in demand by employers. For example, an associate-level degree in manufacturing technology—something many firms need—is an example of a curriculum that is unavailable in most colleges now.[31] States must recognize the economic value of such courses and provide financing and accreditation for them. Students or their employers would pay the tuition.

8. *Employers and schools must develop closer ties.* Schools are often seen as not responsive to labor market demands. Business is seen as not communicating its demands to schools. This must change. For example, Motorola assigns a director to forecast what skills workers will need in 3 to 4 years.[32] It's important that schools learn of these needs so that they can work *with* local businesses to respond to the needs that have been identified. Here is an example of one such partnership.

COMPANY
EXAMPLE

A BUSINESS-SCHOOL PARTNERSHIP AT STIHL, INC.

At Stihl, Inc.'s, Virginia Beach, Virginia, plant, the German-owned maker of chain saws found a shortage of skilled crafts workers in its local and even regional labor markets. So it decided to develop such skills among its current workers by means of an apprenticeship program. Working with Tidewater Community College, it developed a 28-credit curriculum ranging from blueprint reading to industrial mathematics. Initially, the school's curriculum wasn't exactly what Stihl needed, but the college did try to accommodate the company's needs. Blueprint reading, for example, would be taught partly in metric, the European standard. Models are drawn in the three-image German rotation of right-front-top rather than the U.S. style of top-front-left.

The program was begun in the late 1970s, and as of 1993, 36 apprentices had completed the 4-year program. Stihl has lost five of them, including one of the only two African Americans. The program costs the company $50,000 per year per trainee. Most companies would wince at spending that amount, but look at what Stihl has reaped in return. It has tripled productivity and become Virginia Beach's biggest manufacturer. It has 498 workers, up from 40 in 1974. Since 1980, Stihl's U.S. revenue has more than doubled, to $200 million, and the average number of power tools produced per employee has jumped from 800 to 2100. What's the bottom line? All the company's machines are designed, built, and kept running by its apprenticeship graduates.[33]

9. *Organized labor can help.* Unions have developed first-rate apprenticeship programs in a number of crafts. Unions are not opposed to training new apprentices, but they want assurances that the new crafts workers will have jobs at the end of their apprenticeships. Thus the Atlanta Labor Council offered to recruit unemployed youth for construction apprenticeships if city employers would agree to hire union labor for the 1996 Olympics.[34]

CHARACTERISTICS OF EFFECTIVE TRAINING PRACTICE

One survey of corporate training and development practices found that four characteristics seemed to distinguish companies with the most effective training practices.[35]

■ Top management is committed to training and development;[36] training is part of the corporate culture. Thus Xerox Corporation invests about $300 million annually, or about 2.5 percent of revenue, on training. This translates to about $2500 per year per employee. It is an ongoing process for all employees, including the chief executive officer.[37] Hewlett-Packard spends about 5 percent of its revenues, or $250 million, to train its 87,000 workers. Marriott Corporation simply says, "Training is part of our culture."[38]

■ Training is tied to business strategy and objectives and is linked to bottom-line results. More on this shortly.

■ A comprehensive, systematic approach to training exists; training and retraining are done at all levels on a continuous, ongoing basis.

■ There is a commitment to invest the necessary resources, to provide sufficient time and money for training.

The literature on training evaluation shows that while the potential returns from well-conducted training programs can be substantial, there is often considerable variability in the effectiveness with which any given training method or content area is implemented.[39] Considerable planning (through needs analysis) and follow-up program evaluation efforts are necessary in order to realize these returns. To be sure, training is an important component of business strategy for many organizations. To appreciate this more fully, let's examine some alternative competitive strategies.

How Does Training Relate to Competitive Strategies?

The means that firms use to compete for business in the marketplace and to gain competitive advantage are known as *competitive strategies*.[40] As was mentioned briefly in Chapter 2, competitive strategies may differ in a number of ways, including the extent to which firms emphasize speed (time-based competition), innovation, quality enhancement, or cost reduction. Moreover, there is growing recognition that the different types of strategies require different types of HR practices.[41] Training, a key HR practice, is critical to the implementation of several competitive strategies. The important lesson is that *human resources represent a competitive advantage that can increase profits when managed wisely.*

Speed strategy focuses on time-based competition—in every function from product design, development, production, and reaction to customer feedback. Training in team processes and streamlined production methods is critically important. *Innovation strategy* is used to develop products or services that differ from those of competitors. Its primary objective is to offer something new and different. Regular training on new developments in technology and services is a central focus of this strategy. Enhancing product or service quality is the primary objective of the *quality-enhancement strategy*. To do that well, all employees must be trained to provide a consistently high level of service. Finally, the objective of a *cost reduction strategy* is to gain a competitive advantage by being the lowest-cost producer of goods or provider of services.[42]

Speed strategy emphasizes managing people so that they work *faster*; innovation strategy emphasizes managing people so that they work *differently*; quality-enhancement strategy emphasizes managing people so that they work *smarter*; and cost reduction strategy emphasizes managing people so that they work *harder*.

While it is convenient to think of these four competitive strategies as pure types applied to entire organizations, business units, or even functional specialties, the reality is more complex. In practice, most firms and subunits of firms emphasize a combination of these competitive strategies. Training is critical to the implementation of each of them—with the exception of cost reduction, because cost reduction emphasizes tight fiscal and management controls, minimization of overhead, and pursuit of economies of scale. This implies minimal use of training and development.

While the potential returns from well-conducted training programs are hefty, considerable planning and evaluation are necessary in order to realize these returns. The remainder of this chapter examines some key issues that managers need to consider. Let us begin by considering the broad phases that comprise training systems.

ASSESSING TRAINING NEEDS AND DESIGNING TRAINING PROGRAMS

One way to keep in mind the phases of training is to portray them graphically, in the form of a model that illustrates the interaction among the phases. One such model is shown in Figure 8-3.

The *assessment* (or planning) *phase* serves as a foundation for the entire training effort. As Figure 8-3 shows, both the *training and development phase* and the *evaluation phase* depend on inputs from assessment. The purpose of the assessment phase is to define what it is the employee should learn in relation to desired job behaviors. If this phase is not carefully done, the training program as a whole will have little chance of achieving what it is intended to do.

Assuming that the objectives of the training program are carefully specified, the next task is to design the environment in which to achieve those objectives. This is the purpose of the training phase. Methods and techniques must be chosen carefully and delivered systematically in a supportive, encouraging environment, based on sound principles of learning. More on this later.

Finally, if both the assessment phase and the training and development phase have been done competently, evaluation should present few problems. Evaluation is a twofold process that involves (1) establishing indicators of success in training, as well as on the job, and (2) determining exactly what job-related changes have occurred as a result of the training. Evaluation must provide a continuous stream of feedback that can be used to reassess training needs, thereby creating input for the next stage of employee development.

Now that we have a broad overview of the training process, let us consider the elements of Figure 8-3 in greater detail.

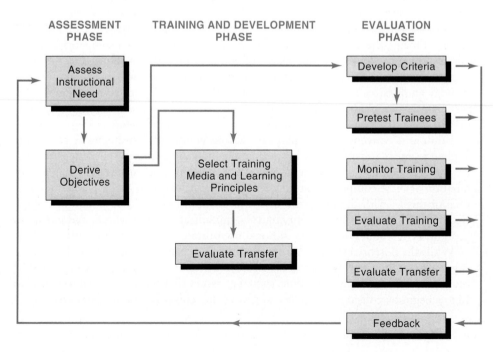

FIGURE 8-3
A general systems model of the training and development process. Note how information developed during the evaluation phase provides feedback, and therefore new input, to the assessment phase. This initiates a new cycle of assessment, training and development, and evaluation.

ASSESSMENT PHASE — TRAINING AND DEVELOPMENT PHASE — EVALUATION PHASE

Assess Instructional Need → Develop Criteria → Pretest Trainees

Derive Objectives → Select Training Media and Learning Principles → Evaluate Transfer

Monitor Training

Evaluate Training

Evaluate Transfer

Feedback

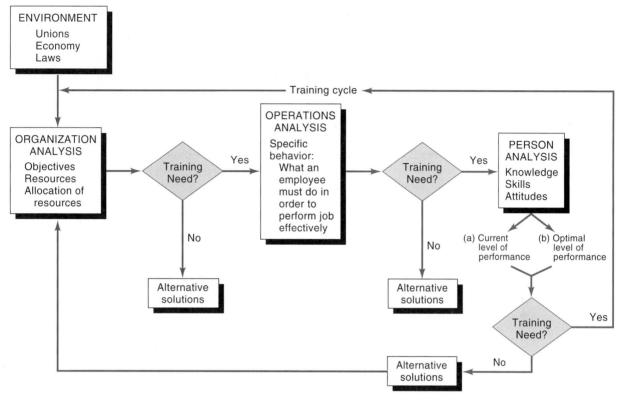

FIGURE 8-4
Training needs assessment model.

Assessing Training Needs

There are three levels of analysis for determining the needs that training can fulfill:[43]

- *Organization analysis* focuses on identifying where within the organization training is needed.
- *Operations analysis* attempts to identify the content of training—what an employee must do in order to perform competently.
- *Individual analysis* determines how well each employee is performing the tasks that make up his or her job.

Training needs might surface in any one of these three broad areas. But to ask productive questions regarding training needs, an "integrative model" such as that shown in Figure 8-4 is needed.

At a general level, training needs must be analyzed against the backdrop of organizational objectives and strategies. Unless this is done, time and money may well be wasted on training programs that do not advance the cause of the company.[44] People may be trained in skills they already possess (as happened to members of a machinists' union of a major airline not long ago); the training budget may be squandered on "rest and recuperation" sessions, where employees are entertained but learn little in the way of required job skills or job knowledge; or the budget may be spent on glittering hardware that meets the training director's needs but not the organization's.

Analysis of the organization's external environment and internal climate is also essential. Trends in the strategic priorities of a business, judicial decisions, civil rights laws, union activity, productivity, accidents, turnover, absenteeism, and on-the-job employee behavior will provide relevant information at this level. The important question then becomes "Will training produce changes in employee behavior that will contribute to our organization's goals?"

In short, the critical first step is to relate the assessment of training needs to the achievement of organizational goals. If that connection cannot be made, the training is probably unnecessary. However, if a training need is identified at this organizational level, an operations analysis is the next step.

Operations analysis requires a careful examination of the job to be performed *after* training. It involves (1) a systematic collection of information that describes exactly *how* jobs are done, so that (2) standards of performance for those jobs can be determined; (3) how tasks are to be performed to meet the standards; and (4) the knowledge, skills, abilities, and other characteristics necessary for effective task performance. Job analyses, performance appraisals, interviews (with jobholders, supervisors, and higher management), and analyses of operating problems (quality control, downtime reports, and customer complaints) all provide important inputs to the analysis of training needs.

Finally, there is *individual analysis*. At this level, training needs may be defined in terms of the following general idea: the difference between desired performance and actual performance is the individual's training need. Performance standards, identified in the operations analysis phase, constitute desired performance. Individual performance data, diagnostic ratings of employees by their supervisors, records of performance kept by workers in diary form, attitude surveys, interviews, or tests (job knowledge, work sample, or situational) can provide information on actual performance against which each employee can be compared to desired job performance standards. A gap between actual and desired performance may be filled by training.

However, assessing the needs for training does not end here. To evaluate the results of training and to assess what training is needed in the future, needs must be analyzed regularly *and* at all three levels.

- At the organizational level, needs must be analyzed by senior managers who set the organization's goals.
- At the operations level, needs must be analyzed by the managers (or teams) who specify how the organization's goals are going to be achieved.
- At the individual level, needs must be analyzed by the managers and workers who do the work to achieve those goals, keeping in mind that performance is a function both of ability (hence, training) and motivation (a worker who wants to perform well).

| COMPANY EXAMPLE | **FROM NEEDS ANALYSIS TO TRAINING TO RESULTS!** |

COMPANY EXAMPLE

FROM NEEDS ANALYSIS TO TRAINING TO RESULTS!

At Pacific Northwest Bell, installers were uncertain about whether and how much they could charge for work on noncompany equipment and wiring, so they were billing very little. The company, in turn, seeing little revenue generated by the labor-hours spent, had stopped marketing the technicians' services.

A team of internal consultants—a company manager, a representative of the International Brotherhood of Electrical Workers, and a representative of the Communications Workers of America—recognized this problem and tried to solve it by involving a cross section of interested parties. The new task force agreed on two goals: increasing revenues and increasing job security.

A subcommittee of two task developers and two technicians developed a training program designed to teach installers *how* and *what* to charge, and also *why* they should keep accurate records: to increase their job security. The committee agreed to measure the revenues generated by time and materials charging so that these revenues could be weighed against labor costs in layoff decisions.

The training consisted of two 6-hour days and was presented by technicians to about 400 installers throughout Washington State and Oregon. In addition to the course, the task force identified a need for a hot line that technicians could call when bidding for a job. The line was set up, and one of the course instructors was promoted to a management position for answering calls.

RESULTS

The results of the training and hot line were phenomenal, as shown by the pattern of revenues from work on noncompany equipment. In January, prior to the training course, the installers had billed for $589. In April, when half the workers had completed the training, they billed for $21,000 in outside work. By the following February, billings for customized work and charges reached $180,000. Total revenues over the 14-month period were about $1.4 million, or nearly twice the task force's projection of $831,000.

In light of these results, the company now markets the installers' services aggressively. For example, if an installation crew drives by a construction site on their way from another job, they stop and bid on the work. The hot line receives about 50 calls per day from systems technicians, installers, the business office, and customers.

The efforts of the task force increased company revenues, as well as the job security of the installers. Demand for their services grew with increased bidding on jobs, and more installers were added, providing union members in other job titles with opportunities for promotions or transfers into this work group. Future layoffs are unlikely, since the savings in labor costs must be weighed against the revenues generated by the installers.[45] Careful assessment of the need for training, coupled with the delivery of a training program that met targeted needs, produced results that startled management, the union, and the installation technicians. Everybody won!

FURTHER ISSUES IN THE DESIGN AND CONDUCT OF TRAINING PROGRAMS

Trainability

Organizations provide training to those who are most likely to profit from it; individuals prefer to be trained in the things that interest them and in which they can improve. To provide instruction for trainees in areas in which they have no aptitude or interest will not benefit them and will certainly not benefit the organization.

From a cost–benefit perspective, the largest cost component of training is the cost of paying the trainees during the training period. Hence, cost savings are possible if training time can be reduced. Perhaps the easiest way to do this is by identifying and training only those employees who clearly are "trainable." *Trainability* refers to how well a person can acquire the skills, knowledge, and behavior necessary to perform a job, achieving its specified outcome within a given time.[46] It is a combination of an individual's ability and motivation.

Can a person's ability to learn a job be predicted? Recent research suggests that the answer is a cautious yes.[47] For example, one study showed that current methods for assigning enlisted navy personnel to specific jobs could be improved by using a concept called "miniature training and evaluation testing."[48] Using this approach, a recruit is trained (and then subsequently tested) on a sample of the tasks that he or she will be expected to perform on the job. The approach is based on the premise that a recruit who demonstrates that he or she can learn to perform a *sample* of the tasks of a navy job will be able to learn and to perform satisfactorily *all* the tasks of that job, given appropriate on-the-job training. Similar results were obtained for seven "minicourses" designed to select personnel for jobs involving new technologies in the telecommunication industry.[49] However, general cognitive ability, as revealed by tests of basic aptitudes (e.g., arithmetic reasoning, mechanical comprehension, electronics information, reading comprehension), is still the best predictor of success in training.[50]

Although "can-do" (ability) factors are necessary, it is important to recognize that "will-do" (motivational) factors also play a vital role in the prediction of trainability. For example, the Navy School for Divers found that a seven-item trainee confidence measure significantly predicted graduation from its 10-week training program in Scuba and Deep Sea Air procedures.[51] Each of the following items is answered on a 6-point scale from "disagree strongly" (score of 1) to "agree strongly" (score of 6):

1. I have a better chance of passing this training than most others do.
2. I volunteered for this training program as soon as I could.
3. The knowledge and experience that I gain in this training may advance my career.
4. Even if I fail, this training will be a valuable experience.
5. I will get more from this training than most people.
6. If I have trouble during training, I will try harder.
7. I am more physically fit for this training than most people.

Trainees most likely to profit from training can be identified reasonably accurately when measures such as these are combined with two other kinds of information: (1) the extent of each potential trainee's job involvement and career planning[52] and (2) each employee's choice to select the training in question.[53] Once these trainees have been identified, it becomes important to structure the training environment for maximum learning. Attention to the fundamental principles of learning is essential.

Principles of Learning

To promote efficient learning, long-term retention, and application of the skills or factual information learned in training to the job situation, training programs should incorporate principles of learning developed over the past century. Which principles should be considered? It depends on whether the trainees are learning skills (e.g., drafting) or factual material (e.g., principles of life insurance).[54]

To be most effective, *skill learning* should include four essential ingredients: (1) goal setting, (2) behavior modeling, (3) practice, and (4) feedback.

PYGMALION IN ACTION: MANAGERS GET THE KIND OF PERFORMANCE THEY EXPECT

To test the Pygmalion effect and to examine the impact of instructors' prior expectations about trainees on the instructors' subsequent style of leadership toward the trainees, a field experiment was conducted at a military training base.[55] One hundred five trainees in a 15-week combat command course were matched on aptitude and assigned randomly to one of three experimental groups. Each group corresponded to a particular level of expectation that was communicated to the instructors: high, average, or no prespecified level of expectation (due to insufficient information). Four days before the trainees arrived at the base, and prior to any acquaintance between instructors and trainees, the instructors were assembled and given a score (known as command potential, or CP) for each trainee that represented the trainee's potential to command others. The instructors were told that the CP score had been developed on the basis of psychological test scores, data from a previous course on leadership, and ratings by previous commanders. The instructors were also told that course grades predict CP in 95 percent of the cases. The instructors were then given a list of the trainees assigned to them, along with their CPs, and asked to copy each trainee's CP into his or her personal record. The instructors were also requested to learn their trainees' names and their CPs before the beginning of the course.

The Pygmalion hypothesis that the instructor's prior expectation influences the trainee's performance was confirmed. Trainees of whom instructors expected better performance scored significantly higher on objective achievement tests, exhibited more positive attitudes, and were perceived as better leaders. In fact, the prior expectations of the instructors explained 73 percent of the variability in the trainees' performance, 66 percent in their attitudes, and 28 percent in leadership. The lesson to be learned from these results is unmistakable: Trainers (and managers) get the kind of performance they expect.

However, when the focus is on *learning facts*, the sequence should change slightly: namely, (1) goal setting, (2) meaningfulness of material, (3) practice, and (4) feedback. Let's consider each of these in greater detail.

Motivating the Trainee: Goal Setting. A person who wants to develop herself or himself will do so; a person who wants to *be* developed rarely is. This statement illustrates the role that motivation plays in training—to learn, you must *want* to learn. And it appears from evidence that the most effective way to raise a trainee's motivation is by setting goals. Goal setting has a proven track record of success in improving employee performance in a variety of settings and cultures.[56] On average, goal setting leads to a 10 percent improvement in productivity, and it works best with tasks of low complexity.[57]

Goal theory is founded on the premise that an individual's conscious goals or intentions regulate her or his behavior.[58] Research indicates that once a goal is accepted, difficult but attainable goals result in higher levels of performance than do easy goals or even a generalized goal such as "do your best."[59] These findings have three important implications for motivating trainees:

1. The objectives of the training program should be made clear at the outset.
2. Goals should be challenging and difficult enough that the trainees can derive personal satisfaction from achieving them but not so difficult that they are perceived as impossible to reach.

3. The ultimate goal of "finishing the program" should be supplemented with sub-goals during training, such as trainer evaluations, work-sample tests, and periodic quizzes. As each hurdle is cleared successfully, trainee confidence about attaining the ultimate goal increases.

While goal setting clearly affects trainees' motivation, so also do the *expectations* of the trainer. In fact, expectations have a way of becoming self-fulfilling prophecies, so that the higher the expectations, the better the trainees perform. Conversely, the lower the expectations, the worse the trainees perform. This phenomenon of the self-fulfilling prophecy is known as the *Pygmalion effect*. Legend has it that Pygmalion, a king of Cyprus, sculpted an ivory statue of a maiden named Galatea. Pygmalion fell in love with the statue, and, at his prayer, Aphrodite, the goddess of love and beauty, gave it life. Pygmalion's fondest wish—his expectation—came true.

Behavior Modeling. Much of what we learn is acquired by observing others. We will imitate other people's actions when they lead to desirable outcomes for those involved (e.g., promotions, increased sales, or more accurate tennis serves). The models' actions serve as a cue as to what constitutes appropriate behavior.[60] A *model* is someone who is seen as competent, powerful, and friendly and has high status within an organization. We try to identify with this model because her or his behavior is seen as desirable and appropriate. Modeling tends to increase when the model is rewarded for behavior and when the rewards (e.g., influence, pay) are things the imitator would like to have. In the context of training (or coaching or teaching), we attempt to maximize trainees' identification with a model. For us to do this well, research suggests the following:

1. The model should be similar to the observer in age, sex, and race. If the observer sees little similarity between himself or herself and the model, it is unlikely that he or she will imitate the model's behaviors.

2. The behaviors to be modeled should be portrayed clearly and in detail. To focus the trainees' attention on specific behaviors to imitate, provide them with a list of key behaviors to attend to when observing the model and allow them to express the behaviors in language that is most comfortable for them. For example, when one group of supervisors was being taught how to "coach" employees, the supervisors received a list of the following key behaviors:[61] (1) focus on the problem, not on the person; (2) ask for the employees' suggestions, and get their ideas on how to solve the problem; (3) listen openly; (4) agree on the steps that each of you will take to solve the problem; and (5) plan a specific follow-up date.

3. The behaviors to be modeled should be ranked in a sequence from least to most difficult; be sure the trainees observe lots of repetitions of the behaviors being modeled.

4. Finally, the behaviors should be portrayed by several models, not just one.[62]

Research continues to demonstrate the effectiveness of behavior modeling over other approaches to training.[63] To a large extent, this is because behavior modeling overcomes one of the shortcomings of earlier approaches to training: telling instead of showing.

Meaningfulness of the Material. Factual material is learned more easily and remembered better when it is meaningful. *Meaningfulness* refers to material that is rich in associations for the trainees and is therefore easily understood by them. To structure material to maximize its meaningfulness:

1. Provide trainees with an overview of the material to be presented during the training. Seeing the overall picture helps trainees understand how each unit of the program fits together and how it contributes to the overall training objectives.[64]

2. Present the material by using examples, terms, and concepts that are familiar to the trainees in order to clarify and reinforce key learning points. Such a strategy is *essential* when training the hard-core unemployed.[65]

3. As complex intellectual skills are invariably made up of simpler ones, teach the simpler skills before the complex ones.[66] This is true whether one is teaching accounting, computer programming, or X-ray technology.

Practice (Makes Perfect). Anyone learning a new skill or acquiring factual knowledge must have an opportunity to practice what is being learned. Practice has three aspects: active practice, overlearning, and the length of the practice session. Let's consider each of these.

- *Active practice.* During the early stages of learning, the trainer should be available to oversee the trainee's practice directly; if the trainee begins to "get off the track," the inappropriate behaviors can be corrected immediately, before they become ingrained in the trainee's behavior. This is why low instructor–trainee (or teacher–pupil) ratios are so desirable. It also explains why so many people opt for private lessons when trying to learn or master a sport such as tennis, golf, skiing, or horseback riding.

- *Overlearning.* When trainees are given the opportunity to practice far beyond the point where the task has been performed correctly several times, the task becomes "second nature" and is said to be "overlearned." For some tasks, overlearning is critical.[67] This is true of any task that must be performed infrequently and under great stress: for example, attempting to kick a winning field goal with only seconds left in a football game. It is less important in types of work where an individual practices his or her skills on a daily basis (e.g., auto mechanics, electronics technicians, assemblers).

- *Length of the practice session.* Suppose you have only 1 week to memorize the lines of a play, and during that week, you have only 12 hours available to practice. What practice schedule will produce the greatest improvement? Should you practice 2 hours a day for 6 days, should you practice for 6 hours each of the final 2 days before the deadline, or should you adopt some other schedule? The two extremes represent *distributed* practice (which implies rest intervals between sessions) and *massed* practice (in which the practice sessions are crowded together). Although there are exceptions, most of the research evidence on this question indicates that for the same amount of practice, learning is better when practice is distributed rather than massed.[68] One exception to this rule is when difficult material, such as hard puzzles or other "thought" problems, must be learned. There seems to be an advantage in staying with the problem for a few massed practice sessions at first, rather than spending a day or more between sessions.

■ *Feedback.* This is a form of information about one's attempts to improve. Feedback is essential both for learning and for trainee motivation.[69] The emphasis should be on *when* and *how* the trainee has done something correctly, for example, "You did a good job on that report you turned in yesterday—it was brief and to the heart of the issues." It is also important to emphasize that feedback affects group, as well as individual, performance.[70] For example, application of performance-based feedback in a small fast-food store over a 1-year period led to a 15 percent decrease in food costs and a 193 percent increase in profits.[71]

To have the greatest impact, feedback should be provided as soon as possible after the trainee's behavior. It need not be instantaneous, but there should be no confusion regarding exactly what the trainee did and the trainer's reaction to it. Feedback need not always be positive, but keep in mind that the most powerful rewards are likely to be those provided by the trainee's immediate supervisor. In fact, if the supervisor does not reinforce what is learned in training, the training will be transferred ineffectively to the job—if at all.

Transfer of Training

Transfer refers to the extent to which knowledge, skills, abilities, or other characteristics learned in training can be applied on the job. Transfer may be *positive* (i.e., it enhances job performance), *negative* (i.e., it hampers job performance), or *neutral*. Long-term training or retraining probably includes segments that contain all three of these conditions. Training that results in negative transfer is costly in two ways—the cost of the training (which proved to be useless) and the cost of hampered performance.

Here's how one company facilitates positive transfer from learning to doing.

COMPANY EXAMPLE

TRW'S STRATEGIC MANAGEMENT SEMINAR

At TRW, *systems learning* helps focus attention on the important concept of "transfer of training."[72] All training activities are designed with a built-in compatibility between what managers are expected to learn and what they are expected to do on their jobs. Here is an example.

Following instruction in the concepts of competitive strategy, a three-phase strategic management seminar was presented to natural business teams within TRW: for example, a division vice president and his or her staff. In phase I, each team receives two things: (1) more instruction in the concepts of competitive strategy and (2) a detailed assignment. The teams must apply the concepts to their business and develop an action strategy. Each team must plan a maximum of six actions that it will take over the next 18 months, and it must designate responsibility to particular team members for each action. The teams then "go home" to work on their strategies for about 8 weeks.

Phase II of the seminar is called the "midterm review." A seminar faculty member visits each team to review its progress on the assignment and provides detailed feedback on how well the team is applying the concepts. Sometimes major changes are made at this point as teams recognize, for example, that their competitive analysis is not thorough enough.

Over the following 8 weeks, phase III of the program, each team prepares its final strategic presentation—to be delivered in the presence of two or three other teams. After each team presents its strategy, the audience provides constructive comments and criticisms. Next, the audience votes on whether to accept or reject the strategy, indicating on their ballots what they like and dislike about the strategy. The votes and comments are collected and offered to the presenting team, along with comments and concerns from the faculty member. What's happening here? A powerful peer review process.

To encourage a tight "fit" between training and application, some changes in TRW's organizational practices were necessary—such as changing the process of developing strategic plans, modifying the compensation system so that long-term success is rewarded, and changing the performance appraisal process to emphasize long-term thinking, planning, and action. However, the biggest change of all was senior management's willingness to encourage the kind of risk taking required to implement some of the strategies. This is the essence of systems learning.

TRW's approach to "systems learning" suggests that transfer of training (that is, the adoption of concepts and practices learned in training to practice on the job) will be greatest when trainees:

- Are confident in using their newly learned skills.
- Are aware of work situations where demonstration of the new skills is appropriate.
- Perceive that their job performance will improve if they use the new skills.
- Believe that the knowledge and skills emphasized in the training program are helpful in solving work-related problems.[73]

Team Training

Up to this point, we have been discussing training and development as an individual enterprise. Yet today there is an increasing emphasis on *team* performance. Management teams, research teams, and temporary task forces are common features of many organizations. *A team is a group of individuals who are working together toward a common goal.* It is this common goal that really defines a team, and if team members have opposite or conflicting goals, the efficiency of the total unit is likely to suffer. For example, consider the effects on a basketball team when one of the players *always* tries to score, regardless of the team's situation.

Research has revealed two broad principles regarding the composition and management of teams. One, the overall performance of a team strongly depends on the individual expertise of its members.[74] Thus individual training and development are still important. But individual training is only a partial solution, for interactions among team members must also be addressed. This interaction is what makes team training unique—it always uses some form of simulation or real-life practice, and it always focuses on the interaction of team members, equipment, and work procedures.[75] For example, Subaru-Isuzu uses a manufacturing simulation in which individuals role play team members of a small-parts assembly firm. Jobs are self-assigned within teams, and team members make their own decisions about planning and allocating resources.[76]

Two, managers of effective work groups tend to monitor the performance of their team members regularly, and they provide frequent feedback to them.[77] In fact, as much as 35 percent of the variability in team performance can be explained by the frequency of use of monitors and consequences. Incorporating these findings into the training of team members and their managers should lead to better overall team performance.

Selecting Training Methods

New training methods appear every year. While some are well founded in learning theory or models of behavior change (e.g., behavior modeling), others result more from technological than theoretical developments (e.g., videotapes, computer-based business games).

Training methods can be classified in three ways: information presentation, simulation methods, or on-the-job training.[78]

- *Information presentation techniques* include lectures, conferences, correspondence courses, motion pictures, reading lists, closed-circuit TV and videotapes, behavior modeling and systematic observation, programmed instruction, computer-assisted instruction, sensitivity training, and organization development—systematic, long-range programs of organizational improvement.
- *Simulation methods* include the case method, role playing, programmed group exercises, the in-basket technique, and business games.
- *On-the-job training methods* include orientation training, apprenticeships, on-the-job training, near-the-job training (using identical equipment but away from the job itself), job rotation, committee assignments (or junior executive boards), understudy assignments, on-the-job coaching, and performance appraisal.

In the context of developing interpersonal skills, training methods are typically chosen to achieve one or more of three objectives:

- Promoting self-insight and environmental awareness—that is, an understanding of how one's actions affect others and how one is viewed by others. For example, at Parfums Stern, staffers act out customer–salesperson roles to better understand customers' emotions. Wendy's International videotapes disabled customers; in one video a blind person asks that change be counted out loud. Meridian Bancorp has workers walk with seeds in their shoes to simulate older customers' corns and calluses.[79]
- Improving the ability of managers and lower-level employees to make decisions and to solve job-related problems in a constructive fashion.
- Maximizing the desire to perform well.

To choose the training method (or combination of methods) that best fits a given situation, *what is to be taught* must first be defined carefully. That is the purpose of the needs assessment phase. *Only then* can the method be chosen that best fits these requirements. To be useful, the chosen method should meet the minimal conditions needed for effective learning to take place; that is, the training method should:

- Motivate the trainee to improve his or her performance.
- Clearly illustrate desired skills.
- Provide for active participation by the trainee.
- Provide an opportunity to practice.
- Provide timely feedback on the trainee's performance.
- Provide some means for reinforcement while the trainee learns.
- Be structured from simple to complex tasks.
- Be adaptable to specific problems.
- Encourage positive transfer from the training to the job.

EVALUATING TRAINING PROGRAMS

Training must be evaluated by systematically documenting the outcomes of the training in terms of how trainees actually behave back on their jobs and the relevance of the trainees' behavior to the objectives of the organization.[80] To assess the utility or value of training, we seek answers to questions such as the following:

1. Have trainees achieved a specific level of skill, knowledge, or performance?
2. Did change occur?
3. Is the change due to training?
4. Is the change positively related to the achievement of organizational goals?
5. Will similar changes occur with new participants in the same training program?[81]

In evaluating training programs, change may be measured in terms of four levels of rigor:[82]

- *Reaction*—how do the participants feel about the training program?
- *Learning*—to what extent have the trainees learned what was taught?
- *Behavior*—what on-the-job changes in behavior have occurred because of attendance at the training program?
- *Results*—to what extent have cost-related behavioral outcomes (e.g., productivity or quality improvements, turnover or accident reductions) resulted from the training?

Since measures of reaction and learning are concerned with outcomes of the training program per se, they are referred to as *internal criteria*. Measures of behavior and results indicate the impact of training on the job environment; they are referred to as *external criteria*.

Measures of reaction typically focus on participants' feelings about the subject and the speaker, suggested improvements in the program, and the extent to which the training will help them do their jobs better. Trainee learning, which may focus on changing knowledge, skills, attitudes, or motivation, can be assessed by giving a paper-and-pencil test (especially when factual information has been presented) or through performance testing following skill training.

Assessing changes in on-the-job behavior is more difficult than measuring reaction or learning because factors other than the training program (e.g., lengthened job

■ **TABLE 8 ▪ 2**

A TYPICAL BEFORE-AFTER DESIGN FOR ASSESSING
TRAINING OUTCOMES

	Trained group	Untrained group
Pretest	Yes	Yes
Training	Yes	No
Posttest	Yes	Yes

experience, outside economic events, changes in supervision or performance incentives) may also improve performance. To rule out these rival hypotheses, it is essential to design a plan for evaluation that includes *before* and *after* measurement of the trained group's performance relative to that of one or more untrained control groups. (However, when it is relatively costly to bring subjects to an evaluation and administration costs are particularly high, after-only measurement of trained and untrained groups is best.[83]) To rule out alternative explanations for the changes that occurred, members of the untrained control group should be matched as closely as possible to those in the trained group. Table 8-2 shows a standard design for such a study. If the outcomes of the training are positive, the untrained control group at Time 1 may become the trained group at a later time. It is important to note that the posttraining appraisal of performance should not be done sooner than 3 months (or more) following the training so that the trainees have an opportunity to put into practice what they have learned.

Finally, the impact of training on organizational results is the most significant but most difficult measure to make. *Measures of results are the bottom line of training success.* Exciting developments in this area have come from recent research showing how the general utility equation (Equation 7-1 on page 227) can be modified to reflect the dollar value of improved job performance resulting from training.[84] Utility formulas are now available for evaluating the dollar value of a single training program compared to a control group, a training program readministered periodically (e.g., annually), and a comparison between two or more different training programs.

**COMPANY
EXAMPLE**

EVALUATING THE BUSINESS IMPACT OF MANAGEMENT TRAINING AT CIGNA CORPORATION

Cigna, an insurance company, set out to demonstrate the impact on productivity and performance of a 7-day training program in basic management skills.[85] The evaluations were based on repeated measures of work-unit performance both before and after training. Some specific features of the program were:

■ Productivity was a central focus of the program.

■ As part of their training, the participants were taught how to create productivity measures.

■ The participants were taught how to use productivity data as performance feedback and as support for performance goal setting.

■ The participants wrote a productivity action plan as part of the training, and they agreed to bring back measurable results to a follow-up session.

■ Individualized productivity measures were put into place as part of the action plan. These plans were tailored to measure results in specific, objective terms.

The results of the training in basic management skills were evaluated, of necessity, in individual work units. Let us consider one such unit—that of a premium collections manager. Collecting premiums on time is important in the insurance business, because late premiums represent lost investment opportunities. Through survey feedback from her subordinates, the manager of this unit found that her problems (only 75 percent of the premiums were collected on time) stemmed from poor HRM skills, coupled with a failure to set clear performance goals.

After being trained, this manager dramatically altered many of her management behaviors. One year later her unit was collecting 96 percent of the premiums on time. This improvement yielded extra investment income of $150,000 per year. What was the return on the fully loaded cost of training her? The training costs included the costs of facilities, program development amortized over 25 programs, trainer preparation time, general administration, corporate overhead, and the salaries plus benefits of the participants over the 7-day program. These came to $1600 per participant. It looks as though the returns generated by the collections manager as a result of the action plan ($150,000) relative to the training's cost ($1600) were phenomenal. But were all these gains due to her training? Probably not.

What would have happened had training not occurred? Extrapolating from the rate of improvement prior to training, the researchers concluded that the collections rate would have been up to about 84 percent, from 75 percent. The additional 12-point improvement that was provided—in part—by the program (which generated about $85,000 in extra investment income) represents the upper boundary of the effects of the training program. (Other economic factors, such as lower unemployment among policy holders, may also have contributed to the gain.) Nevertheless, it represents about a 50-to-1 return on the dollars invested.

IMPACT OF TRAINING AND DEVELOPMENT ON PRODUCTIVITY, QUALITY OF WORK LIFE, AND THE BOTTOM LINE

Recently, quantitative procedures were used to summarize the results of 70 studies that had the following characteristics: (1) each study involved managers, (2) each evaluated the effectiveness of one or more training programs, and (3) each included at least one control or comparison group. Results indicated that management training and development efforts are, in general, moderately effective. In terms of objective measures of training results over all content areas, training improved job performance by almost 20 percent, although there was considerable variability around this estimate.[86] At a more general level, the literature on training evaluation shows that while the potential returns from well-conducted training programs can be substantial, there is often considerable variability in the effectiveness with which any given training method or content area is implemented.[87] As we have seen, considerable planning (through needs analysis) and follow-up program evaluation efforts are necessary in order to realize these returns. Given the pace of change in modern society and technology, retraining is imperative to enable individuals to compete for available jobs (and therefore to maintain their standards of living) and to enable organizations to compete in the marketplace. Continual investment in training and learning is therefore essential, as it has such a direct impact on the productivity of organizations and on the quality of work life of those who work in them.

ETHICAL DILEMMA: DIVERSITY TRAINING—FAD OR HERE TO STAY?

Diversity training is flourishing at the highest reaches of U.S. business. American Airlines, Coca-Cola, Procter & Gamble, and *The New York Times* (which reports that 40 percent of U.S. companies have instituted some form of diversity training) are all engaged in one form or another. All are built on the assumption that "Understanding breeds better relationships."[88] Diversity consultants promise corporations they will increase their profits by "empowering their whole workforce," according to the corporate diversity programs manager at Digital Equipment Corporation. Is there any truth to this claim?

Beyond the rhetoric, there is little evidence that such training can solve the problems it purports to address. Proponents acknowledge that they are unable to document the advantages of diversity training or even describe what "managing-diversity heaven" would look like. To some, the preferred solution to the problems of measurement and description is to declare them irrelevant and proceed on faith alone.[89] Is this ethically justifiable in light of the principles of sound training practice—needs assessment, careful specification of objectives, and then evaluation of training in terms of the original objectives?

HUMAN RESOURCE MANAGEMENT IN ACTION: CONCLUSION

THE NEW EDUCATORS: COMPANY-BASED SCHOOLS

Has Collin's & Aikman's in-house training paid off? The answer is a tentative yes, although the links between training and some measures of performance are somewhat tentative. Within tufting operations, productivity, or the amount of carpet stitched, rose 10 percent over a 2-year period. The company also cut the number of returns—carpets sent back to the plant because of problems—in half over the same period.

Workers at Collins & Aikman say they are more confident about the new machinery. Some 56 of them have earned high school diplomas through courses taught at the plant. Some have stopped constantly asking supervisors for help, because they know the answers themselves—e.g., how to tally the various weights of yarns. Within a year after the program began, 1230 suggestions poured in from workers on ways the company could improve itself. Workers are encouraging their own children to stay in school. Morale is up—and perhaps that is the reason for a sudden outbreak of health. When the program began, an average of 14 workers were absent each day. Two years later, the average was down to 8.

Not all employees are sold on the idea, though. For some, the level of commitment required to complete the training is too high. For others, the idea of going back to school is so unnerving that, even though they know they need to upgrade their skills in order to keep their old jobs, they willingly accept lower-paying jobs instead. As one manager noted, "For capable human beings to take cuts in pay because they don't have the literacy skills they need—that's really sad." For companies to survive, their choices have really come down to two: either they have to compete with higher technology and smart workers or they have to move overseas and compete with cheaper labor.

IMPLICATIONS FOR MANAGEMENT PRACTICE

One of the greatest fears of managers and lower-level employees is obsolescence. Perhaps the Paul Principle expresses this phenomenon most aptly: *Over time, people become uneducated, and therefore incompetent, to perform at a level they once performed at adequately.*[90] Training is an important antidote to obsolescence, but it is important to be realistic about what training can and cannot accomplish.

1. Training cannot solve all kinds of performance problems. In some cases, transfer, job redesign, changes in selection or reward systems, or discipline may be more appropriate.

2. Since productivity (the value of outputs per unit of labor) is a characteristic of a system, such as a firm or an industry, and not of an individual, changes in individual performance are only one possible cause of changes in productivity.[91]

3. As a manager, you need to ask yourself three key questions: "Do we have an actual or a potential performance problem for which training is the answer?"; "Have we defined what is to be learned and what the content of training should be *before* we choose a particular training method or technique?"; and "What kind of evaluation procedure will we use to determine if the benefits of the training outweigh its costs?"

SUMMARY

Clearly, a new employee's initial experience with a firm can have a major effect on his or her later career. To maximize the impact of orientation, it is important to recognize that new employees need specific information in three major areas: (1) *company standards, traditions, and policies*; (2) *social behavior*, and (3) *technical aspects of the job*. This suggests two levels of orientation: company, conducted by an HR representative, and departmental, conducted by the immediate supervisor. To ensure proper quality control plus continual improvement, an *orientation follow-up* is essential (e.g., after 1 week by the supervisor and after 1 month by an HR representative).

The pace of change in our society is forcing both employed and displaced workers continually to acquire new knowledge and skills. In most organizations, therefore, lifelong training is essential. To be maximally effective, training programs should follow a three-phase sequence: *needs assessment, implementation,* and *evaluation. What is to be learned* must first be defined clearly before a particular method or technique is chosen. To define what is to be learned, a continuous cycle of organization analysis, operations analysis, and analysis of the training needs of employees is necessary.

Training needs must then be related to the achievement of broader organizational goals and be consistent with management's perceptions of strategy and tactics. Beyond these fundamental concerns, issues of trainability and principles of learning— goal setting, behavior modeling, meaningfulness of material, practice, feedback, and transfer of training—are essential considerations in the design of any training program. The choice of a particular technique should be guided by the degree to which it fits identified needs and incorporates the learning principles.

In evaluating training programs, we measure change in terms of four categories: *reaction, learning, behavior,* and *results*. Measures of the impact of training on organizational results are the bottom line of training success. Fortunately, advances in utility analysis now make evaluations possible in terms of dollar benefits and dollar costs.

DISCUSSION QUESTIONS

8■1 Why is orientation so often overlooked by organizations?

8■2 Think back to your first day on the latest job you have held. What could have been done to hasten your socialization to the organization and your adjustment to the job?

8■3 Training has been described by some as intensely "faddish." As an advisor to management, describe how the firm can avoid succumbing to training fads.

8■4 How does goal setting affect trainee learning and motivation?

8■5 Outline an evaluation procedure for a training program designed to teach sales principles and strategies.

REFERENCES

1. Gordon, J. (1986). *Training* magazine's industry report, 1986. *Training*, **23**(10), 26–66.
2. Solomon, J. (1988, Dec. 29). Companies try measuring cost savings from new types of corporate benefits. *The Wall Street Journal*, p. B1.
3. Navy worried about growing jet losses (1986, Mar. 23). *Honolulu Star Bulletin*, pp. A1, A4.
4. Brownlee, D. (1983, June). Personal communication.
5. Much of the material in this section is drawn from Lubliner, M. (1978, April). Employee orientation. *Personnel Journal*, pp. 207–208. See also St. John, W. D. (1980, May). The complete employee orientation program. *Personnel Journal*, pp. 373–378.
6. Cappelli, P. (1992). *Is the "skills gap" really about attitudes?* Philadelphia: University of Pennsylvania, National Center on the Educational Quality of the Workforce.
7. St. John, op. cit.
8. Lubliner, op. cit.
9. McGarrell, E. J., Jr. (1984). An orientation system that builds productivity. *Personnel Administrator*, **29**(10), 75–85.
10. Fullerton, H. N., Jr. (1991, November). Labor force projections: The baby boom moves on. *Monthly Labor Review*, pp. 31–44.
11. Uchitelle, L. (1993, Jan. 31). Stanching the loss of good jobs. *The New York Times*, pp. 1F, 6F. See also Cascio, W. F., & Zammuto, R. F. (1989). Societal trends and staffing policies. In W. F. Cascio (ed.), *Human resource planning, employment, and placement*. Washington, DC: Bureau of National Affairs, pp. 2-1 to 2-33.
12. The Perplexing Case of the Plummeting Payrolls. (1993, Sept. 20). *Business Week*, p. 27.
13. Goldstein, I. L., & Gilliam, P. (1990). Training system issues in the year 2000. *American Psychologist*, **45**, 134–143.
14. Wellins, R. S., Byham, W. C., & Wilson, J. M. (1991). *Empowered teams.* San Francisco: Jossey-Bass.
15. Reich, R., in Greenhouse, S. (1992, Feb. 9). Attention America! Snap out of it! *The New York Times*, pp. 1F, 8F.
16. Cascio, W. F. (1993a, November). *Public investments in training: Perspectives on macro-level structural issues and micro-level delivery systems.* Philadelphia: University of Pennsylvania, National Center on the Educational Quality of the Workforce.
17. Brody, M. (1987, June 8). Helping workers to work smarter. *Fortune*, pp. 86–88.
18. Ibid.
19. Kilborn, P. T. (1993, Feb. 21). Wanted: Those high-tech jobs for retrained workers. *The New York Times*, pp. 1D, 3D.
20. Kilborn, P. T. (1990, Feb. 5). Costly pitfalls in worker retraining. *The New York Times*, p. A14.
21. Cascio, op. cit.
22. Labor letter (1991, Oct. 22). *The Wall Street Journal*, p. A1.
23. Hodson, R., Hooks, G., & Rieble, S. (1992). Customized training in the workplace. *Work and Occupations*, **19**(3), 272–292.

24. The literacy gap (1988, Dec. 19). *Time*, pp. 56, 57.
25. Salwen, K. G. (1993, Apr. 19). The cutting edge: German-owned maker of power tools finds job training pays off. *The Wall Street Journal*, pp. A1, A7.
26. Organization for Economic Cooperation and Development (1986). *Flexibility in the labor market: The current debate.* Paris: Author.
27. Ibid.
28. Cascio, W. F. (1993b, February). Downsizing: What do we know? What have we learned? *Academy of Management Executive, 7*(1), 95–104.
29. Kelley, M. R. (1989). An assessment of the skill upgrading and training opportunities for blue-collar workers under programmable automation. *Industrial Relations Research Association: Proceedings of the 39th annual meeting*, Chicago, pp. 301–308.
30. Labor letter, op. cit.
31. Kolberg, W. H., & Smith, F. C. (1992, Feb. 9). A new track for blue-collar workers. *The New York Times*, p. F13.
32. Labor letter, op. cit.
33. Salwen, op. cit.
34. Labor letter, op. cit.
35. Sirota, Alper, & Pfau, Inc. (1989). *Report to respondents: Survey of views toward corporate education and training practices.* New York: Author.
36. Rodgers, R., Hunter, J. E., & Rogers, D. L. (1993). Influence of top management commitment on management program success. *Journal of Applied Psychology, 78*, 151–155.
37. Training is "competitive weapon" in global markets, Xerox chief says (1990, Summer). *BNAC Communicator*, p. 20.
38. Labor letter (1988, Nov. 22). *The Wall Street Journal*, p. A1.
39. Cascio, W. F. (1993c). *Documenting training effectiveness in terms of worker performance and adaptability.* Philadelphia: University of Pennsylvania, National Center on the Educational Quality of the Workforce.
40. Porter, M. E. (1985). *Competitive advantage.* New York: Free Press.
41. Jackson, S. E., & Schuler, R. S. (1990). Human resource planning. *American Psychologist, 45*, 223–239.
42. Schuler, R. S., & Jackson, S. E. (1987). Linking competitive strategies with human resource management practices. *Academy of Management Executive, 1*(3), 207–219.
43. Goldstein, I. L. (1991). Training in work organizations. In M. D. Dunnette & L. M. Hough (eds.), *Handbook of industrial and organizational psychology.* Palo Alto, CA: Consulting Psychologists Press, pp. 507–619. See also Ostroff, C., & Ford, J. K. (1989). Assessing training needs: Critical levels of analysis. In I. L. Goldstein (ed.), *Training and development in organizations.* San Francisco: Jossey-Bass, pp. 25–62.
44. Moore, M. L., & Dutton, P. (1978). Training needs analysis: Review and critique. *Academy of Management Review, 3*, 532–454.
45. Hilton, M. (1987). Union and management: A strong case for cooperation. *Training and Development Journal, 41*(1), 54–55.
46. Robertson, I. T., & Downs, S. (1979). Learning and the prediction of performance: Development of trainability testing in the United Kingdom. *Journal of Applied Psychology, 64*, 42–50.
47. Robertson, I. T., & Downs, S. (1989). Work-sample tests of trainability: A meta-analysis. *Journal of Applied Psychology, 74*, 402–410.
48. Siegel, A. I. (1983). The miniature job training and evaluation approach: Additional findings. *Personnel Psychology, 36*, 41–56.
49. Reilly, R. R., & Israelski, E. W. (1988). Development and validation of minicourses in the telecommunication industry. *Journal of Applied Psychology, 73*, 721–726.
50. Ree, M. J., & Earles, J. A. (1991). Predicting training success: Not much more than *g. Personnel Psychology, 44*, 321–332.
51. Ryman, D. H., & Biersner, R. J. (1975). Attitudes predictive of diving training success. *Personnel Psychology, 28*, 181–188.

52. Noe, R. A. (1986). Trainees' attributes and attitudes: Neglected influences on training effectiveness. *Academy of Management Review,* **11,** 736–749. See also Noe, R. A., & Schmitt, N. (1986). The influence of trainee attitudes on training effectiveness: Test of a model. *Personnel Psychology,* **39,** 497–523.

53. Baldwin, T. T., Magjuka, R. J., & Loher, B. T. (1991). The perils of participation: Effects of choice of training on trainee motivation and learning. *Personnel Psychology,* **44,** 51–65

54. Wexley, K. N., & Latham, G. P. (1991). *Developing and training human resources in organizations.* New York: HarperCollins.

55. Eden, D., & Shani, A. B. (1982). Pygmalion goes to boot camp: Expectancy, leadership, and trainee performance. *Journal of Applied Psychology,* **67,** 194–199.

56. Matsui, T., Kakuyama, T., & Onglatco, M. L. U. (1987). Effects of goals and feedback on performance in groups. *Journal of Applied Psychology,* **72,** 407–415. See also Mento, A. J., Steel, R. P., & Karren, R. J. (1987). A meta-analytic study of the effects of goal setting on performance: 1966–1984. *Organizational Behavior and Human Decision Processes,* **39,** 52–83.

57. Wood, R. E., Mento, A. J., & Locke, E. A. (1987). Task complexity as a moderator of goal effects: A meta-analysis. *Journal of Applied Psychology,* **72,** 416–425.

58. Locke, E. A. (1968). Toward a theory of task motivation and incentives. *Organizational Behavior and Human Performance,* **3,** 157–189.

59. Locke, E. A., Latham, G. P., & Erez, M. (1988). The determinants of goal commitment. *Academy of Management Review,* **13,** 23–39.

60. Bandura, A. (1986). *Social foundations of thought and action: A social cognitive theory.* Englewood Cliffs, NJ: Prentice-Hall.

61. Hogan, P. M., Hakel, M. D., & Decker, P. J. (1986). Effects of trainee-generated versus trainer-provided rule codes on generalization in behavior-modeling training. *Journal of Applied Psychology,* **71,** 469–473.

62. Goldstein, A. P., & Sorcher, M. (1974). *Changing supervisor behavior.* New York: Pergamon Press. See also Latham, G. P., & Saari, L. M. (1979). The application of social learning theory to training supervisors through behavior modeling. *Journal of Applied Psychology,* **64,** 239–246.

63. Cascio, W. F. (1993c), op. cit. See also Baldwin, T. T. (1992). Effects of alternative modeling strategies on outcomes of interpersonal-skills training. *Journal of Applied Psychology,* **77,** 147–154.

64. Wexley & Latham, op. cit.

65. Gray, I., & Borecki, T. B. (1970). Training programs for the hard-core: What the trainer has to learn. *Personnel,* **47,** 23–29.

66. Gagné R. M. (1977). *The conditions of learning.* New York: Holt, Rinehart, & Winston.

67. Driskell, J. E., Willis, R. P., & Copper, C. (1992). Effect of overlearning on retention. *Journal of Applied Psychology,* **77,** 615–622.

68. Goldstein, I. L. (1993). *Training in organizations: Needs assessment, development, and evaluation* (3d ed.). Monterey, CA: Brooks/Cole.

69. Latham, G. P. (1989). Behavioral approaches to the training and learning process. In I. L. Goldstein (ed.), *Training and development in organizations.* San Francisco: Jossey-Bass, pp. 256–295.

70. Pritchard, R. D., Jones, S. D., Roth, P. L., Steubing, K. K., & Ekeberg, S. E. (1988). Effects of group feedback, goal setting, and incentives on organizational productivity. *Journal of Applied Psychology,* **73,** 337–358.

71. Florin-Thuma, B. C., & Boudreau, J. W. (1987). Performance feedback utility in a small organization: Effects on organizational outcomes and managerial decision processes. *Personnel Psychology,* **40,** 693–713.

72. Eastburn, R. A. (1986). Developing tomorrow's managers. *Personnel Administrator,* **31**(3), 71–76.

73. Cascio, W. F. (1991). *Applied psychology in personnel management* (4th ed.). Englewood Cliffs, NJ: Prentice-Hall.

74. Ganster, D. C., Williams, S., & Poppler, P. (1991). Does training in problem solving improve the quality of group decisions? *Journal of Applied Psychology*, **76**, 479–483.

75. Bass, B. M. (1980). Team productivity and individual member competence. *Small Group Behavior*, **11**, 431–504.

76. Wellins et al., op. cit.

77. Komaki, J. L., Desselles, J. L., & Bowman, E. D. (1989). Definitely not a breeze: Extending an operant model of supervision to teams. *Journal of Applied Psychology*, **74**, 522–529.

78. Campbell, J. P., Dunnette, M. D., Lawler, E. E., & Weick, K. E. (1970). *Managerial behavior, performance, and effectiveness*. New York: McGraw-Hill.

79. Labor letter (1990, May 8). *The Wall Street Journal*, p. A1.

80. Kraiger, K., Ford, J. K., & Salas, E. (1993). Application of cognitive, skill-based, and affective theories of learning outcomes to new methods of training evaluation. *Journal of Applied Psychology* (monograph), **78**, 311–328.

81. Sackett, P. R., & Mullen, E. J. (1993). Beyond formal experimental design: Towards an expanded view of the training evaluation process. *Personnel Psychology*, **46**, 613–627. See also Goldstein, I. L., op. cit.

82. Kirkpatrick, D. L. (1983). Four steps to measuring training effectiveness. *Personnel Administrator*, **28**(11), 19–25.

83. Arvey, R. D., Maxwell, S. E., & Salas, E. (1992). The relative power of training evaluation designs under different cost configurations. *Journal of Applied Psychology*, **77**, 155–160.

84. Cascio, W. F. (1989). Using utility analysis to assess training outcomes. In I. L. Goldstein (ed.), *Training and development in organizations*. San Francisco: Jossey-Bass, pp. 63–88. See also Cascio, W. F. (1991). *Costing human resources: The financial impact of behavior in organizations* (3d ed.). Boston: PWS-Kent.

85. Paquet, B., Kasl, E., Weinstein, L., & Waite, W. (1987). The bottom line. *Training and Development Journal*, **41**(6), 27–33.

86. Burke, M. J., & Day, R. R. (1986). A cumulative study of the effectiveness of managerial training. *Journal of Applied Psychology*, **71**, 232–245.

87. Cascio (1993c), op. cit.

88. Lee, M. (1993, Sept. 2). Diversity training grows at small firms. *The Wall Street Journal*, p. B2.

89. MacDonald, H. (1993, July 5). The diversity industry. *The New Republic*, pp. 22–25.

90. Armer, P. (1970). The individual: His privacy, self-image, and obsolescence. *Proceedings of the meeting of the panel on science and technology, 11th "Science and Astronautics."* Washington, DC: U.S. Government Printing Office.

91. Campbell, J. P. (1988). Training design for performance improvement. In J. P. Campbell & R. J. Campbell (eds.), *Productivity in organizations*. San Francisco: Jossey-Bass, pp. 177–215.

CHAPTER 9

APPRAISING EMPLOYEE PERFORMANCE

THE EXECUTIVE APPRAISAL PARADOX*

"It just doesn't make any sense. The higher you climb the ladder in this organization, the less chance you have of getting feedback about your performance. . . . We seem to have time for everything else, but not time to give our top people the kind of reviews they need to help them develop."

This observation from an executive-level controller typifies the type of performance feedback most executives receive. With each promotion, reviews become less frequent, systematic, informative, and useful. At the executive level, there often is almost no regular performance feedback other than superficial praise or criticism for some crisis. This suggests an apparent paradox in performance appraisal: *the higher managers rise in an organization, the lower the likelihood that they will receive quality feedback on their job performance.* For some obscure but apparently pervasive reason, executive appraisal seems to have become a taboo topic in many organizations. This is a serious issue, for executives perform the most uncertain, unstructured, ill defined, and often most important work in an enterprise.

Recent research (a total of 118 hours of in-depth interviews with 84 executives from 11 major organizations spanning 12 different functional areas) suggests that the widespread disappointment with the quality of executive appraisals is traceable to a series of myths surrounding the process. Together, they contribute to the paradox that those who could most use performance feedback to enhance their effectiveness are often the least likely to get it.

---

*Adapted from: C.O. Longenecker & D. A. Gioia, The executive appraisal paradox, *Academy of Management Executive*, **6**(2), 1992, 18–28. Used by permission

The myths turn out to be surprisingly common. We will examine them in the first part of this case, and in the second part, at the end of the chapter, we will identify what can be done to debunk these myths.

Myth #1: Executives neither need nor want structured performance reviews. This belief stems from a widely shared premise that the higher an individual's level in an organization, the lower should be the need for feedback. Paradoxically, this is not the way executives themselves see it. Every executive interviewed said that systematic feedback in some form was crucial in order to help him or her grow.

Myth #2: A formal review is beneath the dignity of an executive. The fallacy here is the presumption that appraisal is somehow a sign that one is still on professional probation, that it is a demeaning, aversive experience that managers mercifully can outgrow. Naturally, appraisal at any level can produce anxiety—"there is a need to know and a fear of knowing." But executives insisted that their need to know far outweighed their fear. They preferred to know where they stood.

Myth #3: Top-level executives are too busy to conduct appraisals. Often "too busy" is a smoke screen for some less mundane reason—such as a belief that appraisals are not worth doing. Said one executive who had been burned by this attitude: "It seems like we have time for lots of things that are a lot less important than talking about improving performance and executive development. There should always be time for a process that contributes to higher performance and productivity and, paradoxically, the saving of time."

Myth #4: A lack of feedback fosters autonomy and creativity in executives. This approach to executive development is attractive because it affirms the admired notion of "pulling yourself up by your bootstraps." To some degree, it can facilitate autonomy and creativity. There is ample evidence, however, that the same goal can be accomplished—faster—with good feedback. Said one executive: "A lack of performance feedback keeps people in the dark about how others view their performance. That breeds doubt and frustration and, maybe worse, allows little problems to fester into big ones."

Myth #5: Results are the only basis for assessing executive performance. As a division manager put it: "Sure, you have to get results; that's why we're in business. But you also need to look at the road you took to get the results. You need feedback on process and style and the intangibles that you can't quantify." Said another VP: "Isolating on results is a formula for long-term trouble." An example from the service industry illustrates this nicely. An executive used hard-nosed methods to build his track record as a troubleshooter, one who could turn divisions around. In one division, however, although he did shore up its bottom line, his severe tactics and caustic style nearly incited an employee rebellion. As a result, he was called to headquarters and given an ultimatum to "improve your human relations skills right now or else." It was the first time he'd received any formal feedback other than praise.

Myth #6: Comprehensive evaluation of executive performance simply cannot be captured via formal performance appraisal. Intuition, gut feelings, flashes of insight, and other nonmeasurable attributes are hallmarks of high-performing managers. As a result, some executives want the evaluation of executive performance to be considered an intangible domain also. Can you appreciate the exasperation of this disgruntled veteran of ambiguous performance standards? "You never really knew where you stood. You could do exactly what you thought you were supposed to do and get burned, or hit the right number in one column, screw up the rest, and be a saint. Performance at the upper levels is subjective, but sometimes it seems like it's kept that way for some suspicious reasons."

Challenges

1. In your opinion, why do these six myths persist?

2. If standards of performance are ambiguous, does this undermine the philosophy that "rewards are based on performance"?

3. Should the process an executive uses be just as important as the outcomes she or he achieves?

Questions This Chapter Will Help Managers Answer

1. What steps can I, as a manager, take to make the performance appraisal process more relevant and acceptable to those who will be affected by it?

2. How can we best fit our approach to performance appraisal with the strategic direction of our department and business?

3. Should managers and nonmanagers be appraised from multiple perspectives—for example, by those above, by those below, by coequals, and by customers?

4. What strategy should we use to train raters at all levels in the mechanics of doing appraisal and the art of giving feedback?

5. What would an effective appraisal process look like?

The chapter opening vignette reveals just how complex performance management can be, for it includes both developmental (feedback) and administrative (pay, promotions) issues, as well as both technical aspects (design of an appraisal system) and interpersonal aspects (appraisal interviews). This chapter's objective is to present a balanced view of the appraisal process, considering both its technical and its interpersonal aspects. Let's begin by examining the nature of the performance appraisal process.

PERFORMANCE APPRAISAL: A COMPLEX AND OFTEN MISUNDERSTOOD PROCESS

Performance appraisal has many facets. It is an exercise in observation and judgment, it is a feedback process, and it is an organizational intervention. It is a measurement process as well as an intensely emotional process. Above all, it is an inexact, human process. While it is fairly easy to prescribe how the process *should* work, descriptions of how it *actually* works in practice are rather discouraging.

Two independent surveys involving more than 9000 employees found that fewer than 50 percent of U.S. workers think their bosses provide regular performance feedback or help solve interpersonal problems. Seventy percent believed that review sessions had not given them a clear picture of what was expected of them on the job or of where they could advance in the company. Only half said their bosses helped them set job objectives, and only one in five said reviews were followed up during the ensuing year.[1] Some managers give short shrift to appraisals—and their subordinates know it.

This chapter examines some of the reasons for common problems in the appraisal process and considers how the application of research findings in the area of performance appraisal can improve the process. Let us begin by defining our terms:

- *Performance* refers to an employee's accomplishment of assigned tasks.
- *Performance appraisal* is the systematic description of the job-relevant strengths and weaknesses of an individual or a group.
- *Appraisal period* is the length of time during which an employee's job performance is observed in order to make a formal report of it.
- *Performance management* is the total process of observing an employee's performance in relation to job requirements over a period of time (i.e., clarifying expectations, setting goals, providing on-the-job coaching, storing and recalling information about performance) and then making an appraisal of it. Information gained from the process may be fed back via an appraisal interview to determine the relevance of individual and work-group performance to organizational purposes, improve the effectiveness of the unit, and improve the work performance of employees.[2]

Before addressing some common problems in performance appraisal, let us first consider the major organizational purposes served by appraisal systems. (A comprehensive list of such purposes is shown in Table 9-3.) In general, appraisal serves a twofold purpose: (1) to improve employees' work performance by helping them realize and use their full potential in carrying out their firms' missions and (2) to provide information to employees and managers for use in making work-related decisions. More specifically, appraisals serve the following purposes:

1. Appraisals provide legal and formal organizational justification for employment decisions to promote outstanding performers; to weed out marginal or low performers; to train, transfer, or discipline others; to justify merit increases (or no increases); and as one basis for reducing the size of the workforce. In short, appraisal serves as a key input for administering a formal organizational reward and punishment system.

2. Appraisals are used as criteria in test validation. That is, test results are correlated with appraisal results to evaluate the hypothesis that test scores predict job performance.[3] However, if appraisals are not done carefully, or if considerations other than performance influence appraisal results, the appraisals cannot legitimately be used for any purpose.

3. Appraisals provide feedback to employees and thereby serve as vehicles for personal and career development.

4. Once the development needs of employees are identified, appraisals can help establish objectives for training programs.

5. As a result of the proper specifications of performance levels, appraisals can help diagnose organizational problems. They do so by identifying training needs and the knowledge, abilities, skills, and other characteristics to consider in hiring, and they also provide a basis for distinguishing between effective and ineffective per-

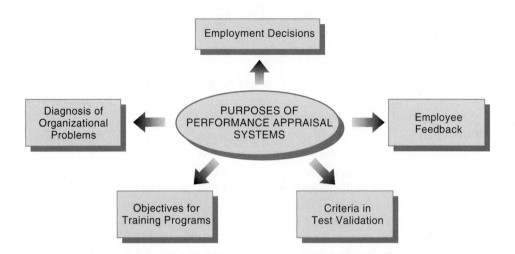

FIGURE 9-1
Purposes of performance
appraisal systems.

formers. Appraisal therefore represents the beginning of a process, rather than an
end product.[4] These ideas are shown graphically in Figure 9-1.

The Organizational and Human Contexts of
Performance Appraisal

Having seen the multiple purposes for which appraisal systems can be used to manage
human resources wisely, let us now consider some enlightening findings from actual
practice:

1. Among U.S. firms, especially large ones, performance appraisal is almost universal.
   Thus a recent survey of 1800 firms in the Rocky Mountain region found that 94
   percent conduct performance appraisals.[5] Other surveys show that more than 90
   percent of such programs ask the immediate supervisor to take the *sole* responsibility for doing the appraisal.[6]

2. A typical manager has limited contact with his or her employees. Studies indicate
   that managers spend only 5 to 10 percent of their workweek with any one subordinate. These contacts are in a limited range of settings, such as formal meetings.[7]
   Managers therefore have access only to a small (and perhaps unrepresentative)
   sample of their subordinates' work.

3. Accuracy in appraisal is less important to managers than motivating and rewarding
   their subordinates. Many managers will not allow excessively accurate ratings to
   cause problems for themselves, and they attempt to use the appraisal process to
   their own advantage.[8]

4. Standards and ratings tend to vary widely and often unfairly. Some raters are
   tough, others lenient. Some departments have highly competent people, others less
   competent people. Consequently, employees subject to less competition or to
   lenient ratings can receive higher appraisals than do equally competent or superior
   associates.

5. Personal values and biases can replace organizational standards. Thus unfairly low
   ratings may be given to valued subordinates so that they will not be promoted out
   of the rater's department, or outright bias may lead to favored treatment for some
   employees.

ETHICAL DILEMMAS IN PERFORMANCE APPRAISAL

Performance appraisal actually encompasses two distinct processes: *observation* and *judgment*. Managers must observe performance if they are to be competent to judge its effectiveness. Yet, as we have noted, some managers assign performance ratings on the basis of small (and perhaps unrepresentative) samples of their subordinates' work. Is this ethical? And further, is it ethical to assign performance ratings (either good or bad) that differ from what a manager knows a subordinate deserves?

6. Sometimes the validity of performance appraisals is reduced by the supervisor's resistance to making them. Rather than confront their less effective subordinates with negative ratings, negative feedback in appraisal interviews, and below-average salary increases, some supervisors take the easy way out and give average or above-average ratings to inferior performers. The result? The average ratings reinforce inferior performance.

7. Some supervisors complain that performance appraisal is pointless paperwork. This author's surveys of more than 1000 supervisors in a county hospital over a 3-year period indicated that fewer than 20 percent could cite *any* use of appraisals in HRM. Is their "pointless paperwork" reaction really a surprise?

8. Performance appraisals interfere with more constructive supervisor–subordinate coaching relationships. Appraisal interviews tend to emphasize the superior position of the supervisor by placing her or him in the role of judge, thus countering her or his equally important roles of teacher and coach. In organizations that are attempting to promote supervisor–subordinate participation in decisions, such situations can be downright destructive. Both IDS Financial Services and Corning handle this problem by separating discussions aimed at employee development from those aimed at administrative decisions (e.g., merit raises, promotions).[9]

It is easy to understand how the foregoing list could engender a sense of hopelessness in any manager or organization thinking about appraisal. However, despite their shortcomings, appraisals continue to be used widely, especially as a basis for tying pay to performance.[10] To attempt to avoid these shortcomings by doing away with appraisals is no solution, for whenever people interact in organized settings, appraisals will be made—formally or informally. The real challenge, then, is to identify appraisal techniques and practices that (1) are most likely to achieve a particular objective and (2) are least vulnerable to the obstacles listed above. Let us begin by considering some of the fundamental requirements that determine whether a performance appraisal system will succeed or fail.

Requirements of Effective Appraisal Systems

Legally and scientifically, the key requirements of any appraisal system are relevance, sensitivity, and reliability. In the context of ongoing operations, the key requirements are acceptability and practicality.[11] Let's consider each of these.

Relevance. This implies that there are (1) clear links between the performance standards for a particular job and an organization's goals and (2) clear links between the

FIGURE 9-2
Relationship of performance standards to job analysis and performance appraisal.

critical job elements identified through a job analysis and the dimensions to be rated on an appraisal form. In short, relevance is determined by answering the question "What really makes the difference between success and failure on a particular job?"

Performance standards translate job requirements into *levels* of acceptable or unacceptable employee behavior. They play a critical role in the job analysis–performance appraisal linkage, as Figure 9-2 indicates. We will have more to say about performance standards later in this chapter.

Relevance also implies the periodic maintenance and updating of job analyses, performance standards, and appraisal systems. Should the system be challenged in court, relevance will be a fundamental consideration in the arguments presented by both sides.

Sensitivity. This implies that a performance appraisal system is capable of distinguishing effective from ineffective performers. If it is not, and the best employees are rated no differently from the worst employees, then the appraisal system cannot be used for any administrative purpose, it certainly will not help employees to develop, and it will undermine the motivation of both supervisors ("pointless paperwork") and subordinates.

A major concern here is the purpose of the rating. One study found that raters process identical sets of performance appraisal information differently, depending on whether a merit pay raise, a recommendation for further development, or the retention of a probationary employee is involved.[12] These results highlight the conflict between appraisals made for administrative purposes and those made for employee development. Appraisal systems designed for administrative purposes demand performance information about differences *between* individuals, while systems designed to promote employee growth demand information about differences *within* individuals. The two different types of information are not interchangeable in terms of purposes, and that is why performance management systems designed to meet both purposes are more complex and costly. In practice, only one type of information is usually collected, and it is used for some administrative purpose.[13] As we have seen, performance appraisal need not be a zero-sum game, but unfortunately it usually is.

Reliability. A third requirement of sound appraisal systems is reliability. In this context it refers to consistency of judgment. For any given employee, appraisals made by raters working independently of one another should agree closely. But raters with different perspectives (e.g., supervisors, peers, subordinates) may see the same individual's job performance very differently.[14] To provide reliable data, each rater must have an adequate opportunity to observe what the employee has done and the conditions under which he or she has done it; otherwise, unreliability may be confused with unfamiliarity.

Note that throughout this discussion there has been no mention of the validity or accuracy of appraisal judgments. This is because we really do not know what "truth" is in performance appraisal. However, by making appraisal systems relevant, sensitive, and reliable—by satisfying the scientific and legal requirements for workable appraisal systems—we can assume that the resulting judgments are valid as well.

Acceptability. In practice, acceptability is the most important requirement of all, for it is true that human resource programs must have the support of those who will use them, or else human ingenuity will be used to thwart them. Unfortunately, many organizations have not put much effort into garnering the front-end support and participation of those who will use the appraisal system. Thus only 62 percent of respondents in an American Productivity & Quality Center survey said that their bosses evaluate them fairly.[15]

Ultimately, it is management's responsibility to define as clearly as possible the type and level of job behavior desired of employees. While this might seem obvious, consider three kinds of behavior that managers might exhibit:

1. Managers may not know what they want, and they may find it extremely painful even to discuss the issue.

2. Managers might fear that when employees find out what they want, the employees may not like it.

3. Some managers feel that they lose flexibility by stating their objectives in advance: "If I tell them what I want, they will do only those things." This is management and appraisal by reaction: "I'll see what they do and then tell them whether I like it or not."

Clearly, these attitudes run counter to research findings in performance appraisal. Under these circumstances we are playing power games with people and undermining the credibility and acceptability of the entire appraisal system. How much simpler it is to enlist the active support and cooperation of subordinates by making explicit exactly what aspects of job performance they will be evaluated on! Instead of promoting secrecy, we should be promoting more openness in human resource management, so that we can say, "This is what you must be able to do in order to perform competently." Only then can we expect to find the kind of acceptability and commitment that is so sorely needed in performance appraisal.

Practicality. This implies that appraisal instruments are easy for managers and employees to understand and use. The importance of this was brought home forcefully to me in the course of mediating a conflict between a county's Metropolitan Transit Authority (MTA) and its human resource (HR) unit. Here's what happened:

PRACTICAL PERFORMANCE APPRAISAL FOR BUS DRIVERS

COMPANY EXAMPLE

The conflict erupted over the HR unit's *imposition* of a new appraisal system on all county departments regardless of each department's need for the new system. MTA had developed an appraisal system jointly with its union 5 years earlier, and it was working fine. In brief, each MTA supervisor (high school–educated) was responsible for about 30 subordinates (a total of 890 bus drivers who were also high school–educated or less). The "old" appraisal system was based on a checklist of infractions (e.g., reporting late for work, being charged with a preventable traffic accident), each of which carried a specified number of points. Appraisals were done quarterly, with each driver assigned 100 points at the beginning of each quarter. A driver's quarterly appraisal was simply the number of points remaining after all penalty points had been deducted during the quarter. Her or his annual appraisal (used as a basis for decisions regarding merit pay, promotions, and special assignments) was simply the average of the four quarterly ratings. Both supervisors and subordinates liked the old system because it was understandable and practical, and also because it had been shown to be workable over a 5-year period.

The new appraisal system required MTA supervisors to write quarterly narrative reports on each of their 30-odd subordinates. The HR unit had made no effort to determine the ratio of supervisors to subordinates in the various departments. Not surprisingly, therefore, objections to the new system surfaced almost immediately. MTA supervisors had neither the time nor the inclination to write quarterly narratives on each of their subordinates. The new system was highly impractical. Furthermore, the old appraisal system was working fine and was endorsed by MTA management, employees, and their union. MTA managers therefore refused to adopt the new system. To dramatize their point, they developed a single, long, detailed narrative on an outstanding bus driver. Then they made 890 copies of the narrative (one for each driver), placed a different driver's name at the top of each "appraisal," and sent the 2-foot-high stack of "appraisals" to the HR unit. MTA made its point. After considerable haggling by both sides, the HR unit backed down and allowed MTA to continue to use its old (but acceptable and eminently practical) appraisal system. That system was not perfect (e.g., drivers could only lose points for poor performance, not earn points for good performance), but it illustrates how strongly the parties in the appraisal process will fight for a system that they find acceptable.

In a broader context, we are concerned with developing decision systems. From this perspective, *relevance, sensitivity,* and *reliability* are simply technical components of a performance appraisal system designed to make decisions about employees. As we have seen, just as much attention needs to be paid to ensuring the *acceptability* and *practicality* of appraisal systems. These are the five basic requirements of performance appraisal systems, and none of them can be ignored. However, since some degree of error is inevitable in all employment decisions, the crucial question to be answered in regard to each appraisal system is whether its use results in less human, social, and organizational cost than is currently paid for these errors. The answers to that question can result only in a wiser, fuller utilization of our human resources.

LEGAL ISSUES IN PERFORMANCE APPRAISAL

There is a rich body of case law on performance appraisal, and three reviews of it reached similar conclusions.[16] To avoid legal difficulties, consider taking the following steps:

1. Conduct a job analysis to determine the characteristics necessary for successful job performance.

2. Incorporate these characteristics into a rating instrument. This may be done by tying rating instruments to specific job behaviors (e.g., BARS, see page 287), but the courts routinely accept less sophisticated approaches, such as simple graphic rating scales. Regardless of the method used, provide written standards to all raters.

3. Train supervisors to use the rating instrument properly, including how to apply performance standards when making judgments. The uniform application of standards is very important. The vast majority of cases *lost* by organizations have involved evidence that subjective standards were applied unevenly to members of protected groups versus all other employees. As we saw earlier, performance appraisal results are used in the selection process to establish the validity of selection instruments. Steps 1, 2, and 3 are identical to those in that process.

4. Formal appeal mechanisms, coupled with higher-level review of appraisals, are desirable.

5. Document the appraisals and the reason for any termination decisions. This information may prove decisive in court. Credibility is enhanced by documented appraisal ratings that describe instances of poor performance.

6. Provide some form of performance counseling or corrective guidance to assist poor performers.

Here is a good example of step 6. In *Stone v. Xerox* the organization had a fairly elaborate procedure for assisting poor performers.[17] Stone was employed as a sales representative and in fewer than 6 months had been given several written reprimands concerning customer complaints about his selling methods and failure to develop adequate written selling proposals. As a result, he was placed on a 1-month performance improvement program designed to correct these deficiencies. This program was extended 30 days at Stone's request. When his performance still did not improve, he was placed on probation and told that failure to improve substantially would result in termination. Stone's performance continued to be substandard, and he was discharged at the end of the probationary period. When he sued Xerox, he lost.

Certainly, the type of evidence required to defend performance ratings is linked to the *purposes* for which the ratings are made. For example, if appraisal of past performance is to be used as a predictor of future performance (i.e., promotions), evidence must be presented to show (1) that the ratings of past performance are, in fact, valid and (2) that the ratings of past performance are statistically related to *future* performance in another job.[18] At the very least, this latter step should include job analysis results indicating the extent to which the requirements of the lower- and higher-level jobs overlap. Finally, to assess adverse impact, organizations should keep accurate records of who is eligible for and interested in promotion. These two factors, *eligibility* and *interest*, define the "applicant group."

In summary, it is not difficult to offer prescriptions for scientifically sound, court-proof appraisal systems, but as we have seen, implementing them requires diligent attention by organizations, plus a commitment to making them work. In developing a performance appraisal system, the most basic requirement is to determine what you want the system to accomplish. This requires a strategy for the management of performance.

The Strategic Dimension of Performance Appraisal

In the study of work motivation, a fairly well established principle is that the things that get rewarded get done. At least one author has termed this "The greatest management principle in the world."[19] So a basic issue for managers is "What kind of behavior do I want to encourage in my subordinates?" If employees are rewarded for generating short-term results, they will generate short-term results. If they are rewarded (e.g., through progressively higher commissions or bonuses) for generating repeat business or for reaching quality standards over long periods of time, then they will do those things.

On a basic level, therefore, managers can emphasize short- or long-term objectives in the appraisal process. Short-term objectives emphasize such things as bottom-line results for the current quarter. Long-term objectives emphasize such things as increasing market share and securing repeat business from customers. To be most useful, however, the strategic management of performance must be linked to the strategies an organization (or strategic business unit) uses to gain competitive advantage—for example, innovation, speed, quality enhancement, or cost control.[20]

Some appraisal systems that are popular in the United States, such as management by objectives (MBO), are less popular in other parts of the world, such as Japan and France. MBO focuses primarily on results, rather than on how the results were accomplished. Typically it has a short-term focus, although this need not always be the case.

In Japan, greater emphasis is placed on the psychological and behavioral sides of performance appraisal than on objective outcomes. Thus an employee will be rated in terms of the effort he or she puts into a job, on integrity, loyalty, and cooperative spirit, and on how well he or she serves the customer. Short-term results tend to be much less important than long-term personal development, the establishment and maintenance of long-term relationships with customers (that is, behaviors), and increasing market share.[21]

Once managers decide what they want the appraisal system to accomplish, the next step is to develop specific standards of performance against which to evaluate employees. Let's consider how this is done.

DEVELOPING PERFORMANCE STANDARDS

Common sense dictates that fair performance appraisal requires a standard against which to compare employee performance. The clearer the performance standard is, the more accurate the appraisal can be. Thus the first step in effectively managing employee or work-group performance is to review existing standards and develop new ones if needed. Unfortunately, many supervisors simply *assume* that employees and work groups know what they are supposed to do on their jobs. Nothing could be further from the truth. At a recent Business Roundtable breakfast, a human resources executive from an insurance company described a study in which his company learned from field interviews with employees that as many as two-thirds could not describe clearly the requirements of their jobs and the performance standards on which they were evaluated!

Performance standards should contain two basic kinds of information for the benefit of both employee and supervisor: *what* is to be done and *how well* it is to be done. The identification of job tasks, duties, and critical elements (see Chapter 5) describes *what* is to be done. This is crucial, for sound human resource management dictates that the content of the appraisal should reflect the nontrivial content of the job; such information provides content-related evidence of the validity of the appraisal system. Performance standards focus on *how well* the tasks are to be done. To be most useful, each standard should be stated clearly enough so that manager and subordinate or work group know what is expected and whether it has been met. Standards should be written to describe *fully satisfactory* performance for critical as well as noncritical tasks.[22]

Since job tasks and performance standards are interrelated, it is common practice to develop them at the same time. Whatever method of job analysis is used should take into account both quantitative and qualitative aspects of performance. Further, each standard should refer to a specific aspect of the job. Examples are:

Quantitative	Qualitative
Number of forms processed	Accuracy, quality of work
Amount of time used	Ability to coordinate (e.g., staff, activities)
Number of errors	Ability to analyze (e.g., data, machine malfunctions)
Number of pages typed	Ability to evaluate (e.g., customer complaints, market research)

Almost all jobs involve both aspects of performance but in varying proportions, depending on the nature of the job. Obviously, it is easier to measure performance against standards that can be described in quantitative terms. However, managerial jobs have an added component. That is, in addition to results that reflect the manager's own performance, other results reflect the performance of the organizational unit for which the manager is responsible. For managerial jobs, therefore, initial performance standards should still be determined by job analysis, even though they may be modified later (as a result of joint agreement by manager and subordinate or work group) to incorporate goals to be achieved. Goals that meet minimum standards are documented in quantitative terms, if possible; for example, a specified kind and amount of work will be done within a certain time limit. Doing so allows managers to assess progress toward goals even before any formal appraisal takes place. An example of a set of performance standards for an electric meter reader is shown in Table 9-1.

Often the first question managers ask is "What's the best method of performance appraisal, which technique should I use?" As in so many other areas of HR management, there is no simple answer. The following section considers some alternative methods, along with their strengths and weaknesses. Since readers of this book are more likely to be *users* of appraisal systems than *developers* of them, the following will focus most on describing and illustrating them. For more detailed information, consult the references at the end of the chapter.

ALTERNATIVE METHODS OF APPRAISING EMPLOYEE PERFORMANCE

Many regard rating methods or formats as *the* central issue in performance appraisal; this, however, is not the case.[23] Broader issues must also be considered—such as *trust* in the appraisal system; the *attitudes* of managers and employees; the *purpose, frequency,* and *source* of appraisal data; and rater *training*. Viewed in this light, rating formats play only a supporting role in the overall appraisal process.

■ **TABLE 9 · 1**

PERFORMANCE STANDARDS FOR AN ELECTRIC-METER READER

Critical (C) or noncritical (NC) tasks	Performance standard (fully satisfactory)
Records readings from residential and commercial meters (C)	Two legibility errors per 480 character entries; one transposition error per 400 meters read as shown by computer and manual checks
Inspects meters for damage or tap-ins (C)	Reports 80 percent of damaged meters found on routes as confirmed by spot checks made by service inspectors
Indicates extremes in usage (NC)	Indicates extremely high or low readings 90 percent of the time as shown by spot computer checks
Complies with safety standards (C)	Complies with safety standards 100 percent of the time
Interacts with customers (C)	No more than two customer complaints per month

Many rating formats focus on employee behaviors, either by comparing the performance of employees to that of other employees (so-called "relative rating systems") or by evaluating each employee in terms of performance standards without reference to others (so-called "absolute rating systems"). Other rating formats place primary emphasis on what an employee produces (so-called "results-oriented systems"); dollar volume of sales, number of units produced, and number of interceptions during a football season are examples. Rating formats that use this results-oriented approach are management by objectives (MBO) and work planning and review.

Evidence indicates that ratings (that is, judgments about performance) are not strongly related to results.[24] Why? Ratings depend heavily on the mental processes of the rater. Because these processes are complex, there may be errors of judgment in the ratings. Conversely, results depend heavily on environmental conditions that may be outside the control of the individual worker, such as the availability of supplies or the contributions of others. Thus most measures of results provide only partial coverage of the overall domain of job performance. With these considerations in mind, let's examine the behavior- and results-oriented systems more fully.

Behavior-Oriented Rating Methods

Narrative Essay. The simplest type of absolute rating system is the narrative essay, in which a rater describes, in writing, an employee's strengths, weaknesses, and potential, together with suggestions for improvement. This approach assumes that a candid statement from a rater who is knowledgeable about an employee's performance is just as valid as more formal and more complicated rating methods. The MTA bus driver case presented earlier illustrated this approach.

If essays are done well, they can provide detailed feedback to subordinates regarding their performance. On the other hand, comparisons across individuals, groups, or departments are almost impossible since different essays touch on different aspects of each subordinate's performance. This makes it difficult to use essay information for employment decisions since subordinates are not compared objectively and ranked relative to one another. Methods that compare employees to one another are more useful for this purpose.

Ranking. *Simple ranking* requires only that a rater order all employees from highest to lowest, from "best" employee to "worst" employee. *Alternation ranking* requires that a rater initially list all employees on a sheet of paper. From this list he or she first chooses the best employee (No. 1), then the worst employee (No. *n*), then the second best (No. 2), then the second worst (No. *n* - 1), and so forth, alternating from the top to the bottom of the list until all employees have been ranked.

Paired Comparisons. This is a more systematic method for comparing employees to one another. Here each employee is compared with every other employee, usually in terms of an overall category such as "present value to the organization." The rater's task is simply to choose the "better" of each pair, and each employee's rank is determined by counting the number of times she or he was rated superior. However, since these comparisons are made on an overall basis (that is, "Who is better?") and not in terms of specific job behaviors or outcomes, they may be subject to legal challenge.[25] On the other hand, methods that compare employees to one another are useful for generating initial rankings for purposes of salary administration.

Forced Distribution. This is another method of comparing employees to one another. As the name "forced distribution" implies, the overall distribution of ratings is forced into a normal, or bell-shaped, curve under the assumption that a relatively small portion of employees is truly outstanding, a relatively small portion is unsatisfactory, and everybody else falls in between. Figure 9-3 illustrates this method, assuming that five rating categories are used.

Forced distribution does eliminate clustering almost all employees at the top of the distribution (rater *leniency*), at the bottom of the distribution (rater *severity*), or in the middle (*central tendency*). However, it can foster a great deal of employee resentment if an entire group of employees *as a group* is either superior or substandard. It is most useful when a large number of employees must be rated and there is more than one rater.

Behavioral Checklist. Here the rater is provided with a series of statements that describe job-related behavior. His or her task is simply to "check" which of the statements, or the extent to which each statement, describes the employee. In this approach raters are not so much evaluators as reporters or describers of job behavior. And descriptive ratings are likely to be more reliable than evaluative (good–bad) ratings.[26] In one such method, the Likert method of *summed ratings*, a declarative statement (e.g., "She or he follows up on customer complaints") is followed by several response categories, such as "always," "very often," "fairly often," "occasionally," and "never." The rater checks the response category that he or she thinks best describes the employee. Each category is weighted, for example, from 5 ("always") to 1

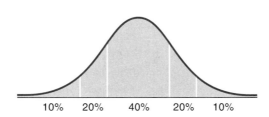

10%   20%   40%   20%   10%

FIGURE 9-3
Example of a forced distribution. Forty percent of the ratees must be rated "average," 20 percent "above average," 20 percent "below average," 10 percent "outstanding," and 10 percent "unsatisfactory."

	Strongly Agree	Agree	Neutral	Disagree	Strongly Disagree
The teacher was well prepared.					
The teacher used understandable language.					
The teacher made me think.					
The teacher's feedback on students' work aided learning.					
The teacher knew his or her field well.					

FIGURE 9-4
A portion of a summed rating scale. The rater simply checks the response category that best describes the teacher's behavior. Response categories vary in scale value from 5 points (Strongly Agree) to 1 point (Strongly Disagree). A total score is computed by summing the points associated with each item.

("never") if the statement describes desirable behavior. An overall numerical rating (or score) for each employee is then derived by *summing* the weights of the responses that were checked for each item. A portion of a summed rating scale for appraising teacher performance is shown in Figure 9-4.

Critical Incidents. These are brief anecdotal reports by supervisors of things employees do that are particularly effective or ineffective in accomplishing parts of their jobs. They focus on behaviors, not traits. For example, a store manager in a retail computer store observed Mr. Wang, a salesperson, do the following:

> Mr. Wang encouraged the customer to try our new word processing package by having the customer sit down at the computer and write a letter. The finished product was full of typographical and spelling errors, each of which was highlighted for the customer when Mr. Wang applied a "spelling checker" to the written material. As a result, Mr. Wang sold the customer the word processing program plus a typing tutor and a spelling checker program.

Such anecdotes force attention onto the ways in which situations determine job behavior and also on ways of doing the job successfully that may be unique to the person described. Hence they can provide the basis for training programs. Critical incidents also lend themselves nicely to appraisal interviews because supervisors can focus on actual job behaviors rather than on vaguely defined traits. Performance, not personality, is judged.

Like other rating methods, critical incidents have their drawbacks. One, supervisors may find that recording incidents for their subordinates on a daily or even a weekly basis is burdensome. Two, the *rater* sets the standards by which subordinates are judged; yet motivation is likely to be enhanced if *subordinates* have some say in setting the standards by which they will be judged. And three, in their narrative form, incidents do not permit comparisons across individuals or departments. To overcome this problem, graphic rating scales may be used.

Graphic Rating Scale. This is probably the most widely used rating method.[27] A portion of one such scale is shown in Figure 9-5.

Many different forms of graphic rating scales exist. In terms of the amount of structure provided, the scales differ in three ways:

1. The degree to which the meaning of the response categories is defined (in Figure 9-5, what does "conditional" mean?)
2. The degree to which the individual who is interpreting the ratings (e.g., a higher-level reviewing official) can tell clearly what response was intended

Rating Factors	Level of Performance				
	Unsatisfactory	Conditional	Satisfactory	Above Satisfactory	Outstanding
Attendance					
Appearance					
Dependability					
Quality of work					
Quantity of work					
Relationship with people					
Job knowledge					

FIGURE 9-5
A portion of a graphic rating scale.

3. The degree to which the performance dimensions are defined for the rater (in Figure 9-5, for example, what does "dependability" mean?)

Graphic rating scales may not yield the depth of essays or critical incidents, but they are less time-consuming to develop and administer, the results can be expressed in quantitative terms, more than one performance dimension is considered, and since the scales are standardized, comparisons can be made across employees. Graphic rating scales have come under frequent attack, but when compared to more sophisticated forced-choice scales, the graphic scales have proven just as reliable and valid and are more acceptable to raters.[28]

Behaviorally Anchored Rating Scales (BARS). These are a variation of the simple graphic rating scale. Their major advantage is that they define the dimensions to be rated in behavioral terms and use critical incidents to describe various levels of performance. BARS therefore provide a common frame of reference for raters. An example of the job knowledge portion of a BARS for police patrol officers is shown in Figure 9-6. BARS require considerable effort to develop,[29] yet there is little research evidence to support the superiority of BARS over other types of rating systems.[30] Nevertheless, the participative process required to develop them provides information that is useful for other organizational purposes, such as communicating clearly to employees exactly what "good performance" means in the context of their jobs.

Results-Oriented Rating Methods

Management by Objectives (MBO). This is a well-known process of managing that relies on goal setting to establish objectives for the organization as a whole, for each department, for each manager within each department, and for each employee. MBO is not a measure of employee behavior; rather, it is a measure of each employee's contribution to the success of the organization.[31]

In theory, objectives are established by having the key people affected do three things: (1) meet to *agree on the major objectives* for a given period of time (e.g., every year, every 6 months, or quarterly), (2) *develop plans* for how and when the objectives will be accomplished, and (3) *agree on the "yardsticks"* for determining whether the objectives have been met. Progress reviews are held regularly until the end of the

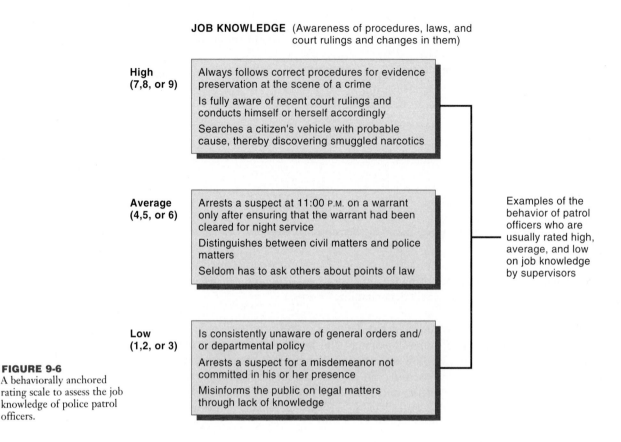

JOB KNOWLEDGE (Awareness of procedures, laws, and court rulings and changes in them)

**High
(7,8, or 9)**

Always follows correct procedures for evidence preservation at the scene of a crime

Is fully aware of recent court rulings and conducts himself or herself accordingly

Searches a citizen's vehicle with probable cause, thereby discovering smuggled narcotics

**Average
(4,5, or 6)**

Arrests a suspect at 11:00 P.M. on a warrant only after ensuring that the warrant had been cleared for night service

Distinguishes between civil matters and police matters

Seldom has to ask others about points of law

**Low
(1,2, or 3)**

Is consistently unaware of general orders and/or departmental policy

Arrests a suspect for a misdemeanor not committed in his or her presence

Misinforms the public on legal matters through lack of knowledge

Examples of the behavior of patrol officers who are usually rated high, average, and low on job knowledge by supervisors

FIGURE 9-6
A behaviorally anchored rating scale to assess the job knowledge of police patrol officers.

period for which the objectives were established. At that time, those who established objectives at each level in the organization meet to evaluate the results and to agree on the objectives for the next period.[32]

To some, MBO is a complete system of planning and control and a complete philosophy of management.[33] In theory, MBO promotes success in each employee because, as each employee succeeds, so do that employee's manager, the department, and the organization. But this is true *only* to the extent that the individual, departmental, and organizational goals are compatible.[34] Very few applications of MBO have actually adopted a formal "cascading process" to ensure such a linkage. An effective MBO system takes from 3 to 5 years to implement, and since relatively few firms are willing to make that kind of commitment, it is not surprising that MBO systems often fail.[35]

Work Planning and Review. This is similar to MBO; however, it places greater emphasis on the periodic review of work plans by both supervisor and subordinate in order to identify goals attained, problems encountered, and the need for training.[36] This approach has long been used by Corning, Inc. Work planning and review are based primarily on each supervisor's judgment about whether a goal has or has not been attained, while MBO relies more on objective, quantifiable evidence. In practice, the two approaches are often indistinguishable. For example, as Table 9-1 illustrates, performance standards are often written with specific percentages to indicate different levels of effectiveness. Even though the standards might be incorporated

■ **TABLE 9 ▪ 2**

A SNAPSHOT OF THE ADVANTAGES AND DISADVANTAGES OF ALTERNATIVE
APPRAISAL METHODS

Behavior-oriented methods

Narrative essay—Good for individual feedback and development but difficult to make comparisons across employees.

Ranking and paired comparisons—Good for making comparisons across employees but provides little basis for individual feedback and development.

Forced distribution—Forces raters to make distinctions among employees but may be unfair and inaccurate if a group of employees, as a group, is either very effective or ineffective.

Behavioral checklist—Easy to use, provides a direct link between job analysis and performance appraisal, can be numerically scored, and facilitates comparisons across employees. However, the meaning of response categories may be interpreted differently by different raters.

Critical incidents—Focuses directly on job behaviors, emphasizes what employees did that was effective or ineffective, but can be very time-consuming to develop.

Graphic rating scales (including BARS)—Easy to use, very helpful for providing feedback for individual development, and facilitate comparisons across employees. BARS are very time-consuming to develop, but dimensions and scale points defined clearly. Graphic rating scales often do not define dimensions or scale points clearly.

Results-oriented systems

Management by objectives—Focuses on results and on identifying each employee's contribution to the success of the unit or organization. However, MBO is generally short-term-oriented, provides few insights into employee behavior, and does not facilitate comparison across employees.

Work planning and review—In contrast to MBO, emphasizes process over outcomes. Requires frequent supervisor–subordinate review of work plans. Is time-consuming to implement properly and does not facilitate comparisons across employees.

---

into an MBO system, if the percentages can be derived only on the basis of judgment, then the supposedly results-oriented MBO method quickly becomes a more process-oriented work planning and review system. Table 9-2 presents a summary of the appraisal methods we have just discussed.

When Should Each Technique Be Used?

You have just read about a number of alternative appraisal formats, each with its own advantages and disadvantages. At this point you are probably asking yourself, "What's the bottom line? I know that no method is perfect, but what should I do?" First, remember that the rating format is not as important as the relevance and acceptability of the rating system. Second, here is some advice based on systematic comparisons among the various methods.

An extensive review of the research literature that relates the various rating methods to indicators of performance appraisal effectiveness found no clear "winner."[37] However, the researchers were able to provide several "if . . . then" propositions and general statements based on their study. Among these are:

■ If employees must be compared across raters for important employment decisions (e.g., promotion, merit pay), MBO and work planning and review should not be used. They are not based on a standardized rating scheme for all employees.

- If a BARS is used, diary keeping should also be made a part of the process. This will improve the accuracy of the ratings, and it also will help supervisors distinguish between effective and ineffective employees.

- If objective performance data are available, MBO is the best strategy to use. Research indicates that work planning and review are not as effective as MBO under these circumstances.

- In general, appraisal methods that are best in a broad, organizational sense—BARS and MBO—are the most difficult to use and maintain. Recognize, however, that no rating method is foolproof.

- Methods that focus on describing, rather than evaluating, behavior (e.g., BARS, summed rating scales) produce results that are the most interpretable across raters. They help remove the effects of individual differences in raters.[38]

- No rating method has been an unqualified success when used as a basis for merit pay or promotional decisions.

- When certain statistical corrections are made, the correlations between scores on alternative rating formats are very high. Hence all the formats measure essentially the same thing.

Which techniques are most popular? A survey of 324 organizations in southern California found that among larger organizations 51 percent use rating scales of some sort, 23 percent use essays, 17 percent use MBO, and 9 percent use all other forms of appraisal systems, which included behavioral checklists, forced choice, and rankings.[39]

WHO SHOULD EVALUATE PERFORMANCE?

The most fundamental requirement for any rater is that he or she has an adequate opportunity to observe the ratee's job performance over a reasonable period of time (e.g., 6 months). This suggests several possible raters.

The Immediate Supervisor. If appraisal is done at all, it will probably be done by this person. She or he is probably most familiar with the individual's performance and, in most jobs, has had the best opportunity to observe actual job performance. Furthermore, the immediate supervisor is probably best able to relate the individual's performance to departmental and organizational objectives. Since she or he also is responsible for reward (and punishment) decisions, it is not surprising that feedback from supervisors is more highly related to performance than that from any other source.[40]

Peers. In some jobs, such as outside sales, law enforcement, and teaching, the immediate supervisor may observe a subordinate's actual job performance only rarely (and indirectly, through written reports). Sometimes objective indicators, such as number of units sold, can provide useful performance-related information, but in other circumstances the judgment of peers is even better. Peers can provide a perspective on performance that is different from that of immediate supervisors. Thus a police officer's partner is in a far better position to rate day-to-day performance than is a deskbound sergeant or lieutenant. However, to reduce potential friendship bias while simultaneously increasing the feedback value of the information provided, it is important to specify exactly what the peers are to evaluate[41]—for example, "the quality of her help on technical problems."

Another approach is to require input from a number of colleagues. Thus, at Harley-Davidson, salaried workers have five colleagues critique their work.[42] Even when done well, however, peer assessments are probably best considered as only part of a performance appraisal system that includes input from all sources that have unique information or perspectives to offer concerning the job performance of an individual or a work group.

Subordinates. Appraisal by subordinates can be a useful input to the immediate supervisor's development. Subordinates know firsthand the extent to which the supervisor *actually* delegates, how well he or she communicates, the type of leadership style he or she is most comfortable with, and the extent to which he or she plans and organizes. Appraisal by subordinates is used regularly by some large firms where managers have many subordinates. In the small firm or in situations where managers have few subordinates, however, it is easy to identify who said what. Thus considerable trust and openness are necessary before subordinate appraisals can pay off. Like peer assessments, they provide only one piece of the appraisal puzzle.

Self-appraisal. There are several arguments to recommend wider use of self-appraisals. The opportunity to participate in the performance appraisal process, particularly if appraisal is combined with goal setting, improves the ratee's motivation and reduces her or his defensiveness during the appraisal interview.[43] On the other hand, self-appraisals tend to be more lenient, less variable, and more biased and to show less agreement with the judgments of others.[44] Since U.S. employees tend to give themselves higher marks than their supervisors do (conflicting findings have been found with mainland Chinese and Taiwanese employees),[45] self-appraisals are probably more appropriate for counseling and development than for employment decisions.

Customers Served. In some situations the "consumers" of an individual's or organization's services can provide a unique perspective on job performance. Examples abound: subscribers to a cable television service, bank customers, clients of a brokerage house, and citizens of a local police or fire-protection district. Although the customers' objectives cannot be expected to correspond completely with the organization's objectives, the information that customers provide can serve as useful input for employment decisions, such as those regarding promotion, transfer, and need for training. It can also be used to assess the impact of training or as a basis for self-development. At General Electric, for example, the customers of senior managers are interviewed formally and regularly as part of the managers' appraisal process. Their evaluations are important in appraisal, but at the same time they also build commitment, because customers are giving time and information to help GE.[46]

Computers. As noted earlier, employees spend a lot of time unsupervised by their bosses. Now technology has made continuous supervision possible—and very real for millions of workers. What sort of technology? Computer software that monitors employee performance.

In summary, several different sources of appraisal information can be used, although they are more useful for some purposes than for others. Twenty such uses are shown in Table 9-3.

■ **TABLE 9 ▪ 3**
TWENTY USES OF PERFORMANCE APPRAISAL

Use	Mean*
Between-person decisions:	
Salary administration	5.58
Recognition of individal performance	5.02
Identification of poor performance	4.96
Promotion	4.80
Retention/termination	4.75
Layoffs	3.51
Within-person decisions:	
Performance feedback	5.67
Identification of individual strengths & weaknesses	5.41
Determination of transfers & assignments	3.66
Identification of individual training needs	3.42
Systems Maintenance:	
Assistance in goal identification	4.90
Evaluation of goal achievement	4.72
Determination of organizational training needs	2.74
Human resource planning	2.72
Reinforcement of authority structure	2.65
Identification of organizational development needs	2.63
Evaluation of HR systems	2.04
Documentation:	
Documentation of employment decisions	5.15
Meeting of legal requirements	4.58
Provision of criteria for validation research	2.30

*Ratings were based on a 7-point rating scale measuring the impact of appraisal on a variety of organizational decisions and actions, where 1 = no impact, 4 = moderate impact, and 7 = primary determinant.
Source: Adapted from J. N. Cleveland, K. R. Murphy, & R. E. Williams, Multiple uses of performance appraisal: Prevalence and correlates, *Journal of Applied Psychology,* **74,** 1989, p. 132.

USING COMPUTERS TO MONITOR JOB PERFORMANCE

To proponents, it is a great new application of technology to improve productivity. To critics, it represents the ultimate intrusion of Big Brother in the workplace. For several million workers today, being monitored on the job by a computer is a fact of life.[47]

Computers measure quantifiable tasks performed by secretaries, factory and postal workers, and grocery and airline reservation sales agents. For example, major airlines regularly monitor the time reservation sales agents spend on each call. Until now, lower-level jobs have been affected most directly by computer monitoring. But as software becomes more sophisticated, even engineers, accountants, and doctors are expected to face electronic scrutiny.

Critics feel that overzealous employers will get carried away with information gathering and overstep the boundary between work performance and privacy. Moreover, being watched every second can be stressful, thereby stifling worker creativity, initiative, and morale.

Not everyone views monitoring as a modern-day version of *Modern Times,* the Charlie Chaplin movie in which the hapless hero was tyrannized by automation. At the Third National Bank of Nashville, for example, encoding clerks can earn up to 25 percent more than their base pay if their output is high—and they like that system.

To be sure, monitoring itself is neither good nor bad; how managers use it determines its acceptance in the workplace. Practices such as giving employees access to data collected on them, establishing procedures for challenging erroneous records, and training supervisors to base actions and decisions on actual observation of employees, not just on computer-generated records, can alleviate the fears of employees.[48] At American Express, for example, monitored employees are given feedback about their performance every 2 weeks.

Managers who impose monitoring standards *without* asking employees what is reasonable may be surprised at the responses of employees. Tactics can include VDT operators who pound the space bar or hold down the underlining bar while chatting, and telephone operators who hang up on customers with complicated problems. The lesson, perhaps, is that even the most sophisticated technology can be thwarted by human beings who feel they are being pushed beyond acceptable limits.[49]

One of the primary sources of information about issues relevant to appraisal is the *attitudes* of those who will be affected by the system. A survey of employees in one federal agency indicated a strong preference for appraisal by immediate supervisors and, to a lesser extent, by the people for whom they provided service. The majority of respondents favored more than one rater, and some felt that peers and subordinates were potentially valid sources of information.[50] Another important consideration is the timing and frequency of performance appraisal.

WHEN AND HOW OFTEN SHOULD APPRAISAL BE DONE?

Traditionally, formal appraisal is done once, or at best twice, a year. Research, however, has indicated that once or twice a year is far too infrequent.[51] Unless he or she

Customers are ofen able to rate important aspects of the performance of employees in front-line customer contact positions.

keeps a diary, considerable difficulties face a rater who is asked to remember what several employees did over the previous 6 or 12 months. This is why firms such as Western Digital, Southern California Gas, and Fluor add frequent, informal "progress" reviews between the annual ones.[52]

Research indicates that if a rater is asked to assess an employee's performance over a 6- to 12-month period, biased ratings may result, especially if information has been stored in the rater's memory according to irrelevant, oversimplistic, or otherwise faulty categories.[53] Unfortunately, faulty categorization seems to be the rule more often than the exception.

For example, consider the impact of prior expectations on ratings.[54] Supervisors of tellers at a large West Coast bank provided predictions about the future job performance of their new tellers. Six months later they rated the job performance of each teller. The result? Inconsistencies between prior expectations and later performance clearly affected the judgments of the raters. Thus when a teller's actual performance disappointed or exceeded a supervisor's prior expectations about that performance, ratings were lower than warranted by actual performance. The lesson to be learned is that it is unwise to assume that raters are faulty, but motivationally neutral, observers of on-the-job behavior.

In the survey of federal employees noted earlier, a majority of the employees were dissatisfied with the use of performance data collected once or twice a year for any important employment decision. A common recommendation was to do appraisals upon the completion of projects or upon the achievement of important milestones in large-scale projects.[55] Such an approach has merit because the appraisals are likely to provide more accurate inputs to employment decisions, and they have the additional advantage of sending clear messages to employees about where they stand. There should be no "surprises" in appraisals, and one way to ensure this is to do them frequently.

PERFORMANCE APPRAISAL AND TOTAL QUALITY MANAGEMENT (TQM)

As we saw in Chapter 1, TQM emphasizes the continuous improvement of products and processes to ensure long-term customer satisfaction. Its group problem-solving focus encourages employee empowerment by using the job-related expertise and ingenuity of the workforce. Cross-functional teams develop solutions to complex problems, often shortening the time taken to design, develop, or produce products and services. Since a team may not include a representative of management, the dividing line between labor and management often becomes blurred in practice, as workers themselves begin to solve organizational problems. Thus adoption of TQM generally requires cultural change within the organization as management reexamines its past methods and practices in light of the demands of the new philosophy.[56]

If the "father of TQM," W. Edwards Deming, had his way, appraisal systems that tie individual performance to salary adjustments would be eliminated. In his view, such systems hinder teamwork, create fear and mistrust, and discourage risk-taking behavior, thereby stifling innovation. Worse yet, Deming argues, most appraisal systems are based on the faulty assumption that individuals have significant control over their own performance—that is, that most individuals can improve if they *choose* to do so by putting forth the necessary effort.[57]

Here is the basis for his argument. Everything done in an organization is done within the framework of one or more systems (e.g., accounting, purchasing, production, sales). The systems provide limits on the activities of machines, processes, employees, and even managers. In a well-designed system, it will be nearly impossible to do a job improperly. Conversely, a poor system can thwart the best efforts of the best employee. If the system itself prevents good work (e.g., outdated technology that makes it impossible to meet current quality standards), performance appraisal cannot serve its intended purpose of differentiating among individuals for purposes of salary adjustments. Further, since employees (and most lower-level managers as well) have little opportunity to change those systems, they may become frustrated and demoralized.

What's the bottom line in all of this? As a basis for implementing a "pay-for-performance" philosophy, performance appraisal is a meaningful tool only if workers have significant control over the variables that affect their individual performance.[58] If not, then it is true, as Deming argues, that appraisals measure only random statistical variation within a particular system.

How Performance Appraisals Can Incorporate Key Elements of TQM

Organizations need not sacrifice their performance appraisal programs on the altar of total quality management. Here are three suggestions for harmonizing these two processes.[59]

1. *Let customer expectations generate individual or team performance expectations.* Start by identifying customer expectations by product or service. Customers may be internal or external. Then individuals or teams can begin to assess their performance against those expectations. Using this baseline of achievement, individuals, teams, and managers can develop continuous improvement targets. Comparing actual performance against expected performance helps avoid detrimental intrateam competition, because individuals or teams are compared against their own benchmarks, rather than against the accomplishments of others.

2. *Include results expectations that identify actions to meet or exceed those expectations.* Employee (or team) and supervisor together consider these customer expectations in conjunction with the business plan and begin to establish priorities for improvement opportunities.

3. *Include behavioral skills that make a real difference in achieving quality performance and total customer satisfaction.* For example, effective customer service requires "attention to detail," "initiative," and "listening skills." These continuous improvement skills are as important to total quality as are results-oriented targets.

When performance expectations focus on process improvements as well as on the behavioral skills needed to provide a product or service, total quality, excellent customer service, and appraisal of individual or team performance become "the way we do business."

APPRAISAL ERRORS AND RATER TRAINING STRATEGIES

The use of ratings assumes that the human observer is reasonably objective and accurate. As we have seen, raters' memories are quite fallible, and raters subscribe to their own sets of expectations about people, expectations that may or may not be valid. These biases produce rating errors, or deviations between the "true" rating an employee deserves and the actual rating assigned.[60] Some of the most common types of rating errors have been discussed previously: leniency, severity, and central tendency. Three other types are halo, contrast, and recency errors.

1. *Halo error* is not as common as is commonly believed.[61] Raters who commit this error assign their ratings on the basis of global (good or bad) impressions of ratees. An employee is rated either high or low on *many* aspects of job performance because the rater knows (or thinks she or he knows) that the employee is high or low on some *specific* aspect. In practice, halo is probably due to situational factors or to the interaction of a rater and a situation (e.g., a supervisor who has limited opportunity to observe her subordinates because they are in the field dealing with customers).[62] Thus halo is probably a better indicator of how raters process cognitive information than it is as a measure of rating validity or accuracy.[63]

2. *Contrast errors* result when several employees are compared to one another rather than to an objective standard of performance.[64] If, say, the first two workers are unsatisfactory while the third is average, the third worker may well be rated outstanding because in contrast to the first two, her or his "average" level of job performance is magnified. Likewise, "average" performance could be unfairly downgraded if the first few workers are outstanding. In both cases, the "average" worker receives a biased rating.

3. *Recency error* results when supervisors assign ratings on the basis of the employee's most recent performance. It is most likely to occur when appraisals are done only after long periods. Here is how one manager described the dilemma of the recency error: "Many of us have trouble rating for the entire year. If one of my people has a stellar three months prior to the review . . . [I] don't want to do anything that impedes that person's momentum and progress."[65] Of course, if the subordinate's performance peaks 3 months prior to appraisal *every year*, that suggests a different problem!

Traditionally, rater training has focused on teaching raters to eliminate errors. Unfortunately, such programs usually have only short-term effects. Worse yet, training raters to reduce *errors* may actually reduce the *accuracy* of the ratings![66] What can be done?

First, emphasis should be placed on training raters to observe behavior more accurately, rather than on showing them "how to" or "how not to" rate. Such an appraisal might proceed as follows:[67]

1. Participants view a videotape of an employee performing his or her job.
2. Participants evaluate the employee on the videotape using rating scales provided.
3. Each participant's ratings are placed on a flip chart.
4. Differences between ratings and reasons for the differences are argued by participants in a discussion led by the trainer.

INTERNATIONAL APPLICATION: THE IMPACT OF NATIONAL CULTURE ON ORGANIZATIONAL PERFORMANCE APPRAISALS

Western expatriate managers are often surprised to learn that their management practices have unintended consequences when applied in non-Western cultures. To illustrate such differences, consider the results of a study of Taiwanese and U.S. business students that examined preferences for various performance appraisal practices.[68]

Compared to Americans, Taiwanese students indicated the following:

- Less support for performance appraisal as practiced in Western cultures
- More focus on group rather than individual performance
- Greater willingness to consider nonperformance factors (e.g., off-the-job behaviors, age) as criteria in appraisal
- Less willingness to attribute performance levels to the skills and efforts of particular individuals
- Less open and direct relations between supervisor and subordinate
- An expectation of closer supervisory styles

These results suggest that U.S. managers will need to modify the performance appraisal process that is familiar to them when working with Taiwanese subordinates in order to make it more consistent with Taiwanese values and culture. Such a process recognizes the importance of groups as well as individuals in the organization and honors the criteria of cooperation, loyalty, and attitudes toward superiors, as well as individual goal accomplishment.

5. Raters reach a consensus regarding performance standards and relative levels of effective or ineffective behavior.

6. The videotape is shown again.

7. Ratings are reassigned, this time on the basis of specific examples of behavior as recorded by each rater.

8. Ratings are evaluated relative to the earlier consensus judgments of participants.

9. Specific feedback is provided to each participant.

Second, a recent review of 24 studies on rater training found that, in general, the more actively involved raters become in the training process, the better the outcome.[69] Third, before raters are asked to observe and evaluate the performance of others, they should be encouraged to discuss the performance dimensions on which they will be rating, and they should be given the opportunity to practice rating a sample of job performance. Finally, they should be provided with "true" (or expert) ratings to which they can compare their own ratings.

In short, application of the basic principles of learning is the key to improving the meaningfulness and usefulness of the performance appraisal process.

SECRETS OF EFFECTIVE APPRAISAL INTERVIEWS

The use of appraisal interviews, at least in terms of company policies on the subject, is widespread. A survey of more than 300 companies found that 89 percent require that appraisal results be discussed with employees.[70] As is well known, however, the existence of a policy is no guarantee that it will be implemented. Thus employees reported the following general reactions to appraisal interviews:[71]

- Employees were less certain about where they stood *after* the interview than before it.
- Employees evaluated supervisors less favorably after the interview than before it.
- Few constructive actions or significant improvements resulted from appraisal interviews.
- Given today's more participative management approaches, the authoritarian tone so common in performance appraisal (PA) interviews is out of date.

These are discouraging findings. The practices they suggest certainly run counter to those espoused in the research literature. Consider just two examples. First, we know that feedback is most effective when it is given immediately following the behavior in question.[72] How effective can feedback be if it is given only once a year during an appraisal interview? Second, for more than 2 decades we have known that when managers use a problem-solving approach, subordinates express a stronger motivation to improve performance than when other approaches are used.[73] Yet evidence indicates that most organizations still use a "tell-and-sell" approach in which a manager completes an appraisal independently, shows it to the subordinate, justifies the rating, discusses what must be done to improve performance, and then asks for the subordinate's reaction and sign-off on the appraisal.[74] Are the negative reactions of subordinates really that surprising?

If organizations really are serious about fostering improved job performance as a result of appraisal interviews, the kinds of activities shown in Table 9-4 are essential *before*, *during*, and *after* appraisals. Let's briefly examine each of these important activities.

■ **TABLE 9 ▪ 4**

SUPERVISORY ACTIVITIES BEFORE, DURING, AND AFTER APPRAISAL

Before:
    Communicate frequently with subordinates about their performance.
    Get training in performance appraisal interviewing.
    Plan to use a problem-solving approach rather than "tell-and-sell."
    Encourage subordinates to prepare for PA interviews.

During:
    Encourage subordinate participation.
    Judge performance, not personality and mannerisms.
    Be specific.
    Be an active listener.
    Set mutually agreeable goals for future improvements.
    Avoid destructive criticism.

After:
    Communicate frequently with subordinates about their performance.
    Periodically assess progress toward goals.
    Make organizational rewards contingent on performance.

Frequent Communication. Research on the appraisal interview at General Electric indicated clearly that once-a-year performance appraisals are of questionable value and that coaching should be a day-to-day activity[75]—particularly with poor performers or new employees.[76] Feedback has maximum impact when it is given as close as possible to the action. If a subordinate behaves effectively (ineffectively), tell him or her immediately. Don't file incidents away so that they can be discussed in 6 to 9 months.

Recent research strongly supports this view. Thus one study found that communication of the appraisal in an interview is most effective when the subordinate already has relatively accurate perceptions of her or his performance before the session.[77]

Training in Appraisal Interviewing. As we noted earlier, more emphasis should be placed on training raters to observe behavior more accurately and fairly than on providing specific illustrations of "how to" or "how not to" rate. Training managers to provide evaluative information and to give feedback should focus on managerial characteristics that are difficult to rate and on characteristics that people think are easy to rate but which generally result in disagreements. Such factors include risk taking and development of subordinates.[78] *Use a problem-solving, rather than a "tell-and-sell," approach* as noted earlier.

Encourage Subordinate Preparation. Research conducted in hospitals, among clerical workers, and in sales organizations has indicated consistently that subordinates who spend more time prior to appraisal interviews analyzing their job responsibilities and duties, problems they encounter on the job, and the quality of their performance are more likely to be satisfied with the appraisal process, more likely to be motivated to improve their performance, and more likely actually to improve.[79]

Encourage Participation. A perception of ownership—a feeling by the subordinate that his or her ideas are genuinely welcomed by the manager—is related strongly to subordinates' satisfaction with the appraisal interview. Participation encourages the belief that the interview was a constructive activity, that some current job problems were cleared up, and that future goals were set.[80]

Judge Performance, Not Personality. In addition to the potential legal liability of dwelling on personality rather than on job performance, supervisors are far less likely to change a subordinate's personality than they are his or her job performance. Maintain the problem-solving, job-related focus established earlier, for evidence indicates that supervisory support enhances employees' motivation to improve.[81]

Be Specific, and Be an Active Listener. By being candid and specific, the supervisor offers clear feedback to the subordinate concerning past actions. She or he also demonstrates knowledge of the subordinate's level of performance and job duties. By being an active listener, the supervisor demonstrates genuine interest in the subordinate's ideas. Active listening requires that you do the following things well: (1) take the time to listen—hold all phone calls and do not allow interruptions; (2) communicate verbally and nonverbally (e.g., by maintaining eye contact) that you genuinely want to help; (3) as the subordinate begins to tell his or her side of the story, do not interrupt and do not argue; (4) watch for verbal as well as nonverbal cues regarding

IMPACT OF PERFORMANCE APPRAISAL ON PRODUCTIVITY, QUALITY OF WORK LIFE, AND THE BOTTOM LINE

Performance appraisal is fundamentally a *feedback* process. And research indicates that feedback may result in increases in performance varying from 10 to 30 percent.[82] That is a fairly inexpensive way to improve productivity; but, to work effectively, feedback programs require sustained commitment. The challenge for managers, then, is to provide feedback regularly to all their employees.

The cost of failure to provide such feedback may result in the loss of key professional employees, the continued poor performance of employees who are not meeting performance standards, and a loss of commitment by *all* employees. In sum, the myth that employees know how they are doing without adequate feedback from management can be an expensive fantasy.[83]

the subordinate's agreement or disagreement with your message; and (5) summarize what was said and what was agreed to. Specific feedback and active listening are essential to subordinates' perceptions of the fairness and accuracy of appraisals.[84]

Avoid Destructive Criticism. Destructive criticism is general in nature, frequently delivered in a biting, sarcastic tone, and often attributes poor performance to internal causes (e.g., lack of motivation or ability). It leads to three predictable consequences: (1) it produces negative feelings among recipients and can initiate or intensify conflict, (2) it reduces the preference of individuals for handling future disagreements with the giver of the feedback in a conciliatory manner (e.g., compromise, collaboration); and (3) it has negative effects on self-set goals and on feelings of self-confidence.[85] Needless to say, this is one type of communication to avoid.

Set Mutually Agreeable Goals. How does goal setting work to improve performance? Studies demonstrate that goals direct attention to the specific performance in question, that they mobilize effort to accomplish higher levels of performance, and that they foster persistence for higher levels of performance.[86] The practical implications of this work are clear: set specific, challenging goals, for this clarifies for the subordinate precisely what is expected and leads to high levels of performance. We cannot change the past, but appraisal interviews that include goal setting and feedback can affect future job performance.

Continue to Communicate, and Assess Progress Toward Goals Regularly. Periodic tracking of progress toward goals (e.g., through work planning and review) has three advantages: (1) it helps keep behavior on target, (2) it provides a better understanding of the reasons behind a given level of performance, and (3) it enhances the subordinate's commitment to perform effectively. All of this helps to improve supervisor–subordinate work relationships. Improving supervisor–subordinate work relationships, in turn, has positive effects on appraisals and performance.[87]

Make Organizational Rewards Contingent on Performance. Research results are clear cut on this point. If subordinates see a link between appraisal results and employment decisions regarding issues like merit pay and promotion, they are more likely to *prepare* for appraisal interviews, to *participate* actively in them, and to be *satisfied* with the overall performance appraisal system.[88] Furthermore, managers who base employment decisions on the results of appraisals are likely to overcome their subordinates' negative perceptions of the appraisal process.

THE EXECUTIVE APPRAISAL PARADOX

DEBUNKING THE MYTHS

HUMAN
RESOURCE
MANAGEMENT
IN ACTION:
CONCLUSION

It is not possible to design a "perfect" or "ideal" performance appraisal program. However, for any such program to be of benefit to all parties in the process, some important items must be in place. These include clearly specified goals and standards, ongoing performance feedback, and an interactive feedback session between superior and subordinate.

Organizations with effective executive appraisals almost invariably cite the involvement of top management as the dominant factor in the success of the process. Senior executives need to articulate and enact the practices discussed below because they are the key players in institutionalizing sound appraisal processes as part of the organization's culture.

1. *Construct a formal, systematic executive appraisal process.* It should be formal so that the process is taken seriously by all parties; it should be systematic so that it provides the executive with useful feedback and guidance.

2. *Incorporate performance planning, which is essential at the executive level, into the executive review and appraisal process.* Essentially, this is strategic planning for people. It should include the following elements: (1) a flexibly framed description of the executive's mission, along with primary and secondary responsibilities; (2) clarification of division/ departmental goals and the executive's role in accomplishing them; (3) discussion of management style issues as well as strategies for accomplishing goals; and (4) agreement about what constitutes "successful" performance, given current strategic and operational goals.

3. *Make performance review and appraisal an ongoing process.* To facilitate this process, senior executives suggest the following four steps: (1) make notes on critical instances of effective and ineffective performance, based on personal observations; (2) obtain regular financial and productivity indicators; (3) check the executive's performance with clients, customers, and other departments to assess external relations and teamwork abilities; and (4) use subordinates' appraisals of executives to provide a different perspective on executive performance.

4. *Focus on process as well as outcomes during the executive review.* Process issues are more difficult to address than bottom-line issues, but they are hallmarks of good executive mentors. Striking a balance between means and ends, processes and outcomes, is a wise strategy.

5. *Be as specific and thorough as possible.* Consider doing the following: (1) to supplement the senior executive's judgments, have subordinate executives provide written self-appraisals that focus on achievements, areas needing improvement, and plans for development; (2) as the basis for the formal review, use the responsibilities, goals, and processes that were agreed upon previously; (3) avoid nebulous language when giving performance feedback; (4) strengthen the link between performance and reward by citing specific reasons for any merit raises, bonuses, or perks; and (5) allow time for the subordinate executive to air concerns and to discuss his or her personal development. After all, the review is a forum for developing a blueprint for the coming year.

Executive appraisal can help to decrease job-role ambiguity. It can also be the key vehicle for communicating the firm's culture, values, and operating philosophy. It gives executives a feel for the firm's bigger picture, how they fit into that picture, and what they have to do to reach their goals. Treating the appraisal of executives as a positive action should be a high priority.

IMPLICATIONS FOR MANAGEMENT PRACTICE

Throughout this chapter we have emphasized the difficulty of implementing and managing performance appraisal systems. Yet studies show repeatedly that while employees and managers are dissatisfied with the appraisal process, efforts by managers to improve it are seldom rewarded.[89] So a basic issue for every manager is "What's in it for me?" If organizations are serious about improving the appraisal process, top management must consider the following policy changes:

- Make "quality of performance appraisal feedback to subordinates" and "development of subordinates" integral parts of every manager's job description.
- Tie rewards to effective performance in these areas.
- Recognize that performance appraisal is a dialogue involving people and data; both political and interpersonal issues are involved. No appraisal method is perfect, but with management commitment and employee "buy-in," performance management can be a very useful and powerful tool.

SUMMARY

Performance appraisal is the systematic description of the job-relevant strengths and weaknesses of an individual or a group. It serves two major purposes in organizations: (1) improving the job performance of employees and (2) providing information to employees and managers for use in making decisions. In practice, many PA systems fail because they do not satisfy one or more of the following requirements: relevance, sensitivity, reliability, acceptability, and practicality. The failure is frequently accompanied by legal challenge to the system based on its adverse impact against one or more protected groups.

Many of the problems of performance appraisal can be alleviated through participative development of performance standards that specify, for each job, *what* needs to be done and *how well* it is being done. Appraisals are usually done by immediate supervisors, although other individuals may also have unique perspectives or information to offer. These include peers, subordinates, the customers served, and the employees themselves.

Performance appraisal is done once or twice a year in most organizations, but research indicates that this is far too infrequent. It should be done upon the *completion* of projects or upon the achievement of important milestones. The rating method used depends on the purpose for which the appraisal is intended. Thus comparisons among employees are most appropriate for generating rankings for salary administration purposes, while MBO, work planning and review, and narrative essays are least appropriate for this purpose. For purposes of employee development, critical incidents or behaviorally anchored rating scales are most appropriate. Finally, rating methods that focus on *describing* rather than *evaluating* behavior (e.g., BARS, behavioral checklists) are the most interpretable across raters.

Rater judgments are subject to various types of biases: leniency, severity, central tendency, and halo, contrast, and recency errors. To improve the reliability and validity of ratings, however, emphasis must be placed on training raters to observe behavior more accurately rather than on showing them "how to" or "how not to" rate. To improve the value of appraisal interviews, systematic training for supervisors is essential.

DISCUSSION QUESTIONS

9■1 The chief counsel for a large corporation comes to you for advice. She wants to know what makes a firm's appraisal system legally vulnerable. What would you tell her?

9■2 Working in small groups, develop a set of performance standards for a cashier in a neighborhood grocery with little technology but lots of personal touch.

9■3 Discuss alternative strategies for controlling rater leniency.

9■4 How can we overcome employee defensiveness in performance appraisal interviews?

9■5 Can discussions of employee job performance be separated from salary considerations? If so, how?

REFERENCES

1. Hymowitz, C. (1985, Jan. 17). Bosses: Don't be nasty (and other tips for reviewing a worker's performance). *The Wall Street Journal*, p. 28. See also Labor letter (1987, Dec. 22). *The Wall Street Journal*, p. 1.

2. *Supervisor's desk guide to performance management* (1988, May). Washington, D.C.: Department of the Navy.

3. Cascio, W. F. (1991). *Applied psychology in personnel management* (4th ed.). Englewood Cliffs, NJ: Prentice-Hall.

4. Jacobs, R., Kafry, D., & Zedeck, S. (1980). Expectations of behaviorally anchored rating scales. *Personnel Psychology*, **33**, 595–640.

5. Total quality and performance appraisal (1992, October). *Mountain States Employers Council Bulletin*, p. 5.

6. Bretz, R. D., Jr., & Milkovich, G. T. (1989). *Performance appraisal in large organizations: Practice and research implications.* Ithaca, NY: Cornell University Center for Advanced Human Resource Studies, Working Paper No. 89–17. See also DeVries, D. L., Morrison, A. M., Shullman, S. L., & Gerlach, M. L. (1981). *Performance appraisal on the line.* New York: Wiley.

7. Ibid.

8. Longenecker, C. O., Sims, H. P., Jr., & Gioia, D. A. (1987). Behind the mask: The politics of employee appraisal. *Academy of Management Executive*, **1**, 183–193.

9. Labor Letter (1990, Oct. 16). *The Wall Street Journal*, p. A1.

10. Cleveland, J. N., Murphy, K. R., & Williams, R. E. (1989). Multiple uses of performance appraisal: Prevalence and correlates. *Journal of Applied Psychology*, **74**, 130–135.

11. Cascio, W. F. (1982). Scientific, legal, and operational imperatives of workable performance appraisal systems. *Public Personnel Management*, **11**, 367–375.

12. Zedeck, S., & Cascio, W. F. (1982). Performance appraisal decisions as a function of rater training and purpose of the appraisal. *Journal of Applied Psychology*, **67**, 752–758.

13. Kavanagh, M. J. (1982). Evaluating performance. In K. M. Rowland & G. R. Ferris (eds.), *Personnel management.* Boston: Allyn & Bacon, pp. 187–226.

14. Borman, W. C. (1991). Job behavior, performance, and effectiveness. In M. D. Dunnette & L. M. Hough, (eds.), *Handbook of industrial and organizational psychology.* Palo Alto, CA: Consulting Psychologists Press, vol. 2, pp. 271–326.

15. Labor letter (1990, Oct. 16), op. cit.

16. Barrett, G. V., & Kernan, M. C. (1987). Performance appraisal and terminations: A review of court decisions since *Brito v. Zia* with implications for personnel practices. *Personnel Psychology,* **40,** 489–503. See also Cascio, W. F., & Bernardin, H. J. (1981). Implications of performance appraisal litigation for personnel decisions. *Personnel Psychology,* **34,** 211–226. See also Feild, H. S., & Holley, W. H. (1982). The relationship of performance appraisal system characteristics to verdicts in selected employment discrimination cases. *Academy of Management Journal,* **25,** 392–406.

17. *Stone v. Xerox* (1982). 685 F. 2d 1387 (11th Cir.).

18. *United States v. City of Chicago* (1978). 573 F. 2d 416 (7th Cir.).

19. LeBoeuf, M. (1987). *The greatest management principle in the world.* New York: Berkley Publishing Co.

20. Beatty, R. W. (1989). Competitive human resource advantage through the strategic management of performance. *Human Resource Planning,* **12,** 179–194.

21. Cascio, W. F., & Serapio, M. G., Jr. (1991, Winter). Human resource systems in an international alliance: The undoing of a done deal? *Organizational Dynamics,* 63–74. See also Schneider, S. C. (1988). National versus corporate culture: Implications for human resource management. *Human Resource Management,* **27,** 231–246.

22. Carlyle, J. J., & Ellison, T. F. (1984). Developing performance standards. In H. J. Bernardin and R. W. Beatty (eds.), *Performance appraisal: Assessing human behavior at work.* Boston: PWS-Kent, Appendix B. See also *Supervisor's desk guide to performance management,* op. cit.

23. Guion, R. M. (1986). Personnel evaluation. In R. A. Berk (ed.), *Performance assessment.* Baltimore: Johns Hopkins University Press, pp. 345–360. See also Bernardin, H. J., & Beatty, R. W. (1984). *Performance appraisal: Assessing human behavior at work.* Boston: PWS-Kent.

24. Murphy, K. R., & Cleveland, J. N. (1991). *Performance appraisal: An organizational perspective.* Boston: Allyn & Bacon. See also Heneman, R. L. (1986). The relationship between supervisory ratings and results-oriented measures of performance: A meta-analysis. *Personnel Psychology,* **39,** 811–826.

25. Cascio & Bernardin, op. cit.

26. Stockford, L., & Bissell, H. W. (1949). Factors involved in establishing a merit rating scale. *Personnel,* **26,** 94–116.

27. Landy, F. J., & Rastegary, H. (1988). Criteria for selection. In M. Smith & I. Robertson (eds.), *Advances in personnel selection and assessment.* New York: Wiley, pp. 68–115.

28. Cascio, W. F. (1991), op. cit.

29. Bernardin, H. J., & Smith, P. C. (1981). A clarification of some issues regarding the development and use of behaviorally anchored rating scales. *Journal of Applied Psychology,* **66,** 458–463.

30. Borman, op. cit.

31. Campbell, J. P., Dunnette, M. D., Lawler, E. E., & Weick, K. E. (1970). *Managerial behavior, performance, and effectiveness.* New York: McGraw-Hill.

32. McConkie, M. L. (1979). A clarification of the goal-setting and appraisal process in MBO. *Academy of Management Review,* **4,** 29–40.

33. Albrecht, K. (1978). *Successful management by objectives: An action manual.* Englewood Cliffs, NJ: Prentice-Hall. See also Odiorne, G. S. (1965). *Management by objectives: A system of managerial leadership.* Belmont, CA: Fearon.

34. Barton, R. F. (1981). An MCDM approach for resolving goal conflict in MBO. *Academy of Management Review,* **6,** 231–241.

35. Kondrasuk, J. N. (1981). Studies in MBO effectiveness. *Academy of Management Review,* **6,** 419–430.

36. Meyer, H. H., Kay, E., & French, J. R. P. (1965). Split roles in performance appraisal. *Harvard Business Review*, **43**, 123–129.
37. Bernardin & Beatty, op. cit.
38. Hartel, C. E. J. (1993). Rating format research revisited: Format effectiveness and acceptability depend on rater characteristics. *Journal of Applied Psychology*, **78**, 212–217.
39. Locher, A. H., & Teel, K. S. (1988, September). Appraisal trends. *Personnel Journal*, pp. 139–145.
40. Becker, T. E., & Klimoski, R. J. (1989). A field study of the relationship between the organizational feedback environment and performance. *Personnel Psychology*, **42**, 353–358.
41. McEvoy, G. M., & Buller, P. F. (1987). User acceptance of peer appraisals in an industrial setting. *Personnel Psychology*, **40**, 785–787.
42. Labor letter (1990, Oct. 16), op. cit.
43. Campbell, D. J., & Lee, C. (1988). Self-appraisal in performance evaluation: Development versus evaluation. *Academy of Management Review*, **13**, 302–314.
44. Fox, S., & Dinur, Y. (1988). Validity of self-assessment: A field evaluation. *Personnel Psychology*, **41**, 581–592. See also Harris, M., & Schaubroeck, J. (1988). A meta-analysis of self-supervisory, self-peer, and peer-supervisory ratings. *Personnel Psychology*, **41**, 43–62.
45. Yu, J., & Murphy, K. R. (1993). Modesty bias in self-ratings of performance: A test of the cultural relativity hypothesis. *Personnel Psychology*, **46**, 357–363. But see also Farh, J. L., Dobbins, G. H., & Cheng, B. S. (1991). Cultural relativity in action: A comparison of self-ratings made by Chinese and U.S. workers. *Personnel Psychology*, **44**, 129–147.
46. Ulrich, D. (1989, Summer). Tie the corporate knot: Gaining complete customer commitment. *Sloan Management Review*, **10**(4), 19–27, 63.
47. Piller, C. (1993, July). Privacy in peril. *Macworld*, pp. 124–130. See also Brophy, B. (1986, Sept. 29). New technology, high anxiety. *U.S. News & World Report*, pp. 54, 55.
48. Nebeker, D. M., & Tatum, C. B. (1993). The effects of computer monitoring, standards, and rewards on work performance and stress. *Journal of Applied Social Psychology*, **28**, 508–534. See also Chalykoff, J., & Kochan, T. A. (1989). Computer-aided monitoring: Its influence on employee job satisfaction and turnover. *Personnel Psychology*, **42**, 807–834.
49. Brophy, op. cit.
50. Bernardin, H. J. (1986). A performance appraisal system. In R. A. Berk (ed.), *Performance assessment*. Baltimore: Johns Hopkins University Press, pp. 277–304.
51. Meyer et al., op. cit.
52. Labor letter (1990, Oct. 16), op. cit.
53. Mount, M. K., & Thompson, D. E. (1987). Cognitive categorization and quality of performance ratings. *Journal of Applied Psychology*, **72**, 240–246.
54. Hogan, E. A. (1987). Effects of prior expectations on performance ratings: A longitudinal study. *Academy of Management Journal*, **30**, 354–368.
55. Bernardin, op. cit.
56. Wiedman, T. G. (1993, October). Performance appraisal in a total quality management environment. *The Industrial-Organizational Psychologist*, **31**(2), pp. 64–66.
57. Deming, W. E. (1986). *Out of the crisis*. Cambridge, MA: MIT Center for Advanced Engineering Study.
58. Wiedman, op. cit.
59. Total quality and performance appraisal, op. cit.
60. Hogan, op. cit.
61. Murphy, K. R., Jako, R. A., & Anhalt, R. L. (1993). Nature and consequences of halo error: A critical analysis. *Journal of Applied Psychology*, **78**, 218–225.
62. Murphy, K. R., & Anhalt, R. L. (1992). Is halo error a property of the rater, ratees, or the specific behavior observed? *Journal of Applied Psychology*, **77**, 494–500.
63. Balzer, W. K., & Sulsky, L. M. (1992). Halo and performance appraisal research: A critical examination. *Journal of Applied Psychology*, **77**, 975–985.
64. Maurer, T. J., Palmer, J. K., & Ashe, D. K. (1993). Diaries, checklists, evaluations, and contrast effects in the measurement of behavior. *Journal of Applied Psychology*, **78**, 226–231.

65. Longenecker et al., op. cit.
66. Murphy, K. R., & Balzer, W. K. (1989). Rater errors and rating accuracy. *Journal of Applied Psychology*, **74**, 619–624. See also Smith, D. E. (1986). Training programs for performance appraisal: A review. *Academy of Management Review*, **11**, 22–40.
67. Latham, G. P., Wexley, K. N., & Pursell, E. D. (1975). Training managers to minimize rating errors in the observation of behavior. *Journal of Applied Psychology*, **60**, 550–555.
68. McEvoy, G. M., & Cascio, W. F. (1990). The United States and Taiwan: Two different cultures look at performance appraisal. *Research in Personnel and Human Resources Management*. suppl. 2, pp. 201–219.
69. Smith, op. cit.
70. Locher & Teel, op. cit.
71. Cederblom, D. (1982). The performance appraisal interview: A review, implications, and suggestions. *Academy of Management Review*, **7**, 219–227.
72. Murphy & Cleveland, op. cit.
73. Wexley, K. N., Singh, V. P., & Yukl, G. A. (1973). Subordinate participation in three types of appraisal interviews. *Journal of Applied Psychology*, **58**, 54–57.
74. Wexley, K. N. (1986). Appraisal interview. In R. A. Berk (ed.), *Performance assessment*. Baltimore: Johns Hopkins University Press, pp. 167–185.
75. Meyer et al., op. cit.
76. Cederblom, op. cit.
77. Ilgen, D. R., Mitchell, T. R., & Frederickson, J. W. (1981). Poor performers: Supervisors' and subordinates' responses. *Organizational Behavior and Human Performance*, **27**, 386–410.
78. Wohlers, A. J., & London, M. (1989). Ratings of managerial characteristics: Evaluation, difficulty, co-worker agreement, and self-awareness. *Personnel Psychology*, **42**, 235–261.
79. Meyer, H. H. (1991). A solution to the performance appraisal feedback enigma. *Academy of Management Executive*, **5**(1), 68–76. See also Burke, R. S., Weitzel, W., & Weir, T. (1978). Characteristics of effective employee performance review and development interviews: Replication and extension. *Personnel Psychology*, **31**, 903–919.
80. Nathan, B. R., Mohrman, A. M., Jr., & Milliman, J. (1991). Interpersonal relations as a context for the effects of appraisal interviews on performance and satisfaction: A longitudinal study. *Academy of Management Journal*, **34**(2), 352–369.
81. Dorfman, P. W., Stephan, W. G., & Loveland, J. (1986). Performance appraisal behaviors: Supervisor perceptions and subordinate reactions. *Personnel Psychology*, **39**, 579–597.
82. Landy, F. J., Farr, J. L., & Jacobs, R. R. (1982). Utility concepts in performance measurement. *Organizational Behavior and Human Performance*, **30**, 15–40.
83. Walther, F., & Taylor, S. (1983). An active feedback program can spark performance. *Personnel Administrator*, **28**(6), 107–111, 147–149.
84. Landy, F. J., Barnes-Farrell, J., & Cleveland, J. N. (1980). Perceived fairness and accuracy of performance evaluation: A follow-up. *Journal of Applied Psychology*, **65**, 355–356.
85. Baron, R. A. (1988). Negative effects of destructive criticism: Impact on conflict, self-efficacy, and task performance. *Journal of Applied Psychology*, **73**, 199–207.
86. Tubbs, M. E. (1986). Goal setting: A meta-analytic examination of the empirical evidence. *Journal of Applied Psychology*, **71**, 474–483.
87. Judge, T. A., & Ferris, G. R. (1993). Social context of performance evaluation decisions. *Academy of Management Journal*, **36**, 80–105.
88. Burke et al., op. cit.
89. Labor letter (1987, Dec. 22), op. cit.

CHAPTER 10

MANAGING CAREERS

CORPORATE CAREER MANAGEMENT COMES OF AGE*

In the past several years companies have begun to take a more active, systematic approach to the career development of their employees. This new approach is based on an underlying assumption that would have been considered heresy 10 or 20 years ago—that each employee is responsible for his or her own career development.

In the past, many companies assumed responsibility for the career pathing and growth of their employees. The company determined to what position, and at what speed, people would advance. That approach worked reasonably well in the corporate climate of the 1950s and 1960s. However, the corporate disruptions of the recent past have rendered this approach to employee career development largely unworkable. Acquisitions, divestitures, rapid growth, and downsizing have left many companies unable to deliver on the implicit career promises made to their employees. Organizations find themselves in the painful position of having to renege on career mobility opportunities their employees had come to expect. In extreme cases, employees who expected career growth no longer even have jobs!

Increasingly, corporations have come to realize that they cannot win if they take total responsibility for the career development of their employees. The old strategy of controlling the career growth of employees from "hire" to "retire" does not work anymore. In today's tur-

---

*For more information on the new approach to career self-management, see J. Fierman, Beating the midlife career crisis, *Fortune*, Sept. 6, 1993, pp. 52–60. See also H. Dennis & H. Axel, *Encouraging employee self-management in financial and career planning*, The Conference Board, New York, Report No. 976, 1991.

307

bulent times, companies have found that they cannot even continue to provide jobs for them. No matter what happens, employees often blame top management or "the company" for their own suboptimal career growth.

One company changed its approach to career growth as a result of pressure from its professional workforce. Employees felt suffocated by 20-plus years of management's determining people's career progress for them. Task teams worked with top management to develop career self-management training for employees and career counseling skills for managers. The resulting increases in employee productivity, enhanced morale, and decreased turnover of key employees have more than justified the new approach to employee career management.

CHARACTERISTICS OF THE NEW APPROACH

A key feature of the new career management concept is that the company and the employee are *partners* in career development. Employees are responsible for knowing what their skills and capabilities are and what assistance they need from their employers, asking for that assistance, and preparing themselves to assume new responsibilities.

Although the primary and final responsibility for career development rests with each employee, the company has complementary responsibilities. The company is responsible for communicating to employees where it wants to go and how it plans to get there (the corporate strategy), providing employees with as much information about the business as possible, and responding to the career initiatives of employees with candid, complete information. One of the most important contributions a company can make to each employee's development is to provide him or her with *honest* performance feedback about current job performance.

This approach to career management can be summed up as follows: assign employees the responsibility for managing their own careers, then provide the support they need to do it. This support takes different forms in different companies but usually contains several core components.

Challenges

1. Should employees be responsible for their own career development?
2. Is the new approach to corporate career management likely to be a passing fad, or is it here to stay?
3. What kinds of support mechanisms are necessary to make career self-management work?

Questions This Chapter Will Help Managers Answer

1. What strategies might be used to help employees "self-manage" their careers?
2. What can supervisors do to improve their management of dual-career couples?
3. Why are the characteristics and environment of an employee's first job so important?
4. What steps can managers take to do a better job of responding to the special needs of workers in their early, middle, and late career stages?
5. How can layoffs be handled in the most humane way?

As the chapter opening vignette demonstrates, corporate career management has come a long way in the last several decades. This chapter presents a number of topics that have sparked this reevaluation. We will consider the impact of mergers, acquisitions, and downsizing on corporate loyalty, the impact of dual-career couples on the career management process, and the major issues that workers and managers must deal with during the early, middle, and late career stages of the adult life cycle. Finally we will examine alternative patterns of career change: promotions, demotions, lateral transfers, relocations, layoffs, and retirements. Career management has many facets, both for the individual and for the organization. The chapter opening vignette emphasized that in the new concept of career management the company and the employee are partners in career development. This theme is emphasized throughout the chapter. Let's begin by attempting to define what is meant by the word "career."

TOWARD A DEFINITION OF "CAREER"

In everyday parlance, the word "career" is used in a number of different ways. People speak of "pursuing a career"; "career planning" workshops are common; colleges and universities hold "career days" during which they publicize jobs in different fields and assist individuals through "career counseling." A person may be characterized as a "career" woman or man who shops in a store that specializes in "career clothing." Likewise, a person may be characterized as a "career military officer." We may overhear a person say, "That movie 'made' his career" (i.e., it enhanced his reputation) or in a derogatory tone, after a subordinate has insulted the CEO, "She can kiss her career good-bye" (i.e., she has tarnished her reputation). Finally, an angry supervisor may remark to her dawdling subordinate, "Watney, are you going to make a career out of changing that lightbulb?"

As these examples illustrate, the word "career" can be viewed from a number of different perspectives. From one perspective *a career is a sequence of positions occupied by a person during the course of a lifetime.* This is the *objective* career. From another perspective, though, *a career consists of the changes in values, attitudes, and motivation that occur as a person grows older.*[1] This is the *subjective* career. Both of these perspectives, objective and subjective, focus on the individual. Both assume that people have some degree of control over their destinies and that they can manipulate opportunities in order to maximize the success and satisfaction derived from their careers.[2] They assume further that HR activities should recognize career stages and assist employees with the development tasks they face at each stage. Career planning is important because *the consequences of career success or failure are linked closely to each individual's self-concept, identity, and satisfaction with career and life.*

Given the downsizing mentality that has characterized most large organizations over the past several years, career development and planning have been deemphasized in some firms as employees wondered if they would even have *jobs,* much less *careers.* Companies that ignore career issues are mistaken if they think the issue will somehow go away. It won't. Here are some reasons why:[3]

1. Rising concerns for quality of work life and for personal life planning
2. Equal employment opportunity legislation and workforce diversity pressures
3. Rising educational levels and occupational aspirations, coupled with
4. Slow economic growth and reduced advancement opportunities

CAREER MANAGEMENT BY ORGANIZATIONS

A career is not something that should be left to each employee; instead, it should be *managed* by the organization to ensure efficient allocation of human and capital resources.[4] But what is the meaning of "career success"?

Toward a Definition of "Career Success"

Workers in the United States want more from their jobs than money; they want to be able to afford a "decent lifestyle." Loyalty to owner, manager, or organization, in many cases, is temporary. Many high-tech workers, with the help of executive search firms, move all over the country. Some industries have developed work styles that stand in stark contrast to traditional work styles. The tradition-oriented "organization man" of the 1950s had a clear definition of success and a stable model for achieving it. However, the "system-oriented" employees of the 1990s have enjoyed sufficient material security to explore alternative models of career success, and they are confronted with a variety of possibilities. As a consequence, organizations are finding today's employees harder to manage. But they are also finding them to be highly motivated and committed to tasks they value.[5]

In practical terms, what does all this mean for the concept of development and success in the work career? Is it occupational success? Job satisfaction? Growth and development of skills? Successful movement through various life stages? Traditionally, career development and success have been defined in terms of *occupational advancement*, which is clear and easy to measure. However, demographers have some unarguable and disturbing news: for people born between 1945 and 1964, the 1990s will be a decade of scarce promotions, frustrated expectations, and job hopping.

Two main forces are behind this trend. Throughout the 1990s, in response to tougher global competition and the threat of being taken over, companies have thinned out their management ranks to become more efficient and profitable. That means less hierarchy and fewer rungs on the corporate ladder.[6] At the same time, the large number of baby boomers (those born between 1945 and 1964), including record numbers of business school graduates, have come of age and are competing for the remaining rungs.[7] The result? Human resource management problems that organizations have never faced before. The impact on employees will be more stress, more burnout, and more psychological withdrawal. Alternative means of satisfying employees' career aspirations will be needed. Ultimately, career success may be defined by each organization in terms of the career programs it creates.[8] The following section examines career management from the individual's perspective; by way of background to this, let's consider the adult life-cycle stages.

Adult Life-Cycle Stages

For years, researchers have attempted to identify the major developmental tasks that employees face during their working lives and to organize these tasks into broader career stages (such as early, middle, and late career). Although a number of models have been proposed, very little research has tested their accuracy. Moreover, there is little, if any, agreement about whether career stages are linked to age or not. Most theorists give age ranges for each stage, but these vary widely. Consequently, it may make more sense to think in terms of career stages linked to time. This would allow

MERGERS, ACQUISITIONS, RESTRUCTURINGS, AND THE DEMISE OF CORPORATE LOYALTY

Thousands of mergers and acquisitions have taken place over the past decade among both large and small companies. In general, after a buyout, the merged company eliminates staff duplications and unprofitable divisions. Restructuring, including downsizing, often leads to similar effects—diminished loyalty from employees. In the wave of takeovers, mergers, downsizings, and layoffs, thousands of workers have discovered that years of service mean little to a struggling management or a new corporate parent. This leads to a rise in stress and a decrease in satisfaction, commitment, intentions to stay, and perceptions of an organization's trustworthiness, honesty, and caring about its employees.[9]

Companies counter that today's competitive business environment makes it difficult to protect workers. Indeed, some companies see the *overly* loyal employee as a detriment: someone who shuns risk, blindly follows corporate policies, and refrains from expressing himself or herself. Understandably, organizations are streamlining in order to become more competitive by cutting labor costs and to become more flexible in their response to the demands of the marketplace. But the rising disaffection of workers at all levels has profound implications for employers.

It may manifest itself in relatively minor matters, such as an employee's refusal to relocate. Or it may result in an employee's departure, now estimated to cost as much as $75,000 in the case of a middle manager, and 3 to 5 times annual salary for a CEO.[10] Such defections are spreading to companies that once had ironclad loyalty to and from their workers. Since the breakup of the Bell System, annual turnover at AT&T has more than tripled, to 13 percent. When Du Pont Company offered a generous early retirement plan to its 113,000 domestic employees, the chemical giant was overwhelmed: 11,200 elected to leave, about twice as many as the company had expected. Among high-tech workers, many are more loyal to their technology than to their employers. In California's Silicon Valley, for example, employee turnover at 231 electronics companies averages 27 percent, more than five times the departure rate for all U.S. manufacturing.[11] The result? Average job tenure fell from 12 years in 1981 to 9 in 1988. Soon managers will hold 7 to 10 jobs in a lifetime, up from 3 to 4 in the 1970s.[12] As one observer noted, "People used to be able to count on the organization and its stability. But the myth that institutions will take care of us has been shattered.[13]

a "career clock" to begin at different points for different individuals, based on their backgrounds and experiences.[14]

Such an approach allows for differences in the number of distinct stages through which individuals may pass, the overlapping tasks and issues they may face at each stage, and the role of transition periods between stages. The lesson for managers is that all models of adult life-cycle stages should be viewed as broad guidelines rather than as exact representations of reality.

CAREER MANAGEMENT: INDIVIDUALS FOCUSING ON THEMSELVES

In thinking about career management, it is important to emphasize the increasingly *temporary* relationships between individuals and organizations. Said a victim of three corporate downsizings in four years: "A job is just an opportunity to learn new skills that you can then peddle elsewhere in the marketplace."[15] While such a view might appear cynical to some, the fact is that responsibility for career development ultimately belongs to each individual. Unfortunately, few individuals are technically prepared (and willing) to handle this assignment. This is not surprising, for very few college programs specifically address the problems of managing one's own career. However, as long as it remains difficult for organizations to match the career expectations of their employees (a following section shows actual corporate examples of this), one option for employees will be to switch organizations. Guidelines for doing this fall into the following three major categories.[16]

Selecting a Field of Employment and an Employer

1. You cannot manage your career unless you have a macro, long-range objective. The first step, therefore, is to think in terms of where you ultimately want to be, recognizing, of course, that your career goals will change over time.

2. View every potential employer and position in terms of your long-range career goal. That is, how well does this job serve to position me in terms of my ultimate objective?

For example, if you aspire to reach senior management by the year 2000, consider the extent to which your current job helps you develop a global orientation, develop public speaking skills, practice the "bring out the best in people" leadership style, and learn to manage cultural diversity. These are now, and will continue to be, key requirements for such senior positions.[17]

3. Accept short-term trade-offs for long-term benefits. Certain lateral moves or low-paying jobs can provide extremely valuable training opportunities or career contacts.

4. Consider carefully whether to accept highly specialized jobs or isolated job assignments that might restrict or impede your visibility and career development.

Knowing Where You Are

1. Always be aware of opportunities available to you in your current position—e.g., training programs that might further your career development.

2. Carefully and honestly assess your current performance. How do you see yourself, and how do you think higher management sees your performance?

3. Try to recognize when you and your organization have outlived your utility for each other. This is not an admission of failure but rather an honest reflection of the fact that there is little more the organization can do for you and, in turn, that your contribution to the organization has reached a point of diminishing returns.

Here are five important symptoms: you're not excited by what you are doing, advancement is blocked, your organization is poorly managed and is losing market share, you feel you are not adequately rewarded for your work, or you are not fulfilling your dreams.[18]

Planning Your Exit

1. Try to leave at *your* convenience, not the organization's. To do this, you must do two things well: (a) know when it is time to leave (as before), and (b) since down-

sizing can come at any time, establish networking relationships while you still have a job.

2. Leave your current organization on good terms and not under questionable circumstances.

3. Don't leave your current job until you've landed another one, for it's easier to find a new job when you're currently employed. Like bank loans, jobs often go to people who don't seem to need them.[19]

Up to this point it may sound as though managing your career is all one-sided. This is not true; the organization should be a proactive force in this process. To do so, organizations must think and plan in terms of shorter employment relationships. This can be done, as it often is in professional sports, through fixed-term employment contracts with options for renegotiation and extension.

A second strategy for organizations is to invest adequate time and energy in job design and equipment. Given that mobility among workers is expected to increase, careful attention to these elements will make it easier to make replacements fully productive as soon as possible. How does the self-management of careers work in practice? If Hewlett-Packard's experience is any indication, we can expect to see more of it in the future.

HELPING EMPLOYEES SELF-MANAGE THEIR CAREERS AT HEWLETT-PACKARD

COMPANY EXAMPLE

A 3-month course in personal career management was developed at Hewlett-Packard's Colorado Springs Division based on two methods: self-assessment and subsequent application of findings to the workplace to chart a career path for each employee.[20]

The idea of self-assessment as the first step toward career planning is certainly not new. Self-help books have flooded the market for years. However, books by themselves lack a critical ingredient for success: *the emotional support of a group setting* in which momentum and motivation can be shared and maintained. Make no mistake about it, self-assessment can be a grueling process.

Hewlett-Packard uses six devices to generate data for self-assessment (based on earlier work for a second-year Harvard MBA course in career development). These include:

- *A written self-interview.* Participants are given 11 questions about themselves, they are asked to provide facts about their lives (people, places, events), and they are asked to discuss the future and the transitions they have made. This autobiographical sketch provides core data for the subsequent analysis.

- *Strong-Campbell Interest Inventory.* Participants complete this 325-item instrument to determine their preferences about occupations, academic subjects, types of people, and so forth. An interest profile is developed for each individual by comparing her or his responses to those of successful people in a wide range of occupations.

- *Allport-Vernon-Lindzey Study of Values.* Each participant makes 45 choices among competing values in order to measure the relative strength of theoretical, economic, aesthetic, social, political, and religious values.

■ *24-hour diaries.* Participants log their activities during one workday and also during one nonworkday. This information is used to confirm, or occasionally contradict, information from the other sources.

■ *Interviews with two "significant others."* Each participant asks a friend, spouse, relative, coworker, or someone else of importance questions about himself or herself. The two interviews are tape-recorded.

■ *Lifestyle representations.* Participants depict their lifestyles using words, photos, drawings, or whatever else they choose.

A key ingredient in this program is its emphasis on an *inductive* approach. That is, the program begins by generating new data about each participant, rather than by starting with generalizations and deducing from them more specific information about each person. The process proceeds from the specific to the general (inductive), rather than from the general to the specific (deductive). Participants slowly recognize generalizations or themes within the large amounts of information they have produced. They come to tentative conclusions about these themes, first in each device individually and then in all the workshop's instruments as a whole, by analyzing the data they have collected.

Following the self-assessment, department managers interview subordinates to learn about their career objectives. They record these objectives and describe the people and positions currently in their departments. This information is then available for senior management to use in devising an overall human resource plan, defining the skills required, and including a timetable. When data on the company's future needs are matched against each employee's career objectives, department managers can help employees chart a career course in the company (e.g., through training or additional job experience). Career development objectives for each employee are incorporated into performance objectives for future performance appraisals. The department head monitors the employee's career progress as part of the review process, and she or he is responsible for offering all possible support.

RESULTS OF THE CAREER SELF-MANAGEMENT PROGRAM

Senior managers at Hewlett-Packard found that after the workshops they had far more flexibility in moving employees than previously. The company was able either to give employees reasons to stay where they were, to develop a new path for them in the company, or to help them move out. Significantly, the Colorado Springs Division's overall turnover rate was unchanged in the year following the workshops. At an estimated $60,000 replacement cost (in 1993 dollars) for a departing middle manager, this was a welcome finding.

Within 6 months after the course, 37 percent of the participants had advanced to new jobs within the company, while 40 percent planned moves within the following 6 months. Of those who advanced, 74 percent credited the program for playing a significant part in their job change. The workshops also promoted workforce diversity since the sessions were open to all employees who expressed an interest in career development.

Perhaps the most persuasive reason for helping employees manage their own careers is the need to remain competitive. Although it might seem like a contradiction, such efforts can enhance a company's stability by developing more purposeful, self-assured employees. As noted earlier, today's employees are more difficult to manage. Companies that recognize the need to provide employees with satisfying opportunities will have the decided advantage of a loyal and industrious workforce.

One of the most challenging career management problems organizations face today is that of the dual-career couple. Let's examine this issue in detail.

Dual-Career Couples: Problems and Opportunities

In 1993, two of every three employed men had wives employed in the workforce.[21] Dual-career couples face the problems of managing work and family responsibilities. Furthermore, it appears that there may be an interaction effect that compounds the problems and stresses of each separate career.[22] This implies that, by itself, career planning and development may be meaningless unless an employee's role as a family member also is considered, particularly when this role conflicts with work activities.[23] What can be done?

Research indicates that if dual-career couples are to manage their family responsibilities successfully, they (and their managers) must be flexible; they must be mutually committed to both careers; they must adopt coping mechanisms (e.g., separating work and nonwork roles clearly, accepting all role demands as given, and finding ways to meet them); and they must develop the competencies to manage their careers through career information and planning, goal setting, and problem solving.[24]

From an organizational perspective, successful management of the dual-career couple requires (1) flexible work schedules, (2) special counseling, (3) training for supervisors in career counseling skills, and (4) the establishment of support structures for transfers and relocations. What have organizations actually done?

As part of a package deal, roughly 50 percent of U.S. companies provide assistance to the "trailing" spouse in finding a suitable job consistent with the spouse's career plans.[25] Unisys pays up to $500 for résumé writing and job-hunting help for a trailing spouse. U.S. West offers as much as $2500, including insuring against home-sale losses. Cigna will cover a month's pay at the spouse's former salary while he or she seeks a new job.[26]

Alternatively, companies that have eliminated the nepotism taboo might hire the trailing spouse themselves. This may be a strategy for attracting and retaining top talent, particularly in technical occupations, which more women are entering. Thus a national survey done for General Electric found that 50 percent of all female technologists were married to technologists. However, another reason for the elimination of no-spouse rules is that they have come under attack in the courts on the grounds that they amount to illegal discrimination on the basis of gender. Women are usually the ones who are forced to leave a company or are not hired in the first place.[27] The hiring of couples seems to work best at large concerns, where more jobs are available and it is easier physically to separate spouses from each other in different offices or buildings. This makes it easier to conform to most firms' policy on this issue: *an employee cannot be placed under the direct or indirect supervision of a spouse.* The advantages of hiring both spouses are:

- It helps lure prospective employees to remote communities where suitable jobs for a spouse might be hard to find.
- It cuts recruiting and relocation costs.
- It encourages executives already on board to accept transfers.
- It makes employees less susceptible to offers from rival firms.

However, as with any other HR policy, the advantages of spouse hiring need to be weighed against the following disadvantages:[28]

- There is considerable risk that disciplining or firing one spouse will cause the other to leave as well.
- Outplacement assistance for one spouse as a result of a layoff may in reality become outplacement assistance for both spouses, if the other voluntarily quits.
- Couples employed by the same firm may encounter tremendous strains when one of them encounters problems at work. The partner cannot just say, "This is between you and your boss; I don't want to get into the middle of it."
- Couples worry that in matters of promotion, transfer, and compensation they will be seen by the company as a team, instead of as individuals.

Although many organizations have been very progressive in the management of dual-career couples, there are also several things organizations have *not* done. Only about 20 firms provide training for supervisors on how to deal with employees who are partners in dual-career couples.[29] Such training is important, for research indicates that when a wife works, the husband often develops lower levels of job and life satisfaction.[30] Wives' employment boosts the mental health of wives but often depresses the mental health of husbands. Why? Some husbands may not yet be ready to abandon the "good provider" role, that is, the traditional role of being sufficiently resourceful as a provider for one's family that one's wife does not *have* to enter the labor force.

In addition to supervisory training, relatively few firms provide job sharing or child care. With regard to child care, demand for the service has never been greater. However, only about 7 percent of U.S. workplaces with 50 or more employees provide on-site or near-site child-care programs.[31] Here are some reasons why employer-supported child care will continue to grow:

- Dual-career couples now comprise a preponderance of the workforce.
- There has been a significant rise in the number of single parents, over half of whom use child-care facilities.[32]
- More and more, career-oriented women are arranging their lives to include motherhood *and* professional goals.

For firms considering child care, here are three options:[33]

1. Set up a clearinghouse for information about child care available in the local community.
2. Refer employees to existing day-care facilities in the community at a reduced rate. The rate can be reduced by negotiating with one or more local providers, by paying a company subsidy of 10 to 50 percent to the providers, or by giving the employees vouchers that reimburse any local center 100 percent of the child-care expenses.
3. The employer may provide a child-care center on or near the worksite.

To assess the quality of child care provided, parents should actually see the facility to be used. Safety, nutritious food, child curriculum and activities, parent involvement, and space and equipment are key areas to probe.[34]

Employers who currently provide some form of child-care assistance report the following *advantages:*

- Tax savings (employers may deduct the cost of child-care benefits, both for on-site and for referral subsidies)
- Reduced turnover
- Improved morale and employer–employee relations
- Effective recruitment tool
- Positive community image

However, there are also *disadvantages* to providing child care. These include:

- The equity of benefits (unless a flexible benefits plan is available, not all employees can take advantage of child care).
- The company expense of voucher and vendor plans.
- The substantial expense of the on-site option.
- Considerable liability exposure for employers providing on-site child care. This disadvantage is probably more myth than reality. Thus one study found that estimates of liability insurance by companies that do not have child-care centers were 6 times higher than the actual amounts. Such costs average about 1 to 3 percent of a center's operating budget. According to the general liability manager of Allstate Insurance Co.: "Businesses are not exposed to any more loss than they have in normal operations."[35]
- Lack of evidence in well-controlled studies that child care increases employee productivity or reduces absenteeism or lateness.[36]

Indeed, the lesson of two recent studies is clear: Don't expect that a day-care center or a flexible schedule will keep women managers from leaving corporations. They may be quite willing to throw corporate loyalty to the wind if they aren't getting adequate opportunities for career growth and job satisfaction.[37]

Managing dual-career couples, from an individual as well as from an organizational perspective, is difficult. But if current conditions are any indication of long-term trends, we can be quite sure of one thing: this "problem" is not going to go away.

CAREER MANAGEMENT: ORGANIZATIONS FOCUSING ON INDIVIDUALS

In this section we will examine current organizational practices used to manage workers at various stages of their careers. Let's begin by considering organizational entry.

Organizational Entry

Once a person has entered the workforce, the next stage is to enter a specific organization, to settle down, and to begin establishing a career there. *Entry* refers to the process of "moving inside," or becoming more involved in a particular organization.[38] To do this well, a process known as socialization is essential. *Socialization* refers to the mutual adaptation of the new employee and the new employer to one another. Learning organizational policies, norms, traditions, and values is an important part of the process. Getting to know one's peers, supervisor, and subordinates is, too. Over

ETHICAL DILEMMA: BRINGING MENTORS AND PROTÉGÉS TOGETHER

Recent research indicates that informal mentorships (spontaneous relationships that occur without involvement from the organization) lead to more positive career outcomes than do formal mentorships (programs that are managed and sanctioned by the organization).[39] Random assignment of protégés to mentors is like a blind date—there is only a small chance that the match will be successful. On the other hand, not all new hires are willing or able actively to seek out opportunities to work with a mentor. For those that do not, is it ethically acceptable to assign them randomly to mentors, or to let them "sink or swim"? How would you advise an organization faced with this dilemma to proceed?

time, organizations adapt to new employees—e.g., the younger generation, the older employee, the hard-core unemployed. Since most turnover occurs early in a person's tenure with an organization, programs that accelerate socialization will tend also to reduce early turnover (i.e., at entry) and therefore reduce a company's overall turnover rate. Two of the most effective methods for doing this are realistic job previews (see Chapter 6) and new-employee orientation (see Chapter 8). A third is "mentoring."

Mentoring. A mentor is a teacher, an advisor, a sponsor, and a confidant.[40] He or she should be bright and well seasoned enough to understand the dynamics of power and politics in the organization and also be willing to share this knowledge with one or more new hires. Indeed, to overcome the potential problems associated with one-on-one, male–female mentoring relationships, some firms have established "quad squads" that consist of a mentor plus three new hires: a male, a female, and one other member of a protected group. Bank of America is typical. It assigns mentors to three or four promising young executives for a year at a time. There are also benefits for the mentor. For example, just being chosen as a mentor, according to one 35-year-old female branch bank manager, boosted her self-esteem. This is a central goal of any mentoring effort.

Organizations should actively promote such relationships and provide sufficient time for mentors and new hires (or promising young executives) to meet on a regularly scheduled basis, at least initially. The mentor's role is to be a "culture carrier," to teach new hires "the ropes," to provide candid feedback on how they are being perceived by others, and to serve as a confidential "sounding board" for dealing with work-related problems. That "sounding board" may even be a computer-based bulletin board, such as America Online or Compuserve, that provides a forum for discussing specific workplace issues.[41] If successful, mentor relationships can help reduce the inflated expectations that newcomers often have about organizations, can relieve the stress experienced by all new hires, and, best of all, can improve the newcomer's chances for survival and growth in the organization.[42]

Early Career: The Impact of the First Job

Many studies of early careers focus on the first jobs to which new employees are assigned. The positive impact of initial job challenge upon later career success and retention has been found many times in a wide variety of settings. Among engineers, challenging early work assignments were related to strong initial performance as well as to the maintenance of competence and performance throughout the engineer's career.[43] In other words, challenging initial job assignments are an antidote to career obsolescence.

The characteristics of the first supervisor are also critical. He or she must be personally secure, unthreatened by the new subordinate's training, ambition, and energy, and able to communicate company norms and values.[44] Beyond that, the supervisor ideally should be able to play the roles of coach, feedback provider, trainer, role model, and protector in an accepting, esteem-building manner.

One other variable affects the likelihood of obtaining a high-level job later in one's career: *initial aspirations*.[45] Employees should be encouraged to "aim high" because, in general, higher aspirations lead to higher performance. Parents, teachers, employers, and friends should therefore avoid discouraging so-called impractical aspirations.

IMPACT OF THE FIRST JOB ON LATER CAREER SUCCESS

COMPANY EXAMPLE

For more than 20 years researchers generally accepted the view that unless an individual has a challenging first job and receives quick, early promotions, the entire career will suffer. This is a "tournament" model of upward mobility. It assumes that everyone has an equal chance in the early contests but that the losers are not eligible for later contests, at least not those of the major tournament. An alternative model is called "signaling" theory. It suggests three cues ("signals") that those responsible for promotion may use: (1) prior history of promotions (a signal of ability), (2) functional-area background, and (3) number of different jobs held.

A study of the patterns of early upward mobility for 180 employees of an oil company over an 11-year period are enlightening.[46] The company's very detailed job classification systems and actual salary grades served as measures of career attainment. The results generally did not support the tournament model of career mobility, because the losers—those passed over in the early periods—were later able to move up quickly. Rather, the results were more analogous to a horse race: position out of the gate had relatively little effect in comparison to position entering the home stretch.

Different mobility patterns for administration and technical personnel helped to explain why the pattern of the early years did not always persist. Those who started early in administrative positions began to move up early but also plateaued early. A technical background meant a longer wait before upward movement, followed by relatively rapid promotion. The number of different positions held also predicted higher attainment.

In summary, one's past position, functional background, and number of different jobs all seem to act as signals to those making decisions about promotions. All were related strongly to career attainment. Together they accounted for more than 60 percent of the variability in promotions.

Managing Men and Women in Midcareer

The theory that a crisis occurs in the lives of U.S. workers between the ages of 35 and 50 is well supported by research. The crisis is variously known as "middlescence," "middle-age crisis," and "midlife transition." The following issues may arise at this stage:[47]

- An awareness of advancing age and an awareness of death
- An awareness of bodily changes related to aging
- Knowing how many career goals have been or will be attained
- A search for new life goals
- A marked change in family relationships
- A change in work relationships (one is now more of a "coach" than a novice or "rookie")
- A growing sense of obsolescence at work (as Satchel Paige once said, "Never look back; someone may be gaining on you")
- A feeling of decreased job mobility and increased concern for job security[48]

One's career is a major consideration during this period. If a person has been in the same job for 10 years or more (sometimes less), he or she must face the facts of corporate politics, changing job requirements, possibilities of promotion, demotion, or job loss altogether. The fact of the matter is, over the next decade promotions will slow down markedly as middle-level managers are put into "holding patterns."

While career success traditionally has been defined in terms of upward mobility, in the 1990s more and more leading corporations are encouraging employees to step off the fast track and convincing them that they can find rewards and happiness in lateral mobility. In lectures and newsletters, the companies are trying to convince employees that "plateauing" is a fact of life, not a measure of personal failure, and that success depends on lateral integration of the business. Does such a move make sense? Yes, if it puts a person into a core business, gives that person closer contact with customers, or teaches new skills that will increase marketability (both inside and outside one's present company) in case the person is fired.[49]

Companies that are moving this way are still a minority, but they include such giants as Monsanto, Motorola, BellSouth, General Electric (GE), and RJR Nabisco. As a senior vice president at GE noted: "You lose the thrill of moving up . . . [but] the trade-off is more of a voice in your work."[50]

Others note that while there are fewer middle managers at medium and large companies as a result of the reductions in layers of managers during the corporate restructurings of the last decade, their jobs are more important. Middle managers now focus less on supervision and more on decision making.[51] However, for those who simply cannot accept lateral mobility, there is still hope. Throughout the 1990s, according to the Bureau of Labor Statistics, many firms will face shortages of managers with leadership and technical knowledge (such as engineers with MBA degrees) and those with expertise in human resource management and computer matters.[52]

What can a middle-aged man or woman do? The rapid growth of technology and the accelerating development of new knowledge require that a person in midlife make some sort of *change* for her or his own survival. A 30-year-old might make the statement "I can afford to change jobs or careers a couple of more times before I have to settle down." But a 50-year-old faces the possibility that there is only one chance left for change, and now may be the time to take it.[53]

Not everyone who goes through this period in life is destined to experience problems, but everyone does go through the transition, and some are better equipped to cope than are others. Why is this so? And how can we cope? Although midcareer might sound as though it is all "gloom and doom," one bright spot is the knowledge that *having realistic expectations about impending crises and transitions can actually ease the stress and pain.*[54] Life planning and career planning exercises are available that encourage employees to face up to feelings of restlessness and insecurity, to reexamine their values and life goals, and to set new ones or to recommit themselves to old ones.

One strategy is to *train midcareer employees to develop younger employees* (i.e., to serve as coaches or mentors). Both parties can win under such an arrangement. The midcareer employee keeps himself or herself fresh, energetic, and up to date, while the younger employee learns to see the "big picture" and to profit from the experience of the older employee. An important psychological need at midcareer is to build something lasting, something that will be a permanent contribution to one's organization or profession.[55] The development of a future generation of leaders could be a significant, lasting, and highly satisfying contribution.

Another strategy for coping with midcareer problems is to *deal with or prevent obsolescence.* To deal with the problem, some firms send their employees to seminars, workshops, university courses, and other forms of "retooling." But a better solution is to prevent obsolescence from occurring in the first place. Research with engineers indicated that this can be done through challenging initial jobs; periodic changes in assignments, projects, or jobs; work climates that contain frequent, relevant communications; rewards that are closely tied to performance; and participative styles of leadership.[56] Furthermore, three personal characteristics tend to be associated with low obsolescence: high intellectual ability, high self-motivation, and personal flexibility (lack of rigidity).

STRATEGIES FOR COPING WITH "PLATEAUED" WORKERS[57]

COMPANY EXAMPLE

Chevron, General Motors, and Chicago's Continental Bank are encouraging employees to move across departmental lines on a horizontal basis since restructuring has made vertical promotions less frequent. In banking, for example, someone from auditing might switch to commercial training; someone from systems research and development might move into international development. The inflexible HRM policies of the past are rapidly fading to accommodate present and future problems. Another strategy is to create dual technical/management ladders. New "technical executive" positions are equal to management jobs in title and dollars. For example, Continental Bank has created senior lending positions and positions for accounting and systems specialists that are equivalent to senior managerial posts in those departments.

An alternative way to placate people who do not move up is to pay them more for jobs well done. For years, companies that rely heavily for growth on creative people—scientists, engineers, writers, artists—have provided incentives for them to stay on. Companies are now offering such incentives to a broader spectrum. For example, at Monsanto, favored scientists can now climb a university-like track of associate fellow, fellow, senior fellow, distinguished fellow. The company has 130 fellows, and they earn from $65,000 a year to well over $100,000.

At General Electric, employees who are "plateaued" (either organizationally, through a lack of available promotions, or personally, through lack of ability or desire) are sometimes assigned to task forces or study teams. These employees have not been promoted in a technical sense, but at least they have gotten a new assignment, a fresh perspective, and a change in their daily work.

Finally, Prudential Life Insurance Company rotates managers to improve their performance. Rockwell International uses task forces, where possible, to "recharge" managers so they do not feel a loss of self-worth if they do not move up as fast as they think they should.

Actually, there may be a bright side to all of this. Because of increased competition for fewer jobs, the *quality* of middle managers should increase. Those unwilling to wait for promotions in large corporations may become entrepreneurs and start their own businesses. Others may simply accept the status quo, readjust their life and career goals, and attempt to satisfy their needs for achievement, recognition, and personal growth off the job. Research at AT&T supports this proposition. By the time managers were interviewed after 20 years on the job, most had long ago given up their early dreams, and many could not even remember how high they had aspired in the first place. At least on the surface, most had accepted their career plateaus and adjusted to them. Midlife was indeed a crisis to some of the managers, but not to the majority.[58]

It is possible to move through the middle years of life without reevaluation of one's goals and life. But it is probably healthier to develop a new or revised "game plan" during this period.

Managing the Older Worker

"Work is life" is a phrase philosophers throughout the ages have emphasized. Today, advances in health and medicine make it possible for the average male to live for more than 72 years and for the average female to live for more than 79 years.[59] Longevity has increased by 27 years in this century! The result: an army of healthy, over-65, unemployed adults. Legally, the elimination of mandatory retirement at *any* age has made this issue even more significant. As managers, what can we expect in terms of demographic trends?

Post–World War II baby boomers (those born between 1946 and 1964) are passing into middle life. The Census Bureau predicts that the number of new workers aged 18 to 24 will drop by 16 percent over the next 20 years. Meanwhile, by the year 2010 all the people born during the baby-boom years will be age 45 and older; those born in 1946 will be 64. In the year 2020, the oldest "baby boomers" will be 75 and the youngest will be 56.[60] Figure 10-1 graphically illustrates these trends. In short, the baby boom of the postwar period will become the "rocking-chair boom" of the twenty-first century.

FIGURE 10-1
Population distribution by age group, ages 16–24 and 45–65. (*Source:* U.S. Bureau of the Census, "Estimates of the Population of the United States, by Age, Sex, and Race: 1980 to 1983," *Current Population Reports,* Series P-25, No. 949, May 1984; U.S. Bureau of the Census, "Projections of the Population of the United States, by Age, Sex, and Race: 1983 to 2080," *Current Population Reports,* Series P-25, No. 952, May 1984.)

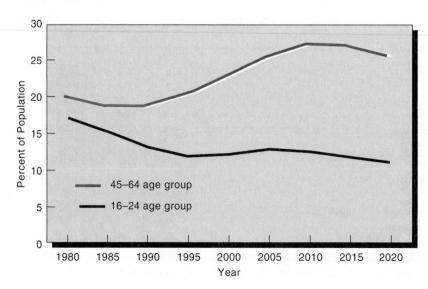

Myths Versus Facts about Older Workers. Age stereotypes are an unfortunate impediment to the continued growth and development of workers over the age of 55. Here are some common myths about age along with the true facts:

Myth. Older workers are less productive than younger workers.
Fact. Cumulative research evidence on almost 39,000 individuals indicates that in both professional and nonprofessional jobs, age and job performance are generally unrelated. However, insufficient evidence is available on the performance of workers over 70 to draw reliable conclusions about this group.[61] Speed of recall and mental performance slow with age, but essential skills remain intact.[62]

Myth. It costs more to prepare older workers for a job.
Fact. Studies show that mental abilities, such as verbal, numerical, and reasoning skills, remain stable into the seventies.

Myth. Older workers are absent more often because of age-related infirmities and above-average rates of illness.
Fact. The average number of workdays lost to all acute conditions (e.g., flu, injuries, colds) for persons aged 18 to 44 was 3.3 days per year, while for persons aged 45 and above the average was 2.6 days per year.[63] Fully half of all people now aged 75 to 84 are free from health problems that require special care or that curb their activities.[64]

Myth. Older workers have an unacceptably high rate of accidents on the job.
Fact. According to a study by the Department of Health and Human Services, persons aged 55 and over had only 9.7 percent of all workplace injuries, even though they made up 13.6 percent of the workforce at the time of the study.[65] One might argue that this is because older workers have more experience on a job. But regardless of length of experience, the *younger* the employee, the *higher* the accident rate (see Chapter 16).

Myth. Older workers do not get along well with other employees.
Fact. Owners of small and large businesses alike agree that older employees bring stability and relate well. Indeed, the over-55 worker's sense of responsibility and consistent job performance provide a positive role model for younger workers.[66]

Myth. The cost of employee benefits outweighs any other possible benefits from hiring older workers.
Fact. True, when older people get sick, the illness is often chronic and requires repeated doctor's visits and hospitalization. However, the costs of health care for an older worker are lower than those for a younger, married worker with several children.[67]

Myth. Older people are inflexible about the type of work they will perform.
Fact. A study of job candidates by Right Associates, placement counselors, found that 55 percent of those under age 50, but 63 percent of those age 50 to 59 and 78 percent of those over age 60, changed industries. Many older workers saw difficulties in being rehired by their old industries.

Myth. Older people do not function well if constantly interrupted.
Fact. Neither do younger people.

In many fields, older workers are especially valuable because they have a lifetime of experience to draw from.

Implications of the Aging Workforce for HRM. Certainly not *all* older workers are model employees, just as not *all* older workers fit traditional stereotypes. What are the implications of this growing group of able-bodied individuals for human resource management?

We know what the future labor market will look like in general terms: both the demand for and the supply of older workers will continue to expand. To capitalize on these trends, one approach is to recruit workers from those individuals who would otherwise retire. *Make the job more attractive than retirement, and keep the employee who would otherwise need replacing.*[68] As the following example illustrates, some companies are doing exactly this.

COMPANY PRACTICES

UNRETIREES

Travelers Corporation is one of a growing number of companies that are finding their own retirees to be a valuable source of experienced, dependable, and motivated help. The retirees meet seasonal or sporadic employment needs for the company, and the company gets a tax break. In 1980, Travelers invited all of its 5000 retirees to enroll in its Retirees

Job Bank in Hartford, Connecticut. By 1990, more than 750 did. They fill a variety of jobs, including typists, data-entry operators, systems analysts, underwriters, and accountants. Working a maximum of 40 hours per month, retirees are paid at the midpoint of the salary range for their job classifications. If they work more than half a standard workweek, they risk losing their pension benefits. Nevertheless, retirees generally like the program, for it keeps them in better physical, mental, and financial shape than full-time retirement does.[69]

With a smaller cohort of young workers entering the workforce, other companies are also seeking workers who once would have been considered "over the hill." McDonald's prints applications for "McMasters" on its tray liners. Days Inns of America holds Senior Power job fairs. One such effort attracted 634 companies and 5000 older people in 26 states. The Polaroid Corporation offers gradual retirement for those who want to continue working part-time.[70] According to Chicago's Harris Trust and Savings Bank, which has been rehiring its retirees since the 1940s, the savings from its program come to $3 to $5 per hour when compared with the fees charged by temporary help agencies.

A second approach is to *survey the needs of older workers and, where feasible, adjust HRM practices and policies to accommodate these needs:*

1. Keep records on why employees retire and on why they continue to work.[71]

2. Implement flexible work patterns and options. For example, older workers might work on Mondays and Fridays and on days before and after holidays, when so many other employees fail to show up.

3. Where possible, redesign jobs to match the physical capabilities of the aging worker.

4. At a broader level, develop career paths that consider the physical capabilities of workers at various stages of their careers.[72]

5. Provide opportunities for retraining in technical and managerial skills. Particularly with older workers, it is important to provide a nonthreatening training environment that does not emphasize speed and does not expose the older learner to unfavorable comparisons with younger learners. Verbal assurances, ample time, and privacy are key ingredients for successfully training older workers.[73]

6. Examine the suitability of performance appraisal systems as bases for employment decisions affecting older workers. To avoid age discrimination suits, be able to provide documented evidence of ineffective job performance.

7. Despite the encouraging findings presented earlier, in the section "Myths Versus Facts about Older Workers," research has indicated no overall improvement in attitudes toward older workers over a 30-year period.[74]

For their part, older workers say their biggest problem is discrimination by would-be employers who underestimate their skills. They say they must convince supervisors and coworkers, not to mention some customers, that they're not stubborn, persnickety, or feeble.[75] To change this trend, workers and managers alike need to know the facts about older workers, so that they do not continue to espouse myths.

CAREER MANAGEMENT: ORGANIZATIONS FOCUSING ON THEIR OWN MAINTENANCE AND GROWTH

Ultimately, it is top management's responsibility to develop and implement a cost-effective career planning program. The program must fit the nature of the business, its competitive employment practices, and the current (or desired) organizational structure. This process is complex because organizational career management combines areas that previously have been regarded as individual issues: performance appraisal, development, transfer, and promotion. Before coaching and counseling take place, however, it is important to identify characteristic career paths that employees tend to follow.

Career paths represent logical and possible sequences of positions that could be held, based on an analysis of what people actually do in an organization.[76] Career paths should:

- Represent real progression possibilities, whether lateral or upward, without implied "normal" rates of progress or forced specialization in a technical area.

- Be tentative and responsive to changes in job content, work priorities, organizational patterns, and management needs.

- Be flexible, taking into consideration the compensating qualities of a particular employee, managers, subordinates, or others who influence the way that work is performed.

- Specify the skills, knowledge, and other attributes required to perform effectively at each position along the paths and specify how they can be acquired. (If specifications are limited to educational credentials, age, and experience, some capable performers may be excluded from career opportunities.)

Data derived from HRM research are needed to define career paths in this manner. Worker-oriented job analyses (see Chapter 5) that can be expressed in quantitative terms are well suited to this task since they focus directly on the behavioral requirements of each job. Clusters or families of jobs requiring similar patterns of behavior can then be identified.

Once this is done, the next task is to identify career paths within and among the job families and to integrate the overall network of these paths into a single career system. The process is shown graphically in Figure 10-2.

Federal guidelines on employee selection require a job-related basis for all employment decisions. Career paths based on job analyses of employee behaviors provide a documented, defensible basis for organizational career management and a strong reference point for individual career planning and development activities.[77]

In practice, organizational career management systems sometimes fail for the following reasons: (1) employees believe that supervisors do not care about their career development, (2) neither the employee nor the organization is fully aware of the employee's needs and organizational constraints, and (3) career plans are developed without regard for the support systems necessary to fulfill the plans.[78] The following section gives examples of several companies that avoided these pitfalls.

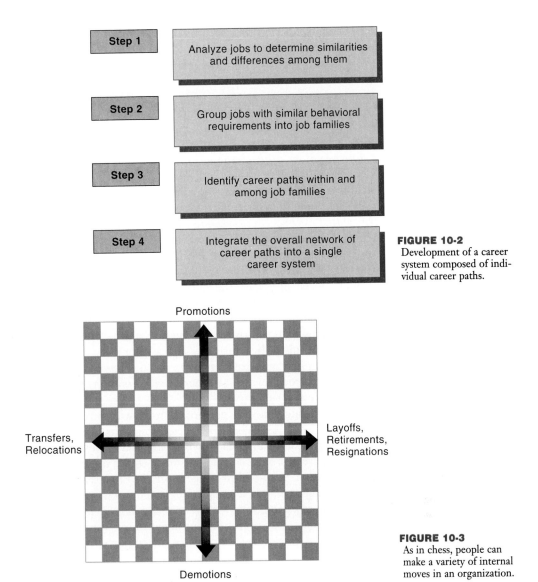

FIGURE 10-2
Development of a career system composed of individual career paths.

FIGURE 10-3
As in chess, people can make a variety of internal moves in an organization.

Internal Staffing Decisions: Patterns of Career Change

From the organization's point of view, there are four broad types of internal moves: up, down, over, and out (Figure 10-3). These moves correspond to promotions (up), demotions (down), transfers and relocations (over), and layoffs, retirements, and resignations (out). Technically, dismissals also fall into the last category, but we will consider them in the context of disciplinary actions and procedural justice. Briefly, let's consider each of these patterns of movement.

Promotions. Promoted employees usually assume greater responsibility and authority in return for higher pay, benefits, and privileges. Psychologically, promotions help satisfy employees' needs for security, belonging, and personal growth. Promotions are important organizational decisions that should receive the same careful attention as any other employment decision. They are more likely to be successful to the extent that:

1. An extensive search for candidates is conducted.
2. Standardized, clearly understandable information is available on all candidates.[79]

Organizations must continue to live with those who are bypassed for promotion. Research indicates that these individuals often feel they have not been treated fairly, their commitment decreases, and their absenteeism increases. Conversely, promoted individuals tend to increase their commitment.[80] To minimize defensive behavior, it is critical that the procedures used for promotion decisions (e.g., assessment centers plus performance appraisals) be acceptable, valid, and fair to the unsuccessful candidates. Further, emphasize the greater merits of the promoted candidates, relative to those who were not promoted.

In unionized situations, the collective bargaining contract will determine the relative importance given to seniority and ability in promotion decisions. Management tends to emphasize ability, while unions favor seniority. Although practices vary considerably from firm to firm, a compromise is usually reached through which promotions are determined by a formula, such as promoting the employee with the greatest seniority *if* ability and experience are equal. However, if one candidate is clearly a superior performer relative to others, many contracts will permit promotion on this basis regardless of seniority.

A further issue concerns promotion from within versus outside the organization. Many firms, such as Delta Air Lines, have strict promotion-from-within policies. However, there are situations in which high-level jobs or newly created jobs require talents that are just not available in-house. Under these circumstances, even the most rigid promotion-from-within policy must yield to a search for outside candidates.

A relatively recent phenomenon is *refusal* of promotions, particularly in dual-career families, where a promotion for one spouse may pose problems for the other.[81] Refusal causes two kinds of organizational problems. First, the company has invested time and money in the career development of an employee for a position that is refused. Second, those who refuse promotions can become deadwood, blocking the career paths of lower-level employees who would normally rise behind them. To avert this problem, firms need to make a variety of career paths available.

COMPANY EXAMPLE

PROMOTIONS TO PARTNER AT GOLDMAN, SACHS & CO.

Goldman, Sachs & Co. is one of the last of Wall Street's major private partnerships. Each year, the firm picks a small number of new partners from among its hundreds of young executives. Winners are set for life and typically retire as multimillionaires after only a decade or so. But it's getting harder to decide who gets the prize.

Exactly what goes on behind the scenes of the 2-month-long competition is a closely held secret. Current partners describe it, of course, as a rigorous but fair process in which politics are unimportant. The process certainly is rigorous. It starts with a winnowing down of the worldwide workforce of 6600 to a list of 50 to 60 serious candidates. Each potential new partner must then be nominated by a current partner.

What do partners look for? In addition to keen business judgment and a proven track record of success, partners look for team players and "culture carriers." Such people fit Goldman's conservative style and its customer-oriented tradition, which dates back to the 1860s, when Marcus Goldman began hawking commercial paper on the streets of New York.

Partners, who are expected to back their nominees' causes throughout the process, then file mountains of endorsement letters. For the next several weeks, an eight-member management committee reviews these materials and checks out the nominees. Members of the committee who are not in a candidate's division grill department heads and other partners about the candidate's qualifications and then report back. Candidates themselves are never interviewed. In fact, they're not even supposed to know that they are candidates. But of course they do.

After a dizzying round of management–committee summit meetings, a final "town meeting" of all current partners is held, at which the management committee presents its final list for discussion and debate—even though it's pretty clear that the committee's list is final. Following the "town meeting," the partners announce the list of newly minted millionaires. In 1990, Goldman added 32 members to its exclusive club, which now numbers 148.[82]

Demotions. Employee demotions usually involve a cut in pay, status, privilege, or opportunity. They occur infrequently since they tend to be accompanied by problems of employee apathy, depression, and inefficiency that can undermine the morale of a work group. For these reasons, many managers prefer to discharge or to move employees laterally rather than demote them. In either case, careful planning, documentation, and concern for the employee should precede such moves.[83]

Aside from disciplinary actions, demotions may result from staff reductions, from the inability of an employee to handle the requirements of a higher-level job, from health problems, or from changing interests (e.g., a desire to move from production to sales). In many cases, demotion is mutually satisfactory to the organization and to the affected employee.

Transfers and Relocations. Who is most likely to be transferred? A survey by Atlas Van Lines found that salesmen 31 to 40 years old earning $30,000 to $50,000 a year are most likely to be transferred by their companies. And they are apt to be moved every 3 to 5 years. Female workers are much less likely to be transferred.[84] Reduced mobility, in turn, tends to retard women's salary progression relative to that of similarly situated men.[85]

With respect to relocations, senior management sometimes faces resistance from employees. The effect of a move on a family can be profound. *For the employee*, relocation often means increased prestige and income. However, the costs of moving and the complications resulting from upsetting routines, loss of friends, and changing schools and jobs are borne by *the family*. Uprooted families often suffer from loss of credentials as well. They do not enjoy the built-in status that awaits the employee at the new job; they must start from scratch. Wives may become more dependent on their husbands for social contacts (or vice versa, depending on who is transferred).

Women now account for about 20 percent of corporate moves, up from 5 percent in 1980. By the year 2000, a third of transferees will be female, and one in four trailing spouses may be men. Do such moves work out? Mobil Corporation finds that a man generally will follow his wife only if she earns at least 25 percent to 40 percent a year more than he does.[86]

There is one bright side to all of this, however. Research has shown that transfers produce little short-term impact on the mental or physical health of children.[87]

Transferred employees who are promoted estimate that it will take them a full 9 months to get up to speed in their new posts. Lateral transfers take an average of 7.8 months. However, the actual time taken to reach competency varies with (1) the degree of similarity between the old and new jobs and (2) the amount of support from peers and superiors at the new job.[88]

To reduce this "downtime," companies are taking some unusual steps. Thus Sprint Corp. spends up to $4000 to replace a relocated spouse's income for 60 days. That has helped transferees to return to full productivity in about 3 months; it had taken 6. Marriott Corp. installed a computerized job-posting system that tracks its managerial vacancies nationwide. Both employees *and* their trailing spouses can apply for the openings.[89] In sum, personal adjustments—not problems with housing—are the biggest obstacles to relocation.[90] As an overall strategy on relocation, some companies have developed frequency standards whereby no manager can be relocated more than once in 2 years or three times in 10 years. Another firm has set up one-stop rotational programs at its larger facilities to replace what used to be four stints of 6 months each at different plants over a 2-year training period.

The financial implications of relocation are another major consideration. In 1970, most relocation programs consisted of a few cost categories: house-hunting trips, the shipment of household goods, temporary living expenses at the new location, and often 1 month's salary bonus to cover other incidentals. In the 1990s, typical relocation expenses and services included all those offered in 1970 plus ongoing cost-of-living differentials; mortgage interest differentials; home disposal and home-finding expenses; expenses to help defray losses on home sales; real estate commissions; home purchase expenses; home maintenance, repair, and refurbishing costs; equity loans; and, for renters, lease-breaking expenses. Employees on temporary assignments often receive home property management expenses. All of this adds up. Thus Chevron estimated that relocation and retraining expenses cost about $75,000 a person in 1993.[91]

Organizations are well aware of these social and financial problems and in many cases they are responding by providing improved support systems. Despite the problems, transfers and relocations are expected to continue. For example, every one of the 10 "best-managed" companies identified in a *Dun's Review* survey said that more moves are in store once an employee demonstrates competence in one managerial position. Annually, over 15 percent of the managers at all levels are likely to be transferred or relocated. This represents about 250,000 families.[92]

Layoffs, retirements, and resignations. These all involve employees moving *out* of the organization.

Layoffs. How safe is my job? For many people, that is the issue of the 1990s. It's becoming clear that corporate cutbacks were not an oddity of the 1980s but rather are likely to persist through the decade.[93]

Involuntary layoffs are never pleasant, and management policies must consider the impacts on those who leave, on those who stay, on the local community, and on the company. For laid-off workers, efforts should be directed toward a rapid, successful, and orderly career transition.[94] How long does it take on average to find a new job? While it depends a great deal on the amount of effort put into the job search, a rough rule of thumb for managers is 1 month for every $10,000 in salary.[95] Outplacement programs that help laid-off employees deal with the psychological stages of career transition (anger, grief, depression, family stress), assess individual strengths and weaknesses, and develop support networks should be emphasized.[96]

Termination is a traumatic experience. Egos are shattered, and employees may become bitter and angry. Family problems may also occur because of the added emotional and financial strain.[97] For those who remain, it is important that they retain the highest level of loyalty, trust, teamwork, motivation, and productivity possible. This doesn't just happen—and unless there is a good deal of face-to-face, candid, open communication between senior management and "survivors," it probably won't. Within the community, layoff policies should consider the company's reputation and image in addition to the impact of the layoff on the local economy and social services agencies. Although layoffs are intended to reduce costs, some costs may in fact *increase*. These include:

Direct costs	Indirect costs
Severance pay, pay in lieu of notice	Recruiting and employment cost of new hires
Accrued vacation and sick pay	Training and retraining
Supplemental unemployment benefits	Increase in unemployment tax rate
Outplacement	Potential charges of unfair discrimination
Pension and benefit payoffs	Low morale among remaining employees
Administrative processing costs	Heightened insecurity and reduced productivity

What are the options? One approach is to initiate a program of *job sharing* to perform the reduced workload. While no one is laid off, everyone's workweek and pay are reduced. This helps the company to reduce labor costs. In an area experiencing high unemployment, it may be better to have all employees share the "misery" rather than to lay off selected ones. Some of the benefits of job sharing are:

■ Twice as much talent and creativity is available.

■ Benefits continue.

■ Overtime is reduced.

■ Workers retain a career orientation and the potential for upward mobility.

■ It eliminates the need for training a temporary employee, for example, when one employee is sick or is on vacation, because the other can take over.[98]

Job sharing is not without its drawbacks:

■ There is a lack of job continuity.

■ Supervision is inconsistent.

IMPACT OF CAREER MANAGEMENT ON PRODUCTIVITY, QUALITY OF WORK LIFE, AND THE BOTTOM LINE

From first-job effects through midcareer transition to preretirement counseling, career management has a direct bearing on productivity, quality of work life, and the bottom line. It is precisely because organizations are sensitive to these concerns that career management activities have become as popular as they are. The saying "Organizations have many jobs, but individuals have only one career" is as true today as it ever was. While organizations find themselves in worldwide competition, most individuals are striving for achievement, recognition, personal growth, and "the good life." Unless careers are managed actively by both individuals and organizations, neither can achieve their goals.

- Accountability is not centered in one person.
- Nonsalary expenses do not decrease, because many benefits are a function of the employee, not the amount of pay.[99]
- When workers are represented by a union, seniority is bypassed, and senior workers may resist sharing jobs.[100]

However, when Motorola reviewed job sharing at its facilities in Arizona, it found that avoiding layoffs saved an average of $1868 per employee—and $975,000 in total.[101]

Retirements. For selected employees, *early retirement* is a possible alternative to being laid off. Early retirement programs take many forms, but typically they involve partial pay stretched over several years along with extended benefits. Early retirement programs are intended to provide incentives to terminate; they are not intended to replace regular retirement benefits. Any losses in pension resulting from early retirement are usually offset by attractive incentive payments.

For example, in 1988, IBM offered workers at its Boca Raton, Florida, plant a voluntary severance program that included up to 2 years' pay, with benefits, plus a $25,000 bonus. In 1990, Digital Equipment offered thousands of workers voluntary severance packages of between 40 weeks and 2 years of pay, plus benefits. Those kinds of packages are disappearing fast. As of 1993, for example, IBM gave departing employees a maximum of 26 weeks of pay plus 6 months of medical coverage.[102]

Yet some voluntary severance and early retirement programs backfire. Both Kodak and IBM lost skilled, senior-level employees in past cutbacks. To overcome that problem, the firms targeted subsequent programs to specific groups of employees, such as those in manufacturing and in some administrative jobs.[103] The keys to success are *to identify, before the incentives are offered, exactly which jobs are targeted for attrition and to understand the needs of the employees targeted to leave.*

Since mandatory retirement at a specified age can no longer be required legally, most employees will choose their own times to retire. More of them are choosing to retire earlier than age 65. In 1948, for example, 50 percent of males and 9 percent of females continued to work past the age of 65. By 2005, those numbers are expected to drop to 16 percent and 8 percent, respectively.[104]

Research indicates that both personal and situational factors affect retirement decisions. Personally, individuals with Type A behavior patterns (hard-driving, aggressive, impatient) are less likely to prefer to retire, while those with obsolete job skills, chronic health problems, and sufficient financial resources are more likely to retire. Situationally, employees are more likely to retire to the extent that they have reached their occupational goals, that their jobs have undesirable characteristics, that home life is seen as preferable to work life, and that there are attractive alternative (leisure) activities.[105]

While retirement is certainly attractive to some, many retirees are returning to the workforce. In fact, retirees are the fastest-growing part of the temporary workforce. Many are bored with retirement, have high energy levels, and can maintain flexible schedules.[106] Others need the money, and they need health benefits to compensate for those they have lost. At a broader level, nearly 2 million nonworking Americans 50 to 64 years old are ready and able to work. Of these, more than 1.1 million would be highly qualified and motivated since they have reasonable wage expectations, would accept difficult working conditions, and have interest in available jobs: managerial, computer, sales, home day care, and as teacher's aides.[107]

Resignations. Resignation, or voluntary worker turnover, has been increasing steadily over the past 15 years, particularly among white-collar and professional workers.[108] Employees who resign should avoid "burning bridges" behind them, leaving anger and resentment in their wake; instead, they should leave gracefully and responsibly, stressing the value of their experience in the company.[109]

CORPORATE CAREER MANAGEMENT COMES OF AGE

Programs of corporate career management often include one or more of the following support mechanisms:

Self-assessment. The goal of self-assessment is to help employees focus on appropriate career goals. Training typically takes the form of workshops designed to help employees walk themselves through the difficult and sometimes emotional self-assessment process. It is a process of identifying and calibrating one's professional aptitudes and capabilities and of identifying improvements that will enhance one's career growth. As we saw in the Hewlett-Packard example, that company has pioneered in offering self-assessment training to its employees at all levels.

Career planning. Workshop training is also used to teach employees how to plan their career growth once they have determined where they want to go. They learn skills for career self-management as well as how to "read" the corporate environment and to become "savvy" about how to get ahead in their own companies. General Electric and Citibank have been leaders in raising this kind of awareness in their employees.

Supervisory training. Employees frequently turn first to their immediate supervisors for help with career management. At Sikorsky Aircraft, for example, supervisors are taught how to provide relevant information and to question the logic of each employee's career plans, but not to give specific career advice. Giving advice relieves the employee of responsibility for managing his or her own career.

Succession planning. Simply designating replacements for key managers and executives is no guarantee that those replacements will be ready when needed. Enlightened compa-

HUMAN RESOURCE MANAGEMENT IN ACTION: CONCLUSION

nies are adopting an approach to succession planning that is consistent with the concept of career self-management. They develop their employees broadly to prepare them for any of several positions that may become available. As business needs change, broadly developed people can be moved into positions that are critical to the success of the business.

The practice of making career self-management part of the corporate culture has spread rapidly over the past several years. Companies are using this approach to build a significant competitive advantage. Given today's turbulent, sometimes convulsive corporate environments, plus workers who seek greater control over their own destinies, it may be the only approach that can succeed over the long term.

SUMMARY

A career is a sequence of positions occupied by a person during the course of a lifetime. Career planning is important because the consequences of career success or failure are closely linked to an individual's self-concept and identity, as well as with career and life satisfaction. This chapter has addressed career management from three perspectives. The first was that of *individuals focusing on themselves:* self-management of one's own career, establishment of career objectives, and dual-career couples. The second perspective was that of *organizations focusing on individuals:* that is, managing individuals during early career (organizational entry, impact of the first job); midcareer, including strategies for coping with midlife transitions and "plateaued" workers; and late career (age 50 and over) stages. We considered the implications of each of these stages for human resource management in both large- and small-business settings. Finally, a third perspective was that of *organizations focusing on their own maintenance and growth.* This requires the development of organizational career management systems based on career paths defined in terms of employee behaviors. It involves the management of patterns of career movement up, down, over, and out.

DISCUSSION QUESTIONS

10∎1 Why is the design of one's first permanent job so important?

10∎2 What practical steps can you suggest to minimize midcareer crises?

10∎3 How can an organization avoid the problems associated with older workers clogging the career paths of younger workers?

IMPLICATIONS FOR MANAGEMENT PRACTICE

To profit from current workforce trends, consider taking the following steps:

- Develop explicit policies to attract and retain dual-career couples.
- Plan for more effective use of "plateaued" workers as well as those who are in midcareer transitions.
- Educate other managers and workers in the facts about older workers; where possible, hire older workers for full-time or part-time work.
- Commit to broadening career opportunities for women and members of protected groups.

10■4 Discuss the special problems faced by dual-career couples.

10■5 Given the trend toward shorter employment relationships, how can the HRM functions of training, performance appraisal, and reward systems integrate HR planning and career planning considerations?

REFERENCES

1. Hall, D. T., & Richter, J. (1990). Career gridlock: Baby boomers hit the wall. *Academy of Management Executive*, **4**(3), 7–22.

2. Greenhaus, J. H. (1987). *Career management.* Chicago: Dryden.

3. Fierman, J. (1993, Sept. 6), op. cit. See also Dennis, H., & Axel, H. (1991), op. cit. See also Quaintance, M. K. (1989). Internal placement and career management. In W. F. Cascio (ed.), *Human resource planning, employment, and placement.* Washington, DC: Bureau of National Affairs, pp. 2-200 to 2-235.

4. Anderson, J. C., Milkovich, G. T., & Tsui, A. (1981). A model of intra-organizational mobility. *Academy of Management Review*, **6**, 529–538. See also Milkovich, G. T., & Anderson, J. C. (1982). Career planning and development systems. In K. M. Rowland & G. R. Ferris (eds.), *Personnel management.* Boston: Allyn & Bacon, pp. 364–389.

5. Deutschman, A. (1990, Aug. 27). What 25-year-olds want. *Fortune*, pp. 42–50. See also Yuppies look beyond corporate, cash success (1989, Jan. 15). *Denver Post*, p. 4H.

6. Byrne, J. A. (1993). Belt-tightening the smart way. *Business Week, Special 1993 Bonus Issue: Enterprise*, pp. 34–38.

7. Rigdon, J. E. (1992, May 26). Using lateral moves to spur employees. *The Wall Street Journal*, pp. B1; B5. See also Kilborn, P. T. (1990, Feb. 27). Companies that temper ambition. *The New York Times*, pp. D1, D6.

8. Hall & Richter, op. cit.

9. Gutknecht, J. E., & Keys, J. B. (1993). Mergers, acquisitions, and takeovers: Maintaining morale of survivors and protecting employees. *Academy of Management Executive*, **7**(3), 26–36. See also Schweiger, D. M., & Denisi, A. S. (1991). Communication with employees following a merger: A longitudinal field experiment. *Academy of Management Journal*, **34**, 110–135.

10. Dalton, D. R., Daily, C. M., & Kesner, I. F. (1993). Executive severance agreements: Benefit or burglary? *Academy of Management Executive*, **7**(4), 69–76.

11. O'Boyle, T. (1985, July 11). Loyalty ebbs at many companies as employees grow disillusioned. *The Wall Street Journal*, p. 29. See also Lohr, S. (1992, Aug. 14). Fewer ties are bonding workers to corporations. *The New York Times*, pp. A1; D2.

12. Fowler, E. M. (1989, Feb. 21). A good side to unwanted job changes. *The New York Times*, p. H1.

13. O'Boyle, op. cit.

14. Milkovich & Anderson, op. cit.

15. Working scared (1993, Apr. 17). *NBC News.*

16. A career survival kit (1991, Oct. 7). *Business Week*, pp. 98–104. See also Baiocchi, D. P. (1991, Fall). Ten key principles of career success. *National Business Employment Weekly*, pp. 5, 6. See also Sikula, A. F., & McKenna, J. F. (1983). Individuals must take charge of career development. *Personnel Administrator*, **28**(10), 89–97.

17. Aburdene, P. (1990, September). How to think like a CEO for the 1990s. *Working Woman*, pp. 134–137.

18. Petras, K., & Petras, R. (1989). *The only job book you'll ever need.* New York: Simon & Schuster.

19. Ibid.

20. Wilhelm, W. R. (1983). Helping workers to self-manage their careers. *Personnel Administrator*, **28**(8), 83–89.

21. Shellenbarger, S. (1993, June 21). So much talk, so little action. *The Wall Street Journal*, pp. R1; R4.

22. Greenhaus, op. cit.
23. London, M., & Stumpf, S. A. (1982). *Managing careers.* Reading, MA: Addison-Wesley.
24. Work & family (1993, June 28). *Business Week,* pp. 80–88. See also Sekaran, U. (1986). *Dual-career families.* San Francisco: Jossey-Bass.
25. Lublin, J. S. (1993, Apr. 13). Husbands in limbo. *The Wall Street Journal,* pp. A1; A8.
26. Labor letter (1989, Apr. 11). *The Wall Street Journal,* p. A1.
27. Labor letter (1987, Sept. 8). *The Wall Street Journal,* p. A1.
28. Ford, R., & McLaughlin, F. (1986). Nepotism: Boon or bane? *Personnel Administrator,* **31**(11), 78–86. See also Couples at same firm—an idea catches on (1983, Sept. 12). *U.S. News and World Report,* p. 71.
29. Shellenbarger, S. (1992, Dec. 7). Managers navigate uncharted waters trying to resolve work-family conflicts. *The Wall Street Journal,* pp. B1; B10.
30. Staines, G. L., Pottick, K. J., & Fudge, D. A. (1986). Wives' employment and husbands' attitudes toward work and life. *Journal of Applied Psychology,* **71,** 118–128.
31. Shellenbarger (1993, June 21), op. cit.
32. Lewin, T. (1992, Oct. 5). Rise in single parenthood is reshaping U.S. *The New York Times,* pp. B1; B6.
33. Friedman, D. E. (1985). *Corporate financial assistance for child care.* New York: The Conference Board.
34. Adolph, B., & Rose, K. (1985). *The employer's guide to child care.* New York: Praeger.
35. Kleiman, C. (1990, Mar. 19). Report dispels child-care liability myth. *Denver Post,* p. 4C.
36. Kossek, E. E., & Nichol, V. (1992). The effects of on-site child care on employee attitudes and performance. *Personnel Psychology,* **45,** 485–509. See also Goff, S. J., Mount, M. K., & Jamison, R. L. (1990). Employer supported child care, work/family conflict, and absenteeism: A field study. *Personnel Psychology,* **43,** 793–810.
37. Trost, C. (1990, May 2). Women managers quit not for family but to advance their corporate climb. *The Wall Street Journal,* pp. B1, B8.
38. Breaugh, J. A. (1992). *Recruitment: Science and practice.* Boston: PWS-Kent.
39. Chao, G. T., Walz, P. M., & Gardner, P. D. (1992). Formal and informal mentorships: A comparison of mentoring functions and contrast with nonmentored counterparts. *Personnel Psychology,* **45,** 619–636.
40. Whitely, W., Dougherty, T. W., & Dreher, G. F. (1991). Relationship of career mentoring and socioeconomic origin to managers' and professionals' early career progress. *Academy of Management Journal,* **34,** 331–351. See also Wilson, J. A., & Elman, N. S. (1990). Organizational benefits of mentoring. *Academy of Management Executive,* **4**(4), 88–94.
41. Rigdon, J. E. (1993, Dec. 1). You're not all alone if there's a mentor just a keyboard away. *The Wall Street Journal,* p. B1.
42. Chao et al., op. cit. See also Whitely et al., op. cit.
43. Northrup, H. R., & Malin, M. E. (1986). *Personnel policies for engineers and scientists.* Philadelphia: Industrial Research Unit, The Wharton School, University of Pennsylvania.
44. Schein, E. H. (1978). *Career dynamics: Matching individual and organizational needs.* Reading, MA: Addison-Wesley.
45. Raelin, J. A. (1983). First-job effects on career development. *Personnel Administrator,* **28**(8), 71–76, 92.
46. Forbes, J. B. (1987). Early intraorganizational mobility: Patterns and influences. *Academy of Management Journal,* **30,** 110–125.
47. Bell, J. E. (1982, August). Mid-life transition in career men. *AMA Management Digest,* pp. 8–10.
48. Bennett, A. (1990, Sept. 11). A white-collar guide to job security. *The Wall Street Journal,* pp. B1, B12.
49. Lublin, J. S. (1993, Aug. 4). Strategic sliding: Lateral moves aren't always a mistake. *The Wall Street Journal,* p. B1. See also Rigdon, op. cit.

50. Kilborn, op. cit.

51. Fowler, op. cit.

52. Richman, L. S. (1993, July 12). Jobs that are growing and slowing. *Fortune*, pp. 52–54. See also Labor letter (1990, Jan. 23). *The Wall Street Journal*, p. A1.

53. Bell, op. cit.

54. Hall, D. T. (ed.). (1986). *Career development in organizations*. San Francisco: Jossey-Bass

55. Bennett, A. (1990, Sept. 11). Layoff victims tell of trials and fulfillment. *The Wall Street Journal*, pp. B1, B12.

56. Northrup & Malin, op. cit.

57. Sources for this section are: Fierman, op. cit. Kilborn, op. cit.; Ference, T. P., Stoner, J. A., & Warren, E. K. (1977). Managing the career plateau. *Academy of Management Review*, **2**, 602–612; Labor letter (1991, Feb. 19). *The Wall Street Journal*, p. A1.

58. Howard, A., & Bray, D. W. (1982, Mar. 21). AT&T: The hopes of middle managers. *The New York Times*, p. F1.

59. American Association of Retired Persons (1990). *The aging work force*. Washington, DC: Author.

60. Belous, R. S. (1991, September). *Demographic currents*. Washington: National Planning Association, Occasional Paper no. 7.

61. McEvoy, G. M., & Cascio, W. F. (1989). Cumulative evidence of the relationship between employee age and job performance. *Journal of Applied Psychology*, **74**, 11–20.

62. Paul, R. J., & Townsend, J. B. (1993). Managing the older worker—Don't just rinse away the gray. *Academy of Management Executive*, **7**(3), 67–74. See also Older—but coming on strong (1988, Feb. 22). *Time*, pp. 76–79.

63. Bureau of National Affairs (1987). Older Americans in the workforce: Challenges and solutions. *Labor Relations Week*, **1**(27), 1–237.

64. Older—but coming on strong, op. cit.

65. Bureau of National Affairs, op. cit.

66. American Association of Retired Persons (1993a). *America's changing work force*. Washington, DC: Author.

67. Bureau of National Affairs, op. cit.

68. American Association of Retired Persons (1993b). *The older workforce: Recruitment and retention*. Washington, DC: Author.

69. Solomon, J., & Fuchsberg, G. (1990, Jan. 26). Great number of older Americans seem ready to work. *The Wall Street Journal*, p. B1. See also Brooks, A. (1985, Dec. 2). Quitting a job gracefully. *The New York Times*, p. B12.

70. More retirees choose to work (1989, Sept. 7). *The New York Times*, p. C13.

71. Lefkovich, J. L. (1992). Older workers: Why and how to capitalize on their powers. *Employment Relations Today*, **19**(1), 63–79.

72. Paul & Townsend, op. cit. See also Labich, K. (1993, Mar. 8). The new unemployed. *Fortune*, pp. 40–49.

73. *Vitality for life: Psychological research for productive aging* (1993). Washington, DC: American Psychological Association.

74. Bird, C. P., & Fisher, T. D. (1986). Thirty years later: Attitudes toward the employment of older workers. *Journal of Applied Psychology*, **71**, 315–317.

75. Hirsch, J. S. (1990, Feb. 26). Older workers chafe under younger managers. *The Wall Street Journal*, pp. B1, B6.

76. Walker, J. W. (1992). *Human resource strategy*. New York: McGraw-Hill.

77. Ibid.

78. Quaintance, op. cit.

79. Stumpf, S. A., & London, M. (1981). Management promotions: Individual and organizational factors influencing the decision process. *Academy of Management Review*, **6**, 539–549.

80. Schwarzwald, J., Koslowsky, M., & Shalit, B. (1992). A field study of employees' attitudes and behaviors after promotion decisions. *Journal of Applied Psychology*, **77**, 511–514.

81. Labor letter (1989, Apr. 11), op. cit.
82. Power, W., & Siconolfi, M. (1990, Oct. 19). Who will be rich? How Goldman, Sachs chooses new partners: With a lot of angst. *The Wall Street Journal*, pp. A1, A8.
83. Geyelin, M. (1989, Sept. 7). Fired managers winning more lawsuits. *The Wall Street Journal*, p. B1. See also Ploscowe, S. A., & Goldstein, M. M. (1987, March). Trouble on the firing line. *Nation's Business*, pp. 36, 37.
84. Labor letter (1990, May 1). *The Wall Street Journal*, p. A1.
85. Stroh, L. K., Brett, J. M., & Reilly, A. H. (1992). All the right stuff: A comparison of female and male managers' career progression. *Journal of Applied Psychology*, **77,** 251–260.
86. Lublin, (1993, Apr. 13). op. cit.
87. Labor letter (1989, Nov. 17). *The Wall Street Journal*, p. A1.
88. Pinder, C. C., & Schroeder, K. G. (1987). Time to proficiency following job transfers. *Academy of Management Journal*, **30,** 336–353.
89. Lublin, (1993, Apr. 13). op. cit.
90. Driessnack, C. H. (1987). Spouse relocation: A moving experience. *Personnel Administrator*, **32**(8), 94–102.
91. Fierman, op. cit.
92. Collie, H. C. (1986). Corporate relocation: Changing with the times. *Personnel Administrator*, **31**(4), 101–106.
93. Richman, L. S. (1993, Sept. 20). When will the layoffs end? *Fortune*, pp. 54–56.
94. Kozlowski, S. W. J., Chao, G. T., Smith, E. M., & Hedlund, J. (1993). Organizational downsizing: Strategies, interventions, and research implications. *International Review of Industrial and Organizational Psychology*, **8,** 263–332.
95. The higher the pay, the longer the job hunt (1989, Dec. 15). *The Wall Street Journal*, p. B1.
96. Collarelli, S. M., & Beehr, T. A. (1993). Selection out: Firings, layoffs, and retirement. In N. Schmitt & W. C. Borman (eds.), *Personnel selection in organizations*. San Francisco: Jossey-Bass, pp. 341–384. See also Sweet, D. H. (1989). Outplacement. In W. F. Cascio (ed.), *Human resource planning, employment, and placement*. Washington, DC: Bureau of National Affairs, pp. 2-236 to 2-261.
97. Collarelli & Beehr, op cit. See also Foderaro, L. W. (1990, Sept. 24). Jobless executives get solace and aid in support groups. *The New York Times*, pp. A1, B2.
98. Owen-Cooper, T. (1990, Oct. 1). Job sharing slowly gaining in appeal. *Denver Post*, pp. 1C, 5C.
99. Work & family, op. cit. See also Hage, J. (ed.). (1988). *Futures of organizations: Innovating to adapt strategy and human resource to rapid technological change*. Lexington, MA: Heath.
100. Noble, K. B. (1988, Mar. 15). Union experiment provokes a fight. *The New York Times*, pp. A1, B20.
101. Labor letter (1986, Apr. 1). *The Wall Street Journal*, p. A1.
102. Lopez, J. A. (1993, Oct. 25). Out in the cold: Many early retirees find the good deals not so good after all. *The Wall Street Journal*, pp. A1, A4.
103. Take the money and run—or take your chances (1993, Aug. 16). *Business Week*, pp. 28, 29. See also Wilke, J. R. (1990, Apr. 13). Firms oust "no layoff" tradition. *The Wall Street Journal*, pp. B1, B2.
104. American Association of Retired Persons (1993a), op. cit.
105. Greene, M. S. (1992). *Retirement: A new beginning*. St. John's, Newfoundland, Canada: Jesperson Press.
106. Andrews, E. S. (1992). Expanding opportunities for older workers. *Journal of Labor Research*, **13**(1), 55–65.
107. Lewin, T. (1990, Jan. 28). For work force, 2 million who'd quit retirement. *The New York Times*, p. 18.
108. Take the money and run—or take your chances, op. cit.
109. Brooks, op. cit.

PART FOUR

COMPENSATION

A CONCEPTUAL VIEW OF
HUMAN RESOURCE MANAGEMENT

STRATEGIC OBJECTIVES, ENVIRONMENTS, FUNCTIONS

STRATEGIC OBJECTIVES
PARTS ONE – SIX · CHAPTERS 1 – 18

Productivity

Quality of Work Life

Profits

ENVIRONMENTS
PART ONE · CHAPTERS 1 – 4

Competitive

Legal

Social

Organizational

FUNCTIONS
PARTS TWO – SIX · CHAPTERS 5 – 18

Employment

Development

Compensation

Labor-Management Accommodation

Support, Evaluation, International Implications

RELATIONSHIP OF HRM FUNCTIONS TO HRM ACTIVITIES

FUNCTIONS	ACTIVITIES
Part Two **Employment**	Job Analysis, Human Resource Planning, Recruiting, Staffing (Chapters 5 - 7)
Part Three **Development**	Orienting, Training, Performance Appraisal, Managing Careers (Chapters 8 - 10)
Part Four **Compensation**	Pay, Benefits, Incentives (Chapters 11 - 13)
Part Five **Labor-Management Accommodation**	Union Representation, Collective Bargaining, Procedural Justice, Ethics (Chapters 14, 15)
Part Six **Support, Evaluation, International Implications**	Job Safety and Health, Costs/Benefits of HRM Activities, International Dimensions of HRM (Chapters 16 - 18)

PART FOUR

COMPENSATION

Compensation, which includes direct cash payments, indirect payments in the form of employee benefits, and incentives to motivate employees to strive for higher levels of productivity, is a critical component of the employment relationship. Compensation is affected by forces as diverse as labor market factors, collective bargaining, government legislation, and top management's philosophy regarding pay and benefits. This is a dynamic area, and Chapters 11, 12, and 13 present the latest developments in compensation theory and examples of company practices. Chapter 11 is a nontechnical introduction to the subject of pay systems, Chapter 12 focuses on employee benefits, and Chapter 13 considers alternative strategies for motivating employees to improve their performance and productivity. You will find that the material in all three chapters has direct implications for sound management practice.

CHAPTER 11

PAY SYSTEMS

THE TRUST GAP*

Among chief executive officers, three of today's most popular buzzwords are "employee involvement" and "empowerment" of employees. CEOs say, "We're a team; we're all in this together." But employees look at the difference between their pay and the CEO's. They see top management's perks—oak dining rooms and heated garages—versus cafeterias for lower-level workers and parking spaces a half mile from the plant. And they wonder, "Is this togetherness?" As the disparity in pay widens (see Table 11-1), the wonder grows. Hourly workers and supervisors indeed agree that "we're all in this together," but what we're in turns out to be a frame of mind that mistrusts senior management's intentions, doubts its competence, and resents its self-congratulatory pay.

Study after study, involving hundreds of companies and thousands of workers, has found evidence of a trust gap—and it is widening. Indeed, the attitudes of middle managers and professionals toward the workplace are becoming more like those of hourly workers, historically the most disaffected group.

Opinion Research Corporation of Chicago found clear evidence of a trust gap when it surveyed 100,000 middle managers, professionals, supervisors, salespeople, and technical, clerical, and hourly workers at *Fortune* 500 companies. With the exception of the sales group, employees believed top management was less willing to listen to their problems now than it had been 5 years earlier. The groups also felt top management now accorded them less respect. Said one observer, "Organizations audit their financial resources regularly but

---

*Adapted from: A. Farnham, The trust gap, *Fortune*, Dec. 4, 1989, pp. 56–78. See also: What, me overpaid? CEOs fight back, *Business Week*, May 4, 1992, pp. 142–148.

■ **TABLE 11 ▪ 1**
THE WIDENING GAP BETWEEN CEO PAY AND WHAT OTHERS MAKE

	1960	1970	1980	1992
Production worker	$4,665	$6,933	$15,008	$24,411
Teacher	$4,995	$8,626	$15,970	$34,098
Engineer	$9,828	$14,695	$28,486	$58,240
CEO	$190,383	$548,787	$624,996	$3,842,247

Source: Executive pay: The party ain't over yet, *Business Week,* April 26, 1993, pp. 56, 57.

fail to take the temperature of their own employees." Such employers are flying blind. As another concluded, the "open doors" of many corporations are only "slightly ajar."

To be sure, much of the trust gap can be traced to inconsistencies between what management says and what it does—between saying "People are our most important asset" and in the next breath ordering layoffs, or between sloganeering about quality while continuing to evaluate workers by how many pieces they push out the door.

The result is a world in which top management thinks it's sending crucial messages but employees never hear a word. Thus another recent survey found that 82 percent of *Fortune* 500 executives believe their corporate strategy is understood by everyone who needs to know. Unfortunately, less than a third of employees in the same companies say management provides clear goals and direction.

Confidence in top management's competence is collapsing. The days when top management could say, "Trust us; this is for your own good" are over. Employees have seen that if the company embarks on a new strategic tack and it doesn't work, employees are the ones who lose their jobs—not management.

While competence may be hard to judge, pay is known, and to the penny. The rate of increase in top management's pay split from workers' in 1979 and has rocketed upward ever since (see Table 11-1). CEOs who make 100 times the average hourly worker's pay are no longer rare. European and Japanese CEOs, who seldom earn more than 15 times the employee average, look on in amazement. Said one observer, "The gap is widening beyond what the guy at the bottom can even understand. . . . There's very little common ground left in terms of the experience of the average worker and the CEO."[1]

While most U.S. workers are willing to accept substantial differentials in pay between corporate highs and lows and acknowledge that the highs should receive their just rewards, more and more of the lows—and the middles—are asking "Just how just is just?"

Challenges

1. To many people, a deep-seated sense of unfairness lies at the heart of the trust gap. What are some of the ways that perceptions of unfairness might develop?

2. What are some of the predictable consequences of a trust gap?

3. Can you suggest alternative strategies for reducing the trust gap?

Questions This Chapter Will Help Managers Answer

1. How can we tie compensation strategy to general business strategy?

2. What economic and legal factors should be considered in establishing pay levels for different jobs?

Michael Eisner, CEO of Disney, is one of the highest paid CEOs in the United States.

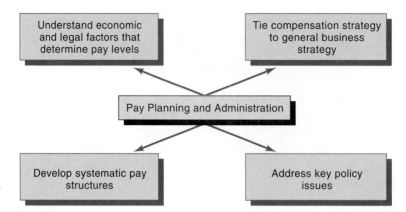

FIGURE 11-1
Four key challenges in planning and administering a pay system.

3. What is the best way to develop pay systems that are understandable, workable, and acceptable to employees at all levels?

4. How can we tie compensation to employee productivity?

5. How can we deal with pay compression in the salaried workforce?

The chapter opening vignette illustrates important changes in the current thinking about pay: levels of pay will always be evaluated by employees in terms of "fairness," and unless pay systems are acceptable to those affected by them, they will breed mistrust and lack of commitment. Pay policies are critically important, for they affect every single employee, from the janitor to the CEO. This chapter explores four major questions: (1) What economic and legal factors determine pay levels within a firm? (2) How do firms tie compensation strategy to general business strategy? (3) How do firms develop systematic pay structures that reflect different levels of pay for different jobs? (4) What key policy issues in pay planning and administration must managers address? These "challenges" are shown graphically in Figure 11-1.

As an educated worker or manager, it is important that you become knowledgeable about these important issues. This chapter will help you develop that knowledge base.

CHANGING PHILOSOPHIES REGARDING PAY SYSTEMS

In 1970, experts made predictions concerning the future of pay systems. The economy of the 1970s was expected to be strong, and median incomes were expected to rise substantially: they did. Inflation was expected to drop from the abnormally high rate of 4 percent: it did not. The male–female ratio in the workforce was expected to remain fairly constant: it did not. The population over the age of 65 was expected to approach 23 million: it did. The average workweek was expected to move to 35 hours (or fewer) per week. By 1990 it did: it fell to 34.3 hours because of increased part-time work by women. These economic and population trends are still with us. They will help shape what occurs in the 1990s and beyond, as they did in the 1980s and 1970s. And they are relevant to a number of factors that will determine the future of pay systems.[2]

One example of this is the continuing move away from policies of "salary entitlement," in which *inflation*, not *performance*, was the driving force. Pay for performance suffered during this time. With budgets for salary increases eroded by inflationary pressures, high performers were awarded raises only slightly larger than those of average performers. Such a policy leads to a predictable effect: *a reduced motivation to perform well*. In the current atmosphere of cost containment, however, we are seeing three major changes in company philosophies concerning pay and benefits:

1. Increased willingness to reduce the size of the workforce and to restrict pay to control the costs of wages, salaries, and benefits.

2. Less concern with pay position relative to that of competitors and more concern with what the company can afford.

3. Implementation of programs to encourage and reward performance. In fact, a recent study revealed that this is one of the most critical compensation issues facing large companies today.[3]

We will consider each of these changes, as well as other material in this and the following chapter, from the perspective of the line manager, not from that of the technical compensation specialist.

Cost Containment Actions

Until the early 1980s, employees were accustomed to receiving hefty annual pay increases and an ever richer banquet of benefits. Now many chief executives are preparing for a future that they think will be characterized by lowered business expectations, tougher competition, and a need for greater productivity. To cope with these changes, they are attempting to contain staff sizes, payrolls, and benefits costs. Some of the cutbacks are only temporary, such as pay freezes and postponements of raises. Other changes are meant to be permanent: firing executives or offering them early retirement; asking employees to work longer hours, to take fewer days off, and to shorten their vacations; reducing the coverage of medical plans or asking employees to pay part of the cost; trimming expense accounts, with bans on first-class travel and restrictions on phone calls and entertainment.

If such a strategy is to work, however, CEOs will first need to demonstrate to employees at all levels, by means of tangible actions, that they are serious about closing the "trust gap" (see chapter opening vignette).

Given that wage and salary payments constitute about 60 percent of the costs of nonfinancial corporations, employers have an obvious interest in controlling them.[4] One example of this is overtime.

CONTROLLING OVERTIME AMONG NEW YORK CITY EMPLOYEES

COMPANY EXAMPLE

Led by a supervising electrician in the Department of Corrections who was paid more than the mayor, New York City employees made $426 million in overtime in one year, a 28.5 percent increase over the previous year's amount and the ninth consecutive increase in overtime spending. The electrician, a 29-year veteran employee, earned more than $84,000 for working 1926 hours of overtime, at a rate of $43.65 per overtime hour. With a base pay of about $52,000 per year, his total income exceeded $136,000—topping the mayor's annual salary of $130,000.

In response the mayor noted: "Overtime is not an inherently dirty word. Some overtime spending is a necessary part of the city's response to short-term emergency situations or special events."[5] But he added that unnecessary overtime drains funds. Then he ordered city agency heads to control overtime. The order prohibits city employees from receiving overtime pay in excess of 5 percent of their base salaries without prior approval from their agency heads, and only for special reasons.

In good times managers did not have to get rid of poor performers or those whose jobs added no real value to their organizations. Bad times made that unpleasant task harder to avoid. Certainly any serious effort to cut management costs must focus on the payroll. This is because an executive costs a company roughly *double* his or her annual salary. Here's why. Benefits cost an average of almost 40 percent of base pay. Office, secretarial, and travel expenses make up the rest. Hence, getting rid of a $75,000-a-year executive and not replacing him or her saves about $150,000 per year.

Paying What the Company Can Afford

To cover its labor costs and other expenses, a company must earn sufficient revenues through the sales of its products or services. It follows, then, that an employer's ability to pay is constrained by its ability to compete. The nature of the product or service market affects a firm's external competitiveness and the pay level it sets.[6]

Key factors in the product and service markets are the degree of competition among producers (e.g., fast-food outlets) and the level of demand for the products or services (e.g., the number of customers in a given area). Both of these affect the ability of a firm to change the prices of its products or services. If an employer cannot change prices without suffering a loss of revenues due to decreased sales, that employer's ability to raise the level of pay is constrained. If the employer does pay more, it has two options: to try to pass the increased costs on to consumers or to hold prices fixed and allocate a greater portion of revenues to cover labor costs.[7]

As is well known, the U.S. steel industry struggled with a host of problems in the 1980s. These ranged from the lofty, uncompetitive wages of unionized employees to the antiquated state of many mills and fabricating plants to the relentless pressure of foreign competitors, who themselves were burdened with bulging capacity and weak domestic markets. Because of excessively generous wage settlements throughout the 1970s, U.S. steelworker employment costs in 1980 averaged $17.46 an hour, versus $9.63 for their Japanese counterparts. Said the chairman of USX: "Our labor costs alone put us out of the ball game."[8] As a result, U.S. steel was not competitive in world markets. While it is true that labor is only one part of overall production costs, unless the cost per unit produced is made lower than the competition's (by reducing costs other than labor), high labor costs will render a company uncompetitive.

To avoid annihilation, U.S. steel companies poured $14 billion into upgrading their mills during the 1980s. At the same time, a massive downsizing effort resulted in 60 percent of the industry's 428,000 workers losing their jobs. Those who remained gave generous pay concessions, so that in 1992 steelworkers earned about $29.00 an hour in wages and benefits ($19.84 in 1980 dollars)—about the same as in Japan. The result? U.S. steel companies are much better positioned to compete in the world markets in the 1990s. It now takes U.S. steelmakers just 5.3 staff-hours to produce a metric ton of cold-rolled steel. That's 44 percent fewer than 10 years ago and bests Japan's 5.6 and Germany's 5.7.[9]

Programs That Encourage and Reward Performance

Firms are continuing to relocate to areas where organized labor is weak and pay rates are low. They are developing pay plans that channel more dollars into incentive awards and fewer into fixed salaries. They are trying to get rid of automatic cost-of-living raises, and they are passing over more employees for raises so that they can award top performers meaningful pay increases. These programs all have a profit and productivity orientation and a commitment to sharing success with employees who produce.

On the other hand, employees will not *automatically* accept this orientation toward improved performance, for, in a sense, firms are changing the rules of the compensation game. The key to a genuine pay-for-performance system is for management to promote this kind of understanding in everything it says and does: *better performance will increase productivity, and outstanding performers will see a share of that benefit in their paychecks.*[10] Chapter 13 will discuss more fully the pay-for-performance theme and how it can be put into effect.

INTERNATIONAL APPLICATION: TYING PAY TO PERFORMANCE IN THE UNITED STATES AND JAPAN[11]

In an effort to hold down labor costs, thousands of U.S. companies are changing the way they increase workers' pay. Instead of the traditional annual increase, millions of workers in industries as diverse as supermarkets and aircraft manufacturing are receiving cash bonuses. For most workers, the plans mean less money. The bonuses take many names: "profit sharing" at Abbott Laboratories and Hewlett-Packard, "gain sharing" at Mack Trucks and Dana Corporation, and "lump-sum payments" at Boeing. All have two elements in common: (1) they can vary with the company's fortunes, and (2) they are not permanent. Because the bonuses are not folded into base pay (as merit increases are), there is no compounding effect over time. They are simply provided on top of a constant base level of pay. This means that both wages and benefits rise more slowly than they would have if the base level of pay was rising each year. The result: a flattening of wages nationally.

Today, 40 percent of all workers covered by major union agreements have bonus provisions in their contracts. How have unions reacted? In the view of the AFL-CIO, "Where there is justification for belt-tightening, then profit sharing is not an unreasonable means of passing on earnings when times improve."[12]

In summary, "flexible pay"—tied mostly to profitability and promising better job security, but not guaranteeing it—is at the heart of the evolving bonus system. Employees are being asked to share the risks of the new global marketplace. How large must the rewards be? MIT economist Martin Weitzman estimates that over the long run the proper bonus level is 20 to 25 percent of total compensation, because that would give workers a pay increase equal to the rate of inflation plus productivity gains. But in the United States most bonus payments have been averaging about 10 percent of a worker's base pay annually. Conversely, the Japanese currently pay many workers a bonus that represents about 25 percent of base pay. For workers in both nations, a significant amount of their pay is "at risk."

Have such plans generated greater productivity in the U.S. manufacturing sector in recent years? Maybe, but an equally plausible explanation is that the gains were due to automation, to company efforts to give workers more of a say in how they do their jobs, and to worker's fear that if they did not improve their productivity, their plants would become uncompetitive and be closed. In short, the jury is still out on the productivity impact of bonus systems as well as on their effect on worker motivation and commitment to the organization.

COMPONENTS AND OBJECTIVES OF ORGANIZATIONAL REWARD SYSTEMS

At a broad level, an organizational reward system includes anything an employee values and desires that an employer is able and willing to offer in exchange for employee contributions. More specifically, the reward system includes both compensation and noncompensation rewards. Compensation rewards include direct financial payments plus indirect payments in the form of employee benefits (see Chapter 12). Noncompensation rewards include everything in a work environment that enhances a worker's sense of self-respect and esteem by others (e.g., work environments that are physically, socially, and mentally healthy; training to improve job skills; and status symbols to enhance individual perceptions of self-worth).

Rewards bridge the gap between organizational objectives and individual expectations and aspirations. To be effective, organizational reward systems should provide four things: (1) a sufficient level of rewards to fulfill basic needs, (2) equity with the external labor market, (3) equity within the organization, and (4) treatment of each member of the organization in terms of his or her individual needs.[13] More broadly, pay systems are designed to attract, retain, and motivate employees. This is the ARM concept. Indeed, much of the design of compensation systems involves working out trade-offs among more or less seriously conflicting objectives.[14]

Perhaps the most important objective of any pay system is fairness, or *equity*. Equity can be assessed on at least three dimensions:

■ *Internal equity:* In terms of the relative worth of individual jobs to an organization, are pay rates fair?

■ *External equity:* Are the wages paid by an organization "fair" in terms of competitive market rates outside the organization?

■ *Individual equity:* Is each individual's pay "fair" relative to that of other individuals doing the same or similar jobs?

Several bases for determining equitable payment for work have been proposed.[15] They have three points in common:

1. Each assumes that employees perceive a fair return for what they contribute to their jobs.

2. All include the concept of *social comparison*, whereby employees determine what their equitable return should be after comparing their inputs (skills, education, effort, etc.) and outcomes (pay, promotion, job status, etc.) with those of their coworkers (comparison persons).

3. The theories assume that employees who perceive themselves to be in an inequitable situation will seek to reduce that inequity. They may do so by mentally distorting their inputs or outcomes, by directly altering their inputs or outcomes, or by leaving the organization.

ETHICAL DILEMMA: SHOULD BOARD MEMBERS WHO SET CEO PAY BE INDEPENDENT?

At Citizens Utilities, based in Stamford, Connecticut, the firm's chief executive officer received $21.6 million in pay in 1992. That's about $26 from each of more than 800,000 Citizens customers in 13 states who get their electricity, water, and gas from the company. All three of the board of directors members who negotiated the CEO's employment contract had close ties to the company. One of them made more than $500,000 in consulting fees. The second benefited from legal work at Citizens. And the third received 7271 stock options in a cellular-phone subsidiary of Citizens that sold stock, netting him a $123,000 paper profit.[16] The board members' actions were legal, but were they ethical? Whose interests should be considered in matters such as these?

Reviews of both laboratory and field tests of equity theory are quite consistent: individuals tend to follow the equity norm and to use it as a basis for distributing rewards. They report inequitable conditions as distressing, although there may be individual differences in sensitivity to equity.[17]

A final objective is *balance*—the optimal combination of direct and indirect compensation, of financial and nonfinancial rewards. Perhaps the major issue is the extent to which benefit dollars, as contrasted with wage and salary dollars, contribute to employee motivation and competitive realities.[18] Another aspect of balance concerns the relative size of pay differentials among different segments of the workforce. If pay systems are to accomplish the objectives set for them, they must ultimately be perceived as adequate and equitable. For example, there should be a balance in relationships between supervisors and the highest-paid subordinates reporting to them. According to the public accounting firm Coopers & Lybrand, among companies judged to be well managed, this differential is generally 15 percent.[19] As the chapter opening vignette illustrated, ratios of 100 to 1 between the highest- and lowest-paid employees are generally regarded as out of balance.

STRATEGIC INTEGRATION OF COMPENSATION PLANS AND BUSINESS PLANS

Unfortunately, the rationale behind many compensation programs is "Two-thirds of our competitors do it" or "That's corporate policy." Compensation plans need to be tied to an organization's strategic mission and should take their direction from that mission. They must support the general business strategy.[20] From a managerial perspective, therefore, the most fundamental question is "What do you want your pay system to accomplish?"

This approach to managing compensation and business strategies dictates that actual levels of compensation should *not* be strictly a matter of what is being paid in the marketplace. Instead, compensation levels derive from an assessment of what *must be paid* to attract and retain the right people, what the organization can *afford*, and what will be *required* to meet the organization's strategic goals. Table 11-2 illustrates how different compensation strategies can be applied in firms that differ in (1) their business strategies and (2) their market positions and maturity.

In firms that are growing rapidly, business strategy tends to be focused on one objective: investing to grow. To be consistent with this business strategy, compensation strategy should stimulate an enterprising, entrepreneurial style of management.

■ **TABLE 11 ▪ 2**

LINKING COMPENSATION STRATEGY TO BUSINESS STRATEGY

Business strategy	Market position and maturity	Compensation strategy	Blend of compensation
Invest to grow	Merging or growing rapidly	Stimulate entrepreneurialism	High cash with above-average incentives for individual performance
			Modest benefits
Manage earnings—protect markets	Normal growth to maturity	Reward management skills	Average cash with moderate incentives on individual, unit, or corporate performance
			Standard benefits
Harvest earnings—reinvest elsewhere	No real growth or decline	Stress cost control	Below-average cash with small incentive tied to cost control
			Standard benefits

Source: Adapted from R. J. Greene & R. G. Roberts, Strategic integration of compensation and benefits, *Personnel Administrator, 28*(5), 1983, 82, Copyright 1983. Reprinted with permission from *HRMagazine* (formerly *Personnel Administrator*), published by the Society for Human Resource Management, Alexandria, VA.

To do this, the firm should emphasize high cash payments with above-average incentives ("high risk, high reward"). In "mature" firms business strategy is oriented primarily toward managing earnings and protecting markets. Compensation strategy should therefore reward management skills, and to do this there should be a blend of average cash payments, moderate incentives, and standard benefits. In the "aging" firm, the most appropriate strategy is to harvest earnings and reinvest them elsewhere. Compensation strategy should thus emphasize control of costs. To implement such a strategy, standard benefits are combined with below-average cash renumeration, and modest incentives are tied directly to control of costs.

Compensation consultants say that currently only about 20 percent of firms tailor their compensation plans to the different stages of development, but that's up from 5 percent in the late 1980s.[21] When compensation is viewed from a strategic perspective, therefore, firms do the following:

1. They recognize compensation as a pivotal control and incentive mechanism that can be used flexibly by management to attain business objectives.
2. They make the pay system an integral part of strategy formulation.
3. They integrate pay considerations into strategic decision-making processes, such as those that involve planning and control.
4. They view the firm's performance as the ultimate criterion of the success of strategic pay decisions and operational compensation programs.[22]

Compensation Strategies for Special Situations

Many companies now recognize that their pay policies must change in response to special situations, such as restructurings linked to takeover attempts or massive divestitures. Restructurings linked to takeover attempts are among the most common triggers of special pay plans. Consider the case of Owens-Corning Fiberglas Corporation.

After the company took on huge debt to ward off a hostile takeover bid from the Wickes Companies, the main objective was to persuade managers to stay with the company and return it to stability. So it installed an all-stock bonus plan for 150 top people that would not pay out for 7 years. The payout was not tied to specific goals, but the managers knew the stock price wouldn't move until they got debt down and profits up.

The scheme paid off: the management team stayed, Owens-Corning is ahead of schedule on paying off its debt, and its stock, which was at $12 when the plan was instituted, traded in the high $40s in late 1993.

Different plans are needed to retain managers during divestitures. In 1987, the Penn Central Corporation spun off Sprague Technologies, its electronics components subsidiary. To persuade a handful of executives to go with Sprague, Penn Central offered a "retention transition bonus." If they stayed with Sprague for a year, their Penn Central stock options, which would normally expire 90 days after an employee's departure, would stay in effect, and they would receive an extra year's salary and bonus. The executives went with Sprague and are still with the company.

Now things have changed at Sprague again. It is liquidating one of its divisions, and it has put in a one-shot bonus plan for the division's three key people, payable after the liquidation is over—and their jobs have been eliminated.

Top managers are generally the beneficiaries of special-situation pay plans. However, some companies (especially those in pharmaceuticals and consumer products) are starting to extend bonus plans to researchers, package designers, and other midlevel people involved in product development. The plans, which usually involve cash bonuses, pay in stages—when a product is developed, when it is introduced, and when it achieves a specified market share. After that, the profits the product generates count toward the general bonus pool.[23] A summary of such plans for these and other special situations is presented in Figure 11-2.

DETERMINANTS OF PAY STRUCTURE AND LEVEL

In the simplest terms, marginal revenue product theory in labor economics holds that the value of a person's labor is what someone is willing to pay for it.[24] In practice, a number of factors *interact* to determine wage levels. Some of the most influential of

TEMPORARY PAY PLANS TO SUIT THE SITUATION		
Situation	**Typical Pay Plan**	**Example**
High debt, as in a leveraged buyout	Cash bonuses or equity based on cash flow, cost cutting	RJR Nabisco, Inc.
Closed plant; liquidated division	Cash bonus payable at end of shut-down operation	Sprague Technologies, Inc.
Start-up division; introduction of new product	Stock or cash awarded first for meeting development deadlines, then for market-share growth	Williams Telecommunications
Divestiture	Stock or cash payable to managers who stay on a year after divestiture	The Penn Central Corporation

FIGURE 11-2
Pay plans for special situations. (*Source:* C. H. Deutch, Revising pay packages, again, *The New York Times*, February 25, 1990, p. F29.)

these are labor market conditions, legislation, collective bargaining, management attitudes, and an organization's ability to pay. Let us examine each of these.

Labor Market Conditions

As noted in Chapter 6, whether a labor market is "tight" or "loose" has a major impact on wage structures and levels. Thus, if the demand for certain skills is high, while the supply is low (a "tight" market), there tends to be an *increase* in the price paid for these skills. Conversely, if the supply of labor is plentiful, relative to the demand for it, wages tend to *decrease*. As an example, consider the following starting salaries for 1993 college graduates with bachelor's degrees:[25]

Area	Average starting salary
Engineering, petroleum	$41,900
Computer science	31,133
Mathematics, statistics	29,287
Chemistry	28,383
Accounting	27,722
Business administration	24,791
Marketing	24,392
Foreign languages	23,914
Journalism	20,049

To a considerable extent, these differences in starting salaries reflect different labor market conditions in the various fields. Another impact of labor market supply-and-demand factors can be seen in the wages paid by companies in different geographic locations. Virtually all large companies, including the federal government, use some kind of geographic adjustment. For example, an employee earning an annual salary of $43,000 in Seattle could expect to receive the following salary by geographic area, in 1993 dollars:[26]

New York City	$78,254	Boulder, CO	$38,689
Boston	50,014	Richmond, VA	38,433
Anchorage	48,114	Houston	36,168
Philadelpha	48,041	Indianapolis	34,816
Los Angeles	47,530	Memphis	34,414

Another labor market phenomenon that causes substantial differences in pay rates, even among people who work in the same field and are of similar age and education, is the payment of wage premiums by employers to attract the best talent available. This is known as the "efficiency wage hypothesis" in labor economics, and it has received considerable support among economic researchers.[27]

A final factor that can affect the supply of labor, and hence tighten the market, is the relative *hazard* level of the work. Consider the following example.

"JUMPERS" WHO MAKE 12 HOURS' PAY FOR 10 MINUTES' WORK

The catch—and there has to be one—is the job site. Every year the nuclear industry recruits hundreds of "jumpers" who fix the aging innards of the nation's nuclear generating stations. The atmosphere is so radioactive that jumpers can stay only about 10 minutes before, in industry parlance, they "burn out." As compensation for their 10 minutes' work, they receive 12 hours' pay. Typically, jumpers are people with few skills or job prospects elsewhere. They crawl into the power plants unsupported by any labor union, health insurance plan, or job security.[28] Repairs often have to do with corrosion or leakage of water pipes, a process that can be slowed but not stopped completely.

What are the risks? The Nuclear Regulatory Commission estimates that if each of 10,000 workers is exposed to 5000 millirems (roughly 250 chest X rays) over the course of a year, three to eight of them will eventually die of cancer as a result of the exposure. If they are exposed to that level for 30 years, 5 percent of them will die of cancer.

The system pleases jumpers because it makes for lots of jobs. Said one, "Last year I think I got over 4000 millirems. I like to work till I get my limit. If you don't reach your limit, you're wasting your time."[29]

Jumpers have a particular incentive to absorb the maximum radiation permitted on a given job: they get a bonus of several hundred dollars each time they "burn out" on an assignment. Between jobs they complete a battery of medical examinations, security checks, and psychological evaluations. "They don't want someone nutty in the reactor, messing things up," said one jumper. "You have to be a little weird to do this job. You just can't be *too* weird."[30]

Highly hazardous work pays well; but then again it has to, in order to attract workers who are willing to take the risks. The forces discussed thus far affect pay levels to a considerable extent. So also does government legislation.

Legislation

As in other areas, legislation related to pay plays a vital role in determining internal organization practices. Although all the relevant laws cannot be analyzed here, a summary of the coverage, major provisions, and federal agencies charged with administering four major federal wage-hour laws is presented in Table 11-3. Wage-hour laws set limits on minimum wages to be paid and maximum hours to be worked.

Of the four laws shown in Table 11-3, the Fair Labor Standards Act (FLSA) affects almost every organization in the United States. It is the source of the terms "exempt employees" (exempt from the overtime provisions of the law) and "nonexempt employees." It established the first national minimum wage (25 cents an hour) in 1938; subsequent changes in the minimum wage and in national policy on equal pay for equal work for both sexes (the Equal Pay Act of 1963) were passed as amendments to this law.

There are many loopholes in FLSA minimum-wage coverage.[31] Certain workers, including casual babysitters and most farmworkers, are excluded, as are employees of small businesses and firms not engaged in interstate commerce. State minimum-wage laws are intended to cover these workers. At the same time, if a state's minimum is higher than the federal minimum, the state minimum applies.

■ **TABLE 11 ▪ 3**
FOUR MAJOR FEDERAL WAGE-HOUR LAWS

	Scope of coverage	Major provisions	Administrative agency
Fair Labor Standards Act (FLSA) of 1938 (as amended)	Employers involved in interstate commerce with two or more employees and annual revenues greater than $500,000. Exemption from overtime provisions for managers, supervisors, executives, outside salespersons, and professional workers.	Minimum wage of $4.25 per hour for covered employees (as of April 1991); time and a half pay for over 40 hours per week; restrictions by occupation or industry on the employment of persons under 18; prohibits wage differentials based exclusively on sex—equal pay for equal work. No extra pay required for weekends, vacations, holidays, or severance.	Wage and Hour Division of the Employment Standards Administration, U.S. Department of Labor
Davis-Bacon Act (1931)	Federal contractors involved in the construction or repair of federal buildings and public works with a contract value over $2000.	Employees on the project must be paid prevailing community wage rates for the type of employment used. Overtime of time and one-half for more than 40 hours per week. Three-year blacklisting of contractors who violate this act.	Comptroller General and Wage and Hour Division
Walsh-Healy Act (1936)	Federal contractors manufacturing or supplying materials, articles, or equipment to the federal government with a value exceeding $10,000 annually.	Same as Davis-Bacon. Under the Defense Authorization Act of 1986, overtime is required only for hours worked in excess of 40 per week, not 8 per day, as previously.	Same as FLSA
McNamara-O'Hara Service Contract Act (1965)	Federal contractors who provide services to the federal government with a value in excess of $2500.	Same as Davis-Bacon.	Same as Davis-Bacon

In the 1980s, the minimum wage really lived up to its name. From 1981, when it was raised to $3.35 an hour, to 1991, when it reached $4.25 an hour, inflation eroded its purchasing power by 27 percent. Moreover, $4.25 per hour was still less than 50 percent of the average hourly wage paid in the United States at that time. How many people earn the minimum wage? Only about 4 million of the nation's 60 million hourly workers. About 40 percent of them are teenagers.[32]

An important feature of the FLSA is its provision regarding the employment of young workers. On school days, 14-year-olds and 15-year-olds are allowed to work no more than 3 hours (no more than 8 hours on nonschool days), or a total of 18 hours a week when school is in session. They may work 40-hour weeks during the summer and during school vacations, but they may not work outside the hours of 7 A.M. to 7 P.M. (or 9 p.m. June 1 to Labor Day). Both federal and state laws allow 16-year-olds and 17-year-olds to work any hours but forbid them to work in hazardous occupations, such as driving or working with power-driven meat slicers.

According to the Department of Labor, the number of child-labor violations has doubled since 1982 as worker shortages in some areas have impelled employers to hire more workers of high school age. Most offenders allow teenagers to work too many hours on school days or to use dangerous equipment.[33]

The remaining three laws shown in Table 11-3 apply only to organizations that do business with the federal government in the form of construction or by supplying goods and services.

Collective Bargaining

Another major influence on wages in unionized *as well as* nonunionized firms is collective bargaining. Nonunionized firms are affected by collective bargaining agreements made elsewhere since they must compete with unionized firms for the services and loyalties of workers. Collective bargaining affects two key factors: (1) the *level* of wages and (2) the *behavior of workers* in relevant labor markets. In an open, competitive market, workers tend to gravitate toward higher-paying jobs. To the extent that nonunionized firms fail to match the wages of unionized firms, they may have difficulty attracting and keeping workers. Furthermore, benefits negotiated under union agreements have had the effect of increasing the "package" of benefits in firms that have attempted to avoid unionization. In addition to wages and benefits, collective bargaining is also used to negotiate procedures for administering pay, procedures for resolving grievances regarding compensation decisions, and methods used to determine the relative worth of jobs.[34]

Managerial Attitudes and an Organization's Ability to Pay

These factors have a major impact on wage structures and levels. It was noted earlier how the labor costs of U.S. steelworkers had to be reduced in order to compete in global markets. This is an important principle. Regardless of an organization's espoused competitive position on wages, its ability to pay ultimately will be a key factor that limits actual wages.

This is not to downplay the role of management philosophy and attitudes on pay. On the contrary, management's desire to maintain or to improve morale, to attract high-caliber employees, to reduce turnover, and to improve employees' standards of living also affect wages, as does the relative importance of a given position to a firm.[35] A safety engineer is more important to a chemical company than to a bank. Wage structures tend to vary across firms to the extent that managers view any given position as more or less critical to their firms. Despite the appearance of scientific precision, compensation administration will always reflect management judgment to a considerable degree. Ultimately, top management renders judgments regarding the overall competitive pay position of the firm (above-market, at-market, or below-market rates), factors to be considered in determining job worth, and the relative weight to be given seniority and performance in pay decisions. Such judgments are key determinants of the structure and level of wages.

AN OVERVIEW OF PAY SYSTEM MECHANICS

The procedures described below for developing pay systems help those involved in the development process to apply their judgments in a systematic manner. The hallmarks of success in compensation management, as in other areas, are understandability, workability, and acceptability. The broad objective in developing pay systems is to assign a monetary value to each job in the organization (a base rate) and an orderly procedure for increasing the base rate (e.g., based on merit, seniority, or some combination of the two). To develop such a system, we need four basic tools:

1. Updated job descriptions
2. A job evaluation method (i.e., one that will rank jobs in terms of their overall worth to the organization)
3. Pay surveys
4. A pay structure

Figure 11-3 presents an overview of this process.

Job descriptions are key tools in the design of pay systems, for they serve two purposes:

1. They identify important characteristics of each job so that the relative worth of jobs can be determined.
2. From them we can identify, define, and weight *compensable factors* (common job characteristics that an organization is willing to pay for, such as skill, effort, responsibility, and working conditions). Once this has been done, the next step is to rate the worth of all jobs using a predetermined system.

A number of job evaluation methods have been developed since the 1920s, and many, if not most, of them are still used. They all have the same final objective—ranking jobs in terms of their relative worth to the organization so that an equitable rate of pay can be determined for each job. Moreover, they all yield similar results.[36]

For example, in the point-factor method of job evaluation, each job is analyzed and defined in terms of the compensable factors an organization has agreed to adopt. Points are assigned to each level (or degree) of a compensable factor, such as responsibility. The total points assigned to each job across each compensable factor are then summed. A hierarchy of job worth is therefore defined when jobs are rank-ordered from highest point total to lowest point total. A brief description of some common approaches to job evaluation, along with their relative advantages and disadvantages, is presented in the technical appendix at the end of this chapter (see Table 11-5a and b).

Job evaluation is used widely, but not universally, among firms. One reason is that several policy issues must be resolved first. These include:[37]

■ Does management perceive meaningful differences among jobs?
■ Can meaningful criteria for distinguishing among jobs be identified and operationalized?
■ Will job evaluation result in meaningful distinctions in the eyes of employees?
■ Are jobs stable, and will they remain stable in the future?
■ Is job evaluation consistent with the organization's goals and strategies? For example, if the goal is to ensure maximum flexibility among job assignments, a knowledge- or skill-based pay system may be most appropriate. We will address that topic more fully in a later section.

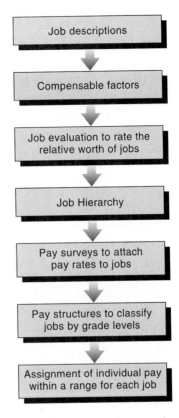

FIGURE 11-3
Traditional job-based compensation model.

The technical appendix following this chapter presents an illustration of one such method, point-factor job evaluation, developed and used by the Hay Group.

Linking Internal Pay Relationships to Market Data

In the point-factor method of job evaluation, the next task is to translate the point totals into a pay structure. Two key components of this process are identifying and surveying pay rates in relevant labor markets. This can often be a complex task since employers must pay attention not only to labor markets but also to *product* markets.[38] Pay practices must be designed not only to attract and retain employees but also to ensure that labor costs (as part of the overall costs of production) do not become excessive in relation to those of competing employers.

The definition of relevant labor markets requires two key decisions: which jobs to survey and which markets are relevant for each job. Jobs selected for a survey are generally characterized by stable tasks and stable job specifications (e.g., computer programmers, purchasing managers). Jobs with these characteristics are known as "key" jobs. Jobs that do not meet these criteria, but that are characterized by high turnover or are difficult to fill, should also be included.

As we noted earlier, the definition of relevant labor markets should consider geographical boundaries (local, regional, national, or international) as well as product-market competitors. Such an approach might begin with product-market competitors as the initial market, followed by adjustments downward (e.g., from national to regional markets) on the basis of geographical considerations.

Once target populations and relevant markets have been identified, the next task is to obtain survey data. Surveys are available from a variety of sources, including the federal government (Bureau of Labor Statistics), employers' associations, trade and professional associations, users of a given job evaluation system (e.g., clients of the Hay Group), and compensation consulting firms.

Managers should be aware of two potential problems with pay survey data.[39] The most serious is the assurance of an accurate job match. If only a "thumbnail sketch" (i.e., a very brief description) is used to characterize a job, there is always the possibility of legitimate misunderstanding among survey respondents. To deal with this, some surveys ask respondents if their salary data for a job are direct matches, or somewhat higher or lower than those described (and therefore worthy of more or less pay).

A second problem has resulted from the explosion of "at-risk" forms of pay, some of which are based on individual performance and some on the profitability of an organization. Base pay is becoming a smaller part of the total compensation package for a broad range of employees. This makes it difficult to determine the actual pay of job incumbents, and can make survey results difficult to interpret. For example, how does one compare salary figures that include only base pay or direct cash payouts with "at-risk" pay that may take the form of a lump-sum bonus, additional time off with pay, or payment into an employee stock ownership plan?

Despite these potential problems, all indications are that pay surveys will continue to be used widely. For example, American Steel & Wire Corporation of Cuyahoga Heights, Ohio, hires employees primarily from its local labor market. It determines "going rates of pay" by studying salaries of comparable jobs at 1200 companies in its county, as well as by studying nationwide salaries.[40] Fortunately, commercial software packages now available allow analysts to design "What if?" scenarios, and estimate the impact of various pay policies, market movements, and organizational changes on total salary costs.

The end result is often a chart, as in Figure 11-4, that relates current wage rates to the total points assigned to each job. For each point total, a trend line is fitted to indicate the *average* relationship between points assigned to the benchmark jobs and the hourly wages paid for those jobs. Once a midpoint trend line is fitted, two others are also drawn: (1) a trend line that represents the *minimum* rate of pay for each point total and (2) a trend line that represents the *maximum* rate of pay for each point total.[41]

Developing a Pay Structure

The final step in attaching dollar values to jobs using the point method is to establish *pay grades*, or ranges, characterized by a point spread from minimum to maximum for each grade. Starting wages are given by the trend line that represents the *minimum* rate of pay for each pay grade, while the highest wages that can be earned within a grade are given by the trend line that represents the *maximum* rate of pay. The pay structure is described numerically in Table 11-4.

For example, consider the job of "administrative clerk." Let's assume that the job evaluation committee arrived at a total allocation of 142 points across all compensable factors. The job therefore falls into pay grade 6. Starting pay is $9.75 per hour, with a maximum pay rate of $12.37 per hour.

The actual development of a pay structure is a complex process, but there are certain rules of thumb to follow:

■ Jobs of the same general value should be clustered into the same pay grade.

■ Jobs that clearly differ in value should be in different pay grades.

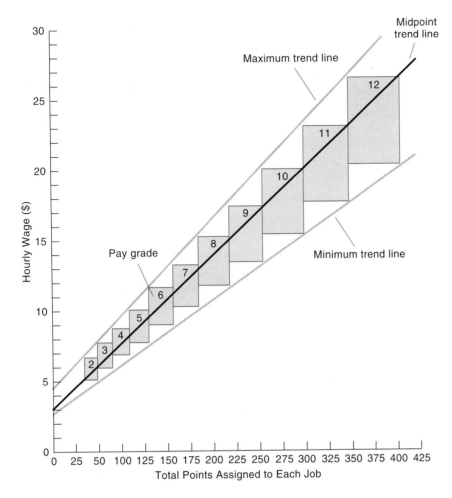

FIGURE 11-4
Chart relating hourly wage rates to the total points assigned to each job. Three trend lines are shown—minimum, midpoint, and maximum—as well as 11 pay grades. Within each pay grade there is a 30 percent spread from minimum to maximum and a 50 percent overlap from one pay grade to the next.

■ **TABLE 11 ▪ 4**
ILLUSTRATIVE PAY STRUCTURE SHOWING PAY GRADES, THE SPREAD OF POINTS WITHIN GRADES, THE MIDPOINT OF EACH PAY GRADE, AND THE MINIMUM AND MAXIMUM RATES OF PAY PER GRADE

Grade	Point spread	Midpoint	Minimum rate of pay	Maximum rate of pay
2	62–75	68	$6.00	$7.50
3	76–91	83	6.75	8.47
4	92–110	101	7.61	9.60
5	111–132	121	8.60	10.89
6	133–157	145	9.75	12.37
7	158–186	172	11.06	14.07
8	187–219	203	12.57	16.03
9	220–257	238	14.30	18.29
10	258–300	279	16.30	20.88
11	301–350	325	18.59	23.87
12	351–407	379	21.23	27.30

■ There should be a smooth progression of point groupings.

■ The new system should fit realistically into the existing allocation of pay within a company.

■ The pay grades should conform reasonably well to pay patterns in the relevant labor markets.[42]

Once such a pay structure is in place, the determination of each individual's pay (based on experience, seniority, and performance) becomes a more systematic, orderly procedure. A compensation planning worksheet, such as that shown in Figure 11-5, can be very useful to managers confronted with these weighty decisions.

Alternatives to Job-Based Pay Systems

There are at least two alternatives to job-based pay. These are market-based pay and skill- or knowledge-based pay. Market-based pay systems use a direct market-pricing approach for all of a firm's jobs. This type of pay structure is feasible if all jobs are benchmark jobs and direct matches can be found in the market. Pay surveys can then

FIGURE 11-5
Annual compensation planning worksheet.

ANNUAL COMPENSATION PLANNING WORKSHEET

ORG. UNIT _____

MGR. OR SUPV. _____

EMPLOYEE NAME	JOB TITLE	LAST SALARY ADJUSTMENT				CURRENT SALARY	RANGE MINIMUM	RANGE MIDPOINT	RANGE MAXIMUM	PERFORMANCE APPRAISAL	FORECAST SALARY ADJUSTMENT (If Any)				
		Amt.	%	Date	Type*						Amt.	%	Date	New Salary	Inter-val

*Code for "Type"
1—Promotion
2—Merit

PREPARED BY _____

be used to determine the market prices of the jobs in question. This type of pay system may be used in entrepreneurial start-up firms, research and development units, and sales organizations.[43] Larger firms with more diverse jobs, however, may have to rely on market pricing only for benchmark jobs and use job evaluation in order to price nonbenchmark jobs.

Skill- or Knowledge-Based Pay. Under such a system, workers are paid not on the basis of the job they currently *are* doing but rather on the basis of the number of jobs they are *capable* of doing, or on their depth of knowledge. In a world of slimmed-down big companies and agile small ones, the last thing any manager wants to hear from an employee is "It's not my job." To see how such a system might work in practice, let's consider Polaroid.

SKILL-BASED PAY AT POLAROID CORPORATION[44]

COMPANY EXAMPLE

Polaroid initiated a companywide, skill-based pay system in April 1990. Polaroid employees are encouraged to form work teams and to redesign their work functions in order to make them more efficient, according to Richard G. Terry, compensation manager at Polaroid, which is based in Cambridge, Mass. Although Polaroid's system includes everyone from the mailroom clerk to the chief executive officer, it has been more effective in the manufacturing part of the business.

Polaroid's manufacturing employees have learned skills in a number of different areas, rather than focusing on a single job. In addition, the work teams have picked up some of the responsibilities of supervisors, such as scheduling assignments and overtime. Employees who have succeeded at the new jobs have received more money. "Their pay has gone beyond what was traditionally the top," Mr. Terry said.

The focus of Polaroid's white-collar employees has been on learning new technologies. But here, the process has not worked as smoothly. Part of the problem is that skills, or competencies, are not so easy to measure in managerial jobs. But that will not stop companies from attempting to apply this scheme to their white-collar workforce. "Slowly, but surely, we're becoming a skill-based society where your market value is tied to what you can do and what your skill set is. . . . In this new world, where skills and knowledge are what really count, it doesn't make sense to treat people as jobholders. It makes sense to treat them as people with specific skills, and to pay them for those skills."

In such a "learning environment," the more workers learn, the more they earn. Nine of 22 Corning plants are on skill-based pay. At one, workers can lift their base pay from $9.50 an hour to almost $13.50. Workers at American Steel & Wire can boost their annual salaries by up to $12,480 by acquiring as many as 10 skills. Is there any impact on productivity or morale? A recent survey of 27 companies with such programs revealed that 70 to 88 percent reported higher job satisfaction, product quality, or productivity. Some 70 to 75 percent reported lower operating costs or reduced turnover.[45]

Although firms such as General Foods, General Motors, Procter & Gamble, and Anheuser-Busch have been experimenting with skill- or knowledge-based pay,[46] job evaluation methods remain more popular. Skill- or knowledge-based pay systems work best when the following conditions exist:[47]

1. A supportive HRM philosophy underpins all employment activities. Such a philosophy is characterized by mutual trust and the conviction that employees have the ability and motivation to perform well.
2. HRM programs such as profit sharing, participative management, empowerment, and job enrichment complement the skill- or knowledge-based pay system.
3. Technology and organization structure change frequently.
4. Employee exchanges (i.e., assignment, rotation) are common.
5. There are opportunities to learn new skills.
6. Employee turnover is relatively high.
7. Workers value teamwork and the opportunity to participate.

In summary, if compensation systems are to be used strategically, it is important that management (1) understand clearly what types of behavior it wants the compensation system to reinforce, (2) recognize that compensation systems are integral components of planning and control, and (3) view the firm's performance as the ultimate criterion of the success of strategic pay decisions and operational compensation programs. Now let us consider some key policy issues.

POLICY ISSUES IN PAY PLANNING AND ADMINISTRATION
Comparable Worth

When women dominate an occupational field (such as nursing or secretarial work), the pay for jobs in that field tends to be lower than the pay men receive when they are the dominant incumbents (such as in construction and skilled trades). Is the market biased against jobs held mostly by women? Should jobs dominated by women and jobs dominated by men be paid equally if they are of "comparable" worth to an employer? Answering this question involves the knotty problem of how to make valid and accurate comparisons of the relative worth of dissimilar jobs. The key difference between the Equal Pay Act and comparable worth is this: the act requires equal pay for men and women who do work that is *substantially equal.* Comparable worth would require equal pay for jobs of *equal value* to an employer (e.g., librarian and electrician).

Typically, job evaluation schemes are used to assess "worth" to an employer. Jobs with roughly equal point totals are considered to be of "comparable worth." While it is reassuring to note that research on alternative job evaluation methods has found them generally to be reliable, to yield comparable results, and to be free of systematic bias for or against jobs dominated by one sex,[48] job pay levels can influence judgments of job content.[49] This means that biased market pay structures can work backward through the job evaluation process to produce deflated evaluations for jobs held predominantly by women without direct bias based on sex having to be present.

Should managers develop pay systems that ensure comparable worth? About 20 states (e.g., Minnesota) have enacted "comparable worth" laws that affect public employees, and in Canada's Ontario Province, all large private as well as public employers are covered by such a law.[50] The State of Washington's program is typical. After several years, the program has run into difficulties. These include:

- The typing pool, once a "pink-collar ghetto," is now a better-paid pink-collar ghetto.
- While no one has taken a pay cut, across-the-board cost-of-living increases have been cut dramatically to pay for the program.
- Men are rejecting offers of employment and also leaving state jobs. Men now hold a minority of the state's jobs.
- Shortages of skilled workers are developing. To attract them, the state has had to grant three special pay increases (thereby fracturing the concept of comparable worth, which is supposed to ignore the marketplace).
- Wages for state jobs are seriously out of line with wages in private industry, with which the state competes.[51]

The state does not know how to address these problems in the context of comparable worth. But wait. Is it possible that the goals of comparable worth can be achieved through normal labor market processes?

Consider that in recent years women have made dramatic inroads in jobs traditionally held by men. Moreover, as women deserted such low-paying jobs as secretary and nurse, the demand for such jobs held steady or increased, and pay rates climbed.[52] These are healthy trends that are likely to continue as long as aggressive enforcement of Title VII and the Equal Pay Act are combined with firm-level actions, such as redesigning jobs to reduce the number of jobs held exclusively by women, career planning and job or project assignments that help women move into male-dominated jobs, and the inclusion of women on job evaluation committees. The objective? To ensure equal job opportunities for women at all levels. The appropriate response is to remove the barriers, not to undermine the market forces that affect labor supply and demand.

Pay Secrecy

The extent to which information on pay is public or private is a basic issue that needs to be addressed by management. Legally, the U.S. courts have generally supported companies in their view that salary information, like a product formula or a marketing strategy, is confidential and the property of management. An employee who ferrets out and releases such data can be discharged for "willful misconduct."[53] However, a 1992 ruling by the National Labor Relations Board makes such a company policy illegal. In its ruling the Board noted:

> It is elemental that these activities encompass the ability of employees to discuss amongst themselves any quarrel that they may have concerning their wages in an effort to obtain a change in this condition of employment. Moreover, this is so regardless of whether a labor organization is on the scene to serve as the proponent of that change.[54]

Pay secrecy is a difficult policy to maintain, particularly as companies look to strengthen the link between pay and performance. For example, research with bank managers found that when pay systems are open, managers tend to award higher pay raises to subordinates on whom they depend heavily. Apparently they do so because they need the subordinates' cooperation, and subordinates can check on pay allocations.[55]

Openness versus secrecy is not an either/or phenomenon. Rather, it is a matter of degree. For example, organizations may choose to disclose one or more of the following: (1) the work- and business-related rationale on which the system is based, (2) pay ranges, (3) pay increase schedules, and (4) the availability of pay-related data from the compensation department.[56] There is also a downside to pay openness:

1. It forces managers to defend their pay decisions and practices publicly. Since the process is inherently subjective, there is no guarantee that satisfactory answers will ever be found that can please all concerned parties.

2. The cost of a mistaken pay decision escalates, since all the system's inconsistencies and weaknesses become visible once the cloak of secrecy is lifted.

3. Open pay might induce some managers to reduce differences in pay among subordinates in order to avoid conflict and the need to explain such differences to disappointed employees.[57]

In general, open-pay systems tend to work best under the following circumstances: individual or team performance can be measured objectively, performance measures can be developed for all the important aspects of a job, and effort and performance are related closely over a relatively short time span.

The Effect of Inflation

All organizations must make some allowance for inflation in their salary programs. Given an inflation rate of 5 percent, for example, the firm that fails to increase its salary ranges at all over a 2-year period will be 10 percent behind its competitors. Needless to say, it becomes difficult to recruit new employees under these circumstances, and it becomes difficult to motivate present employees to remain and, if they do remain, to produce.

How do firms cope? Automatic pay raises for nonunion employees have almost disappeared at most major concerns. Companies such as Corning, Du Pont, Merck, and Santa Fe Pacific are tying pay more to performance.[58] For example, at Commercial Metals Co. of Dallas, cost-of-living adjustments will not be resumed even if inflation zooms. The company found that its employees—*including average performers*—prefer to be paid on the basis of their performance. However, other firms that have adopted this approach, such as Armco and B. F. Goodrich, note that the switch from automatic to merit increases does not necessarily lower labor costs.[59]

Pay Compression

Pay compression is related to the general problem of inflation. It is a narrowing of the ratios of pay between jobs or pay grades in a firm's pay structure.[60] Pay compression exists in many forms, including (1) higher starting salaries for new hires, which lead long-term employees to see only a slight difference between their current pay and that of new hires; (2) hourly pay increases for unionized employees that exceed those of salaried and nonunion employees; (3) recruitment of new college graduates for management or professional jobs at salaries above those of current jobholders; and (4) excessive overtime payments to some employees or payment of different overtime rates (e.g., time and a half for some, double time for others). However, first-line supervisors, unlike middle managers, may actually *benefit* from pay inflation among nonmanagement employees since companies generally maintain a differential between the supervisors' pay and that of their highest-paid subordinates. As we noted earlier, these differentials average 15 percent.[61]

One solution to the problem of pay compression is to institute *equity adjustments;* that is, increases in pay are given to employees to maintain differences in job worth between their jobs and those of others. Some companies provide for equity adjustments through a constantly changing pay scale. Thus Aluminum Company of America (ALCOA) surveys its competitors' pay every 3 months and adjusts its pay rates accordingly. ALCOA strives to maintain at least a 20 percent differential between employees and their supervisors.[62]

Another approach is to grant sign-on bonuses to new hires in order to offer a competitive total compensation package, especially to those with scarce skills. Since bonuses do not increase base salaries, the structure of differences in pay between new hires and experienced employees does not change. Alternatively, some firms provide benefits that increase gradually to more senior employees. Thus, although the difference between the *direct pay* of this group and that of their shorter-service coworkers may be slim, senior employees have a distinct advantage when the *entire* compensation package is considered.

Overtime as a cause of compression can be dealt with in two ways. First, it can be *rotated* among employees so that all share overtime equally. However, in situations where this kind of arrangement is not feasible, firms might consider establishing an overtime pay policy for management employees; for example, a supervisor may be paid an overtime rate after he or she works a minimum number of overtime hours. Such a practice does not violate the Fair Labor Standards Act, for under the law overtime pay is not *required* for exempt jobs, although it may be adopted voluntarily. Finally, a recent survey indicated that one of the most favored solutions by companies is to provide aids to upward mobility, such as training and rapid advancement; strategies of this type keep the pay structure intact while helping individuals to move within it.[63]

Pay compression is certainly a difficult problem—but not so difficult that it cannot be managed. Indeed, it *must* be managed if companies are to achieve their goal of providing pay that is perceived as fair.

Pay Raises

Coping with inflation is the biggest hurdle to overcome in a merit-pay plan. On the other hand, *the only measure of a raise is how much it exceeds the increase in the cost of living:* the 12.4 percent inflation of 1980 more than wiped out the average raise. However, the average 3 percent raise that employees received in 342 collective bargaining agreements in 1993 maintained the purchasing power of employees' dollars, since inflation was also 3 percent.[64]

The simplest, most effective method for dealing with inflation in a merit-pay system is increasing salary ranges. By raising salary ranges (e.g., based on a survey of average increases in starting salaries for the coming year) without giving general increases, a firm can maintain competitive hiring rates and at the same time maintain the merit concept surrounding salary increases. Since a raise in minimum pay for each salary range creates an employee group that falls below the new minimum, it is necessary to raise these employees to the new minimum. Such adjustments technically violate the merit philosophy, but the advantages gained by keeping employees in the salary range and at a rate that is sufficient to retain them clearly outweigh the disadvantages.[65]

The size of the merit increase for a given level of performance should *decrease* as the employee moves farther up the salary range. *Merit guide charts* provide a means for doing this. Guide charts identify (1) an employee's current performance rating and (2) his or her location in a pay grade. The intersection of these two dimensions identifies a percentage of pay increase based on the performance level and location of the employee in the pay grade. Figure 11-6 shows an example of such a chart. The rationale for the merit guide chart approach is that a person at the top of the range is already making more than the "going rate" for that job. Hence she or he should have to demonstrate *more* than satisfactory performance in order to continue moving farther above the going rate.

A final aspect of the program is to increase salaries more than once a year (e.g., every 6 months). By getting a raise every 6 months, employees tend to feel that they are keeping up with inflation. The organization also benefits since the increases will cost less. This is so because rather than giving the entire increase for a full year, employees receive half the increase for 6 months and the rest for the other 6 months.

FIGURE 11-6

Example of a merit guide chart.

EMPLOYEE PERFORMANCE	PERCENT INCREASE				
Distinguished	14%	12%	11%	10%	9%
Commendable	11%	10%	9%	8%	Ceiling
Competent	9%	8%	7%	Ceiling	
Adequate	5%	0	Ceiling		
Provisional	0	Ceiling			
Salary (as % of midpoint) is:	80% ⟶ 88% ⟶ 96% ⟶ 104% ⟶ 112% ⟶ 120%				

For example, if an employee making $25,000 per year gets a 10 percent increase, that increase will cost the employer $2500 for the year. If, instead, the employee gets two 5 percent increases, the total cost for the year is only $1266 ($25,000 × .05 = $1250 or $104.17 per month × 6 months = $625; $25,625 × .05 = $1281.25 or $106.77 per month × 6 months = $640.62; $640.62 + $625 = $1,265.62). Despite this fact, the vast majority of companies continue to award annual raises, either on an employee's anniversary date or on a common review date for all employees.[66] The proposal just outlined will not solve all the compensation problems caused by inflation, but it is important to remember that *it is not an organization's responsibility to pay wages that keep pace with inflation.* The responsibility is merely to pay wages that are competitive. What this merit compensation system will do is allow most employees to stay close until the economy settles down.

IMPACT OF PAY SYSTEMS ON PRODUCTIVITY, QUALITY OF WORK LIFE, AND THE BOTTOM LINE

High salary levels alone do not ensure a productive, motivated workforce. This is evident in the auto industry, where wages are among the highest in the country, yet quality problems and high absenteeism persist. A critical factor, then, is not *how much* a company pays its workers but, more important, *how the pay system is designed, communicated, and managed.* As we have seen repeatedly throughout this chapter, excessively high labor costs, coupled with benefits offered only because "everybody else is doing it," adversely affect productivity, work quality, and the bottom line. Although management's desire to improve the standard of living of all company employees is understandable, excessively high labor costs can bankrupt a company.[67] This is especially likely if, to cover its labor costs, the company cannot price its products competitively. If that happens, productivity and profits both suffer directly, and the quality of work life suffers indirectly. A systematic pay structure helps ensure that each employee is paid equitably and competitively. Current data from a wage survey must then be used to maintain the company's relative position on pay. When sensible compensation policies are established using the principles discussed in this chapter, everybody wins: the company, the employees, and employees' families as well.

THE TRUST GAP

What steps can companies take to sew corporate top and bottom back together? Here are seven suggestions. One, start with the obvious. Tie the financial interests of high- and low-level workers closer together by making exposure to risks and rewards more equitable. Thus, when NUCOR, a steel company in Charlotte, North Carolina, went through tough times, President Ken Iverson took a 60 percent cut in pay. Said a compensation consultant, "How often do you see that? . . . It makes a real difference if employees see that their CEO is willing to take it in the shorts along with them"[68]

Two, consider instituting profit sharing, a Scanlon plan, gain sharing (see Chapter 13), or some other program that lets employees profit from their efforts. Make sure, however, that incentive pay is linked to performance over which the beneficiaries have control.

Three, rethink perquisites. Now that perks come under taxable income, they just don't have the same appeal to executives as they used to. Yet they still have at least the same downside with the rank and file.

HUMAN RESOURCE MANAGEMENT IN ACTION: CONCLUSION

Four, look at the office layout with an eye toward equity. In Sweden, for example, same-size offices are the norm. When an American visitor asked his Swedish corporate hosts how they could give the same amount of space to a secretary as to an engineer, they said, "How can we hire a secretary and expect her to be committed to our company, when, by the size of the office we give her, we tell her she's a second-class citizen?"[69]

Five, make sure your door is really open. If that means meeting with employees at unorthodox times, such as when their shifts end, then do it. Not a single one of the CEOs interviewed by *Fortune* could recall employees ever abusing an open-door policy. The lesson is clear for managers at all levels: employees don't walk through your door unless they have to.

Six, if you don't survey employee attitudes now, start. What you find can help identify problems before they become crises. Share findings, and be sure employees know how subsequent decisions may be related to them. Don't worry about raising expectations too high. As one executive commented, "Employees by and large are reasonable people. They understand you can't do everything they want. As long as they know their views are being considered and they get some feedback from you to that effect, you will be meeting their expectations."[70]

Seven, explain things—personally. While one study found that 97 percent of CEOs believe that communicating with employees has a positive impact on job satisfaction and 79 percent think it benefits the bottom line, only 22 percent do it weekly or more often.

There is no doubt that these seven steps can help close the trust gap that exists in so many U.S. organizations today. On the other hand, virtually all experts cite one important qualification: it is suicidal to start down this road unless you are absolutely sincere.

SUMMARY

Contemporary pay systems (outside the entertainment and professional sports fields) are characterized by cost containment, pay and benefit levels commensurate with what a company can afford, and programs that encourage and reward performance.

Generally speaking, pay systems are designed to attract, retain, and motivate employees; to achieve internal, external, and individual equity; and to maintain a balance in relationships between direct and indirect forms of compensation and between the pay rates of supervisory and nonsupervisory employees. Pay systems need to be tied to the strategic mission of an organization, and they should take their direction from that strategic mission. However, actual wage levels depend on labor market con-

IMPLICATIONS FOR MANAGEMENT PRACTICE

Remember: The *amount* of pay employees receive affects only their decisions about whether to stay or leave. How hard they work, and the productivity resulting from their efforts, is determined by *the way in which pay is administered.* To maximize the productivity gain from pay systems, be sure that the design of the system is consistent with the objectives of the business you are in. Objectives, in turn, are related to the stage of development of the business (e.g., start-up versus mature enterprise), as well as to any special situations, such as restructuring or downsizing. Beyond that, remember that people respond to the world as they perceive it, not as it exists. Internal, external, and individual equity are crucial considerations in all pay systems.

ditions, legislation, collective bargaining, management attitudes, and an organization's ability to pay. Our broad objective in developing pay systems is to assign a monetary value to each job or skill set in the organization (a base rate) and to establish an orderly procedure for increasing the base rate. To develop a job-based system, we need four basic tools: job analyses and job descriptions, a job evaluation plan, pay surveys, and a pay structure.

Finally, the following pay policy issues are important: whether pay systems should be designed to achieve comparable worth, pay secrecy versus openness, the effect of inflation on pay systems, pay compression, and pay raises.

DISCUSSION QUESTIONS

11■1 What steps can a company take to integrate its compensation system with its general business strategy?

11■2 How do the pay practices of unionized firms affect those of nonunionized firms?

11■3 How do management's attitudes and philosophy affect pay systems?

11■4 What can companies do to ensure internal, external, and individual equity for all employees?

11■5 Discuss the advantages and disadvantages of skill-based pay systems.

TECHNICAL APPENDIX

A Brief Look at the Hay Group's Job Evaluation System

At the outset it is important to note two principles: (1) a job evaluation study often becomes an exercise in semantics—trying to express in words perceptible differences in jobs; and (2) jobs have to be explained in response to probing questions about what they require. Usually both tasks are accomplished by a committee comprised of employees who are familiar with company jobs, with guidance from an outside consultant.

The process of job evaluation is an enormously time-consuming, complex, and often frustrating task that is subject to all the political pressures and biases so "natural" among committee members who represent different functional areas. To establish the relationship among jobs in terms of relative worth to the firm, the job evaluation committee uses a systematic procedure that compares one job with another.

Experience has shown that this is easier to do if the committee compares *aspects* of jobs (that is, compensable factors) that are common to all jobs, to various degrees, rather than *whole* jobs. In the Hay system, three compensable factors are analyzed. They are *know-how*, *problem solving*, and *accountability*. Each is defined on a guide chart. An example of the Hay guide chart for the know-how factor is shown in Figure 11-7.

Each guide chart is composed of a point scale, similar to the one shown in Figure 11-7, in which adjacent terms differ by approximately 15 percent. The guide charts themselves reveal what is meant by "know-how," "problem solving," and "accountability." Each of these compensable factors is broken down in terms of more specific "building blocks." For example, know-how (see Figure 11-7) has three components:

1. Scientific disciplines, specialized techniques, and practical procedures

2. Managerial know-how

3. Human relations skills

■ TABLE 11 ▪ 5a

QUANTITATIVE JOB EVALUATION METHODS

Approach	Methodology	Advantages	Disadvantages
Point factor	Select compensable factors. Define the degrees within each factor on a numerical scale. Weight the compensable factors. Analyze and describe the jobs in terms of the compensable factors. Determine which degree definition for each factor best fits the job. Assign points for each factor based on the evaluation. Arrange a job-worth hierarchy based on the total points for each job.	Reliable Relatively objective Easy to evaluate new or revised jobs	Expensive to develop or purchase Difficult to control evaluator bias
Factor comparison	Select compensable factors. Analyze and describe the jobs in terms of the compensable factors. Vertically rank the jobs on each factor. Weight each factor in terms of its relative importance to the organization. Calculate the total points for each job. Develop a job-worth hierarchy based on total points.	Relatively reliable Scales are easy to use Compensable factors tailored to organization Easy to communicate	No degree definitions Difficult to evaluate new or revised job
Job component	In the job component approach, one or more independent variables are related to a "dependent" variable in a statistical equation. Choose a dependent variable and independent variables that are considered important in predicting and explaining pay relationships. Enter the data using a statistical software package. The resulting statistical model can be used for auditing current systems or for assigning pay rates in a new system.	Objective Comprehensive Statistically accurate Management-oriented	Expensive to develop or purchase Time-consuming Complex Difficult to communicate to employees

Within component 1, A, B, C, and D are the degrees of trained skills where know-how is characterized by education plus work experience. The specialized technical and professional skills built on subjects not included in a secondary education are represented by E, F, G, and H.

Management know-how (component 2) deals exclusively with the management process independent of scientific disciplines (component 1) and human relations skills (component 3). The intersection of ratings on components 1, 2, and 3 falls into one of three "slots." Jobs in slot I consist primarily of specialized "on-the-spot" execution; coordination of people or activities is minimal. Jobs in slot II involve coordination and integration of activities (as distinct from merely supervising them). Jobs in slot III emphasize total departmental operations or administration of a strategic corporate function (e.g., the job "director of computer operations").

Human relations (component 3) has three degrees:

■ TABLE 11 ■ 5b
NONQUANTITATIVE, "WHOLE-JOB" JOB CONTENT METHODS

Approach	Methodology	Advantages	Disadvantages
Ranking	Identify the most "important" job in the job set. Identify the next most important job. Continue this process until all jobs are arranged in a hierarchy.	Simple to administer Inexpensive Quickly implemented Little training required	No specific standards No detail or documentation May be superficial Incumbent may unduly influence evaluation
Classification	Create job grades with generic definitions at each grade level. Compare the job descriptions with the grade descriptions. Assign each job to the grade most closely matching the level of work performed.	Simple to administer Inexpensive Quickly implemented Little training required	Jobs may be forced into classes they do not fit Descriptions can be rigged to fit a class
Slotting	Use the existing hierarchy. Compare the new or revised job with the jobs already assigned to existing job grades. Assign the job to the grade containing other jobs that appear similar in overall worth.	Simple to administer Inexpensive Quickly implemented Little training required	Cannot be used as stand-alone method because it is based on a preexisting structure No specific standards

Nonquantitative, whole-job evaluation methods require *each* evaluator individually to (1) determine which compensable factors he or she will use to compare the jobs, (2) "weight" the compensable factors, and (3) define and apply factors to jobs. These may produce inconsistent ratings across evaluators.

1. *Basic*—ordinary courtesy is sufficient.

2. *Important*—being able to handle people in situations where repercussions are anticipated but are not critical considerations in the overall content of the position is important.

3. *Critical*—motivating others to do something is a critical requirement of the job, and the job cannot be done without such emphasis on human relations skills.

Working with job descriptions and the three guide charts, the task of the evaluation committee is to develop a point "profile" of each job on each compensable factor. The total number of points for each job is determined by adding the points assigned to each of the three factors. Note that points are assigned to jobs *independently* of market wage rates.

To provide a structure for evaluating all the jobs in an organization, the committee begins with a group of jobs called "benchmarks." Benchmark jobs:

■ Are well established, with clear job contents

■ Represent each functional area and vary from low to high job content

■ Represent a large number of in-house jobs

GUIDE HAY CHART

KNOW-HOW

© HAY ASSOCIATES 1984

● ● ● **Human Relations Skills** ⟶

DEFINITION: Know-How is the sum total of every kind of skill, however acquired, needed for acceptable job performance. Know-How has three dimensions — the requirements for:

● Practical procedures, specialized techniques, and scientific disciplines.

● ● Know-How of integrating and harmonizing the diversified functions involved in managerial situations occurring in operating, supporting, and administrative fields. This Know-How may be exercised consultatively (about management) as well as executively, and involves in some combination the areas of organizing, planning, executing, controlling and evaluating.

● ● ● Active, practicing, person-to-person skills in the area of human relationships.

MEASURING KNOW - HOW: Know-How has both scope (variety) and depth (thoroughness). Thus, a job may require some knowledge about a lot of things, or a lot of knowledge about a few things. The total Know-How is the combination of scope and depth. This concept makes practical the comparison and weighing of the total Know-How content of different jobs in terms of: "HOW MUCH KNOWLEDGE ABOUT HOW MANY THINGS."

● ● ● **H U M A N   R E L A T I O N S   S K I L L S**
1. **BASIC**: Ordinary courtesy and effectiveness in dealing with others through normal contacts, and request for or providing information.
2. **IMPORTANT**: Understanding, influencing and/or serving people are important considerations in performing the job, causing action or understanding in others.
3. **CRITICAL**: Alternative or combined skills in understanding, selecting, developing and motivating people are important in the highest degree.

PRACTICAL PROCEDURES

SPECIALIZED TECHNIQUES

SCIENTIFIC DISCIPLINES

A. BASIC

Basic work routines plus work indoctrination.

B. ELEMENTARY VOCATIONAL

Familiarization in uninvolved, standardized work routines and/or use of simple equipment and machines.

C. VOCATIONAL

Procedural or systematic proficiency, which may involve a facility in the use of specialized equipment.

D. ADVANCED VOCATIONAL

Some specialized (generally nontechnical) skill(s), however acquired, giving additional breadth or depth to a generally single functional element.

E. BASIC TECHNICAL - SPECIALIZED

Sufficiency in a technique which requires a grasp either of involved practices and precedents; or of scientific theory and principles; or both.

F. SEASONED TECHNICAL - SPECIALIZED

Proficiency, gained through wide exposure or experiences in a specialized or technical field, in a technique which combines a broad grasp either of involved practices and precedents or of scientific theory and principles; or both.

G. TECHNICAL - SPECIALIZED MASTERY

Determinative mastery of techniques, practices and theories gained through wide seasoning and/or special development.

H. PROFESSIONAL MASTERY

Exceptional and unique mastery in scientific or other learned disciplines.

FIGURE 11-7
Illustrative industrial Hay guide charts for the compensable factor "know-how."

Job evaluation committee members make their judgments independently, through secret voting. Differences among members are resolved subsequently in an open discussion. Each member's task is to arrive at a point total for each job on each factor. In the case of know-how, for example, the total is found in the slot that represents the intersection of ratings on components 1, 2, and 3. As an illustration, let's consider the job of "administrative clerk." Here is what compensation specialists call a "thumbnail sketch" (i.e., an abbreviated job description) of the job:

* * B R E A D T H O F M A N A G E M E N T K N O W - H O W															
I. NONE OR MINIMAL Performance or supervision of an activity (or activities) highly specific as to objective and content, with appropriate awareness of related activities.			**II. RELATED** Operational or conceptual integration or coordination of activities which are relatively homogeneous in nature and objective.			**III. DIVERSE** Operational or conceptual integration or coordination of activities which are diverse in nature and objectives, in an important management area.			**IV. BROAD** Integration of major functions in an operating complex, or Company-wide coordination of a strategic function which significantly affects corporate planning or operations.			**V. TOTAL**			
1	2	3	1	2	3	1	2	3	1	2	3	1	2	3	
50	57	66	66	76	87	87	100	115	115	132	152	152	175	200	
57	66	76	76	87	100	100	115	132	132	152	175	175	200	230	A
66	76	87	87	100	115	115	132	152	152	175	200	200	230	264	
66	76	87	87	100	115	115	132	152	152	175	200	200	230	264	
76	87	100	100	115	132	132	152	175	175	200	230	230	264	304	B
87	100	115	115	132	152	152	175	200	200	230	264	264	304	350	
87	100	115	115	132	152	152	175	200	200	230	264	264	304	350	
100	115	132	132	152	175	175	200	230	230	264	304	304	350	400	C
115	132	152	152	175	200	200	230	264	264	304	350	350	400	460	
115	132	152	152	175	200	200	230	264	264	304	350	350	400	460	
132	152	175	175	200	230	230	264	304	304	350	400	400	460	528	D
152	175	200	200	230	264	264	304	350	350	400	460	460	528	608	
152	175	200	200	230	264	264	304	350	350	400	460	460	528	608	
175	200	230	230	264	304	304	350	400	400	460	528	528	608	700	E
200	230	264	264	304	350	350	400	460	460	528	608	608	700	800	
200	230	264	264	304	350	350	400	460	460	528	608	608	700	800	
230	264	304	304	350	400	400	460	528	528	608	700	700	800	920	F
264	304	350	350	400	460	460	528	608	608	700	800	800	920	1056	
264	304	350	350	400	460	460	528	608	608	700	800	800	920	1056	
304	350	400	400	460	528	528	608	700	700	800	920	920	1056	1216	G
350	400	460	460	528	608	608	700	800	800	920	1056	1056	1216	1400	
350	400	460	460	528	608	608	700	800	800	920	1056	1056	1216	1400	
400	460	528	528	608	700	700	800	920	920	1056	1216	1216	1400	1600	H
460	528	608	608	700	800	800	920	1056	1056	1216	1400	1400	1600	1840	

Performs a variety of clerical tasks such as payroll, accounts receivable, accounts payable, or other specialized clerical work requiring knowledge of policies and procedures and a moderate degree of independent judgment.

In terms of Figure 11-7, the job evaluation committee might decide that the job of administrative clerk rates a C-I-1 on the compensable factor know-how. That is, the level of scientific disciplines is a C (vocational), the level of managerial know-how is a

I, and the level of human relations skill involved also merits a 1. Note that within each cell there are three different point totals to choose from. This is done to allow the committee some flexibility in arriving at a point total. In the C-I-1 cell, let's assume that the committee assigned a total of 87 points to know-how.

As judgments accumulate within a slot, the slot assumes a pattern into which new jobs can be fit reliably. The pattern itself is established through the consensus of the committee members. Once set, it should not be tampered with as long as the jobs themselves do not change.

REFERENCES

1. Farnham, A. (1989, Dec. 4). The trust gap. *Fortune*, pp. 58, 62.
2. Look back in wonder: Hits and misses in predictions for 1990 (1990, May). *Money*, p. 22.
3. Bennett, A. (1990, Apr. 18). Pay for performance. *The Wall Street Journal Supplement: Executive Pay*, pp. R7, R8.
4. Mahoney, T. A. (1989). Employment compensation planning and strategy. In L. R. Gomez-Mejia (ed.), *Compensation and benefits*. Washington, DC: Bureau of National Affairs, pp. 3-1 to 3-28.
5. Buder, L. (1990, May 6). With overtime, electrician out-earns mayor. *The New York Times*, p. 39.
6. Milkovich, G. T., & Newman, J. M. (1990). *Compensation* (2d ed.). Homewood, IL: BPI-Irwin.
7. Ibid.
8. Gorman, C. (1989, Feb. 13). Big steel is red hot again. *Time*, p. 61.
9. Milbank, D. (1992, Mar. 9). Minimill inroads in sheet market rouse big steel. *The Wall Street Journal*, pp. B1, B6. See also Why steel is still bent out of shape (1991, July 1). *Time*, pp. 27, 28.
10. Bates, M. W. (1983, March). A look at cash compensation. *Personnel Journal*, pp. 198–200.
11. Uchitelle, L. (1987, June 26). Bonuses replace wage raises and workers are the losers. *The New York Times*, pp. A1, D3.
12. Ibid., p. D3.
13. Lawler, E. E., III (1989). Pay for performance: A strategic analysis. In L. R. Gomez-Mejia (ed.), *Compensation and benefits*. Washington, DC: Bureau of National Affairs, pp. 3-136 to 3-181. See also Lawler, E. E., III (1977). Reward systems. In J. R. Hackman & J. L. Suttle, *Improving life at work: Behavioral science approaches to organizational change*. Santa Monica, CA: Goodyear.
14. Foulkes, F. K., & Livernash, E. R. (1989). *Human resources management: Cases and text* (2d ed.). Englewood Cliffs, NJ: Prentice-Hall.
15. Thierry, H. (1992). Pay and payment systems. In J. F. Hartley & S. M. Stephenson (eds.), *Managing employment relations*. Oxford: Basil Blackwell, pp. 136–160. See also Sweeney, P. D., McFarlin, D. B., & Inderrieden, E. J. (1990). Using relative deprivation theory to explain satisfaction with income and pay level: A multistudy examination. *Academy of Management Journal*, **33**, 423–436.
16. Cowan, A. L. (1993, May 21). At what point is pay too high? *The New York Times*, pp. D1, D2.
17. Huseman, R. C., Hatfield, J. D., & Miles, E. W. (1987). A new perspective on equity theory: The equity sensitivity construct. *Academy of Management Review*, **12**, 222–234.
18. Foulkes & Livernash, op. cit.
19. Labor letter (1990, Oct. 2). *The Wall Street Journal*, p. A1.
20. Gomez-Mejia, L. R., & Balkin, D. B. (1992). *Compensation, organizational strategy, and firm performance*. Cincinnati, OH: South-Western.
21. Deutch, C. H. (1990, Feb. 25). Revising pay packages, again. *The New York Times*, p. F29.

22. Gomez-Mejia & Balkin, op. cit.

23. Ibid.

24. Milkovich & Newman, op. cit.

25. Managing your career (1993, Fall). *The Wall Street Journal Supplement*, pp. 42, 43.

26. Ibid., p. 35.

27. Raff, D. M., & Summers, L. H. (1987, October). Did Henry Ford pay efficiency wages? *Journal of Labor Economics*, **5**(4) (Part 2, Supplement), S57–S87.

28. Williams, M. (1983, Oct. 12). Ten minutes' work for 12 hours' pay? What's the catch? *The Wall Street Journal*, pp. 1, 19.

29. Ibid., p. 19.

30. Ibid.

31. Ormiston, K. A. (1988, May 10). States know best what labor's worth. *The Wall Street Journal*, p. 38.

32. Lacayo, R. (1989, Nov. 13). A pay hike for the poor. *Time*, p. 36.

33. Burger King faces charges it violated child labor laws (1990, Mar. 10). *The New York Times*, p. 8. See also Sleeth, P. (1990, Mar. 25). New child-labor laws to tax strapped system. *Denver Post*, pp. 1G, 7G.

34. Mills, D. Q. (1994). *Labor-management relations* (5th ed.). New York: McGraw-Hill.

35. Pfeffer, J., & Davis-Blake, A. (1987). Understanding organizational wage structures: A resource dependence approach. *Academy of Management Journal*, **30**, 437–455.

36. Gomez, L. R., Page, R. C., & Tornow, W. W. (1982). A comparison of the practical utility of traditional, statistical, and hybrid job evaluation approaches. *Academy of Management Journal*, **25**, 790–809.

37. Gerhart, B., & Milkovich, G. T. (1992). Employee compensation: Research and practice. In M. D. Dunnette & L. M. Hough (eds.), *Handbook of industrial and organizational psychology*. Palo Alto, CA: Consulting Psychologists Press, pp. 481–569. See also Hills, F. S. (1989). Internal pay relationships. In L. R. Gomez-Mejia (ed.), *Compensation and benefits*. Washington, DC: Bureau of National Affairs, pp. 3-29 to 3-69.

38. Rynes, S. L., & Milkovich, G. T. (1986). Wage surveys: Dispelling some myths about the "market wage." *Personnel Psychology*, **39**, 71–90.

39. Fay, C. H. (1989). External pay relationships. In L. R. Gomez-Mejia (ed.), *Compensation and benefits*. Washington, DC: Bureau of National Affairs, pp. 3-70 to 3-100.

40. Rigdon, J. E. (1992, Apr. 22). I want more. *The Wall Street Journal*, pp. R3, R7.

41. Wallace, M. J., Jr., & Fay, C. H. (1988). *Compensation theory and practice* (2d ed.). Boston: PWS-Kent.

42. Sibson, R. E. (1991). *Compensation* (5th ed.). New York: American Management Association.

43. Balkin, D. B., & Logan, J. W. (1988). Reward policies that support entrepreneurship. *Compensation and Benefits Review*, **20**(1), 18–25.

44. Rowland, M. (1993, June 6). It's what you can do that counts. *The New York Times*, p. F17.

45. Skill-based pay boosts worker productivity and morale (1992, Apr. 18). *The Wall Street Journal*, p. A1.

46. Tosi, H., & Tosi, L. (1987). What managers need to know about knowledge-based pay. In D. A. Balkin & L. R. Gomez-Mejia (eds.), *New perspectives on compensation*. Englewood Cliffs, NJ: Prentice-Hall, pp. 43–48.

47. Gomez-Mejia & Balkin, op. cit.

48. Ibid.

49. Rynes, S. L., Weber, C. L., & Milkovich, G. T. (1989). Effects of market survey rates, job evaluation, and job gender on pay. *Journal of Applied Psychology*, **74**, 114–123.

50. Kovach, K. A., & Millspaugh, P. E. (1990). Comparable worth: Canada legislates pay equity. *The Academy of Management Executive*, **4**(2), 92–101.

51. Comparable worth—new problems (1991, October). *Mountain States Employers Council Bulletin*, p. 2.

52. Topolnicki, D. M. (1993, December). Get on the new fast track. *Money*, pp. 142–156.

53. Solomon, J. (1990, Apr. 18). Hush money. *The Wall Street Journal Supplement*, pp. R22–R24.

54. Handbook rule against wage discussion illegal (1992, February). *Mountain States Employers Council Bulletin*, p. 1.

55. Bartol, K. M., & Martin, D. C. (1988). Influences on managerial pay allocations: A dependency perspective. *Personnel Psychology*, **41**, 361–378.

56. Milkovich & Newman, op. cit.

57. Gomez-Mejia & Balkin, op. cit.

58. Rigdon, op. cit. See also Bennett, A. (1991, Sept. 10). Paying workers to meet goals spreads, but gauging performance proves tough. *The Wall Street Journal*, pp. B1, B2.

59. Lublin, J. (1984, Mar. 13). Labor letter. *The Wall Street Journal*, p. 1.

60. Gomez-Mejia & Balkin, op. cit

61. Labor letter (1990, Oct. 2), op. cit. See also Kanter, R. M. (1987, March–April). The attack on pay. *Harvard Business Review*, pp. 60–67.

62. Bergmann, T. J., Hills, F. S., & Priefert, L. (1983, Second Quarter). Pay compression: Causes, results, and possible solutions. *Compensation Review*, **6**, 17–26.

63. Kanter, op. cit.

64. Union wage increases overall below 1992 (1993, September). *Mountain States Employers Council Bulletin*, p. 5.

65. Schwartz, J. D. (1982, February). Maintaining merit compensation in a high-inflation economy. *Personnel Journal*, pp. 147–152.

66. Rigdon, op. cit.

67. Northwest's sigh of relief has rivals groaning (1993, July 26). *Business Week*, p. 84.

68. Farnham, op. cit., p. 66.

69. Ibid.

70. Ibid., p. 70.

CHAPTER 12

INDIRECT COMPENSATION: EMPLOYEE BENEFIT PLANS

THE NEW WORLD OF EMPLOYEE BENEFITS*

As late as 1987, workplace experts were still predicting that benefits packages in the 1990s would become ever more generous as companies competed for a shrinking pool of workers. Today, that forecast seems as outdated as the notion that computers would create a paperless society. Struggling to deal with benefits costs that seem to rise relentlessly, many firms are eliminating benefits or asking employees to pay more for them. Plans that allow employees to choose among alternative benefits choices, so-called flexible benefits, force employees to make trade-offs—and profoundly affect how they think about security, company loyalty, and employment itself. It wasn't always this way.

In the past, major corporations offered their employees a wide array of company-paid insurance and retirement benefits. Corporations decided what was best for their employees. Now, however, most employers are not only changing the range of benefit choices they offer, but also changing the basic structure of their benefits.

Economics and demographics are driving these changes. Economically, most employers realize that the traditional blanket approach to benefits—total coverage for everyone—would subject them to unbearable expense. Benefits are no longer the "fringe" of compensation. Today they often comprise between 20 and 40 percent of wages. As a result of unending increases in the price of medical care, for example, health-care expenses now consume an average of 56 percent of pretax profits of U.S. corporations. Increasing life

---

*Sources: Luciano, L. (1993, May). How companies are slashing benefits. *Money*, 128–138. "The New World of Employee Benefits." (1991, Oct. 21). *Business Week*, Special Advertising Section. Nasar, S. (1992, Apr. 7). Pensions covering lower percentage of U.S. work force. *The New York Times*, pp. A1; D4.

expectancy has made pensions more costly as well. And the combination of increased longevity, rising health-care costs, and a new accounting standard that requires firms to report the cost of future retiree health-care benefits on their balance sheets—thereby reducing profits—has led employers to dramatically rethink their entire approach to employee benefits.

Demographically the United States now has a much more diverse workforce then it has had in the past. As a result, the "one-size-fits-all" approach to employee benefits doesn't work. Employees who have working spouses covered by health insurance have different insurance needs from those who are sole breadwinners. Single parents and childless couples place very different priorities on child-care benefits. So rather than attempt to fashion a single approach that suits all of these interests, many employers determine a sum they'll spend on each employee, establish a menu of benefits, and then let each employee choose the benefits he or she wants or needs. At the same time such plans allow employers to trim benefits merely by raising the prices of the various options on the benefits menu.

These changes reflect more than demographic diversity, however. A fundamental change in philosophy is taking place as employees are forced to take more responsibility. Part of this is a movement toward employee self-management. Indeed, the new approach might well be described as one of "sharing costs, sharing risks."

Challenges

1. Do you think companies should provide a broader menu of "exotic" benefits (e.g., veterinary care, dietary counseling) or improve the menu of "core" benefits (e.g., health care, insurance, pensions)? Why?

2. How might one's preference for various benefits change as one grows older or as one's family situation changes?

Questions This Chapter Will Help Managers Answer

1. What strategic considerations should guide the design of benefits programs?

2. What options are available to help a business control the rapid escalation of health-care costs?

3. Should companies offer a uniform "package" of benefits, or should they move to a flexible plan that allows employees to choose the benefits that are most meaningful to them, up to a certain dollar amount?

4. What cost-effective benefits options are available to a small business?

5. In view of the considerable sums of money that are spent each year on employee benefits, what is the best way to communicate this information to employees?

Benefits currently account for almost 40 percent of the total compensation costs for each employee. Yesterday's "fringes" have become today's (expected) benefits and services. Here are some reasons why benefits have grown:[1]

- The imposition of wage ceilings during World War II forced organizations to offer more benefits in place of wage increases to attract, retain, and motivate employees.

- The interest by unions in bargaining over benefits has grown, particularly since employers are pushing for more cost sharing by employees.[2]

- Internal Revenue Service Code treatment of benefits makes them preferable to wages. Even after the Omnibus Budget Reconciliation Act of 1993, many benefits remain nontaxable to the employee and are deductible by the employer. With other benefits, taxes are deferred. Hence employees' disposable income increases since they are receiving benefits and services that they would otherwise have to purchase with after-tax dollars.

- Granting benefits (in a nonunionized firm) or bargaining over them (in a unionized firm) confers an aura of social responsibility on employers; they are "taking care" of their employees.

STRATEGIC CONSIDERATIONS IN THE DESIGN OF BENEFITS PROGRAMS

As is the case with compensation systems in general, managers need to think carefully about what they wish to accomplish by means of their benefits programs. On average, firms spend over $13,000 in benefits for each worker on the payroll.[3] General Motors, for example, spent about $5700 per worker, almost $4 billion overall, just to provide health benefits to its workers in 1993.[4] It's no exaggeration to say that for most firms, benefits represent substantial annual expenditures. In order to leverage the impact of these expenditures with employees, managers should be prepared to answer questions such as the following:

- Are the type and level of our benefits coverage consistent with our long-term strategic business plans?

- Given the characteristics of our workforce, are we meeting the needs of our employees?

- What legal requirements must we satisfy in the benefits we offer?

- Are our benefits competitive in cost, structure, and value to employees and their dependents?

- Is our benefits package consistent with the key objectives of our total compensation strategy, namely, adequacy, equity, cost control, and balance?

In the following sections, we will discuss each of these points.

Long-Term Strategic Business Plans

Such plans outline the basic directions in which an organization wishes to move in the next 3 to 5 years. One strategic issue that should influence the design of benefits is an organization's stage of development. For example, a start-up venture probably will offer low base pay and benefits but high incentives; a mature firm with well-established products and substantial market share will probably offer much more generous pay and benefits combined with moderate incentives.

Other strategic considerations include the projected rate of employment growth, downsizing, geographic redeployment, acquisitions, centralization or decentralization, and expected changes in profitability.[5] Each of these conditions suggests a change in the optimum "mix" of benefits in order to be most consistent with an organization's business plans.

IBM'S NEW PRODUCT—EMPLOYEE BENEFITS[6]

Like most other companies, IBM has been looking for cost-effective ways to cut its annual cost of employee benefits (more than $1 billion per year). In 1992, it found one that is consistent with its long-term business plan to make each of its independent units a profit center. It spun off its huge human resource operation into a separate company called Workforce Solutions, which is now saving IBM more than $45 million annually in the form of reduced staffing, consolidation of offices, and use of new technology, such as automated telephones. In fact, the overall HR staff has shrunk by about a third, to 1500 employees. The spin-off provides customized services to each of IBM's 13 independent business units. Before, IBM took a one-size-fits-all approach to benefits. In addition, Workforce Solutions also handles business for other companies, such as the National Geographic Society, capitalizing on IBM's reputation for excellence and lots of practical experience in the benefits area. Beginning in 1994, each IBM unit is free to choose its own provider of benefits and HR functions. Workforce Solutions will have to compete for that business. If its early success is any indication, however, marketing internal operations to outsiders could turn benefits departments from drains on the bottom line to profit centers in their own right.

Characteristics of the Workforce

Young employees who are just starting out are likely to be more concerned with direct pay (e.g., for a house purchase) than with a generous pension program. Older workers may desire the reverse. Unionized workers may prefer a uniform benefits package, while single parents, older workers, or workers with disabilities may place heavy emphasis on flexible work schedules. Employers that hire large numbers of temporary or part-time workers may offer entirely different benefits to these groups. Only about 16.5 percent of firms give part-time employees all the health, retirement, and vacation benefits full-timers receive.[7]

Legal Requirements

The government plays a central role in the design of any benefits package. While controlling the cost of benefits is a major concern of employers, the social and economic welfare of citizens is the major concern of government.[8] As examples of such concern, consider the four income-maintenance laws shown in Table 12-1.

Income-maintenance laws were enacted to provide employees and their families with income security in case of death, disability, unemployment, or retirement.

At a broad level, government tax policy has had, and will continue to have, a major impact on the design of benefits programs. Two principles have had the greatest impact on benefits.[9] One is the *doctrine of constructive receipt*, which holds that an individual must pay taxes on benefits that have monetary value when the individual receives them. The other principle is the *antidiscrimination rule*, which holds that employers can obtain tax advantages only for those benefits that do not discriminate in favor of highly compensated employees. According to the Tax Reform Act of 1986, a highly compensated employee is one who owns at least 5 percent of company stock or partnership rights, is a company officer earning more than $45,000 a year, or earns more than $50,000 a year and has income in the top 20 percent of the general workforce. These dollar amounts are adjusted periodically.

■ TABLE 12 ▪ 1
FOUR MAJOR INCOME-MAINTENANCE LAWS

Law	Scope of coverage	Funding	Benefits	Adminstrative agency
Social Security Act (1935)	Full coverage for retirees, dependent survivors, and disabled persons insured by 40 quarters of payroll taxes on their past earnings or earnings of heads of households. Federal government employees hired prior to January 1, 1984, and railroad workers are excluded.	For 1994, payroll tax of 7.65% for employees and 7.65% for employers on the first $60,600 in earnings. Self-employed persons pay 15.3% of this wage base. Of the 7.65%, 6.2% is allocated for retirement, survivors, and disability insurance, and 1.45% for Medicare. The Omnibus Budget Reconciliation Act of 1993 extended the 1.45% Medicare payroll tax to all wages and self-employment income.	Full *retirement payments* after age 65, or at reduced rates after 62, to worker and spouse. Size of pension depends on past earnings. *Survivor benefits* for the family of a deceased worker or retiree. At age 65 a widow or widower receives the full age-65 pension granted to the deceased. A widow or widower of any age with dependent children under 16, and each unmarried child under 18, receives a 75% benefit check. *Disability benefits* to totally disabled workers, after a 5-month waiting period, as well as to their spouses and children. *Health insurance* for persons over 65 (Medicare). All benefits are adjusted upward whenever the consumer price index (CPI) increases more than 3% in a calendar year and trust funds are at a specified level. Otherwise the adjustment is based on the lower of the CPI increase or the increase in average national wages (1983 amendments).	Social Security Administration
Federal Unemployment Tax Act (1935)	All employees except some state and local government workers, domestic and farm workers, railroad workers, and some non-profit employees.	Payroll tax of at least 3.4% of first $7000 of earnings paid by employer. (Employees also taxed in Alaska, Alabama, and New Jersey.) States may raise both the percentage and base earnings taxed through legislation. Employer contributions may be reduced if state experience ratings for them are low.	Benefits average roughly 50% of average weekly earnings and are available for up to 26 weeks. Those eligible for benefits have been employed for some specified minimum period and have lost their jobs through no fault of their own. Most states exclude strikers. During periods of high unemployment, benefits may be extended for up to 52 weeks.	U.S. Bureau of Employment Security, U.S. Training and Employment Service, and the several state employment security commissions

(continues)

■ **TABLE 12 ▪ 1**

FOUR MAJOR INCOME-MAINTENANCE LAWS (*Cont.*)

Law	Scope of coverage	Funding	Benefits	Adminstrative agency
Workers' compensation (state laws)	Generally, employees of nonagricultural, private-sector firms are entitled to benefits for work-related accidents and illnesses leading to temporary or permanent disabilities.	One of the following options, depending on state law: self-insurance, insurance through a private carrier, or payroll-based payments to a state insurance system. Premiums depend on the riskiness of the occupation and the experience rating of the insured.	Benefits average about two-thirds of an employee's weekly wage and continue for the term of the disability. Supplemental payments are made for medical care and rehabilitative services. In case of a fatal accident, survivor benefits are payble.	Various state commissions
Employee Retirement Income Security Act (ERISA) (1974)	Private-sector employees over age 21 enrolled in noncontributory (100% employer-paid) retirement plans who have 1 year's service.	Employer contributions.	The 1986 Tax Reform Act authorizes several formulas to provide vesting of retirement benefits after a certain length of service (5–7 years). Once an employee is "vested," receipt of the pension is not contingent on future service. Authorizes tax-free transfer of vested benefits to another employer or to an individual retirement account ("portability") if a vested employee changes jobs and if the present employer agrees. Employers must fund plans on an actuarially sound basis. Pension trustees ("fiduciaries") must make prudent investments. Employers may insure vested benefits through the federal Pension Benefit Guaranty Corporation.	Department of Labor, Internal Revenue Service, Pension Benefit Guaranty Corporation

These two tax-policy principles define the conditions for the preferential tax treatment of benefits. Together they hold that if benefits discriminate in favor of highly paid or "key" employees, both the employer and the employee receiving those benefits may have to pay taxes on the benefits when they are transferred.

Social Security, which accounts for $1 of every $5 spent by the federal government, has had, and will continue to have, an effect on the growth, development, and design of employee benefits. National health policy increasingly is shifting costs to the private sector and emphasizing cost containment; such pressures will intensify. Finally, national policy on unfair discrimination, particularly through the civil rights laws, has caused firms to reexamine their benefit policies.

The Competitiveness of the Benefits Offered

The issue of benefits program competitiveness is much more complicated than that of salary competitiveness.[10] In the case of salary, both employees and management focus on the same item: direct pay. However, in determining the competitiveness of benefits, senior management tends to focus mainly on cost, while employees are more interested in value. The two may conflict. Thus employees' perceptions of the value of their benefits as competitive may lead to excessive costs, in the view of top management. On the other hand, achieving cost competitiveness provides no assurance that employees will perceive the benefits program as valuable to them.

HOW NIKE MATCHES PEOPLE WITH BENEFITS[11]

COMPANY
EXAMPLE

To attract and retain skilled workers, Nike enlists current employees to help enrich its benefits offerings. It starts by probing workers' fears, needs, and desires in focus groups and surveys, in which employees often express worries about not being able to buy a house, send their children to college, or care for elderly parents. Then Nike asks employee teams to design new benefits packages that offer more choices without raising costs. Some of the choices the teams come up with include company matching funds for college tuition, subsidies for child care or elder care, paid time off for family leave, group discounts on auto or home insurance, discounted mortgages, legal services, and financial planning advice.

Many of the new offerings are relatively cheap for the company. To contain costs further, Nike gives employees incentives to make health-benefits trade-offs, such as pledging to stop smoking or using company-chosen physician networks. By tailoring its benefits to those that employees really need and care deeply about, Nike is maximizing the return on its "benefits bucks."

Total Compensation Strategy

The broad objective of the design of compensation programs (that is, direct as well as indirect compensation) is to integrate salary and benefits into a package that will encourage the achievement of an organization's goals. For example, while a generous pension plan may help retain employees, it probably does little to motivate them to perform on a day-to-day basis. This is because the length of time between performance and reward is too great. On the other hand, a generous severance package offered to targeted segments of the employee population may facilitate an organization's objective of downsizing to a specified staffing level. In all cases, considerations of adequacy, equity, cost control, and balance should guide decision making in the context of a total compensation strategy.

With these considerations in mind, let us now examine some key components of the benefits package.

COMPONENTS OF THE BENEFITS PACKAGE

There are many ways to classify benefits, but we will follow the classification scheme used by the U.S. Chamber of Commerce. According to this system, benefits fall into three categories: security and health, payments for time not worked, and employee services. Within each of these categories there is a bewildering array of options. The following discussions consider only the most popular options and cover only those that have not been mentioned previously.

As we begin, consider how the costs of employer payments for benefits as a percentage of payroll have changed over time:[12]

	1955	1965	1975	1985	1992
PERCENT	20.3	24.7	35.4	37.7	40.2

As the saying goes, "You've come a long way, baby."

Security and Health Benefits

The following are included in the security and health category:

Life insurance

Workers' compensation

Disability insurance

Hospitalization, surgical, and maternity coverage

Health maintenance organizations (HMOs)

Other medical coverage

Sick leave

Pension plans

Social Security

Unemployment insurance

Supplemental unemployment insurance

Severance pay

Insurance is the basic building block of almost all benefits packages, for it protects employees against income loss caused by death, accident, or ill health. Most organizations provide *group* coverage for their employees. The plans may be contributory (in which employees share in the cost of the premiums) or noncontributory.

It used to be that when a worker switched jobs, he or she lost health insurance coverage. The worker had to "go naked" for months until coverage began at a new employer. No longer. Under the Consolidated Omnibus Budget Reconciliation Act (COBRA) of 1986, companies with at least 20 employees must make medical coverage available at group insurance rates for as long as 18 months after the employee leaves—whether the worker left voluntarily, retired, or was dismissed. The law also provides that, following a worker's death or divorce, the employee's family has the right to buy group-rate health insurance for as long as 3 years. Employers who do not comply can be sued and denied corporate tax deductions related to health benefits.[13]

However, since some corporate medical plans do not cover preexisting conditions, some employees have found that when they changed jobs (and health plans), their benefits were reduced sharply. To alleviate that problem, the 1989 budget act allows workers who encounter existing-condition clauses to retain medical coverage at their former jobs for selected periods of time, even if they join the health plan at their new company. Companies are allowed to charge former employees a bit more to retain coverage, but their costs are still likely to go up, since workers apt to take advantage of the law are those with serious medical problems.[14]

With this in mind, let us consider the major forms of security and health benefits commonly provided to employees.

Group Life Insurance. This type of insurance is usually yearly renewable term insurance; that is, each employee is insured 1 year at a time. The actual amounts of coverage vary, but one rule of thumb is to have it equal roughly 2 years' income. This amount provides a reasonable financial cushion to the surviving spouse during the difficult transition to a different way of life. Thus a manager making $40,000 per year may have a group term-life policy with a face value of $80,000 or $100,000. To discourage turnover, almost all companies cancel this benefit if an employee terminates.

Life insurance has been heavily affected by flexible benefits programs. Typically such programs provide a core of basic life coverage (e.g., $25,000) and then permit employees to choose greater coverage (e.g., in increments of $10,000 to $25,000) as part of their optional package.[15] Keep in mind, however, that the Omnibus Budget Reconciliation Act of 1987 imposed Social Security taxes on the cost of group term-life insurance carried by an employer for an employee.[16]

Workers' Compensation. As shown in Table 12-1, these payments vary by state. Disability benefits, which have been extended to cover stress (in four states) and occupational disease, tend to be highest in states where organized labor is strong.[17] With regard to stress, workers' compensation claims for mental stress peaked in 1987 and have been declining since.[18]

A state's industrial structure also plays a big part in setting disability-insurance rates. Thus serious injuries are more common and costly among Oregon loggers and Michigan machinists than among assembly line workers in a Texas semiconductor plant. Sometimes the costs can get out of hand, especially for small businesses. Consider Bartow, Florida, construction contractor Jean Stinson. Her company's liability insurance costs—of which workers' compensation is the biggest part—jumped 187 percent in one year, to $250,000. When she raised her bids to recoup the higher costs, customers put their projects on hold.[19] Trends such as these have prompted high-cost states, such as California, Florida, Michigan, and Maine, to lower workers' compensation premiums so that they can continue to attract and retain businesses in their states.

CONTROLLING THE COSTS OF WORKERS' COMPENSATION

COMPANY EXAMPLE

More than $60 billion is paid out to public and private insurers each year for workers' compensation costs. Some of the driving forces behind these costs are higher medical costs, the increasing involvement of attorneys, and widespread fraud. Recent studies indicate that as much as 20 percent or more of claims may involve cheating.[20] Figure 12-1 shows the differences in medical charges and days of treatment for identical conditions handled by ordinary health insurers, such as Blue Cross, and under the workers' compensation system. For back disorders, for example, the cost under workers' compensation was more than twice as high and treatment lasted more than twice as long. What are companies and insurers doing to control costs?

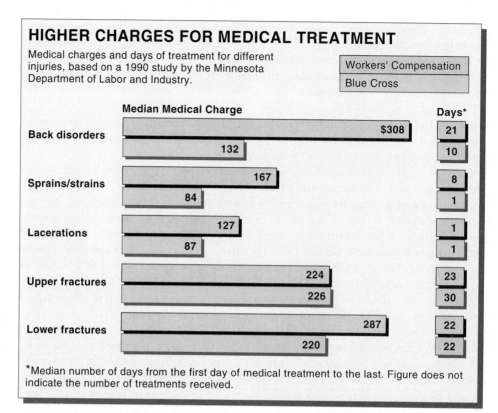

FIGURE 12-1
Comparisons of medical costs: workers' compensation versus Blue Cross. (*Source.* P. Kerr, Vast amount of fraud discovered in workers' compensation system, *The New York Times*, Dec. 29, 1991, p. 14.)

One approach is self-insurance, in which a company establishes its own disability fund. Stereo equipment maker Bose Corporation self-insured in 1991 after watching a 69 percent rise in premiums in only 3 years. Now it saves about $200,000 annually off the $1 million it used to pay in premiums.[21] Travelers Insurance Co. hired more than 600 workers' compensation claims investigators, reducing individual case loads by 50 percent. It also added 350 utilization-review nurses. Continental Insurance Co. uses ergonomists to review tasks at businesses it insures and recommend changes to reduce work-related injuries. ITT Hartford set up a toll-free telephone line for employers to report workplace injuries immediately. Payouts dropped by 33 percent. Finally, Orion Capital Corporation uses teams composed of nurses, attorneys, and investigators to determine whether a prospective client is committed to reducing costs.[22]

Is there an underlying theme in these approaches? Yes, and it's simple: aggressively manage workplace safety, and you will foster less-hostile relationships with injured workers.

At present, all 50 states have a workers' compensation law. While specific terms and levels of coverage vary by state, all state laws share the following features:[23]

■ All job-related injuries and illnesses are covered.

■ Coverage is provided regardless of who caused the injury or illness (i.e., regardless of who was "at fault").

- Payments are usually made through an insurance program financed by employer-paid premiums.
- A worker's loss is usually not covered fully by the insurance program. Most cash payments are at least two-thirds of the worker's weekly wage, but, together with disability benefits from Social Security, the payments may not exceed 80 percent of the worker's weekly wage.

Workers' compensation programs protect employees, dependents, and survivors against income loss resulting from total disability, partial disability, or death; medical expenses; and rehabilitation expenses.

Disability Insurance. Such coverage provides a supplemental one-time payment when death is accidental, and it provides a range of benefits when employees are disabled—that is, when they can't perform the "main functions" of their occupations.[24] Long-term disability (LTD) plans cover employees who are disabled 6 months or longer, usually at no more than 60 percent of their base pay, until they begin receiving pension benefits. Fewer than 50 percent of medium-size and large businesses provide such coverage, but, as one expert noted: "Long-term disability is more important than life insurance. The person is still alive and may have no income at all without such coverage."[25]

Typically, employees are delighted to have their companies pay their insurance premiums. Think again. If the company pays the premium and the day comes when an employee needs to collect benefits, the benefits are taxable to the employee as ordinary income. If the employee paid the premiums, the benefits would be tax-free.[26]

As an example, assume that an employee paid his own premiums (at 2 to 3 percent of annual income per year[27]) from age 40 to 50, then became disabled and remained that way to age 65. His policy would pay him $2000 a month, or $24,000 a year, tax-free. If he had to pay tax on the money at 28 percent, his monthly insurance check would drop from $2000 to $1440. Over the course of 15 years, taxes would consume $100,800 of the $360,000 he got.

LTD costs are extremely high. Based on seven case studies, *direct* nonmedical disability costs (visible plus hidden costs), given as a percentage of annual salary, for a manager earning $40,000 per year were as follows:[28]

	Hidden direct costs
Predisability productivity loss (prior 5 years)	28%
Postdisability productivity loss (until a replacement becomes fully productive)	39%
Replacement cost	30%
Retraining cost	32%
	Visible direct costs
Salary continuance until disability pay begins	48%
Disability payments (percentage of salary to age 65)	62%
Increased pension payments	15%
Increased life insurance	11%

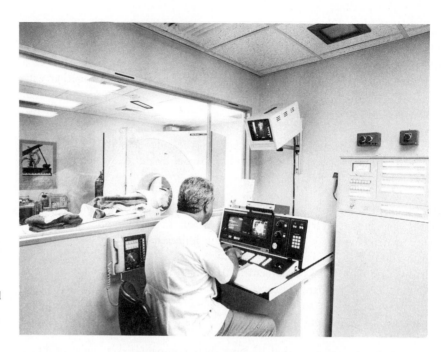

New technology has helped to make medical care better—and more expensive—than ever.

A manager earning $40,000 per year at age 40 who did not previously qualify for pension benefits will cost her or his employer, on average, over $848,000, excluding medical costs, until retirement age. If payment is not required as a lump sum, the net present value of the payments reduces the liability to $511,000.[29] This expenditure is still very large for one, possibly preventable, medical event.

Hospitalization, Surgical, and Maternity Coverage. These are essential benefits for most working Americans. Self-insurance is out of the question since the costs incurred by one serious, prolonged illness could easily wipe out a lifetime of savings and assets and place a family in debt for years to come. The U.S. health insurance system is based primarily on group coverage provided by employers. At a general level, the system is characterized by statistics such as the following:[30]

■ Most Americans have health insurance and receive excellent care. Except for the poor, especially in inner cities, Americans are healthier than ever.

■ Those over age 65 are covered by Medicare, but less than half of those living below the poverty line are covered by Medicaid. About 37 million Americans have no health insurance.[31]

■ Contrary to popular belief, most of the uninsured are jobholders—part-timers and per-day workers—the working poor. Small businesses and service businesses are especially likely not to provide insurance.

■ Insurance rates have climbed faster for small businesses than for large ones.

■ Whether employed or not, younger people, as well as African-American and Hispanic people, are most likely to lack health insurance. Americans with chronic diseases or a history of serious illness have trouble obtaining affordable insurance.

■ Figures on the number of uninsured people understate the extent of vulnerability. Over a recent 28-month period, one in four Americans spent at least a month without health insurance.

■ Polls indicate that most Americans are pleased with their doctors and hospitals. Yet there is widespread anxiety about the reliability of the system, especially as the price of medical care continues to soar at triple the rate of inflation (see Figure 12-2).

In 1993, for example, the United States medical tab exceeded $900 billion, up from $250 billion in 1980. The 14.4 percent of gross domestic product (the total value of retail prices of all goods and services produced in the United States in 1993) that was spent on medical care was about 25 percent higher than in other major industrialized countries, after adjusting for GDP and population differences.[32]

Both management and labor in the United States worry that a gap that large makes U.S. companies less competitive. At the level of the individual firm, General Motors Corp. estimates that health-care costs add $711 to the price of each car and truck it builds in North America.[33] Competitiveness issues arising from health-care costs are particularly acute at companies with the following three characteristics:

1. Their workforces are comprised largely of people in their 40s and 50s, who require more health care than younger workers do.

2. Their health plans cover a much larger number of retired workers than do those of newer companies, like computer or airline concerns.

3. They make products that must compete on world markets.[34]

For workers, the rapid rise in health-care costs has three key consequences. One, there is less money for pay increases. How much less? A study funded by the Service Employees International Union found that working families lost an average of $8398 in forgone wages between 1980 and 1992. In fact, every dollar increase in employer health premiums costs U.S. workers 88 cents in wages.[35] Two, the system promotes

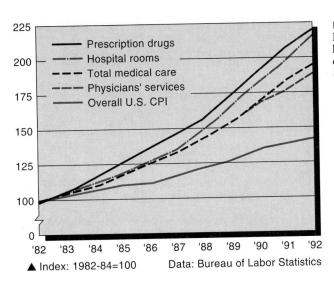

FIGURE 12-2
How health-care prices have risen. (*Source:* A crisis of medical success, *Business Week*, Mar. 15, 1993, p. 79.)

"job lock"—fear of changing jobs because of a medical history that in today's more stringent insurance market probably would prevent a worker's acceptance by a new health plan. Cancer patients and those with chronic diseases are most vulnerable.[36]

Three, because of an accounting regulation that took effect in 1992, companies must estimate health-care costs for both present and future retirees and report them on their balance sheets. The rule, *Statement No. 106*, issued by the Financial Accounting Standards Board, requires all companies to take two steps: they must set up a huge "catch-up" reserve for current and retired employees. And they must set aside a reserve each year to cover the postretirement medical benefits of employees who are currently working.

The impact on corporate profits is a record for any accounting rule change, as much as $1 trillion for major U.S. companies during the next few years.[37] As examples, consider that IBM took a $2.26 billion charge against earnings, Du Pont took a $4.8 billion charge, and GM took a whopping $20.8 billion charge to reflect its liability. Experts predict that as many as 95 percent of employers either are cutting back on retirees' health benefits or will do so eventually. Thus, to cut its $1.5 billion liability, McDonnell Douglas decided to end coverage for its 20,000 retirees by 1996. Unisys, facing a $700 million liability, told most of its 25,000 retirees that they must start bearing the entire cost of their health insurance in 1996.[38] The list goes on and on.

Companies say the changes are necessary if they are to remain profitable, protecting their current employees and stockholders. Advocates of retirees see the changes as nothing less than a betrayal of promises made earlier. Are all retirees so vulnerable? The answer is probably yes, unless one is covered by a union contract or a personal employment contract. Normally, benefit-plan descriptions note that the company can modify or cancel coverage. So far, courts have upheld that right, no matter what verbal assurances company officials may have given workers when they retired.[39]

Why is all this happening? What's driving these increases in the cost of health care? Figure 12-3 shows that, in addition to population changes, general inflation, and excess medical inflation (including administrative costs that absorb one-fifth of the country's health-care spending[40]), a key factor is the cost of new technology.

The United States relies far more heavily on health-care technology than do other advanced nations. On a per capita basis, for example, the United States has four times as many diagnostic imaging machines (magnetic resonance imaging) as Germany and eight times as many as Canada. U.S. doctors perform open-heart surgery 2.6 times as often as Canadian doctors and 4.4 times as often as German doctors. When it comes

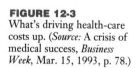

FIGURE 12-3
What's driving health-care costs up. (*Source:* A crisis of medical success, *Business Week*, Mar. 15, 1993, p. 78.)

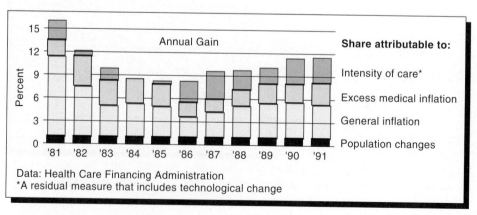

to the use of "smart" machines to perform medical tests, one expert noted: "There's no way to shut it off. The doctors crave it, it's reassuring, and patients crave it."[41] On top of that, hospitals often push to buy the latest machines in order to retain their competitive status as full-service, modern health-care centers.

Cost-Containment Strategies. Strategies to contain the runaway cost of health care are taking center stage in the boardroom as well as in the health-care industry itself. Here are some measures that firms have taken to gain tighter management control over the cost of health care:

1. *Raise deductibles and copayments by employees.* Such steps are a belated adjustment for inflation. Plans with $50 deductibles were established in the 1950s, when that sum paid for 2 days in the hospital; now it does not cover room-only costs for a 4-hour stay in an outpatient clinic. Furthermore, copayments by employees may encourage more responsible use of the health-care system. Employees are clearly bearing more of the economic load. Thus, over a 1-year period, Georgia-Pacific Corp. raised its deductibles 50 percent—to $300 a year for individuals and $600 a year for families.[42]

2. *Induce employees voluntarily to choose reduced medical coverage through flexible benefit plans* (more on this shortly).

3. *Remove the irrational incentives in plans that favor hospitalization over less costly outpatient care.* For example, Sperry Corp. pays 100 percent for home health care but less if an employee checks into a hospital.[43]

4. *Require a second surgical opinion prior to elective surgery.* At Chrysler and J. C. Penney, for example, if an employee fails to get a second opinion, the company will not pay the entire bill. One study of such programs estimates they could save $2.63 for every dollar spent on second opinions.

5. *If employees must go to the hospital, set some rules.* Refuse to let them enter on the weekend if treatment is not scheduled until Monday. Have large hospital bills audited (this could cut expenses by as much as 8 percent). At Texas Utilities, if workers find errors in their hospital bills they get half the savings, up to $500. Require preadmission certification, that is, doctor's clearance for the treatment desired for the employee before he or she enters the hospital. If additional treatment or tests are given, refuse to pay bills unless doctors can confirm that a deviation from the original plan was necessary. For example, Merrill Lynch pays doctors to review other doctors' medical-procedure recommendations.[44]

This strategy has been termed "managed care," and it is being offered by large insurers such as Cigna Corp. One of its clients is Allied-Signal Corp. and its 86,500 employees and their dependents. Managed care relies on a "gatekeeper" system of cost controls. The gatekeeper is a primary-care physician who monitors the medical history and care of each employee and his or her family. The doctor orders testing, makes referrals to specialists, and recommends hospitalization, surgery, or outpatient care, as appropriate. To make this approach pay off, Cigna must deliver high-quality medical care and still keep a tight lid on medical expenses. Yet Allied-Signal embraced the plan. Why? Its health-care bill escalated 39 percent in the year before it adopted managed care.[45] Managed care may take a variety of forms. In our next section we discuss one of the most popular, the health maintenance organization (HMO).

HMOs

An *HMO* is an organized system of health care that assures the delivery of services to employees who enroll voluntarily under a prepayment plan. The emphasis is on preventive medicine, that is, maintaining the health of each employee. Legally, HMOs are authorized under the HMO Act of 1973.

The objective of HMOs is to control health-care costs by keeping people out of the hospital. Deere & Co., the agricultural equipment manufacturer, used to pay for a staggering 1400 hospital days each year for every 1000 workers. Then, in 1980, Deere took the lead in helping local doctors to establish an HMO, and annual hospitalization has since dropped to 500 days per thousand workers. Yet there are drawbacks. Plan members give up the freedom to choose their doctors, and for companies with scattered employment sites, the location of the HMO may be inconvenient.

HMOs covered about 41 million Americans in 1993. By comparison, Medicare and Medicaid covered about 58 million people, and insurance companies insured or administered plans for the 120 million who were not in HMOs. While the HMO industry is dominated by independent companies such as Kaiser Permanente and U.S. Healthcare Corp., insurance companies have invested billions to set up HMOs. In fact, insurance companies operate 4 of every 10 HMOs nationwide. For example, Cigna has the biggest presence in the HMO field. It operates HMOs in 42 markets, covers 2.2 million people, and has 95,000 doctors on contract.[46]

Do HMOs save employers money? A recent study by Northwestern National Life Insurance analyzed $556 million in claims and found that employers saved $400 per employee annually, or as much as 11 percent on health-care costs, if they used HMOs or preferred providers and explored alternative treatments at lower costs.[47] Yet HMOs have not contained the rise in health-care costs as effectively as many had hoped.[48] As Figure 12-4 shows, HMO costs have risen almost as fast as those of private doctors. Nevertheless, their relatively low out-of-pocket costs still make them popular among employees, particularly on the West Coast, where enrollments run as high as 60 percent or more of some employee groups.

To overcome some employees' complaints about the lack of freedom to choose their doctors in an HMO, some firms have contracted with organizations of health-care professionals (including physicians, dentists, and hospitals), so-called preferred provider organizations (PPOs), to deliver health-care services at reduced rates and with close utilization review. In return, the PPO is guaranteed a certain volume of patients.[49] A summary of alternative types of managed care plans, HMOs, PPOs, and point-of-service plans, is presented in Table 12-2.

FIGURE 12-4
How much cheaper are HMOs? This chart tracks the percentage increases in health-care costs and shows that HMO costs have risen almost as fast as those of private doctors. (*Source:* How much cheaper are HMOs? *Time,* Nov. 8, 1992, p. 20.)

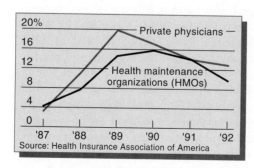

■ TABLE 12 ■ 2
THE ABCs OF MANAGED CARE

Plan	How it works	What you pay	Benefits
Health maintenance organization (HMO)	A specified group of doctors and hospitals provide the care. And a gatekeeper must approve all services before they are performed.	There isn't a deductible. The nominal fees generally range from nothing to $15 a visit depending on the service performed.	Virtually all services are covered, including preventive care. Out-of-pocket costs tend to be lower than for any other managed-care plan.
Preferred-provider organization (PPO)	In-network care comes from a specified group of physicians and hospitals. You can pay extra to get care from outside the network. There generally isn't a gatekeeper.	The typical yearly family deductible is $400. The plan pays 80% to 100% for what's done within the network but only 50% to 70% for services rendered outside it.	Preventive services may be covered. There are lower deductibles and copayments for in-network care than for out-of-network care.
Point-of-service plan (POS)	POSs combine the features of HMOs and PPOs. Patients can get care in or out of the network, but there is an in-network gatekeeper who must approve all services.	In addition to a deductible, there is a flat $5 to $15 fee for in-network care, and you pay 20% to 50% of the bills for care you get outside the network.	Preventive services are generally covered. And there are low out-of-pocket costs for the care you get in the network.

Source: The ABCs of managed care, *Money,* July 1993, p. 115.

Other Medical Coverage

Medical coverage in areas such as dental care, vision care, drug abuse, alcoholism, and mental illness is increasing. For example, mental health and substance abuse treatment cost U.S. companies $245 per employee in 1992. That was nearly 10 percent of their total health-care expenses, up from 5 percent in 1982.[50] As for dental care, dental HMOs are growing fast. As with medical HMOs, a dental plan is usually paid a set annual fee per employee. There were approximately 13.5 million enrollees in dental HMOs in 1993, up from 10.4 million in 1991.[51]

Sick-Leave Programs

These programs provide short-term insurance to workers against loss of wages due to short-term illness. However, in many firms such well-intentioned programs have often *added* to labor costs because of abuse by employees and because of the wide-spread perception that sick leave is a right and that if it is not used, it will be lost ("use it or lose it"). To overcome the negative effects of sick-pay programs, one firm instituted a "well-pay program" that rewards employees for *not* being absent or sick.[52] Over a 1-year period, the firm barely broke even after paying out well-pay bonuses.

Pensions

A *pension* is a sum of money paid at regular intervals to an employee (or to his or her dependents) who has retired from a company and is eligible to receive such benefits. Before World War II, private pensions were rare. However, two developments in the late 1940s stimulated their growth: (1) clarification of the tax treatment of employer contributions and (2) the 1948 Inland Steel case, in which the National Labor

Relations Board ruled that pensions were subject to compulsory collective bargaining.[53]

For a time there were no standards and little regulation, which led to abuses in funding many pension plans and to the denial of pension benefits to employees who had worked many years. Perhaps the most notorious example of this occurred in 1963, when Studebaker closed its South Bend, Indiana, car factory and stopped payments to the seriously underfunded plan that covered the workers. Only those already retired or on the verge of retirement received the pension benefits they expected. Others got only a fraction—or nothing.[54]

Incidents like these led to the passage of the Employee Retirement Income Security Act (ERISA; see Table 12-1) in 1974. Despite increased regulation, ERISA has generally been beneficial. In 1960, only 9 percent of retirees received a private pension. In 1993, about 30 percent did, and by 2004, 88 percent will.[55]

Today, 91 percent of full-time workers at companies with more than 100 employees enjoy pension coverage. Yet only 26 percent of workers at mostly rural companies with 60 or fewer employees are covered.[56] In total, 870,000 pension, profit-sharing, and savings plans cover 76 million participants and retirees.[57] They paid retirees $220 billion in 1988, half again as much as the $148 billion that Social Security paid out.[58]

Money set aside by employers to cover pension obligations has become the nation's largest source of capital.[59] Pension funds hold 26 percent of the company equity and 15 percent of the taxable bonds in the U.S. economy, for a total of $2.5 trillion.[60] That's roughly $8000 for every man, woman, and child in the United States! This is an enormous force in the nation's (and the world's) capital markets.

Pension fund managers tend to invest for the long term, and the big corporate pension funds (95 percent of pension fund assets are covered by 5 percent of the plans) have less than 1 percent of their assets invested in leveraged buyouts or high-risk, high-yield junk bonds.[61]

In general, the financial health of most private pension plans is good.[62] However, to ensure that covered workers will receive their accrued benefits even if their companies fail, ERISA created the Pension Benefit Guaranty Corporation (PBGC). This agency acts as an insurance company, collecting annual premiums from companies with defined-benefit plans that spell out specific payments upon retirement. A company can still walk away from its obligation to pay pension benefits to employees entitled to receive them, but it must then hand over up to 30 percent of its net worth to the PBGC for distribution to the affected employees.

Since 1974, the PBGC has taken over 1476 pension plans of companies that went out of business or could not finance their retirement plans. Payouts increased from $36 million in 1979 to $300 million in 1989.[63] To shore up the PBGC, a 1993 task force recommended that Congress force companies with underfunded pension plans to pay higher insurance premiums until they fund their plans adequately.[64] While that might seem extreme, consider that the PBGC insures the pensions of one out of every three U.S. workers. It is important that, as retirees, most workers end up getting nearly all that is promised to them—and they do.

How Pension Plans Work. Contributions to pension funds are typically managed by trustees or outside financial institutions, frequently insurance companies. As an incentive for employers to begin and maintain such plans, the government defers taxes on the pension contributions and their earnings. Retirees pay taxes on the money as they receive it.

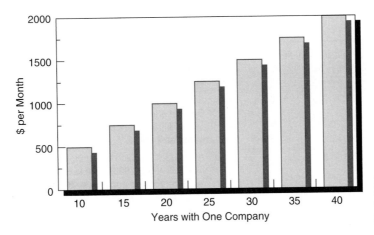

FIGURE 12-5
Monthly pension for a worker whose final average pay is $40,000 per year.

Traditionally, most big corporate plans have been *defined-benefit plans,* under which an employer promises to pay a retiree a stated pension, often expressed as a percentage of preretirement pay. In 1993, 66 percent of medium and large companies (those with 500 or more employees) offered them.[65] The most common formula is 1.5 percent of average salary over the last 5 years prior to retirement ("final average pay") times the number of years employed. In determining final average pay, the company may use base pay alone or base pay plus bonuses and other compensation. Standard Oil of Ohio uses the former method, Standard Oil of California the latter.[66] An example of a monthly pension for a worker earning final average pay of $40,000 a year, as a function of years of service, is shown in Figure 12-5. When combined with Social Security benefits, that percentage is often about 50 percent of final average pay. The company then pays into the fund each year whatever is needed to cover expected benefit payments.

A second type of pension plan, popular as a support to an existing defined-benefit plan, is called a *defined-contribution plan.* Examples include stock bonuses, savings plans, profit sharing, and various kinds of employee stock-ownership plans. Brief descriptions of five types of such plans are shown in Table 12-3.

Defined-contribution plans fix a rate for employer contributions to the fund. Future benefits depend on how fast the fund grows. Such plans therefore favor young employees who are just beginning their careers (because they contribute for many years). Defined-benefit plans favor older, long-service workers.

Defined-contribution plans have great appeal for employers because a company will never owe more than what was contributed. However, since the amount of benefits received depends on the investment performance of the monies contributed, employees cannot be sure of the size of their retirement checks. In fact, regardless of whether a plan is a defined-benefit or defined-contribution plan, employees will not know what the *purchasing power* of their pension checks will be, because the inflation rate is variable.

What appears to be evolving is a system that will make employees (instead of employers) more responsible for how much money they have for retirement. Effective January 1994, the Labor Department adopted rules that protect employers from lawsuits by employees disappointed with the returns on their investments. This obstacle had prevented many companies from offering a wide range of savings and pension plans to their workers. Employers are immune from suits if (1) they give

■ **TABLE 12 ▪ 3**

FIVE TYPES OF DEFINED-CONTRIBUTION PENSION PLANS

Profit-sharing plan	The company puts a designated amount of its profits into each employee's account and then invests the money. ESOPs are a form of profit sharing.
ESOP	An employee stock ownership plan pays off in company stock. Each employee gets shares of company stock that are deposited into a retirement account. Dividends from the stock are then added to the account.
401(k) plan	A program in which an employee can deduct up to $8994 of his or her income (in 1993) from taxes and place the money into a personal retirement account. Many employers add matching funds, and the combined sums grow tax-free until they are withdrawn, usually at retirement.
Money purchase plan	A set percentage of each employee's salary, up to 25% in an incorporated business (20% if self-employed), is contributed by the employer to each employee's account. Employees must be vested. Annual investment earnings and losses are added to or subtracted from the account balances.
Simplified employee pension	Under SEP, a small-business employer can contribute up to 15% of an employee's salary tax-free, but no more than $30,000, to an Individual Retirement Account. The employee is vested immediately for the amount paid into the account. The employee cannot withdraw any funds before age 59-1/2 without penalty.

workers a choice of at least three investment vehicles, each of which differs in risk and return; and (2) they communicate with workers about the relative performance of each option at least quarterly. This allows each employee to decide whether to switch from one vehicle to another if, say, the stock market is slumping and he or she wants to move into fixed-income securities.[67]

The ideal pension plan is one that is adjusted (indexed) each year to maintain the purchasing power of the dollar according to changes in the cost of living. *ERISA does not require indexing.* Although Social Security benefits have been indexed to changes in the consumer price index since 1975, between 1984 and 1989 only 24 percent of all pension plans gave retirees one or more cost-of-living increases.[68] For example, Aetna and Grumman both use the consumer price index as a basis for adjusting pension payments, but they limit the maximum yearly increase to 3 percent. Pension managers strongly resist indexation for two reasons: (1) the amount of money paid out will increase for those already retired and (2) larger reserves have to be set aside to fund future increases on a sound basis. Tying pensions to inflation could add 1 to 2 percent of payroll to an employer's retiree costs, on top of the 4 to 7 percent of payroll that companies now set aside.[69]

Unisex Pensions. Nathalie Norris, an employee of the state of Arizona, paid $199 per month into an annuity retirement plan offered by the state—the amount deducted from the paychecks of both male and female state employees earning the same salary. But Norris discovered that upon retirement she would get $34 per month less than male employees. This figure was based on actuarial tables showing that women, on average, live longer than men. Norris sued the state, and in a 1983 Supreme Court ruling, she won. The Court ruled that federal laws prohibiting sex discrimination in employment also bar employee-sponsored retirement plans that pay men higher benefits than women. Starting August 1, 1983, all contributions to such plans must be used to finance a system of equal payments to employees of both sexes. However, the Court denied retroactive relief to women, which could have cost insurance companies as much as $1.2 billion annually.[70] As a result of this ruling, many insurance companies have developed "merged-gender mortality tables" that show the combined number of persons living, the combined number of persons dying, and the merged-gender mortality rate for each age. The effect on benefits depends on the income option(s) elected at the time retirement income begins. For men aged 65, this could mean a monthly income decrease of up to 8 percent, while for women aged 65, it could mean a monthly income increase of up to 8 percent.[71]

Pension Reforms That Benefit Women. These reforms were incorporated into the Retirement Equity Act of 1984. Corporate pension plans must now include younger workers and permit longer breaks in service. Women typically start work at a younger age than do men, and they are more likely to stop working for several years in order to have and care for children. However, since the new rules apply to both sexes, men also will accrue larger benefits. There are five major changes under the act:[72]

1. As of January 1, 1985, pension plans must include all employees 21 or older (down from 25). This provision extended pension coverage to an additional 600,000 women and 500,000 men.

2. Employers must use 18 rather than 22 as the starting age for counting years of service. Typically employees need 10 years of service to be fully "vested," or entitled to receive their pensions regardless of any future service. Thus a worker hired at age 19 can join a plan at 21 and can be fully vested by age 29.

3. Employees may have breaks in service of as long as 5 years before losing credit for prior years of work. In addition, a year of maternity or paternity leave cannot be considered a break in service.

4. Pension benefits may now be considered a joint asset in divorce settlements. State courts can award part of an individual's pension to the ex-spouse.

5. Employers must provide survivor benefits to spouses of fully vested employees who die before reaching the minimum retirement age.

Social Security

Provisions for this program were outlined in Table 12-1. Social Security is an income-maintenance program, not a pension program. It is the nation's best defense against poverty for the elderly, and it has worked well. Without it, according to one study, the poverty rate among the elderly would have jumped from 12.4 to 47.6 percent.[73] Table 12-4 shows maximum and average Social Security benefits for 1994.

Actually, Social Security beneficiaries get back what they paid with interest by age 71; anything after that is free.[74] Nevertheless, in combination, Social Security and private pensions typically provide just 67 percent of preretirement income for middle-income Americans who are covered by employer pension plans. That's well below the coverage in Western European countries, which ranges from 74 percent in Germany to 92 percent in the Netherlands. In Japan, the rate is 79 percent.[75] Figure 12-6 shows

■ **TABLE 12 ▪ 4**

1994 SOCIAL SECURITY BENEFITS—MONTHLY

Maximum monthly benefit for a person retiring in 1994 at age 65	$1120
Average benefits for:	
All retired workers	660
Retired couples	1120
Young widows with two eligible children	1318
Older widows without children	611

FIGURE 12-6
Where retirees get their income. (*Source: Supplementing Social Security, USA Today,* Apr. 7, 1992, p. 11A.)

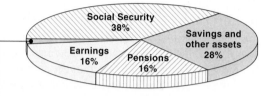

Supplemental Security Income (SSI) 2%

the current distribution of retirees' income, on average. Just over half (54%) comes from Social Security and pensions; the rest comes primarily from personal savings and current earnings in retirement.

The Congressional Budget Office projects that the system will be solvent through the year 2030. At that time, however, given the large number of retirements by baby boomers, Social Security tax outlays will exceed tax revenues. To meet such long-term funding needs, the system will have to be reformed again.

Actually, one element of reform is already in place, thanks to the 1983 Social Security amendments. The normal retirement age will increase from 65 in two stages. It will rise to 66 in 2005 and to 67 in 2022. Actually, the idea of retiring at age 65 is increasingly archaic. If 65 was the proper retirement age in the United States in 1940, then today, based on rising life expectancy, it should be 73.[76]

INTERNATIONAL APPLICATION: SOCIAL SECURITY IN OTHER COUNTRIES

Many countries outside the United States have adopted pension programs that combine Social Security with private retirement accounts. In Britain, for example, workers can opt out of part of the state pension system by applying up to 44 percent of their Social Security tax to their own private individual investment accounts. Japan, Finland, Sweden, France, and Switzerland have similar programs. In these countries, the Social Security component of the pension system remains on a pay-as-you-go basis in which current tax receipts are used to pay for both current benefits and other government programs.

Singapore uses a payroll tax to fund retirement, but it works like a private pension system. The revenues are invested in individually owned accounts; unlike U.S. Social Security taxes, they are tax-deductible and not subject to income taxes.

Employees can withdraw money from their retirement funds to purchase housing, and, as a result, 80 percent of Singapore's citizens own their own residences. If an employee is dissatisfied with the return earned by the public fund, he or she can transfer the account to investments in the

Singapore stock market or other approved vehicles. The asset balance in a Singaporean's retirement fund passes to his or her beneficiaries upon death. Among the countries that have systems similar to Singapore's are India, Kenya, Malaysia, Zambia, and Indonesia.[77]

Unemployment Insurance

Although 97 percent of the workforce is covered by federal and state unemployment-insurance laws, each worker must meet eligibility requirements in order to receive benefits. That is, an unemployed worker must (1) be able and available to work and be actively seeking work, (2) not have refused suitable employment, (3) not be unemployed because of a labor dispute (except in Rhode Island and New York), (4) not have left a job voluntarily, (5) not have been terminated for gross misconduct, and (6) have been employed previously in a covered industry or occupation, earning a designated minimum amount for a specific minimum amount of time. Many claims are disallowed for failure to satisfy one or more of these requirements.

Every unemployed worker's benefits are "charged" against one or more companies. The more money paid out on behalf of a firm, the higher is the unemployment insurance rate for that firm.

The tax in most states amounts to 6.2 percent of the first $7000 earned by each worker. The state receives 5.4 percent of this 6.2 percent, and the remainder goes to the federal government. However, the tax rate may fall to 0 percent in some states for employers who have had no recent claims by former employees, and it may rise to 10 percent for organizations with large numbers of layoffs. Nationwide, the average cost fell throughout the 1980s, to an average of $224 per worker in 1989.[78]

This decline was due partly to the generally buoyant economy that saw fewer people filing claims. However, it was also due to a growing sensitivity by state governments that high unemployment-insurance taxes can be a black eye on a state's business climate. In 1987, for example, unemployment taxes per worker varied from a high of $680 in Alaska to a low of $112 in New Hampshire.[79] Benefit levels have generally kept up with inflation. They average about 35 percent of what workers were earning at their last jobs.[80]

Supplemental Unemployment Insurance

This type of insurance is common in the auto, steel, rubber, flat glass, and farm equipment industries. Employers contribute to a special fund for this purpose. Initially, the primary purpose of such plans was to replace employees' pay during seasonal layoffs, but the provisions also apply in the case of permanent layoffs. Such plans, when combined with unemployment compensation, usually replace nearly all after-tax base wages for 6 months, with extensions under certain conditions. Only 8 percent of employees are covered by supplemental unemployment insurance plans, but most others are protected by some form of severance pay. Both types of arrangements are covered by ERISA, and this point has been affirmed by the Supreme Court.[81]

Severance Pay

Such pay is not legally required, and, because of unemployment compensation, many firms do not offer it. However, severance pay has been used extensively by firms that are downsizing in order to provide a smooth outflow of employees.[82] This is a good example of the strategic use of compensation. Thus Philadelphia Electric Co. gave an extra 9 months' severance pay to 1859 older workers who agreed to stagger their early retirements over a 2-year period. Roughly 17 percent of the workforce took advantage of the offer.[83] Said an executive of the firm: "If we lost all of them at once, we couldn't keep our electricity going."

Length of service, organization level, and the cause of the termination are key factors that affect the size of severance agreements. Most lower-level employees receive 1 week of pay for each year they work for a company.[84] Executives earning $50,000 to $150,000 a year can expect 8 months' pay, and for those making $150,000 to $200,000, the average is 11 months' pay. Chief executive officers with management contracts may receive 2 to 3 years of salary in the event of a takeover.[85] How is severance handled in other countries? In Japan, ousted chief executives receive an average of 2.5 times their annual compensation. They get at least 2 years' pay in the Netherlands, Belgium, and Germany.[86]

Payments for Time Not Worked

Included in this category are such benefits as the following:

Vacations	Personal excused absences
Holidays	Grievances and negotiations
Reporting time	Sabbatical leaves

COMPANY EXAMPLE

PAID PUBLIC-SERVICE LEAVES AT XEROX

Some employees work with persons with disabilities, others do alcohol and drug counseling, and still others do preretirement counseling. All are Xerox employees on 1-year leaves with full pay. Social commitment is a driving force behind the Xerox program, begun in 1971, but it is not the only rationale for the leaves. Public-service leaves boost the morale and skills of employees, according to those responsible for the program, and they make Xerox a more desirable place to work. Former leave takers say their careers were not affected by the leaves, and many feel their careers were advanced. Nevertheless, the program also has its problems. Of 131 leave takers surveyed, 40 percent reported major or moderate reentry difficulties on returning to work. More than one-third have quit, regarding their Xerox work as "not very rewarding or extremely unrewarding," in contrast with their high opinion of volunteer work. Many reported that their Xerox bosses acted as if they had been let down because the employees had left. Despite these problems, Xerox aims to continue the program, at a direct cost of about $500,000 per year. Employees want such a program, and society needs them.[87]

Employee Services

A broad group of benefits falls into the employee services category. Employees qualify for them purely by virtue of their membership in the organization, and not because of merit. Some examples are:

Tuition aid	Thrift and short-term savings plans
Credit unions	Stock purchase plans
Auto insurance	Fitness and wellness programs
Food service	Moving and transfer allowances
Company car	Transportation and parking
Career clothing	Merchandise purchasing
Legal services	Christmas bonuses
Counseling	Service and seniority awards
Child adoption	Umbrella liability coverage
Child care	Social activities
Elder care	Referral awards
Gift matching	Purchase of used equipment
Charter flights	Family leaves

Provisions of the Family and Medical Leave Act were discussed in Chapter 4. That law gives workers up to 12 weeks of unpaid, job-protected leave with health benefits each year to care for a new child, ailing relative, or one's own illness. At a broader level, family-friendly benefits are less expensive and more easily controlled than are open-ended perks like health insurance. As a result, more and more companies are permitting employees to follow flexible schedules, share jobs, or work at home. American Express Travel-Related Services is typical. Its program of "flexible work arrangements" includes flextime, job sharing, gradual return after family leave, compressed workweeks, and telecommuting.[88] RJR Nabisco guarantees college loans for most employees' children; the company also allows workers to put aside tuition money in a tax-deferred savings plan with a dollar-for-dollar company match, up to $1000 a year for 4 years.[89]

Unfortunately, at many companies these benefits go begging, sometimes as a result of employees' lack of knowledge that they exist, sometimes as a result of cultural norms. Consider paternity leave as an example. Very few men ever take advantage of it. Why? Largely because of fear of adverse consequences to their careers. As one

ETHICAL DILEMMA: TO ACCEPT OR NOT TO ACCEPT GIFTS?

Nearly 9 out of every 10 companies surveyed by the Bureau of National Affairs limit employees' abilities to accept gifts from clients and outside business contacts. They do so to avoid even the appearance of a conflict of interest. At Price Waterhouse, such gifts may not exceed $50 in value, while policies at Aetna, 3M, and Motorola do not set specific limits, thus leaving the appropriateness to the judgment of the recipient.

However, even as companies broadcast their policies to the rank and file, some top executives may be participating in golf tournaments, sitting in stadium skyboxes, and riding chartered jets courtesy of clients and suppliers. Said one observer: "People have come to look on these things as perquisites—untaxed compensation that you get when you're in the right job."[90] Is this a double standard? Is it a conflict of interest? If your answer to these questions is "yes," develop a policy that takes into account the interest of all parties and that, in your view, is ethical and just.

manager noted, "No CEO would ever speak out against family leave. It's subtle, unspoken, never in print—it's just the way the game is played. If you're in an environment where the nature of the business is chaotic, you just can't afford to be gone if you want to be a player."[91]

BENEFITS ADMINISTRATION

Benefits and Equal Employment Opportunity

Equal employment opportunity requirements also affect the administration of benefits. Consider as examples health-care coverage and pensions. Effective in 1987, an amendment to the Age Discrimination in Employment Act eliminated mandatory retirement at any age. It also requires employers to continue the same group health-insurance coverage offered to younger employees to employees over the age of 70. Medicare payments are limited to what Medicare would have paid for in the absence of a group health plan and to the actual charge for the services. This is another example of government "cost shifting" to the private sector.

The Older Workers Benefit Protection Act of 1990 restored age discrimination protection to employee benefits, a notion that had been scrapped by a 1989 Supreme Court decision. However, early retirement offers are now legal if they are offered at least 45 days prior to the decision, and, if they are accepted, employees are given 7 days to revoke them. Employers were also granted some flexibility in plant closings to offset retiree health benefits or pension sweeteners against severance pay. That is, an employer is entitled to deny severance pay if an employee is eligible for retiree health benefits.

With regard to pensions, the IRS considers a plan *discriminatory* unless the employer's contribution for the benefit of lower-paid employees covered by the plan is comparable to contributions for the benefit of higher-paid employees. An example of this is a salary reduction plan [known as 401(k)], described briefly in Table 12-3. The plan permits significant savings out of pretax compensation, produces higher take-home pay, and results in lower Social Security taxes. The catch: *the plan has to be available to everyone in any company that implements it.* Maximum employee contributions each year ($8994 in 1993) are indexed to changes in the cost of living, and about 60 percent of those eligible—at all income levels—are salting away part of their earnings in such plans.[92] Currently, 86 percent of employers with 401(k) plans give employees between 50 cents and a dollar for every dollar the employees contribute.[93] Together, the tax deferral and matching features can add up to produce handsome results: a worker making the 1993 maximum contribution with a 50 percent employer match, and earning an annual 9 percent return, would take just under 24 years to reach $1 million.

Costing Benefits

Despite the high cost of benefits, many employees take them for granted. A major reason for this is that employers have failed to do in-depth cost analyses of their benefit programs and thus have not communicated the value of their benefits programs to employees. Four approaches are used widely to express the costs of employee benefits and services. Although each has value individually, a combination of all four often enhances their impact on employees. The four methods are:[94]

■ TABLE 12 ▪ 5
EMPLOYEE BENEFITS: THE FORGOTTEN EXTRAS

Listed below are the benefits for the average full-time employee of Sun, Inc. (annual salary $28,000).

Benefit	Who pays	Sun's annual cost	Percentage of base earnings	What the employee receives
Health, dental, and life insurance	Sun and employee	$2,242.80	8.01	Comprehensive health and dental plus life insurance equivalent to 1 times your annual salary
Holidays	Sun	1,400.00	5.00	13 paid holidays
Annual leave (vacation)	Sun	1,078.00	3.85	10 days vacation per year (additional days starting with sixth year of service)
Sick days	Sun	1,290.80	4.61	12 days annually
Company retirement	Sun	3,060.40	10.93	Vested after 5 years of service
Social Security	Sun and employee	1,876.00	6.70	Retirement and disability benefits
Workers' compensation and unemployment insurance	Sun	280.00	1.00	Compensation if injured on duty and if eligible; income while seeking employment
Total		11,228.00 or $5.40 per hour	40.10	

The dollar amount and percentages will differ slightly depending upon the employee's salary. If an employee's annual salary is less than $28,000, the percentage of base pay will be greater. If the employee's salary is greater than $28,000, the percentage will be less but the dollar amount will be greater. Benefit costs to Sun, Inc., on behalf of 5480 employees are more than $61,500,000 per year.

■ *Annual cost of benefits for all employees*—Valuable for developing budgets and for describing the total cost of the benefits program

■ *Cost per employee per year*—the total annual cost of each benefits program divided by the number of employees participating in it

■ *Percentage of payroll*—the total annual cost divided by total annual payroll (this figure is valuable in comparing benefits costs across organizations)

■ *Cents per hour*—the total annual cost of benefits divided by the total number of hours worked by all employees during the year

A company example of actual benefits costs (for a fictitious firm named Sun, Inc.) is presented in Table 12-5. All four methods of costing benefits have been incorporated into the table. Can you find an example of each?

Cafeteria, or Flexible, Benefits

The theory underlying this approach to benefits is simple: instead of all workers at a company getting the same benefits, each worker can pick and choose among alternative options "cafeteria style." Thus the elderly bachelor might pass up maternity coverage for additional pension contributions. The mother whose children are covered under her husband's health insurance may choose legal and auto insurance instead.

The typical plan works like this: Workers are offered a package of benefits that includes "basic" and "optional" items. Basics might include modest medical coverage, life insurance equal to a year's salary, vacation time based on length of service, and some retirement pay. But then employees can use "flexible credits" to choose among such additional benefits as full medical coverage, dental and eye care, more vacation time, additional disability income, and higher company payments to the retirement fund. Nationwide, about 27 percent of large firms have flexible benefit plans, up from 18 percent in 1987.[95] They were devised largely in response to the rise in the number of two-income families. When working spouses both have conventional plans, their basic benefits, such as health and life insurance, tend to overlap. Couples rarely can use both plans fully. But if at least one spouse is covered by a "flex" plan, the couple can add benefits, such as child care, prepaid legal fees, and dental coverage, that it might otherwise have to buy on its own. A recent study examined employees' satisfaction with their benefits and understanding of them both before and after the introduction of a flexible benefits plan. Results indicated substantial improvements in both satisfaction and understanding after the plan was implemented.[96]

There are advantages for employers as well. Under conventional plans, employers risked alienating employees if they cut benefits, regardless of increases in the costs of coverage. Flexible plans allow them to pass some of the increases on to workers more easily. Instead of providing employees a set package of benefits, the employer says, "Based on your $27,000 annual salary, I promise you $5500 to spend any way you want." If health-care costs soar, the employee—not the employer—decides whether to pay more or to take less coverage.

This is what has happened at PepsiCo ever since "flex" was introduced in 1980. But company surveys show that fully 80 percent of the participants are satisfied with the plan.[97] Besides, there's help for employees even under these circumstances if they work for firms that sponsor "flexible spending accounts" (about 80 percent of all large firms in 1993). Employees can save for expenses such as additional health insurance or day care with pretax dollars, up to a specified amount (e.g., in a dependent-care spending account, up to $5000 for child or elder care). As a result, it's a win-win situation for both employer and employee.[98]

Despite these potential advantages, two disadvantages, neither of which is insurmountable, remain. One, insurers fear that employees' adverse selection of benefits will drive up costs (e.g., the only employees who choose dental insurance coverage are those with bad teeth). But this fear has been eased by new methods of pooling small-business risks and by better ways of predicting (and thus pricing) the benefits employees will choose.[99] Two, major communications efforts are needed to help employees understand their benefits fully. Since employees have more choices, they often experience anxiety about making the "right" choices. In addition, they need benefits information on a continuing basis to ensure that their choices continue to support their changing needs.[100] Careful attention to communication can enhance recruitment efforts, help cut turnover, and make employees more aware of their total package of benefits.

Communicating the Benefits

Try to make a list of good reasons why any company should *not* make a deliberate effort to market its benefits package effectively. It will be a short list. Generally speaking, there are four broad objectives in communicating benefits:

IMPACT OF BENEFITS ON PRODUCTIVITY, QUALITY OF WORK LIFE, AND THE BOTTOM LINE

Generally speaking, employee benefits do not enhance productivity. Their major impact is on attraction and retention and on improving the quality of life for employees and their dependents. Today there is widespread recognition among employers and employees that benefits are an important component of total compensation. As long as employees perceive that their total compensation is equitable and that their benefit options are priced fairly, benefits programs can achieve the strategic objectives set for them. The challenge for executives will be to maintain control over the costs of benefits while providing genuine value to employees in the benefits offered. If they can do this, everybody wins.

1. To make employees *aware* of them. This can be done by reminding them of their coverages periodically and of how to apply for benefits when needed.

2. To help employees *understand* the benefits information they receive in order to take full advantage of the plans.

3. To make employees confident that they can *trust* the information they receive.

4. To convince present and future employees of the *worth* or value of the benefits package. After all, it's their "hidden paycheck."[101]

Traditionally, employers concentrated their communications about benefits at the start of employment and assumed that was sufficient in relation to future events. Today the emphasis is on *event-centered* communications—that is, on providing to employees "the benefits information you need, when you need it."[102] This is done by providing information (1) as new benefits become available and (2) at important milestones [e.g., illness or disability, retirement, death (information to survivors), termination of employment].

Today, we are in what might be called the "third generation of employee benefits communication." Printed materials provided by insurance companies comprised the first generation. The booklets were written from the insurer's viewpoint, not the reader's. Their technical language provided little real communication.

The second generation started when companies began to provide personalized, computer-generated statements of the dollar value of benefits to employees—in plain English (see Table 12-5). Today, with the rapid proliferation of office automation, we are in the third generation of benefits communication. Microcomputers, telephone hotlines, and interactive videos have added a new dimension to this process.[103] Here are some innovative applications:

- A food-processing corporation installed computers at work locations. Now employees can obtain quick answers to "coverage" situations.

- Computer-aided design methods are being used to show how all elements of a benefits program combine to produce an image consistent with a company's culture. This is typically a series of unrelated shapes that, when combined, produce the image of, say, an airplane (for an airline), a company's major product (e.g., a car), or a company symbol (e.g., a pyramid).

■ Aetna has developed a microcomputer system that captures and records employee benefits choices, producing personalized confirmation letters.

Initiating communications technology can be time-consuming and expensive. But so is a benefits plan that no one understands or appreciates.[104]

HUMAN RESOURCE MANAGEMENT IN ACTION: CONCLUSION

THE NEW WORLD OF EMPLOYEE BENEFITS

In this new world of sharing costs and sharing risks, there are four major areas that change has affected most profoundly: health insurance, programs to promote healthy lifestyles, retirement programs, and employee savings programs.

Health Insurance. No more blank checks. Employers and insurers are both taking an aggressive role in shifting from reimbursement plans (in which employees or medical providers receive direct payments for medical expenses) to a managed-care approach (e.g., health maintenance organizations). Half of American workers were in managed-care plans in 1992—and experts predict that by the year 2000 almost all will be.

Keeping Employees Healthier. One of the most important themes in employee benefits is now prevention: limiting health-care claims by keeping employees and their families healthier. The Travelers Insurance Co. thoroughly studied its own programs in this area and found that the funds it spent on health promotion in 1990 helped it save $7.8 million in employee benefits costs. That's a savings of $3.40 for every dollar spent. The biggest payoffs came from education programs, including efforts to discourage smoking and drinking and to encourage healtheir diets.

Some companies have added new benefits, even as they eliminated others. Johnson & Johnson and Hewlett-Packard began paying for routine checkups and tests for infants, while AT&T launched a prenatal care program. Dental insurance is especially popular with employees, and more companies now offer it because it typically constitutes less than 10 percent of total health-care expenditures.

Retirement Programs—Sharing the Risk. More employers are now shifting to defined-contribution pension plans, in which the employee shares the investment risk. In return, however, employees have a larger voice in choosing how the funds will be invested. They also have greater "portability"—due largely to the meteoric growth of 401(k) plans. In 1984, for example, only 36 percent of employers offered such plans. Today, almost all employers offer them. Participation among those eligible exceeds 60 percent at all income levels. Such plans provide a true incentive to save because they are easily funded through payroll deductions, and because many employers provide a partial matching (up to $5000 a year or more) of employees' savings. Meanwhile, some sophisticated companies are developing what IBM calls a "cash balance" plan, combining elements of defined-benefit and defined-contrbution plans.

Expanding the 401(k) Concept. To many observers, the kind of sharing and choice embodied in 401(k) plans is the wave of the future in employee benefits. Companies want plans that give employees choices to suit their needs, incentives to conserve funds, and risks to share with the company. For example, it is possible that the 401(k) concept of individual and corporate partnership will be expanded to assist in saving for long-term medical care.

Of one thing we can be sure, however. During the next decade the number of choices available to employees seems likely to expand and become more complicated. Advice on how to make informed choices will itself become an increasingly popular employee benefit.

IMPLICATIONS FOR MANAGEMENT PRACTICE

As you think about the design and implementation of employee benefit plans, consider three practical issues:

1. What are you trying to accomplish by means of the benefits package? Ensure that the benefits offered are consistent with the strategic objectives of the unit or organization as a whole.

2. Take the time to learn about alternative benefit arrangements. Doing so can save large amounts of money.

3. Develop an effective strategy for communicating benefits regularly to all employees.

SUMMARY

Managers need to think carefully about what they wish to accomplish by means of their benefits programs. At a cost of over $13,000 for every employee and about 40 percent of total payroll costs, benefits represent substantial annual expenditures. Factors such as the following are important strategic considerations in the design of benefits programs: the long-term plans of a business, its stage of development, its projected rate of growth or downsizing, characteristics of its workforce, legal requirements, the competitiveness of its overall benefits "package," and its total compensation strategy.

There are three major benefit components: security and health, payments for time not worked, and employee services. Despite the high cost of benefits, many employees take them for granted. A major reason for this is that employers have not done indepth cost analyses or communicated the value of their benefits programs. This is a multimillion-dollar oversight. Certainly the counseling that must accompany the implementation of a flexible benefits program, or at least a personalized statement of annual benefits, can do much to alleviate this problem.

DISCUSSION QUESTIONS

12■1 What should a company do over the short and long term to maximize the use and value of its benefits choices to employees?

12■2 Should employees have more or less control over how their company-sponsored retirement funds are invested?

12■3 In terms of the "attract-retain-motivate" philosophy, how do benefits affect employee behavior?

12 ∎4 What can firms do to control health-care costs?

12 ∎5 Your company has just developed a new, company-sponsored savings plan for employees. Develop a strategy to publicize the program and to encourage employees to participate in it.

REFERENCES

1. Henderson, R. I. (1989). *Compensation management* (5th ed.). Englewood Cliffs, NJ: Prentice-Hall. See also Wallace, M. J., Jr., & Fay, C. H. (1988). *Compensation theory and practice* (2d ed.). Boston: PWS-Kent.

2. Bennet, J. (1993, Sept. 5). Auto talks hang on health costs, but workers are loath to chip in. *The New York Times*, pp. 1, 8–10.

3. Benefits costs rise faster than pay (1993, April). *MSEC Bulletin*. Denver: Mountain States Employers Council, Inc.

4. Ibid.

5. McCaffery, R. M. (1989). Employee benefits and services. In L. R. Gomez-Mejia (ed.), *Compensation and benefits*. Washington, DC: Bureau of National Affairs, pp. 3-101 to 3-135.

6. Smart, T. (1993, May 10). IBM has a new product: Employee benefits. *Business Week*, p. 58.

7. U.S. Chamber of Commerce (1989). *Employee benefits*. Washington, DC: U.S. Chamber of Commerce.

8. Ledvinka, J., & Scarpello, V. G. (1991). *Federal regulation of personnel and human resource management* (2d ed.). Boston: PWS-Kent.

9. Ibid.

10. McCaffery, op. cit.

11. Shellenbarger, S. (1993, Dec. 17). Firms try to match people with benefits. *The Wall Street Journal*, p. B1.

12. U.S. Chamber of Commerce (1993). *Employee benefits, 1992*. Washington, DC: Author.

13. Peers, A. (1987, June 29). Firms now must offer health insurance to some ex-workers—but at what price? *The Wall Street Journal*, p. 29.

14. Coverage continues when the job doesn't (1990, Mar. 21). *The Wall Street Journal*, p. B1.

15. McCaffery, R. M. (1992). *Employee benefit programs: A total compensation perspective* (2d ed.). Boston: PWS-Kent.

16. Financing and managing public employee benefit plans in the 1990s (1988, October). *Government Finance Review*, pp. 32, 33.

17. Say, does workers' comp cover wretched excess? (1991, July 22). *Business Week*, p. 23. See also Labor letter (1987, Sept. 22). *The Wall Street Journal*, p. 1.

18. A kinder, gentler workplace? (1993, Aug. 31). *The Wall Street Journal*, p. A1.

19. Marsh, B. (1991, Dec. 31). Rising worker compensation costs worry small firms. *The Wall Street Journal*, p. B2.

20. Kerr, P. (1991, Dec. 29). Vast amount of fraud discovered in workers' compensation system. *The New York Times*, pp. 1, 14.

21. Compensating for workers' comp costs (1992, Feb. 3). *Business Week*, p. 72.

22. Making workers' comp work (1993, Oct. 25). *Business Week*, p. 114.

23. McCaffery, R. M. (1992). op. cit.

24. Schultz, E. E. (1990, Apr. 17). Disability coverage? Well, I have some. . . . *The Wall Street Journal*, pp. C1, C23.

25. Slater, K. (1986, May 23). Medical and disability plans: How to tell if a firm's employee benefits measure up. *The Wall Street Journal*, p. 21.

26. Pay your own disability premium (1989, December). *Money*, p. 175.

27. Asinof, L. (1993, Apr. 20). Will your disability policy help when you're helpless? *The Wall Street Journal*, pp. C1; C17.

28. Edwards, M. R. (1981). Permanent disability: What does it cost? *Human Resource Planning,* **4,** 209–220.

29. Ibid.

30. Lewin, T. (1991, Apr. 28). High medical costs affect broad areas of daily life. *The New York Times,* pp. 1, 28–32.

31. Farrell, C. (1993, Mar. 15). Health-care costs: Don't be too quick with the scalpel. *Business Week,* p. 80.

32. Ibid.

33. Bennet, J., op. cit.

34. Uchitelle, L. (1991, May 1). Insurance as a job benefit shows signs of overwork. *The New York Times,* pp. A1, D23.

35. Labor letter (1992, Nov. 3). *The Wall Street Journal,* p. A1.

36. Eckholm, E. (1991, Sept. 26). Health benefits found to deter job switching. *The New York Times,* pp. A1, B12. See also Lewin, op. cit.

37. Berton, L., & Brennan, R. J. (1992, Apr. 22). New medical-benefits accounting rule seen wounding profits, hurting shares. *The Wall Street Journal,* pp. C1, C2.

38. Luciano, L. (1993, May). How companies are slashing benefits. *Money,* pp. 128–138. See also McMurray, S. (1993, Jan. 5). DuPont to cut health care benefits in '94. *The Wall Street Journal,* pp. A3, A6. See also Freudenheim, M. (1992, June 28). Medical insurance is being cut back for many retirees. *The New York Times,* pp. 1, 14.

39. Luciano, op. cit.

40. Eckholm, E. (1991, May 2). Rescuing health care. *The New York Times,* pp. A1, B12–B14.

41. A crisis of medical success (1993, Mar. 15). *Business Week,* pp. 78–80. See also Pollack, A. (1991, Apr. 29). Medical technology "arms race" adds billions to the nation's bills. *The New York Times,* pp. A1, B8–B10.

42. Labor letter (1989, Nov. 28). *The Wall Street Journal,* p. A1.

43. Labor letter (1984, Sept. 18). *The Wall Street Journal,* p. 1

44. Labor letter (1991, Aug. 13). *The Wall Street Journal,* p. A1. See also Richman, L. S. (1983, May 2). Health benefits come under the knife. *Fortune,* pp. 95–110.

45. Garcia, B. E. (1989, Feb. 16). Cigna's "managed" health care is all-or-nothing game. *The Wall Street Journal,* p. A6.

46. Steinmetz, G. (1993, May 18). New treatment. *The Wall Street Journal,* pp. A1, A8.

47. Khanna, P. M. (1992, Aug. 17). Health costs. *The Wall Street Journal,* p. B1.

48. Shellenbarger, S. (1990, Feb. 27). As HMO premiums soar, employers sour on the plans and check out alternatives. *The Wall Street Journal,* pp. B1, B9.

49. Winslow, R. (1989, Sept. 12). Health costs. *The Wall Street Journal,* p. B1.

50. Labor letter (1992, Aug. 25). *The Wall Street Journal,* p. A1.

51. Dental HMO enrollment rising (1993, April). *HRMagazine,* p. 31. See also Freudenheim, M. (1992, May 12). Business and health. *The New York Times,* p. D2.

52. Harvey, B. H., Schultze, J. A., & Rogers, J. F. (1983). Rewarding employees for not using sick leave. *Personnel Administrator,* **28**(5), 55–59.

53. Widder, P. (1982, May 31). Individuals gain more control over their pensions. *Denver Post,* pp. 1C, 8C.

54. Colvin, G. (1982, Oct. 4). How sick companies are endangering the pension system. *Fortune,* pp. 72-78.

55. Topolnicki, D. M. (1993, November). Beat the five threats to your retirement. *Money,* pp. 66–73. See also Widder, op. cit.

56. Labor letter (1988, Nov. 22). *The Wall Street Journal,* p. A1. See also Labor letter (1988, Sept. 13). *The Wall Street Journal,* p. A1.

57. Wallace, A. C. (1989, Aug. 5). Pension experts aren't worried. *The New York Times,* pp. 31, 32.

58. Labor letter (1990, Jan. 16). *The Wall Street Journal,* p. A1.

59. White, J. A. (1990, Mar. 20). Pension funds try to retire idea that they are villains. *The Wall Street Journal,* pp. C1, C8.

60. Salwen, K. G., & Scism, L. (1993, Dec. 14). Corporate pensions face proxy rules. *The Wall Street Journal*, pp. C1, C6. See also Labor letter (1990, May 15). *The Wall Street Journal*, p. A1.

61. White, op. cit.

62. For a real budget buster . . . (1993, Aug. 9). *Business Week*, pp. 64, 65.

63. Wallace, op. cit.

64. Topolnicki, op. cit.

65. Luciano, op. cit.

66. Personal affairs (1982, Nov. 22). *Forbes*, pp. 230–233.

67. Hershey, R. D., Jr. (1993, Fall). Labor Department adopts new rules on pensions. *The New York Times: Themes of the Times*, p. 4.

68. Topolnicki, op. cit.

69. Labor letter (1987, Nov. 10). *The Wall Street Journal*, p. 1.

70. A bow to unisex pensions (1983, July 18). *Newsweek*, p. 66.

71. The *Norris* decision and merged-gender annuity rates (1983, August). TIAA-CREF, Notice to annuity owners.

72. Pension reform has something for everyone (1984, Aug. 27). *U.S. News & World Report*, p. 67.

73. *Older Americans in the workforce: Challenges and solutions* (1987). Washington, DC: Bureau of National Affairs.

74. Shapiro, W. (1993, Dec. 20). The budget: Their turn to pay? *Time*, pp. 36, 37.

75. Labor letter (1992, June 21). *The Wall Street Journal*, p. A1.

76. Hardy, D. R. (1989, Aug. 21). Social Security's insecure future. *The Wall Street Journal*, p. A24.

77. Roberts, P. C. (1990, Feb. 1). Let workers own their own retirement funds . . . that's how it's done in other countries. *The Wall Street Journal*, p. A21.

78. Labor letter (1989, Mar. 21). *The Wall Street Journal*, p. A1.

79. Firms' unemployment taxes fell in most states this year (1987, Dec. 29). *The Wall Street Journal*, p. 17.

80. Rosenbaum, D. E. (1990, Dec. 2). Unemployment insurance aiding fewer workers. *The New York Times*, pp. 1, 38.

81. McCaffery, R. M. (1992). Op. cit.

82. Speck, R. W. (1988). Adapting severance pay practices to today's realities. *Compensation and Benefits Review*, **20**(4), 14–18.

83. Lublin, J. S. (1991, Apr. 1). Bosses alter early-retirement windows to be less coercive—and less generous. *The Wall Street Journal*, pp. B1, B7.

84. Schultz, E. E. (1990, Oct. 17). A financial survival guide for the newly unemployed. *The Wall Street Journal*, pp. C1, C17.

85. Labor letter (1988, Jan. 19). *The Wall Street Journal*, p. A1. See also Labor letter (1987, Sept. 8). *The Wall Street Journal*, p. 1.

86. Labor letter (1988, Nov. 8). *The Wall Street Journal*, p. A1.

87. Tannenbaum, J. A. (1981, May 6). Paid public service leaves buoy workers, but return to old jobs can be wrenching. *The Wall Street Journal*, p. 29.

88. Morrison, E. W., & Herlihy, J. M. (1992). Becoming the best place to work: Managing diversity at American Express Travel-Related Services. In Jackson, S. E. (ed.), *Diversity in the workplace*. New York: Guilford, pp. 203–226.

89. Luciano, op. cit.

90. Jacobs, D. L. (1993, Dec. 5). The rules for giving, and for giving back. *The New York Times*, p. 25.

91. Alexander, S. (1990, Aug. 24). Fears for careers curb paternity leaves. *The Wall Street Journal*, pp. B1, B4.

92. The 401(k) account: A savings carrot that really works (1993, Sept. 27). *Business Week*, p. 28.

93. Schultz, E. E. (1990, Apr. 27). Taking full control of retirement funds. *The Wall Street Journal*, pp. C1, C21.
94. McCaffery, R. M. (1992). Op. cit.
95. Luciano, op. cit.
96. Barber, A. E., Dunham, R. B., & Formisano, R. A. (1992). The impact of flexible benefits on employee satisfaction: A field study. *Personnel Psychology, 45*, 55–75.
97. Reibstein, L. (1986, Sept. 16). To each according to his needs: Flexible benefits plans gain favor. *The Wall Street Journal*, p. 33.
98. Labor letter (1993, Dec. 14). *The Wall Street Journal*, p. A1.
99. Galante, S. P. (1986, July 21). Employers acquiring a taste for providing benefit "menus." *The Wall Street Journal*, p. 17.
100. Anthony, R. J. (1986). A communication program model for flexible benefits. *Personnel Administrator, 31*(6), 65–76.
101. Markowich, M. M. (1992, October). 25 ways to save a bundle. *HRMagazine*, pp. 48–57.
102. McCaffery, R. M. (1992). Op. cit.
103. Labor letter (1991, Jan. 8). *The Wall Street Journal*, p. A1.
104. Watters, D. A. (1986). New technologies for benefits communication. *Personnel Administrator, 31*(11), 110–114.

CHAPTER 13

MOTIVATIONAL STRATEGIES FOR IMPROVING PERFORMANCE AND PRODUCTIVITY

HUMAN RESOURCE MANAGEMENT IN ACTION

HOW *NOT* TO IMPLEMENT AN INCENTIVE-PAY PLAN*

The problem at Sears, Roebuck & Co.'s auto service centers is the same one that retailers grapple with constantly: how to motivate sales forces without making them too pushy. Sears abandoned a commission compensation plan at the auto service centers after New Jersey and California officials alleged that the centers' employees systematically recommended unnecessary repairs to customers. Sears denies that the centers had a systematic plan of recommending unnecessary repairs. It acknowledges, however, that its compensation plan "created an environment where mistakes did occur."

Take Michael Stumpf, for example. He testified before a Senate subcommittee looking into auto fraud that he used to be a walking advertisement for Sears. But when his fiancée took their car to a Sears Automotive Center for an advertised $89.99 strut job, she ended up with a $650 repair bill instead. "Trust shaken is not easily gained back," said Stumpf.

Here's how business was done when the commission plan was in effect at the auto service centers. John Ritucci, manager of the centers in the Northeast, fired off a memo to auto repair "advisers" at the centers in his area. "Nice improvement" in March sales of car suspension springs, he said in a memo in April.

At that time, the advisers, who form the link between customers and mechanics, earned their salaries by drawing commissions on every dollar of parts and labor their customers

---

*Adapted from: G. A. Patterson, Distressed shoppers, disaffected workers prompt stores to alter sales commissions, *The Wall Street Journal*, July 1, 1992, pp. B1–B2. Also, Did Sears take other customers for a ride? *Business Week*, Aug. 3, 1992, pp. 24–25. Also, S. Feison, Sears agrees to pay $8 million to settle auto repair complaints. *The New York Times: Themes of the Times*, Sept. 3, 1992, pp. 1, 10.

Incentive plans may be designed for the right reasons but may reinforce the wrong kinds of behaviors—as the chapter's opening vignette shows.

authorized to be performed on their cars. Sears was pushing the advisers to boost the number of the high-profit-margin car springs they sold customers.

"The goal is still one [set of springs] per day per service adviser," the memo continued, "so we have a long way to go. Let's get as much as we can in April."

At Sears' San Bruno, California, store, Jerry Waddy talked about the "pressure, pressure, pressure to get the dollars." He was fired, he says, for not meeting his quota of 16 oil changes a day. Waddy says that on the advice of his manager he started cheating in the final week to try to save his job. He's now seeking $1 million from Sears in a wrongful discharge suit.

Government investigators, law enforcement officials, and private attorneys representing former Sears auto center employees contend that such policies add up to systematic fraud. "There was a deliberate decision by Sears management to set up a structure that made it totally inevitable that the consumer would be oversold," charged a deputy attorney general in California.

In the wake of these allegations, California officials are moving to force Sears out of the auto repair business in that state. What's more, Sears customers are pursuing a class-action lawsuit based on the auto center allegations.

Challenges

1. What was wrong with the commission compensation plan at Sears?

2. What kinds of management checks and balances should be built into such a system?

3. Can a commission compensation plan be sustained over time? If so, what features should it have?

Questions This Chapter Will Help Managers Answer

1. As a manager, what issues should I consider in choosing one or more strategies to motivate my subordinates?

2. What specific steps should I take to implement my chosen strategy?

3. What can I do as a manager to make self-managing work teams "work"?

4. What costs and benefits might I anticipate from implementing individual, team, or organizationwide incentives?

5. In implementing a merit-pay system, what key traps must I avoid in order to make the system work as planned?

The chapter opening vignette raises an issue that is compelling to many managers—how can we gain and sustain employee motivation for high quality and high productivity? The constant interplay between theory and practice is shown throughout this chapter. Let us begin by reviewing and integrating theories of applied motivation, suggesting a unified motivational framework for management practice, and then illustrating this framework with a company example.

ALTERNATIVE STRATEGIES FOR BUILDING EMPLOYEE TRUST AND PRODUCTIVITY

As pointed out in Chapter 1, to attract both domestic and foreign investment, it is critical for any nation to improve its productivity growth rate, relative to that of other industrialized nations. Both within and outside the United States, some observers question the motivation and work ethic of the U.S. worker. Critics point to the declining role of work in U.S. life, coupled with rising demands for more leisure time.

However, many management policies and practices are at least partly to blame for employees' attitudes. Many firms proudly point to their productivity increases and claim that the increases are due to employees' working smarter, not harder. But in many other firms, managements fail to reward employees for working either harder or smarter.

Many powerful tools lie within management's control, but the tools have to be applied consistently and within the framework of an overall *strategy* for performance improvement. Such a strategy must coordinate the various elements of human resource management into a unified program whose focus is to enhance employees' motivation to work; too often, managers have sacrificed *equitable* treatment for *equality* of treatment.[1] To see how such a strategy might be applied in practice, let's examine three popular categories of motivation theories.

Motivation Theories

A close look at all theories of human motivation reveals a common driving principle: *people do what they are rewarded for doing*. This has been termed "the greatest management principle in the world."[2] In general, the theories can be classified as needs theories, reinforcement theories, expectancy theories, and goal-setting theories. Needs theories focus on *what* motivates people. Hence they are also called "content" theories. Reinforcement, expectancy, and goal setting describe *how* to motivate people. Hence they are also called "process" theories.

Needs Theories. These suggest that individuals have certain physical and psychological needs they attempt to satisfy. *Motivation* is a force that results from an individual's desire to satisfy these needs (e.g., hunger, thirst, social approval). Conversely, a satisfied need is not a motivator. Thus, while a hungry man might well be susceptible to a "Big Mac Attack," after several Big Macs that same individual might find the prospect of yet another to be distinctly uninviting. The most popular needs theories are:

- Maslow's hierarchy of needs, ranging from physiological needs to safety, belonging, esteem, and self-actualization needs.[3]
- Herzberg's two-factor theory, whereby the satisfaction of needs has one of two effects: it either *causes* employees to be *satisfied* with their jobs, or it *prevents* employees from being *dissatisfied* with their jobs.[4]
- McClelland's classification of needs according to their intended effects; that is, they satisfy employee needs for achievement, affiliation, or power.[5]

Reinforcement Theories. Also known as incentive theories or operant conditioning, reinforcement theories are based on a fundamental principle of learning—the Law of Effect.[6] Its statement is simple: *behavior that is rewarded tends to be repeated; behavior that is not rewarded tends not to be repeated.* If management rewards behaviors such as high-quality work, high productivity, timely reports, and creative suggestions, these behaviors are likely to increase. However, the converse is also true: managers should not expect sustained, high performance from employees if they consistently ignore employees' performance and contributions.

Expectancy Theories. While reinforcement theories focus on the *objective relationship* between performance and rewards, expectancy theories emphasize the *perceived relationships*—what does the person expect?

Expectancy concepts form the basis for a general model of behavior in organizational settings, as shown in Figure 13-1.* Working from left to right in the model,

FIGURE 13-1

The expectancy theory of work motivation. (*Source:* E. E. Lawler III, Pay for performance: A strategic analysis. In L. R. Gomez-Mejia (ed.), *Compensation and benfits.* Washington, DC: Bureau of National Affairs, 1989, p. 3-141.)

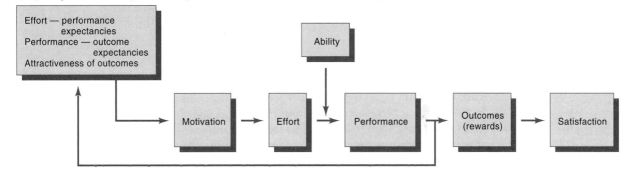

*Much of this section is drawn from the excellent summary presented in E. E. Lawler III, Pay for performance: A strategic analysis. In L. R. Gomez-Mejia (ed.), *Compensation and benefits.* Washington, DC: Bureau of National Affairs, 1989, pp. 3-136 to 3-181.

motivation serves as the force leading to a level of effort by an individual. By itself, however, effort is insufficient to generate performance. Performance is a combination of effort and ability, that is, an individual's skills, training, information, and talents.

Performance, in turn, leads to certain outcomes (rewards). Outcomes (positive or negative) may result either from the environment (e.g., supervisors, coworkers, or the organization's reward system) or from performance of a task itself (e.g., feelings of accomplishment, personal worth, or achievement). Sometimes people perform but do not receive rewards. However, as the performance-reward process occurs again and again, actual events provide further information to support a person's beliefs (expectancies), and beliefs affect future motivation. This influence is shown in Figure 13-1 by the arrow connecting the performance-outcome link with expectancies.

The model also suggests that satisfaction is best characterized as a result of performance rather than as a cause of it. However, satisfaction can increase people's motivation by strengthening their beliefs about the consequences of performance. It can also decrease the importance of outcomes (as with Big Macs, a satisfied need is not a motivator) and, as a result, lower motivation for performances linked to whatever reward has become less important.

Don't be deceived by the simplicity of the model or lulled into believing that all a manager must do to motivate employees is to relate pay and other valued rewards to obtainable levels of performance. Such a link is insufficient on its own, and it is also difficult to establish.

For employees to believe that a pay-for-performance relationship exists, an organization must establish a visible connection between performance and rewards, and it must generate trust and credibility among its workforce. The belief that performance will lead to rewards is a prediction about what will happen in the future. For individuals to make this kind of prediction, they have to trust the system that is promising them rewards. If this occurs, and if they see clear linkages between rewards and their behavior, they will be motivated to perform well.

Goal-Setting Theories. As discussed in Chapter 8, goal setting is one of the best-accepted motivational strategies in organizational science. There are three related reasons why it affects performance. One, it has a *directive* effect—that is, it focuses activity in one particular direction. Two, given that a goal is accepted, people tend to exert *effort* in proportion to the difficulty of the goal. Three, difficult goals lead to more *persistence* (i.e., directed effort over time) than easy goals do. These three dimensions—direction (choice), effort, and persistence—are central to the motivational process.[7]

Rewards That Motivate Behavior

Although some have argued that incentive plans cannot work, especially over long periods of time,[8] managers have long known that individual rewards—such as piece-rate payments, sales commissions, and performance bonuses that tie individual rewards to individual performance—can be effective motivators if they "fit" the type of work performed.[9] They are obviously inappropriate for assembly line jobs, where work is paced automatically, or for team jobs, where outcomes do not depend on the efforts of any single individual.

Nevertheless, research indicates that when incentives geared to reward *individuals* do fit the situation, performance increases an average of 30 percent, while incentives geared to reward *groups* increase performance an average of 18 percent.[10] However, as noted in Chapter 12, the total compensation package each employee receives includes indirect as well as direct financial payments. Benefits, cafeteria privileges, and company-subsidized tuition are examples of indirect payments, or "system rewards," that employees receive simply for being members of the system.[11] They have little impact on the day-to-day performance of employees, but they do tie people to the system. They tend to reduce turnover and to increase loyalty to the company. As you can see, there are a number of alternative strategies available for building employee trust and productivity. However, at this point you are probably also asking yourself "How do I proceed, and when should I use each strategy?"

Integration and Application of Motivation Theories

The intent here is to develop meaningful prescriptions for managers to follow in motivating subordinates, based on the above brief review of motivation theories and types of rewards. Broadly speaking, managers need to focus on three key areas of responsibility in order to coordinate and integrate human resource policy:[12]

1. Performance definition
2. Performance facilitation
3. Performance encouragement

These key areas are shown graphically in Figure 13-2.

Performance Definition. This is a description of what is expected of employees, plus the continuous orientation of employees toward effective job performance. The discussions of job analysis and performance standards in Chapters 5 and 9, respectively, are clearly relevant here. Performance description includes three elements: goals, measures, and assessment.

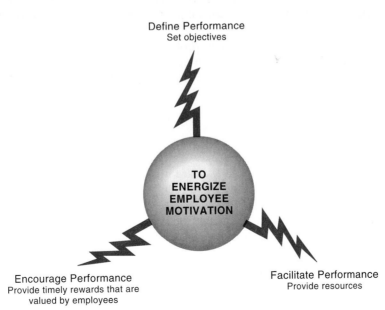

Define Performance
Set objectives

TO ENERGIZE EMPLOYEE MOTIVATION

Encourage Performance
Provide timely rewards that are valued by employees

Facilitate Performance
Provide resources

FIGURE 13-2
Steps that managers can take to motivate employees to improve their performance.

As we have seen, *goal setting* is an effective performance improvement strategy. It enhances accountability and clarifies the direction of employee effort. At Hewlett-Packard, for example, the president commented, "The corporate goals [concerning profit, customers, fields of interest, growth, people, management, and citizenship] provide the basic framework for the management-by-objectives system, which gives individual managers a lot of freedom to be entrepreneurial and innovative. They are a kind of glue—the basic philosophy, the basic sense of direction, sort of a value set— that draws everyone together."[13]

The mere presence of goals, however, is not sufficient. Management must also be able to operationalize and therefore *measure* the accomplishment of goals. This is where performance standards play a vital role, for they specify what "fully successful" performance means. Goals such as "Make the company successful" are too vague to be useful.

The third aspect of performance definition is *assessment*. Regular assessment of progress toward goals encourages a continuing orientation toward job performance. If management takes the time to identify measurable goals but then fails to do assessment, it is asking for trouble. This is so because if there is no assessment of performance on these goals, the goals cannot motivate employees to improve their performance. The goals only send negative messages to employees regarding management's commitment to the goals.

Performance Facilitation. This area of responsibility involves the elimination of roadblocks to performance. Like performance definition, it has three aspects: removing performance obstacles, providing the means and adequate resources for performance, and carefully selecting employees.

Removal of Obstacles. Improperly maintained equipment, delays in receiving supplies, poor physical design of work spaces, and inefficient work methods are obstacles to performance that management must eliminate in order to create highly supportive task environments. Otherwise, motivation will decline as employees become convinced that management does not really care about getting the job done.

Adequate Resources. A similar problem can arise when management fails to provide adequate financial, material, or human resources to get a job done right. Such a strategy is self-defeating and excessively costly in the long run, for employees begin to doubt whether their assigned tasks can be done well.

Careful Selection of Employees. This is essential to employee motivation to perform. Poor staffing procedures ("placing round pegs into square holes") guarantee reduced motivation by placing employees in jobs that either demand too little of them or require more of them than they are qualified to do. Such a strategy results in overstaffing, excessive labor costs, and reduced productivity.

Performance Encouragement. This is the last key area of management responsibility in a coordinated approach to motivating employee performance. It has five aspects:

■ Value of rewards
■ Amount of rewards

- Timing of rewards
- Likelihood of rewards
- Equity, or fairness, of rewards

The *value and amount of the rewards* relate to the choice of rewards to be used. Management must offer rewards to employees (e.g., job redesign, flexible benefits systems, alternative work schedules) that employees personally value. Then a sufficient *amount* of reward must be offered to motivate the employee to put forth the effort required to receive it. How much is enough?

When one manager was asked how much of a raise he gave his top performer, he replied proudly, "Why, I gave him 8 percent." When asked what his worst performer got, the manager responded, "Seven percent, but the difference really was based on merit."[14] Certainly, the belief that a 1 percent differential is sufficient to reward high performance is wishful thinking.

The *timing and likelihood of rewards* relate to the link between performance and outcomes. Whether the rewards are in the form of raises, incentive pay, promotions, or recognition for a job well done, timing and likelihood are fundamental to an effective reward system. If there is an *excessive delay* between effective performance and the receipt of rewards, the rewards lose their potential to motivate subsequent high performance.

Equity, or *fairness,* can also encourage or discourage effective performance. Fairness is related to, but not the same thing as, pay satisfaction.[15] Satisfaction depends on the amount of reward received and on how much is still desired. Satisfaction is comprised of four aspects: the level of pay and benefits, the extent to which workers perceive their earnings as fair or deserved, comparisons with other people's pay, and noneconomic satisfactions, such as intrinsic satisfaction with the content of one's work.[16] Pay satisfaction certainly includes perceptions of fairness or unfairness, but the concepts of fairness and unfairness are distinctly different:

1. Equity, or fairness, depends on a comparison between the rewards one receives and one's contributions to the organization, relative to some comparison standard. Such a standard might be:

Others—a comparison with other people either within or outside the organization

Self—a comparison with one's own rewards and contributions at a different time and/or with one's own evolving views of self-worth

Systems—a comparison with what the organization has promised

These comparison standards are used in varying degrees, depending on the availability of information and the relevance of the standard to the individual.[17] Fairness is also related to employees' understanding of their company's pay system. Those who say they understand the system also tend to perceive it as fair.[18]

2. The practices most likely to produce feelings of unfairness are *adjustments* in pay. However, organizations with carefully designed policies need ensure only that actions match intentions. It probably makes much less difference to employees' perceptions of pay fairness what these policies are than seeing that they are followed con-

sistently. But organizations that say one thing and do another find that pay injustice is one of their most important products.[19]

Thus, while pay satisfaction is important, from the organization's standpoint it is even more important that every employee consider her or his pay to be fair, with some room for improvement. The point is that employees should be encouraged to improve their salaries, presumably by improving their performance. In formulating future human resource policies, therefore, management must:[20]

- Quit relying on employee *indebtedness* to encourage performance and instead consider what the organization *owes* to good performers.
- Consider the *context* of performance and productivity problems.
- Determine whether or not current human resource management policies and practices really do motivate employees to perform their jobs better.

Now, in an extended company example, let's see how these ideas were implemented in practice.

COMPANY EXAMPLE

INCREASING PERFORMANCE AND PRODUCTIVITY AT NORTH AMERICAN TOOL & DIE, INC. (NATD)*

This example is recounted in the words of the president and chief executive officer (in 1983) of NATD, a computer components contract manufacturer in San Leandro, California. His is an old-fashioned philosophy, the belief that *people* make the difference between success and failure.

"My partner and I set three objectives when we bought NATD in June 1978: (1) to expand the company while raising profits, (2) to share whatever wealth was created, and (3) to create an atmosphere that would allow everyone to feel satisfaction and even to have fun on the job. The only way to do this, we decided, was to create an atmosphere of complete trust between us (the owners) and *all* our employees. However, when you say you want such an atmosphere you truly have to believe in it. Then you have to work at improving relations every day in every situation. Otherwise, your employees will sense the hypocrisy and all will be for naught."

GOAL 1: GROWTH AND PROFITS

"We bought a job shop with a reputation for acceptable but not outstanding quality. The only way our quality would improve is if our employees improved it—every day, on every job, on every part. Ours is a highly technical business. We produce hundreds of different parts with a tolerance of 0.019 of an inch. That's about one-fourth the thickness of a human hair. NATD manufactures each of those different parts by the thousands each year. Thus the company's well-being depends entirely on employees caring a great deal about their performance.

---

*From: T. H. Melohn, How to build employee trust and productivity, *Harvard Business Review*, January–February 1983, pp. 56–59.

"To encourage this feeling, we spread the gospel of quality and repeatedly recognize employee efforts to eliminate all rejects. Each month, there's a plantwide meeting—on company time—with a threefold purpose. First, we recognize one employee (no supervisors allowed) who has done a super job of producing good quality during that month. A check for $50 is just a token of what we give. Of much greater import is the `Super Person of the Month' plaque. The employee's name is engraved on the plaque, and it is prominently and permanently displayed in the plant. Second, each employee is given a silver dollar for every year of service if his or her employment anniversary occurs during the month of the meeting. Finally, we share with our `family' where we've been, where we are, and where we're going—in percentages when appropriate. In that way, each employee knows firsthand what's going on at his or her company."

GOAL 2: SHARING THE WEALTH

"We share ownership primarily through our employee stock ownership plan. We give each employee shares of NATD stock each year, according to three simple selection criteria: the employee must be at least 24 years old, work at least 1000 hours a year, and be on the payroll at year end. In our judgment, our people have earned the right to be given company stock without any cash outlay of their own. It's not a warrant, a reduced-price purchase plan, matching dollars, or an option. It's free.

"By the way, my partner and I waived our right to participate in this program. We wanted the number of shares allotted for our employees to be that much larger, that much more meaningful. The shares we grant annually are newly issued—we do not realize any gain by selling our own. NATD's employee stock ownership program has also been instrumental in lowering our rejection rates from customers and improving our productivity and delivery time.

"We also try to stress equitable compensation as a motivational tool. We hold compensation reviews twice annually. This is not a rubber-stamp operation. Each employee has a one-on-one performance review with his or her boss. Each is told, `Here's where you're doing well, and here's where you need to improve, and here's what the company can do to help.'

"Finally, we use cash bonuses to reward innovative employees. In recent months several employees have taken action to help the company and win cash. In one instance, a young employee decided on his own to develop a means to rivet a very difficult part and also to automate the entire process. In another, a department foreman who saw that our labor cost for an important job was too high devised a new method of doing ten operations at one time. He challenged his young associate to `top this' and soon found the entire production step completely automated! Our labor costs were reduced 80 percent."

GOAL 3: SATISFACTION AND FUN

"With our strong belief in the importance of our employees, we pay careful attention to the selection process. We hire a certain kind of person—one who cares about himself, his family, and his company. The person must be honest, willing to speak up, and curious, be it as a sweeper, machine operator, plant foreman, or office manager. That's why I interview each prospective employee myself. My purpose is to determine if the candidate will fit into the NATD family. Perhaps that concept seems old-fashioned, but to us it's pivotal. This process of lengthy evaluation and interviewing is a lot of work, but the results are well worth it.

"Let's face it, the traditional adversary role between management and employees is not productive. In encouraging employee satisfaction at NATD, we follow the tenet that our employees deserve the same treatment we expect from them. They want to know about their future compensation, their potential career paths, how they are contributing, and what they can do to grow. To keep people involved and caring, we work at giving out real compliments—not just the perfunctory `Good job, Smith'—but statements of sincere appreciation for each person's special efforts and accomplishments.

"Compliments don't cost a company anything. We all need them and even crave them. Recognition—both personal and professional—is a major motivating factor. At least two or three times a week we go through the plant chatting with each employee and complimenting those who've worked well. Employees care deeply about their work. If you can tap this well of concern and mesh it with the goals of your corporation, the results will truly stun you.

"To summarize the last 3 years at NATD, our sales have gone from $1.8 million to over $6 million, our pretax earnings have increased well over 600 percent, our stock appreciated 36 percent in 1980 and again in 1981, our customer reject rate has declined from 5 percent to 0.3 percent, our productivity has doubled, our turnover rate has dropped from 27 percent to 6 percent, and we've all had a good time."

EFFECTIVE IMPLEMENTATION

"My job as CEO is to outline the company's objectives and the strategies to attain these goals. To achieve them, we place heavy emphasis on true delegation of responsibility.

"We believe that our managers really want to manage, but we realize that certain conditions must be met before they can become effective managers. First, we work *with* managers to be sure the goals are clear and in fact attainable. Second, we give our employees the tools to reach the goals. Third, we let our managers alone and allow them flexibility. The last thing any manager needs is a second-guessing or a preemptive superior.

"Each supervisor is responsible for on-time production with no rejects and at maximum efficiency. How the supervisor does it is totally up to him or her. We then make sure our managers and employees get credit for their successful accomplishments—from us, from their peers, and in their paychecks.

"Incidentally, we attach no blame to failure. If we have given a job 'our best shot,' there's no problem. If our people are inhibited by the fear of failure, they won't dare to try. If we don't try the unexplored and the untested, then our growth rate and profitability will suffer. And that's no fun."

Update Jim Bradt, current president of NATD, offered the following update in 1994.[21] The company's sales have increased two and a half times since 1983, and, as a result of the employee stock ownership plan, employees now control 38 percent of company stock. The customer reject rate has dropped to an average of 500 parts per million (0.05 percent), and to zero with some customers. Turnover and accidents are both close to zero, and as a result of empowered teams, parts are inspected continuously as they are produced, rather than after final assembly. As a result, parts go directly from "dock to stock," that is, from the loading dock right into a customer's production process. Perhaps even more important, NATD is still a fun place to work.

OVERALL SUMMARY AND INTEGRATION

NATD has applied a logic and a framework to its management practice that has resulted in a coordinated human resource management policy. Such a policy clearly has affected all three of the general themes of this book: productivity, quality of work life, and the bottom line. It also dovetails nicely with the motivation guidelines suggested earlier:

- *Performance definition*—NATD has established goals, measures, and assessments.
- *Performance facilitation*—NATD has removed obstacles to effective performance, it has provided the resources that its employees need to perform their jobs well, and it has emphasized careful personnel selection.
- *Performance encouragement*—NATD has provided rewards employees value (recognition, stock ownership, cash bonuses) in sufficient *amount* to encourage future performance, with a *high likelihood* of actually receiving the rewards, with appropriate *timing* (twice-a-year compensation reviews), and with a genuine concern for employees' perceptions of *fair* treatment.

Performance definition, facilitation, and encouragement "set the stage" for employees to become motivated. Then managers must choose among a range of specific motivational strategies. One of the most popular of these, in recent years, has been job design.

JOB DESIGN

Information, rewards, knowledge, and power are central issues for all organizations. How they are positioned in an organization determines its core management style. When they are concentrated at the top, traditional control-oriented management exists. When they are moved downward, some form of participative management or employee involvement is being practiced.[22] In light of the need for innovation and productivity improvement in our globally interdependent economy, more and more firms are trying to institute some form of high-employee-involvement strategy.

Before examining some current company practices, let's first consider these two fundamental questions:

1. Is there a demonstrable *need* to redesign jobs? Will some other approach to change (e.g., training, selection, performance feedback, financial incentives) or no change at all be appropriate?
2. Is it *feasible* to redesign jobs, given the present structure of the jobs, the technological constraints, and the characteristics of the people who do them?

To begin with, maybe job design is not the problem at all. Managers need to be wary of jumping on the behavioral science bandwagon and adopting a technique simply because "everybody else is doing it." Without hard diagnostic data, implementation of any new change will be premature and may spell failure in the long run.

If it begins to appear that job redesign is needed, there may be larger things to consider first. It just may not be feasible to implement job redesign, given current organizational constraints. Care needs to be taken, for example, in assessing current technology and the cost of proposed modifications (Volvo, for example, built a brand-new plant in Uddevalla, Sweden, before its job redesign ideas could be implemented).

A second consideration is the values and beliefs of key participants. For example, employee involvement requires that managers believe in the capabilities, sense of responsibility, and commitment of people throughout the organization. They need to believe not only that people are a key organizational resource but that people can and will behave responsibly if given the opportunity.[23]

A final consideration is the present organization of work. Is it done by teams, individuals, or some other arrangement? (In this section we will focus on an approach to work redesign for teams, and in the next section we will focus on individually based work redesign.)

Designing Jobs for Teams

In terms of efficiency and practicality, some jobs can be done only by a team. Consider a surgical team in a hospital operating room. Anesthesiologist, surgeon(s), nurse(s), and technicians (those who sterilize and pass instruments) must work interdependently. So also must workers building a ship or a plane, for the sheer weight of the parts and complexity of the task require many heads, hands, and muscles. Knowledge workers also work in teams. For example, the evaluation of a grant or a contract proposal often requires that a group of individuals, each with special expertise, pool their evaluations of various parts of the proposal in order to reach a decision on funding. In fact, more organizations in industrialized countries have implemented work designs with autonomous work teams than have implemented job characteristics approaches oriented to individuals.[24]

Our focus in this section is not on loose aggregations of people with only casual working relationships or on groups that do not have the authority to decide how the members will work together. It is on self-managing work teams.[25] Such teams are defined by three characteristics:[26]

1. They are *real*, meaning that they are intact, identifiable social systems, even if small or temporary.

2. They are *work* teams that have to do a specified piece of work that results in a product, service, or decision whose acceptability is measurable.

3. They are *self-managing* teams whose members have the authority to manage their own task and interpersonal processes as they carry out their work.

Teams with these characteristics are sometimes called "autonomous work groups" or "self-managed work teams," though we also consider temporary task forces, decision-making committees, and many kinds of management teams in this category. All are parts of a broader sociotechnical system.

Key Behaviors Required of Team Members. Not everyone is willing or able to work in a team context. To do so effectively, a person must be able to:[27]

- Ask for ideas
- Offer help without being asked
- Accept suggestions
- Take into consideration the needs, motivations, and skills of other team members when offering help or advice

- Work with other team members to solve a problem
- Recognize and consider the ideas of others

Beware of the Rush to Teamwork! In recent years teams have become popular, and some people view them as the wave of the future. However, before "jumping on the bandwagon," it is important to be able to provide concrete answers to questions such as the following:[28]

- Are teams appropriate for the work to be done?
- What business results will be derived from teams?
- How will those results be measured?
- What are the implications for cross-training based on the degree of specialization or flexibility required?
- Do other company human resource systems (e.g., performance management, compensation) support individuals rather than teams?
- Can boundaries be placed on managerial versus team authority?

Are autonomous work groups worth the substantial time and effort, the break with custom and tradition, required to make them work? A rigorous 3-year evaluation of a nonunion British company that produces confectionery for home and export markets yielded some surprising answers.[29] The autonomous work group design produced a strong, sustained effect on employees' satisfaction with the work itself, as well as a more temporary effect on their satisfaction with the work environment, including pay, but it had no effect on work motivation or job performance. The approach also produced clear economic benefits. With responsibility for decision making delegated to the shop floor, the need for supervision declines, indirect labor costs decrease, and productivity benefits expand.

SELF-MANAGED WORK TEAMS AT GM'S SATURN PLANT

Is this a U.S. auto plant or a factory from another planet? It certainly is different. Situated 35 miles south of Nashville, in the small town of Spring Hill, Tennessee, the Saturn plant and its 3000 team members represent a profound change in the ways GM manages its people. For General Motors, which invested 8 years and $3.5 billion to launch Saturn, the venture has a specific competitive goal: to build small cars as well as the Japanese do—and then some.

Saturn is a medium-tech plant. At its core, however, is one of the most radical labor-management agreements ever developed in the United States, one that involves the United Auto Workers in every aspect of the business—including sharing the executive suite. Beyond sharing power at the top, however, the agreement established 165 work teams, which have been given more power than assembly line workers anywhere else in GM or in any Japanese plant. For example, teams at Saturn do the following:

- Interview and approve new hires for their teams (average size: 10 workers).
- Take responsibility for managing their own areas. When workers see a problem, they can pull a blue handle and shut down the entire line.

■ Assume budget responsibility. For example, one team in Saturn's final-assembly area voted to reject some proposed pneumatic car-assembly equipment and went to another supplier to buy electronic gear that its members believed to be safer.

The workers not only gain a more direct voice in shop-floor operations (as is true in Japan) but also take over managerial duties, such as work and vacation scheduling, ordering materials, and hiring new members. This is how U.S. practices diverge from those used in Japan. Indeed, such divergence is essential to avoid imposing a foreign work culture on U.S. workplaces.

To be sure, many of Saturn's ideas were borrowed from around the world by the Group of 99, a team of Saturn workers who traveled 2 million miles in 1984 to visit some 160 pioneering enterprises, including Hewlett-Packard, McDonald's, Volvo, Kawasaki, and Nissan. Their main conclusions: that most successful companies provide employees with a sense of ownership, have few and flexible guidelines, and impose virtually no job-defining shop rules.

From that blueprint grew the most radical feature of Saturn's philosophy: the provision for consensus decision making. All teams must be committed to decisions affecting them before those changes are put into place—from choosing an advertising agency to selecting an outside supplier. Says the plant's director of human resources: "That means a lot of yelling sometimes, and everything takes a lot longer, but once they come out of that meeting room, they're 100 percent committed."[30]

Saturn's workers were recruited from UAW locals in 38 states and carefully screened. By accepting a job at Saturn, they gave up their rights ever to work for any other GM division. Instead of hourly pay, they work for a salary (average: $34,000), 20 percent of which is at risk. Whether they get that 20 percent depends on a complex formula that measures car quality, worker productivity, and company profits.

Perhaps the most important lesson to be learned from this example is that U.S. companies are now discovering what the Japanese learned long ago: that people—not technology alone or marketing ploys—are the keys to success in global competition. Indeed, U.S. workers can be just as productive as Japanese workers. This has been demonstrated conclusively by the success of Honda, Toyota, and Nissan in using U.S. labor in U.S. plants. Rather than some mystical Asian work ethic, Japan's advantages boil down to teamwork, efficient use of resources, and a tireless effort to improve quality.[31]

Role of the Manager of a Self-managed Work Team

"A self-managed work team's manager!" That may seem like an oxymoron, which you may not remember from English 101 means "a combination of contradictory words" (e.g., "jumbo shrimp"). However, a self-managed work team does need a manager, but one whose tasks and responsibilities are different from those of a manager in the traditional sense. For example, the manager of a self-managed work team is not responsible for initiating, organizing, and directing work processes; the group is. Rather, the kinds of things managers *should* be doing for self-managed work teams include (1) monitoring the basic design of the group and broader organizational events that might affect the group, making alterations as needed for effective group performance, and business planning; and (2) consulting with the group so that it becomes increasingly capable of managing its own affairs in the social, technical, and economic arenas. In short, the managerial roles of "controllers," "planners," and "inspectors" are being replaced by "coaches," "facilitators," and "supporters."[32]

Unfortunately, most first- and second-line managers currently do not have the power that is needed to adjust how a group is set up or to make changes in its working environment (e.g., revising compensation arrangements or task design). Nor is this power delegated to them when they become managers of self-managed work teams. Furthermore, most managers may not be skilled or practiced in interpersonal consulting; a manager without these skills who tries to "help the group over the rough spots" may appear to the group to be "meddling" rather than helping. Managers who experience this feel that their status has been reduced and the meaningfulness of their work eroded.

What can be done to alleviate these kinds of problems for first-line managers? First, it is essential that higher management pay special attention to both the *role* and the *person* of the first-line manager when work is designed for teams.[33] Particularly, the managerial role must ensure the power to do what needs to be done to help the work groups develop into effective teams that fit well with their organizational environment. This includes selecting, training, and supporting the first-line managers so that they can gain the skills they will need in their roles as managers of self-managed groups.

Designing Jobs for Individuals

The dominant approach to job design for individuals over the last decade has been the job characteristics theory of Hackman and Oldham.[34] The model representing this theory is shown graphically in Figure 13-3.

As you can see from the diagram, according to the theory, four positive *personal and work outcomes*—high internal work motivation, high-quality work performance, high work satisfaction, and low absenteeism and turnover—result when an employee works in an environment of three *critical psychological states*—experienced meaningfulness of the work, experienced responsibility for work outcomes, and knowledge of the actual results of work activities. All three of the psychological states must be present for the positive outcomes to be realized.

As the illustration depicts, the three critical psychological states evolve from a job's having five *core dimensions*—(1) skill variety (doing different things at work that require a variety of one's skills), (2) task identity (the opportunity to do a whole piece of work), (3) task significance (the degree to which the job has a substantial impact on the lives or work of other people), (4) autonomy (the opportunity to decide on one's own how to do the work), and (5) feedback (the extent to which managers, coworkers, or the job itself provide information about how well a job is done).

The theory also states that only people who strongly value and desire personal feelings of accomplishment and growth and who are satisfied with the organization's internal environment (pay, security, supervisors, and coworkers) will respond positively to a job that is highly characterized by these five core dimensions.

The strategy for "stimulating" the five core job dimensions to produce an environment of the three critical psychological states is referred to as *"implementing concepts."* As Figure 13-3 shows, these are (1) combining tasks—if possible, to form larger modules of work; (2) forming natural work units—identifying basic work items and grouping them into natural categories; (3) establishing client relationships—that is, by identifying who the client is, establishing the most direct contact possible, and speci-

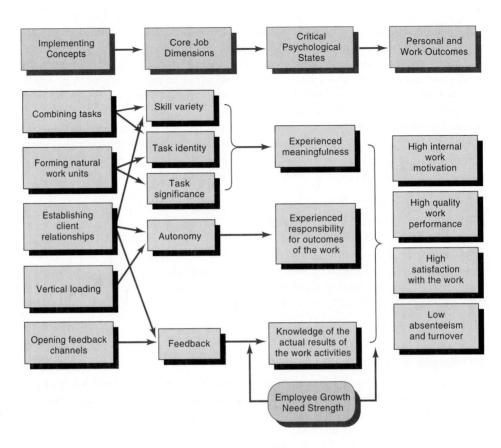

FIGURE 13-3
The full job characteristics model.

fying criteria by which the client can judge the quality of the product or service she or he receives; (4) vertical loading—closing the gap between planning, doing, and controlling the work; and (5) opening feedback channels—by establishing client relationships, placing quality control close to the worker, and providing summaries of performance to the worker.

This overall job characteristics theory was applied to a data-entry operation at the Travelers Insurance Co.[35] Diagnosis of the operation revealed that all five core dimensions were deficient. An experiment was then designed in which the jobs of one group of employees were enriched using all five of the implementing concepts, while a geographically separate control group, similar in size and demographics, was monitored for comparison. After 1 year, the results of the two groups were considerably different. In comparison to the control group, the experimental group showed significant improvements in work quantity and employee attitudes and decreases in error rates, absenteeism, and controls. The supervisor's role likewise changed from merely supervising employees closely and dealing with crises to developing feedback systems and work modules—that is, instead of merely supervising, the supervisor became a manager. In current (1994) dollars, Travelers estimated that the job redesign efforts would save the company about $250,000 *each year.*

Research has generally supported the validity of the job characteristics model.[36] However, the success of any job design effort is likely to depend not only on changes in job content but also on the context in which those changes are implemented.

Characteristics of the reward system (will salaries increase as job responsibility increases?) and management policy (does it support worker participation?) cannot be ignored.

Modifying Work Schedules

Restructuring work schedules is not a job design strategy; it does not change the way jobs are done. Nevertheless, we mention it here for two reasons. One, the positive effects on productivity of the condensed workweek and flexible working hours have been widely touted. Two, since the rigid rules regarding individual work hours are altered, these approaches can at least be considered *secondary job design strategies.*

One of the unpleasant side effects of the cataclysmic changes that have occurred as a result of the massive restructuring and downsizing that seem to characterize the 1990s is that workers feel they have no control over their work. However, companies are finding that giving employees flexibility (and therefore control) over *when* they work can heal morale and increase productivity. It's a kind of shock treatment for stressed-out workers, or, as the executive VP for human resources at Carter Hawley Hale Stores, Inc., noted: "The work force today is screaming for flexibility."[37]

In the 1970s and 1980s, a number of companies experimented with modified work schedules such as the following:

Condensed Workweek. Under this arrangement, employees can work 40 hours in fewer than 5 days. Typically, this is done by having employees work four 10-hour days per week (known as 4/40). Some firms simply do not do business on the fifth day. More commonly, however, organizations stagger work schedules so that they can remain in operation during all normal business days.[38] Advocates of the condensed workweek stress the potential dollar savings from fewer weekly start-ups and lower absenteeism and tardiness. The expected benefits to employees are less commuting time, more leisure time, and heightened job satisfaction. Critics note, however, that employees generally experience more fatigue due to the longer workday (possibly posing a safety risk), and some employees complain that longer workdays infringe on their evening activities.

Flexible Working Hours. A flextime schedule gives control of the work schedule to an employee. Typically, the organization defines a core time (e.g., 10 A.M. to 3 P.M.), during which all employees are expected to work, and then allows a range of time before and after this core period from which employees can choose their own arrival and quitting times. For example, Equifax, Inc., allows workers who enter numbers into data banks to put in their 7.5 hours any time between 7:30 A.M. and 9:30 P.M. US West permits its workers to set any schedule they want—if their supervisors agree.[39]

Two field experiments, one on the impact of condensing the workweek to 4/40, the other on introducing flexible work schedules, revealed some surprising results.[40] In both cases, the changes affected job performance only to the extent that the changed schedule met organizational needs and constraints, such as improved service to customers. Moreover, it was possible to anticipate workers' reactions to the alternative schedules *before* their introduction. Before being placed on the 4/40 or flexible schedules, workers told the researchers (through pretest assessments) the ways they believed they would and would not react to the changed schedules; after 3 to 6 months of experience with the new schedules, these were the reactions that actually emerged. These results suggest that active employee input during the design and implementation of alternative work schedules may provide accurate predictions of the likely impact of the schedules on employees and their organizations.

Telecommuting. For more than 10 million Americans, the daily commute to the office is done without leaving home. Inexpensive personal computers, modems, photocopiers, and facsimile machines allow a much broader range of corporate employees to work out of their homes. Slightly more than half these workers have children in the house or in the office for at least part of the workday.[41] These workers are called "telecommuters." Both low- and high-skill workers are involved, although telecommuting is not for everyone. Research indicates that only 15 percent of U.S. workers react favorably to working alone or independently. "Mix-and-match" programs that let workers and managers prearrange a schedule of days spent at home and in the office are the most common and most popular telecommuting arrangements.[42]

Telecommuting may also cause problems for telecommuters' office colleagues. Some 27 percent say the innovation has increased their workload, for example, by making them have to answer telephones and handle walk-ins for the absent telecommuters. Workers at Apple Computer complained that managers tend to overlook telecommuters when it comes to assigning tasks. Voice mail, better scheduling, and training have helped alleviate such problems.[43] Among managers, many complain that they cannot supervise—much less get to know—employees they cannot see. For example, a Johnson & Johnson manager described the following scene at a meeting: "Half the people are in the office, while the other half are just voices coming out of a little box on the desk. . . . The phone works OK, but it's just not as effective in terms of getting people to feel like a team."[44]

In the mid-1990s, a new generation of experiments reflects an interest in flexibility (i.e., flexible work schedules as well as telecommuting or flexplace) as a way to improve teamwork. Here's a company example.

COMPANY EXAMPLE

LINKING PRODUCTIVITY AND WORK SCHEDULES AT XEROX

At a Xerox administrative center in Dallas, management had long banned flexible work schedules in favor of an 8-to-5 regimen. In an experiment funded by the Ford Foundation, interviewers noted that a high proportion of workers in this division felt stressed by rigid schedules. Many were single parents and dual-career couples with child-care and family problems. When management announced that henceforth workers could set their own hours, many were wary. They hesitated to take advantage of their newfound freedom because they thought that their bosses didn't approve of unusual schedules and that they had to hide personal and family conflicts while they were at work. It was the beginning of a cultural change at the center, and cultural change is always difficult.

Ten months after the announcement, about half the employees chose new starting times or compressed workweeks. They continued to cover their jobs without missing a beat. Absences fell by one-third, teamwork improved, and surveys showed that morale rose. Follow-up interviews by the researchers showed that "employees feel that they have more control over their work . . . and are dealing better with their customers." The lesson: since employees feel committed to getting results so that they can keep the schedules that work best for them, flexibility has turned into a business tool. Other companies, such as GTE,

Stride Rite Corp., and Chicago's Harris Bank have reported similar results. In fact, GTE managers are "constantly astounded at the creativity that employees bring to bear to make nontraditional arrangements work."[45]

Cautions. Few changes unnerve managers more than throwing out the traditional 9-to-5 work schedule. So the first problem is to deal with managers' fears. These include fears that:[46]

- Employees will choose outlandish schedules, coming in at midnight or worse.
- Managers will get bogged down administering offbeat schedules.
- Managers won't know if employees are working if they can't see them.
- Flexibility robs managers of control

To make flexible arrangements work, be prepared to do three things well:

1. Specify work goals and criteria for success.
2. Shift responsibility for performance and team effort to employees
3. Lift all taboos on talking about personal or family needs in the workplace.

At Harris Bank, employees asking for flextime, job sharing, compressed work-weeks, part-time or telecommuting arrangements must explain in writing on a standard form (1) how the change will help the company and (2) how their work should be evaluated. The form is saving managers time by forcing employees to think through their role in meeting company objectives. Of 83 employee requests over a 4-month period, managers turned down only three. Figure 13-4 shows the distribution of requests for flexible work arrangements.

PAY FOR PERFORMANCE

Over the past decade, pay-for-performance plans have boomed in popularity. Between 70 and 80 percent of U.S. companies regard pay for performance as an important compensation objective and offer some form of performance incentive.[47]

Although pay for performance is often treated as a single approach, in fact it is many different approaches. Since the different approaches have different consequences, each needs special treatment.[48] One way to classify them is according to the

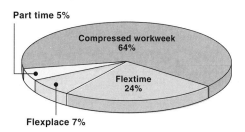

Part time 5%
Compressed workweek 64%
Flextime 24%
Flexplace 7%

Source: Harris Bank

FIGURE 13-4
Requests for flexible work arrangements. (*Source:* S. Shellenbarger, The keys to successful flexibility, *The Wall Street Journal*, Jan. 13, 1994, p. B1.)

level of performance targeted—individual, team, or total organization. Within these broad categories, literally hundreds of different approaches for relating pay to performance exist. In this chapter we will consider the three categories described above, beginning with merit pay for individuals—both executives and lower-level workers. First, however, let's consider some fundamental requirements of *all* incentive programs.

REQUIREMENTS OF EFFECTIVE INCENTIVE SYSTEMS

At the outset it is important to distinguish merit systems from incentive systems. Both are designed to motivate employees to improve their job performance. Most commonly, merit systems are applied to exempt employees in the form of permanent increases to their base pay. The goal is to tie pay increases to each employee's level of job performance. Incentives (e.g., sales commissions, profit sharing) are one-time supplements to base pay. They are also awarded on the basis of job performance, and they are applied to broader segments of the labor force, including nonexempt and unionized employees.

Properly designed incentive programs work because they are based on two well-accepted psychological principles: (1) increased motivation improves performance, and (2) recognition is a major factor in motivation.[49] Unfortunately, however, many incentive programs are improperly designed, and they do not work. They violate one or more of the following rules (shown graphically in Figure 13-5):

- *Be simple.* The rules of the system should be brief, clear, and understandable.
- *Be specific.* It is not sufficient to say, "Produce more," or "Stop accidents." Employees need to know precisely what they are expected to do.
- *Be attainable.* Every employee should have a reasonable chance to gain something.
- *Be measurable.* Measurable objectives are the foundation on which incentive plans are built. Program dollars will be wasted (and program evaluation hampered) if specific accomplishments cannot be related to dollars spent.

FIGURE 13-5
Requirements of effective incentive programs.

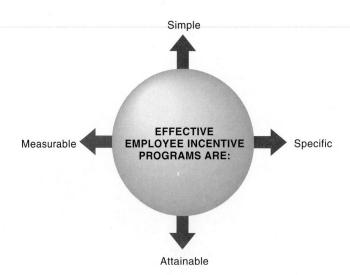

Simple

Measurable

EFFECTIVE EMPLOYEE INCENTIVE PROGRAMS ARE:

Specific

Attainable

MERIT PAY SYSTEMS

In a recent survey of 2400 employers, 94 percent said that at least part of their employees' pay was based on performance.[50] Unfortunately, many of the plans don't work. Here are some reasons why:[51]

1. *The incentive value of the reward offered is too low.* A person earning $2000 per month who gets a 5 percent merit increase subsequently earns $2100 per month. The "stakes," after taxes, are nominal.[52]

2. *The link between performance and rewards is weak.* If performance is measured annually on a one-dimensional scale, employees will remain unclear about just what is being rewarded. In addition, the timing of a merit-pay award may have little or no correlation with the timing of desirable behaviors.[53] If such conditions prevail, and cannot be fixed, financial incentives should not be used. This is consistent with the general philosophy of Total Quality Management.

3. *Supervisors often resist performance appraisal.* Few supervisors are trained in the art of giving feedback accurately, comfortably, and with a minimum likelihood of creating other problems (see Chapter 9). As a result, many are afraid to make distinctions among workers—and they do not. For example, some 2.1 million middle-level employees of the federal government work under a pay system that has a merit component. To be eligible, employees must be rated "fully successful" or better. A full 99.5 percent of them are. The result? The "merit-pay" system has become a de facto seniority system.[54]

4. *Union contracts influence pay-for-performance decisions within and between organizations.* Multiyear contracts (some with cost-of-living provisions) create pressures on pay at other levels and for nonunion employees. Failure to match union wages over a 3- or 4-year period (especially during periods of high inflation) invites dissension and turnover.

5. *The "annuity" problem.* As past "merit payments" are incorporated into an individual's base salary, the payments form an annuity (a sum of money received at regular intervals) and allow formerly productive individuals to slack off for several years and still earn high pay. The annuity feature also leads to another problem: topping out. After a long period in a job, individuals often reach the top of the pay range for their jobs. As a result, pay no longer serves as a motivator because it cannot increase as a result of performance.[55]

These reasons for the failure of merit-pay systems are shown graphically in Figure 13-6.

Barriers Can Be Overcome

Lincoln Electric, a Cleveland-based manufacturer of welding machines and motors, boasts a productivity rate more than double that of other manufacturers in its industry. It follows two cardinal rules:

1. Pay employees for productivity, and only for productivity.
2. Promote employees for productivity, and only for productivity.[56]

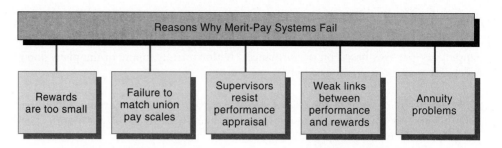

FIGURE 13-6
Why merit-pay systems fail.

Furthermore, research on the effect of merit-pay practices on performance in white-collar jobs indicates that not all merit reward systems are equal.[57] *Those that tie performance more closely to rewards are likely to generate higher levels of performance*, particularly after a year or two. In addition, *merit systems that incorporate a wide range of possible increases tend to generate higher levels of job performance after 1 year.* Some typical ranges used in successful merit systems are: Digital Equipment, 0 to 30 percent; Xerox, 0 to 13 percent; and Westinghouse, 0 to 19 percent.

GUIDELINES FOR EFFECTIVE MERIT-PAY SYSTEMS

Those affected by the merit-pay system must support it if it is to work as designed. This is in addition to the requirements for incentive programs shown in Figure 13-5. From the very inception of a merit-pay system, it is important that employees feel a sense of "ownership" of the system. To do this, consider implementing a merit-pay system on a step-by-step basis (for example, over a 2-year period), coupled with continued review and revision. Here are five steps to follow:

1. *Establish high standards of performance.* Low expectations tend to be self-fulfilling prophecies. In the world of sports, successful coaches such as Landry, Wooden, and Shula have demanded excellence. Excellence rarely results from expectations of mediocrity.

2. *Develop accurate performance appraisal systems.* Focus on job-specific, results-oriented criteria. Consider using multiple raters and appraisal formats that focus on the employees' behavior.

3. *Train supervisors in the mechanics of performance appraisal and in the art of giving feedback to subordinates.* Ineffective performance must be managed constructively.

4. *Tie rewards closely to performance.* Use semiannual performance appraisals to reward or to deny merit increases.

5. *Use a wide range of increases.* Make pay increases meaningful.

Merit-pay systems can work, but diligent application of these guidelines is essential if they are to work effectively. The guidelines are depicted in Figure 13-7.

Merit Pay in the Context of Overall Compensation

Within this framework, managers need to consider the following issues along with merit pay per se.

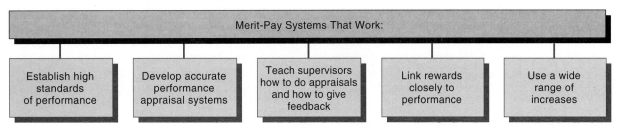

FIGURE 13-7
Guidelines for effective merit-pay systems.

- Consult union contract provisions (if appropriate) concerning *who* must be involved in the design and implementation of merit-pay systems and grievance procedures.

- Do a thorough job analysis to capture the work behaviors and work outcomes used to appraise performance. Share these with job incumbents and reach consensus on job requirements before proceeding further.

- Establish a pay range for each class of jobs.

The midpoint of a pay range (see Figure 11-5) is the basis for comparing employees in terms of their pay levels. It represents a proper rate of pay for an experienced worker performing satisfactorily.

Inexperienced, newly hired employees are normally paid at the minimum of the range. However, market adjustments (based on labor supply and demand) may result in a starting rate above the minimum for certain jobs. Experienced people entering a job class are normally paid a rate consistent with their experience (e.g., at the midpoint of the pay range).

Satisfactory performers may progress from their starting rates to the midpoints of their rate ranges on the basis of merit.

Above-average performers may progress by above-average increments to the midpoint of the pay range (50th percentile) or even to a level midway between the midpoint and the maximum (75th percentile). Ordinarily, no more than 30 percent of employees in a job category are in this group (see Figure 13-8).

Superior performers may progress to the maximum of the pay range. Ordinarily, no more than 20 percent of employees in a job class will fall between the 75th percentile and the maximum (see Figure 13-8).

Once installed, merit-pay systems must be audited periodically to ensure that they are achieving the goals for which they were designed.[58] Questions like the following should be addressed:

- What is the percentage range of pay increases within high, average, and low performance levels?

- What is the increase *by supervisor* within each performance category? Is the same level of performance rewarded similarly across supervisors?

- What is the relationship between merit increases and turnover? Are leavers predominantly from the lower end of the performance scale?

Merit pay represents a significant cost outlay as well as a powerful motivational tool. It pays to check periodically whether it is working as designed.

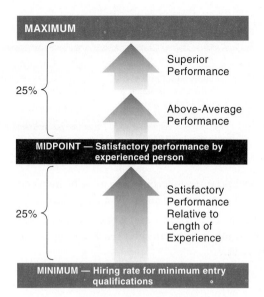

FIGURE 13-8
Performance-based movements within rate ranges characterized by a 25 percent spread from minimum to midpoint and a 25 percent spread from midpoint to maximum.

INCENTIVES FOR EXECUTIVES

"It took me a long while to learn that people do what you pay them to do, not what you ask them to do," says Hicks Waldron, former chairman and CEO of Avon Products, Inc.[59]

Companies with a history of outperforming their rivals, regardless of industry or economic climate, have two common characteristics: (1) a long-term, strategic view of their executives and (2) stability in their executive groups.[60] It makes sense, therefore, to develop integrated plans for total executive compensation so that rewards are based on achieving the company's long-term strategic goals. This may require a rebalancing of the elements of executive reward systems: base salary, annual (short-term) incentives, and long-term incentives.

Regardless of the exact form of rebalancing, base salaries (about $2 million a year for the CEO of a large American corporation[61]) will continue to be the center point of executive compensation.[62] This is because they generally serve as an index for benefit values. Objectives for short- and long-term incentives frequently are defined as a percentage of base salary. However, incentives are likely to become more long- than short-term-oriented. Here's why:

1. Annual, or short-term, incentive plans encourage the efficient use of existing assets. They are usually based on indicators of corporate performance, such as net income, total dividends paid, or some specific return on investment (i.e., net profit divided by net assets). Most such bonuses are paid immediately in cash, with CEOs receiving an average of 48 percent of their base pay, senior management 35 percent, and middle management 22 percent.[63]

2. Long-term plans encourage the development of new processes, plants, and products that open new markets and restore old ones. Hence long-term performance encompasses qualitative progress as well as quantitative accomplishments. Long-term incentive plans are designed to reward strategic gains rather than short-term contributions to profits. They are as common in owner-controlled firms (where at least 5 percent of outstanding stock is held by an individual or organization not involved in

ETHICAL DILEMMA: SHOULD OUTSIDE CEOs HELP SET CEO PAY?

It is not uncommon for chief executive officers to serve as members of the boards of directors of other firms. After all, they are successful businesspeople, and their wisdom and experience are highly prized. Many CEOs know one another, either socially or in the business context. The elements of the CEO's pay package are usually set by the compensation committee, a subgroup of the larger board of directors. Here's the ethical dilemma: should outside CEOs be allowed to serve on compensation committees? Should they have any role in setting CEO pay?

the actual management of a company) as they are in management-controlled firms (where no individual or organization controls more than 5 percent of the stock).[64] This is the kind of view we should be encouraging among executives, for it relates consistently to company success.

In the face of widespread criticism of executive pay practices, some firms are rethinking the way they reward top executives.[65] Take stock options, for example. Executives are granted the right to buy the company's stock sometime in the future at a fixed price, usually the price on the day the options are granted. Options are popular because they allow issuing companies to contend that the executives won't benefit unless the shareholders do. However, even enthusiasts can't prove that options motivate executives to perform better. Critics contend that stock options reward executives not just for their own performance but for a booming stock market. To a large extent, they are right, for as much as 70 percent of the change in a company's stock price depends only on changes in the overall market.[66] In response, some companies now grant stock options not at the market price but at some higher price. Thus executives will profit only after the stock has risen substantially. Here are some company examples of changes in executive-pay practices.[67]

- American Telephone & Telegraph links option awards to stock performance and prices most options at a 20 percent to 50 percent premium.
- ITT requires stock prices to rise by at least 40 percent, or else executives must wait 10 years before they can exercise any options.
- Avon is freezing the salary and slashing by half the bonus of its CEO for 5 years in return for stock options.

Experts in executive compensation expect the current trend toward using long-term performance incentives to continue. However, plans that measure success only in terms of gains in stock prices have been criticized for not rewarding individual or corporate performance. As a result, some employers (56 percent in one survey[68]) are now tying incentive awards to *unit* as well as companywide performance. Here's how one company does it.

COMBINING INCENTIVES AT HONEYWELL

**COMPANY
EXAMPLE**

Honeywell awards incentive pay to 70 of its division managers, based equally on the performance of their units and that of the corporation. The managers receive stock for meeting certain return-on-investment goals for their units over a 3-year period. Says the director of corporate compensation: "We're sending two messages: One is you are a key player and you are responsible for total corporate results. But we also want you to be concerned about improving your own operating units. . . . If you want incentive pay to change [managerial] behavior, a manager has got to believe he has some control over what's being measured."[69]

The plan also reflects Honeywell's diverse, decentralized structure. Its units sell everything from computers to alarm systems, and decision making is pushed down to the various units. Combining corporate and unit incentives makes sense in light of the diverse nature of Honeywell's business. This is a good example of how the company ties its long-term incentives to its long-term business strategy.

Other companies have tried to refine such policies even further, using different measurements to correspond to the unit's strategy. The idea is that executives of a new, risky unit should be judged on, say, building market share, while executives of a stable, mature unit should be judged on generating cash or cutting costs. Given the number of mergers and acquisitions that took place through the 1980s and early 1990s, these kinds of arrangements are likely to be even more popular in the future.

INCENTIVES FOR LOWER-LEVEL EMPLOYEES

As noted earlier in this chapter, a common practice is to supplement employees' pay with increments related to improvements in job performance. Most such plans have a "baseline," or normal, work standard; performance above this standard is rewarded. The baseline should be high enough so that employees are not given extra rewards for what is really just a normal day's work. On the other hand, the baseline should not be so high that it is impossible to earn additional pay.

It is more difficult to specify work standards in some jobs than in others. At the top management level, for instance, what constitutes a "normal" day's output? As one moves down the organizational hierarchy, however, jobs can be defined more clearly, and shorter-run goals and targets can be established.

Setting Workload Standards

All incentive systems depend on workload standards. The standards provide a relatively objective definition of the job, they give employees targets to shoot for, and they make it easier for supervisors to assign work equitably. Make no mistake about it, though, effective performance is often hard to define. For example, when a Corning group set up a trial program to reward workers for improving their efficiency, a team struggled to figure out "What's a meaningful thing to measure? What's reasonable?" The measures finally settled on included safety, quality, shipping efficiency, and forecast accuracy.[70] Once workload standards are set, employees have an opportunity to earn more than their base salaries, often as much as 20 to 25 percent more. In short, they have an incentive to work both harder *and* smarter.

In setting workload standards for production work, the ideal job (ideal only in terms of the ability to measure performance, not in terms of improving work motivation or job satisfaction) should (1) be highly repetitive, (2) have a short job cycle, and (3) produce a clear, measurable output. However, before explicit workload standards can be set, management must do the following:

- Describe the job by means of job analysis.
- Decide *how* the job is to be done (motion study).
- Decide *how fast* the job should be done (time study).

The standards themselves will vary, of course, according to the *type* of product or service (e.g., a hospital, a factory, a cable television company), the *method of service delivery*, the degree to which service can be *quantified*, and *organizational needs*, including legal and social pressures. In fact, the many different forms of incentive plans for lower-level employees really differ only along two dimensions:

1. How premium rates are determined
2. How the extra payments are made

Increasingly, companies are dangling incentive compensation down to lower-level managers and key workers, such as engineers, investment officials, and others who especially aid the company. For example, John Hancock Mutual Life Insurance Co. rewards lower managers with up to 10 percent of their salaries for "extraordinary work." Shawmut Co. has a similar plan for its bank lenders, giving as much as 25 percent of base pay. And Hewlett-Packard gives 200 to 300 special stock options a year to employees who show extra accomplishment.

Indeed, one survey of 644 companies found that fully half offer variable-pay programs to salaried and hourly employees below executive rank.[71] Among companies that provide incentive awards, the average award earned, as a percentage of pay, is 6.8 percent (individual performance awards), 6.4 percent (companywide awards), 5.5 percent (group productivity award), and 4.3 percent (one-time special recognition award).[72] Among companies that give team performance awards, American Greetings Corp. even bases its cost-of-living increases on merit, and bonuses are based on each unit's results. Pacific Gas & Electric has a similar team award program for 8000 management-level workers.[73]

While many firms offer incentives, about one in three is dissatisfied with them. One reason for this is that incentive plans can generate conflict. *Work groups* may impose ceilings on output for the following reasons:

1. Employees may fear that if they earn too much, management will cut premium rates and/or increase workload standards.
2. Employees may fear that as a result of producing excess inventory, they may work themselves out of a job.
3. Unlimited incentives threaten status hierarchies within work groups. That is, older (higher-status) workers may not be able to match the pace of their younger colleagues. So, to protect their social position, work groups establish ceilings, or "bogeys," of what is safe or proper output.

Other firms implement incentive programs only because the competition does it, not for strategic reasons. What are some reasons for implementing incentives? Among firms whose incentive plans "work," they say they implemented them to motivate workers, to keep them focused on specific goals, and to share organizational successes.[74]

Union Attitudes

A unionized employer may establish an incentive system, but it will be subject to negotiation through collective bargaining. Unions may also wish to participate in the day-to-day management of the incentive system, and management ought to consider that demand seriously. As noted earlier, employees often fear that management will manipulate the system to the disadvantage of employees. Joint participation helps reassure employees that the plan is fair.

Union attitudes toward incentives vary with the type of incentive offered. Unions tend to oppose individual piece-rate systems because they pit worker against worker and can create unfavorable intergroup conflict. However, unions tend to support organizationwide systems, such as profit sharing, because of the extra earnings they provide to their members. In one experiment, for example, an electric utility instituted a division-level incentive plan in one division but not in others. The incentive payout was based on equal percentage shares based on salary. Relative to a control division, the one operating under the incentive plan performed significantly better in reducing unit cost, budget performance, and on 9 of 10 other objective indicators. Nevertheless, union employees helped kill the plan for two reasons: (1) negative reactions from union members in other divisions who did not operate under the incentive plan; and (2) a preference for equal dollar shares, rather than equal percentage shares, because the earnings of bargaining-unit employees were lower, on average, than those of managers and staff employees.[75]

**COMPANY
EXAMPLE**

INDIVIDUAL INCENTIVES AT LINCOLN ELECTRIC

From its earliest years, 100-year-old Lincoln Electric Company of Cleveland, Ohio, has charted a unique path in worker-management relations, featuring high wages, guaranteed employment, few supervisors, a lucrative bonus incentive system, and piecework compensation. The company is the world's largest maker of arc-welding equipment; it has 2700 U.S. employees, 23 plants in 17 countries, and no unions. Among the innovative management practices that set Lincoln apart are these:

- Guaranteed employment for all full-time workers with more than 2 years' service, and no mandatory retirement. No worker has been laid off for more than 40 years.

- High wages (an average of $45,000 in 1992), including a substantial annual bonus (up to 75 percent of base pay) based on the company's profits. Wages at Lincoln are roughly equivalent to wages for similar work elsewhere in the Cleveland area, but the bonuses the company pays make its compensation substantially higher. Lincoln has never had a strike and has not missed a bonus payment since the system was instituted in 1934. Individual bonuses are set by a formula that judges workers on four dimensions: ideas and cooperation, output, ability to work without supervision, and work quality.

- Piecework—more than half of Lincoln's workers are paid according to what they produce, rather than an hourly or weekly wage. If a worker is sick, he or she does not get paid.

- Promotion is almost exclusively from within, according to merit, not seniority.

- Few supervisors, with a supervisor-to-worker ratio of 1 to 100, far lower than in much of the industry.

■ No break periods, and mandatory overtime. Workers must work overtime, if ordered to, during peak production periods and must agree to change jobs to meet production schedules or to maintain the company's guaranteed employment program.

While the company insists on individual initiative—and pays according to individual effort—it works diligently to foster the notion of teamwork. And it did so long before the Japanese became known for emphasizing such concepts. If a worker is overly competitive with fellow employees, he or she is rated poorly in terms of cooperation and team play on his or her semiannual rating reports. Thus that worker's bonus will be smaller. Says one company official: "This is not an easy style to manage; it takes a lot of time and a willingness to work with people."[76]

TEAM INCENTIVES

To provide broader motivation than is furnished by incentive plans geared to individual employees, several other approaches have been tried. Their aim is twofold: to increase productivity and to improve morale by giving employees a feeling of participation in and identification with the company. Team incentives are one such plan.

Team incentives provide an opportunity for each team member to receive a bonus based on the output of the team as a whole. Teams may be as small as 4 to 7 employees or as large as 35 to 40 employees. *Team incentives are most appropriate when jobs are highly interrelated.* In fact, highly interrelated jobs are the wave of the future and, in many cases, the wave of the present. In the past, relatively few firms used team incentives. In the future, they will need to be more creative in using team performance appraisal and team incentives.[77] Here's an example of one firm's efforts to do so. At the Saturn plant described earlier, incentives are geared to team performance with respect to car quality. If a team produces fewer defects than the targeted amount, its members receive 100 percent of their salaries. If they exceed a percentage threshold below the targeted amount, they are eligible for a bonus.[78]

Team incentives have the following advantages:

1. They make it possible to reward workers who provide essential services to line workers (so-called indirect labor), yet who are paid only their regular base pay. These employees do things like transport supplies and materials, maintain equipment, or inspect work output.
2. They encourage cooperation, not competition, among workers.

On the other hand, team incentives also have disadvantages, which are as follows:

1. Fear that management will cut rates (or employees) if employees produce too much.
2. Competition between teams.
3. Inability of workers to see their individual contributions to the output of the team. If they do not see the link between their individual effort and increased rewards, they will not be motivated to produce more.

To overcome some of the first two disadvantages of team incentives, many firms have introduced organizationwide incentives.

ORGANIZATIONWIDE INCENTIVES

In this our final section, we consider three broad classes of organizationwide incentives: profit sharing, gain sharing, and employee stock ownership plans. As we shall see, each is different in its objectives and implementation.

Profit Sharing

In the United States, profit sharing is the most common method companies use to provide retirement income for their employees. Firms use it for one or more of the following reasons: to provide a group incentive for increased productivity, to institute a flexible reward structure that reflects a company's actual economic position, to enhance employees' security and identification with the company, to attract and retain workers more easily, and/or to educate individuals about the factors that underlie business success and the capitalistic system.[79]

Employees receive a bonus that is normally based on some percentage (e.g., 10 to 30 percent) of the company's profits beyond some minimum level. In 1994, for example, each of 81,000 Chrysler workers received a profit-sharing bonus of $4,300. Does profit sharing improve productivity? One review of 27 econometric studies found that profit sharing was positively related to productivity in better than 9 of every 10 instances. Productivity was generally 3 to 5 percent higher in firms with profit-sharing plans than in those without plans.[80]

A most ambitious profit-sharing program was started by Du Pont in 1988 for nearly all of its 20,000 managers and employees in the fibers business in the United States. Under the plan, employees can earn up to 12 percent of their base pay if the business exceeds its profit goals, but they can also lose part of their original increase if the profit goals aren't met.[81] In late 1990, when it appeared that workers would lose as much as 4 percent of their base pay as a result of poor sales in the fibers unit, discontent among workers was so high that Du Pont canceled the plan.[82] Although there were many reasons for the plan's failure, two of the most telling were (1) the fact that employees felt powerless to influence profits and (2) employee resentment over loopholes for high-level managers in the fibers unit, who were still able to benefit from Du Pont's companywide bonus program. That program is geared to the company's total profits, not just to the profits of the fibers unit.

This case illustrates the two-sided nature of profit sharing. On the one hand, compensation costs become more variable, since a company pays only if it makes a profit. On the other hand, from the employee's perspective, benefits and pensions are insecure. Certainly, the success of profit-sharing plans depends on the company's overall human resource management policy and on the state of labor-management relations. This is even more true of gain-sharing plans.

Gain Sharing

Gain sharing is a formal reward system that has existed in a variety of forms for more than 50 years. Sometimes known as the Scanlon plan, the Rucker plan, or Improshare (improved productivity through sharing), gain sharing comprises three elements:[83]

1. A philosophy of cooperation
2. An involvement system
3. A financial bonus

The philosophy of cooperation refers to an organizational climate characterized by high levels of trust, two-way communication, participation, and harmonious industrial relations. The involvement system refers to the structure and process for improving organizational productivity. Typically, it is a broadly based suggestion system implemented by an employee-staffed committee structure that usually reaches all areas of the organization. Sometimes this structure involves work teams, but usually it is simply an employee-based suggestion system. The employees involved develop and implement ideas related to productivity. The third component, the financial bonus, is determined by a calculation that measures the difference between expected and actual costs during a bonus period.

The three components mutually reinforce one another.[84] High levels of cooperation lead to information sharing, which in turn leads to employee involvement, which leads to new behaviors, such as offering suggestions to improve organizational productivity. This increase in productivity then results in a financial bonus (based on the amount of the productivity increase), which rewards and reinforces the philosophy of cooperation.

It is important to distinguish gain sharing from profit sharing. The two approaches differ in three important ways:[85]

1. Gain sharing is based on a measure of productivity. Profit sharing is based on a global profitability measure.
2. Gain sharing, productivity measurement, and bonus payments are frequent events, distributed monthly or quarterly, in contrast to the annual measures and rewards of profit-sharing plans.
3. Gain-sharing plans are current distribution plans, in contrast to most profit-sharing plans, which have deferred payments. Hence gain-sharing plans are true incentive plans rather than employee benefits. As such, they are more directly related to individual behavior and therefore can motivate worker productivity.

When gain-sharing plans such as the Scanlon plan work, they work well. For example, consider a 17-year evaluation of such a plan in a manufacturing operation, DeSoto, Inc., of Garland, Texas. The bonus formula, which measures labor productivity, revealed that average bonuses ranged from 2.5 percent to more than 22 percent, with an overall average of 9.6 percent. Moreover, over the 17-year period of the study, output (as measured by gallons of paint) increased by 78 percent.[86] Nevertheless, in the 50 years since the inception of gain sharing, it has been abandoned by firms about as often as it has been retained. Here are some reasons why:

1. Generally, it does not work well in piecework operations.
2. Some firms are uncomfortable about bringing unions into business planning.
3. Some managers may feel they are giving up their prerogatives.[87]

Neither the size of a company nor the type of technology it employs seems to be related to Scanlon plan success. However, employee participation, positive managerial attitudes, the number of years a company has had a Scanlon plan, favorable and realistic employee attitudes, and involvement by a high-level executive are strongly related to the success of a Scanlon plan.[88] To develop an organizationwide incentive plan that has a chance to survive, let alone succeed, careful in-depth planning must precede implementation. It is true of all incentive plans, though, that *none will work well except in a climate of trustworthy labor-management relations and sound human resource management practices.*

Employee Stock Ownership Plans (ESOPs)

ESOPs have become popular in both large and small companies in the United States, as they have in Western Europe, some countries in Central Europe, and China.[89] About 10,000 U.S. firms now share ownership with more than 11 million employees. In at least 1000 companies, employees own the majority of the stock. In fact, if all worker-owned stock is counted, employees have over $150 billion worth. Employee ownership can be found in every industry, in every size firm, and in every part of the country.[90]

Generally, ESOPs are established for any of the following reasons:

- As a means of tax-favored, company-financed transfer of ownership from a departing owner to a firm's employees. This is often done in small firms with closely held stock.[91]

- As a way of borrowing money relatively inexpensively. A firm borrows money from a bank using its stock as collateral, places the stock in an employee stock ownership trust, and, as the loan is repaid, distributes the stock at no cost to employees. Companies can deduct the principal as well as interest on the amount borrowed, and lenders pay taxes on only 50 percent of their income from ESOP loans.

- To fulfill a philosophical belief in employee ownership. For example, at Avis, 12,500 employees bought the company for $1.75 billion as a way of providing stability and ending 10 tumultuous years in which the company had five corporate owners.[92]

- As an additional employee benefit.

Do ESOPs improve employee motivation and satisfaction? Longitudinal research spanning 45 case studies found that stock ownership alone does not make employees work harder or enjoy their day-to-day work more.[93] Nor does it promote an increase in perceived employee influence in company decisions or status on the job. Nevertheless, certain features do affect employee motivation, satisfaction, and commitment through stock ownership.

1. ESOP satisfaction tends to be highest in companies where (a) the company makes relatively large annual contributions to the plan; (b) management is committed to employee ownership, and (c) there are extensive company communications about the ESOP.

2. Employees tend to be most satisfied with stock ownership when the company established its ESOP for employee-centered reasons (management was committed to employee ownership) rather than for strategic or financial reasons (e.g., as an antitakeover device or to gain tax savings).

IMPACT OF INCENTIVES ON PRODUCTIVITY, QUALITY OF WORK LIFE, AND THE BOTTOM LINE

In this area, perhaps more than any other, there is a closer relationship between effective human resource management practice and the three major themes of this book: productivity, quality of work life, and profits. Consider an Improshare plan, for example, in which workers are essentially paid bonuses equal to one-half of any increase in productivity. A study of its use in manufacturing firms found that defect and downtime rates fell by 23 percent each in the first year after its introduction. In the median firm, the overall increase in productivity was more than 5 percent in the first three months and more than 15 percent by the third year. In comparison, productivity increased by only 2 percent, on average, in these manufacturing sectors as a whole.[94] Employees benefit in two ways: (1) from the rewards they receive and (2) from the intrinsic satisfaction that results from a job well done. Organizations also benefit because rewards are granted *only* for increases in productivity and increases in productivity mean improved bottom-line performance. In short, it's a win-win situation.

3. Satisfaction breeds satisfaction. That is, the same individual-level and ESOP characteristics that lead to ESOP satisfaction also lead (somewhat less strongly) to organizational commitment.

How does employee stock ownership affect economic performance? *When the above three conditions are met*, employee-owned firms have been 150 percent as profitable, have had twice the productivity growth, and have generated three times more new jobs than their competitors. High-tech companies that share ownership widely grow two to four times as fast as those that do not. Publicly held companies that are at least 10 percent employee-owned outperform 62 to 75 percent of their competitors, depending on the measure used.[95] On an aggregate level, between 1979 and 1992, a portfolio of companies that were at least 10 percent employee-owned would have produced an annualized return of 27.17 percent, against 16.54 percent for Standard & Poor's 500-stock index.[96]

While such data do not prove that employee stock ownership causes success (it may be that successful firms are more likely to make employees part owners), they do suggest that if implemented properly, such plans can improve employee attitudes and economic productivity. Nevertheless, ESOPs are not risk-free to employees. ESOPs are not insured, and if a company goes bankrupt, its stock may be worthless.

IMPLICATIONS FOR MANAGEMENT PRACTICE

In thinking about how managers motivate their subordinates, expect to see three trends continue:

1. The movement to performance-based pay plans, in which workers put more of their pay "at risk" in return for potentially higher rewards.
2. The movement toward the use of teamwide or organizationwide incentive plans at all levels.
3. Use of a wide range of pay increases, in an effort to make distinctions in performance as meaningful as possible.

HOW *NOT* TO IMPLEMENT AN INCENTIVE-PAY PLAN

Sears executives maintain they've built checks into the system, such as shopping audits and customer response cards, that help prevent overselling. Rather than explain all this in court, Sears settled charges with New Jersey by agreeing to pay $200,000 to the National Association of Attorneys General for an auto repair industry reform fund. Later Sears also settled with California. It agreed to pay $8 million in order to avoid years of costly trials and to speed changes in auto repair practices at Sears, where the state's undercover agents were charged an average of $288 a visit for unnecessary repairs during an 18-month investigation.[97] Sears estimated that the total cost, including lost sales, would be about $15 million.

Sears and others were encouraged to move toward commissions by the growth and success of the Nordstrom, Inc., department store chain, whose sales force works almost strictly on commission. But in copying the example of Nordstrom, which is based in Seattle, the other retailers failed to give their salesclerks the extensive training and the freedom to sell merchandise throughout the entire store that Nordstrom employees enjoy.

Nordstrom says there's a bigger difference in that when retailers switch to a commission-based pay plan, many of their employees have never worked for commissions and don't want the attendant pressure. Commission selling is part of Nordstrom's culture, and people who go to work for the company want to be a part of that culture. In other words, they have self-selected in.

Moreover, while sales success brings high income at Nordstrom, it does not, by itself, lead to promotion. Nordstrom, which promotes strictly from within, considers several other factors in making promotion decisions, including how willing sellers are to perform such tasks as restocking shelves. Sears' commission policy in its automotive centers incorporated none of those things.

SUMMARY

To enhance employees' motivation to work, the various elements of human resource management must be coordinated into a unified program. To do this, managers need to focus on three key areas of responsibility: (1) *performance definition* (describing what is expected of employees, plus the continuous orientation of employees toward effective job performance), (2) *performance facilitation* (eliminating roadblocks to performance, providing adequate resources, and careful personnel selection), and (3) *performance encouragement* (providing a sufficient amount of highly valued rewards in a fair, timely manner).

The most effective incentive programs are simple, specific, attainable, and measurable. One of the most popular is merit pay, and merit pay works best when these guidelines are followed: (1) establish high standards of performance, (2) develop appraisal systems that focus on job-specific, results-oriented criteria; (3) train supervisors in the mechanics of performance appraisal and in the art of giving constructive feedback; (4) tie rewards closely to performance; and (5) provide a wide range of possible pay increases.

Long-term incentives, mostly in the form of stock options, are becoming a larger proportion of the executives' pay package. Finally, there is a wide variety of individual, group, and organizationwide incentive plans (e.g., profit sharing, gain sharing, employee stock ownership plans) with different impacts on employee motivation and economic outcomes.

DISCUSSION QUESTIONS

13■1 What incentives can managers use to motivate subordinates to increase profits?

13■2 Critique the approach to managing people used by North American Tool and Die.

13■3 How has "strategic thinking" affected executive incentives?

13■4 How can union concerns be accommodated in the design and implementation of a gain-sharing plan?

13■5 If you were implementing an employee stock ownership plan, what key factors would you consider?

REFERENCES

1. McFillen, J., & Podsakoff, P. M. (1983). A coordinated approach to motivation can increase productivity. *Personnel Administrator*, **29**(7), 45–53.
2. LeBoeuf, M. (1989). *The greatest management principle in the world.* New York: Berkley Publishing Co.
3. Maslow, A. H. (1954). *Motivation and personality.* New York: Harper.
4. Herzberg, F. (1966). *Work and the nature of man.* New York: Mentor Executive Library.
5. McClelland, D. C. (1961). *The achieving society.* New York: Van Nostrand Reinhold.
6. Skinner, B. F. (1957). *Science and human behavior.* East Norwalk, CT: Appleton-Century-Crofts.
7. Locke, E. A., & Latham, G. P. (1990). *A theory of goal setting and task performance.* Englewood Cliffs, NJ: Prentice-Hall.
8. Kohn, A. (1993, September–October). Why incentive plans cannot work. *Harvard Business Review*, pp. 54–63.
9. Rethinking rewards (1993, November–December). *Harvard Business Review*, pp. 37–49.
10. Locke, E. A., Shaw, K. N., Saari, L. M., & Latham, G. P. (1981). Goal-setting and task performance: 1969–1980. *Psychological Bulletin*, **90**, 125–152.
11. Katz, D., & Kahn, R. L. (1978). *The social psychology of organizations* (2d ed.). New York: Wiley.
12. McFillen & Podsakoff, op. cit.
13. Perry, N. J. (1984, Jan. 9). America's most admired corporations. *Fortune*, p. 55.
14. McFillen & Podsakoff, op. cit.
15. Miceli, M. P., Jung, I., Near, J. P., & Greenberger, D. B. (1991). Predictors and outcomes of pay-for-performance plans. *Journal of Applied Psychology*, **76**, 508–521.
16. Berkowitz, L., Fraser, C., Treasure, F. P., & Cochran, S. (1987). Pay equity, job gratifications, and comparisons in pay satisfaction. *Journal of Applied Psychology*, **72**, 544–551. See also Heneman, H. G., III, & Schwab, D. P. (1985). Pay satisfaction: Its multidimensional nature and measurement. *International Journal of Psychology*, **20**, 129–141.
17. Witt, L. A., & Nye, L. G. (1992). Gender and the relationship between perceived fairness of pay or promotion and job satisfaction. *Journal of Applied Psychology*, **77**, 910–917.
18. Perceptions of pay (1986, July 7). *The Wall Street Journal*, p. 13.
19. Belcher, D. W. (1979, Second Quarter). Pay equity or pay fairness? *Compensation Review*, **2**, 31–37.
20. McFillen & Podsakoff, op. cit.
21. Bradt, J., president of NATD (1994, Jan. 14). Personal communication.

22. Lawler, E. E., III (1988). Choosing an involvement strategy. *Academy of Management Executive*, **2**, 197–204.

23. Ibid.

24. Wall, T. D., Kemp, N. J., Jackson, P. R., & Clegg, C. W. (1986). Outcomes of autonomous workgroups: A long-term field experiment. *Academy of Management Journal*, **29**, 280–304.

25. Wellins, R. S., Byham, W. C., & Wilson, J. M. (1991). *Empowered teams: Creating self-directed work groups that improve quality, productivity, and participation.* San Francisco: Jossey-Bass.

26. Hackman, J. R. (ed.). (1989). *Groups that work (and those that don't): Creating conditions for effective teamwork.* San Francisco: Jossey-Bass.

27. Wellins et al., op. cit.

28. Cohen, S. G. (1992). Transitioning to self-managing work teams in white-collar settings. *Self-Managed Work Teams Newsletter*, **2**(5), 4.

29. Wall et al., op. cit.

30. Gwynne, S. C. (1990, Oct. 29). The right stuff. *Time*, p. 77.

31. Ibid., pp. 74–84. See also Hoerr, J. (1989, July 10). The payoff from teamwork. *Business Week*, pp. 56–62. See also Taylor, A., III (1990, Nov. 19). Why Toyota keeps getting better and better and better. *Fortune*, pp. 66–79.

32. Wellins et al., op. cit.

33. Hackman, J. R., & Oldham, G. R. (1980). *Work redesign.* Reading, MA: Addison-Wesley.

34. Ibid. See also Hackman, J. R., & Oldham, G. R. (1976). Motivation through the design of work: Test of a theory. *Organizational Behavior and Human Performance*, **16**, 250–279.

35. Hackman, J. R., Oldham, G. R., Janson, R., & Purdy, K. A. (1975, Summer). A new strategy for job enrichment. *California Management Review*, pp. 57–71.

36. Campion, M. A., & McClelland, C. L. (1991). Interdisciplinary examination of the costs and benefits of enlarged jobs: A job design quasi-experiment. *Journal of Applied Psychology*, **76**, 186–198. See also Fried, Y., & Ferris, G. R. (1987). The validity of the Job Characteristics Model: A review and meta-analysis. *Personnel Psychology*, **40**, 287–322. See also Graen, G. B., Scandura, T. A., & Graen, M. R. (1986). A field experimental test of the moderating effects of growth need strength on productivity. *Journal of Applied Psychology*, **71**, 484–491.

37. Lambert, R., in Shellenbarger, S. (1994, Jan. 13). More companies experiment with workers' schedules. *The Wall Street Journal*, pp. B1, B2.

38. Cohen, A. R., & Gadon, H. (1978). *Alternative work schedules: Integrating individual and organizational needs.* Reading, MA: Addison-Wesley.

39. Labor letter (1988, Nov. 8). *The Wall Street Journal*, p. A1.

40. Dunham, R. B., Pierce, J. L., & Castaneda, M. B. (1987). Alternative work schedules: Two field quasi-experiments. *Personnel Psychology*, **40**, 215–242.

41. The care and feeding of "lone eagles" (1993, Nov. 15). *Time*, p. 58. See also Kutner, L. (1988, Dec. 8). Working at home, or, the midday career change. *The New York Times*, p. C8.

42. Shellenbarger, S. (1993, Dec. 14). Some thrive, but many wilt working at home. *The Wall Street Journal*, pp. B1, B2.

43. Labor letter (1993, May 18). *The Wall Street Journal*, p. A1.

44. Ansberry, C. (1987, Apr. 20). When employees work at home, management problems often arise. *The Wall Street Journal*, p. 25.

45. Shellenbarger (1994), op. cit.

46. Shellenbarger, S. (1994, Jan. 13). The keys to successful flexibility. *The Wall Street Journal*, pp. B1, B2.

47. Waldman, S., & Roberts, B. (1988, Nov. 14). Grading "merit pay." *Newsweek*, pp. 45, 46.

48. Lawler, E. E., III (1989). Pay for performance: A strategic analysis. In L. R. Gomez-Mejia (ed.), *Compensation and benefits.* Washington, DC: Bureau of National Affairs, pp. 3-136 to 3-181.

49. Rethinking rewards, op. cit. See also Robbins, C. B. (1983). Design effective incentive plans. *Personnel Administrator*, **28**(5), 8–10.

50. Bennett, A. (1991, Sept. 10). Paying workers to meet goals spreads, but gauging performance proves tough. *The Wall Street Journal*, pp. B1, B2.

51. Waldman & Roberts, op. cit.

52. Labor letter (1990, Feb. 20). *The Wall Street Journal*, p. A1.

53. Rollins, T. (1987, June). Pay for performance: The pros and cons. *Personnel Journal*, pp. 104–107.

54. Waldman & Roberts, op. cit.

55. Lawler, E. E., III (1989), op. cit.

56. Wiley, C. (1993, August). Incentive plan pushes production. *Personnel Journal*, pp. 86–91.

57. Kopelman, R. E., & Reinharth, L. (1982, Fourth Quarter). Research results; The effect of merit-pay practices on white-collar performance. *Compensation Review*, **5**, 30–40.

58. Hills, F. S., Madigan, R. M., Scott, K. D., & Markham, S. E. (1987). Tracking the merit of merit pay. *Personnel Administrator*, **32**(3), 50–57.

59. Bennett, A. (1991, Apr. 17). The hot seat: Talking to the people responsible for setting pay. *The Wall Street Journal*, p. R3.

60. Meyer, P. (1983). Executive compensation must promote long-term commitment. *Personnel Administrator*, **28**(5), 37–42.

61. Executive pay (1992, Mar. 30). *Business Week*, pp. 52–58.

62. Bettner, J. (1987, July 28). Executives get bonus for swap in stock options. *The Wall Street Journal*, p. 25.

63. Bigger bonuses (1987, Sept. 17). *The Wall Street Journal*, p. 37.

64. Gomez-Mejia, L. R., Tosi, H., & Hinkin, T. (1987). Managerial control, performance, and executive compensation. *Academy of Management Journal*, **30**, 51–70.

65. White, J. B. (1994, Jan. 5). GM executives won't receive stock bonuses. *The Wall Street Journal*, pp. A2, A5. See also McCarroll, T. (1993, Mar. 1). Rolling back executive pay. *Time*, pp. 49, 50. See also Bennett, A. (1992, Mar. 11). Taking stock: Big firms rely more on options but fail to end pay criticism. *The Wall Street Journal*, pp. A1, A8. See also Linden, D. W. (1991, May 27). Incentivize me. *Forbes*, pp. 208–212.

66. Bennett, A. (1992). op. cit.

67. Executive pay, op. cit.

68. Paying for performance (1991, Apr. 17). *The Wall Street Journal*, p. R5.

69. Reibstein, L. (1987, Apr. 10). More employers link incentives to unit results. *The Wall Street Journal*, p. 29.

70. Bennett, A. (1991, Sept. 10), op. cit.

71. Paying for performance, op. cit.

72. Bennett, A. (1991, Sept. 10), op. cit.

73. Labor letter (1987, Mar. 31). *The Wall Street Journal*, p. 1.

74. Labor letter (1990, June 11). *The Wall Street Journal*, p. A1.

75. Petty, M. M., Singleton, B., & Connell, D. W. (1992). An experimental evaluation of an organizational incentive plan in the electric utility industry. *Journal of Applied Psychology*, **77**, 427–436.

76. Wiley, C. (1993, August). Incentive plan pushes production. *Personnel Journal*, pp. 86–91. See also Serrin, W. (1984, Jan. 15). The way that works at Lincoln. *The New York Times*, p. D1.

77. Norman, C. A., & Zawacki, R. A. (1991, September). Team appraisals—team approach. *Personnel Journal*, pp. 101–104. See also Rowland, M. (1992, Feb. 9). Pay for quality, by the group. *The New York Times*, p. D6.

78. Gwynne, op. cit.

79. Schroeder, M. (1988, Nov. 7). Watching the bottom line instead of the clock. *Business Week*, pp. 134, 136. See also Florkowski, G. W. (1987). The organizational impact of profit sharing. *Academy of Management Review*, **12**, 622–636.

80. Banerjee, N. (1994, Apr. 12). Rebounding earnings stir old debate on productivity's tip to profit-sharing. *The Wall Street Journal*, pp. A2, A12. See also U.S. Department of Labor (1993, August). *High performance work practices and firm performance*. Washington, DC: Author.

81. Hays, L. (1988, Dec. 5). All eyes on Du Pont's incentive-pay plan. *The Wall Street Journal*, p. B1.

82. Koenig, R. (1990, Oct. 25). Du Pont plan linking pay to fibers profit unravels. *The Wall Street Journal*, pp. B1, B5.

83. Collins, D., Hatcher, L., & Ross, T. L. (1993). The decision to implement gainsharing: Role of work climate, expected outcomes, and union status. *Personnel Psychology*, **46,** 77–104. See also Graham-Moore, B., & Ross, T. L. (1990). Understanding gainsharing. In B. Graham-Moore & T. L. Ross (eds.), *Gainsharing*. Washington, DC: Bureau of National Affairs, pp. 3–18.

84. Graham-Moore & Ross, op. cit.

85. Hammer, T. H. (1988). New developments in profit sharing, gainsharing, and employee ownership. In J. P. Campbell & R. J. Campbell (eds.), *Productivity in organizations*. San Francisco: Jossey-Bass, pp. 328–366.

86. Graham-Moore, B. (1990). Seventeen years of experience with the Scanlon plan: DeSoto revisited. In B. Graham-Moore & T. L. Ross (eds.), *Gainsharing*. Washington, DC: Bureau of National Affairs, pp. 139–173.

87. Tyler, L. S., & Fisher, B. (1983). The Scanlon concept: A philosophy as much as a system. *Personnel Administrator*, **29**(7), 33–37. See also Moore, B., & Ross, T. (1978). *The Scanlon way to improved productivity*. New York: Wiley.

88. White, J. K. (1979). The Scanlon plan: Causes and consequences of success. *Academy of Management Journal*, **22**, 292–312.

89. Becker, G. S. (1989, Oct. 23). ESOPs aren't the magic key to anything. *Business Week*, p. 20.

90. Jones, D., & Schmitt, J. (1993, Dec. 20). UAL plan may put industry in new hands. *USA Today*, pp. 1B, 2B. See also Joe Sixpack's grip on corporate America (1991, July 15). *Business Week*, pp. 108, 110.

91. ESOPs offer way to sell stakes in small firms (1988, May 3). *The Wall Street Journal*, p. 33.

92. White, J. A. (1991, Jan. 25). As ESOPs become victims of '90s bankruptcies, workers are watching their nest eggs vanish. *The Wall Street Journal*, pp. C1, C16.

93. Klein, K. J., & Hall, R. J. (1988). Correlates of employee satisfaction with stock ownership: Who likes an ESOP most? *Journal of Applied Psychology*, **73**, 630–638. See also Klein, K. J. (1987). Employee stock ownership and employee attitudes: A test of three models. *Journal of Applied Psychology*, **72,** 319–332. See also Rosen, C., Klein, K. J., & Young, K. M. (1986). When employees share the profits. *Psychology Today*, **20**, 30–36.

94. Kaufman, R. T. (1992). The effects of IMPROSHARE on productivity. *Industrial and Labor Relations Review*, **45,** 311–322.

95. Rosen, et al., op. cit.

96. White, J. A. (1992, Feb. 13). When employees own big stake, it's a buy signal for investors. *The Wall Street Journal*, pp. C1, C9.

97. Faison, S. (1993, Fall). Sears agrees to pay $8 million to settle auto repair complaints. *The New York Times: Themes of the Times*, pp. 1, 10.

PART FIVE

LABOR-MANAGEMENT ACCOMMODATION

A CONCEPTUAL VIEW OF HUMAN RESOURCE MANAGEMENT

STRATEGIC OBJECTIVES, ENVIRONMENTS, FUNCTIONS

STRATEGIC OBJECTIVES — PARTS ONE - SIX — CHAPTERS 1 - 18

Productivity

Quality of Work Life

Profits

ENVIRONMENTS — PART ONE — CHAPTERS 1 - 4

Competitive

Legal

Social

Organizational

FUNCTIONS — PARTS TWO - SIX — CHAPTERS 5 - 18

Employment

Development

Compensation

Labor-Management Accommodation

Support, Evaluation, International Implications

RELATIONSHIP OF HRM FUNCTIONS TO HRM ACTIVITIES

FUNCTIONS	ACTIVITIES
Part Two **Employment**	Job Analysis, Human Resource Planning, Recruiting, Staffing (Chapters 5 - 7)
Part Three **Development**	Orienting, Training, Performance Appraisal, Managing Careers (Chapters 8 - 10)
Part Four **Compensation**	Pay, Benefits, Incentives (Chapters 11 - 13)
Part Five **Labor-Management** **Accommodation**	Union Representation, Collective Bargaining, Procedural Justice, Ethics (Chapters 14, 15)
Part Six **Support,** **Evaluation,** **International** **Implications**	Job Safety and Health, Costs/Benefits of HRM Activities, International Dimensions of HRM (Chapters 16 - 18)

LABOR-MANAGEMENT ACCOMMODATION

Harmonious working relations between labor and management are critical to organizations. Traditionally both parties have assumed a win-lose, adversarial posture toward each other. This must change if U.S. firms are to remain competitive in the international marketplace. Part Five is entitled "Labor-Management Accommodation" to emphasize a general theme: to achieve long-term success, labor and management must learn to *accommodate* one another's needs, rather than *repudiate* them. By doing so, management and labor can achieve two goals at once: increase productivity and improve the quality of work life. In the current climate of wants and needs, there is no other alternative.

The focus of Chapter 14 is on union representation and collective bargaining. Chapter 15 focuses on procedural justice, ethics, and concerns for privacy in employee relations. These are some of the most dominant issues in this field in the 1990s. As is true of all chapters in this book, Chapters 14 and 15 are oriented toward the development of sound human resource management practices by line managers.

CHAPTER 14

UNION REPRESENTATION AND COLLECTIVE BARGAINING

IMPROVING PRODUCTIVITY, QWL, AND PROFITS THROUGH LABOR-MANAGEMENT COOPERATION*

Many managers see unions as a major stumbling block to the implementation of workplace changes that are essential to increased competitiveness. To them, unions are a problem. To others, unions can be and should be part of the solution to problems of workplace competitiveness. Many union leaders and members, in turn, deeply distrust management's motives. They see "enhanced competitiveness" as thinly veiled code words for downsizing. What is right? Is it possible for a well-established union to take a leadership role in workplace innovation and imaginative approaches to enhancing competitiveness? Is it possible for management to allow creative approaches to more efficient operations *without* cutting workers as a result of the increases in efficiency?

To be sure, management and workers have ample reason to distrust each other. Chrysler's union workers grouse that management is demanding ever-faster production while getting bonuses that make their own $4300 profit-sharing checks look paltry. In 1993 Chrysler paid 200 executives bonuses equal to 100 percent of salary.

Many union leaders fear cooperative work systems, because they suspect that management's real intention is to circumvent lawfully designated unions. In some cases this has occurred, as in a recent decision by the National Labor Relations Board that Electromation, Inc., used teams to create a company-dominated union.

---

*Sources: Bernstein, A. (1994, May 23). Why America needs unions—but not the kind it has now. *Business Week*, pp. 70–82. Bernstein. A. (1993, Mar. 1). Now labor can be part of the solution. *Business Week*, p. 35. Simison, R. L. (1994, May 4). Tooling along. *The Wall Street Journal*, pp. A1, A9. Xerox and the ACTWU: Tracing a transformation in industrial relations. In F. K. Foulkes & E. R. Livernash, *Human resources management: Cases and text* (2d ed.), 1989, pp. 348–373, Englewood Cliffs, NJ: Prentice-Hall.

Despite such potential problems, some employee-involvement plans have worked brilliantly. For example, the United Auto Workers played a key role in the improvement of productivity and quality at Ford Motor Co. during the early 1980s. Ford has improved its assembly-line productivity by 36 percent since 1980, at least in part because of its employee-involvement system. Today some Ford plants are as productive as Japanese automakers. Is this just an isolated example, or are there other success stories?

Challenges

1. What are some key obstacles that stand in the way of true cooperation by labor and management?

2. Is labor-management cooperation just a short-term solution to economic problems, or can it become institutionalized into the very culture of an organization?

3. Will widespread labor-management cooperation lead to a loss of union power?

Questions This Chapter Will Help Managers Answer

1. How have changes in product and service markets affected the way labor and management relate to each other?

2. How should management respond to a union organizing campaign?

3. To what extent should labor-management cooperative efforts be encouraged?

4. What kinds of dispute resolution mechanisms should be established in order to guarantee due process for all employees?

WHY EMPLOYEES JOIN UNIONS

Study after study has found consistently that unions form as a result of frustration by employees over their inability to gain important rewards. More specifically, there seem to be two main factors underlying employees' interest in unions.[1] The first of these is *dissatisfaction with working conditions and a perception by employees that they cannot change those conditions.*

One study of more than 87,000 salaried clerical, sales, and technical employees representing 250 units of a national retailing firm found that attitude measures taken 3 to 15 months *prior to* any organizing activity predicted the level of *later* organizing. Consistent with the maxim that "the best union organizer is the boss," this study found that the best predictors of the severity of unionization activity were items dealing with the supervision the workers receive.[2]

Another study of more than 1200 employees who voted in 31 union representation elections supported these findings. Correlations between job satisfaction and votes for or against union representation are shown in Table 14-1.

Dissatisfaction with wages, job security, fringe benefits, treatment by supervisors, and chances for promotion was significantly related to a vote *for* union representation. However, dissatisfaction with the *kind* of work being done did not correlate strongly with a vote for union representation. Hence, *employee interest in unionization was triggered by working conditions, not by the work itself.*

■ **TABLE 14 ▪ 1**

CORRELATIONS BETWEEN JOB SATISFACTION AND VOTES FOR OR AGAINST UNION REPRESENTATION

Item	Correlation with vote*
1. Are you satisfied with your wages?	−.40
2. Do supervisors in this company play favorites?	−.34
3. Are you satisfied with the type of work you are doing?	−.14
4. Does your supervisor show appreciation when you do a good job?	−.30
5. Are you satisfied with your fringe benefits?	−.31
6. Do you think there is a good chance for you to get promoted in this company?	−.30
7. Are you satisfied with your job security at this company?	−.42
8. Taking everything into consideration, are you satisfied with this company as a place to work?	−.36

*The negative correlations indicate that satisfied employees tended to vote against union representation.
Source: Adapted from: J. M. Brett, Why employees want unions. Reprinted, by permission of the publisher, from *Organizational Dynamics, 8*(4), 1980, 51. © 1980 American Management Association, New York. All rights reserved.

The second factor that seems to underlie employee interest in unionization is *the degree to which employees accept the concept of collective action and whether they believe unionization will yield positive rather than negative outcomes for them.* Thus, in the study shown in Table 14-1, dissatisfied employees tended *not* to vote for unionization if they believed the union was unlikely to improve the working conditions that dissatisfied them. Recent research supports the finding that beliefs about the effects of a union at a person's *own workplace* are critical determinants of voting intentions.[3] In addition, employees who hold a negative image of labor unions (i.e., those who feel that unions have too much political influence, abuse their power by calling strikes, cause high prices, misuse union dues and pension funds, and have leaders who promote their own self-interests) tend to vote *against* union representation.[4] In fact, knowing an employee's opinion on these issues allowed researchers to predict with 79 percent accuracy how he or she would vote on the issue of union representation.[5]

On the other hand, it is pure folly to assume that pro-union attitudes are based simply on expected economic gains; much deeper values are at stake.[6] As one author noted:

> If one talks to any worker long enough, and candidly enough, one discovers that his loyalty to the union is not simply economic. One may even be able to show him that, on a strictly cost-benefit analysis, measuring income lost from strikes, and jobs lost as a result of contract terms, the cumulative economic benefits are delusions. It won't matter. In the end, he will tell you, the union is the only institution that insures and protects his "dignity" as a worker, that prevents him from losing his personal identity, and from being transformed into an infinitesimal unit in one huge and abstract "factor of production."[7]

This conclusion that deeper values than money are at stake was illustrated in the 11-year battle to organize workers at the J. P. Stevens plant in North Carolina. The organizing drive was much publicized—the award-winning movie *Norma Rae* was based on it—and the settlement was heralded widely as a historic breakthrough in a decades-old attempt to organize southern industry. Even though the wages at the unionized Stevens plants are not substantially higher now than at the company's nonunionized plants or than the wages at other nonunion textile plants in the south, the wage level was never the biggest issue. The union contract has meant expanded benefits, a seniority system to protect workers when jobs are lost and to provide opportunities when jobs open, and a grievance procedure with access to binding arbitration. For the company, the settlement allowed it to put its past squabbles with the workers behind and to concentrate on battling foreign textile imports. Among union members, however, worker after worker echoes the same sentiment: the collective bargaining agreement has meant that they are treated with new dignity on the job.[8]

UNION MEMBERSHIP IN THE UNITED STATES

Union membership has shrunk from a high of 35 percent of the workforce in 1945 to 22 percent in 1980 to 16 percent in 1993. Excluding public-sector membership, unions represented just 11 percent of private-sector employees in 1993.[9] Figure 14-1 shows the dropoff in membership between 1975 and 1993 in 10 unions.

Several economic and demographic forces favor a resurgence of unions. The same corporate downsizing that has sharply cut union membership has also created a new receptiveness for union organizers among surviving employees, who find themselves overworked and stressed out. Further, while labor productivity has grown in the 1990s, paychecks have gotten smaller. In inflation-adjusted dollars, average weekly wages fell from $272 in 1983 to $254 in 1993.[10] To add insult to injury, the gap between executive pay has grown from 33 times the average income of U.S. workers in 1973 to 157 times the average in 1993. Finally, both women and minority-group members, who are expected to continue entering the workforce at a high rate, tend to favor unions.[11]

FIGURE 14-1
Decline in union membership, 1975 to 1993. (*Source:* K. G. Salwen, What, us worry? Big unions' leaders overlook bad news, opt for status quo, *The Wall Street Journal*, Oct. 5, 1993, p. B.1.

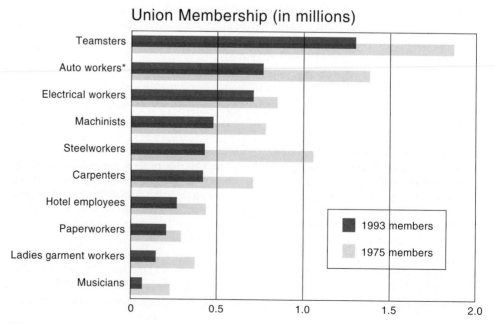

*1975 data are estimated

Source: AFL–CIO, individual unions, Bureau of Labor Statistics

Despite these factors, a large-scale resurgence of unions seems unlikely. What complicates organizing efforts is that many in this new generation are white-collar workers—in fields as diverse as insurance and electronics. Their goals and desires are different from those of labor's traditional blue-collar stalwarts, who seemed to want little more than high wages and steady work. And because so many young workers are highly mobile (workers under 35 stay on a job a median of 2.5 years, compared to 12 years for those over 45), they might not be willing to support a 6-month unionization drive that might culminate in a strike to win a first contract.[12] Finally, many young workers are taking jobs in the rapidly growing service sector—banking, computer programming, financial services—jobs that unions traditionally have not penetrated.

The very nature of high-tech industry also hampers organizing efforts. Many software designers and biotechnical engineers work for small start-up companies that unions find difficult and expensive to organize. Among larger firms like Apple Computer, which has no production unions, workers are often parts of flexible teams that change tasks from month to month and work closely with management. That creates a sense of empowerment that can leave unions with little role to play. As one observer noted: "The new industries in the U.S. are evolving so rapidly that there is no stable craft pattern for a union to represent."[13]

Despite the dropoff in membership, unions are a powerful social, political, and organizational force. In the unionized firm, managers must deal with the union rather than directly with employees on many issues. Indeed, the "rules of the game" regarding wages, hours, and conditions of employment are described in a collective bargaining agreement (or contract) between management and labor. Although it need not always be so, adversarial "us" and "them" feelings are frequently an unfortunate by-product of this process.

Economic and working conditions in unionized firms directly affect those in nonunionized firms, as managers strive to provide competitive working conditions for their employees. Yet the nature of the internal and external environments of most U.S. firms differs dramatically in the 1990s relative to those of earlier periods. This has led to fundamental changes in labor-management relations, as we shall see in the next section.

THE CHANGING NATURE OF INDUSTRIAL RELATIONS IN THE UNITED STATES

Fundamentally, labor-management relations are about power—who's got it and how they use it. As we shall see, both parties are finding that they achieve the best results when they share power rather than revert to a win-lose orientation.[14] In recent years, unions have lost power as a result of three interrelated factors: global competition, corporate downsizing (which has depleted the membership of many unions), and the willingness of firms to move operations overseas. In today's world, firms face more competitive pressures than ever before. That competition arises from abroad (e.g., Toyota, Nissan, Hyundai, Sanyo, Pohang, and third-world steelmakers); from domestic, nonunion operators (e.g., Nucor in steel); and from nonregulated new entities (e.g., dozens of new telecommunications companies).

These competitive pressures have forced business to develop the ability to shift rapidly, to cut costs, to innovate, to enter new markets, and to devise a flexible labor force strategy. As managers seek to make the most cost-effective use of their human resources, the old "rules of the labor-management game" are changing.[15]

Traditionally, the power of unions to set industrywide wage levels and to relate these in "patterns" was based on the market power of strong domestic producers or industries sheltered by regulation. As employers lost their market power in the 1970s and 1980s, union wage dominance shrank and fragmented. One union segment had to compete with another and with nonunion labor both in the United States and abroad. Management's objective was (and is) to get labor costs per unit of output to a point below that of the competition at the product-line level. Out of this approach have come wage-level differences and, with them, the breakdown of pattern bargaining. As a result, even under union bargaining pressures, wages are now far more responsive to economic conditions at the industry and firm levels, and even at the product-line level, than they traditionally have been.[16]

Related to wage-level flexibility is employment-level flexibility. By contracting out work more freely, using subcontracts for business services, and using more part-time and temporary workers, management is trying to make employment levels more fluid and adjustable, to make labor costs even more variable, and to gain power for rapid downsizing and cost cutting. This approach, which may well characterize the 1990s, has been termed "*kanban* employment," using the Japanese term for just-in-time delivery and no stockpiling or inventorying of resources.[17]

The labor relations system that evolved during the 1940s and lasted until the early 1980s was institutionalized around the market power of the firm and around those unions that had come to represent large proportions, if not nearly all, of an industry's domestic workforce. The driving force for change in the 1990s has been business conditions in the firm. Those conditions have changed for good—and so must the U.S. industrial relations system. In order to put that system into better perspective, let us examine the approach taken in other countries. Keep in mind, however, that direct comparisons are difficult. The next section shows why.

DIFFICULTIES IN COMPARING INDUSTRIAL RELATIONS SYSTEMS

It is difficult to compare industrial relations systems across national boundaries for at least three reasons:[18]

1. The same concept may be interpreted differently in different industrial relations contexts. For example, consider the concept of collective bargaining. In the United States it is understood to mean negotiations between a labor union local and management. In Sweden and Germany, however, the term refers to negotiation between an employers' organization and a trade union at the industry level.

2. The objectives of the bargaining process may differ in different countries. For example, European unions view collective bargaining as a form of class struggle, but in the United States collective bargaining is viewed mainly in economic terms.

3. No industrial relations system can be understood without an appreciation of its historical origin. Such historical differences may be due to managerial strategies for labor relations in large companies, ideological divisions within the trade union movement, the influence of religious organizations on the development of trade unions, methods of union regulation by governments, or the mode of technology and industrial organization at critical stages of union development.[19]

To illustrate such differences in industrial relations systems, we will present a brief overview of the Japanese system.

The Japanese Industrial Relations System*

Although the Trade Union Act was passed in December 1945, the basic framework of the industrial relations system was established in 1956 after the economic boom of the Korean War. Workers in the private sector were guaranteed three basic rights: to organize labor unions, to bargain collectively, and to take industrial action to insist on their interests. Union membership peaked in 1949 at 58.9 percent of the workforce. By 1975, it had fallen to 34.4 percent, and to 24.4 percent in 1992. It is expected to fall below 20 percent by the end of the decade, largely due to the growth in nonunion, part-time jobs.[20]

Forms of Trade Unions. Most Japanese unions in the private sector are enterprise unions. This concept, based on the idea of *groupism*, has its roots in the lifestyle and social values of farmers and fishers. Workers moving from rural areas to large cities expected (correctly) that their idea of groupism would be maintained even in the context of manufacturing operations.

Union membership is limited to regular employees of a single company regardless of whether they are blue-collar or white-collar employees. Subcontractors and temporary workers are not eligible for membership, but supervisors of blue-collar workers and subsection heads of white-collar workers may be union members if the company-level collective bargaining agreement permits. Top executives and middle managers are often former members of their company's labor union, because they usually have worked their way up through the ranks.

An enterprise union usually joins one of four so-called national centers of labor unions. These centers play an important role in developing policies of their member labor unions, in coordinating interests of the member unions, and in influencing government economic and industrial relations policies. They also play a leading role in directing the Spring Labor Offensive, which usually determines the main direction of collective bargaining at each company.

The Spring Labor Offensive (*Shunto-hoshiki*) was established in 1956 to overcome the weakness of enterprise unionism. About 80 percent of all labor negotiations take place at the beginning of the spring, especially in March, April, and May. This time was chosen because April is the beginning of the accounting term and the month when new school graduates come into companies. One of the main reasons that employers accept the coordinated wage settlement is that they can avoid severe competition among themselves on wages and other benefits under the guidance of their trade association.

Employers' Organizations. Of the four main employers' associations, Keidanren (Japan Federations of Economic Organization) is the most influential with respect to labor relations issues. It includes 54 trade associations and all the regional employers' associations. Keidanren's main function is to coordinate employers' opinions on economic policies and labor problems and to present these both to the public and to the government.

*Much of the material in this section has been adapted from: K. Okubayashi, The Japanese industrial relations system, *Journal of General Management*, **14**, 67–88 (1989).

The Structure of Collective Bargaining. For the most part, as we have noted, collective bargaining is based on negotiations between an enterprise union and its employer. Contents of the collective agreement include clauses dealing with topics such as wages, annual wage increases, benefits, working hours, and criteria for dismissal. It also includes sections dealing with issues such as union membership as a condition of continued employment, time-card stamping at the beginning and end of work, and the conduct of union activities during working hours. Finally, the agreement includes sections dealing with joint consultation and grievance resolution procedures.

The Joint Consultation System. This system, in addition to collective bargaining, plays a very important role in promoting industrial democracy in Japanese industrial relations. About 71 percent of companies with more than 1000 employees have adopted such a system. Employee representatives at each level of a company (shop floor, factory, and the company as a whole) meet monthly with their counterparts in management to exchange information about the company's policies, production schedule, and changes of practices on the shop floor. At these meetings, management often shares confidential information concerning production plans, financial conditions, staffing plans, and the introduction of new technology, for example. Union representatives can express their opinion of this information and provide counterproposals to management. Differences between the two groups are handled in one of two ways: management subsequently may modify its proposal, or else execution of the original proposal is suspended for a cooling-off period. These mechanisms help avoid severe conflicts or strikes.

In practice, employee representatives are union officials. Therefore rigid differentiation between collective bargaining and the joint consultation system is very difficult in the sense that both work effectively to promote communication between management and employees.

The idea of participative management is supported by labor unions, employers, and workers themselves. However, the main forms of participation in Japanese industrial systems are collective bargaining, the joint consultation system, suggestion systems, and small-group activities such as quality circles. Employee representation on boards of directors and participation in high-level strategic business decisions, which are usual in Germany, are not practiced in Japan.

Worker Participation at Industrial and National Levels. The activities of enterprise unions extend beyond their companies to include joint consultation between representatives of confederations of labor unions and corresponding associations of employers. Such systems exist in mining, textiles, iron and steel, electric power, machinery and metal fabrication, shipbuilding, automobiles, and the chemical, plastics, and oil industries, for example. Representatives exchange opinions on general industrial policies, business trends, and the main strategies of the Spring Labor Offensive, as well as employment security within their own industries, safety, work hours, and minimum wages. These meetings do not have the authority to conclude industrywide collective agreements concerning industrial policies, but they are very effective mechanisms for the exchange of perceptions about industrial situations. This facilitates consensus between enterprise unions and employers.

In summary, the Japanese industrial relations system comprises the following: enterprise unions that work with company managements to conclude collective bargaining agreements during the Spring Labor Offensive and to promote industrial democracy through the joint consultation system, as well as through union-management discussions at the industrial and national levels.

As we noted earlier, examination of another country's industrial relations system, such as that of Japan, helps to put the U.S. system into better perspective. The remainder of this chapter will examine that system in greater detail.

Fundamental Features of the U.S. Industrial Relations System

Six distinctive features of the U.S. system, compared to those in other countries, are as follows:[21]

1. *Exclusive representation*—one and only one union in a given job territory, selected by majority vote. This is in contrast to continental Europe, where affiliations by religious and ideological attachment exist in the same job territory.

2. *Collective agreements* that embody a sharp distinction between *negotiation of and interpretation of an agreement.* Most agreements are of fixed duration, often 2 or 3 years, and they result from legitimate, overt conflict that is confined to a negotiations period. They incorporate no-strike (by employees) and no-lockout (by employer) provisions during the term of the agreement, as well as interpretation of the agreement by private arbitrators or umpires. In contrast, the British system features open-ended, nonenforceable agreements.

3. *Decentralized collective bargaining,* largely due to the size of the United States, the diversity of its economic activity, and the historic role of product markets in shaping the contours of collective bargaining. By contrast, in Sweden the government establishes wage rates, and in Australia, most wages are set by arbitration councils.[22]

4. *Relatively high union dues and large union staffs* to negotiate and administer private, decentralized agreements, including grievance arbitration to organize against massive employer opposition and to lobby before legislative and administrative tribunals.

5. *Opposition by both large and small employers to union organization,* compared to other countries, which has been modified in its forms only slightly by 50 years of legislation.

6. *The role of government* in the U.S. industrial relations system. The government has been relatively passive in dispute resolution and highly legalistic both in administrative procedures and in the courts. As regulation has expanded over health and safety, pension benefits, and equal employment opportunity, the litigious quality of relations has grown in many relationships.

THE UNIONIZATION PROCESS

The Legal Basis

The Wagner, or National Labor Relations Act, of 1935 affirmed the right of all employees to engage in union activities, to organize, and to bargain collectively without interference or coercion from management. It also created the National Labor Relations Board (NLRB) to supervise representation elections and to investigate

■ **TABLE 14 ▪ 2**

UNFAIR LABOR PRACTICES FOR MANAGEMENT AND UNIONS UNDER THE
TAFT-HARTLEY ACT OF 1947

Management

1. Interference with, coercion of, or restraint of employees in their right to organize
2. Domination of, interference with, or illegal assistance of a labor organization
3. Discrimination in employment because of union activities
4. Discrimination because the employee has filed charges or given testimony under the act
5. Refusal to bargain in good faith
6. "Hot cargo" agreements: refusals to handle another employer's products because of that employer's relationship with the union

Union

1. Restraint or coercion of employees who do not want to participate in union activities
2. Any attempt to influence an employer to discriminate against an employee
3. Refusal to bargain in good faith
4. Excessive, discriminatory membership fees
5. Make-work or featherbedding provisions in labor contracts that require employers to pay for services that are not performed
6. Use of pickets to force an organization to bargain with a union, when the organization already has a lawfully recognized union
7. "Hot cargo" agreements: that is, refusals to handle, use, sell, transport, or otherwise deal in another employer's products

charges of unfair labor practices by management. The Taft-Hartley Act of 1947 reaffirmed these rights and, in addition, specified unfair labor practices both for management and for unions. These are shown in Table 14-2. The act was later amended (by the Landrum-Griffin Act of 1959) to add the *secondary boycott* as an unfair labor practice. A secondary boycott occurs when a union appeals to firms or other unions to stop doing business with an employer who sells or handles a struck product.

A so-called free-speech clause in the act specifies that management has the right to express its opinion about unions or unionism to employees, provided that it does not threaten or promise favors to employees to obtain antiunion actions. The Taft-Hartley Act covers most private-sector employers and nonmanagerial employees, except railroad and airline employees (they are covered under the Railway Labor Act of 1926). Federal government employees are covered by the Civil Service Reform Act of 1978. That act affirmed their right to organize and to bargain collectively over working conditions, established unfair labor practices for both management and

ETHICAL DILEMMA

Are the unfair labor practices shown in Table 14-2 also unethical? Are there circumstances under which activities might be legal (e.g., cutting off health-care benefits for striking workers) but at the same time also be unethical?

unions, established the Federal Labor Relations Authority to administer the act, authorized the Federal Services Impasse Panel to take whatever action is necessary to resolve impasses in collective bargaining, and prohibited strikes in the public sector.

DO LABOR-MANAGEMENT TEAMS VIOLATE FEDERAL LABOR LAW?[23]

COMPANY
EXAMPLE

After a year of heavy losses, Electromation, Inc., of Elkhart, Indiana, a small electrical parts maker, skipped wage hikes for its 200 workers. When employees objected, the company set up "action teams"—each with up to six hourly workers and one or two managers—to deal with problems such as absenteeism and pay scales for skilled workers. Soon after, the Teamsters began an organizing drive at the company and filed an objection to the action teams with the NLRB. The Teamsters argued that the teams were simply a company-sponsored union in which management decided who would be on each committee. Such "sham" unions were a common 1930s maneuver by companies to undercut legitimate unions. However, there was no evidence that Electromation knew that the union was organizing its workers when it implemented its "action team" plan.

In late 1992, the full NLRB ruled that such teams violated the National Labor Relations Act. In recent years, of course, teams have become quite popular, and they can be found at 80 percent of the 1000 largest U.S. companies. To be legal, such teams must be structured carefully so as not to interfere with collective bargaining issues over wages, hours, or conditions of employment. Here are three safe approaches:

1. Establishment of teams to deal with issues other than working conditions. These issues could include quality, efficiency, productivity, and safety.

2. Establishment of a team or committee specifically for purposes of communicating with employees. For example, the team solicits suggestions from employees but does not negotiate with management about them.

3. Delegation of management authority to a team. For example, a job enrichment team could be established in which the team decides on the job assignments and overtime scheduling for team members. Alternatively, a team consisting of workers and management that has the authority to resolve grievances could be established.

The Organizing Drive

There are three ways to kick off an organizing campaign: (1) employees themselves may begin it, (2) employees may request that a union begin one for them, or (3) in some instances, national and international unions may contact employees in organizations that have been targeted for organizing. In all three cases, employees are asked to sign *authorization cards* that designate the union as the employees' exclusive representative in bargaining with management.

Well-defined rules govern organizing activities:

1. Employee organizers may solicit fellow employees to sign authorization cards on company premises but not during working time.

2. Outside organizers may not solicit on premises *if* a company has an existing policy of prohibiting all forms of solicitation and if that policy has been enforced consistently.[24]

3. Management representatives may express their views about unions through speeches to employees on company premises. However, they are legally prohibited from interfering with an employee's freedom of choice concerning union membership.

The organizing drive usually continues until the union obtains signed authorization cards from 30 percent of the employees. At that point it can petition the National Labor Relations Board (NLRB) for a representation election. If the union secures authorization cards from more than 50 percent of the employees, however, it may ask management *directly* for the right to exclusive representation. Usually the employer refuses, and then the union petitions the NLRB to conduct an election.

The Bargaining Unit

When the petition for election is received, the NLRB conducts a hearing to determine the appropriate (collective) bargaining unit, that is, *the group of employees eligible to vote in the representation election.* Sometimes labor and management agree jointly on the appropriate bargaining unit. When they do not, the NLRB must determine the unit. The NLRB is guided in its decision, especially if there is no previous history of bargaining between the parties, by a concept called "community of interest." That is, the NLRB will define a unit that reflects the shared interests of the employees involved. Such elements include: similar wages, hours, and working conditions; the physical proximity of employees to one another; common supervision; the amount of interchange of employees within the proposed unit; and the degree of integration of the employer's production process or operation.[25] Under the Taft-Hartley Act, however, professional employees cannot be forced into a bargaining unit with nonprofessionals without their majority consent.

The *size* of the bargaining unit is critical both for the union and for the employer because it is strongly related to the outcome of the representation election. The larger the bargaining unit, the more difficult it is for the union to win. In fact, if a bargaining unit contains several hundred employees, it is almost invulnerable.[26]

The Election Campaign

Emotions on both sides run high during a representation election campaign. However, management typically is unaware that a union campaign is under way until most or all of the cards have been signed. At that point, management has some tactical advantages over the union. It can use company time and premises to stress the positive aspects of the current situation, and it can emphasize the costs of unionization and the loss of individual freedom that may result from collective representation. Supervisors may hold informal meetings to emphasize these antiunion themes. However, certain practices by management are prohibited by law, such as:

1. Physical interference, threats, or violent behavior toward union organizers

2. Interference with employees involved with the organizing drive

3. Discipline or discharge of employees for prounion activities
4. Promises to provide or withhold future benefits depending on the outcome of the representation election

These illegal activities are T.I.P.S.—that is, management may not *t*hreaten, *i*nterrogate, *p*romise, or *s*py.

Unions are also prohibited from unfair labor practices (see Table 14-2), such as coercing or threatening employees if they fail to join the union. In addition, the union can picket the employer *only* if (1) the employer is not currently unionized, (2) the petition for election has been filed with the NLRB in the past 30 days, and (3) a representation election has not been held during the previous year. Unions tend to emphasize two themes during organizing campaigns:

■ The union's ability to help employees satisfy their economic and personal needs
■ The union's ability to improve working conditions

The campaign tactics of management and the union are monitored by the NLRB. If the NLRB finds that either party engaged in unfair labor practices during the campaign, the election results may be invalidated and a new election conducted. However, a federal appeals court has ruled that the NLRB cannot *force* a company to bargain with a union that is not recognized by a majority of the workers, even if the company has made "outrageous" attempts to thwart unionization.[27] Earlier court rulings did allow the NLRB automatically to certify the union as the sole representative of the bargaining unit if evidence showed that management had interfered directly with the representation election process.

The Representation Election and Certification

If management and the union jointly agree on the size and composition of the bargaining unit, a representation election occurs shortly thereafter. However, if management does not agree, a long delay may ensue. Since such delays, sometimes over 3 years, often erode rank-and-file union support, they work to management's advantage.[28] Not surprisingly, therefore, few organizations agree with unions on the size and composition of the bargaining unit.

When a date for the representation election is finally established, the NLRB conducts a *secret ballot* election. If the union receives a majority of the ballots *cast* (not a majority of votes from members of the bargaining unit), the union becomes certified as the exclusive bargaining representative of all employees in the unit. Once a representation election is held, regardless of the outcome, no further elections can be held in that bargaining unit for *1 year*. The entire process is shown graphically in Figure 14-2.

The records of elections won and lost by unions and management have changed drastically since the 1950s. In the 1950s, unions won over 70 percent of representation elections. By the 1990s, that figure had slipped to less than half.[29]

The Decertification of a Union

If a representation election results in union certification, the first thing many employers want to know is when and how they can *decertify* the union. Under NLRB rules,

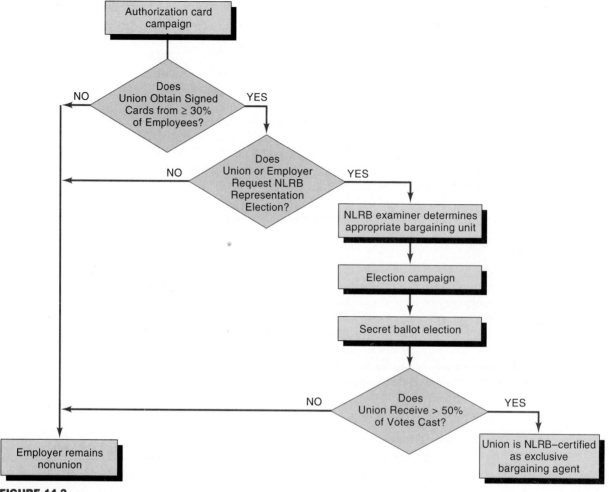

FIGURE 14-2
Steps involved and decisions to be made in a union organizing campaign.

an incumbent union can be decertified if a majority of employees within the bargaining unit vote to rescind the union's status as their collective bargaining agent in another representation election conducted by the NLRB.[30]

Since decertification is most likely to occur the first year or so after certification, unions will often insist on multiyear contracts to insulate themselves against it. Once the terms and duration of the labor contract are agreed to by both parties, the employer is obligated to recognize the union and to follow the provisions of the contract for the stipulated contract period. The American Federation of Labor and Congress of Industrial Organizations (AFL-CIO), a 14-million-member federation of local, national, and international unions in the United States, estimates that even after winning a certification election, unions are unable to sign contracts a third of the time. For example, after the Service Employees International Union won a representation election at the Hyatt Regency Hotel in New Orleans, it took the union 5 years to negotiate its first contract. By then, most of the original workers had left the hotel, and the union was decertified within 7 months.[31]

A petition for decertification must be supported by evidence that at least 30 percent of employees in the bargaining unit *want* a decertification election. NLRB cases indicate that two or more of the following types of evidence are necessary:

■ Employees have verbally repudiated the union.
■ There is a marked decline in the number of employees who subscribe to union dues checkoff, and hence a minority of employees remain on checkoff.
■ A majority of employees did not support the union during a strike.
■ The union has become less and less active as a representative of employees.
■ There was substantial turnover among employees subsequent to certification.
■ The union has admitted a lack of majority support.

As with certification elections, once a decertification election is held, a full year must elapse before another representation election can take place.

Once a union is legally certified as the exclusive bargaining agent for workers, the next task is to negotiate a contract that is mutually acceptable to management and labor. In our next section we examine this process in more detail.

COLLECTIVE BARGAINING: CORNERSTONE OF AMERICAN LABOR RELATIONS

Origins of Negotiation in the United States

The first U.S. strike occurred in the late eighteenth century (the Philadelphia cordwainers), and many other "turnouts" followed during the first half of the nineteenth century. These disputes were neither preceded by nor settled by negotiation. *Negotiation* is a two-party transaction whereby both parties intend to resolve a conflict.[32] Employers unilaterally established a scale of wages. If the wages were unacceptable, journeymen drew up a higher scale, sometimes inserting it into a Bible on which each worker swore that he or she would not work for less. The scale was presented to the employer, and if he or she did not agree, the workers "turned out" and stayed out until one side or the other caved in. There were no counterproposals, no discussions, no negotiations.

Horace Greeley, who was simultaneously a union sympathizer and an employer, found a better way. In 1850, he told a workers' mass meeting in Tammany Hall, "I do not agree that the journeymen should dictate a scale, but they should get the employers to agree to some scale." A few years later, Greeley proposed that workers come to negotiations with statistics and arguments supporting the fairness of their cause. He set the United States on the course known to the twentieth century as collective bargaining.[33]

The Art of Negotiation

What constitutes a "good" settlement? To be sure, the best outcome of negotiations occurs when both parties win. Sometimes negotiations fall short of this ideal. A really bad bargain is when both lose, yet this is a risk that is inherent in the process. Despite its limitations, abuses, and hazards, negotiation has become an indispensable process in free societies in general and in the U.S. labor movement in particular. The fact is that negotiation is the most effective device thus far invented for realizing common interests while compromising conflicting interests.[34] Any practice that threatens the process of collective bargaining will be resisted vigorously by organized labor.

In general, there are two postures that the parties involved in bargaining might assume: win-lose and win-win. In win-lose, or distributive, bargaining, the goals of the parties initially are irreconcilable—or at least they appear that way. Central to the conflict is the belief that there is a limited, controlled amount of key resources available—a "fixed pie" situation. Both parties may want to be the winner; both may want more than half of what is available.[35]

In contrast, in win-win, or integrative, bargaining, the goals of the parties are not mutually exclusive. If one side pursues its goals, this does not prohibit the other side from achieving its own goals. One party's gain is not necessarily at the other party's expense. The fundamental structure of an integrative bargaining situation is that it is possible for both sides to achieve their objectives.[36] While the conflict may initially appear to be win-lose to the parties, discussion and mutual exploration usually will suggest win-win alternatives.

How do skilled negotiators actually behave? In one study skilled negotiators were defined in terms of three criteria: (1) they were rated as effective by both sides, (2) they had a "track record" of significant success, and (3) they had a low incidence of "implementation" failures. Of the 48 skilled negotiators studied, 17 were union representatives, 12 were management representatives, 10 were contract negotiators, and 9 were classified as "other." The behavior of this group was then compared to that of an "average" group over 102 negotiating sessions. The following areas were assessed:[37]

- *Planning time.* There were no significant differences between the groups.
- *Exploration of options.* Skilled negotiators considered a wider range of outcomes or options for action (5.1 per issue) than average negotiators (2.6 per issue).
- *Common ground.* Skilled negotiators gave over three times as much attention to finding common ground areas as did average negotiators.
- *Long-term versus short-term orientation.* The skilled group made twice as many comments of a long-term nature as did the average group.
- *Setting limits.* The average negotiators tended to plan their objectives around a fixed point (e.g., "We aim to settle at 81"). Skilled negotiators were much more likely to plan in terms of upper and lower limits—to think in terms of ranges.
- *Sequence and issue planning.* Average negotiators tended to link issues in sequence (A, then B, then C, then D), whereas skilled negotiators tended to view issues as independent and not linked by sequence. The advantage: *flexibility.*

Face-to-Face Negotiating Behavior

- *Irritators.* Certain words and phrases that are commonly used during negotiations have negligible value in persuading the other party but do cause irritation. One of the most prevalent is "generous offer," used by a negotiator to describe his or her own proposal. Average negotiators used irritators more than 4 times more often than did skilled negotiators.

- *Counterproposals.* Frequently, during bargaining, one party puts forward a proposal and the other party immediately counters. Skilled negotiators make immediate counterproposals significantly less frequently than do average negotiators.

- *Argument dilution.* If one party has five reasons for doing something, is this more persuasive than having only one reason? Apparently not. Skilled negotiators used an average of 1.8 reasons; average negotiators used 3.0.

- *Reviewing the negotiation.* Over two-thirds of the skilled negotiators claimed they *always* set aside some time after a negotiation to review it and to consider what they had learned. In contrast, just under half of average negotiators made the same claim.

What's the bottom line in all this? If you want to become a win-win negotiator, these are the behaviors to imitate or avoid.

Preparation for Negotiations

Like any other competitive activity, physical or mental, the outcome of collective bargaining is influenced significantly by the preparation that precedes actual negotiations. What's worse, mistakes made during union-management negotiations are not easily corrected. Although there is no single "best" set of prebargaining activities or an optimum lead time in which to conduct them, the model shown in Figure 14-3 may provide a useful guide for planning.

In a general sense, planning for subsequent negotiations begins when the previous round of bargaining ends. However, as Figure 14-3 indicates, the formal process begins about 6 months (roughly 24 weeks) prior to the expiration of the current labor agreement. It includes the following 15 activities:[38]

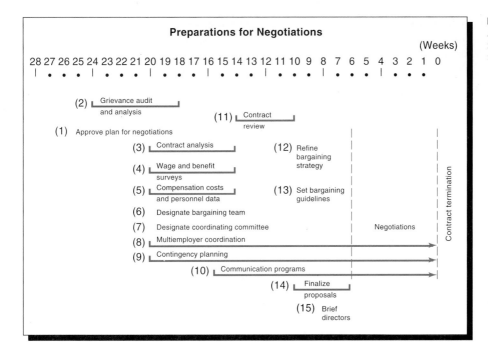

FIGURE 14-3
Activities and lead times involved in preparation for negotiations.

■ **TABLE 14 ▪ 3**
ANALYSIS OF 2 YEARS OF GRIEVANCES IN ONE COMPANY

Type of grievance	Total
Temporary layoff benefits	98
Transfer clause	64
Supervisor working	60
Noncontractual and local agreement	32
Discharge and discipline	27
Discrimination for union activities	26
Overtime pay	20
Overtime equalization	13
Call-out pay	11
Safety and welfare (safety shoes)	9
Contractor doing bargaining-unit work	9
Pension, supplemental unemployment benefits, and insurance	7
New job rate	6
Daily upgrade	5
Holiday pay	4
Schedule change	3
Report pay	3
Timeliness of grievance	2
Seniority	1
Total grievances during contract	400

1. *Approve the plan for negotiation* with top management, identifying management's objectives, intermediate and long-term plans, significant changes in the production mix, major technological innovations, and so forth.

2. *Conduct an audit and analysis of grievances* under the existing contract to provide such information as the number of grievances by section of the contract, interpretations of contract provisions through grievance settlements and arbitration awards, and weaknesses in contract language or provisions. One such analysis is shown in Table 14-3.

3. *Perform a contract analysis,* including a section-by-section comparison with other benchmark collective bargaining agreements. This is particularly important if the agreements tend to establish patterns in an industry. In addition, a review of demands made by the union during prior negotiations may help identify areas of mounting interest.

4. *Conduct wage and benefit surveys of competitors,* both union and nonunion. These are essential. Data on changes in the cost of living should be included, along with an assessment of the structure and operation of employee benefits. These data should be interpreted with respect to the current and projected composition of the workforce: for example, age and sex.

5. *Present compensation costs and employee data* in a form that allows management to determine changes in costs. For example:

Demographic profile of the workforce by sex, age, race, seniority group, shift, and job classification.

■ Wage payments and premiums: current rates, overtime premiums, shift-differential payments, report-in and call-in payments. In recent years employers in aerospace, steel, auto, telephone, and other industries have been trying to substitute annual (or "lump-sum") bonus checks for raises as a way of controlling labor costs.

In companies such as Boeing, workers have been receiving them since 1983, and they have become a way of life.[39]

■ Benefit payments: pay for sickness, vacations, holidays, and civic duties, as well as premiums for pensions, medical, and disability insurance coverage. (An example of one such calculation, costing out a holiday, is shown in Figure 14-4.)

■ The costs of benefits that are required by law: unemployment insurance, workers' compensation, Social Security.

■ Data on worker performance, including absenteeism, layoffs, promotions, transfers, paid time for union activities, and leaves of absence.[40]

6. *Designate a bargaining team* on the basis of technical knowledge, experience, and personality. Include members from line management (not the CEO), human resources–labor relations staff, and finance-accounting (to provide expertise in cost analysis). Unfortunately, evidence indicates that financial officers do *not* negotiate, evaluate, or even participate in major wage and benefit agreements.[41] This is a costly mistake.

7. *Designate a coordinating committee* to develop bargaining guidelines for approval by top management and to monitor progress during negotiations.

FIGURE 14-4
Costing out a holiday.

Average holiday workforce per plant:

   8 first shift, 3 second shift, 3 third shift = 14 workers on, 106 off

     14 <u>workers</u> × 13 plants × 8 hr × $22.00* = $32,032

     106 <u>nonworkers</u> × 13 plants × 8 hr × $11 = $121,264

Total hours worked per year by workforce:

     120 workers/plant × 13 plants × 2080 annual hours/worker = 3,244,800 hr/work year

Cost for holiday workers:

$$\frac{\$32,032}{3,244,800} = .010 \text{ cent}$$

Cost for nonworkers who are paid:

$$\frac{\$121,264}{3,244,800} = .037 \text{ cent}$$

Total cost of each holiday:

     .010 + .037 = .047 cent/hr

   ———————
*Normal $11/hr × double time.

8. *Provide multiemployer coordination* (as appropriate). This may range from a simple information exchange among loosely connected employers to close coordination among organizations (e.g., regional hospitals) that bargain individually with the same union.

9. *Plan for contingencies.* This is essential, for the possibility of a bargaining impasse that may lead to a strike is always present. In the event of a strike, here are the items that one company is prepared to deal with:

Benefits (strikers)	Customer service
Notification of company attorneys	Plant contacts
Continuation of operations	Media communication
Staffing (continuation of production)	Security
Notification responsibilities	Photographic record
General picket report	Strike incident report
Poststrike instructions	Reinstatement of strikers
Treatment of nonstrikers	Vendors
Strike preparation (sales, production)	

10. *Establish communication programs* designed to facilitate two-way communication between the bargaining team and supervisors. These will help bring supervisors' interests into the planning process. During negotiations, informed supervisors can be an effective channel of communication to nonsupervisory employees.

11. *Conduct a contract review.* This should be done by the coordinating committee and, based on all the data assembled thus far, will result in an assessment of contract provisions. Pay particular attention to:

■ Identification of important differences among contract provisions, workplace practices, and human resource policies

■ Identification of contract provisions to be revised, added, or eliminated (examples of ambiguous contract language that can lead to different interpretations are shown in Table 14-4; we might consider these "words to grieve by")

12. *Refine the bargaining strategy* once the preparatory activities are completed. The strategy established at the beginning of the planning process should be modified to reflect such factors as union demands and strategy, management's objectives, experience with multiemployer coordination, and the likelihood of a work stoppage.

13. *Set bargaining guidelines* for top management's approval. Ensure that the chief negotiator has the authority to reach a settlement within the guidelines. A procedure should also be established to modify the guidelines as needed once negotiations are under way.

14. *Finalize proposals* in writing, along with acceptable variations, to provide flexibility. Recheck the data bank for accuracy, comprehensiveness, and ease of access. Ensure that notices required by contract or by labor law have been issued and acknowledged. Compile bargaining aids (e.g., a bargaining book, data reference sheets, and work sheets), and finalize arrangements for note taking and record keeping.

■ TABLE 14 ▪ 4
WORDS TO GRIEVE BY

Ability	Fully	Possible
Absolutely	Habitually	Practical
Adequate	High degree	Properly
Almost	Immediately	Qualification
Capacity	Minimal	Reasonable
Completely	Minimum	Regular
Day	Necessary	Substantially equal
Equal	Normal	Sufficient number
Forthwith	Periodic	With all dispatch
Frequent		

15. *Brief directors*, as necessary, on the planning process, guidelines, and bargaining strategy. Establish a procedure for additional briefings during negotiations and reinforce the principle that governing board members should stay out of the bargaining process.

Successful bargaining results in an agreement that is mutually acceptable to both labor and management. Table 14-5 shows some of the major sections of a typical agreement.

Unfortunately, contract negotiations sometimes fail because the parties are not able to reach a timely and mutually acceptable settlement of the issues—economic, noneconomic, or a combination of both. When this happens, the union may strike, management may shut down operations (a lockout), or both parties may appeal for third-party involvement. Let's examine these processes in detail.

BARGAINING IMPASSES: STRIKES, LOCKOUTS, OR THIRD-PARTY INVOLVEMENT?

In every labor negotiation there exists the possibility of a strike. The right of employees to strike in support of their bargainable demands is protected by the Landrum-Griffin Act. However, there is no *unqualified* right to strike. A work stoppage by employees must be the result of a lawful labor dispute and not in violation of an existing agreement between management and the union. Strikers engaged in activities protected by law may not be discharged, but they may be replaced during the strike. Strikers engaged in activities that are not protected by law need not be rehired after the strike.[42]

Types of Strikes

As you might suspect by now, there are several different types of strikes. Let's consider the major types:

Unfair-labor-practice strikes. These are caused or prolonged by unfair labor practices of the employer. Employees engaged in this type of strike are afforded the highest degree of protection under the act, and under most circumstances they are entitled to reinstatement once the strike ends. Management must exercise great caution in

■ **TABLE 14 = 5**
MAJOR SECTIONS OF A TYPICAL COLLECTIVE BARGAINING AGREEMENT

Unchallenged representation	Protection of employees
Employee rights	Continuous hours of work
Management rights	Recall pay
No strikes	Distribution of overtime
Compensation	Out-of-title work
Travel	No discrimination
Health insurance	Benefits guaranteed
Attendance and leave	Job classifications
Workers' compensation leave with pay	Promotional examinations
Payroll	Employee assistance program
Employee development and training	Employee orientation
Safety and health maintenance	Performance rating procedures
Layoff procedures	Day-care centers
Joint labor-management committees	Discipline
Seniority	Grievance and arbitration procedures
Posting and bidding for job vacancies	Resignation
Employee benefit fund	Job abandonment
Workweek and workday	Duration of agreement

handling unfair-labor-practice strikes because the National Labor Relations Board will become involved and company liability can be substantial.

An economic strike. This is an action by the union of withdrawing its labor in support of bargaining demands, including those for recognition or organization. Economic strikers have limited rights to reinstatement.

Unprotected strikes. All remaining types of work stoppages, both lawful and unlawful, are included. These include sit-down strikes, strikes in violation of federal laws (e.g., the prohibition of strikes by employees of the federal government), slowdowns, wildcat strikes, and partial walkouts. Participants in unprotected strikes may be discharged by their employers.

Sympathy strikes. These are refusals by employees of one bargaining unit to cross a picket line of a different bargaining unit (e.g., when more than one union is functioning at an employer's plant). Although the National Labor Relations Board and the courts have recognized the right of the sympathy striker to stand in the shoes of the primary striker, the facts of any particular situation will ultimately determine the legal status of a sympathy strike.[43]

During a strike, certain rules of conduct apply to *both* parties; these are summarized in Table 14-6. In addition, certain special rules apply to management. *It must not:*

■ Offer extra rewards to nonstrikers or attempt to withhold the "extras" from strikers once the strike has ended and some or all strikers are reinstated

■ Threaten nonstrikers or strikers

■ **TABLE 14 ▪ 6**
RULES OF CONDUCT DURING A STRIKE

- People working in or having any business with the organization have a right to pass freely in and out.
- Pickets must not block a door, passageway, driveway, crosswalk, or other entrance or exit
- Profanity on streets and sidewalks may be a violation of state law or local ordinances.
- Company officials, with the assistance of local law enforcement agents, should make evey effort to permit individuals and vehicles to move in and out of the facility in a normal manner.
- Union officials or pickets have a right to talk to people going in or out. Intimidation, threats, and coercion are not permitted, either by verbal remarks or by physical action.
- The use of sound trucks may be regulated by state law or local ordinance with respect to noise level, location, and permit requirements.
- If acts of violence or trespassing occur on the premises, officials should file complaints or seek injunctions. If you are the object of violence, sign a warrant for the arrest of the person(s) causing the violence.
- Fighting, assault, battery, violence, threats, or intimidation are not permissible under the law. The carrying of knives, firearms, clubs, or other dangerous weapons may be prohibited by state law or local ordinance.

- Promise benefits to strikers in an attempt to end the strike or to undermine the union
- Threaten employees with discharge for taking part in a lawful strike
- Discharge nonstrikers who refuse to take over a striker's job

MORE FIRMS KEEP OPERATING IN SPITE OF STRIKES

COMPANY EXAMPLE

To an increasing number of companies, "strike" is no longer a frightening word, for they are prepared to continue operating right through a labor walkout. Highly automated firms like American Telephone & Telegraph Company have been operating through strikes for years, but in today's economic climate, where many labor-intensive firms such as Magic Chef, Inc., and Whirlpool Corporation truly believe that their survival depends on not giving in to union demands, such a strategy is revolutionary. Although union officials criticize these management tactics, such actions are producing a flourishing business for security firms. The security firms provide companies with armored cars, vans, and guards to protect non-striking workers during labor disputes. For example, one security firm helped Dannon Company, the yogurt maker, maintain operations at several New York area plants during a series of strikes by members of the Teamsters union. The security firm provided about 100 guards to escort company trucks. The guards do not carry weapons, but they are armed with cameras. When strikers know they will be photographed, there tends to be a lot less violence. The cost for the 14-week security service: more than $1 million.[44]

Labor's ultimate weapon, the strike, is mostly failing. The threat of permanent replacement, recent court decisions, growing antiunion sentiment, and a pool of unemployed workers willing to break a strike make it easier for employers to defeat a walkout.[45] As a result, the number of strikes and lockouts has decreased steadily throughout the last two decades. Thus the number of major work stoppages fell to 40 in 1992, compared to 187 in 1980 and 381 in 1970.[46] At Caterpillar, Inc., the maker of construction equipment, management forced an abrupt end to a 5-month strike by 12,500 UAW members by advertising for permanent replacements at six plants in Illinois. With an average wage of $17 an hour and an 8.5 percent state unemployment rate, union members knew they'd be committing economic suicide if they stayed out. The specter of losing jobs forced the union back to the bargaining table.[47]

Proposed alternatives to strikes, including corporate campaigns and in-plant slowdowns, have had mixed success. During a slowdown, while workers adhere to the minimums of their job requirements, they continue to get paid, thereby frustrating management, but such a "work-to-rule" strategy could backfire in the long run; if productivity suffers a prolonged decline and a company fails to meet its production schedules, competitors will move in quickly. Then everybody loses. Companies are fighting back by retaliating in kind, firing activist employees and in some cases locking out the entire workforce. A recent NLRB decision that permits companies to replace locked-out workers with temporary employees has strengthened management's hand.[48]

Management's antiunion tactics have been quite successful, but this does not absolve management of the responsibility to treat workers with dignity and respect, to avoid arrogance, and to recognize that it is hard to give up gains that were so difficult to earn in the first place.

The Increasingly Bitter Nature of Strikes

Although the number of strikes has dropped dramatically during the 1990s, their intensity and general "nastiness" has escalated significantly. Unfair labor practices by both management and labor seem more and more common. For example, when Local 376 of the UAW engaged in a legal strike against Colt Firearms Co., a judge ruled that the company engaged in dozens of unfair labor practices. It changed working conditions, failed to bargain in good faith, offered to settle separately with employees who quit the union, and rejected the union's offer to have strikers return to work under the terms of their old contract. Although the company kept its plants operating by using replacement workers and about 200 union members who crossed the picket lines, a judge ordered that 800 strikers be reinstated in their old jobs.[49]

When the United Mine Workers struck Pittston Co., the company hired replacements and cut off the miners' health-care benefits. Over the course of a bitter 9-month strike, the company was forced to spend about $20 million in security, and the union accumulated $65 million in court fines related to picket-line violence and other violations of court injunctions.[50] By any stretch of the imagination, could this be considered "win-win" negotiating? A similar pattern of violence ensued in the 1990 strikes at Greyhound, Inc., and the New York *Daily News*. When workers see their jobs being lost to replacement workers, violence—including sniper fire, smashed windshields, and threats against substitute workers—often follows. During the *Daily News* strike, the paper itself became a weapon in the war, as one headline pleaded "Call Off the Thugs."[51]

A 1990 Supreme Court decision in *NLRB v. Curtin Matheson Scientific, Inc.*, may undermine a common management strategy. The decision upheld the Board's policy that a company cannot oust a striking union by hiring replacement workers and asserting that the new employees don't support the union. Such a policy had been an effective weapon for management because a company is not required to recognize a

Employees at American Airlines exercised their legal right to strike in November 1993.

union that is not supported by a majority of its employees. In short, employers can't eliminate unions simply by replacing union workers.[52]

What remains unclear is the extent to which the bitterness of strikes will be reduced. In many ways, broader forces are at work, as both companies and their workers are caught in the maw of an economic vise, the jaws of which represent domestic and international competition.

Lockouts

When a collective bargaining agreement has expired and an employer's purpose is to put economic pressure on a union to settle a contract on terms favorable to the employer, it is legal for the employer to lock out its employees.[53] It also is legal for a company to replace the locked-out workers with temporary replacements in order to continue operating during the lockout. However, the use of *permanent* replacements (without first consulting the union) is not permissible, according to the National Labor Relations Board, because such an action would completely destroy the bargaining unit and represent an unlawful withdrawal of recognition of a duly designated union.[54] Thus, when BASF Corp. ended a 5½-year lockout of the Oil, Chemical, and Atomic Workers union from its sprawling chemical complex in Geismar, Louisiana, the two parties agreed to a 3-year contract. The settlement affected 110 workers, who were reinstated in their old jobs. However, 5½ years earlier, the union had represented 370 workers at the 1200-employee plant.[55]

Third-Party Involvement

A bargaining impasse occurs when the parties are unable to move further toward settlement. In an effort to resolve the impasse, a neutral third party may become involved. In most private-sector negotiations, the parties have to agree *voluntarily* before any third-party involvement can be imposed on them. Because employees in the public sector are prohibited by law from striking, the use of third parties is more prevalent there.[56]

Three general types of third-party involvement are common: mediation, fact finding, and interest arbitration. Each becomes progressively more constraining on the freedom of the parties.

Mediation. Mediation is a process by which a neutral third party attempts to help the parties in dispute to reach a settlement of the issues that divide them. It ordinarily does not involve the neutral third party acting as a judge to decide the resolution of the dispute (a process referred to as "arbitration").[57] Rather, mediation involves persuading, opening communications, allowing readjustment and reassessment of bargaining stances, and making procedural suggestions (e.g., scheduling, conducting, and controlling meetings; establishing or extending deadlines).

There is no set time when a mediator will go in and attempt to resolve a dispute. By law the Federal Mediation and Conciliation Service must be notified 30 days prior to the expiration of all labor contracts. However, some unions, such as the United Auto Workers, traditionally refuse mediation, and so many others manage to settle by themselves that the agency estimates that it is involved in only 8000 to 9000 of the country's 100,000 yearly labor negotiations.

Mediators have two restrictions on their power: (1) they are involved by invitation only, and (2) their advice lacks even so much as the umpire's option of throwing someone out of the game. Some will do almost anything to get a settlement.

When 55,000 aerospace workers struck Boeing Corp., Douglas Hammond, the federal mediator, actually stepped outside his usual role as a neutral middleman and devised the agreement that resolved the strike. There was tremendous pressure to do *something:* in the Seattle area, personal income had slid $30 million a week during the strike, the White House cited the stoppage as a factor in lower retail sales and industrial production indicators, and calls from the secretary of labor and the Pentagon were becoming routine. Even the U.S. trade deficit was affected because of Boeing's role as a leading exporter.

Had the effort backfired, Mr. Hammond's standing would have been compromised and negotiations thrown back to square one. Why did he succeed? According to the president of Machinists District 751: "In the negotiating room, Doug Hammond didn't duck. He took a bold stand and I admire him." Added Boeing's top negotiator: "He seems to know the timing, when to separate us and when to get us face-to-face. I trust him, and that's the bottom line."[58]

Fact Finding. Fact finding is a dispute resolution mechanism that is commonly used in the public sector at the state and local government levels. Disputes over the terms of collective bargaining agreements are more common at these levels since such bargaining ordinarily includes subjects such as pay and benefits that are excluded from bargaining with the federal government.

In a fact-finding procedure, each party submits whatever information it believes is relevant to a resolution of the dispute. A neutral fact finder then makes a study of the evidence and prepares a report on the facts. This procedure is often useful where the parties disagree over the truthfulness of the information each is using.[59]

Actually, the term "fact finding" is a misnomer. This is because fact finders often proceed, with statutory authority, to render a public recommendation of a reasonable settlement. In this respect, fact finding is similar to mediation. However, neither fact finding nor mediation necessarily results in a contract between management and labor. Consequently, the parties often resort to arbitration of a dispute, either as a matter of law (compulsory arbitration) or by mutual agreement between union and management (interest arbitration).

Interest Arbitration. Like fact finding, interest arbitration is used primarily in the public sector. However, arbitration differs considerably from mediation and fact finding. As one author noted: "While mediation assists the parties to reach their own settlement, arbitration hears the positions of both and decides on binding settlement terms. While fact finding would recommend a settlement, arbitration dictates it."[60]

Interest arbitration is controversial for at least two reasons. One, imposition of interest arbitration eliminates the need for the parties to settle on their own because if they reach an impasse, settlement by an outsider is certain. Two, many municipal employers apparently feel that arbitrators have been too generous in the awards made to public-employee unions. As a result, some states now specify the factors arbitrators must consider in making awards. Some of these, such as comparable wage rates, are items favored by unions; others, such as productivity and the ability of the employer to pay, are items favored by management.[61]

When the Strike Is Over

The period of time immediately after a strike is critical, since an organization's problems are not over when the strike is settled. There is the problem of conflict between strikers and their replacements (if replacements were hired) and the reaccommodation of strikers to the workplace. After an economic strike is settled, the method of reinstatement is best protected by a written *memorandum of agreement* with the union that outlines the intended procedure. A key point of consideration in any strike aftermath is misconduct by some strikers. To refuse reinstatement for such strikers following an economic strike, management must be able to present evidence (e.g., photographs) to prove the misconduct.

The most important human aspect at the end of the strike is the restoration of harmonious working relations as soon as possible so that full operations can be resumed. A letter or a speech to employees welcoming them back to work can help this process along, as can meetings with supervisors indicating that no resentment or ill will is to be shown toward returning strikers. In practice, this may be difficult to do. However, keep these points in mind:

- Nothing is gained by allowing vindictiveness of any type in any echelon of management.
- The burden of maintaining healthy industrial relations now lies with the organization.
- There is always another negotiation ahead, and rancor has no place at any bargaining table.[62]

TRENDS IN COLLECTIVE BARGAINING

Changes in the Economic Environment

While the impact of foreign competition on U.S. firms is well known, three other changes have also affected the course of collective bargaining in recent years: nonunion domestic competition, deregulation, and recession. New domestic competitors that began and managed to remain unorganized have produced low-cost market competition, which, in turn, has put downward pressure on union wage rates. At nonunion Nucor Corp., workers are paid a base rate below that of union workers at other steelmakers. But they are also paid a production bonus that can exceed 150 percent of base pay. The result: very industrious workers can earn more than $20 an hour—well above union wages. Nucor's total labor costs per hour are about equal to those of other unionized steelmakers, but the company gets higher productivity from its workers because it has lower staffing levels and more flexible work rules.[63]

The deregulation of many product markets created two key challenges to existing union relationships. One, it made market entry very much easier, as in over-the-road trucking, airlines, and telecommunications. Two, under regulation, management had little incentive to cut labor costs, because high labor costs could be passed on to consumers; conversely, labor-cost savings could not be used to gain a competitive advantage in the product market. Under deregulation, however, even major airlines (which are almost entirely organized) found that low costs translated into low fares and a competitive advantage. As a result, all carriers need to match the lowest costs of their competitors by matching their labor contracts.[64] At United Airlines, unions gave $5.5 billion in concessions over 6 years. Why? In return for up to 63 percent of United's stock. This put intense pressure on other airlines to match United's cost structure in order to compete.[65]

Finally, the severity of the recession in the early 1990s put added pressure on firms to reduce labor costs in order to survive. To management, concessions represented a ready means of improving cash flow. To unions, layoffs decimated their ranks, with the United Auto Workers and the United Steelworkers (USW) losing about half their memberships. In many unions, therefore, the focus of bargaining shifted to emphasize job security to reduce the risk of job loss. For example, the USW chose a bold course in 1993, when it set out to negotiate contracts in the steel industry. Instead of the usual demands for better pay, the union stretched out a cooperative hand to management. Companies like Inland, National, and Bethlehem met the union halfway. They gave the union job guarantees and decision-making power, including seats on boards of directors. In exchange, the USW agreed to slash work rules, install teams on the factory floor, and alleviate disruptive strike threats, signing 6-year agreements.[66] These are positive responses to a changing economic environment.

High-Priority Issues for Management and Labor in the 1990s

Given the changes noted above, management's top priority is to control the growth of labor costs. To do so, companies are pushing for greater cost sharing of health-care expenses, weakening of cost-of-living clauses, greater links between pay and corporate performance, and more emphasis on lump-sum bonuses that don't step up the wage base. They are also trying to increase flexibility by securing changes in restrictive work rules. Frequently, such changes lead to reductions in the numbers of employees needed to staff ongoing operations.

Unions, on the other hand, are seeking to phase out two-tier wage schemes (which set lower pay for new employees), to resist cuts in health-care benefits, and to gain improved job security (maintenance of employment at the same firm) and "employment security" for their members. In the latter approach, a company that is laying off a worker would train him or her for another job and try to place that worker in another job.[67] As we shall see, both management and labor have been willing to compromise on these broad goals in specific instances.

Recent Bargaining Outcomes

In general terms, median first-year wage raises decreased to 3.0 percent in collectively bargained contracts in 1993, down from 3.6 percent in 1992. Lump-sum bonuses appeared in only 7 percent of all agreements, down from 42 percent in 1988.[68]

As for specific agreements, consider the pattern bargaining contracts (that run until 1996) between 450,000 UAW workers and GM, Chrysler, and Ford. GM, for example, won the right to eliminate 65,000 blue-collar jobs by 1996 (in an effort to close its yawning $800-a-car labor-cost gap with Ford) and to require laid-off workers to relocate. UAW members have to accept work in plants 100 miles or more away from their former jobs or risk losing their jobless benefits. Before, workers could turn down posts more than 50 miles away and still draw up to 100 percent of their pay. The companies did not succeed in getting UAW members to pay premiums for health insurance.

UAW members got a 3 percent pay increase in 1994 and lump-sum payments in 1995 and 1996, plus sweetened pension benefits of as much as $200 per month. The union did agree, however, to a two-tier pay system whereby newly hired workers will receive 75 percent of the standard UAW base pay of about $18 an hour for 3 years (up from 18 months). Finally, the companies agreed to continue a job- and income-protection program that promises as much as 95 percent of full pay to laid-off workers— even those whose jobs disappeared as long ago as 1987.[69]

As another example, consider the agreement between Rubbermaid, Inc., and the United Rubber Workers Local 302 at the company's 73-year-old plant in Wooster, Ohio. Over a 7-year period the union gave ground on wages and health benefits; it agreed to eliminate automatic cost-of-living increases, reduce overtime pay, and relax rigid work rules. It also agreed to a two-tier wage system that pays people hired since March 1987 substantially less than veteran workers. Why did the union make such concessions? Rubbermaid promised to guarantee the jobs of the workers during the life of the contract.[70] The result: no layoffs in Wooster, despite the fact that the company has 23 other factories that are newer, lower-cost, and nonunion. Both sales and profits have increased substantially at the plant. But instead of wage increases, Rubbermaid earmarks about one-third of its profits for dividends to shareholders and nearly two-thirds for investment in new, more efficient machinery that the company considers vital to ensure its survival.

Labor-Management Cooperation

Make no mistake about it: the recent popularity of cooperation stems largely from the sweeping changes in the economic environment that have occurred over the last decade. Another reason is new technology—factory automation, robotics, and more modern production systems. Cooperation offers a pragmatic approach to problems that threaten the survival of companies, the job and income security of their employees, and the institutional future of their unions.[71] Said a United Steelworkers negotiator: "We ain't going to survive by fighting every three years."[72]

Despite the economic imperatives, however, there is considerable resistance to joint cooperative efforts. Here are four major obstacles: managers who will not accept the legitimacy of a union, union officials who are ideologically opposed to cooperating with management, internal union politics that impede cooperation with an employer, and fears of employees and union officials that their suggestions may lead to the elimination of their jobs.[73]

A final obstacle is lack of trust—on both sides. Consider the auto industry, where each side has good reason to be wary of the other. At GM's big luxury-car assembly plant in Lake Orion, Michigan, more than 120 people work in joint labor-management programs, but the plant has one of the worst labor relations records in the company. In fact, worker opposition forced plant management to abandon an effort to get employees to operate in teams to improve efficiency and quality. Neither is the company without sin, however. In 1987, GM included a plant-closing moratorium in its contract with the UAW. But by calling closedowns "indefinite idlings" instead of "closings," GM closed four car plants and three truck plants. In all, GM has eliminated 1 in 10 of its UAW jobs since 1987.[74]

When cooperation works, however, it works well and often reduces the adversarial confrontations that characterize U.S. labor relations. Consider NUMMI, the joint venture between Toyota and General Motors in Fremont, California. As a result of union-management cooperation, the plant currently has fewer than 30 grievances a year, with an absenteeism rate of less than 6 percent and an unscheduled absenteeism rate of only 1 percent.[75]

Institutionalizing cooperative relationships is no easy task. However, successful efforts have been characterized by features such as the following:[76]

- The reason for the cooperative effort remains strong.
- Benefits derived from the cooperation are distributed equitably.
- The union is perceived as instrumental in attaining program benefits.
- The cooperative effort does not infringe on traditional collective bargaining issues (see the earlier example of Electromation, Inc.).
- The program does not threaten management prerogatives.
- Management has refrained from subcontracting out bargaining-unit work.
- The program does not overlap the grievance procedure.
- Union leaders are not viewed as being co-opted.
- The cooperative effort is protected from the use of bargaining tactics and maneuvers.
- Union leaders continue to pursue member goals on traditional economic issues.

Current Tactics of Management and Labor

Both sides are becoming quite sophisticated in their attempts to win the minds, hearts, and votes of workers during organizing campaigns and also in response to industrial action. For example, when the UAW tried to organize Nissan's car and truck assembly plant in Smyrna, Tennessee, top Nissan officials made no public statements in the contentious organizing campaign. Instead, Nissan made antiunion employees available to journalists to explain their feelings. The company also relied on frequent and forceful antiunion broadcasts on the plant's closed-circuit television network.[77] Workers rejected the union by a 2-to-1 margin.

Management is adopting aggressive antiunion tactics in response to strikes, hiring replacement workers and using lockouts. It has also pitted unionized workers against one another. General Motors did this when it said it would close down either a plant in Arlington, Texas, or one in Ypsilanti, Michigan. The 3200 Arlington workers put cooperation with GM ahead of UAW fellowship, voting to allow a three-shift schedule to build cars around the clock without overtime pay and approving other work-rule changes. Workers in Ypsilanti didn't offer GM much, and the company closed the plant.[78]

In response to these tactics, unions have taken several specific actions. One is in-plant slowdowns. Rather than strike and risk losing jobs to outsiders hired to replace them, workers stay on the job and carry out their tasks "by the book," showing no initiative and taking no shortcuts. Although the AFL-CIO has endorsed this strategy, results thus far are inconclusive.[79] Another tactic is the "rolling strike," which targets one shop at a time. Moving the action keeps management from easily hiring replacements. Rolling strikes recently were used by state employees in Oregon, clerical workers in Los Angeles, and janitors in Washington, D.C. They are difficult to combat because they are more like guerrilla warfare than a full-fledged battle. However, in a recent New Jersey supermarket strike, management locked out union members at one unpicketed store for each store picketed.[80]

Unions are also trying to broaden their base. Thus only about 11 percent of the 1.3 million members of the Teamsters union actually drive trucks. The remainder includes workers as diverse as pilots, zookeepers, and Disney World's Mickey Mouse.

The organizing tactics of unions are becoming more sophisticated as well. Unions such as the Clothing and Textile Workers are using surveys before undertaking expensive organizing campaigns. Unions such as the Airline Pilots Association and the Steelworkers are hiring investment bankers for projects ranging from examining an employer's balance sheet to buying a company, as United, Northwest, and Trans

IMPACT OF UNION REPRESENTATION ON PRODUCTIVITY, QUALITY OF WORK LIFE, AND THE BOTTOM LINE

Is there a link between unionization and organizational performance? Unionization of a workforce often increases control over wage levels by giving monopoly power to the union as the single seller of labor to an enterprise. It also creates a "voice" mechanism for employees by establishing negotiated grievance procedures and the right to bargain collectively.[81]

Economic studies generally show that the existence of a grievance process that acts as a check or balance on management's authority can enhance productivity. One explanation for this is that higher productivity results from lower turnover, which in turn enhances employees' knowledge of the jobs they perform.[82]

If unions actually do raise productivity, why do managements oppose them with such vigor? The answer lies in the impact unions have on corporate profits. A number of studies support the argument that while unions may increase productivity, the wage increases associated with unionization often exceed productivity gains.[83]

IMPLICATIONS FOR MANAGEMENT PRACTICE

Given current conditions in the economic environment, a distributive (win-lose) orientation toward labor is simply inefficient. Rather, view your employees as a potential source of competitive advantage. Treat them with dignity and respect, and they will respond in kind. As for the labor movement itself, it too needs to adjust.

World Airlines' pilots have done.[81] At Harvard University, the scene of two unsuccessful organizing campaigns, the American Federation of State, County, and Municipal Employees finally won over the 3500 workers after it broke with tradition and allowed an open shop and worker-management councils without union participation.[82] Finally, unions are lobbying hard for prolabor legislation; for example, legislation that would outlaw permanent replacement workers. As these few examples demonstrate, it will be a long time before organized labor's obituary is written.

HUMAN RESOURCE MANAGEMENT IN ACTION: CONCLUSION

IMPROVING PRODUCTIVITY, QWL, AND PROFITS THROUGH LABOR-MANAGEMENT COOPERATION

There are lots of success stories of labor-management cooperation in which established unions have taken leading roles. For example, the Amalgamated Clothing and Textile Workers Union, which represents 6200 workers who assemble copiers at Xerox Corporation, has helped cut costs on its machines by millions of dollars. Three tries at teamwork since 1982 have worked out so well that Xerox is bringing 300 jobs from abroad to a new plant in Utica, New York, where it expects higher quality and savings of $2 million a year. Xerox gives union officials internal financial documents and teaches them statistics in the same classes managers take. Cooperative efforts such as these have produced big gains in efficiency at companies such as National Steel Corporation, Scott Paper Company, and LTV Corporation.

Success stories like these will promote further expansion of labor-management cooperation. That is especially likely if the 86 unions of the AFL-CIO follow through on a 1994 report that urges labor to become partners with management in boosting efficiency. As we have seen, the world has changed dramatically in the last decade. If U.S. labor leaders let today's opportunities for labor-management cooperation slip by, they may not get another chance to be part of the solution to the continuing challenge to improve productivity, quality of work life, and profits.

SUMMARY

At a general level, the goal of unions is to improve economic and other conditions of employment. Although they have been successful over the years in achieving these goals, more recently they have been confronted with challenges that have led to membership losses.

Employees join unions for two reasons: (1) dissatisfaction with working conditions and a belief that employees cannot change them and (2) belief that collective action will yield positive outcomes. The National Labor Relations Board, created by the Wagner Act, supervises union organizing campaigns and representation elections. If the union wins, it becomes the *sole* bargaining agent for employees.

Collective bargaining is the cornerstone of the U.S. labor movement. Anything that threatens its continued viability will be resisted vigorously by organized labor. Both sides typically prepare about 6 months in advance for the next round of negotiations. Such preparation involves an analysis of grievances, current wage and benefits costs, and the costs of proposed settlements. Unfortunately, bargaining sometimes reaches an impasse, at which point the parties may resort to a strike (workers) or a lockout (management). Alternatively, the parties may request third-party intervention in the form of mediation, fact finding, or interest arbitration. In the public sector, such intervention is usually required.

Current trends in industrial relations, such as labor-management cooperation, and new tactics used by management and labor are being fueled by changes in the economic climate. These include foreign competition, domestic nonunion competition, changes in technology, and deregulation. In view of these changes, accommodation of labor and management to each other's needs (win-win bargaining) is more appropriate than the old adversarial win-lose approach.

DISCUSSION QUESTIONS

14▪1 Are the roles of labor and management inherently adversarial?

14▪2 Discuss the rights and obligations of unions and management during a union organizing drive.

14▪3 Discuss key differences in the behavior of successful versus average negotiators.

14▪4 Contrast the Japanese system of industrial relations to that of the United States.

14▪5 Compare and contrast mediation, fact finding, and interest arbitration.

REFERENCES

1. Brett, J. M. (1980). Why employees want unions. *Organizational Dynamics*, **8**(4), 47–59.

2. Hamner, W. C., & Smith, F. J. (1978). Work attitudes as predictors of unionization activity. *Journal of Applied Psychology*, **63**, 415–421.

3. Deshpande, S. P., & Fiorito, J. (1989). Specific and general beliefs in union voting models. *Academy of Management Journal*, **32**, 883–897.

4. Kochan, T. A. (1979). How American workers view labor unions. *Monthly Labor Review*, **103**(4), 23–31.

5. Brett, op. cit.

6. Greenwald, J. (1993, Dec. 6). A growing itch to fight. *Time*, pp. 34, 35. See also Ayres, B. D., Jr. (1989, Apr. 27). Coal miners' strike hits feelings that go deep. *The New York Times*, p. A16.

7. Kristol, I. (1978, Oct. 23). Understanding trade unionism. *The Wall Street Journal*, p. 28.

8. Serrin, W. (1985, Dec. 5). Union at Stevens, yes; upheaval, no. *The New York Times*, p. A18.

9. Greenwald, op. cit. See also Salwen, K. G. (1993, Oct. 5). What, us worry? Big unions' leaders overlook bad news, opt for status quo. *The Wall Street Journal*, pp. B1, B4. See also Labor letter (1993, Sept. 21). *The Wall Street Journal*, p. A1.

10. Greenwald, op. cit.

11. Foegen, J. H. (1989). Labor unions: Don't count them out yet! *Academy of Management Executive*, **3**(1), 67–70.

12. Greenhouse, S. (1985, Sept. 1). Reshaping labor to woo the young. *The New York Times*, pp. 1F, 6F.

13. Greenwald, op. cit., p. 35.

14. Schuster, M. (1990). Union-management cooperation. In J. A. Fossum (ed.), *Employee and labor relations*. Washington, DC: Bureau of National Affairs, pp. 4-44 to 4-81.

15. Milbank, D. (1992, May 5). On the ropes: Unions' woes suggest how the labor force in U.S. is shifting. *The Wall Street Journal*, pp. A1, A6.

16. Freedman, A. (1988, May). How the 1980's have changed industrial relations. *Monthly Labor Review*, pp. 35–38.

17. Ibid.

18. Dowling, P. J., & Schuler, R. S. (1993). *International dimensions of human resource management* (2d ed.). Boston: PWS-Kent.

19. Poole, M. (1986). *Industrial relations: Origins and patterns of national diversity*. London: Routledge & Kegan Paul.

20. Japanese union membership (1992, Dec. 30). *The Wall Street Journal*, p. A4. See also Labor letter (1991, Apr. 23). *The Wall Street Journal*, p. A1.

21. Dunlop, J. T. (1988, May). Have the 1980's changed U.S. industrial relations? *Monthly Labor Review*, pp. 29–34.

22. Fossum, J. A. (1990). Employee and labor relations in an evolving environment. In J. A. Fossum (ed.), *Employee and labor relations*. Washington, DC: Bureau of National Affairs, pp. 4-1 to 4-22.

23. Chait, H. N. (1993, Winter). Labor law update. *HRM Update*, pp. 1–3. See also Salwen, K. G. (1992, Dec. 18). NLRB says labor-management teams at firm violated company-union rule. *The Wall Street Journal*, p. A12. See also Putting a damper on that old team spirit (1992, May 4). *Business Week*, p. 60.

24. *NLRB v. Babcock & Wilcox* (1956). 105 U.S. 351.

25. Kilgour, J. G. (1978, April). Before the union knocks. *Personnel Journal*, pp. 186–192, 212, 213.

26. Kilgour, J. G. (1983, March–April). Union organizing activity among white-collar employees. *Personnel*, pp. 18–27.

27. Wermiel, S. (1983, Nov. 16). NLRB can't force companies to bargain with minority unions, U.S. court rules. *The Wall Street Journal*, p. 12.

28. Milbank, op. cit. See also Prosten, W. (1979). The rise in NLRB election delays: Measuring business's new resistance. *Monthly Labor Review*, **103**(2), 39–41.

29. Unions holding fewer, winning more elections (1992, December). *Mountain States Employers Council Bulletin*, p. 4.

30. Swann, J. P., Jr. (1983). The decertification of a union. *Personnel Administrator*, **28**(1), 47–51.

31. Kotlowitz, A. (1987, Apr. 1). Grievous work. *The Wall Street Journal*, pp. 1, 12.

32. Fisher, R., Ury, W., & Patton, B. (1991). *Getting to yes* (2d ed.). New York: Penguin.

33. Ways, M. (1979, Jan. 15). The virtues, limits, and dangers of negotiation. *Fortune*, pp. 86–90.

34. Ibid.

35. Lewicki, R. J., & Litterer, J. A. (1985). *Negotiation*. Homewood, IL: Irwin.

36. Walton, R. E., & McKersie, R. B. (1965). *A behavioral theory of labor negotiations*. New York: McGraw-Hill.

37. Moran, R. T. (1987). *Getting your yen's worth: How to negotiate with Japan, Inc.* Houston: Gulf.

38. Miller, R. L. (1978, January). Preparations for negotiations. *Personnel Journal*, pp. 36–39, 44.

39. Uchitelle, L. (1989, Oct. 12). Boeing's fight over bonuses. *The New York Times*, pp. D1, D6.

40. For more information on labor contract costing, see Cascio, W. F. (1991). *Costing human resources: The financial impact of behavior in organizations* (3d ed.). Boston: PWS-Kent.

41. Fruhan, W. E., Jr. (1985). Management, labor, and the golden goose. *Harvard Business Review*, **63**(5), 131–141.

42. American Society for Personnel Administration (1983). *Strike preparation manual* (rev. ed.). Berea, OH: Author.

43. Ibid.

44. Greenberger, D. (1983, Oct. 11). Striking back. *The Wall Street Journal*, pp. 1, 18

45. Kilborn, P. T. (1992, Apr. 16). Caterpillar's trump card. *The New York Times*, pp. A1, B6. See also Bernstein, A. (1991, Aug. 5). You can't bargain with a striker whose job is no more. *Business Week*, p. 27.

46. Rose, R. L. (1992, Apr. 20). Caterpillar's success in ending strike may curtail unions' use of walkouts. *The Wall Street Journal*, p. A3.

47. Hicks, J. P. (1992, Apr. 21). Still bitter, Caterpillar workers return. *The New York Times*, p. A16.

48. Uchitelle, L. (1993, June 13). Labor draws the line in Decatur. *The New York Times*, pp. F1, F6. See also Kotlowitz, A. (1987, May 22). Labor's shift: Finding strikes harder to win, more unions turn to slowdowns. *The Wall Street Journal*, pp. 1, 7.

49. Colt told to rehire 800 strikers; back pay is to be in millions (1989, Sept. 13). *The New York Times*, p. B3.

50. Swasy, A., & Karr, A. R. (1990, Jan. 2). Pittston, UMW tentatively set labor accord. *The Wall Street Journal*, p. A3.

51. Kifner, J. (1990, Nov. 4). Daily News strike becomes a battle for advertisers. *The New York Times*, pp. 1, 38. See also Kilborn, P. T. (1990, Apr. 9). Money isn't everything in Greyhound strike. *The New York Times*, pp. A1, A12.

52. Wermiel, S. (1990, Apr. 18). Supreme Court upholds policy barring tactic used to oust a striking union. *The Wall Street Journal*, p. A3.

53. Mills, D. Q. (1994). *Labor-management relations* (5th ed.). New York: McGraw-Hill.

54. Ibid.

55. BASF is poised to end 5.5-year U.S. lockout (1989, Dec. 18). *International Herald Tribune*, p. 7.

56. Fossum, J. A. (1989). *Labor relations: Development, structure, process* (4th ed.). Homewood, IL: BPI-Irwin.

57. Mills, op. cit.

58. Wartzman, R. (1989, Nov. 21). Seizing initiative pays off for Boeing strike mediator. *The Wall Street Journal*, pp. B1, B11.

59. Mills, op. cit.

60. Fossum, op. cit., p. 317.

61. Mills, op. cit.

62. American Society for Personnel Administration, op. cit., p. 22.

63. Milbank, op. cit.

64. Cappelli, P. (1990). Collective bargaining. In J. A. Fossum (ed.), *Employee and labor relations*. Washington, DC: Bureau of National Affairs, pp. 4-180 to 4–217.

65. This give-and-take may actually fly (1993, Dec. 27). *Business Week*, p. 37. See also United's unions would rather buy than strike (1993, Aug. 23). *Business Week*, p. 71.

66. Alexander, K. L. (1993, Aug. 16). It's time for USX to take labor's outstretched hand. *Business Week*, p. 30.

67. Karr, A. R. (1988, June 29). Striking out. *The Wall Street Journal*, pp. 1, 17.

68. Union wage increases overall below 1992 (1993, September). *Mountain States Employers Council Bulletin*, p. 5.

69. White, J. B., & Templin, N. (1993, Sept. 17). Auto pact leaves GM hard choice: Go along or confront the union. *The Wall Street Journal*, pp. A1, A4. See also Maybe GM didn't get such a bad deal (1993, Nov. 8). *Business Week*, p. 35.

70. Uchitelle, L. (1992, Apr. 19). Blue-collar compromises in pursuit of job security. *The New York Times*, pp. 1L, 18L, 19L.

71. Schuster, op. cit.

72. Labor deals that offer a break from "us vs. them" (1993, Aug. 2). *Business Week*, p. 30.

73. Pennsylvania task force says cooperation critical for labor, management in "new era" (1988, Feb. 26). *Daily Labor Report*, pp. A6, A7.

74. Patterson, G. A. (1990, Aug. 29). Credibility gap. *The Wall Street Journal*, pp. A1, A10.

75. Brown, C., & Reich, M. (1989). When does union-management cooperation work? A look at NUMMI and GM–Van Nuys. *California Management Review*, **31**, 26–41.

76. Cooke, W. N. (1990). Factors influencing the effect of joint union-management programs on employee-supervisor relations. *Industrial and Labor Relations Review*, **43**, 587–603. See also Schuster, op. cit.

77. Levin, D. P. (1989, July 28). Nissan workers in Tennessee spurn union's bid. *The New York Times*, pp. A1, A6.

78. Patterson, G. A. (1992, Mar. 6). New rules: How GM's car plant in Arlington, Texas hustled to avoid ax. *The Wall Street Journal*, pp. A1, A6.

79. Uchitelle, L. (1993, June 13). Labor draws the line in Decatur. *The New York Times*, pp. 1F, 6F.

80. Labor letter (1993, June 8). *The Wall Street Journal*, p. A1.

81. Freeman, R. B., & Medoff, J. (1984). *What do unions do?* New York: Basic Books.

82. Kleiner, M. M. (1990). The role of industrial relations in industrial performance. In J. A. Fossum (ed.), *Employee and labor relations*. Washington, DC: Bureau of National Affairs, pp. 4-23 to 4-43.

83. Ibid. See also Linneman, P. D., Wachter, M. L., & Carter, W. H. (1990). Evaluating the evidence on union employment and wages. *Industrial and Labor Relations Review*, **44**(1), 34–53.

84. This give-and-take may actually fly, op. cit.

85. Milbank, op. cit.

CHAPTER 15

PROCEDURAL JUSTICE AND ETHICS IN EMPLOYEE RELATIONS

A RADICAL EXPERIMENT AT GE: HOURLY WORKERS CONTROL A GRIEVANCE REVIEW PANEL*

"Are you crazy?" people at General Electric (GE) and other industrial relations organizations ask when they first hear about the new Grievance Review Panel at GE's Appliance Park–East in Columbia, Maryland. They wonder how and why this nonunion facility—one of the largest in the GE chain—allows a rotating panel of three hourly employees to decide the fate of grievances. Yes, it is true that hourly employees, with a 3-to-2 majority over management, can control the results of most grievances submitted by their peers at the facility.

Why did GE undertake such a radical experiment? To answer this question, it is necessary to consider the previous decade of employee relations at the plant. As the second largest nonunion plant in GE, located in the highly unionized Baltimore area, the plant had been a constant target of union organizers.

The production and quality of electric ranges and microwave ovens, as well as sound human relations programs, were severely hampered by extensive time devoted to union campaigns. During the first 8 years of the plant's operations, there were nine campaigns leading to six representation elections. GE's winning majorities were consistently under 60 percent.

More important, each election divided employees into prounion and antiunion camps, causing major morale problems from which it took months to recover. Finally management

*Adapted from: R. T. Boisseau & H. Caras, A radical experiment cuts deep into the attractiveness of unions, *Personnel Administrator*, **28**(10), 76–79, 1983. Copyright 1983. Reprinted with permission from *HRMagazine* (formerly *Personnel Administrator*), published by the Society for Human Resource Management, Alexandria, VA.

493

decided that the best way to put an end to the constant union battles was to make Columbia the best possible place to work.

BACKGROUND ON GRIEVANCES

For years, the Columbia plant had used a formal, written grievance procedure that allowed employees to go immediately to higher levels of management with their grievances. Even though the company had a success rate of over 40 percent (considerably higher than at most union plants), each year there was a steady decline in the use of the formal process. To some extent the decline was due to improved supervision and more consistent application of policies, but some of it also resulted from employees' lack of faith in the process. Many employees admitted honestly that they had a low regard for GE's procedure.

Management brainstormed many different ideas but finally settled on the one recommended by the plant manager at Columbia. At the time, he was the final decision maker in the grievance review process. The plant manager recommended the use of a panel of hourly employees to help him make the best possible decisions. This was the framework:

- Each of five panelists would have an equal vote.
- The two management panelists could be outvoted by the three hourly members of the grievance review panel.
- Review-panel decisions would be final and binding.

SKEPTICAL RESPONSES

The idea was presented to groups of managers, to first-line supervisors, and to employees. Their responses were all about the same—positive about the concept but skeptical that GE was really serious. Even more skepticism came from human resource managers at other local companies and other GE plants: "How can you let yourselves be outnumbered and still maintain your right to run the business?" they invariably asked.

To that question management had a standard response: "If we have a major issue that truly divides the management and hourly members of the panel—and if we cannot convince one of the hourly people that we are right—then we must be wrong."

To explain the new concept to employees and to solicit volunteer panelists, GE scheduled an after-work review of the new procedure. Employees came and listened on their own time. They contributed to the development of the concept, and unofficially they endorsed the plan. Thirty-nine of them volunteered to join an 8-hour program to train panelists. The training was held during off-duty hours, and it emphasized the legal and ethical elements of grievance handling, problem-solving techniques, and effective listening skills. It ended with a role play of an actual grievance.

The response from the panelists was overwhelming. Even some of the most skeptical among them had a totally different perception by the end of the sessions. All were geared up and ready for the first grievance.

ADDITIONAL PUBLICITY

To explain the process further, a special edition of the *GE News*—with full details and comments from a panel of employees who had prior knowledge of the project—announced the grievance-panel idea. Second, the Management Hotline, a 60-second daily telephone commentary on items of interest in the business, encouraged people to take the training. Third, the *GE News* covered the first panel case at the plant. Fourth, an audiovisual program, developed for use at employee roundtable meetings with their supervisors, provided testimonials of how people felt after they had taken the panel training. The panel was then ready to receive its first grievant.

Challenges

1. Discuss two advantages and two disadvantages of the GE grievance review panel.
2. What else needs to be done to improve the overall industrial relations system at the GE plant?
3. The grievance review process at the GE plant is important both for what it is and for what it symbolizes. We know what it is and how it works, but what does it symbolize and what does it say about management's assumptions about workers?

---

1. How can I ensure procedural justice in the resolution of conflicts between employees and managers?
2. How can I administer discipline without at the same time engendering resentment toward me or the company?
3. How do I fire people legally and humanely?
4. What should be the components of a fair information practice policy?
5. What is ethical decision making in employee relations? What steps or considerations are involved?

Questions This Chapter Will Help Managers Answer

The chapter opening vignette illustrates another facet of labor-management accommodation: control of a grievance review panel by hourly workers rather than by management. It is another attempt to enhance the productivity and QWL of employees, although (as the case points out) it evolved only after constant union organizing campaigns. Indeed, the broad theme of this chapter is "justice on the job." We will consider alternative methods for resolving disputes, such as grievance (in union and nonunion settings) and arbitration procedures. We also examine discipline and termination in the employment context. Finally, we will examine the growing concern for employee privacy in these four areas: fair information practice in the computer age, the assessment of job applicants and employees, employee searches, and whistleblowing. Let us begin by defining some important terms.

SOME DEFINITIONS

In this chapter we are concerned with three broad issues in the context of employee relations: (1) procedural justice, (2) due process, and (3) ethical decisions about behavior.

> *Employee relations* includes all the practices that implement the philosophy and policy of an organization with respect to employment.[1]

Justice refers to the maintenance or administration of what is just, especially by the impartial adjustment of conflicting claims or the assignment of merited rewards or punishments.[2]

Procedural justice focuses on the fairness of the procedures used to make decisions. Procedures are fair to the extent that they are consistent across persons and over time, free from bias, based on accurate information, correctable, and based on prevailing moral and ethical standards.[3]

Due process in legal proceedings provides individuals with rights such as the following: prior notice of prohibited conduct; timely procedures adhered to at each step of the procedure; notice of the charges or issues prior to a hearing; impartial judges or hearing officers; representation by counsel; opportunity to confront and to cross-examine adverse witnesses and evidence, as well as to present proof in one's own defense; notice of decision; and protection from retaliation for using a complaint procedure in a legitimate manner. These are constitutional due process rights. They protect individual rights with respect to state, municipal, and federal government processes. However, they do not normally apply to work situations. Hence, employee rights to due process are based on a collective bargaining agreement, on legislative protections, or on procedures provided unilaterally by an employer.[4]

Ethical decisions about behavior concern one's conformity to moral standards or to the standards of conduct of a given profession or group. Ethical decisions about behavior take account not only of one's own interests but also equally of the interests of those affected by the decision.[5]

Procedural Justice in Action: Employee Voice Systems

For most organizations, the most important thing they can do to ensure procedural justice is to provide individuals and groups the capacity to be heard, a way to communicate their interests upward—a voice system. Voice systems serve four important functions:

1. They assure fair treatment to employees.
2. They provide a context in which unfair treatment can be appealed.
3. They help to improve the effectiveness of an organization.
4. They sustain employee loyalty and commitment.[6]

Here are some examples of voice systems that are commonly used:

- Grievance procedures, by which an employee can seek a formal, impartial review of a decision that affects him or her.
- Ombudspersons, who may investigate claims of unfair treatment or act as intermediaries between an employee and senior management and recommend possible courses of action to the parties.
- Open-door policies by which employees can approach senior managers with problems that they may not be willing to take to their immediate supervisor. A related mechanism, particularly appropriate when the immediate supervisor is the problem, is a skip-level policy, whereby an employee may proceed directly to the next higher level of management above his or her supervisor.

■ Participative management systems that encourage employee involvement in all aspects of organizational strategy and decision making.

■ Committees or meetings that poll employee input on key problems and decisions.

■ Senior management visits, where employees can meet with senior company officials and openly ask questions about company strategy, policies, and practices or raise concerns about unfair treatment.

■ Question/answer newsletters, in which employee questions and concerns submitted to a newsletter editor and investigated by that office are answered and openly reported to the organizational community.[7]

■ Toll-free telephone numbers that employees can use anonymously to report waste, fraud, or abuse.

Characteristics of Effective Voice Systems. A thorough review of the literature on voice systems revealed five "core" characteristics of the most effective ones. These are shown in Table 15-1.

The first criterion is *elegance*. That is, the system should be simple to understand, it should be applicable to a broad range of issues (i.e., able to address almost any type of problem that arises), it should use an effective diagnostic framework, and finally, those who manage the system should be able to respond definitively to the issues raised.

The second criterion is *accessibility*. Effective voice systems are easy to use, well advertised, comprehensible, open processes. Information is publicized on how to file a complaint. Indeed, research has found that employees view this feature as a key attribute of an effective dispute-handling system.[8]

The third criterion of effective voice systems is *correctness*, that is, the system should provide the "right" answer to problems by being unbiased, thorough, and effective. The more correct a system, the more likely it is that (1) the complainant can provide relevant input about the problem, (2) the organization can investigate and call for more information if it needs it, (3) a system exists for classifying and coding information in order to determine the nature of the problem, (4) employees can appeal lower-level decisions, and (5) both procedures and outcomes make good sense to most employees.[9]

A fourth criterion is *responsiveness*. At the most basic level, responsive systems let individuals know that their input has been received. Thus IBM's "Speak Up" program requires the manager of the function in question to prepare a written response to the employee within 3 days or face severe sanctions. Responsive systems provide timely responses, are backed by management commitment, are designed to fit an organiza-

■ **TABLE 15 ▪ 1**
CORE CHARACTERISTICS OF EFFECTIVE VOICE SYSTEMS

Elegance—simple procedures, broad application, vested authority, good diagnostic system

Accessibility—easy to use, advertised, comprehensive, open process

Corrrectness—administered well, includes follow-up, self-redesigning, correctable outcomes

Responsiveness—timely, culturally viable, tangible results, management commitment

Nonpunitiveness—appeal system, anonymity, nonretributive

Source: B. H. Sheppard, R. J. Lewicki, & J. W. Minton, *Organizational justice: The search for fairness in the workplace.* New York: Lexington Books, 1992, p. 149.

tion's culture, provide tangible results, involve participants in the decision-making process, and give those who manage the system sufficient "clout" to ensure that it works effectively.

Finally, effective voice systems are *nonpunitive*. This is essential if employees are to trust the system. Individuals must be able to present problems, identify concerns, and challenge the organization in such a way that they are not punished for providing this input, even if the issues raised are sensitive and highly politicized. If the input concerns wrongdoing or malfeasance, the individual's identity must be protected so that direct or indirect retribution cannot occur. Employees as well as managers must be protected.[10]

Now that we've discussed the theory of procedural justice, let's examine how it can be applied in a number of areas of employee relations.

ADMINISTRATION OF THE COLLECTIVE BARGAINING AGREEMENT

To many union and management officials, the real test of effective labor relations comes after the agreement is signed, that is, in its day-to-day administration. At that point, the major concern of the union is to obtain in practice the employee rights that management has granted on paper. The major concern of management is to establish its right to manage the business and to keep operations running.[11] A key consideration for both is the form of union security that governs conditions of employment.

Union Security Clauses

Section 14b of the Taft-Hartley Act enables states to enact "right-to-work" laws that prohibit compulsory union membership (after a probationary period) as a condition of continued employment. Table 15-2 illustrates the forms that such union security provisions can take and indicates that most of them are illegal in the 21 states that have passed right-to-work laws.

Agency shop agreements appear in about 12 percent of all collective bargaining contracts.[12] May the "service charge" for representation be used to pay for activities such as lobbying for prolabor legislation, organizing efforts, and political activities *in addition to* collective bargaining? Non-union-member employees of American Telephone & Telegraph Company sued the Communications Workers of America (CWA) over this issue. The Supreme Court ruled that a union may be violating the rights of nonmembers who are required to pay agency fees for union representation if it uses those fees for political and other activities not directly related to collective bargaining. How much money goes to activities other than collective bargaining? At the trial-court level, a federal judge ordered the CWA to rebate 79 percent of the agency fees it had collected one year, because the union could only prove that 21 percent of its collections were devoted to collective bargaining.[13]

Grievance Procedures in the Unionized Firm

Occasionally during the life of a contract, disputes arise about the interpretation of the collective bargaining agreement, potential violations of federal or state law, violations of past practices or company rules, or violations of management's responsibility (e.g., to provide safe and healthy working conditions). In each instance, an aggrieved party

■ TABLE 15 ▪ 2
FORMS OF UNION SECURITY AND THEIR LEGAL STATUS IN
RIGHT-TO-WORK STATES

	Legal	Illegal
Closed shop Individual must join the union that represents employees in order to be considered for employment.		X
Union shop As a condition of continued employment an individual must join the union that represents employees after a probationary period (typically a minimum of 30 days).		X
Preferential shop Union members are given preference in hiring.		X
Agency shop Employees need not join the union that represents them, but, in lieu of dues, they must pay a service charge for representation.		X
Maintenance of membership Employee must remain a member of the union once he or she joins.		X
Checkoff Employee may request that union dues be deducted from his or her pay and be sent directly to the union.	X	

may file a grievance. A grievance is an alleged violation of the rights of workers on the job.[14] A formal process known as a *grievance procedure* is then invoked to help the parties resolve the dispute. Grievance procedures are the keystone of industrial relations because of their ability to resolve disputed issues while work continues without litigation, strikes, or other radical dispute-resolution strategies.[15]

In addition to providing a formal mechanism for resolving disputes, the grievance procedure defines and narrows the nature of the complaint. Thus each grievance must be expressed in writing. The written grievance identifies the grievant, when the incident leading to the grievance occurred (it could, of course, be ongoing), and where the incident happened. The written statement also indicates why the complaint is considered a grievance and what the grievant thinks should be done about the matter.[16] A typical grievance procedure in a unionized firm works as shown in Figure 15-1. As the figure indicates, unresolved grievances proceed progressively to higher and higher levels of management and union representation and culminate in voluntary, binding arbitration. Specific time limits for management's decision and the union's approval are normally imposed at each step, for example, 3 days for each party at step 1, 5 days for each party at steps 2 and 3, and 10 days for each party at step 4.

It also is important to note that many unions have a policy that up to step 3 of the procedure the grievance "belongs" to the employee. That is, the union will process a grievance through step 2 (and in some cases through step 3) at the grievant's request. However, if the grievance is not settled and reaches step 3, it becomes the union's grievance. At that point, the union will decide whether or not the grievance has merit and whether additional time and financial resources of the union should be spent in carrying it forward. Indeed, many local unions let the membership vote formally to decide whether to take a grievance to arbitration.[17] They do this for good reason: the grievance process is expensive.

Costing a Grievance. One study found that to process 500 grievances (the actual number filed in a single West Coast union local over a 1-year period), 4580 work-

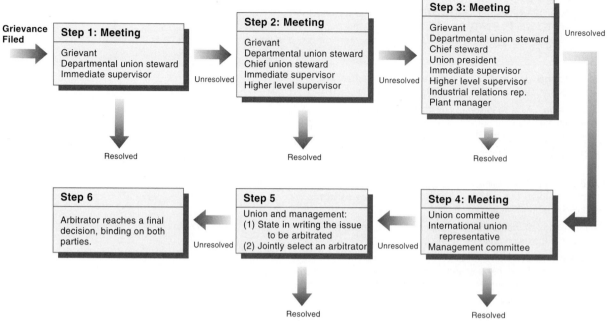

FIGURE 15-1
Example of a formal grievance procedure in a unionized firm.

hours were required, or an average of 9.1 hours per grievance. Assume that the average total compensation (wages plus benefits) for the grievant, union, and management representatives is $120 per hour (in 1994 dollars), or more than $1090 per grievance. This translates into an annual cost of $545,000 to resolve 500 grievances. However, this figure is conservative, for it reflects only the *direct* time used for formal meetings on grievances. It does not include such other factors as preparation time, informal meetings, clerical time, and administrative overhead for management and the union.[18] In complex grievance cases that proceed all the way to arbitration (step 6 in Figure 15-1), the cost to the company or union may exceed $6100 per grievance (in 1994 dollars).[19]

Common Grievances and Their Resolution. For the West Coast local just mentioned, the majority of grievances were filed over disciplinary issues: the introductory disciplinary memorandum, suspensions, and termination. Seniority, the basis of many individual work rights for union employees, is often the basis for a grievance. Beyond that, no single category accounts for a large proportion of the grievances filed.

The majority of grievances filed are resolved without resorting to arbitration. Of these, unions and management each win about half the time. However, *unions* tend to win more grievances related to such issues as the denial of sick benefits, termination, transfer, suspension, and disciplinary memoranda. Ordinarily, the burden of proof in a grievance proceeding is on the union. Since fewer issues of interpretation are involved in the areas that unions usually win, this pattern of grievance resolution is not surprising.[20]

In summary, there are two key advantages to the grievance procedure. One, it ensures that the complaints and problems of workers can be heard, rather than simply allowed to fester. Two, grievance procedures provide formal mechanisms to ensure due process and procedural justice for all parties.

On the other hand, the process is not completely objective in that factors other than merit sometimes determine the outcome of a grievance. Some of these factors include the cost of granting a grievance and the perceived need for management to placate disgruntled workers or to settle large numbers of grievances in order to expedite the negotiation process.[21] In addition, personal factors such as the gender of the grievant (sometimes men and sometimes women are more likely to prevail), the gender composition of the supervisor–union steward dyad that hears cases, or the grievant's work history (good performance, long tenure, few disciplinary incidents) may serve to determine the outcomes of grievance procedures.[22]

What is the role of the line manager in all this? To know and understand the collective bargaining contract, as well as federal and state labor laws. Above all, whether you agree or disagree with the terms of the contract, it is legally binding on both labor and management. Respect its provisions, and manage according to the spirit as well as the letter of the contract.

Does a High Number of Grievances Indicate Poor Labor Relations?

One study examined the impact of a fact-finding program on the grievance process over a 6-year period. A fact-finding team (made up of an appointed union representative and a supervisor, neither of whom could be a party to the grievance under consideration) was given authority to settle disputes in a public utility in the western United States. The program had three objectives: (1) to encourage a more open system of dispute resolution by requiring the revelation of a series of stipulated facts (neither party could subsequently raise a fact not raised in the fact-finding stage), (2) to encourage resolution of disputes at lower levels in the grievance process; and (3) to resolve disputes in a more timely manner.

Measures were obtained in the utility in question as well as in another western utility in which no such intervention occurred. Monthly data were collected for 36 months prior to the intervention, 24 months during it, and 12 months after its removal. All grievances filed by employees of both utilities over the 6-year period (4130 grievances) were examined. The results showed that the introduction of fact-finding led to an increase in the grievance rate and its removal to a decrease back to the baseline level. Fact-finding did not lead to a higher winning percentage for either party, but disputes were resolved at lower levels.

The fact-finding system was discontinued after 2 years at the request of both parties. Management felt it was too expensive and that the benefits of the system did not outweigh its costs. However, the key issue for the union was political—the large difference in authority of the union fact finder (appointed) and the union steward (elected).

Was the program effective? Conventional wisdom suggests that large numbers of grievances signal an unhealthy organizational climate, but these results may suggest the opposite—that a large number of grievances signals the presence of a friendly system that is easily accessible and time-efficient. At a minimum, it seems that high grievance rates do not invariably indicate poor labor relations.[23]

Arbitration

Arbitration is used by management and labor to settle disputes arising out of and during the term of a labor contract. It appears in about 90 percent of all private-sector contracts and in about 75 percent of all public-sector contracts.[24] As Figure 15-1 indicates, compulsory, binding arbitration is the final stage of the grievance process. It is also used as an alternative to a work stoppage, and it is used to ensure labor peace for the duration of a labor contract. Arbitrators may be chosen from a list of qualified people supplied by the American Arbitration Association or the Federal Mediation and Conciliation Service.

Arbitration hearings are quasi-judicial proceedings. Prehearing briefs may be filed by both parties, along with lists of witnesses to be called. Witnesses are cross-examined, and documentary evidence may be introduced. However, *arbitrators are not bound by the formal rules of evidence*, as they would be in a court of law.

Following the hearing, the parties may each submit briefs to reiterate their positions, evidence supporting them, and proposed decisions. The arbitrator then considers the evidence, the contract clause in dispute, and the powers granted the arbitrator under the labor agreement, and finally issues a decision. In the rare instances where a losing party refuses to honor the arbitrator's decision, the decision can be enforced by taking that party to federal court.[25]

Generally an arbitration award cannot be appealed in court simply because one party believes the arbitrator made a mistake in interpreting an agreement. This was recently affirmed by a full federal appeals court in California. A mechanic had been fired for not properly tightening the lug bolts on the wheels of a Mercedes-Benz. An arbitrator ruled that a 120-day suspension, as had been urged by the man's Machinists Union local, was enough discipline. Following extensive precedent, the court ruled

---

PRACTICAL EXAMPLE

FINAL-OFFER ARBITRATION IN MAJOR LEAGUE BASEBALL

The arbitration process allows players with a minimum level of tenure to submit salary disputes to binding arbitration. The final-offer structure requires both the player and the team to submit a salary figure to the arbitrator, who must then select either the player's or the team's offer. In reaching a decision, the arbitrator must use a set of prescribed criteria, including the player's performance, the player's current salary, the performance of other players in the league, and the amount others are paid.

Several studies have examined the impact of arbitration on perceived equity, motivation, and subsequent performance. Among pitchers, those who lost arbitration allowed more batters to get on base, allowed more earned runs, and struck out fewer batters than did arbitration winners. Further, the size of the difference between salary demands and offers was related to subsequent performance changes, but some of this may have been due to player experience.[26]

Among position players, results indicate that (1) all players perform better prior to arbitration; (2) this increase in performance contributes to the propensity to file for arbitration; (3) players who increase their performance more dramatically than others win arbitration; (4) subsequent performance declines for all players, because exceptionally high performance must eventually regress to the player's average level of ability; and (5) more arbitration losers than winners changed teams and left major league baseball. Even though a greater percentage of losers leave baseball, perceived inequity probably has only a small effect on leaving, because few labor market alternatives exist at these pay levels.[27] These results for pitchers and position players indicate the powerful effects of perceived equity or inequity on subsequent performance.

that arbitrator awards are extensions of labor contracts, and court deference is the rule.[28]

Grievance Procedures in Nonunion Companies: Corporate Due Process

Grievance arbitration has generally worked well, and this is why many companies have extended it as an option to their nonunion employees. For example, Federal Express Corporation's "guaranteed fair-treatment process" lets employees appeal problems to a peer review board chosen by the worker involved and management. The board rules for employees about half the time. Bosses cannot appeal decisions, but employees can, to a panel of top executives up to and including the chairman of the board.[29] TWA employees take disputes to a panel comprised of an arbitrator, a representative from the human resources staff, and another employee. One reason for the growing popularity of these programs is that they tend to reduce lawsuits. At Aetna Life & Casualty Co., for example, only one of the almost 300 complaints handled by Aetna's program has gone to litigation.[30]

Figure 15-2 illustrates how such a procedure works in one company. This procedure emphasizes the supervisor as a key figure in the resolution of grievances. As a second step, the employee is encouraged to see the department head, a human resources department representative, or any other member of management. Alternatively, the employee may proceed directly to the roundtable, a body of employee and management representatives who meet biweekly to resolve grievances. Management immediately answers those questions that it can and researches those requiring an in-depth review. The minutes of roundtable meetings, plus the answers to the questions presented, are posted conspicuously on bulletin boards in work areas.[31]

To work effectively, a nonunion grievance procedure should meet three requirements:

1. All employees must know about the procedure and exactly how it operates.

2. They must believe that there will be no reprisals taken against them for using it.

3. Management must respond quickly and thoroughly to all grievances.[32]

FIGURE 15-2

Example of a nonunion grievance procedure. This diagram indicates the possible routes a grievant may take to resolve a complaint. The regular procedural route is designed to resolve the grievance at the lowest possible level—the supervisor. However, if the grievant feels uncomfortable approaching the supervisor, the grievance may be presented directly to any level of management via the open-door policy or the roundtable. [*Source:* Reprinted from D. A. Drost & F. P. O'Brien, Are there grievances against your non-union grievance procedure? *Personnel Administrator*, 28(1), 1983, 37. Copyright 1983. Reprinted with permission from *HRMagazine* (formerly *Personnel Administrator*), published by the Society for Human Resource Management, Alexandria, VA.]

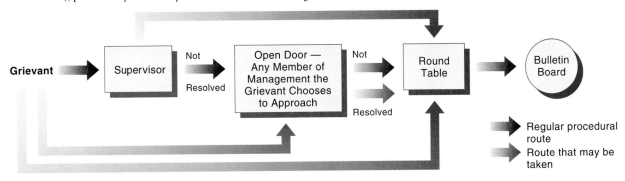

Corporate due process is one of the fastest-developing trends in industry. In the coming decade, a majority of people-oriented firms are likely to adopt it. But how does one begin? Here are four key steps:[33]

1. *Make sure your HR department has lots of expertise in dispute resolution.* It must be able to handle most of the complaints that cannot be resolved by managers and their subordinates; otherwise the "company court" will be inundated with cases. At Bank of America, HR professionals, rather than line managers, investigate cases. They understand the investigation process and the bank's policies better, and they devote the time necessary for a thorough review, which can take as long as a week.[34] At companies such as Polaroid and Citicorp, problem review boards may hear only 12 to 20 cases a year, because of the skill of the HR department in dispute resolution.

2. *Train all managers and supervisors in your company's due process approach.* They simply must know company HR policy because it is the "law" governing company courts and adjudicators. Coach them in how to handle complaints, so that they can resolve problems immediately. And if subordinates take their complaints to the company court, teach your managers to accept reversals as a fact of business life, for in a good due process system, reversals are bound to occur. Three separate studies reported reversal rates that ranged from 20 to 40 percent.[35]

3. *Decide whether you want a panel system or a single adjudicator.* Panel systems, such as the one described in the chapter opening vignette, enjoy high credibility and, for the panelists, mutual support. About 100 companies, including Bank of America, Control Data, Digital Equipment, and Polaroid, now use peer review panels (the roundtable in Figure 15-2) to resolve disputes over firings, promotions, and disciplinary actions. A panel typically consists of three peers and two management representatives. Most companies do not permit grievants to have outside representation; instead, they provide a human resource staff member if help is needed in preparing the case. The panel's decisions are binding on both sides.

An adjudicator system, in which a single investigator first acts as a fact finder and then changes hats and arbitrates the facts, has the advantages of speed, flexibility, and maximum privacy. IBM uses the single-adjudicator approach.

4. *Make your due process system visible.* At a minimum, the system should be described in the employee handbook and publicized by HR specialists. SmithKline Beecham goes even further. Periodically, it features its grievance procedure on closed-circuit television for all company employees.

The trend toward corporate due process represents an effort by companies to broaden employees' rights in disciplinary matters. A position paper at Control Data stated: "It is inherently difficult for the management power structure to concede to a system which allows review of its decision making. . . . But any concept of employee justice is incomplete without the presence of some mechanism to challenge the power system."[36] Due process mechanisms build an open, trusting atmosphere, help deter union organizing, and stem the rising number of costly lawsuits claiming wrongful discharge and discrimination.

Discipline

Make no mistake about it: most employees want to conduct themselves in a manner acceptable to the company and to their fellow employees. Occasionally, problems of absenteeism, poor work performance, or rule violations arise. When informal conversations or coaching sessions fail to resolve these problems, formal disciplinary action is called for.

Employee discipline is the final area of contract administration that we shall consider. Typically, the "management rights" clause of the collective bargaining agreement retains for management the authority to impose *reasonable* rules for workplace conduct and to discipline employees for *just cause*. As developed in thousands of arbitration cases over the past 60 years, the concept of just cause requires an employer not only to produce persuasive evidence of an employee's culpability or negligence but also to provide the employee a fair hearing and to impose a penalty appropriate to the proven offense.[37] Unions rarely object to employee discipline, *provided that* (1) it is applied consistently, (2) the rules are publicized clearly, and (3) the rules are considered reasonable.

Discipline is indispensable to management control. Ideally, it should serve as a corrective mechanism to prevent serious harm to the organization.[38] Unfortunately, some managers go to great lengths to avoid using discipline. To some extent this is understandable, for discipline is one of the hardest HR actions to face. Managers may avoid imposing discipline because of (1) ignorance of organizational rules, (2) fear of formal grievances, or (3) fear of losing the friendship of employees. Yet failure to administer discipline can result in implied acceptance or approval of the offense. Thereafter, problems may become more frequent or severe, and discipline becomes that much more difficult to administer.

As an alternative, some companies are experimenting with a technique called "positive discipline." On its face, it sounds a lot like traditional discipline dressed up in euphemisms. It works as follows: Employees who commit offenses first get an oral "reminder" rather than a "reprimand." Then comes a written reminder, followed by a paid day off—called a "decision-making leave day" (a suspension, in traditional parlance). After a pensive day off, the employee must agree in writing (or orally at some union shops) that he or she will behave responsibly for the next year. The paid day off is a one-shot chance at reform. The process is documented, and if the employee does not change, termination follows.

How has positive discipline worked? At Tampa Electric, which has used it for over 10 years, more employees have improved their job performance than have left the company. Says one power station manager: "Before, we punished employees and treated them worse and worse and expected them to act better. I don't ever recall suspending someone who came back ready to change."[39] These arguments for not imposing punishment are persuasive. But evidence also indicates that discipline (that is, punishment) may be beneficial.[40] Consider that:

- Discipline may alert the marginal employee to his or her low performance and result in a change in behavior.

- Discipline may send a signal to other employees regarding expected levels of performance and standards of behavior.

- If the discipline is perceived as legitimate by other employees, it may increase motivation, morale, and performance.

In fact, statistical reanalyses of the original Hawthorne experiments suggest that managerial discipline was the major factor in increased rates of output.[41] Department managers in a retail store chain who used informal warnings, formal warnings, and dismissals more frequently than their peers had higher departmental performance ratings (in terms of annual cost and sales data and ratings by higher-level managers). This relationship held even when length of service was taken into account. More frequent use of sanctions was associated with improved performance. Why is this so?

The answer may lie in social learning theory.[42] *Individuals in groups look to others to learn appropriate behaviors and attitudes.* They learn them by modeling the behavior of others, by adopting standard operating procedures, and by following group norms. Individuals whose attitudes or behaviors violate these norms may cause problems. Tolerance of such behavior by the supervisor may threaten the group by causing feelings of uncertainty and unfairness. On the other hand, management actions that are seen as maintaining legitimate group standards may instill feelings of fairness and result in improved performance. Failure to invoke sanctions may lead to a loss of management control and unproductive employee behavior.[43] Finally, do not underestimate the *symbolic* value of disciplinary actions, especially since punitive behavior tends to make a lasting impression on employees.[44]

Progressive Discipline. Many firms, both unionized and nonunionized, follow a procedure of progressive discipline that proceeds from an oral warning to a written warning to a suspension to dismissal. However, to administer discipline without at the same time engendering resentment by the disciplined employee, managers should follow what Douglas McGregor called the "red-hot stove rule." Discipline should be:

Immediate. Just like touching a hot stove, where feedback is immediate, there should be no misunderstanding about why discipline was imposed. People are disciplined not because of who they are (personality) but because of what they did (behavior).

With Warning. Small children know that if they touch a hot stove, they will be burned. Likewise, employees must know very clearly what the consequences of undesirable work behavior will be. They must be given adequate warning.

Consistent. Every time a person touches a red-hot stove, he or she gets burned. Likewise, if discipline is to be perceived as fair, it must be administered consistently, given similar circumstances surrounding the undesirable behavior. Consistency *among* individual managers across the organization is essential, but evidence indicates (1) that line managers vary considerably in their attitudes about discipline[45] and (2) that they tend to be less concerned with consistency than with satisfying immediate needs within their work units.[46]

Impersonal. A hot stove is blind to who touches it. So also, managers cannot play favorites by disciplining subordinates they do not like while allowing the same behavior to go unpunished for those they do like.

Documenting Performance-Related Incidents. Documentation is a fact of organizational life for most managers. While such paperwork is never pleasant, it should conform to the following guidelines:

- Describe what led up to the incident—the problem and the setting. Is this a first offense or part of a pattern?
- Describe what actually happened, and be specific: that is, include names, dates, times, witnesses, and other pertinent facts.
- Describe what must be done to correct the situation.
- State the consequences of further violations.

Conclude the warning by obtaining the employee's signature that he or she has read and understands the warning. A sample written warning is shown in Figure 15-3. Note how it includes each of the ingredients just described.

The Disciplinary Interview. Generally, such interviews are held for one of two reasons: (1) over issues of *workplace conduct*, such as attendance or punctuality, or (2) over issues of *job performance*, such as low productivity. They tend to be very legalistic. As an example, consider the following scenario.

You are a first-line supervisor at a unionized facility. You suspect that one of your subordinates, Steve Fox, has been distorting his time reports to misrepresent his daily starting time. While some of the evidence is sketchy, you know that Fox's time reports are false. Accompanied by an industrial relations representative, you decide to confront Fox directly in a disciplinary interview. However, before you can begin the meeting, Fox announces, "I'd appreciate it if a coworker of mine could be present during this meeting. If a coworker cannot be present, I refuse to participate." Your reaction to this startling request is to:

DATE: April 14, 1995

TO: J. Hartwig

FROM: D. Curtis

SUBJECT: Written Warning

On this date you were 30 minutes late to work with no justification for your tardiness. A similar offense occurred last Friday. At that time you were told that failure to report for work on schedule will not be condoned. I now find it necessary to tell you in writing that you must report to work on time. Failure to do so will result in your dismissal from employment. Please sign below that you have read and that you understand this warning.

[Name]   [Date]

FIGURE 15-3
Sample written warning of disciplinary action.

A. Ask Fox which coworker he desires and reconvene the meeting once the employee is present.

B. Deny his request and order him to participate or face immediate discipline for insubordination.

C. Terminate the meeting with no further discussion.

D. Ignore the request and proceed with the meeting, hoping that Fox will participate anyway.

E. Inform Fox that, as his supervisor, you are a coworker and attempt to proceed with the meeting.

Unless your reaction was A or C, you have probably committed a violation of the National Labor Relations Act.[47]

In *NLRB v. J. Weingarten, Inc.*, the Supreme Court ruled that a *union* employee has the right to demand that a union representative be present at an investigatory interview that the employee reasonably believes may result in disciplinary action.[48] However, in *NLRB v. Sears, Roebuck and Co.* (1985), the Court overturned an earlier decision, ruling that *Weingarten* rights do not extend to nonunion employees.[49] To summarize the Weingarten mandate:

1. The employee must *request* representation; the employer has no obligation to offer it voluntarily. If such a request is made, the union representative may meet with the employee privately before the investigatory interview takes place.[50]

2. The employee must reasonably believe that the investigation may result in disciplinary action taken against him or her.

3. The employer is not obligated to carry on the interview or to justify its refusal to do so. The employer may simply cancel the interview and thus effectively disallow union or coworker representation.

4. The employer has no duty to bargain with any union representative during the interview, and the union representative may not limit the employer's questioning.[51]

If the National Labor Relations Board determines that these rights were violated and that an employee was subsequently disciplined for conduct that was the subject of the unlawful interview, the board will issue a "make-whole" remedy. This may include (1) restitution of back pay, (2) an order expunging from the employee's personnel records any notation of related discipline, or (3) a cease-and-desist order. To avoid these kinds of problems, top management must decide what company policy will be in such cases, communicate that policy to first-line supervisors, and give them clear, concise instructions regarding their responsibilities should an employee request representation at an investigatory interview.[52]

Having satisfied their legal burden, how should supervisors actually conduct the disciplinary interview? They must do *nine* things well:

1. Come to the interview with as many facts as possible. Check the employee's personnel file for previous offenses as well as for evidence of exemplary behavior and performance.

2. Conduct the interview in a quiet, private place. "Praise in public, discipline in private" is a good rule to remember. Whether the employee's attitude is truculent or contrite, recognize that he or she will be apprehensive. In contrast to other interviews, where your first objective is to dispel any fears and help the person relax, a "light touch" is inappropriate here.

3. Avoid aggressive accusations. State the facts in a simple, straightforward way. Be sure that any fact you use is accurate, and never rely on hearsay, rumor, or unconfirmed guesswork.

4. Be sure that the employee understands the rule in question and the reason it exists.

5. Allow the employee to make a full defense, even if you think he or she has none. If any point the employee makes has merit, tell him or her so and take it into consideration in your final decision.

6. Stay cool and calm; treat the subordinate as an adult. Never use foul language or touch the subordinate. Such behaviors may be misinterpreted or grossly distorted at a later date.

7. If you made a mistake, be big enough to admit it.

8. Consider extenuating circumstances, and allow for honest mistakes on the part of the subordinate.

9. Even when corrective discipline is required, try to express confidence in the subordinate's worth as a person and ability to perform acceptably in the future. Rather than dwelling on the past, which you *cannot* change, focus on the future, which you *can*.

Employment-at-Will

For the more than 70 percent of U.S. workers who are not covered by a collective bargaining agreement or an individual employment contract, dismissal is an ever-present possibility. *Employment-at-will* is created when an employee agrees to work for an employer but there is no specification of how long the parties expect the agreement to last. Under a century-old common law in the United States, employment relationships of indefinite duration can, in general, be terminated at the whim of either party.[53] Furthermore, under certain situations, successful victims of unjust dismissal can collect sizable punitive and compensatory damages from their former employers. Thus an analysis of 120 wrongful discharge cases that went to trial in California found that the average salary of fired employees was $36,254. Plaintiffs won 67.5 percent of their cases and were awarded an average of $646,855. About 40 percent of the awards were for punitive damages.[54] It's important to note, however, that initial jury awards, while frequently high, are almost always reduced after trial, according to a study by the Rand Institute for Civil Justice. Half of all damage awards in California, for example, are for less than $177,000.[55]

COMPANY
EXAMPLE

FIRED EMPLOYEE SHOWS CHARACTER DEFAMATION[56]

A $15.6 million Texas jury verdict against Procter & Gamble Co. illustrates just how costly such suits can be. The case involved Don Hagler, a 41-year company employee who claimed P&G fired him after publicly accusing him of stealing a $35 company telephone. Mr. Hagler proved that the phone was his property and that P&G libeled him by posting notices accusing him of theft on 11 bulletin boards and on the plant's electronic-mail system. He testified that P&G used him as an example to stop a rash of thefts at the plant. After his firing, he applied for more than 100 jobs, only to be turned down when prospective employers learned why he had been fired by P&G. The state-court jury agreed with Mr. Hagler and awarded him $1.6 million in actual damages and $14 million in punitive damages.

In recent years, several important exceptions to the "at-will" doctrine have emerged. These exceptions provide important protections for workers. The first—and most important—is legislative. Federal laws limit an employer's right to terminate at-will employees for such reasons as age, race, sex, religion, national origin, union activity, reporting of unsafe working conditions, or disability.[57] However, employment-at-will is primarily a matter of state law.[58]

Such suits are now permitted in 46 states, and in many of them courts have shown a willingness to apply traditional causes of action—such as defamation, fraud, intentional infliction of emotional distress, and invasion of privacy—to this area of employment law.[59]

State courts have carved out three judicial exceptions. The first is a *public policy exception.* That is, an employee may not be fired because he or she refuses to commit an illegal act, such as perjury or price fixing. Second, when an employer has promised not to terminate an employee except for unsatisfactory job performance or other good cause, the courts will insist that the employer carry out that promise. This includes *implied* promises (such as oral promises and implied covenants of good faith and fair dealing) as well as explicit ones.[60] For example, in *Fortune v. National Cash Register Company*, a salesperson (Mr. Fortune) was fired after he sold a large quantity of cash registers. Under the terms of his contract, Mr. Fortune would not receive a portion of his commission until the cash registers were delivered. He claimed he was fired before delivery was made to avoid payment of the full $92,000 commission on the order. The court held that terminating Mr. Fortune solely to deprive him of his commissions would breach the covenant of good faith implied in every contract.[61]

The third exception allows employees to seek damages for outrageous acts related to termination, including character defamation (see earlier Company Example). This includes so-called retaliatory discharge cases, where a worker is fired for actions ranging from filing a workers' compensation claim to reporting safety violations to government agencies. The Supreme Court has ruled that where state law permits (as it does in 34 states), union as well as nonunion employees have the right to sue over their dismissals, even if they are covered by a collective bargaining contract that provides a grievance procedure and remedies.[62]

For some employers, however, relief is in sight. Since 1988, the California Supreme Court has disallowed thousands of lawsuits by employees seeking punitive damages for wrongful discharge.[63] On the other hand, courts in many states—notably Illinois, Massachusetts, Michigan, and New York—expressly permit punitive damages in certain instances.[64]

To avoid potential charges of unjust dismissal, managers should scrutinize each facet of the human resource management system. They should look, for example, at the following:

Recruitment. Beware of creating implicit or explicit contracts in recruitment advertisements. Ensure that no job duration is implied and that employment is not guaranteed or "permanent."

Interviewing. Phrases intended to entice a candidate into accepting a position, such as "employment security," "lifelong relationship" with the company, "permanent" hiring, and so forth, can create future problems.

Applications. Include a statement that describes the rights of the at-will employee, as well as those of the employer. However, do not be so strident that you scare off applicants.

Handbooks and manuals. A major source of company policy statements regarding "permanent" employment and discharge for "just cause" is the employee handbook. According to a growing number of state laws, such handbook language constitutes an *implied contract* for employment. Courts have upheld an employer's prerogative to refrain from making any promises to employees regarding how a termination will be conducted or the conditions under which they may be fired. However, if an employer does make such a promise of job security, whether implied verbally or in writing in an employment document or employee handbook, the employer is bound by that promise.[65]

Performance appraisals. Include training and written instructions for all raters, and use systems that minimize subjectivity to the greatest extent possible. Give employees the right to read and comment on their appraisals, and require them to sign an acknowledgment that they have done so whether or not they agree with the contents of the appraisal.[66] Encourage managers to give "honest" appraisals; if an employee is not meeting minimum standards of performance, "tell it like it is" rather than leading the employee to believe that his or her performance is satisfactory.

Document employee misconduct and poor performance, and provide a progressive disciplinary policy, thereby building a record establishing "good cause."[67]

Employment Contracts

Earlier we noted that employees with contracts (bargained collectively or individually) are not at-will employees. More and more executives, professionals, and even middle managers are demanding contracts. Thus a survey of 560 of the nation's largest companies revealed that 48 percent of them have written understandings with their high-ranking employees.[68] While getting a contract can be a wise career move, when is the proper time to ask for one—and how?

You should consider asking for a contract in any business where the competition for talent is intense, where ideas are at a premium, or when the conditions of your employment differ in unusual ways from a company's standard practices. A contract assures you of a job and a minimum salary for some period of time, usually 2 to 3 years, during which you agree not to quit. Other typical provisions include your title, compensation (salary, procedures for salary increases, bonuses), benefits, stock options, length of vacation, the circumstances under which you can be fired, severance pay, and, in some cases, no-compete agreements.[69]

No-compete agreements are most common in such highly competitive industries as computers, pharmaceuticals, toys, biotechnology, and electronics. However, whether or not a contract has been signed, executives are still required to maintain all trade secrets with which their employers have entrusted them. This obligation, often called a "fiduciary duty of loyalty," cannot keep the executive out of the job market, but it does provide the former employer with legal recourse if an executive joins a competitor and tells all. Indeed, this is precisely what McDonald's claimed when it succeeded in muzzling a former market researcher.[70]

COMPANY EXAMPLE

McLITIGATION

The former employee (we'll call him McEx) was an expert in market research. He quit to join a competitor a few years ago, taking with him a large batch of papers. McDonald's filed suit, alleging that he walked away with company secrets.

Before filing suit and within a few days of his leaving, McDonald's sent a letter to McEx warning him not to divulge any "confidential information" regarding activities such as marketing, advertising, training methods, profit margins, raw materials prices, selling prices, and operating procedures.

The letter further requested a meeting with McEx, during which he would be asked to return any written materials he had taken from McDonald's and also to sign an agreement not to divulge any company trade secrets to his new employer.

When McEx declined to attend the meeting, McDonald's promptly filed suit in McEx's new home state. The company managed to win a temporary restraining order that McEx says effectively meant he could not perform *any* market research for his new employer. He was thereafter relegated to less important work.

Finally, about 6 months after the suit was filed, the case was settled out of court. McEx agreed not to use information gained on the job with McDonald's in his new job. But the issue had become academic. Disenchanted with his new nonjob and aware that his new employer was viewing him more as a problem than as an asset, McEx left his new job. He is now employed by another food chain, not involving fast-food restaurants. In short, companies are now playing hardball when it comes to the disclosure of trade secrets. For both parties, the stakes are high.

Companies say they need no-compete agreements now that growing numbers of acquisitions, bankruptcies, mergers, and layoffs regularly set loose employees with access to trade secrets and other sensitive information. Increasingly, however, judges are finding that the agreements go too far in restraining employees. In some cases they are modifying terms to make them less restrictive (e.g., with respect to geographical boundaries or the length of time an employee is barred from competing). In others they are invalidating the agreements altogether, viewing them as illegal restraints of trade. While some kinds of no-compete pacts stand a better chance in court than others (e.g., those in which the seller of a business promises not to compete with the buyer), closer scrutiny reflects a broader trend in which courts are viewing employee rights more favorably.[71]

Now back to employment contracts. In dealing with a prospective employer, do not raise the issue of a contract until you have been offered a job and have thoroughly discussed the terms of your employment. How do you broach the subject? Calmly. Say, for example, "I'd appreciate a letter confirming these arrangements." If the employer asks why, you might point out that both of you are used to putting business agreements on paper and that it's to your mutual benefit to keep all these details straight.[72]

Here are some tips on how to negotiate an employment contract:

1. Keep the tone upbeat. Don't use the words "I" and "you"; talk about "we"—as though you're already aboard.

2. Decide beforehand on three or four "make or break" issues (e.g., salary, job assignment, location). These are your "need to haves." Also make a list of secondary issues, so-called "nice to haves" (e.g., company car, sign-on bonus).

3. Negotiate the entire package at one time. Don't keep coming back to nitpick.

4. Be flexible (except on your "make-or-break" issues); let the company win on some things.

Once you receive the proposed contract, have an attorney review it before you sign. As one executive recruiter noted: "We seem to be drifting toward a point where no executive will move without some form of legal protection."[73]

Termination

We discussed layoffs in Chapter 10. The focus here is on *how* to terminate employees when it becomes necessary to do so. Termination is one of the most difficult tasks a manager has to perform. As we learned in our discussion of employment-at-will, disgruntled former employees are winning about two-thirds of court cases contesting their dismissals. Clearly, there is room for improvement on the part of managers. For those fired, the perception of inequity, of procedural injustice, is often what drives them to court.

Sometimes termination is done for disciplinary reasons, sometimes for economic reasons (i.e., "downsizing"). It is not an infrequent occurrence, since some 2 million workers in the United States are fired every year,[74] and that doesn't include large-scale layoffs, which claimed 600,000 U.S. jobs in 1993.[75] With respect to layoffs, while the Plant Closing Law of 1988 requires employers of more than 100 workers to grant 60 days' written notice before closing a plant or before laying off more than one-third of a workforce in excess of 150 people, very few firms provide any training to supervisors on *how* to conduct terminations.

While termination may be traumatic for the employee, it is often no less so for the boss. Faced with saying the words "Your services are no longer required," even the strongest person can get the "shakes," sleepless nights, and sweaty palms.[76] So how should termination be handled? Certainly not the way it was at one company that was trying to downsize. At 8:30 A.M. all employees were ordered to their offices. Between then and 10:30 A.M., like angels of death, managers accompanied by security guards knocked on doors, brusquely informed employees that their services were no longer required, gave affected employees a box in which to place their personal articles, and asked the employees to leave the premises within 15 minutes, accompanied by a security guard. Is this procedural justice? Certainly not.

THE TERMINATION CHECKLIST

Documentation

_____ If the job is eliminated, gather supporting evidence of a company or department reduction in head-count.

_____ If poor performance is the reason, the file should contain copies of several successive poor appraisals that were transmitted to (and usually signed by) the candidate at the time they were prepared.

Clearances

_____ Who needs to approve the termination?

Prior Notices

_____ Safeguards to prevent leaks to the public

_____ Key staff members

_____ Board members

_____ Key customers

_____ Regulatory agency officers

Precautions for New Leaks

_____ Ignore the leak

_____ Advance the date of termination to immediate

_____ Delay the termination with no comment

Terms of Termination

_____ Resignation

_____ Transfer to special assignment

_____ Early retirement

_____ Outright termination

Legal Precautions

_____ Salary

_____ Bonuses

_____ Benefits

_____ Other obligations

_____ Scientists and inventors

_____ No-compete agreements

Public Announcements

_____ Should it be a standard press release?

_____ What should the content of the statement be?

Personal Considerations

_____ Medical data

_____ Significant dates

_____ Family circumstances

_____ Personal emotional state

FIGURE 15-4
The termination checklist.
(_Source:_ D. H. Sweet,
Outplacement. In W. F.
Cascio (ed.), _Human resource
planning, employment, and
placement._ Washington,
DC: Bureau of National
Affairs, 1989, pp. 246, 247.)

As an alternative, more humane procedure, companies should familiarize all supervisors with company policies and provide a termination checklist to use when conducting dismissals. One such checklist is shown in Figure 15-4.

Before deciding to dismiss an employee, managers should conduct a detailed review of all relevant facts, including the employee's side of the story. To ensure consistent treatment, the supervisor should also examine how similar cases have been handled in the past. Once the decision to terminate has been made, the termination interview should minimize the trauma for the affected employee. Prior to conducting such an interview, the supervisor should be prepared to answer three basic questions: who, when, and where.

Who. The responsibility for terminating rests with the manager of the individual who is to be released. No one else has the credibility to convey this difficult message.

The Termination Interview

_____ Think through details.
_____ When? Not late on Friday.
_____ Who? It's the line manager's responsibility.
_____ Where? Best place is in a neutral area or the candidate's office.
_____ Outplacement consultant on hand?
_____ Termination letter prepared?

Orderly Transitions of Commitments

_____ Reassign internal assignments and projects.
_____ External activities to be reassigned:
  • Customer servicing
  • Convention or professional meetings
  • Speeches and public relations commitments
  • Civic and professional commitments
  • Club memberships
  • Board memberships, e.g., of subsidiaries

Regrouping the Staff

_____ Announcement to immediate colleagues and support staff
_____ What they are to be told
_____ Transfer of assignments
_____ References
_____ Reassurances

Termination Letters

_____ Written evidence to verify the termination
_____ Summary of important information the candidates may not have listened to, or
_____ remembered
_____ Brief and business-like confirmation of the facts and the details
_____ Include:
  • Termination date
  • Severance or bridging pay allowance
  • Vacation pay
_____ Continuation of benefits:
  • Regular benefits
  • Special benefits, such as pension rights
_____ Job search support:
  • Logistical
  • Financial
  • Outplacement
  • Transfer of responsibilities
  • Continuation of responsibilities
  • Return of company property
  • Legal documents
  • Conditions of termination?

Source: Reprinted with permission from James J. Gallagher, chairman, J. J. Gallagher Associates, New York, N.Y.

When. This decision may be crucial to the success of the termination process. First of all, consider personal situations—birthdays, anniversaries, family illnesses. Further, most experts agree that Friday is the worst day of the week for terminations. That leaves the employee with the entire weekend to brood before any positive action can be taken.[77]

Where. Neutral territory—not the manager's or employee's office. The firing manager should arrange a neutral location so that each party is easily able to leave after the interview.

Following these activities, the firing manager should follow five rules for the termination interview:[78]

1. *Present the situation in a clear, concise, and final manner.* Don't confuse the message to be delivered, and don't drag it out. "Tom, no doubt you are aware that the organization has eliminated some jobs, and one of them is yours." Remember: spend only a few minutes, don't make excuses, don't bargain, and don't compromise. Get to the point quickly and succinctly. As one outplacement executive noted: "It's not cruel to cut clean."[79]

2. *Avoid debates or a rehash of the past.* Arguments about past performance may only compound bad feelings that already exist. Don't shift responsibility; the person is your responsibility, and you must accept that as a fact.

3. *Never talk down to the individual.* Your objective should be to remove as much of the emotion and trauma as possible. Emphasize that it's a situation that isn't working and that the decision is made. It's a business decision—don't make excuses or apologies. Be tactful, and by all means, avoid insulting (and unlawful) remarks, such as "At your age I'd be thinking of early retirement."

4. *Be empathetic but not compromising.* "I'm sorry that this has to happen, but the decisions are made. We are going to provide assistance to you [or to each of the people affected]."

5. *What's the next step?* "I'm going to give you this letter outlining the severance arrangements. I suggest you take the rest of the day off and plan on being here tomorrow at 9 A.M. to talk with the benefits people. Also, we have engaged a very successful outplacement firm, and I would like to introduce you to Fred Martin, who, if you wish, will be working with you through your transition."[80]

Be prepared for a variety of reactions from disbelief to silent acceptance to rage. The key is to remain calm and focus on helping the employee confront the reality of the situation. This is best done by maintaining your distance and composure. It does no good to argue or cry along with the employee.

After terminations or layoffs, the work attitudes and behaviors of remaining employees ("survivors") may suffer. If the layoff (or its management, or both) is perceived to be unjust, survivors are likely to feel angry. In addition, they may feel guilty that they, rather than their laid-off coworkers, could have been dismissed just as easily. This layoff-induced stress, with its attendant feelings of anger, guilt, and job insecurity, can be reduced in two ways. One, provide extra social support (e.g., from coworkers and supervisors) to those survivors who are perceived as especially "at risk." Two, organizations that provide outplacement support to those who are dismissed enjoy, as a secondary benefit, reduced postlayoff stress among survivors.[81]

Finally, public disclosure of termination practices (e.g., in the case of layoffs) may actually help displaced employees, since it assures potential employers that economic factors—not individual shortcomings—caused the dismissals.[82] Having examined a very public issue, termination, let us now turn our attention to a related issue, employee privacy.

EMPLOYEE PRIVACY AND ETHICAL ISSUES

Privacy refers to the interest employees have in controlling the use that is made of their personal information and in being able to engage in behavior free from regulation or surveillance.[83] Attention centers on three main issues: the kind of information collected and retained about individuals, how that information is used, and the extent to which it can be disclosed to others. These issues often lead to ethical dilemmas for managers, that is, situations that have the potential to result in a breach of acceptable behavior.

But what is "acceptable" behavior? The difficulty lies in maintaining a proper balance between the common good and personal freedom, between the legitimate business needs of an organization and a worker's feelings of dignity and worth.[84] Although we cannot prescribe the *content* of ethical behavior across all conceivable situations, we can prescribe *processes* that may lead to an acceptable (and temporary) consensus among interested parties regarding an ethical course of action. In the remainder of this chapter, we will examine several areas that pose potential ethical dilemmas for employers and privacy concerns for employees or job applicants. Let us begin by considering fair information practice policies.

Fair Information Practices in the Computer Age

The Electronic Communications Privacy Act of 1986 prohibits "outside" interception of electronic mail by a third party—the government, the police, or an individual—without proper authorization (such as a search warrant). Information sent on public networks, such as Compuserve and MCI Mail, to which individuals and companies subscribe, is therefore protected. However, the law does not cover "inside" interception, and, in fact, no absolute privacy exists in a computer system, even for bosses.[85] They may view employees on closed-circuit TV; tap their phones, e-mail, and network communications; and rummage through their computer files with or without employee knowledge or consent 24 hours a day.[86] Safeguards to protect personal privacy are more important than ever. However, as we noted in Chapter 5, only about 20 percent of U.S. companies have written policies regarding electronic privacy for employees. What should managers do?

First, *periodically and systematically review record-keeping practices* such as the following:

- The number and types of records maintained on employees, former employees, and applicants
- The specific information retained in each record
- The uses made of information in each type of record
- The disclosures made to parties outside the organization
- The extent to which individuals are aware and informed of such uses and disclosures of information about them

After reviewing their current practices, managers should *articulate, communicate, and implement fair information practice policies* by taking the following actions:

- Limiting the collection of information about individuals to that which is relevant to specific decisions
- Informing individuals of the types of information being maintained and the uses to be made of it
- Adopting procedures to ensure the accuracy, timeliness, and completeness of such information

ETHICAL DILEMMA: DO EMPLOYEES HAVE A RIGHT TO ELECTRONIC PRIVACY?[87]

When Alana Shoars arrived for work at Epson America, Inc., one morning, she discovered her supervisor reading and printing out electronic-mail messages between other employees. Ms. Shoars was appalled. When she had trained employees to use the computerized system, she had told them their mail was private. Now a company manager was violating that trust.

When she questioned the practice, Ms. Shoars says she was told to mind her own business. A day later, she was fired for insubordination. Then she filed a $1 million lawsuit for wrongful termination. Although she soon found a job as e-mail administrator at another firm, she still bristles about Epson: "You don't read other people's mail, just as you don't listen to their phone conversations. Right is right, and wrong is wrong."

Michael Simmons, chief information officer at the Bank of Boston, disagrees completely. "If the corporation owns the equipment and pays for the network, that asset belongs to the company, and it has a right to look and see if people are using it for purposes other than running the business." At a previous job, for example, Mr. Simmons discovered that one employee was using the computer system to handicap horse races, and another was running his Amway business on his computer. Both were fired immediately. "The guy handicapping horses was using 600 megabytes of memory," Mr. Simmons said. What do you think? Do employees have a right to electronic privacy?

- Permiting individuals to see, copy, correct, or amend records about themselves
- Taking adequate security precautions to limit internal access to records (e.g., physical security, passwords, system audit trails, read/write authentication routines)
- Limiting external disclosures of information, particularly those made without the individual's authorization
- Conducting regular reviews of compliance with these fair information practice policies.[88]

Companies that have taken such measures, such as IBM, Bank of America, AT&T, Cummins Engine, Avis, and TRW, report that they have not been overly costly, produced burdensome traffic in access demands, or reduced the general quality of their HR decisions. Furthermore, they receive strong employee approval for their policies when they ask about them on company attitude surveys. By matching words with deeds, companies such as these are weaving their concerns for employee privacy into the very fabric of their corporate cultures.

Assessment of Job Applicants and Employees

Decisions to hire, promote, train, or transfer are major events in individuals' careers. Frequently, such decisions are made with the aid of tests, interviews, situational exercises, performance appraisals, and other assessment techniques. Developers and users of these instruments must be concerned with questions of fairness, propriety, and individual rights, as well as with other ethical issues.

Developers, if they are members of professional associations such as the American Psychological Association, the Society for Human Resource Management, or the Academy of Management, are bound by the ethical standards put forth by those bodies. Managers who use assessment instruments are subject to other ethical principles, beyond the general concerns for accuracy and equality of opportunity. These include:[89]

- Guarding against invasion of privacy
- Guaranteeing confidentiality
- Obtaining informed consent from employees and applicants before assessing them
- Respecting employees' rights to know (e.g., regarding test content and the meaning, interpretation, and intended use of scores)
- Imposing time limitations on data (i.e., removing information that has not been used for HR decisions, especially if it has been updated)
- Using the most valid procedures available, thereby minimizing erroneous acceptances and erroneous rejections
- Treating applicants and employees with respect and consideration (i.e., by standardizing procedures for all candidates)

What can applicants do when confronted by a question they believe is irrelevant or an invasion of privacy? Some may choose not to respond. However, research indicates that employers tend to view such nonresponse as an attempt to conceal facts that would reflect poorly on an applicant. Hence applicants (especially those who have nothing to hide) are ill advised not to respond.[90] Clearly, it is the employer's responsibility to (1) know the kinds of questions that are being asked of candidates and (2) to review the appropriateness and job-relatedness of all such questions.

Whistle-Blowing

Like a referee on a playing field who can blow the whistle to stop action, whistle-blowing refers to disclosure by former or current organization members of illegal, immoral, or illegitimate practices under the control of their employers to persons or organizations that may be able to do something about it.[91] Research indicates that individuals can be conditioned to behave unethically (if they are rewarded for it), especially under increased competition,[92] but that the threat of punishment has a counterbalancing influence.[93] More important, when a formal or informal organizational policy is present that favors ethical behavior, ethical behavior tends to increase.[94]

Research with almost 8600 employees of 22 federal agencies and departments revealed that those who had observed alleged wrongdoing were more likely to "blow the whistle" if they:

- Were employed by organizations perceived by others to be responsive to complaints
- Held professional positions, had long service, and had positive reactions to their work
- Were recently recognized for good performance
- Were male (although race was unrelated to whistle-blowing)
- Were members of large work groups[95]

IMPACT OF PROCEDURAL JUSTICE AND ETHICS ON PRODUCTIVITY, QUALITY OF WORK LIFE, AND THE BOTTOM LINE

As we have seen throughout this chapter, employees and former employees are very sensitive to the general issue of "justice on the job." On a broad range of issues, they expect to be treated justly, fairly, and with due process. Doing so certainly contributes to improved productivity and quality of work life, for grievances are both time-consuming and costly. On the other hand, organizations that disregard employee rights can expect two things: (1) to be hit with lawsuits and (2) to find courts and juries to be sympathetic to tales of employer wrongdoing. Employment-at-will cases illustrate this trend clearly. As for employers contesting such suits, one corporate attorney noted: "Even a victory isn't a victory because the [defendant's] attorneys' fees are at least $50,000 for a typical case."[96] As in so many other areas of employee relations, careful attention to procedural justice and ethical decision making yields direct as well as indirect benefits. The old adage "an ounce of prevention is worth a pound of cure" says it all.

These findings are consistent with other research that has destroyed the myth that whistle-blowers are social misfits. A study of nearly 100 people who reported wrongdoing in public and private-sector organizations found that the average whistle-blower was a 47-year-old family man employed for 7 years before exposing his company's misdeeds.[97]

Despite retaliation, financial loss, and high emotional and physical stress,[98] there are at least two reasons why more whistle-blowers are likely to come forward in the future. One, some 30 states (and the federal government) now protect the jobs of workers who report wrongdoing by their companies.[99] Two, disclosure of fraud, waste, and abuse by federal contractors can lead to substantial financial gains by whistle-blowers. As a result of recent amendments to the federal False Claims Act of 1863, private citizens may sue a contractor for fraud on the government's behalf and share up to 25 percent of whatever financial recovery the government makes as a result of the charges. Thus a federal judge awarded $11.5 million to a former General Electric Co. employee for exposing a defense contract fraud. That was almost 20 percent of the $59.5 million GE paid to settle the civil portion of the charges.[100] If you have a tale to tell, here are some do's and don'ts:[101]

Do make sure your allegation is correct, keep careful records, research whether your state provides protection for whistle-blowers, and be realistic about your future. Do talk to your family, and be prepared for a worst-case scenario.

Don't assume a federal or state law will protect you as the "good guy." Legal protection for private-sector workers is often inadequate and varies from state to state.

Don't run to the media (check with an attorney first), and *don't* expect a windfall if you're fired. Although some states allow punitive damages, you may be eligible only for back pay and reinstatement—in a place where you probably don't want to work anyway.

Conclusion

Ethical behavior is not governed by hard-and-fast rules. Rather, it adapts and changes in response to social norms. This is nowhere more obvious than in human resource management. What was considered ethical in the 1950s and 1960s (deep-probing selection interviews; management prescriptions of standards of dress, ideology, and lifestyle; refusal to let employees examine their own personnel files) would be considered improper today. Indeed, as we have seen, growing concern for employee rights has placed organizational decision-making policies in the public domain. The beneficial effect of this, of course, is that it is sensitizing both employers and employees to new concerns.

To be sure, ethical choices are rarely easy. The challenge in managing human resources lies not in the mechanical application of moral prescriptions but rather in the process of creating and maintaining genuine relationships from which to address ethical dilemmas that cannot be covered by prescription.[102]

A RADICAL EXPERIMENT AT GE: HOURLY WORKERS CONTROL A GRIEVANCE REVIEW PANEL

HUMAN RESOURCE MANAGEMENT IN ACTION: CONCLUSION

Shortly after the procedure went into effect, a grievant took the first case to the panel. By policy, he was allowed to choose the names of four hourly-worker panelists through a random-selection procedure and to put one name back, leaving three hourly-worker panelists to hear the case with the two managers.

The case was an intriguing one. It involved a job promotion that had been denied because of a rule prohibiting a person from downgrading to a lower-level job and then upgrading back to the same job within 6 months. The grievant felt that extenuating circumstances should have allowed him to bypass the 6-month rule.

After hearing all the evidence and investigating precedents, the panel ruled against the grievant. One of the hourly members of the panel said, "We sympathize with the guy, but a rule is a rule and it's the same for everyone." The message in that statement is that the panelists have taken their responsibility seriously.

Is the expanded grievance procedure with the review panel a cure-all for GE's employee relations concerns? Certainly not. But the company has proven itself correct in its belief that employees can be trusted to make wise decisions. As a result, both management and employees agree, the Columbia plant is now a better place in which to work.

IMPLICATIONS FOR MANAGEMENT PRACTICE

Individual managers who disregard employee rights to procedural justice do so at their peril. If you are operating in a unionized setting, know the collective bargaining agreement inside and out. More important, follow both the letter and the spirit of its provisions. In nonunion settings, be sure that decisions about selection, assignment, promotion, discipline, and discharge are based on clear standards and recorded judgments that can be examined when a dispute arises. Study after study confirms the beneficial effects on employee attitudes and performance of procedural justice safeguards.[103] Provide explicit procedures for resolving conflicts and be sure that all employees know how to use them. Finally, treat all people with dignity and respect; think win-win rather than win-lose.

SUMMARY

The broad theme of this chapter is "justice on the job." This includes procedural justice, due process, and ethical decision making. Each of these processes should guide the formulation of policy in matters involving dispute resolution (e.g., through union or nonunion grievance procedures), arbitration, discipline, employment contracts, and termination for disciplinary or economic reasons. Indeed, such concerns for procedural justice and due process form the basis for many challenges to the employment-at-will doctrine.

Two of the most important employment issues of our time are employee privacy and ethical decision making. Three areas that involve employee privacy are receiving considerable emphasis: fair information practices in the computer age, the assessment of job applicants and employees, and whistle-blowing. Although it is not possible to prescribe the *content* of ethical behavior in each of these areas, *processes* that incorporate procedural justice can lead to an acceptable (and temporary) consensus among interested parties regarding an ethical course of action.

DISCUSSION QUESTIONS

15■1 Discuss the similarities and differences in these concepts: procedural justice, corporate due process, and ethical decisions about behavior.

15■2 What advice would you give to an executive who is about to negotiate an employment contract?

15■3 Is it ethical to tape-record a conversation with your boss without his or her knowledge?

15■4 How can a firm avoid lawsuits for employment-at-will?

15■5 What are some guidelines to follow in determining a reasonable compromise between a company's need to run its business and employee rights to privacy?

REFERENCES

1. Fossum, J. A. (1990). Employee and labor relations in an evolving environment. In J. A. Fossum (ed.), *Employee and labor relations.* Washington, DC: Bureau of National Affairs, pp. 4-1 to 4-22.
2. *Webster's new collegiate dictionary* (1976). Springfield, MA: Merriam-Webster.
3. Greenberg, J. (1987). Reactions to procedural injustice in payment distributions: Do the means justify the ends? *Journal of Applied Psychology, 72,* 55–61.
4. Wesman, E. C., & Eischen, D. E. (1990). Due process. In J. A. Fossum (ed.), *Employee and labor relations.* Washington, DC: Bureau of National Affairs, pp. 4-82 to 4-133.
5. Cullen, J. B., Victor, B., & Stephens, C. (1989). An ethical weather report: Assessing the organization's ethical climate. *Organizational Dynamics, 18,* 50–62. See also Nielsen, R. P. (1989). Changing unethical organizational behavior. *Academy of Management Executive,* 3(2), 123–130.
6. Sheppard, B. H., Lewicki, R. J., & Minton, J. W. (1992). *Organizational justice: The search for fairness in the workplace.* New York: Lexington.
7. Ibid.
8. Ibid.
9. Tyler, T. R., & Bies, R. J. (1990). Beyond formal procedures: The interpersonal context of procedural justice. In J. S. Carroll (ed.), *Applied psychology and organizational settings.* Hillsdale, NJ: Erlbaum, pp. 77–98.
10. Sheppard et al., op. cit.
11. Mills, D. Q. (1994). *Labor-management relations* (5th ed.). New York: McGraw-Hill.
12. Ibid.

13. Noble, K. B. (1988, June 30). Unions limited in use of dues and fees. *The New York Times*, p. 13.

14. Mills, op. cit.

15. Labig, C. E., & Greer, C. R. (1988). Grievance initiation: A literature survey and directions for future research. *Journal of Labor Research*, **9**, 1–27.

16. Ibid.

17. Ibid.

18. Dalton, D. R., & Todor, W. D. (1981). Win, lose, draw: The grievance process in practice. *Personnel Administrator*, **26**(3), 25–29.

19. Kotlowitz, A. (1987, Aug. 28). Labor's turn? *The Wall Street Journal*, pp. 1, 14. See also Kotlowitz, A. (1987, Apr. 1). Grievous work. *The Wall Street Journal*, pp. 1, 12.

20. Mesch, D. J., & Dalton, D. R. (1992). Unexpected consequences of improving workplace justice: A six-year time series assessment. *Academy of Management Journal*, **35**, 1099–1114. See also Dalton & Todor, op. cit.

21. Meyer, D., & Cooke, W. (1988). Economic and political factors in the resolution of formal grievances. *Industrial Relations*, **27**, 318–335.

22. Klaas, B. S. (1989). Managerial decision making about employee grievances: The impact of the grievant's work history. *Personnel Psychology*, **42**, 53–68. See also Dalton, D. R., Todor, W. D., & Owen, C. L. (1987). Sex effects in workplace justice outcomes: A field assessment. *Journal of Applied Psychology*, **72**, 156–159. See also Dalton, D. R., & Todor, W. D. (1985). Gender and workplace justice: A field assessment. *Personnel Psychology*, **38**, 133–151.

23. Mesch & Dalton, op. cit.

24. Staudhar, P. D. (1976). Grievance arbitration in public employment. *The Arbitration Journal*, **31**, 116–124.

25. Hill, M., Jr., & Sinicropi, A. V. (1980). *Evidence in arbitration*. Washington, DC: Bureau of National Affairs.

26. Hauenstein, M. A., & Lord, R. G. (1989). The effects of final-offer arbitration on major league baseball players: A test of equity theory. *Human Performance*, **2**, 147–165.

27. Bretz, R. D., Jr., & Thomas, S. L. (1992). Perceived equity, motivation, and final-offer arbitration in major league baseball. *Journal of Applied Psychology*, **77**, 280–287.

28. Labor letter (1989, Nov. 14). *The Wall Street Journal*, p. A1.

29. Ewing, J. B. (1989, Oct. 23). Corporate due process lowers legal costs. *The Wall Street Journal*, p. A14.

30. Taking it to arbitration (1985, July 16). *The Wall Street Journal*, p. 1.

31. Drost, D. A., & O'Brien, F. P. (1983). Are there grievances against your non-union grievance procedure? *Personnel Administrator*, **28**(1), 36–42.

32. Ibid.

33. Ewing, op. cit.

34. Seeley, R. S. (1992, July). Corporate due process. *HRMagazine*, pp. 46–49.

35. Ibid. See also Reibstein, L. (1986, Dec. 3). More firms use peer review panel to resolve employees' grievances. *The Wall Street Journal*, p. 33. See also Olson, F. C. (1984). How peer review works at Control Data. *Harvard Business Review*, **62**(6), 58–61.

36. Seeley, op. cit., p. 49.

37. Wesman & Eischen, op. cit.

38. Belohlav, J. (1983). Realities of successful employee discipline. *Personnel Administrator*, **28**(3), 74–77, 92.

39. Baum, L. (1986, June 16). Punishing workers with a day off. *Business Week*, p. 80.

40. O'Reilly, C. A., III, & Weitz, B. A. (1980). Managing marginal employees: The use of warnings and dismissals. *Administrative Science Quarterly*, **25**, 467–484.

41. Franke, R., & Karl, J. (1978). The Hawthorne experiments: First statistical interpretation. *American Sociological Review*, **43**, 623–643. See also O'Reilly & Weitz, op. cit.

42. Bandura, A. (1986). *Social foundations of thought and action: A social cognitive theory.* Englewood Cliffs, NJ: Prentice-Hall.

43. Trevino, L. K. (1992). The social effects of punishments in organizations: A justice perspective. *Academy of Management Review*, **17**, 647–676.

44. O'Reilly, C. A., III, & Puffer, S. M. (1989). The impact of rewards and punishments in a social context: A laboratory and field experiment. *Journal of Occupational Psychology*, **62**, 41–53.

45. Klaas, B. S., & Feldman, D. C. (1994). The impact of appeal system structure on disciplinary decisions. *Personnel Psychology*, **47**, 91–108. See also Klaas, B. S., & Dell'omo, G. G. (1991). The determinants of disciplinary decisions: The case of employee drug use. *Personnel Psychology*, **44**, 813–835.

46. Klaas, B. S., & Wheeler, H. N. (1990). Managerial decision making about employee discipline: A policy-capturing approach. *Personnel Psychology*, **43**, 117–134.

47. Israel, D. (1983). The Weingarten case sets precedent for co-employee representation. *Personnel Administrator*, **28**(2), 23–26.

48. *NLRB v. Weingarten* (1975). 420 U.S. 251, 95 S. Ct. 959.

49. *NLRB v. Sears Roebuck and Co.* (1985, Feb. 27). *Daily Labor Report*, **39**, D1–D5.

50. Weingarten rights include prior consultation (1992, August). *Mountain States Employers Council Bulletin*, p. 4.

51. Employee's "Weingarten" rights limited by NLRB (1993, January). *Mountain States Employers Council Bulletin*, p. 4.

52. Israel, op. cit.

53. Lorber, L. Z., Kirk, J. R., Kirschner, K. H., & Handorf, C. R. (1984). *Fear of firing: A legal and personnel analysis of employment-at-will*. Alexandria, VA: American Society for Personnel Administration.

54. Geyelin, M. (1989, Sept. 7). Fired managers winning more lawsuits. *The Wall Street Journal*, p. B13.

55. Geyelin, M., & Moses, J. M. (1992, Apr. 7). Rulings on wrongful firing curb hiring. *The Wall Street Journal*, p. B1.

56. Stern, G. (1993, May 5). Companies discover that some firings backfire into costly defamation suits. *The Wall Street Journal*, pp. B1, B7.

57. Spurgeon, Haney, & Howbert, P. A. (1985). *Ready, fire! (aim): A manager's primer in the law of terminations*. Colorado Springs, CO: Author.

58. Koys, D. J., Briggs, S., & Grenig, J. (1987). State court disparity on employment-at-will. *Personnel Psychology*, **40**, 565–577.

59. Stern, op. cit. See also Geyelin, op. cit.

60. Heshizer, B. (1984). The implied contract exception to at-will employment. *Labor Law Journal*, **35**, 131–141.

61. Bakaly, C. G., Jr., & Grossman, J. M. (1984, August). How to avoid wrongful discharge suits. *Management Review*, pp. 41–46.

62. Wermiel, S. (1988, June 7). Justices expand union workers' right to sue. *The Wall Street Journal*, p. 4.

63. Yoder, S. K., & Lambert, W. (1990, Dec. 21). California rulings may limit worker suits. *The Wall Street Journal*, p. B6. See also Schlender, B. R. (1988, Dec. 30). California ruling curtails damages in dismissal suits. *The Wall Street Journal*, p. B1.

64. Geyelin, op. cit.

65. Handbooks (1994, January). *Mountain States Employers Council Bulletin*, p. 2. See also Fulmer, W. E., & Casey, A. W. (1990). Employment at will: Options for managers. *Academy of Management Executive*, **4**(2), 102–107.

66. Lorber, L. Z. (1984). Basic advice on avoiding employment-at-will troubles. *Personnel Administrator*, **29**(1), 59–62.

67. Engel, P, G. (1985, Mar. 18). Preserving the right to fire. *Industry Week*, pp. 39–40.

68. Stickney, J. (1984, December). Settling the terms of employment. *Money*, pp. 127, 128, 132.

69. Johnson, R. K. (1988, May). Employment contracts. *The Advisor*, pp. 6, 7.

70. Personal affairs (1983, June 6). *Forbes*, pp. 174, 178.

71. Wadman, M. K. (1992, June 26). More firms restrict departing workers. *The Wall Street Journal*, pp. B1, B3. See also You'll never eat lunch in this industry again (1991, Nov. 11). *Business Week*, p. 44. See also Green, W. B. (1989, Jan. 11). Courts skeptical of "noncompete" pacts. *The Wall Street Journal*, p. B1.

72. Stickney, op. cit.

73. Stickney, op. cit., p. 132.

74. Geyelin, op. cit.

75. Greenwald, J. (1994, Jan. 10). The economy: Picking up speed. *Time*, pp. 18–21.

76. Sweet, D. H. (1989). *A manager's guide to conducting terminations*. Lexington, MA: Lexington Books.

77. Youngblood, D. (1987, June 22). Supervisors offered guidelines to "humane" firing. *Rocky Mountain News*, p. 62.

78. Stern, op. cit. See also Sweet, op. cit.

79. Youngblood, op. cit.

80. Sweet, op. cit., p. 56.

81. Brockner, J., Grover, S., Reed, T. F., & Dewitt, R. L. (1992). Layoffs, job insecurity, and survivors' work effort: Evidence of an inverted-U relationship. *Academy of Management Journal*, **35**, 413–425. See also Brockner, J. (1988). The effect of work layoffs on survivors: Research, theory, and practice. In B. M. Staw & L. L. Cummings (eds.), *Research in organizational behavior*. Greenwich, CT: JAI Press, vol. 10, pp. 213–255.

82. Sweet, D. H. (1989). Outplacement. In W. F. Cascio (ed.), *Human resource planning, employment, and placement*. Washington, DC: Bureau of National Affairs, pp. 2-236 to 2-261.

83. Piller, C. (1993, July). Privacy in peril. *Macworld*, pp. 124–130.

84. Privacy (1988, Mar. 28). *Business Week*, pp. 61–68.

85. Elmer-Dewitt, P. (1993, Jan. 18). Who's reading your screen? *Time*, p. 46.

86. Piller, C. (1993, July). Bosses with X-ray eyes. *Macworld*, pp. 118–123.

87. Rifkin, G. (1991, Dec. 8). Do employees have a right to electronic privacy? *The New York Times*, p. 8F.

88. Cascio, W. F. (1991). *Applied psychology in personnel management* (4th ed.). Englewood Cliffs, NJ: Prentice-Hall.

89. London, M., & Bray, D. W. (1980). Ethical issues in testing and evaluation for personnel decisions. *American Psychologist*, **35**, 890–901.

90. Stone, D. L., & Stone, E. F. (1987). Effects of missing application-blank information on personnel selection decisions: Do privacy protection strategies bias the outcome? *Journal of Applied Psychology*, **72**, 452–456.

91. Miceli, M. P., & Near, J. P. (1992). *Blowing the whistle*. New York: Lexington.

92. Nielsen, op. cit.

93. Jansen, E., & Von Glinow, M. A. (1985). Ethical ambivalence and organizational reward systems. *Academy of Management Review*, **10**, 815–822.

94. Hegarty, W. H., & Sims, H. P., Jr. (1979). Organizational philosophy, policies, and objectives related to unethical decision behavior: A laboratory experiment. *Journal of Applied Psychology*, **64**, 331–338.

95. Miceli, M. P., & Near, J. P. (1988). Individual and situational correlates of whistle-blowing. *Personnel Psychology*, **41**, 267–281.

96. Barrett, A., cited in Schlender, B. R. (1988, Dec. 30). California ruling curtails damages in dismissal suits. *The Wall Street Journal*, p. B1.

97. Farnsworth, C. H. (1987, Feb. 22). Survey of whistle blowers finds retaliation but few regrets. *The New York Times*, p. 22.

98. Greenwald, J. (1993, June 21). A matter of honor. *Time*, pp. 33, 34. See also Hilts, P. J. (1991, Mar. 22). Hero in exposing science hoax paid dearly. *The New York Times*, pp. A1, B6.

99. Wald, M. L. (1990, Mar. 11). Whistle-blowers in atomic plants to be aided. *The New York Times*, p. 28.

100. Kumar Naj, A. (1993, Apr. 26). Whistle-blower at GE to get $11.5 million. *The Wall Street Journal*, pp. A3, A8.

101. Dunkin, A. (1991, June 3). Blowing the whistle without paying the piper. *Business Week*, pp. 138, 139.

102. Cascio, op. cit.

103. Gilliland, S. W. (1993). The perceived fairness of selection systems: An organizational justice perspective. *Academy of Management Review*, **18**, 694–734. See also Saal, F. E., & Moore, S. C. (1993). Perceptions of promotion fairness and promotion candidates' qualifications. *Journal of Applied Psychology*, **78**, 105–110. See also Schwarzwald, J., Koslowsky, M., & Shalit, B. (1992). A field study of employees' attitudes and behaviors after promotion decisions. *Journal of Applied Psychology*, **77**, 511–514. See also Konovsky, M. A., & Cropanzano, R. (1991). Perceived fairness of employee drug testing as a predictor of employee attitudes and job performance. *Journal of Applied Psychology*, **76**, 698–707.

PART SIX

SUPPORT, EVALUATION, AND INTERNATIONAL IMPLICATIONS

A CONCEPTUAL VIEW OF
HUMAN RESOURCE MANAGEMENT

STRATEGIC OBJECTIVES, ENVIRONMENTS, FUNCTIONS

Productivity

Quality of Work Life

Profits

Competitive

Legal

Social

Organizational

Employment

Development

Compensation

Labor-Management Accommodation

Support, Evaluation, International Implications

RELATIONSHIP OF HRM FUNCTIONS TO HRM ACTIVITIES

FUNCTIONS	ACTIVITIES
Part Two **Employment**	Job Analysis, Human Resource Planning, Recruiting, Staffing (Chapters 5 - 7)
Part Three **Development**	Orienting, Training, Performance Appraisal, Managing Careers (Chapters 8 - 10)
Part Four **Compensation**	Pay, Benefits, Incentives (Chapters 11 - 13)
Part Five **Labor-Management Accommodation**	Union Representation, Collective Bargaining, Procedural Justice, Ethics (Chapters 14, 15)
Part Six **Support, Evaluation, International Implications**	Job Safety and Health, Costs/Benefits of HRM Activities, International Dimensions of HRM (Chapters 16 - 18)

SUPPORT, EVALUATION, AND INTERNATIONAL IMPLICATIONS

This capstone section deals with three broad themes: organizational support for employees, evaluation of human resource management activities, and the international implications of human resource management activities. Chapter 16 examines key issues involved in employee safety and health, both mental and physical. Chapter 17 presents the latest methods of assessing the costs and benefits of human resource management activities in a number of areas. Finally, Chapter 18 considers key issues in international human resource management; given the rapid growth of multinational corporations, it is perhaps in this area more than any other that employees and their families need special social and financial support from their firms.

CHAPTER 16

SAFETY, HEALTH, AND EMPLOYEE ASSISTANCE PROGRAMS

SUBSTANCE ABUSE ON THE JOB PRODUCES TOUGH POLICY CHOICES FOR MANAGERS*

Experts estimate that 5 to 10 percent of employees in any company have a substance abuse problem (alcohol or drugs) serious enough to merit treatment. The situation may be even worse. Thus, in 1984 and 1985, unbeknown to employees and job applicants, Chevron Corp. carried out anonymous drug testing. About 30 percent of all applicants and 20 percent of all employees tested positive for illegal drug use.

What is an appropriate policy for managers to adopt in these circumstances? Certainly cost pressures are forcing some employers to reexamine their drug and alcohol treatment programs. After noting that the cost of a 21-day detoxification program runs from $4000 to $14,000, one health care professional commented, "People want to fire other people because they consume a lot of health-care dollars. Those of us in the . . . field are feeling [pressure]. We were feeling it before *Valdez,* and we'll feel it after. In terms of cutting their costs, they go for the most visible, and clearly the most visible are chemically dependent people."

Another professional in the field says that more hard-line companies simply demote people who have been in treatment. "They won't have a written policy, but they'll guide that person into a position of no strategic importance. If asked, the companies won't acknowledge it. They don't want the bad publicity of being a mean guy."

---

*Adapted from: Firms debate hard line on alcoholics, *The Wall Street Journal*, Apr. 13, 1989, p. B1. Reprinted by permission of *The Wall Street Journal*, © 1989 Dow Jones & Company, Inc. All rights reserved worldwide.

Buoying these hard-liners are some very public drug- and alcohol-related accidents, of which the Exxon *Valdez* oil spill is probably the best known. According to federal regulators, the rate of railroad employees who failed drug or alcohol tests following accidents rose to 6 percent in the first 11 months of 1988, from 4.6 percent in 1986. More recently, three Northwest Airlines pilots were convicted of operating a commercial airliner while intoxicated. What should firms do? While dismissal and demotion are two obvious policy choices, rehabilitation is a third.

Among companies that endorse rehabilitation, however, there is considerable debate about whether employees should be returned to their jobs if they are successfully rehabilitated. Standard industry practice is to return people to their jobs after treatment. Exxon, however, bucked the industry trend following the wreck of its oil tanker Exxon *Valdez* (and the environmental disaster that followed). The ship's captain had previously been treated for alcoholism and returned to work. After the accident, a blood test revealed a high level of alcohol in his system. Exxon therefore adopted the policy that, following treatment, known alcohol and drug abusers won't be allowed to return to so-called critical jobs such as piloting a ship, flying a plane, or operating a refinery, although they will be given other jobs.

Those who favor returning people to work after rehabilitation argue that it is not only more humane but also more effective. Refusing to return people to work—even in safety-sensitive positions—would be "short-sighted. It will make sure that no one who's an alcoholic ever gets help," according to the medical director of United Airlines (which regularly returns pilots to their jobs after treatment). "As ubiquitous a disease as alcoholism is, you have two choices: you either have practicing alcoholics in the cockpits, or you have recovering ones." Those who take a more hard-line attitude toward drug and alcohol abuse point out that many companies are thinking through their policies, wondering how much criticism from the community they can tolerate.

Challenges

1. What are some arguments for and against each of these policies: dismissal, demotion, return to the same job following rehabilitation, return to a different job following rehabilitation?

2. Should follow-up be required after rehabilitation? If so, how long should it last and what form should it take?

Questions This Chapter Will Help Managers Answer

As the chapter opening vignette shows, managers face tough policy issues in the area of workplace health and safety. As we shall see, a combination of external factors (e.g., the spiraling cost of health care) and internal factors (e.g., new technology) are making these issues impossible to ignore. Here are some decisions that managers will have to grapple with:

1. What is the cost-benefit trade-off of adopting measures to enhance workplace safety and health?

2. Which approaches to job safety and health really work?

3. What should an informed, progressive AIDS policy look like?

4. What are some key issues to consider in establishing and monitoring an employee assistance program?

5. Does it make sound business sense to institute a worksite wellness program? If so, how should it be implemented and what should it include?

This chapter begins by examining how social and legal policies on the federal and state levels have evolved on this issue, beginning with workers' compensation laws and culminating with the passage of the Occupational Safety and Health Act. The chapter then considers enforcement of the act, with special emphasis on the rights and obligations of management. It also examines prevailing approaches to job safety and health in other countries. Finally it considers the problems of AIDS and business, employee assistance programs, and corporate "wellness" programs. Underlying all these efforts is a conviction on the part of many firms that it is morally right to improve job safety and health—and that doing so will enhance the productivity and quality of work life of employees at all levels.

THE EXTENT AND COST OF SAFETY AND HEALTH PROBLEMS

Consider these startling facts. Every year in U.S. workplaces:[1]

- Roughly 1 of every 12 workers is injured or becomes ill on the job.
- Almost 10,000 workers die in workplace accidents.
- More than 6 million workers either get sick or are injured because of their jobs.
- Being hit by an object is the most common workplace injury, followed by sprains, strains, slips, and falls.[2]
- 35 million workdays are lost.

This figure balloons to 75 million workdays lost when permanently disabling injuries that occurred in prior years are included. The cost? A staggering $40 billion in lost wages, medical costs, insurance administration costs, and indirect costs. At the level of the individual firm, a Du Pont safety engineer determined that a disabling injury costs an average of almost $23,000 (in 1994 dollars). A company with 1000 employees could expect to have 27 lost-workday injuries per year. With a 4.5 percent profit margin, the company would need $13.8 million of sales to offset that cost.[3]

Regardless of one's perspective, social or economic, these are disturbing figures. In response, public policy has focused on two types of actions: *monetary compensation* for job-related injuries and *preventive measures* to enhance job safety and health. State-run workers' compensation programs and the federal Occupational Safety and Health Administration are responsible for implementing public policy in these areas. Let's examine each of them.

WORKERS' COMPENSATION: A HISTORICAL PERSPECTIVE

State governments introduced workers' compensation laws in the early 1900s. Such laws are based on the principle of *liability without fault*, under which employers contribute to a fund providing compensation to employees involved in work-related accidents and injuries. The scale of benefits is related to the nature of the injury. The benefits are not provided because of liability or negligence on the part of the employer; rather, they are provided simply as a matter of social policy. Since the premiums paid reflected the accident rate of the particular employer, states hoped to provide an incentive for firms to lower their premium costs by improving work conditions. The Supreme Court upheld the constitutionality of such laws in 1917, and by 1948 all states had adopted them in one form or another.[4]

For the more than 80 million workers, or 88 percent of the nation's workforce, who are covered, workers' compensation provides three types of benefits: (1) payments to replace lost wages while an employee is unable to work, (2) payments to cover medical bills, and (3) if an individual is unable to return to his or her former occupation, financial support for retraining. To replace lost wages, the legislation typically allows for some percentage of regular wages (60 to 67 percent) up to a maximum amount. However, the benefits actually received are often less than half of regular wages.[5]

By the 1960s, it was becoming apparent that neither the workers' compensation laws nor state safety standards were acting to reduce occupational hazards. Evidence began to accumulate that there were health hazards (so-called silent killers) in the modern work environment that either had not been fully recognized previously or were not fully understood. Research on industrial diseases was beginning to disclose that even brief exposure to certain toxic materials in a work environment could produce disease, sterility, and high mortality rates. This new concern was dramatized by revelations of "black lung" (pneumoconiosis) among coal miners, of "brown lung" (byssinosis) among textile workers, and of the toxic and carcinogenic (cancer-causing) effects of substances such as vinyl chloride and asbestos in other work environments.

Today, stress-related awards account for nearly 14 percent of occupational disease claims, up from less than 5 percent just 8 years ago. Workers' compensation has also been awarded for certain adverse physiological reactions to computer monitors, such as eyestrain.[6] Thus, in addition to *compensation* for work-related injuries, it became clear that a federally administered program of *prevention* of workplace health and safety hazards was essential. This concern culminated in the passage of the Williams-Steiger Occupational Safety and Health Act of 1970.

THE OCCUPATIONAL SAFETY AND HEALTH ACT

Purpose and Coverage

The purpose of the act is an ambitious one: "To assure so far as possible every working man and woman in the Nation safe and healthful working conditions and to preserve our human resources." Its coverage is equally ambitious, for the law extends to any business (regardless of size) that *affects* interstate commerce. Since almost any business affects interstate commerce, about 6 million U.S. workplaces and 93 million workers are included.[7] However, employers in low-hazard industries with 10 or fewer employees are exempt from regular safety inspections.[8] Federal, state, and local government workers are also excluded since the government cannot easily proceed against itself in the event of violations.

Administration

The 1970 act established three government agencies to administer and enforce the law:

- *The Occupational Safety and Health Administration* (OSHA) to establish and enforce the necessary safety and health standards
- *The Occupational Safety and Health Review Commission* (a three-member board appointed by the President) to rule on the appropriateness of OSHA's enforcement actions when they are contested by employers, employees, or unions
- *The National Institute for Occupational Safety and Health* (NIOSH) to conduct research on the causes and prevention of occupational injury and illness, to recommend new standards (based on this research) to the secretary of labor, and to develop educational programs

Safety and Health Standards

Under the law, each employer has a "general duty" to provide a place of employment "free from recognized hazards." Employers also have the "special duty" to comply with all standards of safety and health established under the act.

OSHA has issued a large number of detailed standards covering numerous environmental hazards. These include power tools, machine guards, compressed gas, materials handling and storage, and toxic substances such as asbestos, cotton dust, silica, lead, and carbon monoxide.

As an example, consider OSHA's bloodborne pathogen standard, which took effect in 1992. Workers exposed to blood and bodily fluids (e.g., health-care providers, first-aid providers) are covered by the rule, but it does not apply to workers who give first aid as "good Samaritans." It requires facilities to develop exposure control plans, implement engineering controls and worker training, provide personal protective equipment and hepatitis B vaccinations, and communicate hazards to workers.[9]

To date, NIOSH has identified more than 15,000 toxic substances based on its research, but the transition from research findings to workplace standards is often a long, contentious process. In 1992, for example, a federal court overturned OSHA's plan to set exposure standards for 400 toxic substances. Currently, it takes 38 to 46 months to set a standard.[10]

Record-Keeping Requirements

A good deal of paperwork is required of employers under the act. Specifically:

- A general log of each injury or illness (OSHA Form 200) (see Figure 16-1)
- Supplementary records of each injury or illness (OSHA Form 101)

Employees are guaranteed access, on request, to Form 200 at their workplace, and the records must be retained for 5 years following the calendar year they cover. The purpose of these reports is to identify where safety and health problems have been occurring (if at all). Such information helps call management's attention to the problems, as well as that of an OSHA inspector, should one visit the workplace. The annual summary must be sent to OSHA directly, to help the agency determine which workplaces should receive priority for inspection.

FIGURE 16-1
OSHA Form 200, log and summary of occupational injuries and illnesses.

OSHA Enforcement

In administering the act, OSHA inspectors have the right to enter a workplace and to conduct a compliance inspection. However, in its *Marshall v. Barlow's, Inc.* decision, the Supreme Court ruled that employers could require a search warrant before allowing the inspector onto company premises.[11] In practice, only about 3 percent of employers go that far, perhaps because the resulting inspection is likely to be especially "close."[12]

Since it is impossible for the roughly 1100 agency inspectors (most of whom are either safety engineers or industrial hygienists) to visit the nation's 6 million workplaces, a system of priorities has been established. In the past, OSHA made inspections mostly in response to employee complaints that safety or health standards had been violated. Employers are prohibited from discriminating against employees who file such complaints, and an employee representative is entitled to accompany the OSHA representative during the inspection.

As of 1994, however, OSHA has assigned top priority to worksites that are exposed to three risks: confined-space problems, lead in construction materials, and tuberculosis. Businesses particularly affected include health-care facilities, nursing homes, construction companies, and manufacturers whose plants contain potentially dangerous chemicals. Many of these enterprises are small.[13]

Considerable emphasis has been given to OSHA's role of *enforcement*, but not much to its role of *consultation*. Employers in nearly every state who want help in recognizing and correcting safety and health hazards can get it from a free, on-site consultation service funded by OSHA. The service is delivered by state governments or private-sector contractors using well-trained safety and/or health professionals (e.g., industrial hygienists). Primarily targeted for smaller businesses, this program is penalty-free and completely separate from the OSHA inspection effort. An employer's only obligation is a commitment to correct serious job safety and health hazards.

Penalties. Fines are mandatory where serious violations are found. If a violation is willful (one in which an employer either knew that what was being done constituted a violation of federal regulations or was aware that a hazardous condition existed and made no reasonable effort to eliminate it), an employer can be assessed a civil penalty of up to $70,000 for each violation. An employer who fails to correct a violation (within the allowed time limit) for which a citation has been issued can be fined up to $7000 for each day the violation continues. Finally, a willful first violation involving the death of a worker can carry a criminal penalty as high as $70,000 and 6 months in prison. A second such conviction can mean up to $140,000 and a full year behind bars.[14]

Executives can also receive criminal penalties. Thus, after a fire at Imperial Food Products in Hamlet, North Carolina, killed 25 workers in 1991, investigators learned that the high death count had been the result of illegally locked plant doors and the absence of a sprinkler system. Prosecuted under criminal statutes, the owner was sentenced to 19 years, 11 months in jail.[15]

Appeals. Employers can appeal citations, proposed penalties, and corrections they have been ordered to make through multiple levels of the agency, culminating with the Occupational Safety and Health Review Commission. The commission presumes the employer to be free of violations and puts the burden of proof on OSHA.[16] Further appeals can be pursued through the federal court system.

The Role of the States. Although OSHA is a federally run program, the act allows states to develop and administer their own programs if they are approved by the Secretary of Labor. There are many criteria for approval, but the most important is that the state program must be judged "at least as effective" as the federal program. Currently, 23 states have approved plans in operation.

Workers' Rights to Health and Safety. Both unionized and nonunionized workers have walked off the job when subjected to unsafe working conditions.[17] In unionized firms, walkouts have occurred during the term of valid collective bargaining agreements that contained no-strike and grievance and/or arbitration clauses.[18] Are such walkouts legal? Yes, the Supreme Court has ruled, under certain circumstances:[19]

- Objective evidence must be presented to support the claim that abnormally dangerous working conditions exist.
- If such evidence is presented, a walkout is legal *regardless* of the existence of a no-strike or arbitration clause.
- It is an unfair labor practice for an employer to interfere with a walkout under such circumstances. This is true whether a firm is unionized or nonunionized.
- Expert testimony (e.g., by an industrial hygienist) is critically important in establishing the presence of abnormally dangerous working conditions.
- If a good-faith belief is not supported by objective evidence, employees who walk off the job are subject to disciplinary action.

OSHA's Impact

From its inception, OSHA has been both cussed and discussed, and its effectiveness in improving workplace safety and health has been questioned by the very firms it regulates. Controversy has ranged from disagreements over the setting of health standards to inspection procedures.[20] Employers complain of excessively detailed and costly regulations that, they believe, ignore workplace realities. Investigations by Congress and by outside researchers have found that OSHA has made no significant, lasting reductions in lost workdays or injury rates.[21] In the opinion of the AFL-CIO, this is due to a lack of enforcement of safety standards and regulations by OSHA. The directors of OSHA argue exactly the opposite: It's precisely because of better record keeping, brought about in part by stiff fines levied against companies by OSHA, that injury rates haven't shown a sustained decline. Another reason is that employers sometimes try to improve their competitiveness at the expense of safety. Here's an example.

**COMPANY
EXAMPLE**

MAINTAINING PRODUCTIVITY AT THE EXPENSE OF SAFETY

Preoccupied with staying in business, many small businesses skimp on safety information and worker training. That can be especially risky because such companies rely more heavily than do big companies on workers who are young or who speak little English.

In 1992, Everardo Rangel-Jasso was crushed to death at Denton Plastics, Inc., in Portland, Oregon. The 17-year old was backing up a forklift, with a box high on its fork, when he cut the rear wheels sharply and the vehicle tipped over. A posted sign, in English, warned forklift drivers to wear seat belts—but the Mexican youth didn't speak English. According to an OSHA investigator, a seat belt might have saved his life.

Employees told OSHA that Hispanic workers learned their jobs through "hand signals and body gestures." Mr. Rangel-Jasso hadn't received any forklift training and lacked a driver's license and a juvenile's work permit. Federal and state officials levied more than $150,000 in fines against the company, and two senior managers faced criminal indictments. This is not an isolated incident. A computer analysis of 500,000 federal and state safety inspection records from 1988 to 1992 shows that 4337 workers died at inspected workplaces with fewer than 20 workers, but only 127 died at companies with more than 2500 workers. According to an OSHA administrator: "[At many small businesses] it takes a serious accident or fatality for them to wake up."[22]

Despite these problems, even OSHA's critics have agreed that simply by calling attention to the problems of workplace safety and health, OSHA has caused a lot more *awareness* of these dangers than would otherwise have been the case. Management's willingness to correct hazards and to improve such vital environmental conditions as ventilation, noise levels, and machine safety is much greater now than it was before OSHA. Critics also agree that, because of OSHA and the National Institute for Occupational Safety and Health, we now know far more about such dangerous substances as vinyl chloride, PCBs, asbestos, cotton dust, and a host of other carcinogens. As a result, management has taken at least the initial actions needed to protect workers from them.

Finally, any analysis of OSHA's impact must consider the fundamental issue of the *causes* of workplace accidents. OSHA standards govern potentially unsafe *work conditions* that employees may be exposed to. There are no standards that govern potentially unsafe *employee behaviors*. And while employers may be penalized for failure to comply with safety and health standards, employees are subject to no such threat. Research suggests that the enforcement of OSHA standards, directed as it is to environmental accidents and illnesses, can hope *at best* to affect 25 percent of on-the-job accidents.[23] The remaining 75 percent require *behavioral* rather than *technical* modifications.

ASSESSING THE COSTS AND BENEFITS OF OCCUPATIONAL SAFETY AND HEALTH PROGRAMS

Let's face it: accidents are expensive. Aside from workers' compensation costs, consider the "indirect" costs of an accident:

1. Cost of wages paid for time lost
2. Cost of damage to material or equipment
3. Cost of overtime work by others required by the accident
4. Cost of wages paid to supervisors while their time is required for activities resulting from the accident
5. Costs of decreased output of the injured worker after she or he returns to work
6. Costs associated with the time it takes for a new worker to learn the job

7. Uninsured medical costs borne by the company
8. Cost of time spent by higher management and clerical workers to investigate or to process workers' compensation forms

On the other hand, safety pays, as the following examples illustrate.

COMPANY EXAMPLES

SAFETY PAYS AT DU PONT AND ALCOA

At Du Pont Corp., safety experts provide feedback while engineers observe workers and then redesign valves and install key locks to deter accident-causing behavior. When injuries do happen, the company reports them quickly to workers to provide a sense of immediacy, trying to show the behavior that caused the accident without naming the offender. It also fosters peer pressure to work safely by giving units common goals—that way workers are working together instead of independently. Du Pont offers carrots, too. Its directors regularly give safety awards, and workers win $15 to $20 prizes if their divisions are accident-free for 6 to 9 months. The company's incentive for doing this is not altogether altruistic—it estimates its *annual* cost savings to be $150 million.

At Aluminum Company of America, Inc. (Alcoa), which introduced a "brother's keeper" slogan in the workplace, all employees must submit safety improvement suggestions, and even the lowest-level workers can stop production lines if they suspect a safety problem. The company's chairman has made safety a top priority as well. At a plant visit, a vice president discovered a truck that didn't beep when it backed up. He told the manager to shut down the entire facility until the truck's alarm was fixed. Have these efforts paid off? You bet. Alcoa improved its safety record by 25 percent in three years and estimates it saves $10,000 to $12,000 in workers' compensation for each accident avoided.[24]

Like many other problems of the marketplace, safety and health programs involve what economists call "externalities"—the fact that not all the social costs of production are necessarily included on a firm's profit and loss statement. The employer does not suffer from the worker's injury or disease and therefore lacks the full incentive to reduce it. As long as the outlays required for preventive measures are less than the social costs of disability among workers, higher fatality rates, and the diversion of medical resources, the enforcement of safety and health standards is well worth it and society will benefit.[25]

ORGANIZATIONAL SAFETY AND HEALTH PROGRAMS

As noted earlier, accidents result from two broad causes: *unsafe work conditions* (physical and environmental) and *unsafe work behaviors.* Unsafe physical conditions include defective equipment, inadequate machine guards, and lack of protective equipment. Examples of unsafe environmental conditions are noise, radiation, dust, fumes, and stress. In one study of work injuries, 50 percent resulted from unsafe work conditions, 45 percent resulted from unsafe work behaviors, and 5 percent were of indeterminate origin.[26] However, accidents often result from an *interaction* of unsafe conditions and unsafe acts. Thus, if a particular operation forces a worker to lift a heavy part and twist around to set it on a bench, the operation itself forces the worker to perform an unsafe

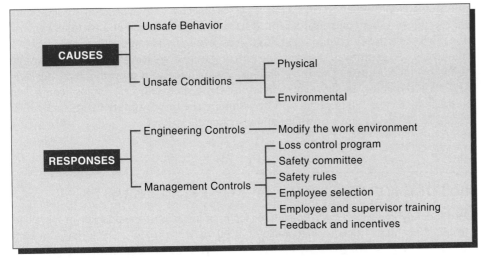

FIGURE 16-2
Causes of and responses to workplace accidents.

act. Telling the worker not to lift and twist at the same time will not solve the problem. The *unsafe condition itself* must be corrected, either by redesigning the flow of material or by providing the worker with a mechanical device for lifting.

To eliminate, or at least reduce, the number and severity of workplace accidents, a combination of management and engineering controls is essential. These are shown in Figure 16-2.

Engineering controls attempt to eliminate unsafe work conditions and to neutralize unsafe worker behaviors. They involve some modification of the work environment: for example, installing a metal cover over the blades of a lawn mower to make it almost impossible for a member of a grounds crew to catch his or her foot in the blades. *Management controls* attempt to increase safe behaviors, and in the following sections we shall discuss each of the elements shown in Figure 16-2.

Loss Control

Management's first duty is to formulate a safety policy. Its second duty is to implement and sustain this policy through a *loss control program*. Such a program has four components: a safety budget, safety records, management's personal concern, and management's good example.[27]

To reduce the frequency of accidents, management must be willing to spend money and to budget for safety. As we have seen, accidents involve *direct* as well as *indirect* costs. Since the national average for indirect costs is 4 times higher than the average for direct costs, it is clear that money spent to improve safety is returned many times over through the control of accidents. Detailed analysis of accident reports, as well as management's personal concern (e.g., meeting with department heads over safety issues, on-site visits by top executives to discuss the need for safety, as Alcoa did in the previous company example, and publication of the company's accident record), keeps employees aware constantly of the need for safety.

Study after study has shown the crucial role that management plays in effective safety programs.[28] Such concern is manifest in a number of ways: appointment of a high-level safety officer, rewards to supervisors on the basis of their subordinates' safety records, and comparison of safety results against preset objectives. Management's good example completes a loss control program. If hard hats are required at a particular operation, then executives should wear hard hats even if they are in business suits. If employees see executives disregarding safety rules or treating hazardous situations lightly by not conforming with regulations, they will feel that they, too, have the right to violate the rules. In short, organizations show their concern for loss control by establishing a clear safety policy and by assuming the responsibility for its implementation. Here's an example of what happens when they don't.

COMPANY EXAMPLE

CUTTING CORNERS IN THE MEATPACKING INDUSTRY

IBP, formerly known as Iowa Beef Processors, is the largest meatpacker in the United States. It operates 12 plants that employ 17,000 workers. In 1987, OSHA levied a $2.59 million fine against the company for failing willfully to report more than 1000 job-related injuries and illnesses over a 2-year period. Among the unreported injuries and illnesses cited by the agency were knife cuts and wounds, concussions, burns, hernias, and fractures.

OSHA determined that 1 week before it subpoenaed IBP's records, the company assembled 50 people to "revise" injury and illness logs. According to OSHA, IBP added more than 800 injuries and illnesses that had not been recorded when they occurred. How did OSHA know this to be true? Company workers had previously obtained the unrevised logs and had given them to agency investigators.[29]

In 1988, OSHA tacked on an additional $3.1 million in fines against IBP for requiring employees to perform repetitive motions that can cause nerve damage (carpal tunnel syndrome) that may cripple the hand or wrists so that the victim is unable to grip or pick up objects. The matter was settled in 1989, when IBP agreed to pay a reduced fine ($975,000), while establishing a model job redesign program to combat repetitive-motion injuries.[30]

The Role of the Safety Committee

Representation of employees, managers, and safety specialists on the safety committee can lead to a much higher commitment to safety than might otherwise be the case. Indeed, merely establishing the committee indicates management's concern. Beyond that, however, the committee has important work to do:

- Recommend (or critique) safety policies issued by top management
- Develop in-house safety standards and ensure compliance with OSHA standards
- Provide safety training for employees and supervisors
- Conduct safety inspections
- Continually promote the theme of job safety through the elimination of unsafe conditions and unsafe behaviors

As an example of recommendations that such a committee might make, consider some possible policies to reduce the incidence of repetitive-motion injuries that have afflicted not only meatpackers and pianists but also telephone and computer operators and supermarket checkout clerks who repeatedly slide customers' purchases over price scanners. Aetna Life & Casualty Co. installed ergonomically designed chairs with lower-back supports, adjustable seats, and armrests. U.S. West created "Worksmart," a one-on-one telephone operator-training program. Operators' work habits are videotaped and analyzed for work speed and posture. Exercises help stretch hands and wrists, and a metronome helps operators work at a smooth pace.[31]

Safety Rules

Safety rules are important refinements of the general safety policies issued by top management. To be effective, they should make clear the consequences of not following the rules, for example, progressive discipline. Evidence indicates, unfortunately, that in many cases the rules are not obeyed. Take protective equipment, for example. OSHA standards require that employers *furnish* and employees *use* suitable protective equipment (e.g., hard hats, goggles, face shields, earplugs, respirators) where there is a "reasonable probability" that injuries can be prevented by such equipment. However, as the following data show, "You can lead a horse to water, but you can't make it drink":[32]

■ Hard hats were worn by only 16 percent of workers who sustained head injuries, although 40 percent were required to wear them.

■ Only 1 percent of workers suffering facial injuries were wearing facial protection.

■ Only 23 percent of workers with foot injuries were wearing safety shoes or boots.

■ Only 40 percent of workers with eye injuries were wearing protective equipment.

Perhaps the rules are not being obeyed because they are not being enforced. But it is also possible that they are not being obeyed because of flaws in employee selection practices, because of inadequate training, or because there is simply no incentive for doing so.

Employee Selection

To the extent that keen vision, dexterity, hearing, balance, and other physical or psychological characteristics make a critical difference between success and failure on a job, they should be used to screen applicants. However, there are two other factors that also relate strongly to accident rates among workers: *age* and *length of service*.[33] Regardless of length of service, the younger the employee, the higher the accident rate. In fact, accident rates are substantially higher during the *first month* of employment than in all subsequent time periods, regardless of age. And when workers of the same age are studied, accident rates decrease as length of service increases. Thus, in mining, the disabling injury rate for miners 18 to 24 years of age is about 3 times that of miners over 45, and it is about twice that of miners between the ages of 25 and 45.[34] The same general pattern holds true in industries as diverse as retail trade, transportation, public utilities, and services. The lesson for managers is clear: *New worker equals high risk!*

Training for Employees and Supervisors

Accidents often occur because workers lack one vital tool to protect themselves: information. Consider the following data collected by the Bureau of Labor Statistics:[35]

■ Nearly 1 out of every 5 workers injured while operating power saws received no safety training on the equipment.

■ Of 724 workers hurt while using scaffolds, 27 percent had received no information on safety requirements for installing the kind of scaffold on which they were injured.

■ Of 554 workers hurt while servicing equipment, 61 percent were not told about lockout procedures that prevent the equipment from being turned on inadvertently while it is being serviced.

In nearly every type of injury that researchers have studied, the same story is repeated over and over. Workers often do not receive the kind of safety information they need, *even on jobs that require them to use dangerous equipment.* This is unfortunate, but a problem that is just as serious occurs when safety practices that are taught in training are not reinforced on the job. Regular feedback and incentives for compliance are essential.

Feedback and Incentives

Previous chapters have underscored the positive impact on the motivation of employees when they are given feedback and incentives to improve productivity. The same principles can also be used to improve safe behavior. Thus, in one study of a wholesale bakery that was experiencing a sharp increase in work accidents, researchers developed a detailed coding sheet for observing safe and unsafe behaviors. Observers then used the sheets to record systematically both safe and unsafe employee behaviors over a 25-week period before, during, and after a safety training program. Slides were used to illustrate both safe and unsafe behaviors. Trainees were also shown data on the percentage of safe behaviors in their departments, and a goal of 90 percent safe behaviors was established. Following all of this, the actual percentage of safe behaviors was posted in each department. Supervisors were trained to use positive reinforcement (praise) when they observed safe behaviors. In comparison to departments that received no training, workers in the trained departments averaged almost 24 percent more safe behaviors. Not only did employees react favorably to the program, but the company was able to maintain it. One year prior to the program, the number of lost-time injuries per million hours worked was 53.8. Even in highly hazardous industries, this figure rarely exceeds 35. One year after the program, it was less than 10.[36]

Similar results were found in a farm machinery manufacturing firm.[37] Behavioral safety rules were obeyed more when employees received frequent feedback concerning their performance in relation to an accepted standard. Although the implementation of a training session to teach employees exactly what was expected of them also resulted in a significant increase in performance, it did not produce optimum performance. Assigning employees specific, difficult, yet acceptable safety goals and providing information concerning their performance in relation to these goals produced the maximum reduction in lost-time injuries. The results of these studies suggest that training, goal setting, and feedback provide useful alternatives to disciplinary sanctions to encourage compliance with the rules. As one safety consultant noted: "It's better to recognize a guy for success than to beat him up for failure."[38]

Job Safety and Health: What Are Companies Doing?

Traditionally, managers tended to think of safety as an important issue in manufacturing. Today, however, 84 percent of U.S. employees work in service-based industries, as well as in high-technology jobs.[39] Many of the new jobs involve video display terminals (VDTs), semiconductor production, or exposure to chemicals. Some companies are proactively dealing with these new challenges.

Between 40 and 50 percent of the U.S. workforce deals with VDTs on a daily basis. Many users complain of a variety of syndromes, including blurred vision, eyestrain, repetitive motion disorders, and muscular pains in the shoulder, back, or neck.[40] To deal with this, the St. Paul Companies, a large insurance company, recently introduced a program designed to teach VDT users relaxation techniques, workstation organization, and health awareness, including the need for regular eye checkups. The company reported significantly lowered technostress levels following the program.[41] Apple Computer, trying to make its computer screens more user-friendly, uses an antiglare treatment that scatters light. Other firms are purchasing antiglare filters for their employees.[42]

Another new technology that may produce adverse health consequences is semiconductor production, which involves acids and gases. Such consequences may include a higher rate of miscarriages among women who work in the production process, as well as higher rates of nausea, headaches, and rashes. Digital Equipment, AT&T, Intel, and Texas Instruments all have adopted policies that allow pregnant women to transfer out of production operations without sacrificing pay or seniority.[43]

Another thing that companies are doing is alerting workers exposed to high levels of chemicals or other possible causes of disease. The notification rules come under

For many officeworkers, video display terminals are essential tools.

OSHA's "hazard communication" standard, put into effect in 1988. The rules apply to about 575,000 hazardous chemicals and 320,000 manufacturing businesses and affect some 32 million workers.[44] They require *every* workplace in the country to identify and list hazardous chemicals being used ("from bleach to bowl cleaner")[45] and to train employees in their use. Such "right-to-know" requirements have helped to avoid situations like the following.

COMPANY
EXAMPLE

RIGHT-TO-KNOW RULES IN THE CHEMICAL INDUSTRY

Cathy Zimmerman, a 26-year-old lab technician at Hercules, Inc., in Wilmington, Delaware, was pouring chemicals last year when she noticed that the bottles were labeled "mutagen" and "teratogen." She went to her dictionary, which said that a mutagen can alter chromosomes and a teratogen can cause malformations in fetuses. "I said, 'O, my God!' " she recalls. "When I saw that, I talked to my boss and told him I was scared. I didn't want to take a chance."

Mrs. Zimmerman, who is expecting her first child, has since been transferred to Hercules' flavoring division, where she works with less hazardous materials. But she hopes that a new right-to-know training program required by OSHA will prevent such surprises in the future. "With right-to-know, we'd have gone over it first, before it came into the lab," she says. "We didn't have that before."

Some employees are alarmed to discover that they have been working with certain hazardous chemicals. Others are overwhelmed by the detailed labeling, which they say makes it even harder to distinguish really dangerous materials. Meanwhile some businesses claim that fearful workers are demanding unnecessary and costly changes. At the same time, however, OSHA defends the measure, arguing that heightened awareness, and even anxiety, will help reduce work-related accidents. As one spokesperson for OSHA commented, "I'd rather be anxious and alive than calm and dead."[46]

In the United States there is considerable pressure to improve plant safety. Now let's consider the situation in other countries.

INTERNATIONAL APPLICATION: HEALTH AND SAFETY—THE RESPONSE BY GOVERNMENTS AND MULTINATIONAL FIRMS IN LESS DEVELOPED COUNTRIES

In 1984, 45 tons of lethal methyl isocyanate gas leaked from the Union Carbide (India) Ltd. pesticide plant in the central Indian city of Bhopal, killing more than 3800 people and disabling more than 20,000 in history's worst industrial disaster. Subsequently, several events occurred: (1) in 1991, the Indian Supreme Court upheld an earlier ruling and ordered Union Carbide to pay $470 million in damages to victims of the disaster (although dissatisfied survivors could still file claims in the United States as well);[47] (2) in 1992, an Indian judge ordered the seizure of all of Carbide's Indian assets as part of continuing criminal proceedings against the company;[48] and (3) India formed committees in every state to identify potential factory hazards as government and public awareness of environmental hazards skyrocketed. However, the committees inspect only major factories, not the thousands of small chemical factories, many of which are illegal.

These events produced important consequences. U.S. multinational firms found out that liability for any Bhopal-like disaster could be decided in U.S. courts. This, more than pressure from third-world governments, has forced companies to tighten safety procedures, upgrade plants, supervise maintenance more closely, and educate workers and communities in their far-flung empires.[49]

In India, despite the outcry against Union Carbide, the country continues to welcome foreign investment and technology. However, the government is insisting that it know more about the risks involved, including potential manufacturing hazards. New factories must carry out environmental impact studies and install safety equipment. As a government spokesman noted, "If there is a lesson to learn, it is when we buy black boxes we must know the entire consequences."[50]

In Mexico, a gas explosion at Pemex, the state-owned oil monopoly, killed at least 500 people and wounded thousands of others at about the same time as the Bhopal disaster. One year later, little had been done to improve the conditions that caused the explosion. After years of neglect and rampant pollution at Pemex facilities, the government was loath to clamp down because that would focus attention on the main culprit: the Mexican government itself.[51]

Neither the Bhopal nor the Pemex incident had any noticeable effect on multinational investment in Mexico. In fact, all the developing countries in one survey seem to rely on the multinationals, rather than on draconic new regulations, to prevent a repeat of Bhopal. This is true in South Korea, Taiwan, Egypt, and Thailand, for example. In Thailand, a 1993 fire at a toy factory killed more than 240 workers. There were no fire escapes, fire alarms, sprinkler systems, or other safety features. Experts say such negligence is common throughout the region, where labor unions are weak and corruption is often endemic.[52] As these few examples make clear, in many of the less developed countries around the world, foreign investment is a political and economic issue, not a safety issue.

In at least one newly industrialized country, South Korea, government, management, and unions are becoming aware of the human cost of unsafe conditions. In 1989, 2 out of every 100 mine and factory workers were injured, and 26 out of every 100,000 were killed. (In the United States, the death rate is 10 per 100,000 workers.) In 1990, the death rate jumped 43 percent and the accident rate 3 percent. Twenty percent of Korean workers have suffered an accident. Yet government efforts to educate workers have fallen flat. Why? Many regard the wearing of welding masks or hard hats as unmanly.[53]

HEALTH HAZARDS AT WORK

The National Institute of Occupational Safety and Health has identified more than 15,000 toxic substances, of which some 500 might require regulation as carcinogens (cancer-causing substances). The list of harmful chemical, physical, and biological hazards is a long one. It includes carbon monoxide, vinyl chloride, dusts, particulates, gases and vapors, radiation, excessive noise and vibration, and extreme temperatures. When present in high concentrations, these agents can lead to respiratory, kidney, liver, skin, neurological, and other disorders. Scary, isn't it?

There have been some well-publicized lawsuits against employers for causing occupational illnesses as a result of lack of proper safeguards or technical controls.[54] Thus the U.S. Supreme Court ruled in the case of Karen Silkwood, a former laboratory analyst at a plutonium plant in Oklahoma, that the federal government's interest in nuclear safety didn't prevent a jury from awarding damages to Mrs. Silkwood's family for injuries arising from exposure to radiation at her workplace.[55] In another decision, a jury in Cleveland awarded $520,000 to a former government employee who sued the maker of a fireproofing material that contained asbestos after she was diagnosed as having an asbestos-related disease. The woman had worked in the building for 12 years and sued the original seller of the material 3 years after that.[56]

The U.S. Supreme Court has ruled that the states can prosecute company officials under criminal statutes for endangering the health of employees, even if such hazards are also regulated by OSHA.[57] Nevertheless, some of the criticism against employers is not fair. To prove negligence, it must be shown that management *knew* of the connection between exposure to the hazards and negative health consequences and that management *chose* to do nothing to reduce worker exposure. Yet few such connections were made until recent years. Even now, alternative explanations for the causes of disease or illness cannot be ruled out in many cases. Responsibility for regulation has been left to OSHA.

The primary emphasis to date has been on installing engineering controls that *prevent* exposure to harmful substances. In fact, in a sweeping move in 1989, OSHA established or toughened workplace exposure limits for 376 toxic chemicals. The rules cost employers $788 million a year. While this figure might sound steep, consider that an estimated $30 billion is spent annually just to *treat* preventable cancer. The benefits? According to OSHA, the new limits should save nearly 700 lives a year and reduce work-related illnesses such as cancer, liver and kidney impairments, and respiratory and cardiovascular illnesses, by about 55,000 cases a year.[58] But is cost-benefit analysis appropriate when lives are literally at stake?

The Supreme Court recognized this problem in its 1981 "cotton dust" decision. It held that OSHA need not balance the costs of implementing standards against the benefits expected. OSHA has to show only that it is *economically feasible* to implement the standards. The decision held that Congress had already decided the balance between costs and benefits in favor of the worker when it passed the law.[59] On one issue all parties agree: *the nature of cancer itself makes it virtually impossible for workers to protect themselves from exposure to cancer-causing substances.* In recent years, another killer has entered the workplace. While its origins lie outside the workplace, businesses cannot ignore either its costs or its consequences. That killer is AIDS.

AIDS and Business

AIDS (acquired immune deficiency syndrome) is a medical time bomb. With 340,000 diagnosed cases in the United States and 1.5 million people infected with the human immunodeficiency virus (HIV) that causes AIDS, employers are fast having to deal with increasing numbers of AIDS victims in the workplace. Unlike other life-threatening illnesses, such as Alzheimer's or heart disease, the vast majority of those with HIV or AIDS are of working age—between 22 and 45. It's a bottom-line business issue.[60] Consider these facts and prognoses about the disease:

■ The World Health Organization estimates that by the year 2000, 30 million people will be infected with HIV. Yet AIDS, a killer, can itself be killed through education and the adoption of safe behavior.[61]

■ Non-AIDS public-health programs will be curtailed in cities hit hard by the epidemic.

■ With no cure in sight for at least 20 years, the Health Insurance Association of America estimates that the AIDS medical bill may be as much as $11 billion a year after 1994. The disease has already killed more than 200,000 Americans.[62]

■ The cost of treating an AIDS patient from diagnosis to death was $102,000 in 1993. This is higher than the average cost of treating leukemia, cancer of the digestive system, a heart attack, or paraplegia from an auto crash.

■ The cumulative costs of long-term disability payments to people with AIDS through 1995 are expected to exceed $2 billion.

■ Direct costs to companies will escalate in three ways: through (1) increased medical premiums to cover their employees with AIDS, (2) increased medical premiums to cover AIDS victims without insurance, and (3) an increased Medicaid burden.

■ Indirect costs will also affect the bottom line in at least three ways. One is through lost work time of AIDS patients. Since jobs held by AIDS-affected persons are protected by the Americans with Disabilities Act, others have to do their work while they are out, and they may be less productive. Two, productivity may suffer if coworkers refuse to work with an AIDS-infected employee (as happened in 1985 at New England Telephone). Three, recruitment costs will increase because AIDS is a lethal disease that is always fatal. Those employees (or coworkers who quit rather than work with an AIDS-infected employee) must be replaced.[63]

■ The ADA also prohibits discrimination against job applicants who have the disease.

LEVI STRAUSS & CO.'S AIDS-RELATED CORPORATE PHILOSOPHIES[64]

COMPANY EXAMPLE

1. There is no special AIDS policy. Instead, the company addresses the needs of employees with AIDS and their coworkers within the framework of its general approach to employee relations.

2. There is no preemployment testing of any sort for AIDS, and there are no AIDS screening questions on employment applications.

3. Employees with AIDS are treated with compassion and understanding—as are employees with any other life-threatening disease.

4. Employees with AIDS can continue to work as long as they are medically cleared to do so; they are also eligible for work accommodation.

5. Employees are assured of confidentiality when seeking counseling or medical referral.

6. Company medical coverage, disability leave policy, and life insurance do not distinguish between AIDS and any other life-threatening disease.

7. The company's medical plan supports home health and hospice care for the terminally ill.

8. A case management strategy is implemented whenever an employee becomes critically ill.

9. Managers are held accountable for creating a work environment that is supportive of an employee with AIDS.

10. The company has assumed responsibility for educating employees so that neither unwarranted fear nor prejudice affects the work environment of people with AIDS.

11. Individual, family, or group counseling is available to employees and their families through the company's Employee Assistance Program (EAP) or through outside agencies.

12. The EAP staff conducts department and management counseling sessions on request about issues such as how to handle rumors about AIDS, how to deal directly with people's feelings when a colleague becomes ill with AIDS, what colleagues can do to be helpful to a person with AIDS, and how to deal with grief associated with the death of a colleague.

How do these policies work in practice? According to CEO Robert Haas: "It's a kaleidoscope of combined efforts with literally thousands of people in Levi Strauss & Co. [worldwide] contributing to our broad commitment to employee education, to humane care, to outreach, and to our various publics; and that's a model for how we do business here . . . it creates enormous commitment, better decisions, a lot of energy, and results that speak for themselves."[65]

EMPLOYEE ASSISTANCE PROGRAMS

Another (brighter) side of the employee health issue is reflected in employee assistance programs (EAPs). Such programs represent an expansion of traditional work in occupational alcoholism treatment programs. From a handful of programs begun in the 1940s (led by Du Pont), today more than 70 percent of the largest companies in the United States, and many others in Canada, offer EAPs.[66] EAPs have been developed and applied in other countries as well, but exact transfer from one culture to another simply will not work. Rather, it is necessary to "fit" the EAP to the social, cultural, economic, and political climates of the countries in question.[67]

By its very title, "employee assistance program" signals a change both in application and in technique from the traditional occupational alcoholism treatment program. Modern EAPs extend professional counseling and medical services to all "troubled" employees. A troubled employee is *an individual who is confronted by unresolved personal or work-related problems.*[68] Such problems run the gamut from alcoholism, drug abuse, and high stress to marital, family, and financial problems. While some of these may originate "outside" the work context, they most certainly will have spillover effects to the work context.

Do Employee Assistance Programs Work?

Companies like Monsanto, Kodak, Xerox, and Kennecott Copper have instituted EAPs based on an awareness of their social responsibility. By offering assistance to troubled employees, the companies promote positive employee relations climates.[69] They also contribute to their employees' well-being and to their ability to function productively at work, at home, and in the community.

From a business perspective, too, well-run programs seem to pay off handsomely. In one study, for example, 70 percent of the 17,743 employees who were referred to EAPs for alcoholism were back on the job and performing adequately.[70] At the level of the individual firm, Du Pont found that about 80 percent of its alcoholic workers with long service recover with treatment. General Motors Corp., whose EAP counsels more than 6500 employees with alcohol problems each year, reports a 65 to 75 percent success rate and estimates that it gains $3 for every $1 spent on care. In addition, blue-collar workers who resolve their alcohol and drug abuse problems through an EAP file only half as many grievances as they did before treatment. McDonnell Douglas, which dramatically expanded its EAP in 1985 by hiring more counselors, serves about 5 percent of its workforce every year. It estimates a 4-to-1 return on its investment. Says the director of its EAP: "Our feeling is that if you do the job right the first time, it's cheaper in the long run."[71]

EAPs run by outside firms cost from $12 to $35 per employee per year,[72] but, as we have seen, recent data on their effects are impressive. Nevertheless, it is important to be cautious. Often there is a "rush to evaluate" EAPs and other occupational programs. This can lead to premature claims of success or, equally likely, premature condemnation. *Beware of making strong statements about a program's impact at least until repeated evaluations have demonstrated the same findings for different groups of employees.*[73]

How Employee Assistance Programs Work

There are five steps involved in starting an EAP:[74]

1. *Develop a written statement* of the objectives of the program, consistent with organizational policy. Confirm the company's desire to offer help to employees with behavioral or medical problems, and emphasize that such help will be offered on a *personal and confidential* basis.

2. *Teach managers, supervisors, and union representatives what to do*—and what not to do—when they confront the troubled employee and when they use the program to resolve job performance problems.

3. *Establish procedures for referral* of the troubled employee to an in-house or outside professional who can take the time to assess what is wrong and arrange for treatment.

4. *Establish a planned program of communications* to employees to announce (and periodically to remind them) that the service is available, that it is confidential, and that other employees are using it.

5. *Continually evaluate* the program in terms of its stated objectives.

With respect to step 2 above, employee confrontation, it is important to stress that a certain amount of performance failure must be expected in any program that relies on a large and changing group of relatively untrained supervisors to handle the initial confrontation. Some managers or supervisors may allow feelings of sympathy or concern to delay appropriate action. This is "killing with kindness." If the same manager suspected that the employee had symptoms of a heart attack or cancer, she or he would probably insist that the employee get an immediate checkup. Similarly, a union steward may be reluctant to confront a fellow union member in a way that may sound threatening. Both the supervisor and the steward need to be trained to recognize that they are helping, not hurting, the employee by referring her or him to the EAP.

More on the Role of the Supervisor. In the traditional alcoholism treatment program, the supervisor has to look for symptoms of alcoholism and then diagnose the problem. Under an EAP, however, the supervisor is responsible *only* for identifying declining work performance. If normal corrective measures do not work, the supervisor confronts the employee with evidence of his or her poor performance and offers the EAP. Here are some recommendations on how to proceed.[75]

1. Once you suspect a problem, begin documenting instances in which job performance has fallen short. Absenteeism (leaving early, arriving late for work, taking more days off than allowed by policy), accidents, errors, and a rise in conflicts with other employees (due to changes in mood swings) may become evident.

2. Having assembled the facts, set up a meeting. However, don't get right to the point; that's the last thing experts recommend. Don't even mention the problem you suspect (e.g., alcoholism, drug abuse, excessive stress), let alone diagnose it. Instead, keep the discussion focused on performance. Outline the employee's

shortcomings, insist on improvement, and then ask if there is anything you can do to help.

3. At this point, the employee will probably promise to improve. But almost inevitably, performance problems will recur, often within just a few weeks. Now it's time for a tougher session. At this meeting, still avoid the issue you suspect is causing the performance problems and say, "I don't know what's wrong with you, but I want you to see an employee assistance counselor." To give the employee an extra push, experts advise setting up the appointment yourself.

This approach leaves the diagnosis and treatment recommendations to trained counselors. But you can increase the odds of success, according to the medical director of United Airlines, by "telling them that if performance doesn't improve they'll be disciplined."[76]

By using declining work performance or a particular disruptive incident as the *sole* basis for referral to the EAP, management is able to maintain high work standards and consistent practices. Employees know that participation in the program is voluntary. But they also know that continued poor work performance will result in disciplinary action and, ultimately, in termination. In the contemporary view, therefore, the supervisor need not become involved in the employee's personal problem—or even know what it is. Rather, *the supervisor's focus is on job performance, attitude, and productivity.*

Now that we understand what EAPs are, their effects, and how they work, let us examine three of today's most pressing workplace problems. These are alcoholism, drug abuse, and violence.

Alcoholism

Management's concern over the issue is understandable, for alcohol misuse by employees is costly in terms of productivity, time lost from work, and treatment. How prevalent is alcoholism, and how costly is it? At the outset we should note that while many figures are bandied about, a critical review of the development and reporting of knowledge about employee alcoholism treatment programs has shown these estimates to be supported by limited empirical data.[77] Nevertheless, according to the National Council on Alcoholism and Drug Dependence:[78]

- About 18 million Americans have a serious drinking problem.
- Annual deaths due to alcohol number about 105,000.
- Of all hospitalized patients, about 25 percent have alcohol-related problems.
- Alcohol is involved in 47 percent of industrial accidents.
- Fully half of all auto fatalities involve alcohol.

The cost? A staggering $86 billion in costs due to lower productivity and treatment, premature death, and accidents, crime, and law enforcement.

Alcoholism affects employees at every level, but it is costliest at the top. Experts estimate that it afflicts at least 10 percent of senior executives. As an example, consider an executive who makes $100,000 per year, is unproductive, and files large health claims. That cost is certainly far higher than a $10,000 inpatient treatment program.

A study done for McDonnell Douglas Corp. shows how expensive it is to ignore substance abuse problems in the workplace. The company found that in the previous

5 years each worker with an alcohol (or drug) problem was absent 113 more days than the average employee and filed $23,000 more in medical claims. Their dependents also filed some $37,000 more in claims than the average family. As we have seen, however, intervention works. Recovered alcoholics frequently credit such programs with literally saving their lives. Companies win, too—by reclaiming employees whose gratitude and restored abilities can result in years of productive service.

Drug Abuse

Drug abuse is no less insidious. It cuts across all job levels and types of organizations and, together with employee alcohol abuse, costs U.S. businesses more than $30 billion in annual productivity losses.[79]

Evidence clearly shows that drug abuse affects on-the-job behaviors.[80] Here is a profile of the "typical" recreational drug user in today's workforce. He or she:

- Is late 3 times as often as fellow employees
- Requests early dismissal or time off during work 2.2 times as often
- Has 2.5 times as many absences of 8 days or more
- Uses 3 times the normal level of sick benefits
- Is 5 times as likely to file a workers' compensation claim
- Is involved in accidents 3.6 times as often as other employees
- Is one-third less productive than fellow workers

A longitudinal study of 5465 applicants for jobs with the U.S. Postal Service found that after an average of 1.3 years of employment, employees who had tested positive for illicit drugs had an absenteeism rate 59.3 percent higher than employees who had tested negative. Those who had tested positive also had a 47 percent higher rate of involuntary turnover than those who had tested negative. However, there was no relationship between drug test results and measures of injury and accident occurrence.[81] This may not be true in other occupations, however.

Said a construction union leader in California: "Sometimes 90 percent of the crew's been doing uppers. I just leave the jobs when the guys are dopers. Would you want to work on a four-story building knowing the guy with the blowtorch next to you is doing drugs?"[82]

Remember, the Americans with Disabilities Act protects rehabilitated alcohol and drug abusers from discrimination in employment. However, the ADA Technical Assistance Manual specifically states: "Employees who use drugs or alcohol may be required to meet the same standards of performance and conduct that are set for other employees."[83] As we have seen, rehabilitation under an EAP can be effective. From an employment perspective, however, the key issue is documented evidence of decreased job performance.

Violence at Work

What do General Dynamics, Circle K Corporation, and the U.S. Postal Service have in common? They have employees who died violently while at work. Nationally, 7603 Americans were slain on the job between 1983 and 1993.[84] Those most at risk are taxi drivers, police officers, retail workers, people who work with money or valuables, and people who work alone or at night.

Violence disrupts productivity, causes untold damage to those exposed to the trauma, is related to workplace abuse of drugs or alcohol and absenteeism, and costs employers millions of dollars. In a stressed-out, downsized business environment, people are searching for someone to blame for their problems. With the loss of a job or other event the employee perceives as unfair, the employer may become the focus of a disgruntled individual's fear and frustration. Although security measures cannot prevent all harm, there are steps organizations can take to reduce the risk of violence.[85] First, be alert to warning signs. These include:

- *Verbal threats*—take seriously remarks from an employee about what he or she may do. Experts say that individuals who make such statements usually have been mentally committed to the act for a long period of time. It may take very little provocation to trigger the violence.

- *Physical actions*—employees who demonstrate "assaultive" physical actions at work are dangerous. The employer, working with experts trained to assess a possibly violent situation, needs to investigate and intervene. Failure to do so may be interpreted as permission to do further or more serious damage.

- *Behaviors*—watch for changes such as irritability and a short temper. Is the employee showing a low tolerance to work stress or frustrations?[86]

Prevention strategies include the following.[87]

- Consult specialists—professionals in the area of facility security, violence assessment, EAP counseling, community support services, and local law enforcement—to formulate a plan for identifying, defusing, and recovering from a violent event.

- Create and communicate to all employees a written policy that explains the organization's position on intimidating, threatening, or violent behavior and establishes a procedure for investigating any potentially violent talk or action.

- Establish a Threat Assessment/Violence Management team with the authority to make decisions quickly. This group will evaluate problems, select intervention techniques, and coordinate follow-up activities.

- Offer training and employee orientation—train supervisors and managers in how to recognize aggressive behavior, identify the warning signs of violence, be effective communicators, and resolve conflict. (Untrained supervisors often escalate violent situations.) Orient all employees on facility security procedures and on how to recognize and report threats of violence in the workplace.

- Help employees adjust to change—for example, in the event of a downsizing, a merger, or an acquisition give employees advance notice. Under the Worker Adjustment and Retraining Act (WARN) of 1988, covered employers are required to give 60 days' notice to employees affected by mass layoffs or plant closings. A 1993 study found, unfortunately, that most employers fail to do so.[88] Keeping employees informed about impending changes and providing additional benefits, such as severance pay or counseling, can help employees adjust to the change.

- Be aware of potential risks and respond appropriately. Remarks such as "I'll kill you" or "I'd like to put out a contract on him" should not be taken lightly. Experts say that in many cases an individual who becomes violent has given multiple clues of potentially violent behavior to a number of people within the organization.

However, these warnings were overlooked or dismissed. Be proactive; don't assume the employee doesn't mean it, because when employees feel powerless there is a greater likelihood of violence. Report the incident to management for investigation.

IMPACT OF SAFETY, HEALTH, AND EAPs ON PRODUCTIVITY, QUALITY OF WORK LIFE, AND THE BOTTOM LINE

We know that the technology is available to make workplaces safe and healthy for the nation's men and women. We also know that legislation can never substitute for managerial commitment to safe, healthy workplaces based on demonstrated economic and social benefits. Consider just one example. Based on an analysis of 3896 disability cases, Northwestern National Life Insurance Company calculated that the average cost of rehabilitating an employee disabled because of stress was $1925. If he or she is not rehabilitated, companies will need to hold in reserve an average of $73,270 or more to cover disability payments for employees disabled by job-related stress.[89] On balance, commitment to job safety, health, and EAPs is a win-win situation for employees and their companies. Productivity, QWL, and the bottom line all stand to gain.

CORPORATE HEALTH PROMOTION: THE CONCEPT OF "WELLNESS"

Consider these sobering facts:

■ U.S. companies spend, on average, about 26 percent of their earnings (13.6 percent of their payrolls) on health-care costs.[90]

■ Business today pays half the nation's health-care bill. Common backaches alone account for about 25 percent of all workdays lost per year, for a total cost of $15 to $20 billion in lost productivity, disability payments, and lawsuits.[91]

■ Business spends some $700 million per year to replace the 200,000 employees aged 45 to 65 who are killed or disabled by heart disease.

Keep in mind that health plans do not promise good health. They simply pay for the cost of ill health and the associated rehabilitation. Because 8 of the 10 leading causes of death are largely preventable, however, managers are beginning to look to *disease prevention* as one way to reduce health-care spending. The old saying "an ounce of prevention is worth a pound of cure" is certainly true when one compares the costs of a workshop to help employees stop smoking with the price tag on an average coronary bypass operation.[92]

Is it possible that health-care costs can be tamed through on-the-job exercise programs and health promotion efforts? Convinced that if people were healthier, they would be sick less often, two out of three U.S. businesses with more than 50 employees have some form of health-promotion program in place.[93] Do such programs work? In a moment we will consider that question, but first let's define our terms and look at the overall concept.

The process of corporate health promotion begins by promoting *health awareness*, that is, knowledge of the present and future consequences of behaviors and lifestyles and the risks they may present. The objective of "wellness programs" is not to eliminate symptoms and disease; it is to help employees build lifestyles that will enable them to achieve their full physical and mental potential. Wellness programs differ from EAPs in that *wellness focuses on prevention, while EAPs focus on rehabilitation.* Health promotion is a four-step process:[94]

1. Educating employees about health-risk factors—life habits or body characteristics that may increase the chances of developing a serious illness. For heart disease (the leading cause of death), some of these risk factors are high blood pressure, cigarette smoking, high cholesterol levels, diabetes, a sedentary lifestyle, and obesity. Some factors, such as smoking, physical inactivity, stress, and poor nutrition, are associated with many diseases.[95]

2. Identifying the health-risk factors that each employee faces.

3. Helping employees eliminate or reduce these risks through healthier lifestyles and habits.

4. Helping employees maintain their new, healthier lifestyles through self-monitoring and evaluation. The central theme of health promotion is "No one takes better care of you than you do."

To date, the most popular programs are smoking cessation, blood pressure control, cholesterol reduction, weight control and fitness, and stress management. In well-designed programs, 40 to 50 percent of employees can be expected to participate.[96] However, it's the 15 percent to 20 percent of high-risk employees who account for up to 80 percent of all claims that are the most difficult to reach.[97] Here is one company's approach.

COMPANY EXAMPLE

CONTROL DATA'S "STAY WELL" PROGRAM

Control Data Corporation has an ambitious health promotion program. It is called "Stay Well," and it reaches 22,000 employees and their families in 14 cities. A key ingredient of the program is the recruitment of informal "opinion leaders" to promote the program at each plant. Stay Well includes physiological tests, computerized health-risk profiles, wellness education classes, and courses in lifestyle change. The lifestyle courses cover such areas as stress, fitness, weight control, nutrition, and smoking cessation.

Stay Well also features follow-up worker support groups to help make the lifestyle changes stick and employee task forces to promote health-enhancing changes in the workplace. Such task forces have won stretch breaks, showers, no-smoking areas, and fresh fruit in vending machines. Said the director of the company's health-care services division: "We want to produce cultural changes in the workplace. We want to change the norms of health-related behavior."[98]

A 4-year study of 15,000 Control Data employees showed dramatic relationships between employees' health habits and insurance claim costs. For example, people whose weekly exercise was equivalent to climbing fewer than five flights of stairs or walking less than half a mile spent 114 percent more on health claims than those who climbed at least 15 flights of stairs or walked 1.5 miles weekly. Health-care costs for obese people were 11 percent higher than those for thin ones. And workers who routinely failed to use seat belts spent 54 percent more days in the hospital than those who usually buckled up. Finally, people who smoked an average of one or more packs of cigarettes a day had 118 percent higher medical expenses than nonsmokers. This study was the first to tie health costs to workers' behavior. It was corroborated in another longitudinal study that appeared at about the same time.[99] Together, such results may form the basis for incentive programs to (1) improve workers' health habits and (2) reduce employees' contributions to health-insurance costs or increase their benefits.[100]

The success of Stay Well and its companion EAP has prompted Control Data to market them to other firms. Buyers of Stay Well include 3M and Northeastern Mutual Life Insurance. Philip Morris and the National Basketball Association are two of the many organizations that have signed up for the company's EAP.

Evaluation: Do Wellness Programs Work?

Few controlled studies exist,[101] and the movement's doctrines remind some medical doctors of earlier measures that also seemed as unassailable as apple pie—annual physicals, annual Pap smears, and mass health screening. Unfortunately, none of these provided the huge health benefits that seemed almost guaranteed.

Wellness programs are especially difficult to evaluate, for at least six reasons:[102]

1. Health-related costs that actually decrease are hard to identify.
2. Program sponsors use different methods to measure and report costs and benefits.
3. Program effects may vary depending on *when* they are measured (immediate versus lagged effects).
4. Program effects may vary, depending on *how long* they are measured.
5. Few studies use control groups.
6. Data on effectiveness are limited in the choice of variables, estimation of the economic value of indirect costs and benefits, estimation of the timing and duration of program effects, and estimation of the present value of future benefits.

At a general level, four key questions need to be answered:

1. Do health promotion programs in fact eliminate or reduce health-risk factors?
2. Are these changes long-lasting?
3. If the changes are long-lasting, will illness and its subsequent costs be reduced?
4. Are the savings great enough to justify the expense?

Based on a number of independent studies, the answers to the first two questions appear to be yes—especially when programs incorporate systematic outreach and follow-up counseling.[103] For example, one longitudinal study measured the following health-risk factors: blood pressure, cholesterol levels, number of pounds over ideal mean weight, seat belt usage, salt intake, dietary fat intake, smoking, alcohol intake, exercise, and stress.

Although there was some variation in improvement in various categories and between age groups, there was nearly a 20 percent improvement in health-risk scores after 18 months, and the gains were sustained at 30 months. While the effect of age on the rate of change diminished over time, the effect of educational level did not. Those with more education had lower health-risk scores at the beginning of the study and also made the most improvement. In general, these results suggest that participation in an organized health promotion program results in improved health.[104]

ETHICAL DILEMMA: SHOULD EMPLOYEES BE PUNISHED FOR UNHEALTHY LIFESTYLES?[105]

Johnson & Johnson Health Management, Inc., which sells wellness programs to companies, estimates that 15 to 25 percent of corporate health care costs stem from employees' unhealthy lifestyle conditions. As a result, individuals may not be hired, might even be fired, and could wind up paying a monthly penalty based on their after-hours activities. Here are some examples:

- Texas Instruments imposes a $10 monthly surcharge on health insurance for employees and dependents who smoke.

- Turner Broadcasting won't hire smokers.

- U-Haul International imposes a biweekly $5 charge for health insurance for employees who smoke or chew tobacco or whose weight exceeds guidelines.

- Multi-Developers won't hire anyone who engages in what the company views as high-risk activities: skydiving, piloting a private aircraft, mountain climbing, or motorcycling.

Existing civil rights laws generally don't protect against "lifestyle discrimination" because smokers and skydivers aren't named as protected classes. Should employers be able to implement "lifestyle policies"?

The answer to the third question also appears to be positive, based on a 1993 analysis of 200 corporate wellness programs. The best such programs cut medical claims by up to 20 percent. If such "demand reduction" could be extended to all Americans, according to the researchers, the nation could cut $180 billion from its health-care bill.[106]

With respect to the fourth question, several studies have focused on costs that would have been incurred if a wellness program had not been available. This was the approach taken by the Adolph Coors Co. in evaluating its mammography screening program for breast cancer. By calculating exactly how many examinations showed breast cancer in the early stages, Coors was able to calculate the costs avoided, assuming that without mammography the problem would have gone undetected and the cancer would have matured. Coors spent $232,500 to perform 2500 screenings and avoided $828,000 in health-care costs. This yielded a net saving of $595,500, or an ROI of greater than 3.5 to 1.[107]

The medical director at Eli Lilly & Co. estimated that an advanced case of breast cancer costs Lilly more than $100,000 a case in lost work time and medical costs. Mammography equipment costs about $80,000. While it might appear that a compelling case can be made for purchasing such equipment, experts estimate that a company needs to employ at least 1000 to 2000 women to justify starting such a program. For smaller companies that cannot afford to buy their own equipment, one option is to contract with mobile mammography screening programs to bring vans to company premises once a year.[108] Here are some other company examples of cost-benefit analyses of wellness programs:

- Travelers Insurance reported saving $7.8 million in benefit costs by using its "Taking Care" program for its 34,700 participating employees. Each dollar spent yielded a return of $3.40.[109]

■ Pillsbury claims that every dollar spent on its "Be Your Best" wellness program produced $3.63 in health-related cost savings.[110]

■ Adolph Coors Co., which has blazed the health promotion trail, claims an average dollar return on investment of more than 6 to 1. Its cardiac rehabilitation program alone saved the company $4.2 million over a 10-year period.[111]

■ Small businesses too are saving money by claiming insurance discounts for group-life premiums if they offer some type of wellness program to their employees. Thus Babson Brothers, a dairy-farm equipment maker in Naperville, Illinois, saved $5000, or 5 percent, on its group-life premiums because it has a no-smoking policy and fitness programs.[112]

Results such as these make the "wellness" concept well worth looking into.

Wellness Programs and the Americans with Disabilities Act (ADA)

Employers that require employees to submit to wellness initiatives, such as health-risk appraisals (questionnaires about one's health history and current lifestyle) and assessments (physical and biomedical tests that screen for specific health conditions), are violating the ADA. This is so because the act forbids employers from conducting mandatory medical exams once an employee is hired, unless the inquiry is "job-related and consistent with business necessity."

Employers also must be careful when tying financial incentives or disincentives (e.g., cash bonuses, lower health insurance contributions) to test results. The employer can offer an incentive only upon verification that the employee went for the test. The incentive cannot be tied to the test results. Under the ADA, employers cannot discriminate in pay or benefits based on a legally protected disability. In addition, any test results from wellness screening must be kept confidential.

What type of wellness programs do not violate the ADA? Educational wellness programs that encourage people to sign up for tests and instruct them on how to improve their lifestyles.[113] By helping employees to take an interest in their future health, employers should ultimately be able to keep at least a loose lid on claims and major expenses.

SUBSTANCE ABUSE ON THE JOB PRODUCES TOUGH POLICY CHOICES FOR MANAGERS

Given the amounts of time and money invested in employees, especially highly skilled knowledge workers, many firms try to rehabilitate those with substance abuse problems. But how do firms get "problem" employees into rehabilitation programs? The most popular approaches are self-referral and referral by family and friends. Among pilots who have gone through the airline industry's alcohol rehabilitation program, in effect since 1973, 85 percent were initially turned in by family, friends, or coworkers.

According to the Air Line Pilots Association, one of the hallmarks of the industry's program is a willingness of people to turn in an alcoholic pilot. That willingness, in turn, depends on knowing that the pilot can return to work. If people know that by turning in a pilot they will also be taking away his or her livelihood, they may not do it.

The key to returning to work, in the opinion of most professionals in the field of sub-stance abuse, is follow-up, because substance abuse is a recurring disease. Prior to the Exxon *Valdez* accident, the company really had no systematic policy on how to handle employees after treatment. The company depended solely on the judgments of local man-agers.

Under United's program, rehabilitated pilots are monitored for at least 2 years. During this time, the pilot is required to meet monthly with a committee comprising counselors and representatives of both union and management in a kind of group therapy session with other recovering pilots. They may also be required to undergo periodic surprise alcohol or drug tests. United has never had an alcohol-related accident.

Although experts don't always agree on how long follow-up should last, programs most commonly require 6 months of intensive contact, such as weekly meetings, and 1 year after that of monthly contact. Longer-term follow-up may last as long as 4 years.

IMPLICATIONS FOR MANAGEMENT PRACTICE

In the coming years, we can expect to see three developments in occupational safety and health:

1. More widespread promotion of OSHA's consultative role, particularly as small businesses rec-ognize that this is a no-cost, no-penalty option available to them

2. Wider use of cost-benefit analysis by regulatory agencies; industry is demanding it, and Executive Order 12292 endorses it

3. Broadening of the target group for EAPs and wellness programs to include dependents and retirees

The high costs of disabling injuries and occupational diseases, together with these three trends, suggest that the commitment of resources to enhance job safety and health makes good business sense *over and above* concerns for corporate social responsibility.

SUMMARY

Public policy regarding occupational safety and health has focused on state-run work-ers' compensation programs for job-related injuries and federally mandated preven-tive measures to enhance job safety and health. OSHA enforces the provisions of the 1970 Occupational Safety and Health Act, under which employers have a "general duty" to provide a place of employment "free from recognized hazards." Employers also have the special duty to comply with all standards of safety and health established under the act. OSHA's effectiveness has been debated for more than a decade, but it is important to note that workplace accidents can result either from *unsafe work condi-tions* or from *unsafe work behaviors.* OSHA can affect only unsafe work conditions. There are no standards that govern potentially unsafe employee behaviors.

A major concern of employers today is with the possible health hazards associated with high technology, such as video display terminals and semiconductors, with dis-eases related to radiation or carcinogenic substances that may have long latency peri-ods, and with AIDS.

In response, OSHA has established or toughened workplace exposure limits for many carcinogenic substances. Management's first duty in this area is to develop a safety and health policy. Management's second duty is to establish controls that include a loss control program, a safety committee, safety rules, careful selection of employees, extensive training, and feedback and incentives for maintaining a safe work environment.

Employee assistance programs represent a brighter side of the health issue. Such programs offer assistance to all "troubled" employees. Under an EAP, supervisors need be concerned only with identifying declining work performance, not with involving themselves in employee problems. Treatment is left to professionals. Finally, health promotion, or "wellness," programs differ from EAPs in that their primary focus is on prevention, not rehabilitation. Both EAPs and wellness programs hold considerable promise for improving productivity, quality of work life, and profits.

DISCUSSION QUESTIONS

16 ■1 Should OSHA's enforcement activities be expanded? Why or why not?

16 ■2 What advantages and disadvantages do you see with workers' compensation?

16 ■3 Discuss the relative effectiveness of engineering versus management controls to improve job safety and health.

16 ■4 If the benefits of EAPs cannot be demonstrated to exceed their costs, should EAPs be discontinued?

16 ■5 Should organizations be willing to invest more money in employee wellness? Why or why not?

REFERENCES

1. *Accident facts* (1993). Chicago: National Safety Council.
2. Labor letter (1993, Sept. 14). *The Wall Street Journal*, p. A1.
3. Labor letter (1987, Apr. 14). *The Wall Street Journal*, p. 1.
4. Burtt, E. J. (1979). *Labor in the American economy.* New York: St. Martin's Press.
5. Ledvinka, J., & Scarpello, V. G. (1991). *Federal regulation of personnel and human resource management* (2d ed.). Boston: PWS-Kent.
6. Olian, J. D. (1990). Workplace safety and employee health. In J. A. Fossum (ed.), *Employee and labor relations.* Washington, DC: Bureau of National Affairs, pp. 4-218 to 4-285.
7. Salwen, K. G. (1993, Nov. 22). White House to proffer ergonomic rule for workplaces, employers' liabilities. *The Wall Street Journal*, p. B6.
8. Marsh, B. (1994, Feb. 3). Workers at risk. *The Wall Street Journal*, pp. A1; A8.
9. New OSHA bloodborne pathogen standards (1992, September). *Mountain States Employers Council Bulletin*, p. 4.
10. Salwen, op. cit. See also Stepping into the middle of OSHA's muddle (1993, Aug. 2). *Business Week*, p. 53.
11. *Marshall v. Barlow's, Inc.* (1978). 1978 OSHD, Sn. 22,735. Chicago: Commerce Clearing House.
12. Elliott, S. (1984, June 27). OSHA Region III area director, personal communication.
13. Bowers, B. (1994, Feb. 1). OSHA to mix a little mercy with latest crackdown. *The Wall Street Journal*, p. B2.
14. OSHA penalties increased (1991, February). *Mountain States Employers Council Bulletin*, p. 2.

15. The price of neglect (1992, Sept. 28). *Time*, p. 24.

16. U.S. Department of Labor (1983, March). *Program highlights: Job safety and health.* Washington, DC: U.S. Government Printing Office, Fact Sheet No. OSHA-83-01 (rev.).

17. *NLRB v. Jasper Seating Co.* (1988). CA 7, 129 LRRM 2337. See also *Whirlpool Corporation v. Marshall* (1981, Feb. 26). *Daily Labor Report*, Washington, DC: Bureau of National Affairs, pp. D3–D10.

18. *Gateway Coal Co. v. United Mine Workers of America* (1974). 1974 OSHD, Sn. 17,085. Chicago: Commerce Clearing House.

19. Ledvinka & Scarpello, op. cit.

20. Davis, B. (1992, Aug. 6). What price safety? *The Wall Street Journal*, pp. A1, A7.

21. Marsh, op. cit. See also Trost, C. (1988, Apr. 22). Occupational hazard: A much-maligned OSHA confronts rising demands with a reduced budget. *The Wall Street Journal Supplement*, p. 25R. See also McCaffrey, D. P. (1983). An assessment of OSHA's recent effects on injury rates. *Journal of Human Resources*, **18**(1), 131–146.

22. Marsh, op. cit., p. A1.

23. Cook, W. N., & Gautschi, F. H. (1981). OSHA plant safety programs and injury reduction. *Industrial Relations*, **20**(3), 245–257.

24. Milbank, D. (1991, Mar. 29). Companies turn to peer pressure to cut injuries as psychologists join the battle. *The Wall Street Journal*, pp. B1, B3.

25. Ashford, N. A. (1976). *Crisis in the workplace: Occupational disease and injury.* Cambridge, MA: MIT Press. See also Burtt, op. cit.

26. Follmann, J. F., Jr. (1978). *The economics of industrial health.* New York: AMACOM.

27. *Inside OSHA: The role of management in safety* (1975, Nov. 1). New York: Man and Manager, Inc.

28. Getting business to think about the unthinkable (1991, June 24). *Business Week*, pp. 104–107. Smith, M. J., Cohen, H. H., Cohen, A., & Cleveland, R. J. (1978). Characteristics of successful safety programs. *Journal of Safety Research*, **10**, 5–15. See also Cohen, A. (1977). Factors in successful occupational safety programs. *Journal of Safety Research*, **9**, 168–178.

29. Shabecoff, P. (1987, Oct. 11). Industry is split over disclosure of job dangers. *The New York Times*, p. 28.

30. Swoboda, F. (1990, Jan. 12). OSHA targets repetitive motion injuries. *Washington Post*, p. A10. See also U.S. fines meatpacker $3.1 million over injuries (1988, May 12). *The New York Times*, p. A20.

31. Repetitive stress: The pain has just begun (1992, July 13). *Business Week*, pp. 142, 143. See also Crippled by computers (1992, Oct. 12). *Time*, pp. 70, 71.

32. U.S. Department of Labor, op. cit.

33. Siskind, F. (1982). Another look at the link between work injuries and job experience. *Monthly Labor Review*, **105**(2), 38–41. See also Root, N. (1981). Injuries at work are fewer among older employees. *Monthly Labor Review*, **104**(3), 30–34.

34. Leary, W. E. (1982, Aug. 2). Management concern affects mine safety. *Denver Post*, p. 1C.

35. U.S. Department of Labor, op. cit.

36. Komaki, J., Barwick, K. D., & Scott, L. R. (1978). A behavioral approach to occupational safety: Pinpointing and reinforcing safe performance in a food manufacturing plant. *Journal of Applied Psychology*, **63**, 434–445.

37. Reber, R. A., & Wallin, J. A. (1984). The effects of training, goal setting, and knowledge of results on safe behavior: A component analysis. *Academy of Management Journal*, **27**, 544–560.

38. Milbank, op. cit.

39. The perplexing case of the plummeting payrolls (1993, Sept. 20). *Business Week*, p. 27.

40. Eyestrain tops American office workers' lists of job-related complaints (1991, Nov. 19). *The Wall Street Journal*, p. A1. See also Lorber, L. Z., & Kirk, R. J. (1987). *Fear itself: A legal and personnel analysis of drug testing, AIDS, secondary smoke, and VDTs.* Alexandria, VA: ASPA Foundation.

41. Olian, op. cit.

42. Eyestrain tops American office workers' lists of job-related complaints, op. cit.

43. Olian, op. cit.

44. *Chemical hazard communication* (1988). Washington, DC: U.S. Department of Labor, OSHA #3084 (rev. ed.).

45. Jacobs, S. L. (1988, Nov. 22). Small business slowly wakes to OSHA hazard rule. *The Wall Street Journal*, p. B2.

46. Hays, L. (1986, July 8). New rules on workplace hazards prompt intensified on-the-job training programs. *The Wall Street Journal*, p. 31.

47. McMurray, S. (1991, Oct. 4). India's high court upholds settlement paid by Carbide in Bhopal gas leak. *The Wall Street Journal*, p. B3. See also Damages for a deadly cloud (1989, Feb. 27). *Time*, p. 53.

48. McMurray, S., & Harlan, C. (1992, May 1). Indian judge orders seizure of Carbide assets in country. *The Wall Street Journal*, p. B5.

49. Foreign firms feel the impact of Bhopal most (1985, Nov. 26). *The Wall Street Journal*, p. 24.

50. Miller, M. (1985, Nov. 26). Words still speak louder than deeds: India hasn't come to grips with plant safety. *The Wall Street Journal*, p. 24.

51. Foreign firms feel the impact of Bhopal most, op. cit.

52. Thailand fire shows region cuts corners on safety to boost profits (1993, May 13). *The Wall Street Journal*, p. A13.

53. Risk capital: Korea suffers the highest rate of industrial accidents (1990, Sept. 11). *The Wall Street Journal*, p. A1.

54. *Illinois v. Chicago Magnet Wire Corp.* (1990, Oct. 24). 126 Ill. 2d 356, 534 N.E., 2d 962, 128 Ill.

55. Marcus, A. D., & de Cordoba, J. (1990, Oct. 17). New York court rules employers can face charges in worker safety. *The Wall Street Journal*, p. B9.

56. $520,000 awarded in an asbestos-related illness (1987, Oct. 8). *The New York Times*, p. A21.

57. Wermiel, S. (1989, Oct. 3). Justices let states prosecute executives for job hazards covered by U.S. law. *The Wall Street Journal*, p. A11.

58. Karr, A. R. (1989, Jan. 16). OSHA sets or toughens exposure limits on 376 toxic chemicals in workplace. *The Wall Street Journal*, p. C16.

59. Stead, W. E., & Stead, J. G. (1983, January). OSHA's cancer prevention policy: Where did it come from and where is it going? *Personnel Journal*, pp. 54–60.

60. Alliton, V. (1992, February). Financial realities of AIDS in the workplace. *HRMagazine*, pp. 78–81. See also Businesses break through some barriers (1991, Dec. 11). *USA Today*, pp. 1B, 2B.

61. Tedlow, R. S. (1993, June 18). Levi Strauss & Co. and the AIDS crisis. *Harvard Business School*, Case #9-391-198.

62. Alliton, op. cit.

63. Ibid.

64. Levi Strauss & Co. See also Tedlow, op. cit.

65. Tedlow, op cit., p. 17.

66. Is business bungling its battle with booze? (1991, Mar. 25). *Business Week*, pp. 76–78. See also Sperling, D. (1989, Mar. 9). More employers help foot the detox bill. *USA Today*, p. 5D.

67. Balgopal, P. R., Ramanathan, C. S., & Patchner, M. A. (1987, December). *Employee assistance programs: A cross-cultural perspective.* Paper presented at the Conference on International Personnel and Human Resource Management, Singapore.

68. Berg, N. R., & Moe, J. P. (1979). Assistance for troubled employees. In D. Yoder & H. G. Heneman, Jr. (eds.), *ASPA handbook of personnel and industrial relations.* Washington, DC: BNA, pp. 1.59–1.77.

69. Stone, D. L., & Kotch, D. A. (1989). Individuals' attitudes toward organizational drug testing policies and practices. *Journal of Applied Psychology*, **74**, 518–521.

70. Substance abuse in the workplace (1987, June 20). *Hospitals*, pp. 68–73.

71. Is business bungling its battle with booze?, op. cit.

72. French, H. W. (1987, Mar. 26). Helping the addicted worker. *The New York Times*, pp. 29, 34.

73. Foote, A., & Erfurt, J. (1981, September–October). Evaluating an employee assistance program. *EAP Digest*, pp. 14–25.

74. Ray, J. S. (1982). Having problems with worker performance? Try an EAP. *Administrative Management*, **43**(5), 47–49.

75. How is drinking affecting the workplace? (1993, August). *Mountain States Employers Council Bulletin*, p. 5. See also How to confront—and help—an alcoholic employee (1991, Mar. 25). *Business Week*, p. 78.

76. How to confront—and help—an alcoholic employee, op cit.

77. Weiss, R. M. (1987). Writing under the influence: Science versus fiction in the analysis of corporate alcoholism programs. *Personnel Psychology*, **40**, 341–356.

78. Is business bungling its battle with booze?, op. cit.

79. Farkas, G. M. (1989). The impact of federal rehabilitation laws on the expanding role of employee assistance programs in business and industry. *American Psychologist*, **44**, 1482–1490.

80. Lehman, W. E. K., & Simpson, D. D. (1992). Employee substance abuse and on-the-job behaviors. *Journal of Applied Psychology*, **77**, 309–321.

81. Normand, J., Salyards, S. D., & Mahoney, J. J. (1990). An evaluation of preemployment drug testing. *Journal of Applied Psychology*, **75**, 629–639.

82. Taking drugs on the job (1983, Aug. 22). *Newsweek*, p. 55.

83. How is drinking affecting the workplace?, op. cit.

84. Murder tops job deaths in 5 states (1993, Nov. 29). *The Denver Post*, p. 4A.

85. Violent employees (1994, February). *Mountain States Employers Council Bulletin*, p. 5. See also Violence goes to work (1993, September). *Mountain States Employers Council Bulletin*, pp. 1, 3.

86. Kilborn, P. T. (1993, May 17). Inside post offices, the mail is only part of the pressure. *The New York Times*, pp. A1, A15.

87. Violent employees, op. cit.

88. Most firms fail to warn workers of plant closings (1993, Feb. 23). *The Wall Street Journal*, p. A2.

89. Brody, J. E. (1991, July 10). As benefits and staff shrink, job stress grows. *The New York Times*, p. C11.

90. Lombino, P. (1992, February). An ounce of prevention. *CFO*, pp. 15–22. See also Winslow, R. (1991, Jan. 29). Medical costs soar, defying firms' cures. *The Wall Street Journal*, p. B1

91. Hollenbeck, J. R., Ilgen, D. R., & Crampton, S. M. (1992). Lower back disability in occupational settings: A review of the literature from a human resource management view. *Personnel Psychology*, **45**, 247–278.

92. Lombino, op. cit.

93. Ibid.

94. Epstein, S. S. (1989). *A note on health promotion in the workplace*. Boston: Harvard Business School.

95. Stolberg, S. (1993, Nov. 10). Top underlying cause of death: Tobacco use. *The Denver Post*, p. 2A. See also Kahn, R. L., & Byosiere, P. (1992). Stress in organizations. In M. D. Dunnette & L. M. Hough (eds.), *Handbook of industrial and organizational psychology* (2d ed., vol. 3). Palo Alto, CA: Consulting Psychologists Press, pp. 571–650.

96. Mavis, B. E. (1992). Issues related to participation in worksite health promotion: A preliminary study. *American Journal of Health Promotion*, **7**(1), 53–63. See also Alexy, B. B. (1991). Factors associated with participation or nonparticipation in a workplace wellness center. *Research in Nursing and Health*, **14**(1), 33–39.

97. Lombino, op. cit.

98. American business is bullish on "wellness" (1982, Mar. 29). *Medical World News*, pp. 33–39.

99. Parkes, K. R. (1987). Relative weight, smoking, and mental health as predictors of sickness and absence from work. *Journal of Applied Psychology*, **72**, 275–286.

100. James, F. B. (1987, Apr. 14). Study lays groundwork for tying health costs to workers' behavior. *The Wall Street Journal*, p. 37.

101. Falkenberg, L. E. (1987). Employee fitness programs: Their impact on the employee and the organization. *Academy of Management Review*, **12**, 511–522.

102. Cascio, W. F. (1991). *Costing human resources: The financial impact of behavior in organizations* (3d ed.). Boston: PWS-Kent.

103. Erfurt, J. C., Foote, A., & Heirich, M. A. (1992). The cost-effectiveness of worksite wellness programs for hypertension control, weight loss, smoking cessation, and exercise. *Personnel Psychology*, **45**, 5–27. See also Viswesvaran, C., & Schmidt, F. L. (1992). A meta-analytic comparison of smoking cessation methods. *Journal of Applied Psychology*, **77**, 554–561. See also Gebhardt, D. L., & Crump, C. E. (1990). Employee fitness and wellness programs in the workplace. *American Psychologist*, **45**, 262–272.

104. Fries, J. F. (1992). Health risk changes with a low-cost individualized health promotion program: Effects at up to 30 months. *American Journal of Health Promotion*, **6**(5), 367–380.

105. If you light up on Sunday, don't come in on Monday (1991, Aug. 26). *Business Week*, pp. 68–72.

106. Fries, J. F., Koop, C. E., Beadle, C. E., Cooper, P. P., England, M. J., Greaves, R. F., Sokolov, J. J., & Wright, D. (1993). Reducing health care costs by reducing the need and demand for medical services. *New England Journal of Medicine*, **329**(5), 321–325.

107. Johnson, S. (1988, June). Breast screening's bottom line—lives saved. *Administrative Radiology*, p. 4.

108. Petty, A. (1993, Sept. 17). More women get mammograms at work. *The Wall Street Journal*, pp. B1, B6.

109. Lombino, op. cit.

110. Rothman, H. (1992). Wellness works for small firms. *Nation's Business*, **77**(12), 42–46.

111. Lombino, op. cit.

112. Wellness can mean a trim bottom line (1993, Aug. 16). *Business Week*, p. 112.

113. Matthes, K. (1992, December). ADA checkup: Assess your wellness program. *HR Focus*, **69**(12), p. 15.

CHAPTER 17

COMPETITIVE STRATEGIES, HUMAN RESOURCE STRATEGIES, AND THE FINANCIAL IMPACT OF HUMAN RESOURCE MANAGEMENT ACTIVITIES

HUMAN RESOURCE MANAGEMENT IN ACTION

ATTITUDE SURVEY RESULTS: CATALYST FOR MANAGEMENT ACTIONS*

Attitude surveys can yield far more than a measure of morale. By relating specific management actions and styles to high employee turnover and lowered profitability, the results of an attitude survey in one company led to concrete directions for change. The changes implied improved productivity, quality of work life, and bottom-line financial gain.

The company is a nationwide retail operation with an exceptional record of growth and profitability. To staff its rapidly expanding management positions, the company hires large numbers of men and women as trainees in store management. However, despite attractive salaries and promotion opportunities, the company was having trouble retaining the new hires. Top management was at a loss to explain why. Turnover among store managers accelerated beyond the most recent hires; managers in whom the company had invested considerable time and money were also quitting. Moreover, there was no apparent pattern to the turnover—some locations were experiencing a great deal, others very little.

Despite continued profitability, there was growing concern among top management that the level of turnover might be detrimental to the company's long-term success. The actual dollar outlay for the cost of turnover was only one aspect of the problem. An additional consideration was the possibility of poor public relations resulting from unhappy former employees. As a consumer-oriented company, the firm was concerned about its public image and the effect that a "bad employer" reputation could have on the patronage of its stores.

---

*Adapted from: B. Goldberg and G. G. Gordon, Designing attitude surveys for management action, *Personnel Journal*, October 1978, pp. 546–549. Used by permission.

THE PROBLEM: TURNOVER VERSUS PROFITABILITY

As turnover worsened, the company conducted various statistical analyses and reviewed reports from field managers in an attempt to locate the source of the problem. Several theories were proposed, such as low pay and inconvenient scheduling of work, but none was supported by sufficient evidence to produce change. Indeed, most of the proposed solutions to the turnover problem (e.g., hiring more employees to work fewer hours) were rejected because their anticipated costs would reduce company profitability.

Top management initially felt that high turnover was acceptable because it did not have much of an adverse effect on profits. In fact, many managers believed that turnover actually increased profitability because it kept overall salary costs down. Vacancies caused stores to operate understaffed until replacements were hired, and these new hires were paid lower salaries than their predecessors.

WHY AN ATTITUDE SURVEY?

Despite attempts to find it, the root cause of the turnover of store managers remained elusive. The problem could lie anywhere in the management system, in the types of employees hired, in how they were trained, in how they were managed, or in how their performance was rewarded.

Top management decided to conduct a broad survey among the store managers themselves to determine the cause of the high turnover. The survey's intent was not to determine how to improve morale and thereby to reduce turnover. It was to help management discover the factors contributing to turnover and the concrete and constructive actions that might reduce it. And, because top management believed that high turnover had a positive effect on profitability, another objective of the survey was to determine what could be done to reduce turnover without reducing profitability! This part of the survey yielded some very enlightening results.

DESIGNING THE SURVEY

The company first rank-ordered its profit centers in two ways—(1) according to turnover and (2) according to profitability—based on the results for the most recent 12-month period. A questionnaire was developed through personal interviews with a number of store managers, and hypotheses were advanced concerning the relationship between the attitudes of store managers and turnover. The hypotheses produced further guides for questionnaire design; they also yielded an outline for subsequent data analyses.

The resulting questionnaire covered a broad range of management issues, including:

- Store characteristics (location and volume)
- Biographical characteristics of the store managers
- Recruitment and selection practices
- Training activities
- Working conditions
- Management climate
- Rewards system

The questionnaire was sent to every store manager then working in one of the profit centers identified earlier.

SURVEY RESULTS

The survey revealed significant differences in the ways store managers were selected, managed, and treated. It also identified a number of fundamental management practices that were counterproductive. For example, some higher-level supervisors never made field visits to work with their store managers.

However, the most revealing part of the survey results had to do with turnover and profitability. Many factors contributing to high turnover were also contributing to lower profitability. The survey revealed six critical areas of human resource management, all interrelated and each related to turnover and profitability.

Challenges

1. What are some of the advantages and disadvantages of a low turnover rate?

2. How can attitude surveys help orient managers toward more effective performance?

3. In the survey design phase, why do you think the company first ranked each store in terms of its profitability and turnover rate?

Questions This Chapter Will Help Managers Answer

1. Does our firm's HR strategy follow from our firm's competitive business strategy?

2. What kinds of employee behaviors and HR activities should we encourage, given our firm's competitive business strategy?

3. How can HR research be useful to a line manager?

4. If I want to know how much turnover is costing us each year, what factors should I consider?

5. Is there evidence that high-performance work policies are associated with improved financial performance?

In business settings, it is hard to be convincing without data. If the data are developed systematically and comprehensively and are analyzed in terms of their strategic implications for the business or business unit, they are more convincing. The chapter opening vignette demonstrates how a systematic procedure (an attitude survey) designed to collect data on a broad range of management issues could be used to improve management practices. This chapter will first present several alternative competitive strategies and then identify the kinds of employee behaviors and human resource (HR) activities that are most consistent with each one. Then we will discuss the need for audit and evaluation of HR activities and how HR research can help in this effort. Finally, we will present examples of methods used to assess the costs and benefits of HR activities in some key areas.

ORIENTATION

As emphasized earlier, the focus of this book is *not* on training HR specialists. Rather, it is on training line managers who must, by the very nature of their jobs, manage people and work with them to accomplish organizational objectives. Consequently, the purpose of this chapter is not to show how to measure the effectiveness of the human resources department; the purpose is to show how to align HR strategies with general business strategies and, having done so, to assess the costs and benefits of relevant HR activities. The methods can and should be used in cooperation with the human resources department. But they are not the exclusive domain of that department. They are general enough to be used by any manager in any department to measure the costs and benefits of employee behavior.

This is not to imply that dollars are the only barometer of the effectiveness of human resource activities. The payoffs from some activities, such as managing diversity and child care, must be viewed in a broader social context. Furthermore, the firm's strategy and goals must guide the work of each business unit and of that unit's human resource management activities. For example, to emphasize its outreach efforts to the disadvantaged, a firm might adopt a conscious strategy of *training* workers for entry-level jobs, while *selecting* workers who already have the skills to perform higher-level jobs. To make the most effective use of the information that follows, it is important always to keep these points in mind.

In Chapter 2 we identified strategic HR management as a process of getting everybody from the top of the organization to the bottom to do things to implement the strategy of the business effectively—to use people most wisely with respect to the organization's strategic needs. We presented a systematic framework for doing this (the "5-P" model), and noted that strategic business needs, or competitive strategies, set the 5-P model into motion. In the following sections, we'll describe some alternative competitive strategies and then link HR processes to each one.

Alternative Competitive Strategies

The means that firms use to compete for business in the marketplace and to gain competitive advantage are known as *competitive strategies.*[1] Competitive strategies may differ in a number of ways, including the extent to which firms emphasize innovation, quality enhancement, cost reduction, and speed.[2] Moreover, there is growing recognition that the different types of strategies require different types of HR practices.[3] Hence the assessment of outcomes associated with HR activities should focus on those activities that are most crucial to the implementation of the competitive strategy chosen. The important lesson for managers is that *human resources represent a competitive advantage that can increase profits when managed wisely.*

Innovation strategy is used to develop products or services that differ from those of competitors. Its primary objective is to offer something new and different. Enhancing product or service quality is the primary objective of the *quality-enhancement strategy,* while the objective of a *cost reduction strategy* is to gain competitive advantage by being the lowest cost producer of goods or provider of services. Finally, the objective of a *time-based, or speed, strategy* is to be the fastest innovator, producer, distributor, and responder to customer feedback. Innovation strategy emphasizes managing people so that they work *differently*; quality-enhancement strategy emphasizes managing people so that they work *smarter*; cost reduction strategy emphasizes managing people so that they work *harder*; and speed strategy emphasizes managing people so that they work *more efficiently* by changing the way work is done.

While it is convenient to think of these four competitive strategies as pure types applied to entire organizations, business units, or even functional specialties, the reality is more complex. As the following statement illustrates, various combinations of the four strategies are often observed in practice.

As is well known, Ford Motor Co. has emphasized employee involvement since the early 1980s. In October 1978, Philip Caldwell, then president of Ford, made the following statement at a meeting of top executives: "Our strategy for the years ahead will come to nothing unless we ask for greater participation of our work force. Without motivated and concerned workers, we're not going to lower our costs as much as we need to—and we aren't going to get the product quality we need."[4] Elements of both cost reduction and quality-enhancement strategies are evident in Caldwell's statement.

Employee Behaviors and Human Resource Strategies Appropriate to Each Competitive Business Strategy

Innovation Strategy. Under a competitive strategy of innovation, the implications for managing people may include selecting highly skilled individuals, giving employees more discretion, using minimal controls, making greater investments in human resources, providing more resources for experimentation, allowing and even rewarding occasional failure, and appraising performance for its long-run implications. Innovative firms such as Hewlett-Packard, 3M, Raytheon, and PepsiCo illustrate this strategy.[5]

Because the innovation process depends heavily on individual expertise and creativity, employee turnover can have disastrous consequences.[6] Moreover, firms pursuing this strategy are likely to emphasize long-term needs in their training programs for managers and to offer training to more employees throughout the organization.[7] HR strategy should therefore emphasize the use of highly valid selection and training programs as well as the reduction of controllable turnover, especially among high performers, who are not easy to replace.

The latter approach is being used more and more by firms that are trying to hang on to valued employees as they steer through bankruptcy reorganizations. Such "employee-retention plans" offer incentive bonuses for managers who stay for 1 or 2 years and who meet certain performance criteria. They also offer lucrative severance packages if jobs are cut. Federated Department Stores and Allied Stores, Campeau Corporation's U.S. retailing subsidiaries, used this approach, as did the Braniff, L. J. Hooker, LTV, and Wickes companies. Although the programs are relatively new, early indications are that they work. Why do companies adopt them? Because it does little good for a firm to fight its way out of bankruptcy court if essential employees don't stay around to guide the restructured operations.[8]

Quality-Enhancement Strategy. The profile of behaviors appropriate under this strategy includes relatively repetitive and predictable behaviors; a longer-term focus; a modest amount of cooperative, interdependent behavior; a high concern for quality with a modest concern for quantity of output; a high concern with *how* goods or services are made or delivered; low risk-taking activity; and commitment to the goals of the organization.[9]

Quality enhancement typically involves greater commitment from employees and fuller use of their abilities. As a result, fewer employees may be needed to accomplish the same amount of work. This phenomenon has been observed at firms such as L. L. Bean, Corning Glass, Honda, and Toyota.[10]

It is well known that the gains in productivity that result from more valid selection or training programs can be expressed in various ways: in dollars, increases in output, decreases in hiring needs, or savings in payroll costs.[11] Since fewer workers *may* be needed after the implementation of more valid selection or training programs, managers may wish to focus on the change in staffing requirements (as well as the associated cost savings) as one outcome of a quality-enhancement strategy.

Since reliable, predictable behavior is important to the implementation of this strategy, another objective is to minimize absenteeism, tardiness, and turnover. Cost savings associated with any HR programs designed to control these undesirable behaviors should therefore be documented carefully. In a later section of this chapter, we will present methods for doing this.

Commitment to the goals of the organization and flexibility to change can both be increased by constant formal and informal training programs. Changes in commitment and flexibility can then be assessed by measuring employee attitudes over multiple time periods. Finally, other ways to signal concern for the long-term welfare of employees are by actively promoting day-care, employee assistance, wellness, and smoking-cessation programs.

In summary, to be consistent with a quality-enhancement strategy, HR strategy should focus on the use of highly valid selection and training programs, on promoting positive changes in employees' attitudes and lifestyles, and on decreasing absenteeism and controllable turnover. To assess the effectiveness of strategy implementation, managers must then examine costs and benefits in each of these areas.

Cost Reduction Strategy. Firms pursuing this strategy are characterized by tight fiscal and management controls, minimization of overhead, and pursuit of economies of scale. The primary objective is to increase productivity by decreasing the unit cost of output per employee. Strategies for reducing costs include reducing the number of employees; reducing wages; using part-time workers, subcontractors, or automation; changing work rules; and permitting flexibility in job assignments.[12]

The profile of employee behaviors under this strategy includes relatively repetitive and predictable behaviors, a comparatively short-term focus, primarily autonomous or individual activity, a modest concern for quality coupled with a high concern for quantity of output (goods or services), emphasis on results, low risk taking, and stability. In addition, there is minimal use of training and development.

Sometimes managements adopt cost reduction strategies in rather desperate situations, as their firms struggle to survive.[13] More commonly, though, cost reduction is used in combination with other strategies to keep companies prosperous. As an example, consider the response to international competition of Cummins Engine Co., a $2.5 billion manufacturer of diesel engines and related products and services headquartered in Columbus, Indiana. The company has about 22,000 employees worldwide, and its sales mix is 70 percent U.S. business and 30 percent international. It powers about 60 percent of the trucks on U.S. highways.

Cummins watched with deep concern throughout the 1970s as foreign competition won nearly 100 percent of the U.S. motorcycle market, 30 percent of the U.S. auto market, and a big chunk of the U.S. steel market—all in about 10 years. In the company's view, those gains in market share were mostly won fairly and squarely with better products, quality, prices, and responsiveness to the customer.[14] Those industries are close to Cummins's, and the company vowed to compete aggressively.

To do so, it focused on the variables of product, prices, costs, and performance. It spent nearly a billion dollars on product development through the 1980s—triple the company's market value in 1980! To meet world price levels, the company swore off price increases for 5 years. As for performance, managers at every level developed specific goals in the areas of quality, cost, and delivery and allocated them to work groups throughout the company. Every quarter the president provided videotaped progress reports to all employees.

What were the results? Financially, the company has lost no domestic business to international competition. Its domestic market share has grown, as has its success in international markets. As one executive noted: "We have experienced, and managed, a full range of human emotions during these years. . . . Our people have been stretched, pulled, and at times really shaken up trying to meet all these challenges; facilities have been closed as operations were consolidated, and many jobs were lost despite our successful efforts to create new ones. . . . This process, of course, continues . . . for it is a game—or war—that can be won but never finished."[15]

Speed Strategy. "The computer, the fax, and the microwave are not going to go away; they are going to get faster or be replaced by new technologies that do even more than they do and faster yet. Demands by consumers for more choices, and faster, more comprehensive services . . . would seem to underline the need for speed in development, production, and delivery of products and services."[16]

The first imperative under such a strategy is to select highly skilled individuals who are committed to speed management and whose beliefs, attitudes, and values related to time are consistent with those the organization is seeking. Both workers and managers must embrace change, rather than resist it, company culture must support their efforts, and both work groups and cross-functional teams must share the same norms about time. A fluid, networked organizational structure, rather than the old "command, control, and compartmentalization" system, is most appropriate. Finally, *all* HR systems, including staffing, training, reward, and performance management, must support the speed management philosophy.

To appreciate the importance of speed in every function, consider the following changes in development time: new cars—Honda, from 5 years to 3; telephones—AT&T, from 2 years to 1; computer printers—Hewlett-Packard, from 4.5 years to 22 months; and trucks—Navistar, from 5 years to 2.5. When it comes to production, consider these world-class time standards from receipt of the customer's order to finish: General Electric (circuit-breaker boxes)—from 3 weeks to 3 days; Motorola (pagers)—from 3 weeks to 2 hours; Hewlett-Packard (electronic testing equipment)—from 4 weeks to 5 days; and Brunswick (fishing reels)—from 3 weeks to 1.[17] In terms of services, consider the bank that decreased the time for loan approval from several days to 30 minutes by creating a team composed of a credit analyst, an experienced collateral appraiser, and a bank procedures expert. The team is empowered to draw on its collective knowledge and experience to respond to the customer almost at once.[18]

General Electric CEO Jack Welch summed up the challenge well: "We have to get faster if we are to win in a world where nothing is predictable except the increasingly rapid pace of change."[19] Managing people effectively in such an environment is a continuing challenge.

HUMAN RESOURCES RESEARCH—THE BASIS FOR AUDIT AND EVALUATION OF HUMAN RESOURCES ACTIVITIES

One of the classic functions of management is that of control. In a small business, managers are close to the scene of operations. They can see for themselves exactly what is happening. However, the need for management control becomes greater as managers are further removed from the scene of operations, as is the case in many firms that do business in multiple locations. As we have stressed, it is important for managers to assess the degree of "fit" between their firm's competitive strategies and its human resource strategies. Beyond that, it is important to conduct HR research—to assess the outcomes of the HR activities undertaken at different levels of analysis.

Types of Outcomes

Outcomes may be expressed in quantitative terms (e.g., cost-benefit analysis) or in qualitative terms (e.g., indicators of overall morale, job satisfaction, or reaction to a training program). Alone, each type of outcome is incomplete; both are necessary to describe the rich results of HR programs. Later in this chapter, we will illustrate how quantitative outcomes can be determined. Now, however, let's consider a qualitative HR research tool that is becoming quite popular—the attitude survey.

To a large extent, the growing popularity of attitude surveys is due to an idea stressed in many popular books on management: that it is important to listen to employees. This idea has taken on added significance as more companies endure the organizational trauma of mergers and restructurings or adopt more participative management styles.

As employee surveys become more common, the range of issues on which opinions are solicited is expanding considerably. At Wells Fargo & Co. in San Francisco, for instance, employees have been asked about such things as the effectiveness of the bank's advertising, the quality of innovation of its products, and its responsibility to the community.

It is one thing to ask employees for their opinions—it shows that management is willing to listen. But surveys can backfire; employees become angry and resentful if their expectations are raised but management fails to react to their comments or complaints. When facing employees who feel they are underpaid, for example, one manager noted that firms "had better be prepared with facts to tell them that their perception is incorrect or perhaps that there are reasons. That can get very sensitive."[20] As a result of its own survey, Hewlett-Packard found out that engineers were concerned about their lack of communication with peers in other units. After listening to the engineers at a postsurvey meeting, the company accelerated development of an electronic-mail system.

After mergers and acquisitions, many companies try to move quickly to evaluate the morale of the acquired company and to discover any differences in operating styles. Just 2 months after it acquired Crocker National Corp., for example, Wells Fargo surveyed 1500 Crocker employees. As a Wells Fargo vice president noted: "There's a lot of organizational change going on. . . . Wells Fargo was in a major downsizing, and now [there is] the acquisition. This helps us know what's going on . . . we really didn't know what the silent majority felt."[21]

Surveys are most effective when they are aligned with competitive strategy—that is, when they tap issues that are important to strategy implementation at all levels and when managers commit *up front* to take action based on survey findings. Doing so helps to build bridges between survey feedback and existing change strategies such as total quality management, reengineering, or continuous improvement.[22]

Attitude surveys represent just one type of HR research tool. In addition, the wide availability of computerized employee databases makes it possible to answer a variety of other questions, such as factors that relate consistently to the retention of engineers, the productivity and turnover of salespeople, and the personal characteristics of employees who accept offers of early retirement. Finally, detailed, sophisticated research is being conducted on issues as diverse as the impact of plant shutdowns, worker participation in management decisions, worker ownership, and the impact of quality-improvement efforts. As these few examples show, the range of HR research topics and the methods used to investigate them are limited only by the imagination and ingenuity of the managers and researchers involved.

The Level of Analysis

It is important to distinguish HR activities performed at the corporate level from those performed at the middle-management level or at the operating level.[23] At the corporate level, HR decisions involve the design of policies that meet an organization's strategic challenges, such as business objectives, corporate values or culture, technology, structure, and responses to environmental constraints (e.g., health and safety policies).

At the middle-management level, key HR decisions involve the design of systems or programs that are consistent with policy guidelines and will facilitate the cost-effective achievement of business goals. The primary objective is management control, and it is accomplished by assessing the cost-effectiveness of HR programs.

At the operating level, managers implement HR policies and programs, making decisions that affect the attraction, retention, and motivation of employees. This level includes the hands-on HR practices of line managers (e.g., to reduce absenteeism or controllable turnover) and the day-to-day services provided by the HR function (e.g., recruiting, staffing, training) that directly affect HR outcomes.

Assuming that a manager appreciates the need to align competitive and human resource strategies and desires to assess the costs and benefits of the HR activities that are most relevant to the chosen strategy, how does he or she proceed? Let us begin by distinguishing human resource accounting from behavior costing.

Human Resource Accounting

In the mid-1960s, the first attempts were made to account for the costs of human resource management activities. This accounting has come to be known generally as human resource accounting (HRA).

The first firm to report HRA results was the R. G. Barry Corp. of Columbus, Ohio, which did so in its 1967 annual report.[24] The company's objective was to report accurate estimates of the worth of the human assets in its employ. For each manager, costs were accumulated in five subsidiary accounts: (1) recruiting and acquisition, (2) formal orientation and training, (3) informal orientation and training, (4) experience, and (5) development. The costs for each manager were amortized over his or her expected working lifetime; unamortized costs (such as for a manager who left the company) were written off.

Valuing managers in this way is what accountants call the "asset model of accounting," which uses the historical cost of the asset. That is, the organization's investment in each manager (the asset) is measured by the expenses actually incurred (the historical cost) in developing each manager as an asset.

Such an approach considers only the investments made in managers and not the returns on those investments. This is one reason why asset models of HRA never caught on widely.[25]

A newer approach focuses on dollar estimates of the behaviors, such as the absenteeism, turnover, and job performance, of managers. This approach measures not the value of a manager as an asset, but rather the economic consequences of his or her behavior. This is an *expense model* of HRA.[26] It is the approach taken in this chapter to assessing the costs and benefits of the activities of all employees, managerial as well as nonmanagerial. We will apply standard cost accounting procedures to employee behavior. To do this, we must first identify each of the elements of behavior to which we can assign a cost; each behavioral cost element must be separate and mutually exclusive from the others. To begin, let's define some key terms.

The Behavior Costing Approach

Contrary to popular belief, there are methods for determining the costs of employee behavior in *all* human resource management activities—behaviors associated with the attraction, selection, retention, development, and utilization of people in organizations. These costing methods are based on several definitions and a few necessary assumptions.

To begin with, there are, as in any costing situation, both controllable and uncontrollable costs, and there are direct and indirect measures of these costs.

- *Direct measures* refer to actual costs, such as the accumulated, direct cost of recruiting.
- *Indirect measures* do not deal directly with cost; they are usually expressed in terms of time, quantity, or quality.[27] In many cases indirect measures can be converted to direct measures. For example, if we know the length of time per preemployment interview plus the interviewer's hourly pay, it is a simple matter to convert time per interview into cost per interview.

Indirect measures have value in and of themselves, and they also supply part of the data needed to develop a direct measure. As a further example, consider the direct and indirect costs associated with mismanaged organizational stress, as shown in Table 17-1.[28] The direct costs listed in the left-hand column of Table 17-1 can all be expressed in terms of dollars. To see this, consider just two items: the costs associated with work accidents and grievances. Figure 17-1 presents just some of the direct costs associated with accidents; it is not meant to be exhaustive, and it does not include such items as lost time, replacement costs, institution of "work to rule" by coworkers if they feel the firm is responsible, the cost of the safety committee's investigation, and the costs associated with changing technology or job design to prevent future accidents. The items shown in the right-hand column of Table 17-1 cannot be expressed as easily in dollar terms, but they are no less important, and the cost of these indirect items may in fact be far larger than the direct costs. Both direct and indirect costs, as well as benefits, must be considered to apply behavior costing methodology properly.

Controllable Versus Uncontrollable Costs. In any area of behavior costing, some types of costs are controllable through prudent HR decisions, while other costs are simply beyond the control of the organization. Consider employee turnover as an example. To the extent that people leave for reasons of "better salary," "more opportunity for promotion and career development," or "greater job challenge," the costs associated with turnover are somewhat controllable. That is, the firm can alter its human resource management practices to reduce the voluntary turnover. However, if

DIRECT AND INDIRECT COSTS ASSOCIATED WITH MISMANAGED
STRESS

Direct costs	Indirect costs
Participation and membership:	Loss of vitality:
Absenteeism	Low motivation
Tardiness	Dissatisfaction
Strikes and work stoppages	Communication breakdowns:
Performance on the job:	Decline in frequency of contact
Quality of productivity	Distortions of messages
Quantity of productivity	Faulty decision making
Grievances	Quality of work relations:
Accidents	Distrust
Unscheduled machine downtime	Disrespect
and repair	Animosity
Material and supply overutilization	Opportunity costs
Inventory shrinkages	
Compensation Awards	

Source: B. A. Macy & P. H. Mirvis, Evaluation Review, *6*(3), Figure 4-5. Copyright ©
1982 by Sage Publications, Inc. Reprinted by permission.

FIGURE 17-1
The costs of accidents and
grievances.

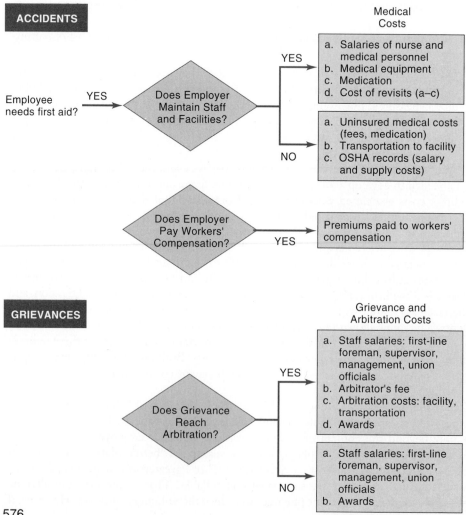

the turnover is due to such factors as death, poor health, or spouse transfer, the costs are uncontrollable.

The point is that in human resource costing, our objective is not simply to *measure* costs but also to *reduce* the costs of human resources by devoting resources to the more "controllable" factors. To do this, we must do two things well:

1. Identify, for each HR decision, which costs are controllable and which are not
2. Measure these costs at Time 1 (prior to some intervention designed to reduce controllable costs) and then again at Time 2 (after the intervention)

Hence the real payoff from determining the cost of employee behaviors lies in being able to demonstrate a financial gain from the wise application of human resource management methods.

The next three sections present both hypothetical and actual company examples of behavior costing in the areas of absenteeism, turnover, and training. Following that, we will present three macrolevel assessments of the financial impact of high-performance work practices. Our focus will be on methods and outcomes rather than on alternative HR management approaches that might be used to reduce costs or increase profits in each area. These have been discussed elsewhere in the book.

COSTING EMPLOYEE ABSENTEEISM

In any human resource costing application, it is important first to define exactly what is being measured. From a business standpoint, *absenteeism is any failure of an employee to report for or to remain at work as scheduled, regardless of reason.* The term "as scheduled" is very significant, for this automatically excludes vacations, holidays, jury duty, and the like. It also eliminates the problem of determining whether an absence is "excusable" or not. Medically verified illness is a good example of this. From a business perspective, the employee is absent and is simply not available to perform his or her job; that absence will cost money. How much money? In 1993, the cost of unscheduled absences in U.S. workplaces varied from about $250 to $550 *per employee per year.*[29]

A flowchart that shows how to estimate the total cost of employee absenteeism over any period is shown in Figure 17-2.[30] To illustrate the computation of each cost element in Figure 17-2, let us use as an example a hypothetical 1800-employee firm called Mini-Mini-Micro Electronics; dollar figures are shown in Table 17-2. An item-by-item explanation of each of them follows.

Item 1: Total hours lost. If we assume a 2.1 percent monthly absenteeism rate (slightly above the average for manufacturing firms in 1993),[31] we can apply this figure to *total scheduled work hours.* Hours of *scheduled work time* per employee may be determined as follows:

2080 hours of work per year

−80 hours of vacation (2 weeks)

−40 hours (5 days) paid holidays

This equals 1960 hours of scheduled work time per employee × 1800 employees = 3,528,000 total scheduled work hours per year. If 2.1 percent of total scheduled

■ **TABLE 17 ▪ 2**

COST OF EMPLOYEE ABSENTEEISM AT MINI-MINI-MICRO
ELECTRONICS

Item	Mini-Mini-Micro Electronics
1. Total hours lost to employee absenteeism for the period	74,088 hr
2. Weighted-average wage or salary per hour per employee	$10.159/hr
3. Cost of employee benefits per hour per employee	$3.556/hr
4. Total compensation lost per hour per absent employee:	
(a) if absent workers are paid (wage or salary plus benefits;	$13.715/hr
(b) if absent workers are not paid (benefits only)	—
5. Total compensation lost to absent employees [total hours lost × 4(a) or 4(b), whichever applies]	$1,016,116.92
6. Total supervisory hours lost on employee absenteeism	8820 hr
7. Average hourly supervisory wage, including benefits	$18.225/hr
8. Total supervisory salaries lost to managing problems of absenteeism (hours lost × average hourly supervisory wage—item 6 × item 7)	$160,744.50
9. All other costs incidental to absenteeism not included in the preceding items	$50,000
10. Total estimated cost of absenteeism—summation of items 5, 8, and 9	$1,226,861.42
11. Total estimated cost of absenteeism per employee: Total estimated costs ÷ total number of employees	$681.59 per employee absence

work hours are lost to absenteeism, a total of 3,528,000 × 0.021, or 74,088, hours are lost.

Item 2: Weighted-average wage or salary per hour per absent employee. In 1993, two out of every three employers had a system in place for employees to report their absences.[32] Thus they can determine the exact wage or salary per hour per absent employee. Others might use the following procedure to estimate a weighted-average wage or salary per hour per absentee:

Occupational group	Approximate percentage of total absenteeism	Average hourly wage	Weighted average wage
Blue collar	0.55	$10.45	$ 5.747
Clerical	0.35	8.15	2.852
Management	0.10	15.60	1.560
Total weighted average pay per employee per hour			$10.159

Item 3: Cost of employee benefits per hour per absent employee. We include the cost of benefits in our calculations because benefits consume, on average, more than a third of total compensation (see Chapter 12). Ultimately, we want to be able to cal-

1. Compute total employee-hours lost to absenteeism for the period.

2. Compute weighted average wage or salary/hr per absent employee.

3. Compute cost of employee benefits/hr per employee.

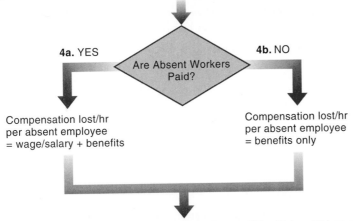

4a. YES   Are Absent Workers Paid?   **4b.** NO

Compensation lost/hr per absent employee = wage/salary + benefits

Compensation lost/hr per absent employee = benefits only

5. Compute total compensation lost to absent employees [(1) x (4a) or (4b) as applicable].

6. Estimate total supervisory hours lost to employee absenteeism.

7. Compute average hourly supervisory salary + benefits.

8. Estimate total supervisory salaries lost to managing absenteeism problems [(6) x (7)].

9. Estimate all other costs incidental to absenteeism.

10. Estimate total cost of absenteeism [(5) + (8) + (9)].

11. Estimate total cost of absenteeism/employee [(10) ÷ Total no. of employees].

FIGURE 17-2
Total estimated cost of employee absenteeism. (*Source:* Wayne F. Cascio, *Costing human resources: the financial impact of behavior in organizations,* 3d ed., 1991. © PWS-Kent Publishing Co., Boston. Reprinted by permission of PWS-Kent Publishing Co., a division of Wadsworth, Inc.)

culate the total compensation lost due to absenteeism. Since our primary interest is in the cost of benefits per absentee, we take the weighted-average hourly wage multiplied by benefits as a percentage of base pay. (If benefits differ as a function of union-nonunion or exempt-nonexempt status, a weighted-average benefit should be computed in the same manner as was done to compute a weighted-average wage.) For Mini-Mini-Micro, this figure is

$$\$10.159 \times 35\% = \$3.556 \text{ per hour}$$

Item 4: Total compensation lost per hour per absent employee. This equals the weighted-average hourly wage plus the hourly cost of benefits (assuming that absent workers are paid). Some firms (e.g., Honda USA) do not pay absentees: "No work, no pay." In such instances, only the cost of benefits should be included in the estimate of total compensation lost per hour per absent employee. For Mini-Mini-Micro, the compensation lost per hour for each absent employee is

$10.159 + $3.556 = $13.715

Item 5: Total compensation lost to absent employees. This is simply total hours lost multiplied by total compensation lost per hour:

74,088 hr × $13.715/hr = $1,016,116.92

Note that the first five items shown in Figure 17-2 refer to the costs associated with absentees themselves. The next three items refer to the firm's costs of *managing* employee absenteeism.

Item 6: Total supervisory hours lost in dealing with employee absenteeism. Three factors determine this lost time, which is the product of $A \times B \times C$, where:

A = Estimated average number of hours lost per supervisor per day managing absenteeism problems

The supervisor's time is "lost" because, instead of planning, scheduling, and troubleshooting productivity problems, he or she must devote time to nonproductive activities associated with managing absenteeism problems. The actual amount of time lost can be determined by having supervisors keep diaries indicating how they spend their time or by conducting structured interviews with experienced supervisors.

B = Total number of supervisors who deal with absenteeism problems
C = Total number of working days in the period for which absentee costs are being analyzed (including all shifts and weekend work).

For Mini-Mini-Micro Electronics, the data needed for this calculation are:

Estimate of A =   30 min, or 0.50 hr, per day

Estimate of B =   1800 employees (10%, or 180, are supervisors, and 40% of the 180, or 72, of the supervisors deal regularly with absenteeism problems)

Estimate of C =   245 days per year

Supervisory hours lost in
dealing with absenteeism = 0.50 hr/day × 72 supervisors × 245 days/year

                          = 8820 supervisory hours lost per year

Item 7: Average hourly supervisory wage, including benefits. For those supervisors who deal regularly with absenteeism problems, assume that their average hourly wage is $13.50 plus 35 percent benefits ($4.725), or $18.225 per hour.

Item 8: Total cost of supervisory salaries lost to managing problems of absenteeism. To determine this cost, multiply the total supervisory hours lost by the total hourly supervisory wage:

8820 hr lost × $18.225/hr = $160,744.50

Item 9: All other absenteeism-related costs not included in items 1 through 8. Assume that Mini-Mini-Micro spends $50,000 per year in absenteeism-related costs that are not associated either with absentees or with supervisors. These costs are associated with elements such as overtime premiums, wages for temporary help, machine downtime, production losses, inefficient materials usage by temporary substitute employees, and, for very large organizations, permanent labor pools to "fill in" for absent workers.

Item 10: Total cost of employee absenteeism. This is the sum of the three costs determined thus far: costs associated with absent employees (item 5) plus costs associated with the management of absenteeism problems (item 8) plus other absenteeism-related costs (item 9). For Mini-Mini-Micro Electronics, this figure is

$1,016,116.92 + $160,744.50 + $50,000 = $1,226,861.42

Item 11: Per-employee cost of absenteeism. This is the total cost divided by 1800 employees, or $681.59.

Perhaps the first question management will ask upon seeing absenteeism cost figures is "What do they mean? Are we average, above average, or what?" Unfortunately, there are no industry-specific figures on the costs of employee absenteeism. Certainly, these costs will vary depending on the type of firm, the industry, and the level of employee that is absent (unskilled versus skilled or professional workers). Remember that the dollar figure just determined (we will call this the "Time 1" figure) becomes meaningful as a *baseline* from which to measure the financial gains realized as a result of a strategy to reduce absenteeism. At some later time (we will call this "Time 2"), the total cost of absenteeism should be measured again. The difference between the Time 2 figure and the Time 1 figure, minus the cost of implementing the strategy to reduce absenteeism, represents *net gain.*

Another question that often arises at this point is "Are these dollars real? Since supervisors are drawing their salaries anyway, what difference does it make if they have to manage absenteeism problems?" True, but what is the best possible gain from them for that pay? Let's compare two firms, A and B, identical in regard to all resources and costs—supervisors get paid the same, work the same hours, manage the same size staff, and produce the same kind of product. But absenteeism in A is very low, and in B it is very high. The paymasters' records show the same pay to supervisors, but the accountants show higher profits in A than in B. Why? Because the supervisors in firm A spend less time managing absenteeism problems. They are more productive because they devote their energies to planning, scheduling, and troubleshooting. Instead of putting in a 10- or 12-hour day (which the supervisors in firm B consider "normal"), they wrap things up after only 8 hours. In short, reducing the number of hours that supervisors must spend managing absenteeism problems has two advantages: (1) it allows supervisors to maximize their productivity, and (2) it reduces the stress and wear and tear associated with repeated 10- to 12-hour days, which in turn enhances the quality of work life of supervisors.

COSTING EMPLOYEE TURNOVER

Turnover may be defined as *any permanent departure beyond organizational boundaries*[33]—a broad and ponderous definition. Not included as turnover within this definition, therefore, are transfers within an organization and temporary layoffs. The rate of turnover in percent over any period can be calculated by the formula:

Number of turnover incidents per period/Average workforce size × 100%

Nationwide in 1993, for example, monthly turnover rates averaged about 0.7 percent, or 8.4 percent annually.[34] However, this figure most likely represents both controllable turnover (controllable by the organization) and uncontrollable turnover. Controllable turnover is "voluntary" on the part of the employee, while uncontrollable turnover is "involuntary" (due, e.g., to retirement, death, or spouse transfer). Furthermore, turnover may be *functional*, where the employee's departure produces a benefit for the organization, or *dysfunctional*, where the departing employee is someone the organization would like to retain.

High performers who are difficult to replace represent dysfunctional turnovers; low performers who are easy to replace represent functional turnovers. The crucial issue in analyzing turnover, therefore, is not how many employees leave but rather the performance and replaceability of those who leave versus those who stay.[35]

In costing employee turnover, we first determine the total cost of all turnover and then estimate the percentage of that amount that represents controllable, dysfunctional turnover—resignations that represent a net loss to the firm and that the firm could have prevented. Thus, if total turnover costs $1 million and 50 percent is controllable and dysfunctional, $500,000 is our Time 1 baseline measure. To demonstrate the net financial gain associated with the strategy adopted prior to Time 2, the total gain at Time 2, say $700,000, minus the cost of implementing the strategy to reduce turnover, say $50,000, must be compared to the cost of turnover at Time 1 ($500,000). In this example, the net gain to the firm is $150,000. Now let's see how the total cost figure is derived.

Components of Turnover Costs

There are three broad categories of costs in the basic turnover costing model: separation costs, replacement costs, and training costs. In this section, we present only the cost elements that comprise each of these three broad categories. For those who wish to investigate the subject more deeply, more detailed formulas are available.[36]

Separation Costs. There are four cost elements in separation costs. These are:

- *Exit interview*, including the cost of the interviewer's time and the cost of the terminating employee's time.

- *Administrative functions related to termination*: for example, removal of the employee from the payroll, termination of benefits, and turn-in of company equipment.

- *Separation pay*, if applicable.

- *Increased unemployment tax*. Such an increase may come from either or both of two sources. First, in states that base unemployment tax rates on each company's turnover rate, high turnover will lead to a higher unemployment tax rate. Suppose a company with a 10 percent annual turnover rate was paying unemployment tax at a rate of 5 percent on the first $7000 of each employee's wages in 1993. But in 1994, because its turnover rate jumped to 15 percent, the company's unemployment tax rate may increase to 5.5 percent. Second, replacements for those who leave will result in extra unemployment tax being paid. Thus a 500-employee firm with no turnover during the year will pay the tax on the first $7000 (or whatever the state maximum is) of each employee's wages. The same firm with a 20 percent annual turnover rate will pay the tax on the first $7000 of the wages of 600 employees.

The sum of these four cost elements represents the total separation costs for the firm.

Replacement Costs. The eight cost elements associated with replacing employees who leave are:

- *Communicating job availability*
- *Preemployment administrative functions:* for example, accepting applications and checking references
- *Entrance interview,* or perhaps multiple interviews
- *Testing* and/or other types of assessment procedures
- *Staff meetings,* if applicable, to determine if replacements are needed, to recheck job analyses and job specifications, to pool information on candidates, and to reach final hiring decisions
- *Travel and moving expenses:* travel for all applicants and travel plus moving expenses for all new hires
- *Postemployment acquisition and dissemination of information:* for example, all the activities associated with in-processing new employees
- *Medical examinations,* if applicable, either performed in-house or contracted out

The sum of these eight cost elements represents the total cost of replacing those who leave.

Training Costs. This third component of turnover costs includes three elements:

- *Informational literature* (e.g., an employee handbook)
- *Instruction in a formal training program*
- *Instruction by employee assignment* (e.g., on-the-job training)

The sum of these three cost elements represents the total cost of training replacements for those who leave.

Two points should be noted: First, if there is a formal orientation program, the per-person costs associated with replacements for those who left should be included in the first cost element, *informational literature.* This cost should reflect the per-person, amortized cost of developing the literature, not just its delivery. Do not include the total cost of the orientation program unless 100 percent of the costs can be attributed to employee turnover.

Second, probably the major cost associated with employee turnover, *reduced productivity during the learning period,* is generally not included along with the cost elements *instruction in a formal training program* and *instruction by employee assignment.* The reason for this is that formal work-measurement programs are not often found in employment situations. Thus it is not possible to calculate accurately the dollar value of the loss in productivity during the learning period. If such a program does exist, then by all means include this cost. For example, a major brokerage firm did a formal work-measurement study of this problem and reported the results shown in Table 17-3. The bottom line in all of this is that we want to be conservative in our training cost figures so that we can defend every number we generate.

■ **TABLE 17 ▪ 3**

PRODUCTIVITY LOSS OVER EACH THIRD OF THE LEARNING PERIOD FOR
FOUR JOB CLASSIFICATIONS

Classification	Weeks in learning period	Productivity loss during learning		
		1	2	3
Management and partners	24	75%	40%	15%
Professionals and technicians	16	70	40	15
Office and clerical	10	60	40	15
Broker trainees	104	85	75	50

Note: The learning period for the average broker trainee is 2 years, although the cost to the firm is generally incurred only in the first year. It is not until the end of the second year that the average broker trainee is fully productive.

The sum of the three component costs—separation, replacement, and training—represents the total cost of employee turnover for the period in question. Other factors could also be included in our tally, such as the uncompensated performance differential between leavers and their replacements, but that is beyond the scope of this book.[37]

Remember, *the purpose of measuring turnover costs is to improve management decision making.* Once turnover figures are known, managers have a sound basis for choosing between current turnover costs and instituting some type of turnover reduction program (e.g., job enrichment, realistic job previews).

As examples, consider the results Corning, Inc., found when it tallied *only* its out-of-pocket expenses for turnover, such as interview costs and hiring bonuses. That number, $16 to $18 million annually, led to an investigation into the causes of turnover and, in turn, to new policies on flexible scheduling and career development.[38]

Merck & Company, the pharmaceutical giant, found that, depending on the job, turnover costs were 1.5 to 2.5 times the annual salary paid.[39] In the retail automobile industry, the cost of turnover averages more than $18,000 per salesperson.[40] Finally (in 1994 dollars), at a major brokerage firm the cost per terminating employee was about $7500,[41] and the cost per terminating store manager at a large retail department store chain was more than $11,000.[42] Obviously, there are opportunities in this area for enterprising managers to make significant bottom-line contributions to their organizations. Indeed, one way to reduce turnover, especially among employees who seek opportunities for personal growth and professional development, is to provide training. At firms such as Hewlett-Packard, IBM, and Skyway Express, training is an important component of the competitive strategies of innovation, quality enhancement, and speed.[43] Methods of assessing the costs and benefits of training are described next.

COSTING THE EFFECTS OF TRAINING ACTIVITIES

At the most basic level, the task of evaluation is counting—counting clients, counting errors, counting dollars, counting hours, and so forth. The most difficult tasks of evaluation are deciding *what* things should be counted and developing routine *methods* for counting them. Managers should count the things that will provide the most useful feedback. As noted in Chapter 8, we assess the results of training to determine whether it is worth the cost. Training valuation (in financial terms) is not easy, but the technology to do it is available and well developed.[44] A manager may have to value training in two types of situations: one in which only indirect measures of dollar outcomes are available and one in which direct measures of dollar outcomes are available.

Indirect Measures of Training Outcomes

Indirect measures of training outcomes are more common than direct measures. That is, many studies of training outcomes report improvements in job performance or decreases in errors, scrap, and waste. Relatively few studies report training outcomes directly in terms of dollars gained or saved. Indirect measures can often be converted into estimates of the dollar impact of training, however, by using a method known as utility analysis. While the technical details of the method are beyond the scope of this chapter,[45] here's a summary of one such study.

In a study of the effects of behavior modeling skills on the performance of supervisors (see Chapter 8 for a fuller description of behavior modeling), the performance of a trained group of supervisors was compared to that of an untrained group. The two groups were matched as closely as possible on characteristics such as job requirements, geographical location, salary, experience, and age. When posttraining performance appraisal scores for the two groups were compared, the trained group was rated about 12 percent higher than the untrained group.[46]

Using utility analysis to translate the gain in performance into economic terms, the authors found the 1-year net benefit for the 65 supervisors who were trained to be about $35,000. This represents the dollar gain in performance, minus the cost of the training program, adjusted for variable costs (those that rise and fall with changes in productivity, such as sales commissions), taxes, and discounting. These benefits were assumed to accumulate over time, and, assuming that obsolescence did not negate the effect of the training, a net benefit of almost $150,000 was estimated by year 5. Now let's focus on direct measures of training outcomes—a study that examined the impact of training on sales performance.

Direct Measures of Training Outcomes

When direct measures of the dollar outcomes of training are available, standard valuation methods are appropriate. The following study valued the results of a behavior-modeling training program for sales representatives in relation to the program's effects on sales performance.[47]

Study Design. A large retailer conducted a behavior-modeling program in two departments, Large Appliances and Radio/TV, within 14 of its stores in one large metropolitan area. The 14 stores were matched into seven pairs in terms of size, location, and market characteristics. Stores with unusual characteristics that could affect their overall performance, such as declining sales or recent changes in management, were not included in the study.

The training program was then introduced in seven stores, one in each of the matched pairs, and not in the other seven stores. Other kinds of ongoing sales training programs were provided in the control-group stores, but the behavior-modeling approach was used only in the seven experimental-group stores. In the experimental-group stores, 58 sales associates received the training, and their job performance was compared to that of 64 sales associates in the same departments in the control-group stores.

As in most sales organizations, detailed sales records for each individual were kept on a continuous basis. These records included total sales as well as hours worked on the sales floor. Since all individuals received commissions on their sales and since the value of the various products sold varied greatly, it was possible to compute a job performance measure for each individual in terms of average commissions per hour worked.

There was considerable variation in the month-to-month sales performance of each individual, but sales performance over 6-month periods was more stable. In fact, the average correlation between consecutive sales periods of 6 months each was about .80 (where 1.00 equals perfect agreement). Hence the researchers decided to compare the sales records of participants for 6 months before the training program was introduced with the results achieved during the same 6 months the following year, after the training was concluded. All sales promotions and other programs in the stores were identical, since these were administered on an areawide basis.

The Training Program Itself. The program focused on specific aspects of sales situations, such as "approaching the customer," "explaining features, advantages, and benefits," and "closing the sale." The usual behavior-modeling procedure was followed. First the trainers presented *guidelines* (or "learning points") for handling each aspect of a sales interaction. Then the trainees *viewed a videotaped situation* in which a "model" sales associate followed the guidelines in carrying out that aspect of the sales interaction with a customer. The trainees then *practiced* the same situation in role-playing rehearsals. Their performance was *reinforced* and shaped by their supervisors, who had been trained as their instructors.

Study Results. Of the original 58 trainees in the experimental group, 50 were still working as sales associates 1 year later. Four others had been promoted during the interim, and 4 others had left the company. In the control-group stores, only 49 of the original 64 were still working as sales associates 1 year later. Only 1 had been promoted, and 14 others had left the company. Thus the behavior-modeling program may have had a substantial positive effect on turnover since only about 7 percent of the trained group left during the ensuing year, in comparison to 22 percent of those in the control group. (This result had not been predicted.)

Figure 17-3 presents the changes in average per-hour commissions for participants in both the trained and untrained groups from the 6-month period before the training was conducted to the 6-month period following the training. Note in Figure 17-3 that the trained and untrained groups did not have equal per-hour commissions at the start of the study. While the *stores* that members of the two groups worked in were matched at the start of the study, *sales commissions* were not. Sales associates in the trained group started at a lower point than did sales associates in the untrained group. Average per-hour commissions for the trained group increased over the year from $9.27 to $9.95 ($14.20 to $15.24 in 1994 dollars); average per-hour commissions for the untrained group declined over the year from $9.71 to $9.43 ($14.87 to $14.44 in 1994 dollars). In other words, the trained sales associates increased their average earnings by about 7 percent, whereas those who did not receive the behavior-modeling training experienced a 3 percent decline in average earnings. This difference was statistically significant. Other training outcomes (e.g., trainee attitudes, supervisory

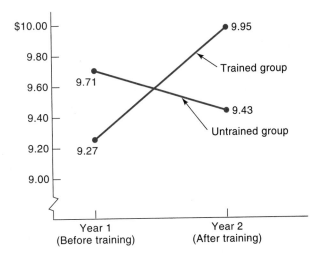

FIGURE 17-3
Changes in per-hour commissions before and after the behavior modeling training program.

behaviors) were also assessed, but, for our purposes, the most important lesson was that the study provided objective evidence to indicate the dollar impact of the training on increased sales.

The program also had an important secondary effect on turnover. Since all sales associates are given considerable training (which represents an extensive investment of time and money), it appears that the behavior modeling contributed to *cost savings* in addition to *increased sales*. As noted in the previous discussion of turnover costs, an accurate estimate of these cost savings requires that the turnovers be separated into controllable and uncontrollable because training can affect only controllable turnover.

Finally, the use of objective data as criterion measures in a study of this kind does entail some problems. As pointed out earlier, the researchers found that a 6-month period was required to balance out the month-to-month variations in sales performance resulting from changing work schedules, sales promotions, and similar influences that affected individual results. It also took some vigilance to ensure that the records needed for the study were kept in a consistent and conscientious manner in each store. According to the researchers, however, these problems were not great in relation to the usefulness of the study results. "The evidence that the training program had a measurable effect on sales was certainly more convincing in demonstrating the value of the program than would be merely the opinions of participants that the training was worthwhile."[48]

MACROLEVEL ASSESSMENTS OF THE FINANCIAL IMPACT OF HIGH-PERFORMANCE WORK PRACTICES

More and more business leaders seem to recognize that investments in workers are keys to their future competitiveness. Here are some representative comments from two of them at a recent conference on the future of the U.S. workplace:[49]

■ "For years many of us invested in new machinery to deskill operations and speed things up. I think the lesson today is we need to start investing in people, for the real technology of the 1990s and the 21st century is our people." (CEO of Levi Strauss & Co.)

■ "Technology can be copied and moved readily. If we are going to win, it will be because of the asset of our people, and those people working together are absolutely crucial to our future." (CEO of Boeing, Inc.)

The Growing Use of High-Performance Work Practices

In an effort to enhance their competitiveness, some firms have instituted "high-performance work practices." Sometimes this is done in an effort to avoid downsizing, and sometimes it is done in conjunction with downsizing. Such practices provide workers with the information, skills, incentives, and responsibility to make decisions that are essential for innovation, quality improvement, and rapid response to change. They seem particularly appropriate given the attributes that characterize today's economic environment: an unusual reliance on front-line workers; the treatment of workers as assets to be developed, not costs to be cut; new forms of worker-management collaboration that break down adversarial barriers; and the integration of technology and work in ways that will cause machines to serve human beings and not vice versa.[50] In a nationally representative sample of 700 private-sector establishments in the United States, 37 percent had a majority of frontline workers engaged in two or more high-performance work practices.[51] Thus, while the absolute number of firms that have adopted such practices is still a minority, if managers are to be able to argue forcefully for greater investments in people, they must be able to demonstrate that the benefits of implementing such practices outweigh the costs. Do such programs pay off?

High-Performance Work Practices and Organizational Performance

A substantial amount of research has been conducted on the relationship between productivity and high-performance work practices, such as the use of valid staffing procedures, organizational cultures that emphasize team orientation and respect for people, employee involvement in decision making, compensation linked to firm or worker performance, and training. The evidence indicates that such practices are usually associated with increases in productivity (defined as output per worker), as well as with a firm's long-term financial performance. However, these effects are most pronounced when such work practices are implemented *together as a system*.[52] In the following sections we will briefly consider the impacts of staffing practices and organizational culture on productivity and financial performance.

Use of Valid Staffing Practices. In a 1993 study, survey data were collected from the heads of the HRM departments of 201 organizations regarding the extent of their use of five staffing practices recommended in the academic literature: (1) follow-up studies of recruiting sources, (2) validation studies on the use of predictors of job performance, (3) structured preemployment interviews, (4) cognitive ability tests, and (5) biographical information blanks or weighted application blanks.[53]

The authors found that the use of more of these practices was related both to annual profits and to a growth in annual profits across all industries. However, the strength of the relationships varied considerably across industries, with the strongest relationships in service and financial industries. In these industries, correlations ranged from .71 to .86 between the total number of progressive staffing practices used and the following outcome measures: average annual profit over the previous 5 years, average annual profit growth, sales growth, and overall performance.

The authors speculated that the relationships were particularly strong in the service and financial industries because good staffing practices should help firms to secure the best talent available, and human resources are the primary inputs in those industries, as opposed to capital-intensive industries such as manufacturing.

Organizational Culture, Employee Retention, and HR Costs. Another recent study investigated the retention rates of 904 college graduates hired by six public accounting firms over a 6-year period.[54] Organizational culture values varied considerably across the six firms, from high task orientation (i.e., high orientation toward detail and stability) to high interpersonal orientation (i.e., high concern for a team orientation and respect for individuals).

New employees stayed an average of 45 months in the cultures emphasizing interpersonal relationships but only 31 months in the cultures emphasizing work task values (see Figure 17-4). This is a 14-month difference in median survival time. The next task was to translate the difference in time into a measure of profits forgone (i.e., opportunity losses).

Using the firms' average billing fees, along with hiring, training, and compensation costs, mean profits per professional employee ranged from $58,000 during the first year of employment to $67,000 during the second year and $105,000 during the third. A firm therefore incurs an opportunity loss of only $9,000 ($67,000 − $58,000) when a new employee replaces a 2-year employee but a $47,000 loss ($105,000 − $58,000) when it replaces a 3-year employee.

Assuming that both strong and weak performers generated the same average level of profits in each year of employment and that annual profits were distributed uniformly between 31 and 45 months' seniority, it is possible to estimate the opportunity loss associated with the 14-month difference in median survival time. This difference translated into an opportunity loss of approximately $44,000 per new employee [($47,000 − $9,000/12) × 14] between the firms having the two different

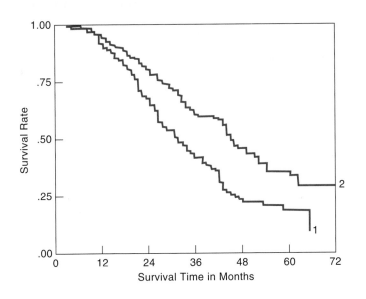

1. Emphasis on work task values

2. Emphasis on interpersonal relationship values

FIGURE 17-4
Voluntary survival rates in two organizational cultures. (*Source:* J. E. Sheridan, Organizational culture and employee retention, *Academy of Management Journal,* **35,** 1992, 1049.)

types of cultural values. Considering the total number of new employees hired by each office over the 6-year period of the study, a firm emphasizing work-task values incurred opportunity losses of approximately $6 to $9 million more than a firm emphasizing interpersonal relationship values.

High-Performance Work and Financial Performance

The most comprehensive study of work practices and financial performance is based on a survey of over 700 publicly held firms in all major industries. This study examined the use of "best practices" in the following areas:

- Personnel selection
- Job design
- Information sharing
- Performance appraisal
- Promotion systems
- Attitude assessment
- Incentive systems
- Grievance procedures
- Labor-management participation

Based on an index of "best practice" prevalence, firms using more progressive policies in these areas were generally found to have superior financial performance. The 25 percent of firms scoring highest on the index performed substantially higher on key performance measures, as shown below:

Performance Measure	Bottom 25%	2nd 25%	3rd 25%	Top 25%
Annual Return to Shareholders	6.5%	6.8%	8.2%	9.4%
Gross Return on Capital	3.7%	1.5%	4.1%	11.3%

The top 25 percent of firms—those using the largest number of "best practices"—had an annual shareholder return of 9.4 percent versus 6.5 percent for firms in the bottom 25 percent. Firms in the top 25 percent had an 11.3 percent gross rate of return on capital, more than twice as high as that of the remaining firms. After accounting for other factors likely to influence financial performance (such as industry characteristics), the human resource index remained significantly related to both performance measures.[55]

As these examples show, investments in people can pay off handsomely. The extent to which they actually will pay off depends on the skill and care with which the many HR practices available are implemented in practice.

IMPACT OF HUMAN RESOURCE MANAGEMENT ACTIVITIES ON PRODUCTIVITY, QUALITY OF WORK LIFE, AND THE BOTTOM LINE

There is a rapidly growing awareness in the business community of the need for HR research. Indeed, there is a growing consensus among managers in many industries that the future success of their firms may depend more on the skill with which human problems are handled than on the degree to which their firms maintain leadership in technical areas. Consider family leave costs as an example. Survey research has shown that the average cost of parental leave is 32 percent of annual salary (39 percent for management employees and 28 percent for nonmanagement employees). The alternative, permanently replacing the employee, costs at least 75 percent of salary.[56] Awareness alone, however, will not improve productivity, and there are no quick-fix solutions. Nevertheless, as General Motors found in the gradual turnaround of its problem plants at Tarrytown and Lordstown, when HR research results get translated into operating management practices, everybody wins. Labor-management relations improve, productivity goes up, quality goes up, profitability goes up, reworks go down, and the quality of work life becomes more tolerable.

The head of Mazda Motor Corporation captured the essence of HRM when he said: "The most important element in management is the human being, whatever his or her job happens to be." Another executive went a step further, saying: "The corporation that is not in the business of human development may not be in any business. At least not for long."[57]

ATTITUDE SURVEY RESULTS: CATALYST FOR MANAGEMENT ACTIONS

HUMAN RESOURCE MANAGEMENT IN ACTION: CONCLUSION

The survey highlighted six areas of human resource management that were related to effective company performance in terms of turnover and profitability:

1. *Recruitment and selection.* High-profit locations were recruiting many more management trainees from among the nonmanagement employees already working for the company. Hence the high-profit locations were getting store manager trainees who already had experience and an understanding of what the job entailed.

2. *Training.* Classroom instruction was rated favorably by everyone and was not a factor in turnover. The training that did make a difference was *on-the-job training.* Store managers in high-profit, low-turnover areas reported that they received better in-store training than did their counterparts in lower-profit areas.

3. *Staffing.* Keeping management staff at a minimum was not producing greater profits. It was producing overworked, disenchanted managers who could neither run their stores effectively nor provide the training found to be so important for new store managers. Less effective profit centers had fewer managers, who worked many more hours, had fewer days off, and were bothered more frequently at home about work-related matters when they had a scheduled day off.

4. *Performance management.* Managers in the high-profit, low-turnover areas received performance reviews on a quarterly basis. Store managers throughout the system who received performance reviews less than quarterly wanted to see them conducted more

often. In addition, everyone expressed a desire for more informal feedback from superiors about his or her performance.

A second aspect of performance management and control was regular store visits by higher-level supervisors. Supervisors in high-profit areas visited their stores more frequently than did their counterparts in low-profit areas.

5. *Climate.* Job security in this company's environment was not associated with compensation or with promotion opportunities. However, it was associated with the needs of the store managers to be treated fairly, to be kept informed, and to have superiors available when needed to help the store managers solve their problems. In less effective profit centers, store managers saw their superiors as less competent at handling problems, they had less confidence that their superiors would back them up in their actions, and they felt that their superiors neglected them in terms of the frequency of store visits and formal performance reviews. They also indicated that they were more apt to hear things first through the grapevine rather than directly from their superiors.

6. *Management style.* The areas described thus far all point to some basic differences in how the store managers were being managed in different parts of the company. These distinctions became clearer when comparisons were made between high- and low-turnover centers that were highly profitable. In fact, two styles of management seemed to result in high profitability. In high-profit, low-turnover centers, store managers felt that they worked in a delegative and supportive climate, with a strong emphasis on performance and the control of performance; however, these emphases were balanced by a demonstrated concern for the store managers and their needs. In contrast, high-profit, high-turnover areas were characterized as directive and overcontrolling in style; considerable emphasis was placed on the achievement of bottom-line results *without* a strong emphasis on the personal and developmental needs of the store managers.

TOP MANAGEMENT'S RESPONSE TO THE SURVEY FINDINGS

Based on the survey results, top management established a task force to deal with the problems identified. The task force recommended 28 specific actions with time frames for accomplishment that varied from 1 month to 1 year. These actions ranged from close enforcement of staffing guidelines to development of an improved in-store training package. In time, as expected, turnover began to trend downward.

This study illustrates two important aspects of ensuring the effectiveness of an attitude survey as a management tool. First, the survey dealt with the operational aspects of working life in the company, and it focused on issues over which top management had some control. Hence top management found it an easy task to translate survey findings into direct actions. Second, an attitude survey's credibility with top management rests squarely on its ability to demonstrate that *the results are important in some meaningful business sense.* In the present study, the message that provoked significant actions was the proof that if certain management practices were adopted, greater profitability *and* reduced turnover could be expected.

While it is not always possible to relate survey results directly to profits (as it was here), it is possible to approach any survey from the perspective of how the results can contribute to organizational effectiveness. This perspective is a key step in establishing the credibility of the survey.

ETHICAL DILEMMA: SURVEY FEEDBACK—NICE OR NECESSARY?

Is it unethical to ask employees for their opinions, attitudes, values, or beliefs on an attitude survey and then subsequently not to give them any feedback about the results? We know that survey results that are not fed back to employees are unlikely to be translated into action strategies[58] and that it is poor management practice to fail to provide feedback. Is it unethical as well? (Hint: See the definition of ethical decision making in Chapter 15.)

IMPLICATIONS FOR MANAGEMENT PRACTICE

Many managers do not realize the magnitude of their firm's investment in employees until they adopt a systematic framework for costing human resources. However, to be most useful, such a framework must include three key steps:

1. Understanding your organization's, department's, and operating unit's competitive strategies— innovation, quality enhancement, cost reduction, speed, or some combination of these

2. Making sure that HR activities are consistent with your chosen competitive strategy; for example, if innovation is the objective, don't skimp on training and development activities

3. Using behavior costing methods to assess the costs and benefits of the HR activities that are most relevant to your chosen competitive strategy

SUMMARY

In assessing the costs and benefits of HR activities, managers must first understand the competitive strategies of their organizations, departments, and operating units. Some possible strategies are innovation, quality enhancement, cost reduction, and speed. The next task is to align HR strategy with competitive strategy and to emphasize the kinds of employee behaviors that are most appropriate to the chosen strategy. In order to assess the outcomes of HR activities, HR research (which includes both qualitative and quantitative outcomes) may be conducted at corporate, middle management, or operating levels.

One approach to HR research that is growing in popularity is called behavior costing. To apply behavior costing methodology properly, both direct and indirect costs must be considered. However, our objective is not simply to *measure* these costs; it is also to *reduce* them by devoting resources to those costs that are controllable. We discussed behavior costing methods in three key areas of employee behavior—absenteeism, turnover, and employee training—and then considered the financial impact of high-performance work practices on organization-level outcomes. Firms that implement more such practices tend to be more profitable and provide higher returns to shareholders than those that implement fewer or none of them.

Assessing the costs and benefits of human resource management activities is just one aspect of the broader subject of HR research. The objective of HR research is to contribute to the development and application of improved solutions to employee relations problems and to the more effective use of people in organizations. When

HR research results that are targeted on operational problems get translated into practice, everybody wins.

DISCUSSION QUESTIONS

17∎1 Discuss three controllable and three uncontrollable costs associated with absenteeism.

17∎2 Why should efforts to reduce turnover focus only on controllable costs?

17∎3 Discuss the HR activities that are most relevant to the following competitive strategies: innovation, quality enhancement, cost reduction, and speed.

17∎4 Given the positive financial returns from high-performance work practices, why don't more firms implement them?

17∎5 If attitude surveys are to be taken seriously by management, what key issues should be considered in their design, implementation, and evaluation?

REFERENCES

1. Porter, M. E. (1985). *Competitive advantage.* New York: Free Press.
2. Vinton, D. E. (1992). A new look at time, speed, and the manager. *Academy of Management Executive*, **6**(4), 7–16. See also Schuler, R. S., & Jackson, S. E. (1987). Linking competitive strategies with human resource management practices. *Academy of Management Executive*, **1**(3), 207–219.
3. Jackson, S. E., & Schuler, R. S. (1990). Human resource planning. *American Psychologist*, **45**, 223–239.
4. Banas, P. A. (1988). Employee involvement: A sustained labor/management initiative at the Ford Motor Company. In J. P. Campbell and R. J. Campbell (eds.), *Productivity in organizations.* San Francisco: Jossey-Bass, pp. 388–416. (Quotation source: p. 391.)
5. Schuler & Jackson, op. cit.
6. Kanter, R. M. (1985, Winter). Supporting innovation and venture development in established companies. *Journal of Business Venturing*, **1**, 47–60.
7. Jackson, S. E., Schuler, R. S., & Rivero, J. C. (1989). Organizational characteristics as predictors of personnel practices. *Personnel Psychology*, **42**, 727–736.
8. Pollock, E. J. (1990, Mar. 20). Beleaguered firms dangle lures to retain employees. *The Wall Street Journal*, pp. B1, B2.
9. Schuler & Jackson, op. cit.
10. Taylor, A., III. (1990, Nov. 19). Why Toyota keeps getting better and better and better. *Fortune*, pp. 66–79.
11. Cascio, W. F. (1989). Using utility analysis to assess training outcomes. In I. L. Goldstein (ed.), *Training and development in organizations.* San Francisco: Jossey-Bass, pp. 63–88.
12. Touby, T. (1993, November/December). The business of America is jobs. *Journal of Business Strategy*, **14**(6), 20–31.
13. Richman, L. S. (1993, Sept. 20). When will the layoffs end? *Fortune*, pp. 54–56.
14. White, B. J. (1988). The internationalization of business: One company's response. *Academy of Management Executive*, **2**(1), 29–32.
15. Ibid., p. 31.
16. Vinton, op. cit., p. 14.
17. Dumaine, B. (1989, Feb. 13). How managers can succeed through speed. *Fortune*, pp. 54–74.
18. Stalk, G., Jr., & Hout, T. M. (1990). *Competing against time.* New York: Free Press.
19. Dumaine, op. cit., p. 55.
20. Reibstein, L. (1986, Oct. 27). A finger on the pulse. Companies expand use of employee surveys. *The Wall Street Journal*, p. 27.
21. Ibid.
22. Does survey feedback make a difference? (1993, Fall). *Decisions . . . Decisions*, pp. 1, 2.

23. Tsui, A. S., & Gomez-Mejia, L. R. (1988). Evaluating human resource effectiveness. In L. Dyer (ed.), *Human resource management: Evolving roles and responsibilities.* Washington, DC: Bureau of National Affairs, pp. 1-187 to 1-227.

24. Woodruff, R. C., Jr. (1970). Human resources accounting. *Canadian Chartered Accountant*, **97**, 156–161.

25. Scarpello, V., & Theeke, H. A. (1989). Human resource accounting: A measured critique. *Journal of Accounting Literature*, **8**, 265–280. See also Baker, G. M. N. (1974). The feasibility and utility of human resource accounting. *California Management Review*, **16**(4), 17–23.

26. Mirvis, P. H., & Macy, B. A. (1976). Measuring the quality of work and organizational effectiveness in behavioral-economic terms. *Administrative Science Quarterly*, **21**, 212–226.

27. Fitz-enz, J. (1984). *How to measure human resources management.* New York: McGraw-Hill.

28. For an up-to-date treatment of this issue, see Kahn, R. L., & Byosiere, P. (1992). Stress in organizations. In M. D. Dunnette & L. M. Hough (eds.), *Handbook of industrial and organizational psychology* (2d ed., vol. 3). Palo Alto, CA: Consulting Psychologists Press, pp. 571–650.

29. Unscheduled absence costs up. (1993, June). *HRMagazine*, p. 22.

30. Cascio, W. F. (1991). *Costing human resources: The financial impact of behavior in organizations* (3d ed.). Boston: PWS-Kent.

31. *Bulletin to management* (1993, 4th Quarter). Washington, DC: Bureau of National Affairs.

32. Unscheduled absence costs up, op. cit.

33. Macy, B. A., & Mirvis, P. H. (1983). Assessing rates and costs of individual work behaviors. In S. E. Seashore, E. E. Lawler, P. H. Mirvis, & C. Camann (eds.), *Assessing organizational change.* New York: Wiley, pp. 139–177.

34. *Bulletin to management*, op. cit.

35. Martin, D. C., & Bartol, K. M. (1985). Managing turnover strategically. *Personnel Administrator*, **30**(11), 63–73.

36. Cascio (1991), op. cit.

37. For more on this, see Cascio (1991), op. cit.

38. Solomon, J. (1988, Dec. 29). Companies try measuring cost savings from new types of corporate benefits. *The Wall Street Journal*, p. B1.

39. Ibid.

40. Ashbach, N. W. (1989, April). *The cost of turnover in the retail automobile industry.* Unpublished manuscript, Executive MBA Program, University of Colorado, Denver.

41. Cascio, W. F. (1983, August). One year's turnover costs in a major brokerage firm. In M. Quaintance, *Cost analyses of human resource interventions: Are they worth it?* Symposium conducted at the meeting of the American Psychological Association, Anaheim, CA.

42. Weekley, J., & Champagne, B. (1983). *Employee turnover costs in the Zale division.* Unpublished manuscript, Zale Corporation, Irving, TX.

43. Watson, J. (1993, Feb. 8). CEO of Skyway Express, speech to IBM employees, Denver, Co.

44. Cascio (1989), op. cit.

45. For more information see Boudreau, J. W. (1991). Utility analysis for decisions in human resource management. In M. D. Dunnette & L. M. Hough (eds.), *Handbook of industrial and organizational psychology* (vol. 2). San Francisco: Jossey-Bass, pp. 621–745. For a contrarian view, see Latham, G. P., & Whyte, G. (1994). The futility of utility analysis. *Personnel Psychology*, **47**, 31–46.

46. Mathieu, J. E., & Leonard, R. L., Jr. (1987). Applying utility concepts to a training program in supervisory skills: A time-based approach. *Academy of Mangement Journal*, **30**, 316–335.

47. Meyer, H. H., & Raich, M. S. (1983). An objective evaluation of a behavior modeling training program. *Personnel Psychology*, **36**, 755–761.

48. Ibid., p. 761.

49. Forecasting the future of the American workplace (1993, September). *American Workplace*, **1**(1), 1, 4.

50. Ibid., comments by U.S. Secretary of Labor Robert Reich.

51. Osterman, P. (1994). How common is workplace transformation, and can we explain who adopts it? *Industrial and Labor Relations Review,* **47**(2), 173–188.

52. *High performance work practices and firm performance.* (1993, August). Washington, DC: U.S. Department of Labor.

53. Terpstra, D. E., & Rozell, E. J. (1993). The relationship of staffing practices to organizational-level measures of performance. *Personnel Psychology,* **46,** 27–48.

54. Sheridan, J. E. (1992). Organizational culture and employee retention. *Academy of Management Journal,* **35,** 1036–1056.

55. Huselid, M. A. (1993, June 15). *Human resource management practices and firm performance.* Working paper, Institute of Management and Labor Relations, Rutgers University, New Brunswick, NJ.

56. Survey calculates family leave costs. (1993, January). *HRMagazine,* p. 40.

57. Gilmour, A. D. (1988). Changing times in the automotive industry. *Academy of Management Executive,* **2**(1), 23–28

58. Does survey feedback make a difference?, op. cit.

CHAPTER 18

INTERNATIONAL DIMENSIONS OF HUMAN RESOURCE MANAGEMENT

A DAY IN THE LIFE OF TOMORROW'S MANAGER*

The time is 6:10 A.M., the year is 2010, and another Monday morning has begun for Linda Smith. The marketing VP for a major U.S. appliance manufacturer is awakened by her computer alarm. She saunters to her terminal to check the weather outlook in Madrid, Spain, to which she'll fly late tonight, and to send an electronic voice message to a supplier in Thailand.

Meet the manager of the future, a different breed from her contemporary counterparts. She lives in an international business world shaped by competition, collaboration, and corporate diversity. Comfortable with technology, she's been logging on to computers since she was 7 years old. A literature honors student with a joint MBA–advanced communications degree, the 38-year-old joined her current employer 4 years ago after stints at two other corporations—one abroad—and a marketing consulting firm. Now she oversees offices in a score of countries on four continents.

Is this realistic? Absolutely, say chief executives and management consultants. Tomorrow's managers will have to know how to operate in an anytime, anyplace universe. They may land on London time and leave on Tokyo time. While managers who aren't cost-conscious and productive won't survive any better in the future than they do now, in the future they'll also have to be more flexible, more responsive, and smarter. Managers will have to be nurturers and teachers, instead of police officers and watchdogs.

---

* Adapted from C. Hymowitz, A day in the life of tomorrow's manager, *The Wall Street Journal*, Mar. 20, 1989, p. B1. Reprinted by permission of *The Wall Street Journal*, © 1989 Dow Jones & Company, Inc. All rights reserved worldwide.

7:20 A.M.: Ms. Smith and her husband, who heads his own architecture firm, organize the home front before darting to the supertrain. They leave instructions for their computer to call the housecleaning service as well as the gourmet carryout service that will prepare dinner for eight guests Saturday. And they quickly review the schedules for their two small daughters with their nanny.

On the train during a speedy 20-minute commute from suburb to city, Linda Smith checks her electronic mailbox and reads her favorite trade magazine via her laptop computer.

The jury is still out on how dual-career couples will juggle high-pressure work and personal lives. While some experts predict that the frenetic pace will only quicken, others believe that more creative uses of flexible schedules as well as technological advances in communications and travel will allow more balance. Said one expert: "In the past, nobody cared if your staff had heart attacks, but in tomorrow's knowledge-based economy we'll be judged more on how well we take care of people."

Challenges

1. What kinds of employee relations, compensation, and career management issues will Linda Smith encounter at the office?

2. Given the globalization of companies, will managers intent on rising to the top still be judged largely on how well they articulate ideas and work with others?

Questions This Chapter Will Help Managers Answer

1. What factors should I consider in "sizing up" managers, employees, and customers from a different culture?

2. What should be the components of expatriate recruitment, selection, orientation, and training strategies?

3. How should an expatriate compensation package be structured?

4. What kinds of career management issues should a manager consider before deciding to work for a foreign-owned firm in the United States?

5. What special issues deserve attention in the repatriation of overseas employees?

Increasingly, the world is becoming a "global village" as multinational investment continues to grow. All the human resource management issues that have been discussed to this point are interrelated conceptually and operationally and are particularly relevant in the international context: human resource planning, recruitment, selection, orientation, training and development, career management, compensation, and labor relations. In examining all these issues, as well as considering the special problems of repatriation (the process of reentering one's native culture after being absent from it), this chapter thus provides a capstone to the book. As usual, numerous practical examples will illustrate important issues.

THE GLOBAL CORPORATION: A FACT OF MODERN ORGANIZATIONAL LIFE

In order to maintain a leadership position in any one developed country, any business, whether large or small, increasingly has to attain and hold leadership positions in all developed markets worldwide. It has to be able to do research, to design, to develop, to engineer, to manufacture in any part of the developed world, and to export from any developed country to any other. It has to go global.[1]

The vehicle for doing this is often not an acquisition or a financial transaction but what the Germans call a "community of interest": an international alliance, a collaboration between two or more multinational companies designed to let them jointly pursue a common goal. However, alliances cover only *some* of the activities of the partners. The partners therefore maintain their individual identities and engage in other activities, separate from those of the alliance. As an example, consider the joint venture between Chrysler and Mitsubishi, called Diamond Star Corp., in Normal, Illinois. The plant, managed by Mitsubishi, produces the Plymouth Laser and the Eagle Talon for Chrysler Motors and the Eclipse for Mitsubishi.

This characteristic distinguishes an international alliance from an international merger or acquisition, in which the identities and activities of the partners are fully merged. Such alliances may take several forms, for example, joint ventures, marketing and distribution agreements, research and development partnerships, or licensing agreements.[2] In the opinion of many, such alliances are an essential component of global business strategy.[3]

One reason that leadership in any one developed market increasingly requires leadership in all is that the developed world has become one in terms of technology. All developed countries are equally capable of doing everything, doing it equally well, and doing it equally fast. All developed countries also share instant information. Companies can therefore compete just about everywhere the moment that economic conditions give them a substantial price advantage. In an age of sharp and violent currency fluctuations, this means that a leader must be able to innovate, to produce, and to market in every area of the developed world—or else be defenseless against foreign competition should currency exchange rates shift sharply.[4] Besides, when customers vote with their pocketbooks, they leave the trappings of nationalism behind.[5]

Signs of Globalization

In this emerging economic order, foreign investment by the world's leading corporations is a fact of modern organizational life. Today foreign investment is viewed not just as an opportunity for U.S. companies investing abroad but also as an opportunity for other countries to develop subsidiaries in the United States and elsewhere. Indeed, a single marketplace has been created by factors such as the following:[6]

- Global telecommunications enhanced by fiber optics, satellites, and computer technology[7]
- Giant multinational corporations such as Gillette, Unilever, and Nestlé, which have begun to lose their national identities as they integrate and coordinate product design, manufacturing, sales, and services on a worldwide basis
- Growing free trade among nations (exemplified by the 1993 North American Free Trade Agreement among Mexico, the United States, and Canada)
- Financial markets' being open 24 hours a day around the world
- Foreign investment in the United States, which now exceeds $2 trillion
- Foreign control of more than 12 percent of U.S. manufacturing assets and employment of 3 million U.S. workers[8]

■ The emergence of global standards and regulations for trade, commerce, finance, products and services

Before proceeding further, let's define some terms that will be used throughout the chapter:

■ A *global corporation* is one that has become an "insider" in any market or nation where it operates and is thus competitive with domestic firms operating in local markets.[9] Unlike domestic firms, however, the global corporation has a global strategic perspective and claims its legitimacy from its effective use of assets to serve its far-flung customers.

■ An *expatriate* or *foreign-service employee* is a generic term applied to anyone working outside her or his home country with a planned return to that or a third country.

■ *Home country* is the expatriate's country of residence.

■ *Host country* is the country in which the expatriate is working.

■ A *third-country national* is an expatriate who has transferred to an additional country while working abroad. A German working for a U.S. firm in Spain is a third-country national.

One of the most important determinants of a company's success in an international venture is *the quality of its executives*. In the words of one international executive: "Virtually any type of international problem, in the final analysis, is either created by people or must be solved by people. Hence, having the right people in the right place at the right time emerges as the key to a company's international growth. If we are successful in solving that problem, I am confident we can cope with all others."[10]

Globalization as a Growth Strategy

Consider these startling facts:

■ Over 100,000 U.S. companies are engaged in global ventures, valued at over $1 trillion. U.S. corporations have invested more than $400 billion abroad and employ more than 60 million overseas workers.[11]

■ One-third of U.S. profits come from international business, and one-sixth of the nation's jobs are created by foreign trade.[12]

■ McDonald's operates almost 14,000 restaurants in 70 countries and added 900 new restaurants in 1993 alone.

■ Gillette holds 60 percent of the U.S. razor-blade market, but more than 75 percent of its employees work outside the United States. In 1992, it entered into joint ventures with razor-blade companies in Russia, Poland, and China, and it is rolling out its Braun and Oral-B products in eastern Europe and Asia.[13]

■ Foreigners hold top management positions in one-third of large U.S. firms and one-fourth of European-based firms. They are even more conspicuous in third-world, developing countries.

It should be clear by now that today's world economy is governed by an entirely new set of rules and that to compete effectively firms must abandon such outdated assumptions and behaviors as these:

- Believing that there is "one best way" to approach all problems or that for each problem there is only "one best answer"

- Attending only to immediate short-term problems and issues, focusing on details, seeing only the parts and not the whole, ignoring the long term, failing to put problems into a context, and losing sight of the objectives of the overall organization and the economy as a whole

- Failing to be aware of the implicit and unstated assumptions that have guided individual behavior and organizational policies in the past and failing to change them when they are no longer appropriate in the current environment[14]

To take an example of the "one best way" approach, many U.S. executives were surprised to find out how well Japanese ways worked at Nissan's car and truck plant in Smyrna, Tennessee. The plant features Japanese-style quality controls (small work groups with a big say in problem solving, job rotation every 2 hours, and statistical quality control techniques), just-in-time delivery of parts, and widespread use of industrial robots. Painting is done with West German technology, using robots from Norway. Fiber-optic communications, developed by U.S. aerospace firms, monitor 3000 points in the paint process. The result? After producing 500,000 vehicles, the plant showed two things: (1) U.S. workers are just as productive and skilled as the Japanese, and (2) the plant is one of the most efficient, highest-quality plants in the world.[15]

In the 1980s, as the United States lost market share and jobs in important industries like steel, autos, and electronics, both labor and management in many firms grudgingly acknowledged that they had to change, that they could not continue doing business as usual. They had to "reach out" to the broader world at large. Thus, as we saw in Chapter 13, many ideas for managing the General Motors Saturn plant were borrowed from around the world as a result of plant visits by the Group of 99, a team of Saturn workers who traveled 2 million miles to visit some 160 pioneering enterprises, including Hewlett-Packard, McDonald's, Volvo, Kawasaki, and Nissan.[16] As is well known, all these firms have operations in many countries around the globe. It is also well known that when expatriates staff overseas operations, costs can be astronomical.

The Costs of Overseas Executives

One of the first lessons global corporations learn is that it is far cheaper to hire competent host-country nationals (if they are available) than to send their own executives overseas, for foreign-service employees typically cost *2 to 3 times* their annual home-country salaries.[17] Table 18-1 illustrates some of these costs.

In 1993, the cost of maintaining an executive in western Europe averaged two to three times base salary because of such added costs as a housing allowance and tuition for children's private school. It was even steeper in Japan, where cost-of-living adjust-

■ **TABLE 18 ▪ 1**

TYPICAL U.S. EXPATRIATE COMPENSATION PACKAGE (ANNUAL EXPENSE):
MARRIED WITH ONE CHILD

Category	U.S. compensation	Overseas compensation
Base salary	$85,000	$85,000
Overseas incentive		15%
Hardship		10%
Housing differential		35%
Furniture		12%
Utilities differential		20%
Car and driver		15%
Cost-of-living adjustment		40%
Club membership		2%
Education		12%
Total	$85,000	$221,850
U.S. tax	24,000	24,000
Net annual compensation	$61,000	$197,850

Note: A complete expatriate package also includes the following: (1) annual transportation to the United States for home leave, (2) storage of U.S. household goods, (3) shipment of some goods to the foreign location, (4) U.S. auto disposal, (5) U.S. house management, (6) interim living expenses, (7) travel to new assignment and return, and (8) annual tax equalization

ments sometimes equal 80 percent of base salaries and where employers must subsidize a visiting executive's rent, which typically costs $11,000 a month for a modest house in a Tokyo suburb. Altogether, General Motors typically spends $750,000 to $1 million on an executive and his or her family during a 3-year stint abroad.[18]

Even for executives who do not relocate overseas, daily allowances are high. For example, in 1993, daily living costs (hotel, meals, and incidentals) were $575 in Tokyo, $484 in Buenos Aires, $436 in Hong Kong, $407 in London, $250 in Toronto, and $237 in Sydney.[19] Of course, these costs fluctuate with international exchange rates relative to the U.S. dollar. On top of the high costs, there is a high failure rate among overseas personnel—between 16 and 40 percent of all Americans sent overseas.[20] For all levels of employees, the costs of mistaken expatriation include the costs of initial recruitment, relocation expenses, premium compensation, repatriation costs (i.e., costs associated with resettling the expatriate), replacement costs, and the tangible costs of poor job performance. When an overseas assignment does not work out, it *still* costs a company, on average, twice the employee's base salary.

Although the costs of expatriates are considerable, there are also compensating benefits to multinational firms. In particular, overseas postings allow managers to develop international experience outside their home countries—the kind of experience needed to compete successfully in the global economy that we now live in.

Nevertheless, it is senseless to send people abroad who do not know what they are doing overseas and cannot be effective in the foreign culture. As the manager of international human resources at Hewlett-Packard remarked: "When you are sending someone abroad to work on an important agreement, it is terribly important that they have as much information as possible about how to do business in that country. The cost of training is inconsequential compared to the risk of sending inexperienced or untrained people."[21]

For all these reasons, companies need to consider the impact of culture on international human resource management. But what is culture? *Culture* refers to characteristic ways of doing things and behaving that people in a given country or region have evolved over time. It helps people to make sense of their part of the world and provides them with an identity. Thus their part of the world is foreign only to strangers, not to those who live there.

THE ROLE OF CULTURAL UNDERSTANDING IN INTERNATIONAL MANAGEMENT PRACTICE

Managers who have no appreciation for cultural differences have a *local* perspective. They believe in the inherent superiority of their own group and culture, and they tend to look down on those considered "foreign." Rather than accepting differences as legitimate, they view and measure alien cultures in terms of their own.

By contrast, *cosmopolitan* managers are sensitive to cultural differences, respect the distinctive practices of others, and make allowances for such factors when communicating with representatives of different cultural groups. Recognizing that culture and behavior are relative, they are more tentative and less absolute in their interactions with others.[22]

Such cultural understanding can minimize "culture shock" and allow managers to be more effective with both employees and customers. The first step in this process is increasing one's general awareness of differences across cultures, for they deeply affect human resource management practices.

HUMAN RESOURCE MANAGEMENT PRACTICES AS A CULTURAL VARIABLE

Particularly when business does not go well, Americans returning from overseas assignments tend to blame the local people, calling them irresponsible, unmotivated, or downright dishonest. Such judgments are pointless, for many of the problems are a matter of fundamental cultural differences that profoundly affect how different people view the world and operate in business. This section presents a systematic framework, 10 broad classifications, that will help managers assess any culture and examine its people systematically. It does not consider every aspect of culture, and by no means is it the only way to analyze culture. Rather, it is a useful beginning for cultural understanding. The framework is comprised of the following 10 factors.[23]

- Sense of self and space
- Dress and appearance
- Food and eating habits
- Communication: verbal and nonverbal
- Time and time sense
- Relationships
- Values and norms
- Beliefs and attitudes
- Work motivation and practices
- Mental processes and learning

Sense of Self and Space

Self-identity may be manifested by a humble bearing in some places, by macho behavior in others. Some countries (e.g., the United States) may promote independence and creativity, while others (e.g., Japan) emphasize group cooperation and conformity. Americans have a sense of space that requires more distance between people, while Latins and Vietnamese prefer to get much closer. Each culture has its own unique ways of doing things.

Dress and Appearance

This includes outward garments as well as body decorations. Many cultures wear distinctive clothing—the Japanese kimono, the Indian turban, the Polynesian sarong, the "organization-man-or-woman" look of business, and uniforms that distinguish wearers from everybody else. Cosmetics are more popular and accepted in some cultures than in others, as is cologne or after-shave lotion for men.

Food and Eating Habits

The manner in which food is selected, prepared, presented, and eaten often differs by culture. Most major cities have restaurants that specialize in the distinctive cuisine of various cultures—everything from Afghan to Zambian. Utensils also differ, ranging from bare hands to chopsticks to full sets of cutlery. Knowledge of food and eating habits often provides insights into customs and culture.

Communication: Verbal and Nonverbal

The axiom "Words mean different things to different people" is especially true in cross-cultural communication. When an American says she is "tabling" a proposition, it is generally accepted that it will be put off. In England, "tabling" means to discuss something now. Translations from one language to another can generate even more confusion as a result of differences in style and context. Coca-Cola found this out when it began marketing its soft-drink products in China.

The traditional Coca-Cola trademark took on an unintended translation when shopkeepers added their own calligraphy to the company name. "Coca-Cola," pronounced "ke kou ke la" in one Chinese dialect, translates as "bite the wax tadpole." Reshuffling the pronunciation to "ko kou ko le" roughly translates to "may the mouth rejoice."[24]

In many cultures, directness and openness are not appreciated. An open person may be seen as weak and untrustworthy, and directness can be interpreted as abrupt, hostile behavior. Providing specific details may be seen as insulting to one's intelligence. Insisting on a written contract may suggest that a person's word is not good.

Nonverbal cues may also mean different things. In the United States, one who does not look someone in the eye arouses suspicion and is called "shifty-eyed." In some other countries, however, looking someone in the eye is perceived as aggression.[25] Just as communication skills are key ingredients for success in U.S. business, such skills are basic to success in international business. There is no compromise on this issue; ignorance of local customs and communications protocol is a high-risk strategy.

Time and Time Sense

To Americans, time is money. We live by schedules, deadlines, and agendas; we hate to be kept waiting, and we like to "get down to business" quickly. In many countries, however, people simply will not be rushed. They arrive late for appointments, and business is preceded by hours of social rapport. People in a rush are thought to be arrogant and untrustworthy.

In the United States, the most important issues are generally discussed first when making a business deal. In Ethiopia, however, the most important things are taken up last. While being late seems to be the norm for business meetings in Latin America, the reverse is true in Sweden, where prompt efficiency is the watchword.[26] The lesson for Americans doing business overseas is clear: *Be flexible about time and realistic about what can be accomplished.* Adapt to the process of doing business in any particular country.

Relationships

Cultures designate human and organizational relationships by age, gender, status, and family relationships, as well as by wealth, power, and wisdom.[27] Relationships between and among people vary by category—in some cultures the elderly are honored; in others they are ignored. In some cultures women must wear veils and act deferentially; in others the female is considered the equal, if not the superior, of the male.

In some cultures (e.g., Japan, Korea, and to some extent the United States and Great Britain), *where* one went to school may affect one's status. Often, lifelong relationships are established among individuals who attended the same school. In other cultures (e.g., Switzerland), one's rank in the military may affect one's job level and prospects for promotion. Finally, the issue of nepotism is viewed very differently in different parts of the world. While most U.S. firms frown upon the practice of hiring or contracting work directly with family members, in Latin America or Arab countries, it only makes sense to hire someone you can trust.[28]

Values and Norms

From its value system, a culture sets norms of behavior, or what some call "local customs." International managers ignore them at their peril.[29] For example, consider the impact of values and norms on negotiating styles.

COMPANY EXAMPLE

BARGAINING WITH THE JAPANESE[30]

The knot tightens in the Western businessman's stomach as he peers glumly at the Japanese negotiating team across the table. The executive's flight leaves early tomorrow. His home office has been pressing him to complete a deal quickly. But although the talks have dragged on for days, the key issues have barely been discussed. "What is this?" the frustrated businessman wonders. "Don't these people know that time is money?"

Such questions arise frequently when Western executives confront the Japanese. Foreigners eager to do business must often endure endless rounds of what seem to be aimless talks, dinners, and drinks. Still, they have little choice but to put up with the ceremony if they hope to gain access to Japan's vast domestic market.

The exotic set of rituals seen during negotiations is the face Japan presents to the world of business. Japanese negotiators are exquisitely polite and agonizingly vague, yet at the same time they are determined to win the best possible deal. Perhaps the most striking feature of this system of bargaining is the huge amount of time it consumes. One Australian attorney offers the following rule of thumb: *Allow five times as long as usual when doing business in Japan.*

Japanese companies negotiate slowly because everyone from junior management to major shareholders must approve a deal, in keeping with the national tradition of consensus. Startled Western executives may therefore find themselves confronting negotiating teams of 10 to 15 Japanese. Moreover, this may be only the beginning. The faces can change from session to session as new experts are added for different topics.

The Japanese are usually minutely well informed about their prospective partners. Said one former official of British Leyland who worked on a joint agreement with Honda, "The Japanese negotiators seemed to know more about our labor and managerial problems than we did."

At first the Japanese seem to have remarkably little interest in the business at hand. Their conversation is likely to dwell at length on social and family concerns rather than on products and prices. They stress personal relations because they are interested in the long-term implications of an agreement. Western executives, on the other hand, may tend to look more at the shorter term. Said one expert, "The American feeling is that it's the horse buyer's fault if he fails to ask whether a horse is blind; . . . for the Japanese, however, a deal is more of a discussion of where mutual interests lie."[31]

GUIDELINES FOR NEGOTIATING WITH THE JAPANESE

Experts on Japanese business methods offer the following guidelines for foreign negotiators:[32]

1. Before sending a woman to take part in formal talks, be sure she understands that while foreign women will generally be accepted by their male counterparts in Japan, Japanese women are all but barred from the management of big companies, and the important

after-hours socializing in Japan is exclusively stag. (This situation is changing slowly,[33] and, understandably, it is difficult for U.S. professional women to accept.)

2. Do not send anyone under age 35 to conduct negotiations. Said a U.S. manager with a high-tech firm, "You are insulting the Japanese by sending a young man to deal with a senior executive, who is likely to be 65."

3. Be wary of mistaking Japanese politeness for agreement. A Japanese negotiator may frequently nod and say "*hai*" (yes) during talks. But the word also is used to let the listener know that the conversation is being followed, as with the English "uh-huh" or "I see." In short, "yes" does not always mean "yes."

4. Japanese negotiators may confuse outsiders by lapsing into silence to mull a point. Western businesspeople may then jump into that pool of silence, much to their regret. Thus the head of a Japanese firm did nothing when a contract from International Telephone and Telegraph (ITT) was presented for his signature. The ITT manager hastily sweetened the deal by $250,000. If he had waited just a few more minutes, he would have saved the company a quarter of a million dollars.

5. Evasiveness is another characteristic of Japanese negotiators. They hate to be pinned down, and they often suppress their views out of deference to their seniors. Add to this the Japanese tendency to tell listeners what they seem to want to hear, and a foreign negotiator can easily go astray.

To be successful, a visiting executive never lets on what he is really thinking, he has unending patience, and he is unfailingly polite. In short, he acts very Japanese.

Beliefs and Attitudes

To some degree, religion expresses the philosophy of a people about important facets in life. While Western culture is largely influenced by Judeo-Christian traditions and Middle Eastern culture by Islam, Oriental and Indian cultures are dominated by Buddhism, Confucianism, Taoism, and Hinduism. In cultures where a religious view of work still prevails, work is viewed as an act of service to God and people and is expressed in a moral commitment to the job or quality of effort.[34] In Japan, the cultural loyalty to family is transferred to the work organization. It is expressed in work-group participation, communication, and consensus.[35]

T. Fujisawa, cofounder of Honda Motor Co., once remarked: "Japanese and American management is 95 percent the same, and differs in all important respects." In other words, while organizations are becoming more similar in terms of structure and technology, people's behavior within those organizations continues to reveal culturally based differences.[36]

Work Motivation and Practices

Knowledge of what motivates workers in a given culture, combined with (or based on) a knowledge of what they think matters in life, is critical to the success of the international manager. Europeans pay particular attention to *power and status*, which results in more formal management and operating styles in comparison to the *informality* found in the United States. In the United States individual *initiative and achievement* are rewarded, but in Japan managers are encouraged to seek *consensus* before acting, and employees work as teams. In one comparison of motivating factors for middle-aged Japanese and U.S. business managers, the Japanese showed more interest in advancement, money, and forward striving. Since these characteristics tend to be closely associated with success, it may be that achievement and advancement motivation are driving forces behind Japanese productivity and "team" action only their method of disciplining and rewarding it.[37] When a similar survey was conducted among German workers, 48 percent said higher income was the key motivating factor for them, followed by opportunities for promotion (25 percent) and more independence (25 percent).[38]

The determinants of work motivation may not be all that different in developing countries. In Zambia, for example, work motivation seems to be determined by six factors: the nature of the work itself, opportunities for growth and advancement, material and physical provisions (i.e., pay, benefits, job security, favorable physical work conditions), relations with others, fairness or unfairness in organizational practices, and personal problems. The effect of personal problems is totally negative. That is, *their presence impairs motivation, but their absence does not enhance it.*[39]

Mental Processes and Learning

Linguists, anthropologists, and other experts who have studied this issue have found vast differences in the ways people think and learn in different cultures. While some cultures favor abstract thinking and conceptualization, others prefer rote memory and learning. The Chinese, Japanese, and Korean written languages are based on ideograms, or "word pictures." On the other hand, English is based on precise expression using words. Western cultures stress linear thinking and logic, that is, A, then B, then C, then D. Among Arabic and Oriental cultures, however, nonlinear thinking prevails. This has direct implications for negotiation processes. That is, A may be followed by C; then back to B and on to D. Such an approach, in which issues are treated as independent and not linked by sequence, can be confusing and frustrating to Westerners because it does not appear "logical." What can we conclude from this? What seems to be universal is that each culture has a reasoning process, but each manifests the process in its own distinctive way.[40] Managers who do not understand or appreciate such differences may conclude (erroneously and to their detriment) that certain cultures are "inscrutable."

**COMPANY
EXAMPLE**

CULTURAL DIFFERENCES AMONG IBMers WORLDWIDE

Geert Hofstede, a Dutch researcher, identified four dimensions of cultural variation in values among IBM employees in 60 countries.[41] He analyzed 116,000 questionnaires completed by respondents matched by occupation, gender, and age at different time periods. The four dimensions were power distance, uncertainty avoidance, individualism, and masculinity.

Power distance refers to the extent that members of a culture accept inequality and whether they perceive much distance between those with power (e.g., top management) and those with little power (e.g., rank-and-file workers). Hofstede found the top power distance countries to be the Philippines, Mexico, and Venezuela; the bottom ones were Austria, Israel, and Denmark.

Uncertainty avoidance is reflected in an emphasis on ritual behavior, rules, and stable employment. Countries that score high on this dimension tend to be more ideological and less pragmatic than those that score low. The countries highest in uncertainty avoidance were Greece, Portugal, Belgium, and Japan; the lowest were Singapore, Denmark, Sweden, and Hong Kong. The United States is low on this dimension.

Individualism reflects the extent to which people emphasize personal or group goals. If they live in nuclear families that allow them to "do their own thing," individualism flourishes. However, if they live with extended families or tribes that control their behavior, collectivism—the essence of which is giving preference to in-group over individual goals—is more likely.[42] The most individualistic countries are the United States and the other English-speaking countries. The most collectivist countries are Venezuela, Colombia, and Pakistan.

Hofstede's fourth dimension, *masculinity,* is found in societies that differentiate very strongly by gender. Femininity is characteristic of cultures where sex-role distinctions are minimal. While the centrality of work in a person's life is greater in masculine cultures, feminine cultures emphasize quality of life and give more of their GNP to the third world. Hofstede found the most masculine cultures to be Japan, Austria, and Venezuela, while the most feminine were Sweden, Norway, and the Netherlands.

This work is valuable because it provides a set of benchmarks against which other studies can be organized conceptually. It also helps us to understand and place into perspective current theories of motivation, leadership, and organizational behavior.

Lessons Regarding Cross-Cultural Differences

There are three important lessons to be learned from this brief overview of cross-cultural differences. One, it is critically important that managers *guard against exportation of headquarters-country bias.* As we have seen, the human resource management approach that works well in the headquarters country might be totally out of step in another country. Managers who bear responsibility for international operations need to understand the cultural differences inherent in the management systems of the countries in which their firms do business. Two, *think in global terms.* We live in a world in which a worldwide allocation of physical and human resources is necessary for continued survival. Three, *recognize that no country has all the answers.* Flexible work hours, quality circles, and various innovative approaches to productivity have arisen outside the United States. Effective multinational managers must not only think in global terms but also be able to synthesize the best management approaches to deal with the complex problems at hand.

HUMAN RESOURCE MANAGEMENT ACTIVITIES OF GLOBAL CORPORATIONS

Before we consider recruitment, selection, training, and other international human resource management issues, it is important that we address a fundamental question: is this subject worthy of study in its own right? The answer is yes, for two reasons—scope and risk exposure.[43] In terms of scope, there are at least five important differences between domestic and international operations. International operations have:

1. More functions, such as taxation and coordination of dependents

2. More heterogeneous functions, such as coordination of multiple-salary currencies

3. More involvement in the employee's personal life, such as housing, health, education, and recreation

4. Different approaches to management, since the population of expatriates and locals varies

5. More complex external influences, such as from societies and governments

Heightened risk exposure is a second distinguishing characteristic of international human resource management. Companies are vulnerable to a variety of legal issues in each country, and the human and financial consequences of a mistake in the international arena are much more severe. On top of that, terrorism is now an ever-present risk for executives overseas. Indeed, it is estimated that firms spend 1 to 2 percent of their revenues on protection against terrorism.[44] This has had an important effect on how people are prepared for and moved to and from international assignment locations. In light of these considerations, it seems reasonable to ask, "Why do people accept overseas assignments?" Why do they go? As companies' global ambitions grow, fast-track executives at companies such as Gerber, Procter & Gamble, General Electric, and Dell Computer see foreign tours as necessary for career advancement. As senior executives with years of overseas experience move into top management positions at these companies, they are redefining the image of a successful U.S. executive.[45]

Japanese executives have long accepted the fact that a stint overseas is often necessary for career advancement. After all, their companies depend on exports. Fully 50 percent of Mitsubishi's $160 billion in 1993 revenues were earned abroad, and, at any one time, 1000 of the company's roughly 9800 Japanese employees are posted abroad.[46]

Organizational Structure

Businesses tend to evolve from domestic to international to multinational to global organizational structures.[47] These structures, in turn, have significant implications for the management of people within them. An *international* (or *multidomestic*) company transports its business outside of its own country although, in general, each of its operations is a replication of the company's domestic experience. Typically, an international company is structured geographically and involves subsidiary general managers. A *multinational* company, by contrast, grows and defines its business on a worldwide basis but continues to allocate its resources among national or regional areas. Companies with multiple product lines often find it difficult to remain geographically organized for a variety of reasons, such as the need to have a common accounting system, common financial and management controls, and interrelated marketing programs. As a result, such companies tend to evolve into multinational structures with combinations of product-line and solid-line responsibilities.[48]

Global organizations treat the entire world as though it were one large country. A global organization may be an entire company or one or more of its product lines. Some firms operate with a mixture of two or even three of these models of organizational structure simultaneously. The choice and combination of structure directly impact on all human resource management functions from recruitment through retirement. Thus effective HR management does not exist in a vacuum but must be integrated into the overall strategy of the organization. Indeed, from the perspective of strategic management, the fundamental problem is to keep the strategy, structure, and human resource dimensions of the organization in direct alignment.[49]

Human Resource Planning

This issue is particularly critical for firms doing business overseas, for they need to analyze both the local *and* the international external labor markets as well as their own internal labor markets in order to estimate the supply of people with the skills that will be required at some time in the future. Six other key issues in international HR planning are:[50]

1. Identifying top management potential early
2. Identifying critical success factors for future international managers
3. Providing developmental opportunities
4. Tracking and maintaining commitments to individuals in international career paths
5. Tying strategic business planning to HR planning and vice versa
6. Dealing with multiple business units while attempting to achieve globally and regionally focused (e.g., European, Asian) strategies.

In developed countries, national labor markets can usually supply the skilled technical and professional people needed. However, developing countries are characterized by severe shortages of qualified managers and skilled workers and by great surpluses of people with little or no skill, training, or education.[51] The bottom line for companies operating in developing countries is that they must be prepared to develop required skills among their own employees.

Recruitment

Broadly speaking, companies operating outside their home countries follow three basic models in the recruitment of executives: (1) They may select from the national group of the parent company only, (2) they may recruit only from within their own country and the country where the branch is located, or (3) they may adopt an international perspective and emphasize the unrestricted use of all nationalities.[52] Each of these strategies has both advantages and disadvantages.

Ethnocentrism: Home-Country Executives Only. This strategy may be appropriate during the early phases of international expansion, because firms at this stage are concerned with transplanting a part of the business that has worked in their home country. Hence, detailed knowledge of that part is crucial to success. On the other hand, a policy of ethnocentrism, of necessity, implies blocked promotional paths for local executives. And if there are many subsidiaries, home-country nationals must recognize that their foreign service may not lead to faster career progress. Finally, there are cost disadvantages to ethnocentrism as well as increased tendencies to impose the management style of the parent company.[53]

Limiting Recruitment to Home- and Host-Country Nationals. This may result from acquisition of local companies. In Japan, for instance, where the labor market is tight, most people are reluctant to switch firms. Thus use of a local partner may be extremely important. Hiring nationals has other advantages as well. It eliminates language barriers, expensive training periods, and cross-cultural adjustment problems of managers and their families. It also allows firms to take advantage of (lower) local salary levels while still paying a premium to attract high-quality employees.

Yet these advantages are not without cost. Local managers may have difficulty bridging the gap between the subsidiary and the parent company, for the business experience to which they have been exposed may not have prepared them to work as part of a global enterprise.[54] Finally, consideration of *only* home- and host-country nationals may result in the exclusion of some very able executives.

Geocentrism: Seeking the Best Person for the Job Regardless of Nationality. At first glance it may appear that this strategy is optimal and most consistent with the underlying philosophy of a global corporation. Yet there are potential problems. Such a policy can be *very* expensive, it would take a long time to implement, and it requires a great deal of centralized control over managers and their career patterns. To implement such a policy effectively, companies must make it very clear that cross-national service is important and that it will be rewarded.

Colgate-Palmolive is an example of a such a company. It has been operating internationally for more than 50 years, and its products (e.g., Colgate toothpaste, Ajax cleanser) are household names in more than 170 countries. Fully 60 percent of the company's expatriates are from countries other than the United States, and two of its last four CEOs weren't U.S. nationals. In addition, all the top executives speak at least two languages, and important meetings routinely take place all over the globe.[55] Let's now consider a very serious problem that confronts many executives offered overseas assignments.

PRACTICAL EXAMPLE

JOB AID FOR SPOUSES OF OVERSEAS EXECUTIVES

In 59 percent of all U.S. families, both the husband and the wife hold jobs. About 41 percent of employees transferred abroad have spouses who worked before relocating. At the same time, global companies are expanding into areas such as central and eastern Europe and the Middle East, where spouses of expatriates face particularly tough obstacles to finding jobs. Here is a scenario likely to become more and more common in the future. A company offers a promotion overseas to a promising executive. But the executive's spouse has a flourishing career in the United States. What should the company—and the couple—do?

Employers and employees are wrestling with this dilemma more often these days. As noted in Chapter 10, job aid for the so-called trailing spouse is already a popular benefit for domestic transfers. Now, 47 percent of employers are also providing informal or formal job help to the spouses of international transferees.[56]

HR officers may try to find a job for the spouse within the company, press a spouse's current employer for a foreign post, provide job leads through customers and suppliers, or plow through costly government red tape to get work permits. This kind of aid usually occurs in industries like banking, financial services, pharmaceuticals, and computers, all of which have significant numbers of high-level women executives.

Despite company efforts, it is often very difficult to place spouses abroad. Where there are language barriers or barriers of labor laws, tradition, or underemployment, it can be almost impossible. Certain Middle Eastern nations frown on women working or even driving. Moreover, an international assignment can slow a spouse's professional progress and sometimes stir resentment. And when both husband and wife work for the same employer, nepotism rules can interfere with the pursuit of their careers overseas because one is more likely to have to supervise the other. For example, a Citibank lending officer decided to get married just before the bank moved him to a small, 40-person office in Maracaibo, Venezuela. His wife, also a Citibank lending officer, had to go on unpaid leave.[57] Not surprisingly, many experts believe that spousal income loss will be *the* overseas compensation issue of the 1990s and the single most important factor determining an executive's decision to accept or reject an overseas position.[58]

International Staffing

There are two important guidelines in this area: (1) do not assume that a job requires the same skills from one location to another, and (2) do not underestimate the effect of the local culture and physical environment on the candidate.[59] In many cultures, tribal and family norms take precedence over technical qualifications in hiring employees. African managers often hire relatives and members of their tribes.[60] Likewise, in India, Korea, and Latin America, family connections are frequently more important than technical expertise. For an expatriate, technical competence along with other factors, such as the ability to relate well to others, may increase her or his chances of successful performance abroad.

Selection criteria for international jobs cover five areas: *personality*, *skills*, *attitudes*, *motivation*, and *behavior*.[61] Personality traits related to success include perseverance and patience (for when everything falls apart); initiative (because no one will be there to indicate what one should try next); and flexibility (to accept and to try new ways).

Highly developed technical skills, of course, are the basic rationale for selecting a person to work overseas. In addition, however, candidates should possess skills in communication (both home- and host-country languages, verbal, nonverbal, and written);[62] interpersonal relations (in developing countries, native people will simply walk off the job rather than continue to work with disagreeable outsiders), and stress management (to overcome the inevitable "culture shock"—frustration, conflict, anxiety, and feelings of alienation—that accompanies overseas assignments).

Tolerant attitudes toward people who may differ significantly in race, creed, color, values, personal habits, and customs are essential for success in overseas work. People who look down smugly on other cultures as inferior to their own simply will not make it overseas.

High motivation has long been acknowledged as a key ingredient for success in missionary work. Who, for example, can forget the zeal of the Protestant missionaries in the book *Hawaii*, by James Michener, as they set out from their native New England? While motivation is often difficult to assess reliably, firms should at the very least try to eliminate from consideration those who are only looking to get out of their own country for a change of scenery.

The last criterion is behavior—especially concern for other members of a group, tolerance for ambiguity, displays of respect, and nonjudgmental behavior. These characteristics may be determined from tests or interviews. For example, the Foreign Assignment Selection Test (FAST) appraises candidates in terms of six critical criteria: cultural flexibility, willingness to communicate, ability to develop social relationships, perceptual abilities, conflict resolution style, and leadership style. Research indicates that most of the FAST criteria are indeed related to expatriate adjustment at work and outside of work in a new cultural environment.[63]

COMPANY
EXAMPLE

INTERVIEWING POTENTIAL EXPATRIATES AT AT&T

AT&T is a new worldwide player, having experienced exponential growth in overseas markets. At the end of 1986, this U.S. giant had 50 people in 10 countries, and about 1 percent of its revenue came from outside the United States. In 1993, it had more than 52,000 overseas employees in 105 countries and earned 26 percent of its revenue abroad![64] Here are some typical questions used by AT&T to screen candidates for overseas transfers:[65]

- Would your spouse be interrupting a career to accompany you on an international assignment? If so, how do you think this will affect your spouse and your relationship with each other?
- Do you enjoy the challenge of making your own way in new situations?
- How able are you in initiating new social contacts?
- Can you imagine living without television?
- How important is it for you to spend significant amounts of time with people of your own ethnic, racial, religious, and national background?
- As you look at your personal history, can you isolate any episodes that indicate a real interest in learning about other peoples and cultures?
- Has it been your habit to vacation in foreign countries?
- Do you enjoy sampling foreign cuisines?
- What is your tolerance for waiting for repairs?

A final issue involves government regulation of staffing activities in foreign countries. In several western European countries, for example, employment offices are operated by the government, and private agencies are not permitted. And in countries such as Holland, Poland, and Sweden, prospective employees have the right to prior knowledge of psychological tests. If they so choose, they can insist that test results not be reported to an employer. In fact, in Sweden, employer, union, peers, and subordinates all participate in the entire selection process for managers—from job analysis to the hiring or promotion decision.[66] These kinds of HR practices and regulations may require global corporations to modify their human resource and industrial relations policies to operate successfully overseas.

Orientation

Orientation is particularly important in overseas assignments, both before departure and after arrival. Formalized orientation efforts—for example, elaborate audiovisual presentations for the entire family, supplemented by presentations by representatives of the country and former expatriates who have since returned to the United States— are fine, to a point. Instead of trying to convey the "truth about Tokyo," overseas orientation programs should make quite clear that employees and family members will each experience their *own* Tokyos. No matter what they may have heard or read, each of their experiences will be unique.

Some firms go further. Federal Express, for example, actually sends prospective expatriates and their families on familiarization trips to the foreign location in question. While there, they have to "live like the natives" do by taking public transportation, shopping in local stores, and visiting prospective schools and current expatriates. A recent survey found that 71 percent of firms now pay for such trips, up from 16 percent in 1985.[67]

In fact, there may be three separate phases to orientation.[68] The first is called *initial orientation*, which may last as long as 2 full days. Key components are:

- *Cultural briefing.* Traditions, history, government, economy, living conditions, clothing and housing requirements, health requirements, and visa applications. (Drugs get a lot of coverage, both for adults and for teenagers—whether they use drugs or not. Special emphasis is given to the different drug laws in foreign countries. Alcohol use also gets special attention when candidates are going to Muslim countries, such as Saudi Arabia.)
- *Assignment briefing.* Length of assignment, vacations, salary and allowances, tax consequences, and repatriation policy.
- *Relocation requirements.* Shipping, packing, or storage; and home sale, rental, or acquisition.

During this time, it is important that employees and their families understand that there is no penalty attached to changing their minds about accepting the proposed assignment. It is better to bail out early than reluctantly to accept an assignment that will be regretted later.

The second phase is *predeparture orientation*, which may last another 2 or 3 days. Its purpose is to make a more lasting impression on employees and their families and to remind them of material that may have been covered months earlier. Topics covered at this stage include:

- Introduction to the language
- Further reinforcement of important values, especially open-mindedness
- En route, emergency, and arrival information

The final aspect of overseas orientation is *arrival orientation.* Upon arrival, employees and their families should be met by assigned company sponsors. This phase of orientation usually takes place on three levels:

- *Orientation toward the environment.* Language, transportation, shopping, and other subjects that—depending on the country—may become understandable only through actual experience.
- *Orientation toward the work unit and fellow employees.* Often a supervisor or a delegate from the work unit will introduce the new employee to his or her fellow workers, discuss expectations of the job, and share his or her own initial experiences as an expatriate. The ultimate objective, of course, is to relieve the feelings of strangeness or tension that the new expatriate feels.
- *Orientation to the actual job.* This may be an extended process that focuses on cultural differences in the way a job is done. Only when this process is complete, how-

IMPACT OF GLOBAL HUMAN RESOURCE MANAGEMENT ON PRODUCTIVITY, QUALITY OF WORK LIFE, AND THE BOTTOM LINE

The impact of effective (or ineffective) recruitment, selection, orientation, training and development, compensation, and industrial relations practices is magnified when overseas assignments are involved. The *downside* risk associated with poor performance (regardless of cause) and reduced morale of subordinates is huge, given the costs (roughly 2 to 3 times annual salary) associated with sending managers abroad. On the other hand, firms such as Gillette, Colgate-Palmolive, and AT&T have found that there is potential for great gains in productivity and QWL and, consequently, bottom-line profits when the processes discussed in this chapter are implemented properly.

ever, can we begin to assess the accuracy and wisdom of the original selection decision.

Cross-Cultural Training and Development

Until June 1990, AT&T had no formal process for choosing people for international positions, or for providing training to them. This oversight resulted in a crushing 40 percent of expatriates leaving the company during or after their assignments. Subsequently, the company created an international HR department to handle selection, orientation, training, relocation, legal, and labor procedures. It also created an International Career Development Program to maximize the payoffs of overseas assignments.[69]

To survive, cope, and succeed, managers need training in three areas: the culture, the language, and practical, day-to-day matters.[70] Recent reviews of research in this area found that cross-cultural training has a positive impact on the individual's development of skills, on his or her adjustment to the cross-cultural situation, and on his or her performance in such situations.[71] These results suggest that sending a manager overseas without training is like sending David to meet Goliath without even a slingshot.

To a very great extent, expatriate failure rates can be attributed to the culture shock that usually occurs 4 to 6 months after arrival in the foreign country. The symptoms are not pleasant: homesickness, boredom, withdrawal, a need for excessive amounts of sleep, compulsive eating or drinking, irritability, exaggerated cleanliness, marital stress, family tension and conflict (involving children), hostility toward host-country nationals, loss of ability to work effectively, and physical ailments of a psychosomatic nature.[72]

To be sure, many of the common stresses of everyday living become amplified when a couple is living overseas with no support other than from a spouse. To deal with these potential problems, spouses are taught to recognize stress symptoms in each other, and they are counseled to be supportive. One exercise, for example, is for the couples periodically to list what they believe causes stress in their mates, what the other person does to relieve it, and what they themselves do to relieve it. Then they compare lists.[73] Some companies have taken a different tack to grooming global talent. Gillette, Inc., is a good example.

GILLETTE'S INTERNATIONAL TRAINEE PROGRAM[74]

Gillette competes in three major consumer businesses: personal grooming products for men and women, stationery products, and small electrical appliances. Some of its brand names include Braun, Oral-B, Liquid Paper, and Paper Mate. International markets generate approximately 70 percent of Gillette's total sales and operating profit. More than 75 percent of its employees work outside the United States, in one of the more than 200 countries and territories in which Gillette does business. Global deployment of people has created the need for individuals trained specifically to work in Gillette operations. The International Trainee Program is designed to do just that.

The company seeks top business graduates from prestigious universities internationally. In addition, trainees must be:

- Adaptable, having good social skills
- Younger than 30 years old
- Mobile and internationally career-oriented
- Single
- Fluent in English
- Enthusiastic and aggressive

Junior trainees typically work at the Gillette subsidiaries in their home countries for 6 months. After that, Gillette management may choose to transfer them to one of the firm's three international headquarters (Boston, London, or Singapore) for 18 months. Assignments usually depend on which world region their subsidiaries are part of. Current trainees come from Argentina, Brazil, China, Colombia, Egypt, Guatemala, India, Indonesia, Malaysia, Morocco, New Zealand, Pakistan, Peru, Poland, Russia, South Africa, Turkey, and Venezuela.

Upon completion of their terms, graduates return to their home countries to assume entry-level managerial positions. If they are successful, they move on to other assignments in other countries. Eventually, they end up back in their home countries as general managers or senior operating managers.

The intent of the program is not to fill short-term vacancies. Rather, the objective is to hire and develop people who want careers with global proportions. As this example shows, the global workforce is a reality now, and it will continue to be so into the twenty-first century.

Integration of Training and Business Strategy

Earlier, we noted that firms tend to evolve from domestic (exporters) to international (or multidomestic) to multinational to global. Not surprisingly, the stage of globalization of a firm influences both the type of training activities offered and their focus. Table 18-2 summarizes some key design issues that emerge at each stage of globalization.

■ **TABLE 18 ▪ 2**

TRAINING DESIGN RELATED TO STAGE OF GLOBALIZATION

Domestic (export) stage	International stage	Multinational stage	Global stage
Degree of rigor required is low to moderate.	Degree of rigor required is moderate to high.	Degree of rigor required is moderate to high.	Degree of rigor required is moderate to high.
Content emphasis is on interpersonal skills, local culture, consumer values, and behavior.	Content emphasis is on interpersonal skills, local culture, technology transfer, stress management, local business practices, and laws.	Content emphasis is on interpersonal skills, two-way technology transfer, corporate value transfer, international strategy, stress management, local culture, and business practices.	Content emphasis is on global corporate operations/systems, corporate culture transfer, multiple cultural values and business systems, international strategy, socialization tactics.
Low to moderate training of host nationals to understand home country products and policies.	Low to moderate training of host nationals; primary focus on production/service procedures.	Moderate to high training of host nationals in technical areas, product/service systems, and corporate culture.	High training of host nationals in global corporate production/efficiency systems, corporate culture, multiple cultural and business systems, and headquarters policy.

Source: J. S. Black, H. B. Gregersen, & M. E. Mendenhall, *Global assignments.* San Francisco: Jossey-Bass, 1992, p. 109.

In general, the more a firm moves away from the export stage of development, the more rigorous the training should be, and its breadth of content also increases. At the multinational and global stages, managers need to be able to socialize host-country managers into the firm's corporate culture and other firm-specific practices. This added managerial responsibility intensifies the need for rigorous training.[75]

International Compensation

Compensation policies can produce intense internal conflicts within a company at any stage of globalization. Indeed, few other areas in international human resource management demand as much top-management attention as does compensation.

The principal problem is straightforward: *Salary levels for the same job differ among countries in which a global corporation operates.* Compounding this problem is the fact that fluctuating exchange rates require constant attention in order to maintain constant salary rates in U.S. dollars.[76]

Ideally, an effective international compensation policy should meet the following objectives:

■ Attract and retain employees who are qualified for overseas service

■ Facilitate transfers between foreign affiliates and between home-country and foreign locations

■ Establish and maintain a consistent relationship between the compensation of employees of all affiliates, both at home and abroad

■ Maintain compensation that is reasonable in relation to the practices of leading competitors[77]

As firms expand into overseas markets, it is important to establish a worldwide compensation system so that cultural variables can be dealt with systematically. The following two principles have helped establish such systems in many global corporations:

The Home-Country Concept. All expatriates are tied to their respective home-country payrolls regardless of where they are working. Doing so provides, in essence, a cultural frame of reference within which to make compensation decisions. Also, it keeps the overseas employee thinking in terms of her or his home-country compensation values. This can help make repatriation less traumatic.

The Modular Approach. This approach breaks the compensation package down into its separate elements and, relative to home-country and host-country laws, modifies those elements so that the expatriate neither loses nor gains. Specific "modules" of the compensation package are therefore set up to balance out the total package. The philosophy underlying this approach is to keep the employee "whole" in terms of home-country purchasing power.[78]

In analyzing the international compensation package, there are two major components: direct salary payments (with their associated tax consequences) and indirect payments in the form of (1) benefits and (2) adjustments and incentives. Let's consider each of these.

Salaries. To be competitive, global corporations normally follow local salary patterns in each country. Is there any other alternative? A firm that tried to maintain the same salary levels in all countries would "cost itself out" of markets where lower salary levels prevail, and it would be unable to attract managers in high-salary countries. To deal with this problem, one approach is to establish base salaries relative to those of the home country (this is the *home-country concept*) and then to add to these various types of premiums (see Table 18-1). One of the most common is the *foreign-service premium*, which typically ranges from 10 to 25 percent or more of base pay.[79] Some companies offer this premium tax-free. Its purpose also varies. In firms that take a modular approach to international compensation, it represents a combination of compensation for living away from the home country plus an inducement to accept an overseas assignment. In this case, the percentage is usually low. However, in firms that intend the expatriation premium to compensate for *all* overseas problems, it is much higher.

Another adjustment usually made in international compensation is *income tax equalization* with the home country. Its objective is to ensure that when the expatriate is assigned overseas, she pays neither more nor less tax than she would have paid had she remained in her home country. There are several benefits to tax equalization. One, it reduces repatriation problems. Thus, if a U.S. employee were sent to Saudi Arabia (which has essentially no personal income tax) and allowed to keep the tax windfall, upon repatriation he or she would realize a drop in disposable income of 30 to 50 percent!

Two, tax equalization makes it easier to motivate employees to move from low-tax countries (such as Saudi Arabia) to high-tax countries (such as Sweden). Third, if a majority of employees sent on global assignments originate from high-tax countries, the firm often receives a net benefit (or cost reduction) due to differential tax rates.[80]

Benefits. These may vary drastically from one country to another. For example, in Europe it is common for employees to get added compensation in proportion to the number of family members or unpleasant working conditions. In Japan, a supervisor whose weekly salary is modest (by U.S. standards) may also get benefits that include family income allowances, housing or housing loans, subsidized vacations, year-end bonuses that can equal 3 months' pay, and profit sharing.[81]

Global corporations commonly handle benefits coverages in terms of the "best-of-both-worlds" benefits model. Figure 18-1 illustrates the approach. Wherever possible, the expatriate is given home-country benefits coverage. However, in areas such as disability insurance, where there may be no home-country plan, the employee may join the host-country plan.

Another benefit provided by most U.S. multinationals is the *cost-of-living allowance* (COLA). Its purpose is to provide for the difference in living costs (that is, the costs of goods, services, and currency realignments) between the home country and the host country. COLAs may include any one or more of the following components:

- *Housing allowance.*
- *Education allowance* to pay for schools, uniforms, and other educational expenses that would not have been incurred had the expatriate remained in the United States.
- *Income tax equalization allowance* (as described earlier).
- *Hardship pay*, which is usually a percentage of base pay provided as compensation for living in an area with climactic extremes, political instability, or poor living conditions.
- *Hazardous-duty pay* to compensate for living in an area where physical danger is present, such as a war zone. Such a premium can be as high as 25 percent of base pay in some Middle Eastern and African countries.[82]
- *Home leave*—commonly one trip per year for the entire family to the expatriate's home country. Hardship posts normally include more frequent travel for rest and relaxation.
- *School allowance*—as a rule, companies will pay for private schooling for the children of their expatriates.[83]

Finally, it is common practice for companies to pay for security guards in many overseas locations, such as in Middle Eastern countries, in the Philippines, and in Indonesia.

Pay Adjustments and Incentives. In the United States, adjustments in individual pay levels are based, to a great extent, on how well people do their jobs, as reflected in a performance appraisal. In most areas of the third world, however, objective measures for rating employee or managerial performance are uncommon. Social status is

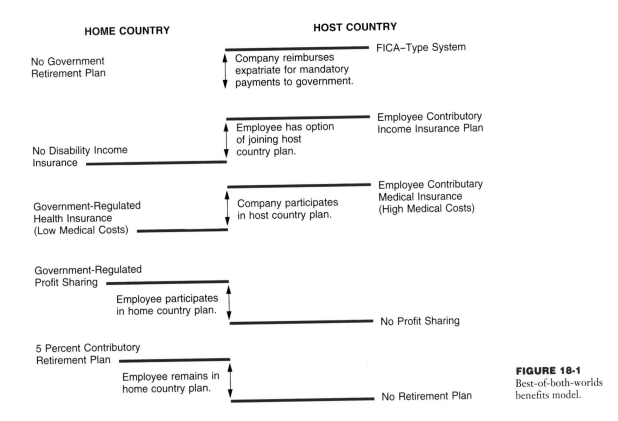

HOME COUNTRY

HOST COUNTRY

FICA–Type System

No Government
Retirement Plan

Company reimburses
expatriate for mandatory
payments to government.

Employee Contributory
Income Insurance Plan

Employee has option
of joining host
country plan.

No Disability Income
Insurance

Employee Contributary
Medical Insurance
(High Medical Costs)

Company participates
in host country plan.

Government-Regulated
Health Insurance
(Low Medical Costs)

Government-Regulated
Profit Sharing

Employee participates
in home country plan.

No Profit Sharing

5 Percent Contributory
Retirement Plan

Employee remains in
home country plan.

No Retirement Plan

FIGURE 18-1
Best-of-both-worlds
benefits model.

based on characteristics such as age, religion, ethnic origin, and social class. Pay differentials that do not reflect these characteristics will not motivate workers. For example, consider Japan. Rewards are based less on the nature of the work performed or individual competence than on seniority and personal characteristics such as age, education, or family background. A pay system based on individual job performance would not be acceptable since group performance is emphasized, and the effect of individual appraisal would be to divide the group.[84] Needless to say, exportation of U.S. performance appraisal practices to these kinds of cultures can have disastrous effects.

Despite such differences, research indicates that there are also important similarities in reward allocation practices across cultures. The most universal of these seems to be the equity norm, according to which rewards are distributed to group members based on their contributions.[85]

When implementing performance appraisal overseas, therefore, first determine the *purpose* of the appraisal. Second, whenever possible, set standards of performance against quantifiable assignments, tasks, or objectives. Third, allow more time to achieve results abroad than is customary in the domestic market. Fourth, keep the objectives flexible and responsive to potential market and environmental contingencies. Table 18-3 illustrates characteristics of performance appraisal in a Western culture (the United States), a Middle Eastern culture (Saudi Arabia), and a Far Eastern culture (Korea). Perhaps the most important lesson of this table is that a foreign man-

■ **TABLE 18 ▪ 3**

SOME CHARACTERISTICS OF PERFORMANCE APPRAISAL SYSTEMS IN THE UNITED STATES, SAUDI ARABIA, AND KOREA

Issue	United States	Saudi Arabia	Korea
Objective	Administrative decisions, employee development	Placement	Develop relationship between supervisor and employee
Done by?	Supervisor	Manager several layers up who knows employee well	Mentor and supervisor
Authority of appraiser	Presumed in supervisor role	Reputation (prestige determined by nationality, age, sex, family, tribe, title, education)	Long tenure of supervisor with organization
Style	Supervisor takes the lead, with employee input	Authority of appraiser is important; never say "I don't know"	Supervisor takes the lead, with informal employee input
Frequency	Usually once/year	Once/year	Developmental appraisal once/month for 1st year; annually thereafter
Assumptions	Objective—appraiser is fair	Subjective appraisal more important than objective; connections are important	Subjective appraisal more important than objective; no formal criteria
Feedback	Criticisms are direct, may be in writing	Criticisms more subtle; not likely to be given in writing	Criticisms subtle and indirect; may be given verbally
Employee acknowledgment and possible rebuttal	Employee acknowledges receipt; may rebut in writing	Employee acknowledges receipt; may rebut verbally	Employee does not see or sign formal appraisal; would rarely rebut
How praised	Individually	Individually	Given to entire group
Motivators	Money, upward mobility, career development	Loyalty to supervisor	Money, promotion, loyalty to supervisor

Note: Characteristics of the Saudi Arabian approach to appraisal come from P. R. Harris & R. T. Moran, *Managing cultural differences* (3d ed.). Houston: Gulf Publishing, 1990.
Source: W. F. Cascio & E. Bailey, International HRM: The state of research and practice. In O. Shenkar (ed.), *The human factor: Managing people in the global century,* New York: Macmillan, in press.

ager could be completely misled by assuming that the approach that "works" in his or her own culture will work elsewhere.[86]

More and more U.S. companies that are exploring strategic compensation approaches at home are beginning to adopt similar approaches for their senior executives worldwide. They are beginning to introduce local and regional performance criteria into these plans, and they are attempting to qualify the plans under local tax laws. Why are they doing this? In order to create stronger linkages between executives' performance and long-term business goals and strategies, to extend equity ownership to key executives (through stock options), and in many instances to provide tax benefits.[87]

MULTINATIONAL COLLECTIVE BARGAINING

Labor relations structures, laws, and practices vary considerably among countries. Unions may or may not exist. Management or government may dictate terms and conditions of employment. Labor agreements may or may not be contractual obligations. Management may conclude agreements with unions that have little or no membership in a plant or with nonunion groups that wield more bargaining power than the established unions do. And principles and issues that are relevant in one context may not be in others, for example, seniority in layoff decisions or even the concept of a layoff.[88]

In general, unions may constrain the choices of global companies in three ways: (1) by influencing wage levels to the extent that cost structures may become noncompetitive, (2) by limiting the ability of companies to vary employment levels at their own discretion, and (3) by hindering or preventing global integration of such companies (i.e., by forcing them to develop parallel operations in different countries).[89]

One of the most intriguing aspects of international labor relations is multinational collective bargaining. Unions have found global corporations particularly difficult to deal with in terms of union power and difficult to penetrate in terms of union representation.[90] Here are some of the special problems that global corporations present to unions:

1. While national unions tend to follow the development of national companies, union expansion typically cannot follow the expansion of a company across national boundaries, with the exception of Canada. Legal differences, feelings of nationalism, and differences in union structure and industrial relations practices are effective barriers to such expansion.

2. The nature of foreign investment by global corporations has changed. In the past, they tended to invest in foreign sources of raw materials. As a result, the number of processing and manufacturing jobs in the home country may actually have increased. However, in recent years there has been a shift toward the development of parallel, or nearly parallel, operations in other countries.[91] Foreign investment of this type threatens union members in the home country with loss of jobs or with a slower rate of job growth, especially if their wages are higher than those of workers in the host country. This threat is very real in Germany, for example, where labor costs in 1993 were 25 percent higher than in the United States, and 33 percent higher than in Japan.[92]

3. When a global corporation has parallel operations in other locations, the firm's ability to switch production from one location shut down by a labor dispute to another location is increased. This, of course, assumes that the same union does not repre-

sent workers at each plant or that, if different unions are involved, they do not coordinate their efforts and strike at the same time. Another assumption is that the various plants are sufficiently parallel that their products are interchangeable.

One solution to the problems that global corporations pose for union members is multinational collective bargaining. For this to work, though, coordination of efforts and the cooperation of the unions are required. What is called for is an "international union" with the centralization of authority characteristic of U.S. national unions. Yet two persistent problems stand in the way of such an international union movement:[93]

1. National and local labor leaders would have to be willing to relinquish their autonomy to an international level. This is a major stumbling block because the local union or enterprise union is essentially an autonomous organization.

2. Political and philosophical differences pose a further barrier to any international union movement. For example, a French labor leader committed to a communist form of economic organization is unlikely to yield authority willingly to an international union patterned after the United Auto Workers or any other union committed to the capitalist economic system. Conversely, the leaders of the United Auto Workers are unlikely to relinquish their autonomy to a communist international labor union.

As an example of the difficulties such cooperation poses, consider the role of labor unions in the New Europe (the 12-member European Community, which unified into a common market for goods, services, capital, and labor in 1992). To the unions the issue is clear: it's a question of jobs, pay, and standard of living. The threat to organized labor is clear, for higher unemployment has characterized the early stages of a more efficient Europe.[94] Attempts to cut back on benefits and job security have resulted in violent labor protests in Italy and massive demonstrations in Germany. In Paris, a crippling walkout by Air France employees forced the government to back down on plans to cut 4000 jobs.[95] Prospects for a unified "European union" that might negotiate with employers are weak.

Alternative Union Strategies

Since the prospects for effective multinational collective bargaining by unions are not very promising, unions must consider alternative strategies. These include:

■ Independent bargaining by unions with global corporations within each country
■ Securing legislation to protect union members' jobs within each country
■ Attempting to coordinate multinational collective bargaining

For example, in an effort to address the increasing importance of global companies in the telecommunications industry, the U.S. and Canadian unions most involved have signed an alliance promising to cooperate in organizing and bargaining efforts not only in the two countries but wherever in the world telecommunications companies operate. According to the president of the U.S. union, such companies "will have

ETHICAL DILEMMA: CROSS-NATIONAL WHIPSAWING

In an era of reduced resources, firms often have to make choices about where to produce goods. Suppose that identical products are produced in plants in two countries. Is it ethical for management to pit workers (or unions) in one country against workers (or unions) in another in an effort to extract concessions? Is there a point beyond which such "whipsawing" becomes unethical?

no place to flee. Wherever they go around the world, there will be a union waiting, and support from others."[96] Industry-specific arrangements like these may play a key role in twenty-first-century capitalism. So also will regional trading blocks.

The North American Free Trade Agreement (NAFTA)

Economic competition in the twenty-first century will consist not of scattered countries nibbling at one another but of major regions operating as economic units on the global playing field.[97] Beginning in 1994, NAFTA combines U.S., Canadian, and Mexican economic strengths, reduces or eliminates trade barriers on goods and services within the three countries, and creates a region of 370 million consumers and $6.5 trillion in output. It is North America's strategic response to the global economy. Farming, autos, consumer goods, telecommunications, financial services, textiles, and energy industries all stand to gain as North America, Inc., takes shape.[98]

In Mexico, labor, management, and the government are working together toward a common goal: world-class levels of productivity. To illustrate this, consider the recent case of Volkswagen de México.

DEALING WITH UNION DISSIDENTS AT VOLKSWAGEN DE MÉXICO[99]

COMPANY EXAMPLE

Conflict erupted when the government-controlled union at VW, based in Puebla, Mexico, agreed with management on a massive restructuring plan to raise productivity. VW management insisted the new agreement was vital for global competitiveness. This was hardly idle talk, since VW supplies the entire North American market from Puebla. Fearing layoffs, however, a group of dissidents opposed the plan. After weeks of a bitter strike, the government gave VW permission to rip up the union contract. The company promptly fired 14,000 workers and rehired all of them, minus some 300 dissidents, under a new contract. Within days, VW instituted a new HR management system; seniority as a basis for promotion is out, while training, and lots of it, is in. Workers are now promoted according to skills and performance.

Today, the most favored union leaders in Mexico preach the gospel of productivity—and it's paying off. Already Nissan de México is exporting Sentras to Canada and light trucks back to Japan, while Ford's super-efficient Hermosillo plant builds Escorts and Tracers for U.S. consumption.[100]

REPATRIATION

The problems of repatriation, for those who succeed abroad as well as for those who do not, have been well documented. *All* repatriates experience some degree of anxiety in three areas: personal finances, reacclimation to the U.S. lifestyle, and readjustment to the corporate structure.[101] They also worry about the future of their careers and the location of their U.S. assignments. Precisely the same issues were found in a study of Japanese and Finnish expatriates.[102]

Financially, repatriates face the loss of the foreign-service premium and the effect of inflation on home purchases. Having become accustomed to foreign ways, upon reentry they often find home-country customs strange and, at the extreme, annoying. Such "reverse culture shock" may be more challenging than the culture shock experienced when going overseas![103] Finally, many repatriates complain that their assignments upon return to their home country are mundane and lack status and authority in comparison to their overseas positions. Possible solutions to these problems fall into three areas: planning, career management, and compensation.

Planning

Both the expatriation assignment and the repatriation move should be examined as parts of an integrated whole—not as unrelated events in an individual's career.[104] To do this, it is necessary to define a clear strategic purpose for the move. *Prior* to the assignment, therefore, the firm should define one or more of the three primary purposes for sending a particular expatriate abroad: executive development, coordination and control between headquarters and foreign operations, and transfer of information and technology.[105] Research shows that unless there is a planned purpose in repatriation, the investment of over $1 million to send an expatriate overseas is likely to be squandered completely.

Increasingly, multinational corporations are seeking to improve their human resource planning and also to implement it on a worldwide basis. Careful inclusion of expatriation and repatriation moves in this planning will help reduce uncertainty and the fear that accompanies it.

Career Management

Firms such as 3M, IBM, Ford, and Disney appoint a "career sponsor" (usually a group vice president or higher)[106] to look out for the expatriate's career interests while she or he is abroad and to keep the expatriate abreast of company developments. The development of global electronic-mail networks certainly has made that job faster and easier than it used to be. Sponsors also must be sensitive to the "job shock" the expatriate may suffer when she or he gets back and must be trained to counsel the returning employee (and her or his family as well) until resettlement is deemed complete.[107] To accelerate this process, some firms assemble a group of former expatriates to give advice and offer insights based on their own experiences.[108]

Compensation

The loss of a monthly premium to which the expatriate has been accustomed is a severe shock financially, whatever the rationale. To overcome this problem, some firms have replaced the monthly foreign-service premium with a onetime "mobility premium" (e.g., 3 months' pay) for each move—overseas, back home, or to another overseas assignment. A few firms also provide low-cost loans or other financial assistance so that expatriates can get back into their hometown housing markets at a level at least equivalent to what they left. Finally, there is a strong need for financial counseling for repatriates. Such counseling has the psychological advantage of demonstrating to repatriates that the company is willing to help with the financial problems that they may encounter in uprooting their families once again to bring them home.[109]

A DAY IN THE LIFE OF TOMORROW'S MANAGER

8:15 A.M.: In her high-tech office that doubles as a conference room, Ms. Smith reviews the day's schedule with her executive assistant (traditional secretaries vanished a decade ago). Then it's on to her first meeting: a conference via video screen between her division's chief production manager in Cincinnati and a supplier near Munich.

While today's managers spend most of their time conferring with bosses and subordinates in their own companies, tomorrow's managers will be intimately hooked to suppliers and customers and will be well versed in competitors' strategies.

10:30 A.M.: At a staff meeting, Ms. Smith finds herself refereeing between two subordinates who disagree vehemently on how to promote a new appliance. One, an Asian manager, suggests that a fresh campaign begin much sooner than envisioned. The other, a European, wants to hold off until results from a test market are received later that week.

Linda Smith quickly recognizes that this is a cultural, not strategic, clash, pitting a let's-do-it-now, analyze-it-later approach against a more cautious style. She makes them aware that they're not really far apart, and the European manager agrees to move swiftly.

By 2010, managers will have to handle greater cultural diversity with subtle human relations skills. Managers will have to understand that employees don't think alike about such basics as handling confrontation or even what it means to do a good day's work.

12:10 P.M.: Lunch is in Ms. Smith's office today, giving her time to take a video lesson in conversational Japanese. She already speaks Spanish fluently and wants to master at least two more languages. After 20 minutes, she moves to her computer to check her company's latest political-risk assessment on Spain. Although the report indicates that the recent student unrest is not anti-American, she decides to have a bodyguard meet her at the Madrid airport anyway.

Technology will provide managers with easy access to more data than they can possibly use. The challenge will be to synthesize the data to make effective decisions.

2:20 P.M.: Two of Ms. Smith's top lieutenants complain that they and others on her staff feel that a bonus payment for a recent project wasn't divided equitably. Bluntly, they note that while Ms. Smith received a hefty $20,000 bonus, her 15-member staff had to split $5000, and they threaten to defect. Smith quickly calls her boss, who says he'll think about increasing the bonus for staff members.

With skilled technical and professional managers likely to be in short supply, tomorrow's managers will have to share more authority with their subordinates and, in some cases, pay them as much as or more than the managers themselves earn.

While yielding more to their employees, managers in their thirties in 2010 may find their own climb up the corporate ladder stalled by superiors—older baby boomers who don't want to retire. Nevertheless, despite the globalization of companies and the speed of overall change, some things will stay the same. Managers intent on rising to the top will still be judged largely on how well they articulate ideas and work with others. In addition, different corporate cultures will still encourage and reward different qualities—for example, risk taking versus caution and predictability.

6:00 P.M.: Before heading to the airport, Ms. Smith uses her videophone to give her daughters a good-night kiss and to talk about the next day's schedule with her husband. Learning that he must take an unexpected trip himself the next evening, she promises to catch the SuperConcord home in time to put the kids to sleep herself.

IMPLICATIONS FOR MANAGEMENT PRACTICE

No one has discovered a single best way to manage. But before a company can build an effective management team, it must understand thoroughly its own culture, the other cultures in which it does business, and the challenges and rewards of blending the best of each.

In the immediate future, there will certainly be international opportunities for managers at all levels, particularly those with the technical skills needed by developing countries. In the longer run, global companies will have their own cadres of "globalites," sophisticated international executives drawn from many countries, as firms like Gillette, Nestlé, and Sumitomo do now. There is a bright future for managers with the cultural flexibility to be sensitive to the values and aspirations of foreign countries.

Finally, there is one thing of which we can be certain. Talent—social, managerial, and technical—is needed to make global business work. Competent human resource management practices can find that talent, recruit it, select it, train and develop it, motivate it, reward it, and profit from it. This will be the greatest challenge of all in the years to come.

SUMMARY

Foreign investment by the world's leading corporations is a fact of modern organizational life. For executives transferred overseas, the opportunities are great, but the risks of failure are considerable. This is because there are fundamental cultural differences that affect how different people view the world and operate in business. The lesson for companies doing business overseas is clear: guard against the exportation of home-country bias, think in global terms, and recognize that no country has all the answers.

Recruitment for overseas assignments is typically based on one of three basic models: (1) ethnocentrism, (2) limiting recruitment to home- and host-country nationals, or (3) geocentrism. Selection is based on five criteria: personality, skills, attitudes, motivation, and behavior. Orientation for expatriates and their families often takes place in three stages: initial, predeparture, and postarrival. Cross-cultural training may incorporate a variety of methods and techniques, but to be most effective it should be integrated with the firm's long-range global strategy and business planning. International compensation presents special problems since salary levels differ among countries. To be competitive, firms normally follow local salary patterns in each country. Expatriates, however, receive various types of premiums (foreign service, tax equalization, and COLAs) in addition to their base salaries. Benefits are handled in terms of the best-of-both-worlds model. An overseas assignment is not complete, however, until repatriation problems have been resolved. These fall into three areas: personal finances, reacclimation to the U.S. lifestyle, and readjustment to the corporate structure. Finally, since global companies operate across national boundaries while unions typically do not, the balance of power in the multinational arena clearly rests with management.

DISCUSSION QUESTIONS

18■1 What advice would you give to a prospective expatriate regarding the application of his management style in Japan?

18■2 Discuss the special problems that women face in overseas assignments.

18■3 How can the balance of power between management and labor be restored in international labor relations?

18■4 Describe the conditions necessary in order for a geocentric recruitment policy to work effectively.

18■5 Should foreign language proficiency be required for executives assigned overseas? Why or why not?

REFERENCES

1. Drucker, P. F. (1987, Aug. 25). The transnational economy. *The Wall Street Journal*, p. 38.

2. Cascio, W. F., & Serapio, M. G., Jr. (1991, Winter). Human resources systems in an international alliance: The undoing of a done deal? *Organizational Dynamics*, pp. 63–74.

3. Wysocki, B., Jr. (1990, Mar. 26). Cross-border alliances become favorite way to crack new markets. *The Wall Street Journal*, pp. A1, A6. See also Ohmae, K. (1989, March–April). The global logic of strategic alliances. *Harvard Business Review*, pp. 143–154.

4. Drucker, op. cit.

5. Ohmae, op. cit.

6. Marquardt, M. J., & Engel. D. W. (1993). *Global human resource development*. Englewood Cliffs, NJ: Prentice-Hall.

7. Revzin, P., Waldman, P., & Gumbel, P. (1990, Feb. 1). World view: Ted Turner's CNN gains global influence and a "diplomatic" role. *The Wall Street Journal*, pp. A1, A10.

8. McWhirter, W. (1989, Oct. 9). I came, I saw, I blundered. *Time*, pp. 72, 73.

9. Ohmae, K. (1990). *The borderless world*. New York: Harper Business.

10. Dueer, M., in Greene, W. E., & Walls, G. D. (1984). Human resources: Hiring internationally. *Personnel Administrator*, **29**(7), 61.

11. Marquardt, op. cit.

12. Farney, D. (1992, Oct. 28). Turning point: Even U.S. politics are being reshaped by a global economy. *The Wall Street Journal*, pp. A1, A8.

13. Laabs, J. J. (1993, August). How Gillette grooms local talent. *Personnel Journal*, pp. 65–76.

14. Mitroff, I. I., & Mohrman, S. A. (1987). The slack is gone: How the United States lost its competitive edge in the world economy. *Academy of Management Executive*, **1**, 65–70.

15. Golden, S. B., Jr., Manager, training and organization development, Nissan Motor Manufacturing Corp. U.S.A. (1994, Feb. 19). Personal communication. See also Hillkirk, J. (1987, Oct. 28). Nissan gears up in USA. *USA Today*, p. 4B.

16. Gwynne, S. C. (1990, Oct. 29). The right stuff. *Time*, pp. 74–84.

17. The fast track leads overseas (1993, Nov. 1). *Business Week*, pp. 64–68.

18. Ibid.

19. Firms ease the reins on foreign-trip costs (1993, Oct. 18). *The Wall Street Journal*, p. B1.

20. Black, J. S., Mendenhall, M., & Oddou, G. (1991). Toward a comprehensive model of international adjustment: An integration of multiple theoretical perspectives. *Academy of Management Review*, **16**, 291–317.

21. Copeland, L. (1984). Making costs count in international travel. *Personnel Administrator*, **29**(7), 47.

22. Hesketh, B., & Bochner, S. (1994). Technological change in a multicultural context: Implications for training and career planning. In H. C. Triandis, M. D. Dunnette, & L. M. Hough (eds.), *Handbook of industrial and organizational psychology*, vol. 4. Palo Alto, CA: Consulting Psychologists Press, pp. 191–240.

23. Harris, P. R., & Moran, R. T. (1990). *Managing cultural differences* (3d ed.). Houston: Gulf Publishing.

24. Ricks, D. A. (1993). *Blunders in international business*. Oxford, England: Blackwell.

25. Copeland, op. cit.

26. Thorsberg, F. (1984, June 17). Culture gap hurts American workers overseas. *Honolulu Star Bulletin & Advertiser*, p. B5.

27. Harris & Moran, op. cit.

28. Copeland, op. cit.

29. Ralston, D. A., Gustafson, D. J., Elsass, P. M., Cheung, F., & Terpstra, R. H. (1992). Eastern values: A comparison of managers in the United States, Hong Kong, and the People's Republic of China. *Journal of Applied Psychology*, **77**, 664–671.

30. Negotiation waltz (1983, Aug. 1). *Time*, pp. 41–42.

31. Ibid., p. 42.

32. Ibid. See also Moran, R. T. (1985). *Getting your yen's worth: How to negotiate with Japan, Inc.* Houston: Gulf Publishing.

33. Japan: Women changing at work (1993, Dec. 10). *The Denver Post*, p. 28A.

34. Ibrahim, Y. M. (1994, Feb. 3). Fundamentalists impose culture on Egypt. *The New York Times*, pp. A1, A10.

35. Harris & Moran, op. cit.

36. Adler, N. J., Doktor, R., & Redding, S. G. (1986). From the Atlantic to the Pacific century: Cross-cultural management reviewed. *Journal of Management*, **12**, 295–318.

37. Howard, A., Shudo, K., & Umeshima, M. (1983). Motivation and values among Japanese and American managers. *Personnel Psychology*, **36**(4), 883–898.

38. Employee motivation in Germany (1989, March). *Manpower Argus*, no. 246, p. 6.

39. Machungwa, P. D., & Schmitt, N. (1983). Work motivation in a developing country. *Journal of Applied Psychology*, **68**(1), 31–42.

40. Harris & Moran, op. cit.

41. Hofstede, G. (1991). *Cultures and organizations*. London: McGraw-Hill. See also Hofstede, G. (1980). *Culture's consequences*. Beverly Hills, CA: Sage.

42. Triandis, H. C. (1994). Cross-cultural industrial and organizational psychology. In H. C. Triandis, M. D. Dunnette, & L. M. Hough (eds.), *Handbook of industrial and organizational psychology*, vol. 4. Palo Alto, CA: Consulting Psychologists Press, pp. 103–172.

43. Schuler, R. S., Dowling, P. J., & De Cieri, H. (1993). An integrative framework of strategic international human resource management. *Journal of Management*, **19**(2), 419–459. See also Morgan, P. V. (1986). International HRM: Fact or fiction? *Personnel Administrator*, **31**(9), 43–47.

44. Dowling, P. J., & Schuler, R. S. (1990). *International dimensions of human resource management*. Boston: PWS-Kent.

45. The fast track leads overseas, op. cit. See also Lublin, J. S. (1992, Dec. 9). Firms ship unit headquarters abroad. *The Wall Street Journal*, pp. B1, B8.

46. Why Japan's execs travel better (1993, Nov. 1). *Business Week*, p. 68.

47. Adler, N. J. (1992). Managing globally competent people. *Academy of Management Executive*, **6**(3), 52–65. See also Zeien, A. (1991, 4th Quarter). International, multinational, and/or global? *Prism*, pp. 85–88.

48. Zeien, op cit.

49. Schuler, Dowling & De Cieri, op. cit. See also Bartlett, C. A. (1986). Building and managing the transnational: The new organizational challenge. In M. E. Porter (ed.), *Competition in global industries*. Boston: Harvard Business School Press, pp. 367–404.

50. Cascio, W. F. (1993). International human resource management issues for the 1990s. *Asia-Pacific Journal of Human Resource Management*, **30**(4), 1–18. See also Dowling & Schuler, op. cit.

51. Marquardt & Engel, op. cit. See also Safavi, F. (1981). A model of management education in Africa. *Academy of Management Review*, **6**(2), 319–331.

52. Shahzad, N. (1984). The American expatriate manager. *Personnel Administrator*, **29**(7), 23–30.

53. Greene & Walls, op. cit.

54. Solomon, C. M. (1994, January). Staff selection impacts global success. *Personnel Journal*, pp. 88–101.

55. Ibid.

56. Lublin, J. S. (1992, Aug. 19). Spouses find themselves worlds apart as global commuter marriages increase. *The Wall Street Journal*, pp. B1, B4.

57. Lublin, J. S. (1984, Jan. 26). More spouses receive help in job searches when executives take positions overseas. *The Wall Street Journal*, p. 29.

58. Adkins, L. (1990, October–November). Innocents abroad? *World Trade*, pp. 70–76. See also Overman, S. (1989, October). Shaping the global workplace. *Personnel Administrator*, pp. 41–44, 101.

59. Black, J. S., Gregersen, H. B., & Mendenhall, M. E. (1992). *Global assignments*. San Francisco: Jossey-Bass.

60. Marquardt & Engel, op. cit. See also Safavi, op. cit.

61. Cascio, W. F. (1991, September). *International assessment and the globalization of business: Riddle or recipe for success?* Keynote address prepared for the National Assessment Conference, Minneapolis, MN.

62. Ronen, S. (1989). Training the international assignee. In I. L. Goldstein (ed.), *Training and development in organizations*. San Francisco: Jossey-Bass, pp. 418–453.

63. Black, J. S. (1990). Personal dimensions and work-role transitions: A study of Japanese expatriate managers in America. *Management International Review*, **30**(2), 119–134.

64. Solomon, op. cit.

65. Fuchsberg, G. (1992, Jan. 9). As costs of overseas assignments climb, firms select expatriates more carefully. *The Wall Street Journal*, pp. B1, B5.

66. Lévy-Leboyer, C. (1994). Selection and assessment in Europe. In H. C. Triandis, M. D. Dunnette, & L. M. Hough (eds.), *Handbook of industrial and organizational psychology*, vol. 4. Palo Alto, CA: Consulting Psychologists Press, pp 173–190.

67. Odds and ends (1992, Nov. 11). *The Wall Street Journal*, p. B1.

68. Black, Gregersen & Mendenhall, op. cit. See also Solomon, op. cit. See also Conway, M. A. (1984). Reducing expatriate failure rates. *Personnel Administrator*, **29**(7), 31–38.

69. Solomon, op. cit.

70. Dowling & Schuler, op. cit.

71. Harrison, J. K. (1992). Individual and combined effects of behavior modeling and the cultural assimilator in cross-cultural management training. *Journal of Applied Psychology*, **77**, 952–962. See also Black, J. S., & Mendenhall, M. (1990). Cross-cultural training effectiveness: A review and a theoretical framework for future research. *Academy of Management Review*, **15**, 113–136.

72. Linowes, R. G. (1993). The Japanese manager's traumatic entry into the United States: Understanding the American-Japanese cultural divide. *Academy of Management Executive*, **7**(4), 21–40. See also Black, Gregersen, & Mendenhall, op. cit.

73. Chronis, P. G. (1983, Feb. 6). They're learning how to live overseas . . . in Boulder. *Denver Post*, pp. 1C, 8–9C.

74. Laabs, op. cit.

75. Black, Gregersen, & Mendenhall, op. cit.

76. Capdevielle, P. (1989). International comparisons of hourly compensation costs. *Monthly Labor Review*, **112**(6), 10–12.

77. Greene & Walls, op. cit.

78. Black, Gregersen, & Mendenhall, op. cit.

79. Ibid. See also Adkins, op. cit.

80. Black, Gregersen, & Mendenhall, op. cit.

81. Greene & Walls, op. cit.

82. U.S. Department of Labor (1993, July). *U.S. Department of State indexes of living costs abroad, quarters allowances, and hardship differentials*. Washington, DC: U.S. Government Printing Office.

83. Black, Gregersen, & Mendenhall, op. cit. See also Adkins, op. cit.

84. Sekimoto, M. (1983). Performance appraisal in Japan, past and future. *The Industrial/ Organizational Psychologist*, **20**(4), 52–58.

85. Kim, K. I., Park, H. J., & Suzuki, N. (1990). Reward allocations in the United States, Japan, and Korea: A comparison of individualistic and collectivistic cultures. *Academy of Management Journal*, **33**, 188–198.

86. Cascio, W. F., & Bailey, E. (in press). International HRM: The state of research and practice. In O. Shenkar (ed.), *The human factor: Managing people in the global century*. New York: Macmillan.

87. Ibid. See also Brooks, B. J. (1988). Long-term incentives: International executives need them too. *Personnel*, **65**(8), 40–42.

88. Gaugler, E. (1988). HR management: An international comparison. *Personnel*, **65**(8), 24–30. See also Kujawa, D. (1982). International labor relations. In I. Walter & T. Murray (eds.), *Handbook of international business*. New York: Wiley.

89. Dowling & Schuler, op. cit.

90. Mills, D. Q. (1994). *Labor-management relations* (5th ed.). New York: McGraw-Hill. See also Levine, M. J. (1988). Labor movements and the multinational corporation: A future for collective bargaining? *Employee Relations Law Journal*, **13**, 382–403.

91. Sera, K. (1992). Corporate globalization: A new trend. *Academy of Management Executive*, **6**(1), 89–96.

92. Time to leave the cocoon? (1993, Oct. 18). *Business Week*, pp. 46, 47.

93. Levine, op. cit.

94. Europe's economic agony (1993, Feb. 15). *Business Week*, pp. 48, 49.

95. Farewell to welfare (1993, Nov. 22). *Time*, pp. 51, 52.

96. Ibid. See also Union effort to deal with transnational firms (1990, June 12). *Daily Labor Report*, No. 113, p. A6.

97. Bradley, B. (1993, Sept. 16). NAFTA opens more than a trade door. *The Wall Street Journal*, p. A14.

98. Border crossings (1993, Nov. 22). *Business Week*, pp. 40–42.

99. The Mexican worker (1993, Apr. 19). *Business Week*, pp. 84–92.

100. Border crossings, op. cit.

101. Black, J. S., & Gregersen, H. B. (1991). When Yankee comes home: Factors related to expatriate and spouse repatriation adjustment. *Journal of International Business Studies*, **22**(4), 671–695. See also Clague, L., & Krupp, N. B. (1978). International personnel: The repatriation problem. *Personnel Administrator*, **23**(4), 29–33, 45.

102. Black, Gregersen, & Mendenhall, op. cit.
103. Gregersen, H. B. (1992). Commitments to a parent company and a local work unit during repatriation. *Personnel Psychology,* **45,** 29–54.
104. Clague & Krupp, op. cit.
105. Black, Gregersen, & Mendenhall, op. cit.
106. Taking steps can cut risk of rocky return from overseas stint (1993, Aug. 25). *The Wall Street Journal,* p. B1.
107. Ibid. See also Black, Gregersen, & Mendenhall, op. cit.
108. Savich, R. S., & Rodgers, W. (1988). Assignment overseas: Easing the transition before and after. *Personnel,* **65**(8), 44–48.
109. Clague & Krupp, op. cit.

CREDITS

ILLUSTRATION CREDITS

Books. **Fig. 17-1:** J. C. Quick & J. D. Quick, *Organizational stress and preventative management*, McGraw-Hill, 1984. B. A. Macy & P. H. Mirvis, "Organizational change efforts: Methodologies for assessing organization effectiveness and program costs versus benefits," *Evaluation Review*, **6**(3), 1982. Copyright © 1982 by Sage Publications, Inc. Reprinted by permission. **Fig. 17-3:** H. H. Meyer & M. S. Raich, "An objective evaluation of a behavior modeling training program," *Personnel Psychology*, **36**, 1983. Used by permission of the publisher. **Fig. 17-4:** J. E. Sheridan, "Organizational culture and employee retention," *Academy of Management Journal*, **35** (1992). Used by permission of the publisher. **Table 17-1:** B. A. Macy & P. H. Mirvis, "Direct and indirect costs associated with mismanaged stress," *Evaluation Review*, **6**(3), Fig. 4-5. Copyright © 1982 by Sage Publications, Inc. Reprinted by permission of Sage Publications, Inc. **Fig. 18-1:** D. M. Noer, *Multinational people management*, The Bureau of National Affairs, Inc., Washington, DC, 1975. **Table 18-2:** J. Stewart Black, Hal B. Gegersen, & Mark E. Mendenhall, *Global assignments: Successfully expatriating and repatriating international managers*, Table 4.2. Copyright © 1992 by Jossey-Bass, Inc., Publishers. Code 9271. Used by permission. **Table 18-3:** W. F. Cascio & E. Bailey, "International HRM: The state of research and practice." In O. Shenkar (ed.), *The human factor: Managing people in the global century* (Englewood Cliffs, NJ: Prentice-Hall), in press. Used by permission of the publisher.

TEXT CREDITS

45–47 (Company Examples: Using Human Resources for Competitive Advantage at Federal Express and United Parcel Service): Adapted from P. Cappelli & A. Crocker-Hefter, *Distinctive human resources are the core competencies of firms* (Philadelphia: National Center on the Educational Quality of the Workforce, Working Paper WP18), 1993. **69–70** (Company Example: Commitment to Diversity at Xerox): Adapted from V. J. Sessa, "Managing diversity at the Xerox Corporation: Balanced workforce goals and caucus groups." In S. E. Jackson (ed.), *Diversity in the workplace*, Chap. 3 (New York: Guilford), 1992. Used by permission. **71–72** (Company Example: Management Diversity at Pacific Bell): Adapted from L. Roberson & N. Gutierrez, "Beyond good faith: Commitment to recruiting management diversity at Pacific Bell." In S. E. Jackson (ed.), *Diversity in the workplace*, Chap. 4 (New York: Guilford), 1992. Used by permission. **151–153** (Company Example: Succession Planning in the Ministry of Transportation and Communications, Province of Ontario): Used by permission. **157–158** (Company Example: Managing the Merger between Harris Semiconductor and General Electric Solid State): Adapted from D. M. Schweiger, J. R. Ridley, Jr., & D. M. Marini, "Creating one from two: The merger between Harris Semiconductor and General Electronic Solid State." In S. E. Jackson (ed.), *Diversity in the workplace* (New York: Guilford), 1992. Used by permission. **176** (Company Example: How Bristol-Myers Squibb Uses Computer Technology to Find Top MBA Students): Adapted from J. Koch, "Desktop recruiting," *Recruitment Today*, **3** (Winter 1990). Used by permission. **203–204** (Company Example: Performance Factors Inc.): "A video game that tells if employees are fit for work," *Business Week*, June 3, 1991. Reprinted from June 3, 1991 issue of Business Week by special permission, copyright © 1991 by McGraw-Hill, Inc. **220–221** (International Application: The Japanese Approach to Personnel Selection): Adapted from R. Koenig, "Exacting employer: Toyota takes pains, and time, filling jobs at its Kentucky plant," *The Wall Street Journal*, Dec. 1, 1987. Reprinted by permission of *The Wall Street Journal*, © 1987 Dow Jones & Company, Inc. All rights reserved worldwide. **250** (Company Example: A Business-School Partnership at Stihl, Inc.): Adapted from K. G. Salwen, "The cutting edge: German-owned maker of power tools finds job training pays off," *The Wall Street Journal*, Apr. 19, 1993. Reprinted by permission of *The Wall Street Journal*, © 1993 Dow Jones & Company, Inc. All rights reserved worldwide. **260–261** (Company Example: TRW's Strategic Management Seminar): Adapted from Richard A. Eastburn, "Developing tomorrow's managers," *Personnel Administrator*, **31**(3), March 1986. Reprinted with the permission of *HRMagazine* (formerly *Personnel Administrator*) published by the Society for Human Resource Management, Alexandria, VA. **313–314** (Company Example: Helping Employees Self-Manage Their Careers at Hewlett-Packard): Adapted from Warren R. Wilhelm, "Helping workers to self-manage their careers," *Personnel Administrator*, **28**(8), August 1983. Reprinted with the permission of *HRMagazine* (formerly *Personnel Administrator*) published by the Society for Human Resource Management, Alexandria, VA. **321** (Company Example: Strategies for Coping with "Plateaued" Workers): Adapted from "Labor letter," *The*

Wall Street Journal, Feb. 19, 1991. Reprinted by permission of *The Wall Street Journal*, © 1991 Dow Jones & Company, Inc. All rights reserved worldwide. **363** (Company Example: Skill-Based Pay at Polaroid Corporation): From M. Rowland, "It's what you can do that counts," *The New York Times*, June 6, 1993. Copyright © 1993 by The New York Times Company. Reprinted by permission. **363** (Note 45): Adapted from "Labor letter," *The Wall Street Journal*, Apr. 18, 1992. Reprinted by permission of *The Wall Street Journal*, © 1992 Dow Jones & Company, Inc. All rights reserved worldwide. **422–425** (Company Example: Increasing Performance and Productivity at North American Tool & Die, Inc.): Reprinted by permission of *Harvard Business Review*. An excerpt from T. H. Melohn, "How to build employee trust and productivity," *Harvard Business Review*, January-February 1983. Copyright © 1982 by the President and Fellows of Harvard College; all rights reserved. **427–428** (Company Example: Self-Managed Work Teams at GM's Saturn Plant): S. C. Gwynne, "The right stuff," *Time*, Oct. 29, 1990. Copyright 1990 Time Inc. Reprinted by permission. **432–433** (Company Example: Linking Productivity and Work Schedules at Xerox): Adapted from S. Schellenbarger, "More companies experiment with workers' schedules," *The Wall Street Journal*, Jan. 13, 1994. Reprinted by permission of *The Wall Street Journal*, © 1994 Dow Jones & Company, Inc. All rights reserved worldwide. **433** (Note 46): Adapted from S. Schellenbarger, "The keys to successful flexibility," *The Wall Street Journal*, Jan. 13, 1994. Reprinted by permission of *The Wall Street Journal*, © 1994 Dow Jones & Company, Inc. All rights reserved worldwide. **538–539** (Company Example: Maintaining Productivity at the Expense of Safety): Adapted from B. Marsh, "Workers at risk," *The Wall Street Journal*, Feb. 3, 1994. Reprinted by permission of *The Wall Street Journal*, © 1994 Dow Jones & Company, Inc. All rights reserved worldwide. **540** (Company Examples: Safety Pays at Du Pont and Alcoa): Adapted from D. Milbank, "Companies turn to peer pressure to cut injuries as psychologists join the battle," *The Wall Street Journal*, Mar. 29, 1991. Reprinted by permission of *The Wall Street Journal*, © 1991 Dow Jones & Company, Inc. All rights reserved worldwide. **549–550** (Company Example: Levi Strauss & Co.'s AIDS-Related Corporate Philosophies): Courtesy of Levi Strauss & Co. **614** (Company Example: Interviewing Potential Expatriates at AT&T): Adapted from G. Fuchsberg, "As costs of overseas assignments climb, firms select expatriates more carefully," *The Wall Street Journal*, Jan. 9, 1992. Reprinted by permission of *The Wall Street Journal*, © 1992 Dow Jones & Company, Inc. All rights reserved worldwide. **617** (Company Example: Gillette's International Trainee Program): Adapted from J. J. Laabs, "How Gillette grooms local talent," *Personnel Journal*, August 1993. Used by permission.

PHOTO CREDITS

12: AP/Wide World Photos. **46:** Angel Franco/Woodfin Camp. **78:** Mark Richards. **109:** AP/Wide World Photos. **131:** Courtesy IBM. **179:** Courtesy Novosad and Co., Inc. **203:** Courtesy Performance Factors Inc. **208:** Randy Matusow. **293:** Jon Feingersh/The Stock Market. **324:** Richard Wood/The Picture Cube. **345:** AP/Wide World Photos. **390:** Guy Gillette/Photo Researchers. **415:** Jeff Jacobson/Archive Pictures. **481:** AP/Wide World Photos. **545:** Gerard Fritz/Monkmeyer. **604:** Liu Heung Sh'ing/Woodfin Camp.

INDEXES

NAME INDEX

SUBJECT INDEX